M000236602

This book provides a distinctive and rich conception of methodology within international studies. From a rereading of the works of leading Western thinkers about international studies, Hayward Alker rediscovers a "neo-classical" conception of International Relations which is both humanistic and scientific. He draws on the work of classical authors such as Aristotle and Thucydides; modern writers like Machiavelli, Leibniz, Vico, Marx, Weber, Deutsch and Bull; and post-modern writers like Havel, Connolly and Toulmin. The central challenge addressed is how to integrate "positivist" or "falsifica-tionist" research styles within humanistic or interpretive ones. The author argues that appropriate, philosophically informed reformula-tions of conventional statistical and game-theoretic analyses are possible. He describes a number of humanistic methodologies for International Relations, including argumentation analysis, narrative modeling, computationally assisted explications of practical political understanding, and the reconstructive analysis of historical connec-tions and possibilities.

CAMBRIDGE STUDIES IN INTERNATIONAL RELATIONS: 41

Rediscoveries and Reformulations

Cambridge Studies in International Relations is a joint initiative of Cambridge University Press and the British International Studies Association (BISA). The series will include a wide range of material, from undergraduate textbooks and surveys to research-based monographs and collaborative volumes. The aim of the series is to publish the best new scholarship in International Studies from Europe, North America and the rest of the world.

CAMBRIDGE STUDIES IN INTERNATIONAL RELATIONS

Series list continues after index

Rediscoveries and Reformulations

Humanistic methodologies for International Studies

Hayward R. Alker

CAMBRIDGE UNIVERSITY PRESS

Published by the Press Syndicate of the University of Cambridge
The Pitt Building, Trumpington Street, Cambridge CB2 1RP
40 West 20th Street, New York, NY 10011–4211, USA
10 Stamford Road, Oakleigh, Melbourne 3166, Australia

First published 1996

Printed in Great Britain at the University Press, Cambridge

A catalogue record for this book is available from the British Library

Library of Congress cataloguing in publication data

Alker, Hayward R.
   Rediscoveries and reformulations: humanistic methodologies for interna-
tional studies / Hayward R. Alker.
       p.   cm.
   ISBN 0 521 46130 8 (hb). – ISBN 0 521 46695 4 (pbk).
   1. Political science – Philosophy. 2. International relations – Philosophy.
I. Title.
JA71.A474 1996
320/.01–dc20   95–18925 CIP

ISBN 0 521 46130 8 hardback
ISBN 0 521 46695 4 paperback

CE

To my coworkers in the vineyards of knowledge –
Teachers, students, coauthors, critics and friends –
Whose persistent efforts at cultivation
May yet make more bountiful this present harvest

Contents

Contents

Figures

Tables

Acknowledgments

In earlier forms, the present essays have benefited from the essential contributions of several coauthors. Wendy Lehnert and Daniel Schneider shared in the rediscovery and reformulation of "Toynbee's Jesus", the essay in Chapter 3 below which appeared in a somewhat different form in vol. 6 (1985) of the *Quaderni di Ricerca Linguistica* (Alker, Lehnert, Schneider 1985). Roger Hurwitz and Karin Rothkin shared in the authorship of an earlier version of Chapter 9 ("Beneath Tit-for-Tat"), i.e. (Alker, Hurwitz, Rothkin 1993); Chapter 9's previously unpublished graphic Appendix is basically the work of Erik Devereux. That Appendix reflects Devereux's crucial earlier synthetic role in establishing the equivalence of different argumentation graphing approaches illustrated in Chapter 1. Once these contributions have rightfully been acknowledged, I must absolve any and all of these coauthors from the revisions I have made of our previously agreed upon texts and the uses I have made of them; these scholars may or may not agree with my changes.

With various differences from the texts presented here, a version of Chapter 1 appeared as "The Dialectical Logic of Thucydides' Melian Dialogue," in the *American Political Science Review*, 82/3, 1988. "The Humanistic Moment in International Studies," Chapter 4, appeared in *International Studies Quarterly*, 36 (1992), 347–371, while "Rescuing 'Reason' from the 'Rationalists,'" Chapter 6, came out first in *Millennium*, 19/2 (1990), 161-184. Chapter 7 appeared in a slightly earlier version as "An Orwellian Lasswell for Today," in Robert L. Savage, James Combs, Dan Nimmo, eds., *The Orwellian Moment: Hindsight and Foresight in the Post-1984 World*, University of Arkansas Press, Fayetteville, 1989, 131–155.

"Fairy Tales, Tragedies and World Histories," Chapter 8 below, appeared in *Behaviormetrika*, 21 (1987), 1–28. In particular, thanks to Jean M. Mandler and Nancy S. Johnson for their permission to reprint Tables 8.2 and 8.3, as well as Figure 8.1, taken from their "Remembrance of Things Parsed: Story Structure and Recall," *Cognitive Psychology*, 9 (1977), 111–151; and to Cambridge University Press for permission to reprint the text of Table 8.7 from Ernest Mandel's *Long Waves of Capitalist Development: The Marxist Interpretation*, Cambridge, 1980. I am grateful as well to the Rand Corporation, for permission to reprint in Chapter 9 from their RM 789, "Some Experimental Games," by Merrill Flood, the text of the annotations and moves associated with the first Prisoner's Dilemma game. "Emancipatory Empiricism," Chapter 10 below, appeared in Peter Wallenstein, ed., *Peace Research: Achievements and Challenges*, Boulder and London, Westview Press, 219–241. All are reprinted with the appropriate permissions.

More generally, as students and colleagues, Jim Bennett, Tom Biersteker, Cheryl Christensen, Erik Devereux, Gavan Duffy, Tad Homer-Dixon, Karen Rothkin, Roger Hurwitz, John Mallery and Dwain Mefford have shared, sustained and amplified the vision of rigorous hermeneutical and dialectical methodologies entertained here. Roger Karapin and David Simson helped with argumentation theory formalisms as well.

As Political Science colleagues in the Boston area, Lincoln Bloomfield, Nazli Choucri, Zhiyuan Cui and Joshua Cohen at MIT, and Craig Murphy at Wellesley, were helpfully critical, as well as encouraging. From among my teachers at Yale and MIT, I am glad especially to acknowledge the contributions of Robert P. Abelson, Noam Chomsky, Robert Dahl, Karl W. Deutsch, Robert Lane, Harold Lasswell, Charles Lindblom and Herbert Marcuse, whose different but overlapping visions of a humane social science I have shared. As research assistant and secretary, Peter Kubaska shared in this project as much as these others.

Working in Cambridge gave me the opportunity to clarify and sharpen my views in dialogue with Stanley Hoffmann, Herbert Kelman, Gary King, Joseph Nye and Sheldon White at Harvard, and Noam Chomsky, Marvin Minsky and Ken Haase at MIT. Visits from, and discussions with, James Der Derian and Wendy Lehnert have been similarly illuminating. If I have often agreed with Karl Deutsch and disagreed with Robert Keohane, it is to the credit of both holders of the Stansfield Professorship of International Peace at Harvard that the only person who clearly outshines their influence in these pages is Jürgen Habermas. Fortunately, I had the chance to meet him through the good auspices of Thomas McCarthy, then at Boston University.

Institutionally, I am indebted. The work discussed here has directly or indirectly received support at MIT (the Department of Political Science and the Center for International Studies) from the United States National Science Foundation, and the John D. and Catherine R. MacArthur Foundation. In Switzerland, I benefited from associations with the Center for Research on International Institutions at Hautes Etudes and the Department of Political Science at the University of Geneva, with the assistance of Jean Siotis, Dusan Sidjanski, Charles Roig and Urs Luterbacher. My two visits to Sweden, and the associated time for teaching and reflection benefited considerably from associations with the Swedish Collegium for Advanced Studies in the Social Sciences, the Olof Palme Professorship funded by the Swedish Humanities and Social Science foundation, and the Department of Peace and Conflict Research at Uppsala University. Peter Wallensteen, Björn Wittrock and Tom Burns were the most important of many stimulating colleagues in my stays in Uppsala. Kjell Goldmann, his colleagues and the students there made my weekly teaching trips to Stockholm and the University there also memorable. Jim Richardson and the Department of International Relations, RSPACS, ANU, Canberra, helped stimulate this volume's final chapter, The VKI fund of the School of International Relations at USC financed the preparation of the index. None of these organizations or institutions or individuals is responsible, of course, for what I have to say.

If foreign sojourns brought perspective to the MIT endeavors reported on here, summers on Block Island, Rhode Island gave me the time, the beautiful walks, the gardener's detachment and the serenity sufficient to write many of the chapters presented here. Carried in bulging suitcases on the Block Island ferry or obtained from the Block Island Library, the works of authors from long ago and far away have crept back to life in that peaceful place.

From afar, with or without their knowledge, many acquaintances and coworkers have contributed in a more general fashion to these essays. Tahir Amin, Tony Giddens, Ijaz Gilani, Rom Harré, Jürgen Habermas, Takashi Inoguchi, George Lakoff, Kinhide Mushakoji, Bertell Ollman, Livia Polanyi, Victor Sergeev, David Sylvan, Jim Richardson, Stephen Toulmin and Anna Wierzbicka have all been inspirations. Beyond those already cited, John Burton, Johan Galtung,

Acknowledgments

Harold Guetzkow, Anatol Rapoport, Peter Wallensteen and Elise Boulding have been my most important teachers in peace research.

At home, my wife and collaborator Ann Tickner, our daughters Joan, Heather and Gwendolyn, as well as my mother Dorothy Alker, my late father-in-law Fred J. Tickner, my brother Henry and my sister Charity, have all shaped my ability to understand and resonate with the contributions of those acknowledged above.

Introduction
Voyages of rediscovery

From my writings over the last twenty years, I have selected and present here twelve essays with two common elements: first, my philosophical, methodological and disciplinary preoccupation as a social scientist with somehow voyaging between, connecting up, or finding a bridging place between the humanities and the sciences; secondly, their focus on the methodological and discipline-defining ideas of leading Western thinkers about International Studies[1] since classical antiquity. Despite being professionally trained in a contradictorily named discipline called Political Science, I have resisted the temptation of attempting to resolve by fiat the problem of meaningful disciplinary coherence raised in the minds of my fellow ordinary language users by such a disciplinary label: how can a field of study deeply concerned with things that are so passionate, so value-laden, so personal and so encompassing as "politics" or "society" be a science? Is not the need to answer such a question even more difficult, but no less important when the goings and comings of international relations

---

[1] Three conventions need clarifying here. First, I shall capitalize International Relations (and other such disciplinary names) to refer to the disciplines in question, leaving uncapitalized disciplinary names to refer to their subject phenomena. Secondly, International Relations is, in my preferred usage, an inter-disciplinary field of research, training and rationally guided practice concerning relations among or across the major groups, nations, states and cross-border agencies (including individuals). I shall label the subfield of Political Science dealing with international affairs International, or World, Politics. Thirdly, when capitalized, International Studies refers to the most inclusive, regionally or globally oriented, interdisciplinary version of International Relations, emphasizing within its scope – as some scholars do not – normative, legal or humanistic concerns as well as more strictly naturalistic and social scientific ones. When a multidisciplinary cluster of comparative and internationally oriented disciplines is intended, I shall not capitalize international studies.

and world politics, as seen from many different vantage points, are the focus of attention?

My subtitle suggests a fresh attempt at social scientific synthesis, uniting the inclusive subject matter, the concern with discovering and shaping meaning, and the value orientations of the humanities with the methodological discipline, the formal rigor and the explanatory concerns one normally associates with the natural sciences. It suggests, as I shall try to demonstrate, the possibility of developing and deploying, with scientific rigor and international subject matter, methodologies appropriate for humanistic analytic purposes, which I take to include the comparative development and evidence-linked testing of explanatory historical generalizations. The disciplinary foci of these essays range from Political Science to International Relations to, more inclusively, international studies, and, more generally, the social sciences as a whole.

In the chapters of the present collection, the main connecting links result from voyages to the past, and back. I have found astonishing resonances between my own recent, modest conceptual, theoretical and methodological discoveries and similar, but much earlier and more important – indeed, discipline-constituting – contributions by the giants of philosophy, history, linguistic and literary analysis, political science, sociology and international relations. Even in the last part of the book, reporting on contemporary research paradigms and programs, links with an historical and disciplinary past are evident. My discoveries are thus rediscoveries; my methodological formulations, reformulations. This book reports how my own rediscoveries of discipline-constituting analyses have suggested humanistic methodological reformulations for contemporary and future International Studies.

These chapters do not complete a task which, most broadly, shapes the self-understandings of entire culture and civilizations. They do not even precisely define the task of inter-disciplinary linkage and possible synthesis, although redefined disciplinary foci and less sharply defined boundaries distinguishing the social sciences from the humanities would be a desirable result. Nor do they conclusively determine the sometimes difficult political choices that well funded research and its application necessarily raise. Indeed, their chief virtue as a collection may be the growing recognition they contain as to the nature of the problems generated by exaggerated perceptions as to the distances separating the humanities from the social and the natural sciences, together with their offering of some modest illustrations as to how interdisciplinary connections can be reestablished within a society and civilization mature and sophisticated enough to recognize these disciplines' various but related contributions.

I thus follow the lead of my late teacher and friend, Karl W. Deutsch. In the early years of the Cold War, he re-raised the issue of the "philosophic synthesis of the sciences and the humanities." Modestly, he attempted "to survey a number of problems that might be relevant to the development of such a synthesis in the future, and perhaps to indicate a number of pathways along which it might be approached by further research" (Deutsch 1958). In the same essay, Deutsch quotes Winston Churchill's November 3, 1953 speech to the effect that "It may be that ... when the advance of destructive weapons enables everyone to kill everybody else, nobody will want to kill anyone at all." Deutsch suggests that science may thus be forcing humankind to "reappraise its humanistic heritage and to restructure some of the fundamental habits and institutions of humanistic civilization." In addition to the contribution of the methods and results of science to such rethinking, he suggests "that the vividness, the multiplicity, the intuitive sophistication, and the presentational vitality of the humanistic approach would be no less essential."[2] This book similarly attempts to cumulate in an accessible, organized, relatively sustained fashion some of the conceptual, methodological and inter-disciplinary insights I have gained concerning humanistic approaches to international studies over the last two decades.

An initial preoccupation with generative narrative models

Having broadly sketched the focus of these essays, I would like now briefly to recollect certain elements of their originating context. Although I had begun to write on the methodological implications for political scientists of Kuhn's systematic historical account of paradigmatic revolutions (Kuhn 1970) in the early 1970s, my first public lecture on a clearly humanistic subject – on narrative modeling – was

---

[2] How different this attitude is, and how praiseworthy, when compared with the serious, if conditional, advocacy by both Bertrand Russell and Jon von Neumann of a preventive American nuclear attack on the Soviet Union during the early years of the Cold War! (Poundstone 1993: 70–80, 142–143, 195–196).

given in 1975 in Geneva.[3] A recollection of some specific elements of my early interest in generative narrative modeling will motivate a recollection of the more general framework of competing philosophies of sociopolitical inquiry with which I started the present collection of essays. Both thematics set the tone for many of the essays included here, including the most difficult of these to unpack: "Can the End of Power Politics be Part of the Concepts with which its Story is Told?", reprinted in close to its 1977 version as Chapter 5 below.

Tired of the limited repertoire of accounts possible with mechanistic causal models, I had for some time looked toward more complex ways of modeling, simulating and understanding human activities. This led to a fascination with the creative, generative, monad-like, Propp-Abelson-Chomsky style story scripts or plots and their associated plot-elaborating, rewrite-rule grammars. Epistemologically I would now describe these as testable structuralist models of historical possibilities, and note that perhaps the earliest example of the kind of modeling I had in mind was by George Lakoff (1962).[4] I had recently been exposed to Chomsky's formal demonstration (Chomsky 1956; Miller and Chomsky 1963) that all but the most degenerative of the language generation and understanding models in the Chomsky hierarchy of formal grammars transcended the generative and the interpretive (i.e., parsing) power of *all* the considerable variety of statistical models I had written or read about. As a mathematically trained social scientist, I was fascinated by the infinite generative power of Chomskean grammatical rewrite rules applied either to sentence components or to intersentential relationships.

Having been early exposed to Robert Abelson's highly suggestive generative modeling of political belief systems dynamics,[5] I was

---

[3] The French title I used then – "Contes de fé et histoires du monde" – has evolved into Chapter 8 below, entitled "Fairy Tales, Tragedies and World Histories."

[4] The reference is to Lakoff's unpublished MIT BS thesis, accepted in September 1962, supervised by Norman Holland (Lakoff 1962). I didn't read the thesis until "Fairy Tales, Tragedies and World Histories" (Alker 1987) was first in press.

[5] Especially Abelson and Reich 1969 and Abelson 1973. With acknowledgment, I taught for years from Abelson's unpublished notes from a 1973 lecture entitled "Grammar of Plans, Interventions & Adventures ("Venches"): A component of the nested structures model of beliefs." The first paragraph starts out with a conscious, if humorous, reference to the Aristotelian roots of the Schank–Abelson language/beliefs modeling approach:

> *Elementary classes of nouns* (Thank you, Aristotle)
> AME, animate objects, e.g., prince, dragon, horse, princess

already intrigued by Abelson's Aristotelian-Chomskean-Schankean incorporation of generative/interpretive capacities (Alker 1976, 1984). This work suggested how people could make, within limits, their own meaningful histories.

If the original version of the "Fairy Tales" lecture included references to Propp's, Abelson's and Chomsky's work, it did not then include the current version's introduction to Wendy Lehnert's similar, but affectively oriented, and more individually varying mode of plot unit analysis. Then both a colleague and former student of Abelson and Schank at Yale, Lehnert presented her recent work (1981) at the MIT Artificial Intelligence Laboratory, a talk I was fortunate enough to attend. This approach, which in a post-structuralist manner flexibly develops interpretive constructions responsive to convergent or divergent reader/listener reactions, is used in Chapter 3 by Lehnert, Schneider and myself to explore specific meanings associated with, or triggered in the receiver's mind by, Toynbee's generalized Jesus story framework.

Another of the attractions of Chomsky's writing on language was his concern to develop what he called a mathematics of creativity, of freedom. If the scholars mentioned above had helped me to see how it could be extended to multi-sentential narrative or textual accounts, for a long time, I did not see very clearly how an emancipatory social science could be defined in such terms, or by analogy with Kuhn's writing on paradigmatic revolutions. Indeed, until I read Habermas on the subject of human knowledge interests (Habermas 1971), I was unaware of what an emancipatory knowledge interest – a deeply ingrained disposition or tendency to learn how to remove unnecessary structures of domination – might look like.

THG, inanimate concrete "things," e.g., sword, poison apple
LOC, fixed geographic locations, e.g., castle, pond
QUA, qualities of objects, e.g., redness, beauty, death
STE, states, e.g., knowing, having, being an agent
(ING, tangibles, the union of the sets AME and THG)
Its key generating relationship is a rewrite rule for creating meaningful "Venches":
An initial vench-generating purpose molecule:
V = W(ant)-A(ction)-S(tate)
is recursively rewritable in 4 different ways:
A -> ASA or B(eginning intent)-H(elp)-A or B-D(ifficulty)-F(ailure)-A or concrete ACT.

The originating methodological conflict addressed by these chapters

My engagements with narrative modeling were parts of a larger, more generally defined, philosophical complexity about the nature and direction of the social sciences. Should they look like formal logic, mathematics or physics, or were they to be more engaged and committed to social change, as Marxians regularly said they were? For me these issues came to a boil in the tension between the logical empiricist, or logical positivist, philosophies of science and the more politically engaged and historically conceived modes of interpretive and emancipatory inquiry associated with Kant, Marx, Freud, Adorno, Marcuse, Habermas, Apel and the Frankfurt School. Habermas' writing about "hermeneutics" and "dialogics" fascinated and troubled me. Having written a BS thesis on formal logic, I had never heard of what he called "dialogics"! Rather than practical, humanistic textual interpretation, I first thought hermeneutics was the philosophy of spiritual hand holding! Having been trained in Yale's outstanding graduate Political Science program about the many methodological limitations of Adorno *et al.*'s *The Authoritarian Personality*, I could not remember hearing as a graduate student about the existence of "critical theory," nor of any serious philosophic rationale for the Frankfurt School!

Updated from a 1976 paper on "Learning About Political and Social Science," which saw abbreviated publication as Alker (1982), Table Intro.1 contrasts these positions, largely on the basis of Radnitzky's contrast of logical-empiricist and hermeneutic-dialectic schools of contemporary "metascience"[6] (Radnitzky 1973, which includes several of his earlier volumes). The table merges Radnitzky's broadly Popperian perspective with Habermas' early writings (especially Habermas 1971). It summarizes different positions in two remarkably similar epistemological controversies: the Kuhnian knowledge cumulation controversy (Lakatos and Musgrave, eds. 1970), and the "Positivism

---

[6] Radnitzky uses "metascience" rather like I would say "philosophy of science"; his "metascience" includes the discussion of human knowledge interests and natural or social ontologies. I recall with approval his suggestion that in addition to Habermas' positive, hermeneutic and emancipatory knowledge interests, he would suggest a cosmological knowledge interest in world picture painting. Having read Wright (1955) on thinking of the world alternatively as a plan, equilibrium, organization, community or field, I immediately liked, and still like, this suggestion.

Controversy" in German Sociology (Adey and Frisby, eds. 1976). The table suggests how I was beginning to fill in and order intermediate philosophical and methodological orientations between "positivist" and "dialectical-hermeneutic" extremes (see Alker and Hurwitz 1980; Alker 1982). It embodies Lakatos's suggestive treatment of "methodology" as applied philosophy of research, i.e. applied epistemology. It only hints at *the deeper, narratively oriented, integrative possibility, with which I have become seized, that of adapting the logically informed analytical-empirical philosophies of research to humanistic, dialectical-hermeneutic purposes.*[7]

Indeed, the hope of resolving such a conflict of applied philosophical views has energized the present volume; it seems clear enough today, however, that such resolutions will only be possible by a transformation in the social or "human" sciences that recognizes the appropriateness of a more inclusive set of knowledge aims and interests than naturalistic scientists usually allow. For me, writing "Can the End of Power Politics be Part of the Concepts with Which its Story is Told?" (Chapter 5 below, written in 1977) first pointed toward a way out of this extreme opposition of research philosophies. It suggested what a peace-oriented, emancipatory, humanistic science might look like. The use of empirically testable and revisable Schank–Abelson story-generating computer models made this possible. At the level of specific research methodologies, the paper also prefigures my specific concerns throughout these chapters with argumentation processes, other dialectically subsumptive theoretical and historical developments, the interpretation and generation of narratively generated meaning structures, and the sustained development and redeployment of classical notions of reason and action.

Written in part like the "causal modelers vs. voluntaristic social action theorists" debate at the end of Alker (1974), "Can the End of Power Politics ..." simulates an ontological encounter of Marxian and Leibnizian perspectives on how potentially emancipatory world

---

[7] Perhaps the most important contribution of the subsequent chapters in this regard is to propose synthetic disciplinary approaches that integrate across, and go beyond, the axis of Figure Intro.1. Scholars like Aron, Berlin, Bull, Chomsky, Deutsch, Lasswell, Rescher, Ricoeur and Toulmin have all been familiar with the writings of the Frankfurt school, but they have not motivated their own developments primarily in its terms. The reader may be encouraged to explore more multidimensional typologies; my own papers along those lines, either associated with a project on the Dialectics of World Order or a series of papers going from "causal modeling to artificial intelligence," are not included here.

Table Intro.1 *Some contrasting views on various issues of social science relevance in the paradigms and positivism debates*

Issue	Positivistic Logical Empiricism (Russell, Vienna Circle, Carnap, Nagel?)	Critical Rationalism or Methodological Falsificationism (Popper, Lakatos, Albert, D.T. Campbell)	The Hermeneutics of Scientific Revolutions (Kuhn) or Methodological Anarchism (Feyerabend)	Dialectics (Adorno, Habermas) or Dialectical Hermeneutics (Apel, Habermas, Giddens?)
Attitude toward metaphysics	Anti-metaphysical, favoring ontological reductionism toward analytical (logical) and synthetic (sense-based) truth	Critical of historicist, and essentialist metaphysics yet cognizant of positive methodological role of atomistic and other ontologies, nonfalsifiable core assumptions, rational standards and positive research heuristics. Truth exists forever in an objective third world of subjectless knowledge.	Emphatic on cosmological component in scientific revolutions, analogies and associated exemplary new ways of seeing associated with disciplinary communities.	Insistent on the primacy of social totalities acting through individuals; these exhibit contextual historicity, embodied transindividual subjects, the partial identity of subject and object, and the material unity of thought and action. Constructive linguistic reflexivity is an essential human characteristic.
On the unity of the sciences and scientific progress	Strongly favors such unity and typically employs probabilistic verificationism: knowledge cumulation is typically incremental.	Emphasize methodological principles of falsificationism and the rationally reconstructible internal history of science, including its revolutions when they occur.	Share with Popper *et al.* the values of truth, simplicity, consistency, fruitfulness, which are however of varying importance; emphasize the discontinuous nature of progress and consider rational reconstructions inadequate accounts thereof.	See a basic disunity of technical, hermeneutic and emancipatory knowledge-constituting interests; progress is dialectical – ultimately the increase of man's autonomy *vis-à-vis* nature and other (groups of) men.

On naturalism and physical reductionism	Strongly favors physicalism and the reduction of science to statements in an ideal logical language.	Against inductive scientism, also nonfalsifiable psychoanalysis and falsified Marxist historiography. Popper sees sociology as governed by a weakly hermeneutic logic – a situational approach not used in physics.	Kuhn sees hermeneutics as distinct from natural science. Like Adorno, Feyerabend refuses to identify the boundaries of valid knowledge with contemporary Western science (citing Voodoo, acupuncture, etc.). Both oppose reductionism.	Oppose historiography or psychoanalysis to physics, and humanism to naturalism; existentialist rather than historicist hermeneutics is preferred. The constructive appreciation of social-natural totality contrasts with "atomistic" social science in the service of administrative or technocratic interests.
On logic, deduction, extensionality	Approves of Russellian logic or extensionalist metamathematics as the ideal language of hypothetical-deductive scientific theorizing.	Deductive logic is the truth-or-error preserving organon of rational criticism, but there is no necessary fit of mathematics to nature.	Deny the *logical* nature of criteria for theory choice. Make problematical both the top-down and bottom-up application of mathematical formalisms.	Against absolutizing, extensional deductive logic; favor dialectical tacking between part and whole, subject and object, theory and practice using discursive logic or "dialogic."
On empiricism and truth	Approves either a positivistic version in terms of observational primitives or scientifically verifiable perceptions. Typically a correspondence theory of objective truth is offered.	Denounces the purely observational character of facts (basic propositions), opposes inductivism and objects to the verifiability conception of scientific perception; Popper accepts Tarski on the logical nature of truth, but grounds basic observations in "convent-ional" decisions by scientists.	Emphasize the tacit, nonlogical, consensually accepted knowledge embedded in basic observational statements; Kuhn's exemplary ways of seeing which prefigure puzzle solutions are closer to the hermeneutic circle than Popper's or Lakatos' similar views.	Dialectical treatments of observations seek societal explanations and critique beneath hermeneutic meanings and empiricist pseudo-objectifications. Truth is the totality. A consensual theory of truth is given both scientific and political applications.

Table Intro.1   *contd*

Issue	*Positivistic Logical Empiricism* (Russell, Vienna Circle, Carnap, Nagel?)	*Critical Rationalism or Methodological Falsificationism* (Popper, Lakatos, Albert, D.T. Campbell)	*The Hermeneutics of Scientific Revolutions* (Kuhn) or *Methodological Anarchism* (Feyerabend)	*Dialectics* (Adorno, Habermas) or *Dialectical Hermeneutics* (Apel, Habermas, Giddens?)
On scientific autonomy, insulation and value	The logical systems ideal of science seeks autonomy by minimizing value relevance and insulating all stages of theory development.	Falsificationism doesn't deny societal inputs, but tries to correct for them through rational social criticism.	Kuhn usually defends insulation of science, but recognizes cosmological overlaps with social philosophies; Feyerabend defends some violations of autonomy.	Science is seen as subordinate to organized practical interests; autonomy/neutrality claims are criticized in the light of social structures preventing genuine consensus and making autonomy less than it could be. Theory and practice are internally related.
On social reform	Commitment to a restricted form of enlightenment makes bureaucratic utilization easier; but this is not always expressed.	Prefer "piecemeal social engineering" or experimentally corroborated reforms in open societies to violent social revolutions, i.e., "reason" over revolution (Popper).	Feyerabend, but not Kuhn, argues that anarchistic violence can be helpful in changing social epistemology.	On some occasions violent revolutions are appropriate; but a preference for democracy over totalitarianism is expressed.

Source: Alker 1982.

histories should be narratively generated. In my mind the debate was mediated by Aristotle from the past and Norbert Weiner – Leibniz's cybernetic descendent – from the future! At the time when I wrote "Can the End of Power Politics …," I thought of it as an attempt to confront, choose between or synthesize "Marx vs. Monads"! "Marx vs. Leibniz" might have been a better description. This book attempts to catch, unpack, deepen, connect, integrate, learn from, and projectively generalize upon that exhilarating experience.

In particular, the dialectical opposition between naturalistic "explanatory" and humanistic "interpretive" or "emancipatory" models of social scientific inquiry is a major focus of Table Intro.1 and of these chapters. This creative tension is evident in all three of the chapters on classical antiquity; it reappears with particular force in later discussions of Abelson–Schank interpretive belief system models, my Vico–Habermas inspired attempt to "Rescue Reason from the Rationalists" (Chapter 6), and my concluding discussion of "The Return of Practical Reason to International Theory" (Chapter 12).

Only when stimulated by post-modern critics to reread Immanuel Kant's "What is Enlightenment," did I finally realize how much Enlightenment goals of freedom from immature dependency, of mature and rational self-determination, fit in with a social tradition valuing autonomous self-sufficiency going back to Aristotle and the Greek city-state (Chapter 3) and forward to contemporary "critical and reflective" social theory (especially as reviewed in Chapter 6). Moreover, over the millennia from Plato and Aristotle to Chomsky, Habermas and Donald Campbell, with Leibnizian lenses I have been able to see repeated reworkings of the methodologically instructive, directional ontological premise of the plenitude immanent in Nature, or what Leibniz might call Nature's plan, viz. the "Great Chain of Being" (Lovejoy 1936). With roots going back to Plato's *Republic*, Aristotle's teleology of nature and cosmopolitan Stoic utopias, reinterpreted as objective tendency, subjective necessity, or architectonic design possibility, Leibniz's metaphysically sublime "monad of monads" can be interpreted as both source and end of world history. In the eighteenth century Leibniz's follower Wolff saw in the voluntary agreements of the laws of nations evidence for the existence of an objective but virtual reality, a Great Republic of Republics; it was a *civitas maxima* linking many *civitates* like individual citizens, an international "society among all nations." It suggested evidence of humanity's ultimate end within the Great Chain of Being, in a time and place where anarchical power politics has come to an end (Onuf 1994, as discussed further, in Chapters 5, 11 and 12).

This Grotian ideal prefigures Kant's, Hegel's and Marx's writings about the End of History. The early modern ideal of a global republic of autonomous republics constituted by autonomous citizens underlines the idea of an international world community. Always presenting social science as if it were a value-neutral enterprise obscures these great ancestral commonalities (and their variants) shared by Western "critical and reflective" social science and the more naturalistically oriented work they frequently criticize.

This book itself falls short of such an ideal, however, staying mostly within the Western tradition. But when one's focus has been more narrowly on contemporary International Studies' discipline-constituting analyses and debates, some interrelated rediscoveries of specific professional utility are also more likely to develop. Indeed, my sense of professional identity with International Studies has been broadened, deepened and strengthened by the process: for example, I have found that the debates between so-called "realists" and "idealists," and between "constructivists" and "naturalists" have existed in Western sociopolitical thought at least since Thucydides' time.

Voyages of rediscovery can be endless. More importantly, I have rediscovered a shareable way – which might be called the imaginative reliving of discipline-constituting moments – of teaching humanistic disciplinary conceptions, and their associated research methodologies. What has been possible for me in this way should be possible for others: the innovative development of context-sensitive, humanistic, yet reliable and truthful, methodological reformulations appropriate for contemporary International Studies.

A chapter by chapter outline

A more concrete anticipation of the specific chapters below may also be helpful. Part I contains three such contemporally oriented voyages of discovery into the pasts of dialectical argumentation, of Aristotelian ethical-political inquiry, and of the affective-moral content of the Jesus story. Each chapter introduces new ways of reading the classics. While my suggestion of Thucydides' employment of pre-Socratic dialectical reasoning tools is certainly not original, the claim that he was writing *both* a dramatic, but historical Greek tragedy *and* a partly formalizable scientific account of Athenian self-destruction does have more originality. It is not new, however, as Raymond Aron and other well read traditional scholars doubtless knew. I find Aristotle's *Nicomachean Ethics* – taken together with his *Politics* and *Rhetoric*, his *Metaphysics* and his methodological *Organon* – an impressive, but not tension free, ethical-political-cosmological vision of practical and theoretical socio-political inquiry. Although not a Straussian believer in the timeless superiority of esoteric Aristotelian theory, I nevertheless argue for the enormous fecundity of Aristotle's interdisciplinary, publicly oriented conception of truth-seeking, and the teleologically oriented, methodologically rich literatures to which the Aristotelian tradition has given birth. Similarly, my exploration of the affective, emotional-moral plot structures discoverable within (or regularly associated with) Toynbee's generalized version of the Jesus story finds in classical Mediterranean culture an enduring, if contradictorily interpreted, source of meaning in Western civilization; the generalized strategy for empirically discovering various action-engendering life projects derived from Lehnert's plot unit analysis methodology is clearly linked back to concerns evident in Thucydides' dramatic historical interpretations and Aristotle's *Poetics*.

Reconstructions of past methodological formulations and disciplinary definitions require lots of hermeneutical effort at reading texts from long ago. Nonetheless, Part II of this book focuses on relevant contributions by early modern writers like Machiavelli, Las Casas, Leibniz and Vico, as well as later modern writers Marx, Weber and Lasswell. The early modern Renaissance both rediscovered and invented ways of understanding, explaining and deciding upon actions. Situated within both contemporary explanatory traditions and humanistic constructivist perspectives, I nonetheless feel a sense of exhilarating rebirth and novelty in rereading modern giants like these. Even if later modern writers like Weber and Lasswell are easier to understand, what they have to say about combining scientific and moral traditions of critical inquiry may still be a novel experience, of value to others.

This book's title emphasizes such naturalistic discovery and humanistic invention themes, both treated as recurrences. For example, the reconceptualization of Renaissance humanism in Chapter 4, with links to later chapters in Part II, was personally extremely revelatory. Without the opportunity to review early modern international political and legal theory, I would not have discovered the common root – the neo-classical clustering of the "Humanities" – of the "distant" disciplines whose insights and approaches I kept trying to bring (back) into

Political Science, International Relations and the social sciences more generally. Moreover, I rediscovered that the distant descendants of the Melians and the Athenians – Las Casas and Machiavelli – both combined humanistic and scientific concerns in ways that seem to have been nearly forgotten, but are nonetheless of direct relevance to the issue whether our current era has become a post-modern one.

I have already suggested above how many of the essays chosen for inclusion may be described as following the model of Chapter 5's Leibnizian *reconciliations* of supposedly contrasting, "practical," "humanistic" and "scientific" approaches. In Leibnizian, cybernetic terms, the chapter responds to neo-Marxist and communitarian critiques by Bertell Ollman and John Burton of J. David Singer's positivistic, statistically implemented peace research. Characteristically, I cut across the cleavages mentioned above, suggest a more "humanistic" or "historicist" way of appropriating the "classics" – in this case proposing a variant of Leibnizian peace research sensitive both to his ontological syntheses, the contextually oriented critics of formal modeling, and the innovative, emancipatory possibilities of contemporary Artificial Intelligence models of story-linked human understanding.

The answers suggested in Chapter 5 to the question "Can the End of Power Politics...?" remain for me provocative because they, like the Vico–Habermas reading of Weber in Chapter 6, suggest a missed pathway in modernity's troubled development, the path of explicitly humanistic social sciences. Quite unexpectedly, I have found my own earlier analysis of Leibniz's thought to be broadly complementary to that given by Toulmin in one of the key citations of my ISA Presidential Address (Chapter 4), his *Cosmopolis* (Toulmin 1990).

Toulmin's account of the order-seeking desperation behind the ontological and epistemological inventiveness of Descartes, Newton and Leibniz nearly converges with my own. In more general terms than I am able to argue, Toulmin suggests that the shift toward written, formalized, axiomatic, deductive reasoning was a kind of epistemological counter-revolution against the secular, skeptical, tolerant, context-specific, but not finally conclusive reasoning of the post-Italian European Renaissance and, I might add, of classical dialectical logic. Toulmin further suggests that Newton, Descartes and Leibniz reacted against the horrors of religious total war by attempting to construct a new, more certain, ontologically grounded, logically rigorous, balanced and equilibrated world view, or cosmopolis. Like Stephen Toulmin, I have tried to recover the use of less completely formalized, more open-ended variants of dialectical logic and practical reasoning; perhaps I am more optimistic than he is about the potentials of creatively and humanistically deployed new technologies for humanistic social science; but I believe our motivations and historical analyses to be remarkably similar.[8]

The third chapter in Part II, Chapter 6 on "Rescuing Reason from the Rationalists," elaborates my own understanding of the "critical or reflective" tradition of international social theorizing, as evidenced in different retellings of the contributions of Vico, Marx and Weber. Starting from Isaiah Berlin's immensely provocative account of Vico's metaphorically defined interpretive/constructivist social science, it treats both Marx and Weber as exemplary writers in this tradition. It thus carries into later periods the earlier discussions of Renaissance thought. Moreover, it provides another example of humanistic-naturalistic rediscovery, concerning the important roles of narrative construction in the creation of civilizational historicity. It connects the earlier discussions of narrative structure and functioning in Chapters 3–5 with the more contemporary and formal technical treatment of Chapter 8.

Chapter 7's sympathetic review of Lasswell's contingent, "configurative," Weberian and Freudian mode of social scientific analysis picks up, and recapitulates, the contextual, dialectical, skeptical epistemological themes of the previous chapters. The convergence of his psychoanalytic, humanistic, emancipatory approach towards Orwell's more literary style of writing catches as well the humanistic rediscovery and methodological reformulation themes of earlier classical and early modern writers. Chapter 7 provides as well a hopefully accessible summary and application of the major themes of the entire section – and therefore much of modernity – of the literary *and* scientific ideal of a humanistic science. Its concrete applications are drawn from the recent time of Ronald Reagan's first term as president of the United States.

The third and last section of the book is even more focused on the current, or contemporary, period. It contains both more specific methodological suggestions – as, for example, how to study the UN

---

[8] Sheldon White has reminded me of a related but different interpretive argument, less grounded in the horrors of early modern total warfare. It sees the shift evident in Descartes and Leibniz and Bacon toward more rigorous foundations for philosophy and science as a step in a "Great Instauration." When Francis Bacon wrote his *Novum Organum* he could be seen as calling for a new beginning, rather than a rebirth (or renaissance) of philosophy, science and society.

Collective Security System or to reanalyze Prisoner's Dilemma games –
and discipline-redefining suggestions. Each chapter addresses particular, ongoing, contemporary research programs. As elaborations on
the themes of earlier chapters, the essays there have also, I hope, some
current and future value for International Studies more generally.
From a Kuhnian perspective, knowledge cumulation has both incremental – research program based – and more encompassing and
sometimes discontinuous, paradigm changing aspects.

Accepting that human action, as informed by the creativity of
linguistically mediated thought, can produce a variety of hard-to-
predict responses to complex situations, how can we scientifically
assess our rationalized understanding of this creativity? I begin the
third section of this work with an exploration of different ways of
empirically fitting, or testing for, models of this generativity (Chapter
8: "Fairy Tales, Tragedies, and World Histories"). These grammatical
models are extended to oversimplified but provocative textual models
of collective historical accounts. Formal grammatical devices help us
better *testably* to specify the ways we *understand* our past and imagine
our future. Examples of such generative structures include underlying
oral (Russian) fairy tale traditions, the classic tragedies of antiquity
through the Renaissance, and similarly heroic Christian, Greek,
Roman, Malthusian and Marxist frameworks for making sense of
world history. As we learn about the biological or cultural universals
underlying such competences, we can also be more sensitive to the
ways different individuals, cultures or civilizations distinctively shape
such meanings as well.

My recent joint paper on Mandeville's and others' "fairy tale"
accounts of the conflict-ameliorating properties of capitalist self-interested action (Chapter 9) fits this sectional thematic of the book as well.
Just as the formal grammars of Chapter 8 can be thought of as
embodying Leibniz's practically oriented, monad-like "active principles of unity," the next chapter finds past political-economy fairy
tales contained inside present protocols of Sequential Prisoner's
Dilemma (SPD) interchanges. Beneath behavioral regularities – summarized nowadays usually in Tit-for-Tat terms – one finds cultural
residues of much earlier contested worldviews concerning appropriate
interest-maximizing behavior.

Making deeper, more precise and appropriately particularistic sense
of such SPD behavioral patterns requires knowledge of what individual SPD players are trying to do with their moves. The undelivered

thoughts experimentally recorded along with behavioral cooperation and defection decisions help make these behaviors intelligible; they turn behavior into action. Within such actions one finds the previously mentioned cultural residues of centuries of previous practical argumentation about how one ought to behave in mixed interest situations.

Going back to Aristotle's focus on practical reasoning, von Wright and Olafson have proposed that such interactive behavior-payoff sequences can be *explained* by quasi-causal chains of practical reasons and their effects. When thought of as improvised mini-historical dramas, SPD games gain in significance and in depth from an awareness of multiple, deep or shallow, action-interpreting possibilities. Such reconstructions nicely further illustrate the Toulmin–Alker understanding of contingent, dialogical, order-construction practices; they are illustrated with some reconstructions of practical reasoning in a specific SPD protocol suggested by Erik Devereux.

Chapter 10, "Emancipatory Empiricism," unpacks and explicates for a peace research audience, the ways since I first wrote "Can the End of Power Politics ..." that I have tried to do empirical but emancipatory international relations research. While many of my colleagues have remained fascinated (and, I would say, trapped) by the positivistic or instrumentalist temperament and methodologies of the natural and economic sciences, I have been more and more drawn to, and stumbled into, the insights and rigorous methodological formulations of linguistic, philosophical, historical and even literary inquiry.

Indeed, as elaborated upon in Chapter 10 ("Emancipatory Empiricism"), the repeated empirical failures of technically advanced statistical models early convinced me of the methodological import of the maxim that history is (ontologically and epistemologically, as well as methodologically) much more than a time series or econometric time series analysis. Driven toward the lived, rewritten and still living history of practicing politicians and historians, I have increasingly been fascinated by the extreme methodological demands of the professional historian. What dialectical philosophers of history describe as the internal relations of historical processes, others refer to as the temporally organized, collectively shared, self-understanding of a continuing human society: its historicity or historicality. Both individual, group, disciplinary, national, international and civilizational versions of this search for identity and reproduction have preoccupied me. This cluster

17

of concerns, I now see, may be reflectively generalized and described in humanistic terms as an engaged, but disciplined form of emancipatory peace research.

Generalizing on the different ways of generating narrative accounts formally reviewed in Chapter 8 ("Fairy Tales ..."), Chapter 10 also applies and develops the "Leibnizian" perspective of Chapters 5 and 8 to the United Nations Collective Security system. Here is the second example, after Chapter 5, where I have suggested an Aristotelian style analysis of the enhancements and decays of a constitution-like system, here defined at the international level of analysis. Moreover, Chapter 10 fulfills as well the Aristotelian–Habermasian concern with a multiplicity of human knowledge construction interests. Specifically, it is the clearest vision I have had to date of the methodological implications of an emancipatory knowledge interest for data-making, data analysis and data anticipation.

Chapter 11, "The Presumption of Anarchy in World Politics," synthesizes many of the methodological insights of the previous chapters. Moving up from the micro-worlds of Sequential Prisoner's Dilemmas to the "Cooperation under Anarchy" problematique of contemporary neorealist international relations theory, Chapter 11 recalls Hobbes' richer appreciation of the dilemmas involved in this and other similar historical situations. It invokes the considerable organizing power of Hedley Bull's sophisticated historical understanding of the development of an international society of states. The seminal idea, discussed above, of using narrative interpretive structures to make collectively shareable historical sense of the past and the future is also explored. A focus on constructed meanings of human social-historical interactions reappears in the guise of a general discussion of the ways major international theorists of the past have contributed to the historicity of world society. Here the concern with artificially intelligent models of belief dynamics and decision-making in Chapter 5 also comes to further fruition.

Finally, Chapter 12 ("The Return of Practical Reason to International Theory") interprets the contribution of recent International Relations texts by Kratochwil, Onuf, Hollis and Smith as embodiments of a new attentiveness to practical reasoning. Moreover, I find a reopening of the British-American-Australian realism-idealism debate from thirty years earlier in the ways the present authors reconstruct practical judgments as key components of a newer, humanistically richer version of international theory. It is an extremely recent treatment of exciting new – and at the same time quite old! – prospects for international theory.

Towards reconciling a divided interdiscipline

It has become a common subject of agreement among scholars of international relationships that International Relations is not only a dividing discipline, it is also a divided one. As Quincy Wright, Raymond Aron, Michael Banks, James Dougherty and Robert Pfaltzgraff, K.J. Holsti and Michael Banks have described it, International Relations is a divided field of study, an interdiscipline, a clustering of disciplines, traditions, approaches, paradigms and research programs loosely related by their subject matter. With the exception of scholarly issues directly linked to the major conflicts of our times, we appear to reserve our most bitter disputes for a different aspect of our disciplinary orientations: our related, if often more abstract and theoretical, research orientations. It is toward those disagreements that the present chapters are addressed. Given the direction my rediscoveries and reformulations of the field have moved in, I find Quincy Wright's relatively early discussions of the component disciplines of International Relations particularly enlightening.

Thinking of International Relations as an attempted union of internationally oriented disciplines, rather than as a subfield of Political Science, Quincy Wright saw International Relations as a discipline seeking to give due weight to logical, efficacious, subjective and objective truths. As a result it has encountered difficulties in retaining disciplinary unity and coherence. Wright called for the synthesis or unification of the theoretical and practical component disciplines of International Relations. He groups them (Wright 1955: Chs. 1–3, 30–33) into arts, philosophies, histories and sciences.

Although one might well place the particular disciplines, or parts of them, in different boxes, and one might be tempted to think of contemporary international administration or governance as other than "Colonial 'Government,'" I find this constitutive conception of International Relations highly suggestive. Isn't the treatment of politics as "applied" and of International Relations as a synthesis of abstract, concrete, theoretical and applied disciplines provocative? I hope others will also think so. The discriminating use of such terms was for a long time puzzling to me. The present collection of essays should help the

	Theoretical disciplines	Applied disciplines
Abstract	Psychology, sociology, Ethics, and other similar SCIENCES	Politics Colonial government Organization, Law Economics, Communications Education & other PHILOSOPHIES
Concrete	Geography Demography Technology, and other similar HISTORIES	War, Diplomacy, conduct of foreign relations & other ARTS

Figure Intro.1
Wright's grouping of International Relations' component disciplines

Source: Wright 1955: 502

reader better understand and reformulate Wright's own integrative vision of the field (1955).

The most obvious, and perhaps the most important, additional division for international relations scholars claiming to seek and to report globally valid truths, is the division of the field apparent across the language worlds, the ethnic communities, the nations and/or states, the diplomatic groupings and the cross-boundary private and public organizations. If Stanley Hoffmann once (1977), with considerable ironic force, referred to "An American Social Science" of International Relations, I no longer think such contradictory narrowness to be the case. Certainly before "the American Century," International Relations was not only, or mostly, an American social science. Even in present day America, however, we relive many pasts from outside our hemisphere. The world we inhabit is becoming more closely connected. A truly global interdiscipline of International Relations is beginning to emerge.

Part I
Recovering Western antiquity

1   The dialectical logic of Thucydides' Melian Dialogue

> The Melian Dialogue is *"at the same time . . .*
> the result of art . . . [and] the reflection of reality"
>
> R. Aron (1984: 28)

In writing his classic study of the Peloponnesian War, Thucydides sought "an exact knowledge of the past as an aid to the interpretation of the future, which in the course of human things it must resemble if it does not reflect it" (I.22).[1] For twentieth-century British and American realists, e.g., Wight (1978: 24) and Morgenthau (1978: 8–9, 38), this has typically meant seeking supreme, timeless or even eternal truths – perhaps even expressible as mathematical laws – about the state's eternal, self-interested search for power and the need to balance against it. Werner Jaeger's reference to "This political necessity, the *mere mathematics of power politics*" conveyed a similar realist message to the German-speaking world of the 1930s; indeed, in a book widely renowned for its penetrating and inspirational account of Greek civic culture, Jaeger asserts that this "necessity" "is defined [by Thucydides] as the true cause . . . of the war" (Jaeger 1976: 488, my emphasis).[2]

---

[1]   I follow the customary form of citations to the Books, paragraphs (and sometimes even sentences) in the standardized Greek text. I like the Rex Warner translation (Thucydides 1972), which sometimes explicitly uses the terminology of dialectical philosophy. Since to use a translation that abets my interpretation may be said to stack the deck in my favor, my reliance on the Crawley translation (Thucydides 1910, 1950) in Table 1.1 below (which is in the public domain) is intended as a self-checking move.

[2]   Jaeger cites Thucydides' famous argument (I.23, 6) about the necessity of the war: "The growth of the power of Athens, and the alarm which this inspired in Lacedaemon, made war inevitable." Hobbes' translation (Schlatter 1975) uses the dialectical metaphor of a quarrel: "And the truest quarrel, though least in speech, I conceive to be the growth of the Athenian power; which putting the Lacedaemonians into fear necessitated the war." Cogan (1981: 4–21) and White (1984: 60) like "causes

Would not any other social scientist in our own century, if desirous of emulating the increasingly universal validity of the natural sciences and committed to building up reliable knowledge grounded in the deductive certainty of axiomatic formal argument and the "positive" evidence of our senses, also want to claim to "have written my work, not as an essay which is to win the applause of the moment, but as a possession for all time"? (I.23) Neither immune to such broader epistemological trends (developmentally described as "positivistic," "logical positivism," "logical or analytical empiricism" and "critical rationalism" in Alker 1982),[3] nor slavishly imitative of them, the more literate of our "quantitative" or "scientific" professors of international politics[4] must also have approvingly cited – for the benefit of their students –Thucydides' search for "the clearest data," or his standard of objective precision: "the accuracy of the report being always tried by the most severe and detailed tests possible." (I.23)

Contemporary neorealists similarly appreciate Thucydides' classic analyses of state actions, extended to include the structural determinants of these actions (Keohane 1983, 1986; Waltz 1979). Despite their logical empiricist objections to the imprecision, logical inconsistency, and empirical nontestability of too much traditional realism, scientifically aspiring neorealists seem to share with their ancient predecessor an aspiration to discover timeless laws of power politics, independent of moral praise or blame, objectively and falsifiably delineated with what Jaeger took to be mathematical precision. Surely, it would seem, these were the goals of Thucydides' "scientific history" or "scientific politics."

Beyond its realist preoccupation with the unchanging motivational bases for, and causal dynamics of power politics, Thucydides' work is

for action" better. Cogan suggests that the growth of the Athenian empire was a necessary, but not a sufficient cause of the war: one needed to look at the "grievances" or "alleged causes," the decisive moments and the deliberate choices – the universal capacity for communication and persuasion is the Thucydidean "human thing" – before the war decisions of both sides can be adequately accounted for. The Corinthians drew a line on the Corcyrean matter and the Athenians crossed it knowingly. It was this action that caused the Corinthians to change their perception of Athens from a growing imperial state to a hostile one! (Similarly, see Patomäki 1992.)

3   See as well the schematic versions of these positions in Table Intro.1 of the Introduction to the present volume.
4   "Quantitative International Politics" and the "Scientific Study of International Politics" have been terms used to cluster behaviorally oriented international politics research by J. David Singer, Dina Zinnes, among others, e.g., Zinnes (1975).

as well known for the equally fatalistic moral cynicism of the Athenian statement in the Melian Dialogue (or Conference) that "right, as the world goes, is only in question between equals in power, while the strong do what they can and the weak suffer what they must" (V89). Surely this quotation continues to dazzle, to shock and sometimes to subdue students in introductory courses on International Politics around the world.

With similar practical import, but an apparently more detached and scientific tone, structurally oriented neorealists often deny that some policies or states have a more moral character than others (Waltz 1979: 127, 187n). They express doubts about the possibility of learning lessons from history: "classical realism, with its philosophical roots in a tragic conception of the human condition, directs our attention in the twentieth century to the existential situation of modern humanity.... But Realism, whether classical or structural, has little to say about how to deal with that situation" (Keohane 1983: 519).

These or similar views of Thucydides' aspirations and contributions I take still to be held by the majority of contemporary Anglo-American students of international relations. They were my own, in large part, until I began regularly to assign, reread and critically teach Thucydides' great work on "human things" in an historically oriented class on international relations theories, supplementing that reading with an additional week of selections from a variety of secondary commentaries.

Although I still agree that Thucydides is one of the first[5] "scientific historians" (Jaeger 1976; Strauss 1978: Ch. 3; Keohane's 1983 arguments for continuity in the "hard core" of the realists' research program from Thucydides to Waltz), I now think his philosophy of inquiry was neither logical positivism, nor a naturalistic logical empiricism seeking eternal mathematical laws, nor the amoral realism in

---

[5] Jaeger (1976: 483n) argues Hecataeus was the first Greek taking "the scientific and rational approach to the facts of human life as the essence of history," while Herodotus gets the credit (among Greeks) for introducing "the religious and dramatic element" into history.

From a dialectical-hermeneutic world order perspective (Alker and Biersteker 1984), it is more interesting that somewhat similar traditions existed in China (and perhaps elsewhere) at about the same time. The punitive realism of the Athenians at Melos has its clearest parallel in Lord Shang's legalist writings. But neither Chinese legalism (the closest to Greek realism) nor Confucian communitarianism nor Sun Zi's extraordinarily dialectical (and Daoist) *Art of War* exactly match the Greek traditions (compare Freiberg 1977).

terms of which I as an undergraduate and so many of my teachers and professional peers were trained to see the past. Nor should Thucydides' view be equated with the cynical ambassadorial sophistry to which some of Thucydides' contemporaries (and some of our own) still aspire.

I now believe that his painstaking commitment to factual accuracy was an expression of a naturalistic-humanistic synthesis, a dialectical historiography combining philosophical, scientific and dramaturgical elements. In contemporary terms, Thucydides' "scientific history" can be reconstructed with an overlap and synthesis of historical concerns, naturalistic medical thinking (Cochrane 1929), an ancient but also modern dialectical philosophy of argumentatively rational inquiry (Rescher 1977; van Eemeren, Grootendorst and Kruiger 1987), ethno-methodological social science (Harré and Secord 1972), and systematic literary theory or poetics (Burke 1969). Indeed, I now think – and shall try to show – that a dramatic-historical conception of mathematical political science is much closer to Thucydides' actual viewpoint than Jaeger's cited remarks – so prototypical of twentieth-century perspectives. Ignoring its artistic and philosophical origins, we seem almost to have forgotten that his scientific political history is at the same time one of the greatest "morality plays" ever written,[6] in essence a Greek tragedy.

To better understand what Thucydides actually thought he was doing in writing his history, and to try and preserve the relevance of Thucydides' insights and historical-political science for today's problems,[7] I shall focus on the dialectical ways – now thought to have been learned from the Sophists[8] – in which he presents, reconstructs

[6]   The Keohane quotation above correctly links classical realism and a tragic, dramatic, sensibility; the contrary view – that "morality plays" are written by "idealists," but not modern political *scientists* – was the view of the teacher of my first international politics course. Classical realists are predisposed to link tragedies to events beyond one's control, to fatal flaws in character or, more generally, human nature. The rather fatalistic Greek medical view of the endogenously determined passage of a disease through its natural stages gives a scientific flavor to this pessimistic, yet eminently dramatic, sense of historical possibility. The prophetic and horrifying plague at Athens can thus be seen as symbolizing a natural tragedy. Cochrane (1929) argues the influence of Greek medicine in Thucydides' analysis.

[7]   Garst (1989) and Bagby (1994) give revealing, complementary accounts of neorealists' substantive misreadings of Thucydides. They allow me to continue the broader, more epistemologically oriented focus of the 1981 and 1988 versions of this article. Garst's treatment of Cogan (1981) and White (1984) was especially helpful in this regard.

[8]   Thucydides' use of sophistic dialectic has been noted by classical scholars, but in a

and uses the Melian Dialogue. Since the specifics of Thucydides' philosophical-methodological training are incompletely known, I shall find useful for my purposes Nicholas Rescher's recent (1977), but classically informed, reconstruction of the dialogical bases of disputation-like inquiry. I shall argue that Thucydides consciously used a very similar rational dialectic of inquiry in the reporting, reconstruction or composition[9] of this dialogue.

Contrary to neorealist complaints, he did so with a degree of rigor approaching, and in some ways exceeding, contemporary modes of logical and empirical analysis. The most appropriate epistemological standards and formal tools for detecting, understanding and criticizing his methodological discipline are those suggested by recent work on dialectical logic and argumentation theory.

Correlatively, but in ways not fully anticipated by his best commentators, in the Melian Dialogue – and to a lesser extent, the other debates he reports – Thucydides employed a partly formalizable dialectic of composition/reconstruction, a penetrating investigative mode of situationally specific dramatic interpretation grammatically grounded in an ontology of opposed inner dispositions and characters. There was, as well, a larger conception of the ways speeches and subsequent actions interrelated with one another, a larger sense of structure and unity in the composition of his history. In contemporary language, his polimetrics was one of seeking to uncover – through critical, partly formalizable, rational argumentation – the determinative structures, the characteristic contrasts, the syntheses and transformations practically constitutive of Greek politics.

Finally, I want to suggest that although relatively detached from the partisan politics of his time, Thucydides did take sides on the key issue of moral-political responsibility for the war. Indeed, Thucydides was consciously a participant in the ongoing "great debates" of his era about the proper conduct of international affairs, debates which find

---

less formal way than I present it (e.g., Finley 1939; 1942: 250ff.). More generally, the dialectical character of Thucydides' realism has (with credits to de Romilly 1963) been well argued in Aron (1978: 20–46).

9   Defending the relative accuracy of Thucydides' reconstructions, Kagan (1975: 77) argues that, in the voluminous literature on the subject, "no one has shown that there is a single speech in the *History* that could not have been given in something like its Thucydidean form." As will be illustrated below, Cogan (1981: 92ff.) similarly argues that the speeches have important reporting functions, selectively presented by Thucydides to increase precise understanding of the motives and rationales associated with decisive moments in the history.

many echoes in contemporary conflicts of theoretical traditions. Through a critical, contextualized appreciation of Thucydides' dialectical realism, our own scholarly political argumentation can, and should, advance.

The Melian Dialogue as classical dialectic

The Melian Dialogue, or Conference, occurs at a pivotal point in Thucydides' history; the subjects debated there, the ensuing actions and the lessons drawn in and from this episode contribute significantly to the book's enduring value. It breaks into two parts – a debate about Athenian and Melian interests, which I shall analyze, followed by one about the folly of the Melians' hope that the Spartans would come to their assistance. For realist historians the Melian Dialogue has become the "mother" of all diplomatic debates. Accepting the expert view that the Dialogue is Thucydides' reconstruction, based at most on incomplete, but truthful reports of its having occurred, I shall focus on its situation-respecting compositional practice.

In discerning how Thucydides proceeds methodologically it must first be noted that there are three recurring levels of discussion in the Melian Conference (Sections 85–116) and of the stylized dialogue or debate (Sections 87–111) that takes place within that terminal episode of Book V of Thucydides' history.

Neither popular rhetoric nor apodictic, but formal debate

The first level of discussion concerns the type of negotiation to take place between the Melians and the Athenians – whether it will be a logical and analytical investigation of the sort we would call deductive science, merely a rhetorical exchange before a large group of people, or a formal disputation allowing interruptions at any point, i.e., a serious debate. Both parties clearly have in mind some kind of uncoerced formal disputation before a judge and an audience; Habermas' "dia-logic" (1971), Barth and Krabbe's Formal Dialectics (1982), and the ideal models of argumentative discourse (van Eemeren, Grootendorst, Jackson and Jacobs 1993) would be comparable contemporary versions of this idea. A second level intersects with this one: it concerns the possible contradiction between standards of conduct defined in terms of power or interest and those defined in terms of justice or fairness. Not only does this theme reappear in the body of the Melian Dialogue, it arises concerning the fairness of the proceedings themselves and the mutual determination of a subject about which to have a serious debate. The third level of discussion is the debate proper, once the topic of national/imperial interests has been reluctantly agreed upon.

The evidence for treating the Melian Dialogue as – at least in form – a classical disputation is explicit within Thucydides' text. Consistent with their oligarchic political character, initially derived from Sparta, their parent state, the Melians "did not invite [the Athenian] representatives to speak before the people [as would be the custom in a democratic state like Athens], but asked them to make the statement for which they had come in front of the governing body and the [oligarchic] few" (V84). The Athenians put a good face on this choice by treating it as a preference for serious argument rather than the set speeches of popular rhetoric by which the masses might be "led astray": they philosophically propose that the Melians "should instead interrupt us whenever we say something controversial and deal with that before going on to the next point" (V85).

The kind of argument envisioned is also not what Aristotle would later call apodictic (deductive, demonstrative or necessary) reasoning. Before Aristotle's discovery of all the valid syllogisms, I suspect their model of such reasoning was geometric deduction, which already had achieved significant results by the end of the fifth century BC. My evidence is the Melian statement that disputants "should be allowed to use and to profit by arguments that fall short of a mathematical accuracy" (V90). Since their lives depend upon their persuasiveness, they wanted to be able to make arguments that they could not strictly prove, but against which effective counter-arguments might not be made. Clearly, we are in the realm of dialectical inferences which "must start from premises that command general assent [i.e., are "probable"] rather than universal or necessary truths" (Aristotle 1964: 83).[10] Except for his somewhat more positive – more democratically respectful – conception of rhetoric, Aristotle's great collection of writings on formal and informal logic, his *Organon*, will soon make similar distinctions (Arnhart 1981: Ch. 2).

---

[10] To allay confusion, I give Aristotle's decidedly non-parametric definition of the probable: "A probability is a generally approved proposition, something known to happen, or to be for the most part thus and thus" (Aristotle 1964: 158). See Chapter 2 below for more on Aristotelian logic.

Coercive irrationalities in the Dialogue

This agreement on a dialectical mode of political discussion – the Athenians do not object – occurs in the realm of practical reasoning pointed toward action in concrete situations, where arguments start from reasonable assumptions not the necessary truths of geometry, where strict deductions are often not possible or appropriate, where better arguments still do not claim deductive certainty. But this realm is not completely "dialogically logical" in any ideal sense; nor does agreement extend to a second level of argument about the topic of discussion. The Athenian proposal only to discuss matters of self-interest is described without objection as "scarcely consistent with" the expectation of a reasonable exchange of views in "a calm atmosphere." The Melians see the Athenian invasion of their island as a "present threat" of "making war" against them, evidence that they have come "prepared to judge the argument yourselves" (V86). The Athenians do not deny the coercive element of their proposal, turning the subject to the matter of Melian survival. A similar response occurs when, later in the debate (V90), the Melians note that the Athenians "force us to leave justice out of account and to confine ourselves to self-interest" right after the Athenians have asserted that for "practical people, the standard of justice depends on the equality of power to compel...." Evidently, Thucydides thinks like contemporary argumentation theorists who would consider this conduct "irrational in [such a] dialectical situation" (Barth and Krabbe 1982: 58).[11]

Despite the coercive irrationalities – which may be said to threaten the adequacy, coverage and truthfulness of the debate's conclusions – I now want to show that the third level of substantive discussion in the Melian debate, the debate proper, can be formally reconstructed as largely consistent with Nicholas Rescher's pragmatic, yet scientifically

---

[11] As Popperian "critical rationalists," Barth and Krabbe (1982) associate with the opponent's role "an *unconditional* right to criticize" proponent assertions (p. 58), and reconstruct the pragmatic rules of logical argumentation non-coercively, explicitly, to include rule FD E5super: "When party N performs a speech act that is not among those permitted to N by the rules of this system of formal dialectics, or if it performs a nonpermitted, nonverbal action that reduces the other party's chances of winning the discussion, then N has lost all its rights in the discussion and N's behavior is to be called *irrational with respect to the present dialectical situation* by the company that has adopted this system of formal3 dialectics" (p. 63). More broadly, see Becker and Essler (1981).

rationalized, version of dialectical inquiry (Rescher 1977;[12] another application is Alker 1984). To explicate the methodological rigor and subsequently to defend the scientific character of the analysis of the debate, I shall first summarize Rescher's controversy-oriented approach to knowledge cumulation, and then show how well, how rigorously and how insightfully the Melian Dialogue conforms to his model. I shall emphasize the practical, creative, truth-revealing contribution of this mode of disputational discourse.

Except for her neglect of formalizability, Jacqueline de Romilly makes the same point about dialectical creativity in clarifying Thucydides' achievement: "Thanks to the dialogue form, the particular and the general mingle together. This form enables maieutics to take the place of formal [strictly deductive] demonstration, so that the complete pattern Thucydides has in mind is revealed little by little, in all its aspects down to its deepest foundations" (de Romilly 1963: 274). The practical and fecund root meaning of *maieutics* in classical Greek is particularly apt: "midwifery."

Rescher's dialectical logic

To many, Thucydides' Athenian and Melian diplomatic arguers sound rather like contemporary lawyers, not the students of the pre-Socratic Sophists, with whom they probably would have studied. All well-trained lawyers – those contemporary descendants of ancient sophists, philosophers, dialecticians and rhetoricians – know better than many formal logicians and not a few political scientists the many ways human claims and counterclaims can be supported, qualified, excepted, revised or distinguished. The achievement of most, if not all, natural language arguers, of successful lawyers and diplomats, and especially of ordinary language philosophers like Rescher, is to be able carefully, provisionally, argumentatively, specifically, persuasively to make and defend their case and/or to reconstruct and criticize someone else's. If it is to be scientific, Thucydides' own dialectical approach must be seen as a systematizing and institutionalizing improvement on such practices and capabilities.

Rescher is very aware that other, more or less formal, characterizations of rational argumentation exist; but his simplified version is

---

[12] My partial summary of Rescher's argument, including quotations, is taken primarily from his first chapter, pp. 1–34; see also his second and fifth chapters.

adequate for his primary purpose: to exhibit the "social nature of the ground rules of probative reasoning," the establishing of our factual knowledge through a social process of controversy-oriented, yet still rational and cumulative argumentation. Coincident with his social process orientation, Rescher's dialectical logic starts from, and fits, a social-legal scenario involving four unequal roles: the proponent, the opponent, a rational and rule-enforcing judge or "determiner" and an audience. We too shall find Rescher's formalization highly useful for our primary purposes: to argue for, and learn from, the dialectical, yet logical, partly formalizable and scientific character of the pre-Socratic natural philosophy employed in Thucydides' reconstruction, presentation and uses of the Melian Dialogue.

Rescher's formalization

A compact graphical summary of Rescher's formalization of the proponent's move and the opponent's countermove possibilities within formal disputation is given in Figure 1.1.[13] In making sense of the figure, I shall focus first on the different roles, repertoires and move relationships indicated there, leaving the specific form of the claims and counter-claims until later. The theoretically anticipated "history" of the debate is that it will go from left to right, along one of the theoretically anticipated paths. Since protagonists normally make only one of the specified moves at a time, and the moves are grouped into separate columns, or rounds, in a left-to-right sequence, under one interpretation of Figure 1.1, the debate history always moves to the right. But in another sense, there is the possibility of the debate "returning" at a later time to challenge or develop assertions made within earlier moves, and perhaps not yet elaborated upon by the originator or responded to by the other. In another, more complex, "grammar-like" version of Figure 1.1 – not actually drawn – such back-and-forth movements would certainly be anticipated and are clearly allowed by Rescher's theory.

As one would expect, Rescher's formal "grammar" of dialectical possibilities requires focused back-and-forth argumentation. It starts with a proponent's "Categorical assertion" of the main thesis he is to defend; a *prima facie* case – a provisoed assertion of support for that

---

[13] This figure and my textual summary are based on Rescher (1977: 1–34; see also Chs. 2 and 5).

claim – may also be initially made. Each round, including the first, the proponent is required to make a new categorical assertion. In Rescher's world, the focus of such categorical claims is on putative "facts"; I take it that these could include analytical truths, categorical qualities claimed to be characteristic of some entity, more or less reliable generalizations, or claims about appropriate conduct in a particular situation.[14]

The proponent, like a legal claimant under Greco-Roman law, both takes the initiative and bears the burden of proof – the responsibility appropriately to develop a persuasive and defensible argument for the major thesis he is arguing. The proponent's role is thus a "strong" one, but with a harder task than that of his skeptical or critical opponent. Symbolically each of his categorical assertions is preceded by an exclamation point.

Taking her turn, as shown in the figure the opponent has three possible counter-moves associated with her role in the second round of the debate; there is also a fourth. She attempts to discredit the proponent either by an insightful challenge or "cautious denial" of the proponent's prior claim (move (2)), a provisoed denial of the proponent's claim associated with a cautious assertion of her own (move (3)), or a "weak distinction" – that special version of a provisoed denial where the provisoed supporting proposition is rewritten to include additional circumstances, combined with the cautious assertion of the truthfulness of those circumstances (move (4)).[15] The development of her own counter-argument – as begun in moves (3) and (4) – is an option, not a requirement; technically each of these possibilities fits the requirement for a new assertion every move. In any case, these countermoves should be directed at the proponent's categorical asser- tions – in this case, !P or !Q – or – and this is the fourth countermove possibility – these assertions' analytical presuppositions or deductive entailments.[16] Normally a turn or round will consist of only one of these moves.

[14] In Chapter 2, I introduce a few more complicating steps in the possible formalization of action-oriented argumentation, including a focus on Aristotelian practical syllogisms.

[15] Distinction-making is a key creative move in dialectical logic: "Recognition of the central role of distinctions in the dialectical enterprise – based on the division (*dihairesis*) of key concepts – goes back at least to the Socrates of Plato's *Phaedrus* and is doubtless present in the theory and practice of the early Sophists." (And their students, as we shall see!) (Rescher 1977: 12n13.)

[16] Only the later of these possibilities is mentioned in Figure 1.1, at the bottom. The intriguing former possibility – to my knowledge not explicitly mentioned by Rescher – will prove to be a crucial move in the Melian Dialogue, as analyzed below.

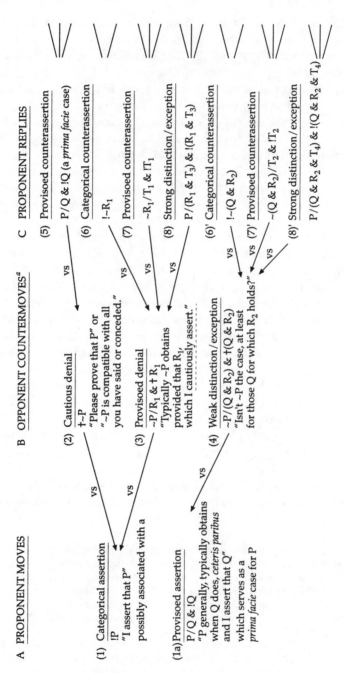

Figure 1.1 Rescher's simplified formulation of dialectical move sequences.

Source: Rescher 1977 (6–15): "It would also be possible to claim an entailment, such as P ⊢ S₁ or (*vis-à-vis* move 1a) Q ⊢ S₂, and then indirectly attack either P or Q with cautious or 'provisoed' denials of S₁ or S₂."

Characteristically, each opponent's countermove is, or can be easily rephrased as, a question, as is already the case for move (4) in the figure. Thus move (2) can also be read as "Isn't the opposite of your thesis consistent with everything you have so far asserted or conceded?" Notationally, all of the opponent's allowed countermoves include a denial or an assertion of fact; since the focus of debate is on the proponent's claims, the provisional, cautious, weak but still opposed quality of these claims is symbolized by a preceding dagger (†). Given these various limitations, the opponent's position is, relatively speaking, a "weaker" one in Rescher's theory.

Following Rescher, I symbolically indicate that each of the opponent's three graphed move possibilities is a focused attack using a corresponding solid-headed arrow. Moving from the second column to the first column, these are labeled with a "vs." in the figure. The same type of labeling is applied to his list of possible proponent replies in the third column of Figure 1.1. But note that the positioning of such a "versus" arrow is in some cases more complex: buttressing or supporting reference to the earlier claims of the first round is also intended. Thus proponent's moves (5), (8) and (8)′ explicitly cite P, and move (8)′ strengthens the earlier supporting claim Q of his *prima facie* case with a strongly asserted further distinction or exception. In developing a way of graphing actual argument flows, an awareness of these more complex possibilities will be important.

We are now far enough along in the exposition of Rescher's adversarial social process model to discuss what those with formal training are likely to think of as its major surprise and innovation. Any contemporary who previously learned something about elementary logic's sentential calculus – i.e., their "Ps," "not-Ps," "if-then horseshoes" "ands," "ors" and "Qs" – is likely to expect a formalizer of argumentation processes to use its symbolism. Although Rescher's approach *subsumes* the possibility of such formal relations,[17] its focus is different.

Within the context of strong and weak assertions, Rescher's key formal, dialogical connectives are "~", "/" and "&". Like its mono-

---

[17] Indeed, Rescher (1977: 13–14f) suggests that his formal dialectics fits nicely with classical (univariate) quantitative logic – Aristotle's formal syllogistic reasoning – modified to include an "all-things-being-equal" operator. He follows Aristotle's argument here that syllogistic principles apply both to demonstrations involving universal, necessary truths and dialectical exchanges concerning less certain matters (Aristotle 1964: 153ff.).

logical counterpart, the first of these dialogical connectives, "~", negates the propositional symbol which follows, as in "~P", read "not-P" or "the negation of P"; but for Rescher the weak assertion †~P pragmatically suggests a need for substantive "refinement," not necessarily total rejection. The second key dialogical connective refers to "presumptive, or provisoed, support *by* the expression on its right *for* the expression asserted on its left," as in "P/Q". "P/Q" is read as: "P generally (or *usually* or *typically*) obtains provided that Q," or "P obtains, other things being equal, when Q does."[18] The third key connective in Rescher's dialectical logic – ...&... – should not be confused with its much simpler special case, logical *and*; it might be translated as "[the expression on the left] additionally rewritten to accommodate [the proposition to the right]." We have already seen its use in the discussion of distinction making. Go back through the examples in Figure 1.1 to see other ways in which all of these dialogical connectives are used.

Combined with ! or †, located somewhere in an evolving debate, along with additional propositional content, Rescher's ~ has a performative quality to it: it refers to an act of denying specifically focused on what has previously been asserted. Even more unusual, for the formally trained, is the open-ended, contingent, tentative, revisable quality of the "provisoed assertion" and "provisoed denial" relationships: P/Q and ~P/Q, respectively. The way Rescher has focused and simplified his dialectical logic, these tentative, ideal typical relationships are not ever directly challenged, they are presumptive support relationships: the focus is instead on the probative, on the dialogically connected evidential bases of "facts," "distinctions" and "exceptions" supporting or undermining the major ! or † claims.

The associated meta-linguistic claim, however, is very important: *most human argumentation relies on revisable, tentative, ideal typical, ceteris paribus (other things being equal) forms of inference*. Like Toulmin's earlier, quasi-legal analyses of an argument's components (Toulmin 1958), Rescher's "/" is built on this understanding. In contemporary lan-

18 The provisoed or presumptive inference from Q to P, P/Q, is very different from either the Q ⊃ P ("Q implies P") or Q ⊢ P ("Q entails P") of standard, modern symbolic logic. Because this key inferential relation is only *presumptive*, it does *not* unconditionally support detachment of a conclusion Q from P & (Q/P). Hence, "in *dialectical* (as opposed to *deductive*) reasoning an assessment of the cognitive standing of a thesis never leaves its probative origins behind altogether." Alternatively, without detachment each dialectical argument requires inspection of the entire history of its derivation.

guage, Rescher's dialectics is a partly formalized, philosophically supported, adversarial methodology for moving imperfect, but plausible initial opinions about "facts" closer to the truth. The compatible, but more ambitious, route of attempting partly to formalize the rules and linkages of valid natural language argumentation is a major area of informal argumentation theory research (van Eemeren, Grootendorst, Jackson and Jacobs 1993).[19] To recognize that such informal practice doesn't directly conform to the standards of modern deductive logic or computer science raises the possibility of further formalizing the bases for its validity.[20]

The role of the determiner or judge

Putting aside for now a discussion of the historical embodiments of an audience and a judge, to be fairly representative, this summary account of Rescher's dialectical logic must now address the role of the determiner or judge. It is also a crucial role in scientific assessment. How indeed ought one to assess relative and absolute performance in a disputation?

The judge both evaluates the substantive and the procedural[21]

---

[19] An even more ambitious semi-formal synthesizing move between the dialectical and standard, i.e., formal and deductive, logical traditions is Lorenzen and Lorenz (1978). They define the standard logical constants – &, v, ~, if ... then – dialectically, i.e., argumentationally, in terms of tabular rules for their use in *critical dialogues* between Proponents and Opponents! Barth and Krabbe (1982: 12–55) see this work as part of a linguistic-pragmatic, social respecification of the foundations of logic and mathematics, as an elaboration of Wittgenstein's notion of a *language game*. Their own set of twenty-one definitions and forty plus rules proposed for bringing both Cartesian monological axiomatics and post-Hegelian associative thinking into the discursive, socially and rationally arguable, realm is given in their Chapter 3, from which one anti-coercive rule was cited above. Both cooperative and competitive language game versions are explored.

[20] Indeed, "deviant" logicians within Artificial Intelligence have made major contributions to formalizing revisable inferences. The relevant literature contains breathtaking flashes of insight, and provocative formal innovations concerning "non-monotonic," "autoepistemic," and "defeasible" reasoning – reasoning that leads both to new conclusions and, occasionally, the retraction of old ones (Winograd 1980; Pollock 1992). Pollock clearly recognizes strong fits between his formal model of defeasible reasoning and the rationality invoked in formal disputation. There remain, however, deep but not unsolvable problems of the formalizability of the pragmatics of situation-specific human communication (Winograd and Flores 1986; Reichman 1985).

[21] A major initial simplification (presumably adequate for Rescher's purposes) is the assumption that erroneous evidential inferences using the provisoed assertion con-

performance of the proponent and opponent, and he or she addition-ally oversees other related behavioral aspects of the disputation. To ensure progress, the judge should expect not only that assertions in the second and later rounds are new and not repetitive, but that the proponent's new assertions non-trivially or non-tautologically *develop* the argument with new grounds, distinctions, supportive theses or conditional reformulations. Similarly, an opponent must be judged for success or failure in finding, and successfully elaborating upon, weak initial and supporting claims in the proponent's arguments.

In adversarial terms, a judge may measure progress in terms of "commitments" and "concessions." If we think of the proponent's initial and subsequent categorical assertions as "commitments," every unattacked assertion of the proponent becomes, at least temporarily, a "concession" by the opponent. Proponent reformulations, such as moves (1a), (5) and (8) and (8)' in Figure 1.1, are said formally to "discharge" the proponent's responsibility to defend previously made categorical "commitments." Whenever the opponent makes a distinc-tion as a way of limiting the scope of strong assertion, the stronger form of the assertion is also treated as a "concession." The proponent should honor his initial (and subsequent, unconceded "living") "com-mitments" by strongly defending and developing them, making minimal concessions in the face of opponent's queries, perhaps ex-tracting significant concessions from her as well. The opponent succeeds when she convincingly argues how the proponent has failed to do so.

As we have seen, Rescher's determiner role makes judgments on either *formal* or *material* criteria, which the proponent and opponent too have at least partially internalized. Formal failures include illicit circularities in reasoning, inconsistencies and incoherences within one's expressed beliefs, and formal logical errors; material failures include increasingly implausible commitments, as well as concessions that undermine initial claims and subsequent commitments. Appro-priate evidential plausibility standards mentioned by Rescher for participants, judges and others include: source reliability and author-itativeness; the relative strengths of supportive evidence for rival theses; and the ease (simplicity, regularity, uniformity with other cases,

nective ("/") are either not made by the participants or immediately corrected by the judge. This limitation has the important consequence that the parties primarily address themselves to matters of evidential substance – their factual/categorical assertions and challenges.

presumptive normality) with which such theses are supportive of inductive systematization.

A partial, Rescherian formalization of the Melian Dialogue

To see if Rescherian dialectics will help us to recover Thucydides' sophistic dialectic, consider the first major substantive debate in the Melian Dialogue: whether the submission of Melos to Athens, either voluntarily or through coercion, can be said to be in either or both of their interests. Table 1.1 and Figure 1.2 fulfill this expectation. Either in Rescher's dialogical formalism or in a closely related argumentation graphing approach initially developed in Devereux (1985),[22] these representations show how the first part of the Melian Debate can be formalized. With numbering corresponding to the move turns evident in the Crawley text, aided by various interpolations indicated in square brackets, the flow of argumentation evident in both the table and the figure remarkably fits Rescher's rules of dialectical logic.

Several arguments for the relative adequacy of Rescher's formalization of this text are quite straightforward. First, in the Crawley translation text given in the table and the revised version thereof used in the figure (from Thucydides 1951), there is the clear and repeated use of the specialized terminology of argumentation: "proceed to show," "and how, pray, . . .?," "argument," "category," "distinction," and "therefore" are terms of argumentative art that any broadly literate philosophical scholar will recognize. Moreover, the argument

[22] With support from a MacArthur Foundation grant to the Center for International Studies at MIT, and under my supervision, Anne Quadraas and Roger Karapin developed, with examples from the international security realm, a student-oriented exposition of a corrected version of Devereux's thesis approach. Including some nice equivalence theorems across Rescher, Toulmin and Birnbaum's slightly different earlier approaches, Devereux's impressive 1985 thesis was a response to my teaching and writing on the subject, including the conjecture of equivalence which he strongly confirmed. Devereux's thesis also shows how a generalized version of Rescher's dialogical algebra – including attacks on provisoed inferences – allows isomorphic translations between it and a graphical representation strategy very close to that illustrated in Figure 1.2. Karapin and Alker (unpublished, written in the summer and fall of 1985) is a revised version of the earlier, primarily student effort. Homer-Dixon and Karapin (1989) further describe and illustrate this effort, citing Karapin and Alker (unpublished) but not Devereux (1985). The GMATS computerized graphing routines used to create Figure 1.1 were written by David L. Simson as part of a 1986 MIT Electrical Engineering and Computer Science Bachelor's thesis.

Table 1.1 *Should the Melians submit to the Athenians?* A partial reconstruction and Rescherian formalization of the Melian Dialogue. (V. 91–97)

Athenians ... We will now proceed to show you that we are come here [seeking Melian submission, voluntarily, if possible] in the interest of our empire, and that we are going to say [is in your interest, i.e., is] for the preservation of your country;

LET P_1 = MELIAN SUBMISSION IS IN ATHENIAN IMPERIAL INTEREST, AND P_2 = VOLUNTARY MELIAN SUBMISSION IS IN HER (AND ATHENS') INTEREST

$$! P = ! (P_1 \text{ \& } P_2) \tag{1}$$

as [a two part *prima facie* case] we would fain [preferably] exercise that empire over you without trouble [through Melos' voluntary submission],

LET Q = IMPERIALLY, MELOS' VOLUNTARY SUBMISSION IS DESIRABLE

$$P_1 / Q \text{ \& } ! Q \tag{1a}$$

and see you preserved for the good of us both.

LET R = PRESERVATION OF MELOS VIA VOLUNTARY SUBMISSION

$$P_2 / R \text{ \& } ! R \tag{1b}$$

Melians And how, pray, could it turn out as good for us to serve [voluntarily submit] as [it is] for you to rule?

LET $P_2 = P_{21} \text{ \& } P_{22}$, WHERE P_{21} = ATHENIAN INTEREST IN RULE AND P_{22} = MELIAN GOOD FROM VOLUNTARY SUBMISSION

$$\dagger \, (\sim P_{21} \text{ \& } P_{22}) \tag{2}$$

Athenians Because you would [avoid] ... suffering the worst, and

LET W = MELOS' AVOIDING THE WORST

$$P_{22} / W \text{ \& } ! W \tag{3a}$$

we should gain [a more valuable tributary] by not destroying you.

LET X = GREATER ATHENIAN TRIBUTARY GAIN

$$P_{21} / X \text{ \& } ! X \tag{3b}$$

Melians [Why could we not remain] neutral, friends instead of enemies, but allies of neither side?

LET N = MELOS' FRIENDLY NEUTRALITY, AND I = ATHENS' INTEREST

$$\sim P_1 / (I \text{ \& } N) \text{ \& } \dagger \, (I \text{ \& } N) \tag{4}$$

Athenians No; for your hostility cannot so much hurt us as your

$$! \sim (I \text{ \& } N) \tag{5}$$

friendship will [; it would] be an argument to our subjects of our weakness,

LET S = SUBJECTS' REGARD FOR ATHENIAN POWER

$$\sim I / (\sim S / N) \quad \& \quad ! (\sim S / N) \qquad (5a)$$

and your enmity of our power.

$$I / (S / \sim N) \quad \& \quad ! (S / \sim N) \qquad (5b)$$

Melians Is that your subjects' idea of equity, to put those ...

LET T = $(\sim S / N)$ & $(S / \sim N)$, i.e., "that"

[unconnected] with you in the same category with ... your own colonists, and some conquered rebels?

LET $\sim$ D = (MAKING) NO DISTINCTION ...

$$T \vdash \sim D \quad \& \quad \dagger D \qquad (6), \text{ a logical entailment}$$

Athenians [Yes!] ...they think one has as much of [right] as another,...

$$! \sim D \qquad (7)$$

if any maintain their independence, it is because they are strong, and that if we do not molest them it is because we are afraid;

LET N_1 = STILL BEING INDEPENDENT, $\sim S_1$ = THEIR STRENGTH;
AND N_2 = NOT BEING ATTACKED BY ATHENS, $\sim S_2$ = ATHENS' BEING AFRAID TO ATTACK

$$\sim D / (N_1/\sim S_1 \& N_2/\sim S_2) \quad \& \quad ! (N_1/\sim S_1 \& N_2/\sim S_2) \quad (7a)$$

so that besides extending our empire we should gain in security by your subjection; the fact that you are islanders and weaker than others rendering it all the more important that you should not succeed in baffling the masters of the sea.

LET I_1 = INCREASE IN IMPERIAL SIZE AND SECURITY,
I_2 = ATHENIAN INTEREST AS SEA RULER VIS-À-VIS ISLANDERS, AND
I_3 = PARTICULAR ATHENIAN INTEREST VIS-À-VIS WEAKER ISLANDERS

$$I \vdash I_2 \qquad (7b), \text{ an analytical entailment}$$
$$P_1 / (I_1 \& I_2 \& I_3) \quad \& \quad ! (I_1 \& I_2 \& I_3) \quad (7c)$$

Notes: Lower case texts are from the Crawley translation; interpretive insertions are indicated by square brackets – [ ]. Upper case definitions and formulae represent a Rescherian formalization.

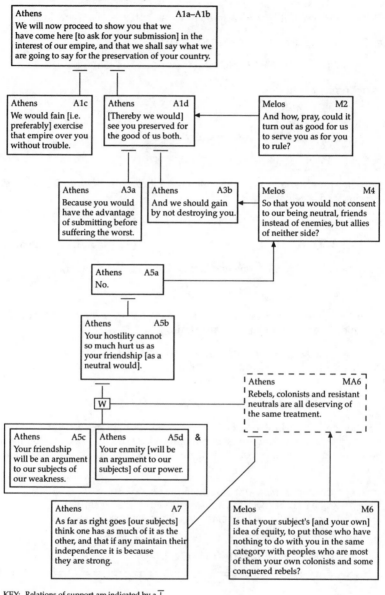

Athens   A1a–A1b

We will now proceed to show you that we have come here [to ask for your submission] in the interest of our empire, and that we shall say what we are going to say for the preservation of your country.

Athens   A1c

We would fain [i.e. preferably] exercise that empire over you without trouble.

Athens   A1d

[Thereby we would] see you preserved for the good of us both.

Melos   M2

And how, pray, could it turn out as good for us to serve you as for you to rule?

Athens   A3a

Because you would have the advantage of submitting before suffering the worst.

Athens   A3b

And we should gain by not destroying you.

Melos   M4

So that you would not consent to our being neutral, friends instead of enemies, but allies of neither side?

Athens   A5a

No.

Athens   A5b

Your hostility cannot so much hurt us as your friendship [as a neutral would].

Athens   MA6

Rebels, colonists and resistant neutrals are all deserving of the same treatment.

W

Athens   A5c

Your friendship will be an argument to our subjects of our weakness.

Athens   A5d   &

Your enmity [will be an argument to our subjects] of our power.

Athens   A7

As far as right goes [our subjects] think one has as much of it as the other, and that if any maintain their independence it is because they are strong.

Melos   M6

Is that your subject's [and your own] idea of equity, to put those who have nothing to do with you in the same category with peoples who are most of them your own colonists and some conquered rebels?

KEY: Relations of support are indicated by a ⊤
Relations of attack are indicated by ⟶
The symbol "&" is a dialogical "and"
Unlike the actual claims in solid boxes [with interpolations in square brackets],
dotted boxes contain claims inferred by disputants
A boxed W refers to a "warranting" principle used to justify a support connective

Figure 1.2   A graphic rendition of the first part of the Melian Debate

forms in Table 1.1, from categorical assertions like (1) to the provisoed counter-assertions of (3a,b) and the weak distinctions of move (4), clearly conform to Figure 1.1's evolving grammar of move, counter-move and subsequent reply possibilities. Secondly, there is the explicitly indicated turn-taking required by Rescher, involving asymmetrically defined roles. Coincident with their arriving with a major show of force, the Athenians have the proponent role, articulating the major theses of this discussion, and offering a *prima facie* argument sketch for them. As opponents, the Melians regularly question, or weakly assert their views (formulae 2, 4, 6). Thirdly, the stringent requirement of always responding to previous arguments with new and focused argumentation is also met.

Deeper analyses also support the goodness of fit. The work reported on in Table 1.1 shows how subsequent parts of the debate are in fact critical, sustained, increasingly penetrating elaborations of theses directly spun off from the Athenians' main arguments of their first move. Thus both P_1 and P_2 are attacked and defended in a provisoed way, with (7c) being a very significant restatement of probative grounds for P_1, clearly more persuasive than those offered in the preliminary argument sketch. Moreover, in the substructure of the elaborated theses, and the use of distinction-based respecifications of positions, one finds here strong support for the centrality of *ceteris paribus* inference in (at least classical) political argumentation, thought of as a kind of provisoed assertion that subsumes standard formal inference[23] and encourages novel, more adequate substantive reformulations. With some interesting variations, Figure 1.2 suggests a parsimonious graphical treatment of the syntactic and focusing aspects of these structural dependencies.[24] The approach has, moreover, recently

---

[23] As for Figure 1.1's, and Rescher's, subsumptive approach toward standard formal logic, the fit is pretty good, considering the distances involved. Allowing speakers to make several arguments in one turn is required to fit Thucydides' texts, but it is not a fundamental problem. There are at least several cases where roughly equivalent versions of the same proposition, e.g., P_1, P_2, I, S, N, T and D (and their negations) are logically substituted for each other in a modern way. Moreover, an apparently analytic entailment claim appears when the Athenian interest in controlling islands is inferred without further evidence from her interest and internal nature as a "master of the seas" (7b). Only fragments of the sentential calculus were recognized, however, in Classical Greek times.

[24] In addition to using a variant of the Crawley translation – a way of gauging the variability of translations and their dialogical consequences – Figure 1.2 generalizes the provisoed support and attack relations of Figure 1.1. Moreover, the debatable simplifying methodological requirement of having each move focused on only one

been applied with apparent success to the rest of the debate (Patomäki 1992: 303).[25]

Let me elaborate more fully on two places where the attempt to fit Rescher's formalism to Thucydides' text not only supports the goodness of fit, but helps us extend Rescher's analysis. First of all, the Melian attempt to reformulate Athenian imperial interest so that it is consistent with Melian neutrality – the weak distinction of move (4) in the table and M4 in the figure – is an especially creative, revealing (as well as practically crucial) reformulation.[26] Note that in the subsequent round, the Athenians are put on the defensive, to the extent that they are induced explicitly to assert the denial of the Melian neutrality thesis. The argumentative requirement to support this new, negative claim produces moves (5a,b) in the table (A5c, A5d in the figure), which in turn allow the most revealing – and for a relatively neutral Greek determiner, probably decisive – move by the Melians: their inferential assertion of the Athenians' underlying warrant of no difference, no differentiation, no distinction in conduct expected from

---

[25] earlier move of the other side led – in the presence of Thucydides' obviously lengthier texts – to the breaking down into smaller components of the argument of the original texts. Thus whereas for round 5, Table 1.1 has the Athenians uttering three separable claims, Figure 1.2 separates out four. Adding a separate, "No"-supporting, box A5b including "Your hostility cannot so much hurt us ..." allows the earlier "No" to attack Melian move 4, and move fragments A5a and A5b to be treated as (elaborating) supports for A5b. But there is no separately numbered formula corresponding to the intermediate formulation of A5b in Table 1.1; hence the formal expression numbering system of the table has different subscripts than those used for labeling figure boxes. Both approaches handle explicitly the Melian's creative anaphora in intuiting the implicit warranting premise of the Athenians (formula 6 and the two preceding LET definitions) in the table and the inferred, dotted box MA6 in the figure, but the Devereux style graph of Figure 1.2 seems to do a more suggestive representational job here. Rescherian dialogic and Devereux–Alker style graphing still need better ways of handling elaborations and sequences of arguments.

[25] Patomäki's impressive reformulation of the previously published parts of this chapter deserves further discussion at greater length than is possible here. His most ambitious misspecification treats the entire Melos episode as iconically modeled history, with different actors, possessing different resources, conducting themselves according to modes of communicative and strategic interaction governed by regulative and constitutive rules (Patomäki 1992: 307–325).

[26] Rescher's description (1977: 66f) of "constructive negation" exactly fits the creativity of Melian distinction making: "When P/Q is succeeded by ~P / (Q & R), there is not just the displacement from P to ~P", but also the refinement (amplification, improvement) from Q to (Q & R) ... it advances the discussion and shifts the issue onto a more sophisticated ground."

neutrals, colonists and rebels, which at move 7 the Athenians clearly accept.

For a society in which (according to Aristotle) justice is defined among educated citizens in terms of proportionality, or appropriate distinction, not only does this admission speak against the Athenians on this point, it contradicts their own expressed preference not to talk of the justice of their actions. Seen through neorealist lenses, external insecurity is pressuring the Athenians to take actions decreasing the security (and independent existence) of others. More dialectically, the Athenians who once fought the Persians to set free Greek city states under their sway are now following the same expansive imperial logic of subjugation, or worse, without the Melians having given any offense. The side which has "won" the debate at this point must soon, tragically, pay with their lives.[27]

As a second example of its deep fit with the creative powers of discovery implicit in Thucydides' use of Rescher-like procedures, let us look more closely at formulae (7a,b,c), which are not graphed in Figure 1.2. Although the Athenians may not at that moment recognize it, at this point Thucydides reports that Athens has moved into an especially insecure and cruel phase of the war.[28] In steps (7b,c) there occurs a new, more revealing, corresponding redefinition of the components of the Athenians' interest. Being a sea power especially worried about vitally damaging potential revolts by her subjects now constitutes the nature of Athens' fundamental interests in a new way. Such identifying interests are now defined expansively and imperialistically with respect to neutrals, without regard to previously relevant distinctions. Thucydides here reports/reconstructs/discovers underlying generic features of the Athenian state and its conduct at a new stage of its existence. The debate has succeeded in identifying what are called

[27] In work in progress, David Sylvan disputes the existence, in classical Greece, of what Hedley Bull calls an "anarchical society of states" in which a right to independence is mutually recognized. Therefore I have resisted making here the even more dialectical claim that the Athenians are acting in ways that contradict the social principles constituting their own identity and independence.

[28] Cogan (1981: 92ff.) gives more specifics: "What is 'new' in this Athenian argument [at Melos] is an urgent anxiety about the solidity of their hold on their allies." Neutrality of islands like Melos can no longer be tolerated; a neutral middle ground is destroyed and "truly total war" develops. Although, as David Sylvan (1994) and others have argued, enslavement of Greek losers and killing of defeated soldiers was not new to the war, the degeneration in rationales from that of Pericles' funeral oration – treating colonials equally in the law courts – to that of Diodotus in the Mytilene debate – treating subjects moderately by only killing ringleaders of the revolt – is palpable.

identity-modifying or identity-sustaining "internal relations" in the Hegelian, Marxist and European analytical traditions.[29]

On the basis of these two extended examples, I can enthusiastically support Rescher's claim that his controversy-oriented dialectics can, and has, produced new knowledge. Each of the formulae (7, 7a, 7b and 7c) of the seventh round of the debate is part of such an argument.[30] Rescher's preference for a dialectics of probative reasoning, one that does not challenge provisoed assertions *per se*, however, seems somewhat too restrictive.[31]

With Rescher's mediating assistance, I have now shown how the "mother of all idealist-realist debates" was recorded, reconstructed and/or composed according to a remarkably sophisticated version of dialectics. By demonstrating that Thucydides' rigorous reconstructive discipline – which appears to have been developed through his exposure to teachers working in the traditions of the Sophists – corresponds in detail with a philosophically sophisticated contemporary theory of controversy-based knowledge cumulation, I have strengthened arguments both for the seriousness and the worth of his version of classical dialectical inquiry as at least a potential contributor to scientific knowledge.[32]

---

[29] Rescher understandably sidesteps the difficult issue of how formally to represent internal relations in his *Dialectics*. Briefly, "internal relations," like Hegel's master-bondsman relationship, are those relations (partially) constitutive of the generic features, the identities (or defining essences) of the entities being related. Without slavery (an internal relations), it has often been said, there would not be any masters. Elster (1978) argues that power is an "internal relation." Ollman (1977) shows how central they are to the Marxist tradition. Relevant formalisms are further discussed in Chapter 5 below.

[30] Because dialectical negation is not just displacement, but *refinement*, the classical, formally correct, law of double negation ($\sim\sim P = P$) is pragmatically abandoned, replaced by the possibility (seen in the seventh round of the debate) of "constructive negation" – an original thesis being *aufgehoben*, preserved in a refined form that arises out of constructive, critical debate. Rescher (1977: 66–72) refers to this as a knowledge enhancing "cycle of probative dialectic" with an Hegelian aspect, revealed with the help of "inconsistency tolerant logic."

[31] If one recognizes that P_1 might aptly be respecified as I/M , where M = (Melian) SUBMISSION, one sees more clearly the intimate connections between the earliest and later stages of the argumentation. Indeed, the challenges to P_1 can all be said to challenge this implicit assertive connective.

[32] Finley (1942: 37–73) has several things to say about the Sophistic movement that support my use of Rescher's more fully articulated dialectics. First, it is "obvious" that they are the main figures in Thucydides' background, and that they led the Greeks away from poetic to more naturalistic, realistic, truer if less moral explanations. Next, the Sophists reflected the change in mood in Athens away from heroic

The rebirth of a methodology

Because of the centrality of formal schematizations in Rescher's approach, my considerable success in using these and their derivatives in formally representing the Athenian–Melian exchange entitles me to describe the resulting formalizations as successful qualitative measurements. This is an unanticipated additional result of an effort to respecify as formally as possible, and illustrate, the workings of Thucydides' dialectically interpretive methodology.

Two special problems with reading Rescher's approach to dialectics in a methodologically suggestive way should be mentioned. Observe that the stated interpretation of P_1 is based on an interpolation in Thucydides' text, rather than its actual words. Perhaps one approaches the limits of Rescher's rather elementary formalism when one recognizes the need, in the interests of coherence, to interpolate such context-sensitive theses concerning Athenian and Melian interests in the first round of the argument. The question of what perspective to bring to bear in making such context-sensitive sense remains a difficult hermeneutic challenge in the making of such interpolations, and more generally. Also, given the need for this particularly complex anaphoric linguistic capacity (Ristad 1993), this kind of interpolation is not yet (and may never be) an easy, reliably automated procedure: taken literally, the Athenians are both powerfully and synthetically *allusive* (e.g., "what we are now going to say" is the same kind of demonstrative anaphora as the "that" of move 6) and *elliptical* (e.g., "we are come here" as a substitute for an explicit statement of purposes only inferable from common knowledge, indexical situation descriptions and the larger body of Thucydides' text).

Although much needs to be done in further specifying how

efforts of liberation of the Greeks from the Persians toward a subtly darker, more realist vision of human beings preoccupied with the struggle for power. Thirdly, Cogan's excellent point that Thucydides introduced debates into his text in order most precisely to clarify moments of decision fits the Sophist Protagoras' dialectics, his "method of searching antithesis," which as part of Thucydides' training probably left the "habit of grasping ideas by pairs and in contrasts fixed in his mind." Fourth, the Sophists introduced the arguments from "likelihood," from "advantage," from "expediency" or interest, from the "generic" or "typical" or "probable" aspects of human "nature" into public discourse. "No other trait of the Greek mind more clearly reveals the humanistic character of their civilization" than the "ability to convey the generic without falsifying the unique." Here is the deep, ontological basis for using revisable claims or Rescherian dialogic, and searching for more penetrating formulations, allowing *ceteris paribus* exceptions!

rigorously, reliably and validly this methodology of adversarial inquiry should be taught, applied and further developed,[33] the reborn Protagoras-Thucydides-Rescher mode of analysis is at the very least, a rigorous, informed, generalizable methodology for representing important aspects of the content, structure and flow of political argumentation processes, whose relevance extends across at least 2,400 years of Western civilization! I have thus discovered within Thucydides' most famous debate, a specific dialectical logic, data theory and methodology generally relevant for reconstructing, formally representing, and scientifically assessing, the content and form of political and diplomatic arguments. Others, cited along the way, have helped this reformulation. From the womb of classical, dialectical realism has appeared a new modality of political methodology, or poli(s)metrics.

Reconstructing the Melian Dialogue as part of a scientific process

The disciplined way Thucydides probes for possibly general underlying causes and reasons for action surely conforms to an important sense of the scientific character of the work. Illustrative application of a revealing, modestly replicable, politics-appropriate, "data-making" methodology surely qualifies as a scientific accomplishment. What more of a scientific character does Thucydides' dialectical approach to the Melian Dialogue have to offer?

Rescher (1977: 54–58) proposes a common input-output structure for rational inquiry that includes an Albert–Popper model of science as a possibly endless cycle of explanatory conjectures, flaw-probing experimental tests that sometimes produce refutations, and revised theories and conjectures. I have just shown how formula (7c) at the end of the formalized section of the Melian Dialogue instantiated this notion of a "cycle of probative inquiry." Probative inquiry and disputation, if they too are allowed to recycle, possibly with different participants, have a similar feedback-like structure, where "flaw-probing counter-argument" can have either an intellectual or an empirical cast. That way provisoed presuppositions can be revised in a later round, just as scientific and philosophical theories often are.

The polite, cautious, carefully questioning, cooperative yet critical

---

[33] The textually oriented literature on the formal modeling of conversational argumentation suggests many improvements beyond the relative simplicity of the present exercise. See especially Ashley (1990) and Reichman (1985).

truth-seeking style of Melian interventions suggests another aspect of an iterative, more comprehensive, social-historical conception of science. That style fits well the formal manner of public dissertation criticism (and defense) still practiced in European universities 2,400 years later![34]

In scientific discussions, failures of serious efforts at testing one's hypotheses are considered valuable. Whether or not the student successfully defends his or her thesis, he or she is expected – like audiences and judges alike – to have learned from that experience. Overall knowledge has increased. One can successfully defend the falsification of someone else's thesis. Of course, we suspect that the Melian arguers eventually paid with their lives – of greater value than a successful thesis defense – and gained an uncertain immortality, thanks to Thucydides, by doing so. But in Thucydides' history, the Melians and the Athenians were their own, very practically concerned judges. Subsequent readers, Thucydides' audience, are thus the necessary, hopefully more impartial judges of his political science.

A single chapter or a book of consistently argued chapters does not make a science; the Melian Dialogue is at best a vivid part of a larger scientific enterprise. A continuing community attempting to test its hypotheses further and revising them when they fail, is required. Given schools where they were regularly taught and used as bases for making critical interpretive sense of other historical events, the movement from Homer to Herodotus to Thucydides may well have evidenced such progress; perhaps it is better described as an evolving *tradition* of investigation. Probably Livy and Tacitus can be seen in these lights as well. But it is not until the Islamic/European Renaissance that such a line of writers can be reidentified. Stricter definitions of disciplinarity see International Relations as a separate discipline

---

[34] Having been a member of the audience for (Uppsala, 1987) Lars Udehn's sociological Ph.D. defense, having thus participated in an ancient but living dialectical institution whose history is very little known to North Americans, I am emboldened to suggest that a more scientifically oriented version of Rescher's formalization in Table 1.1 should be extended to include the reflective, cooperative, role-reversing requirements that opponents summarize the proponent's argument to the proponent's satisfaction before proceeding to criticize it, and that the proponent thank the opponent for his/her valued, yet critical contributions before the judges vote on the acceptability of the thesis. These, and other, ways in which "debates" supersede "games" have been ably argued in the largely ignored final chapters of Rapoport (1960), the only assigned sympathetic methodological discussion of dialectics oriented toward its potential contributions to social science I encountered as a graduate student, thanks to Karl W. Deutsch.

claiming Thucydides as a founder only coming into existence in the present century. We, his readers interested in historical, theoretical and practical lessons, are thus the living, if uncertain and frequently contradictory, proofs of his scientific success.

Other dialectical elements in Thucydides' Melian Dialogue

Of the twenty-six speeches and one dialogue in Thucydides' history, seventeen plus the one dialogue occur as parts of political debates on eight different occasions, which Cogan (1981: 3–8) cogently suggests are those decisive moments, the beginnings of new intentions, aims, policies, actions whose deliberative aspects deserve special analytical attention. Consistent with Protagoras' "method of searching antitheses," why does the most penetrating of these spoken encounters – the dialogue allowing focused interruptions – occur only here, at what many would say was a strategically insignificant incident in the war?[35] I accept Jaeger's, Finley's and Cogan's answers as far as they go: Thucydides used the most penetrating tool in his scholarly repertoire uniquely at this point: to convey new motivational information; to probe deeply into the deepest moral issue of the war;[36] to delineate the third, the cruellest and most active, post-truce phase of the war, and a phase where "military actions assumed prime importance" (Cogan

[35] That a somewhat looser form of continuing, past-reflective, but still formalizable argumentation exists in other deliberations than the Melian Dialogue is convincingly argued in Mefford (1985). Although his PROLOG implemented examples of reflective argumentation processes have several technical advantages when compared to Rescher's simpler formalisms, even they might be more rigorous reanalyzed in terms of second order quantified predicate calculus, raising the deeper issue of the representational adequacy of standard logical formalisms for pragmatic-linguistic purposes.

[36] Jaeger (1976: 401–402) argues that in the Melian Dialogue, Thucydides uses the dialogue form – a

> sophistic device which occurs nowhere else in his book – to show the two opponents parrying argument by argument ... and to eternalize the painful conflict of might and right in all its inescapable necessity. It is impossible to doubt that he composed this [private] debate ... with entire freedom of intervention, to express the conflict of two unreconcilable principles ... the right of the stronger through the law of nature ... and the forces of religion and morality. The very nature of the form he chooses to expand the conflict shows that it can never reach a final decision, for the strength of the sophistic debates ... lay not in finding the solution to a problem but in stating both sides as clearly as possible.

1981: 158–158); and, dramatically, to show Athens is at her self-destructive worst, pursuing an aggressively expansive imperial policy while increasingly divided at home by leadership cabals. From the point of view of writing more dramatically compelling history, many have noted that the slaughter of the Melians is followed immediately by a new book (Book VI) beginning Thucydides' dramatic account of Athens' fateful, self-defeating effort to conquer all of Sicily (Cornford 1971).

Even Jaeger grudgingly admits that the literary form of Thucydides' history is tragic, but how does this connect to any general account (like Burke's given below) of the "dialectics of tragedy?" Surely, too, the dramaturgy claimed to exist here must be related to his argumentative science and his dialectical ontology. Beyond referring to the ontological ground of his scientific analysis of the Athenians, the Spartans and the other war parties, I shall try more generally to connect Thucydides' "dialectical" approach to the manner in which Thucydides most penetratingly conveys the most important "lessons" contained in the multiple success and failure stories, the tragedies and comedies of *The Peloponnesian War*.

Events data, speeches and judgments in Thucydides' approach

Let us begin with the way Thucydides interrelates events and speeches. As Finley observes in his Introduction to the updated Crawley edition (Thucydides 1951: xii, my emphasis), Thucydides' historiography "uniquely *combined* opposite tendencies of dialectic and observation, of generalization and observation ..." Throughout the book, there are speeches which regularly come before the great actions (or "motions") of his story. This sequencing is an explicit aspect of his interpretive, explanatory methodology mentioned previously and now quoted explicitly: "my habit has been to make the speakers say what was in my opinion demanded of them by the various occasions, of course adhering as closely as possible to the general sense of what they really said" (I.21).

When speeches reporting alternative ways of one side's responding to a situation are reported, Cogan's detailed discussions make clear that the speeches are included to help clarify shared or contrasting perceptions, interpretations, deliberative or justifying rationales, and the resulting actions and their (often unanticipated) consequences at the main turning points in the war. As White (1984: 59–71) argues concerning the interstate diplomacy, these speeches reflect a changing "culture of argument," a performable repertoire or grammar of arguments and counter-arguments focused on justice, expediency and gratitude. The bearers of this diplomatic community of argument derive from it a presentable sense of self, as well as a vocabulary for defining their interests in a justifiable fashion.

Given his evolving understanding of the significance of various events, and even the likelihood that many of the speeches were written or rewritten after the narrative was nearly finished, it is not surprising that they reveal a remarkable artistic unity (Jaeger 1976: 342–347; Kagan 1975: 77). It is highly plausible, therefore, to look for Thucydides' own interpretations and analysis of events and their motives in the contents and oppositions apparent in almost all his speeches.

Just such a series of contrasts, noted by many commentators, is the difference between Pericles, Diodotus, Nicias, Cleon and Alcibiades. Alcibiades is described by Plutarch, but not by Thucydides, as the principal mover of the degrees ordering the slaughter of the Melians (Cornford 1971). He appears to be a most influential advocate of an invasion of Sicily. Thucydides himself makes a rare explicit judgment, not in a speech, but in comments that constitute his encomium for Pericles at his death, two and a half years after the war began.

> The correctness of his previsions ... became better known by his death. He told them to wait quietly ... to attempt no new conquests.... [Rather,] what they did was the very contrary, allowing private ambitions ... to lead them into projects whose success would only conduce to the honour and advantage of private persons. [Moreover,] committing even the conduct of state affairs to the whims of the multitude ... produced a host of blunders, and amongst them the Sicilian expedition; though this failed not so much through a miscalculation of the power [of the Sicilians] ... as through a fault in the senders ... choosing rather [than continuing to help] ... to occupy themselves with private cabals for the leadership of the commons ... [which] first introduced civil discord at home.   (II.65–66)

Historically, these last remarks refer at least in part to the public's love-hate relationship with Alcibiades, whose beauty, passion and "can do" daring they idolized, but whom they distrusted as a possible tyrant. He was recalled from Sicily under false suspicions of treason, weakening the war leadership and provoking his defection to the Spartans, whom he then mobilized against Athens. Further civil strife after the disaster of the Sicilian expedition also helped pave the way for the final defeat of Athens.

The above, extensive and rather exceptional quote confirms, then, the interpretation we have made on other grounds, that speeches like the Melian Dialogue are to be considered comparatively for their implicit judgmental implications about the motives of the principal actors in Thucydides' history. To use more contemporary language, major event data sequences must be supplemented by dialectically interpretive, even judgmental, accounts of the principal actors' reasoning, standards of action and motivations – if Thucydides' model historiography is to be revived by contemporary analysts. This view is a far cry from any positivist perspectives calling for mathematical, value-free, historical-political science.

Thucydides' symbolic oppositions and principled contradictions

In Rescher's suggestive view, the dialectic of the Melian Debate points toward a controversy-based path of knowledge cumulation. I have accepted Jaeger's similar claim that the format of that debate fits a penetrating investigative purpose, augmenting this analysis by stressing the complementary value of both clinically observed event sequences and judgmentally contrasted speeches from related occasions.

But the dialogue form points further for our understanding: in the manner of the Sophists, it highlights the contradictions, literally the speakings-against-one-another, articulated in his analytically reconstructed debates. As we have just seen again, the reader is induced to see the personae of such debates as articulating contradictory principles or forces, viz. moderation vs. excess, might vs. right. Frequently the debaters are leaders of different city-states or their contending factions; sometimes they are spokespersons for, or symbols of, a frail but larger collective will politically composed out of contradictory inputs.

Cornford, Finley, Jaeger and Strauss, among others, have all stressed Thucydides' stylistic or methodological appeal to symbolic, articulated oppositions. Finley (Thucydides 1951: xii–xiii) argues that the contrasts of Athens to Sparta starts off Thucydides' work, reaching a climax in the victory of Athens at Pylos in Book Four, based on the following of a Periclean harassment strategy, and dies away in the Sicilian disaster of Books Six and Seven (with the Melian conference as prologue). Elaborating a theme we have already seen in the Melian Dialogue's explanatory account, Athens is characterized as a naval power, based on an extensive commercial economy and political democracy (excluding women and slaves, but typically including many of the militarily and economically necessary oarsmen); Sparta's nature is that of a land power, based on helot agriculture, controlled by a conservative oligarchy and a weak, rotating monarchy. Athens "encourages enterprise and initiative; Sparta emphasizes tenacity and tradition." These differences are discussed at length in the introductory sections (V84 and V85) and the later parts (V97, 99, 107–111) of the Melian Conference that have only briefly been referred to heretofore.

A second principled contrast, also suggested above, includes and extends beyond the Melian Dialogue. It contrasts "the wisely led democracy of Pericles to the corrupt democracy of his successors ... [first visible in the] symptoms of mistake and misgovernment in the Mytilenian debate ... generalized in the fearful analysis of revolution [a brutal Corcyrean class war] ... made operative in the refusal of Sparta's offer of peace after Pylos, and reaching its height in the Melian Dialogue at the end of Book Five and the Sicilian disaster of Book Seven" (Cornford 1971: Chs. 10–12, also the source of some of the above translations).

On the basis of a close but sometimes controversial reading of Thucydides' text, Leo Strauss also stresses major, principled oppositions as a fundamental preoccupation of Thucydides' writing: Athens represents "daring, progress, and the arts"; Sparta, "moderation and the divine law." The Alcibiades vs. Nicias debate over Sicily contrasts motion and rest, seen by Strauss (very dialectically) as internal reflections of the larger opposition of Athenian activism and Sparta's relative passiveness (Strauss 1978: 145–162, 192–209; also Finley in Thucydides 1951: xiii; Thucydides I.68ff.).

Moreover, there is the opposition between the Hobbesian "original and universal insecurity" and the later "security, power, and wealth" of state success resulting for some in "Greekness, the union of freedom and love of beauty." The Greek vs. Barbarian theme Strauss sees in the lavish Alcibiades–Nicias expedition to Sicily, with its parallels in Herodotus' history of Xerxes' fated attack on all of Greece. Virtually the same critical characterization of Athenian remarks in the Melian Dialogue was made by a classical commentator Dionysus, cited at length by Cornford: "Such words would be appropriate to an oriental monarch addressing Greeks" (Cornford 1971: 176). Surely this opposition is meant to be a condemnatory one.

Strauss puts some of the above oppositions into a partial hierarchy of dialectical distinctions: "Just as humanity divides itself into Greeks and barbarians, Greekness in its turn has two poles, Sparta and Athens. The fundamental opposition of motion and rest returns on the level of Greekness; Sparta cherishes rest whereas Athens cherished motion" (Strauss 1978: 157). Interestingly, figures like the agile Spartan Brasidas and the moderate and hesitant Athenian Nicias combine such traits in differing degrees. Even more remarkable (and extreme) is Strauss' argument:

> [In] the Peloponnesian War ... one sees Greeks at their peak in motion; one sees the beginning of the descent. The peak of Greekness is the peak of humanity. The Peloponnesian War and what it implies exhausts the possibilities of man.... All human life moves between the poles of war and peace, and between the poles of barbarism and Greekness. By studying the Peloponnesian War Thucydides grasps the limits ... the nature of all human things. It is for this reason that his work is a possession for all times. (Strauss 1978: 157)

Despite an ethnocentric excess, these truly remarkable quotations may be said provisionally to complete[37] the quest signaled by Thucydides' own words, and well begun in the Melian Dialogue's searching pursuit of the deeper bases of Athenian action (and Spartan inaction, since at the end of the Melian Episode they do not come to the aid of their descendants).

By way of additional commentary, note the claim that substantial oppositions grounded in human nature limit or exhaust the possibilities of historical observation. The thought is at once dialectical – in its revelatory search for fundamental oppositions – and grammatical – in its suggestion of a grammar of motives, or of opposed organizing principles spanning or generating the space of possible human political activity. The notion of Thucydides' science in this respect remarkably parallels what I have called the dialectical-hermeneutic orientation in recent philosophy of social science; Habermas would

---

[37] Comparisons of gendered differences in "manliness" orientations, Helot/slave dependencies, degrees of militarism, and the effects of different personalities, *inter alia*, are plausible extensions of these self-constituting explanatory distinctions. Additionally, if falsifiable interpretations are our goal, comparable ways of arguing from action reports to their principled bases, including measures of degrees of fit, are required. This topic receives further discussion in Chapters 3 and 8 below.

similarly characterize Thucydides as doing *reconstructive-research* rather than *empirical-analytical science.*[38]

If the opposed generative principles of Greekness and barbarism, war (motion) and peace (rest), etc., delimit human possibilities, they also show why history contains both novelty and a tendency to repeat itself. It should be clear that Thucydides the Athenian, proud of Pericles' "school of Hellas," but equally sensitive to, and appreciative of, Spartan "moderation," certainly preferred "Greek" to "barbarian" conduct. Both a Hobbesian state of nature *and* more civilized behavior exist within this restricted catalogue of human potentialities. Thus, rather than advocating the cynical realism of "might vs. right," we may interpret Thucydides' own view of human nature and politics as closer to E.H. Carr's variant: realism without idealism is sterile; idealism without realism is utopian (Carr 1946).

The ontological foundations of Thucydides' oppositions

Thucydides' contrasts and oppositions have cultural roots, grounded in civilizational ontologies. Perhaps the most adequate modern reconstruction of Thucydides' ontology is a dramatist one, in the sense of Kenneth Burke.[39] In his *A Grammar of Motives*, Burke systematically explores possible answers to "What is involved when we say what people are doing and why they are doing it?" (Burke 1969: xv–xxiii). In an Aristotelian vein, he argues that "any complete statement about motives will offer *some kind* of answers to these five questions: What was done (act), when or where it was done (scene), who did it (agent), how he did it (agency), and why (purpose)." Besides invoking "necessary" or "internal" links from action components to basic human characteristics, the search for motivational explanations in Thucydides' speeches, although never finally adequate, also seeks enlightenment in the interrelationships of human acts, scenes, agencies and purposes. "Dialectical substance ... derives its character from the systematic contemplation of the antinomies attendant upon the fact that we necessarily define a thing in terms of something else" (Burke 1969: 33).

Therefore the many ironies of Thucydides' dialogues may well be grounded in a dialectical concept of substance linking but contrasting

---

[38] See the relevant discussion of Table Intro.1 in the Introduction above, and associated citations.

[39] For a lucid introduction to, and systematization of, Burke's approach by a political scientist, see Roig (1977).

one motivational element in terms of another. Thus the idea of dialectical substance expressing itself in different ways in the previously reviewed opposition of Sparta and the Athenians, plus their allies and colonies, suggests a deeper cause of the "necessity" of the Peloponnesian War: the events there are not all unavoidable, but they do reflect the underlying, internally related characteristics of its principal antagonists.

Thucydides' dialectics of tragedy and science

At last we come to a central argument about Thucydides' historical-political science: his study of power politics is essentially dramatic. Specifically it is a dramatic collection of tragedies and comedies, written with the constraint of being objectively true to historical facts and to human nature, as he understood it. More technically put, his use of dialectical substance, "the overall category of dramatism," conforms to the dramatist's search for the roots of human action in the terms of verbal action (Burke 1969: 33).

Early on, we noted the distinctions between Thucydides' naturalistic narratives and his probing, interpretative speeches. "When men are treated in terms of other things, men may even be said to speak for the dumb objects [or forces] of nature." Burke then goes on to characterize his dialectical conception of tragedy (and science):

> Galileo speaks of experimental testing as an "ordeal." Stated broadly, the dialectical (agonistic) approach to knowledge is through the act of assertion, whereby one suffers or calls forth as counter-assertions the kind of knowledge that is the reciprocal of his act. This is the process embodied in tragedy, where the agent's action involves a corresponding passion, and from the sufferance of the passion [by the original agent or the empathetic observer] there arises an understanding of the act, an understanding that transcends the act. In this final state of tragic vision, intrinsic and extrinsic motivations are merged ... [A]lthough purely circumstantial factors participate ... they bring about a *representative* kind of accident ... that belongs with the agent's particular kind of character. (Burke 1969: 38)

How does this dramatic conception of tragedy, which fits so closely Rescher's probative dialectic of knowledge seeking, apply to Thucydides' work in general, and to the Melian Dialogue in particular? Several strands of affirmative argument converge.

First, Leo Strauss emphasizes in his commentary Thucydides' effort to prove the Peloponnesian War a greater one than all previous ones experienced by the Greeks, e.g., their war against Xerxes and the Persians. Thucydides is quite clear why this is the case: because of the exceptional level of earthquakes, plagues and other "natural" calamities associated with it, and, less religiously, because of the magnitude of "misfortunes" associated with it (I.24). Or, as Strauss says, the "war surpassed the Persian War in regard to human suffering, caused (intrinsically) by men and (extrinsically) by nature" (Strauss 1978: 150).

I suggest that this strange list makes sense in terms of Burke's above notion of the dialectics of tragedy and science, which even has a mathematical aspect. Two relevant "commonsense" Greek proverbs cited by Burke (1969: 39f) are: *ta patemata mathemata* (roughly, "the suffered is the learned") and *poiemata, pathemata, mathemata* (roughly, "an action or deed or poem produces a passive suffering, followed by learning"). Quite opposite from Jaeger's quotation at the beginning of this chapter, Burke argues that in these sayings: "We can ... catch glimpses of a relation between dialectics and [Platonic] mathematics ... in the fact that *mathemata* means both things learned ... and the mathematical sciences ..." Thus, in an inherently tragic dialectic, "the act organizes the opposition (brings to the fore whatever factors resist or modify the act), that the agent 'suffers' this opposition, and as he learns to take the oppositional motives into account, widening his terminology accordingly, he has arrived at a higher order of understanding." Similarly, Strauss (1978: 162) refers to war as a "violent teacher." Living through the history, showing the passions of the major players (especially as their motives are revealed in Thucydides' carefully constructed speeches), we learn valuable lessons from it.

The suffering theme reappears in the Sicilian tragedy, to which the Melian Debate is prologue. Alcibiades' rhetoric incites the popular assembly with remarks about warlike Athens, following her nature, her true character, attempting to conquer all of Sicily. Like Thucydides, Athens and the reader "suffer" the kind of knowledge resulting from this act. As a Burkean "representative anecdote," the Melian episode reveals in advance this tragedy. In the moral psychology of the time, the blindness of "tyrannical Eros," of blind Athenian Hybris and its insolent defiance of the gods. Besides paralleling Herodotus' moral-laden history of Xerxes' over-extension, it instances the Aeschylian mythic notion that God "uses the tragic passions themselves as agents of punishment" (Cornford 1971: 234). The dramatic irony of the Athenians' criticism of the *Melians'* blind hope in the second substantive argument of the Dialogue is devastating with respect to their own eventual end, and because it extends indirectly to Athens' bitter capitulation at the end of the Peloponnesian War.

How does this sense of the tragic in the Melian Dialogue link to the larger history? At the fateful turning point of the war, "The dialogue on Melos separates the Spartan comedy from the Athenian tragedy" (Strauss 1978: 225). Arguing much like Cornford, Strauss continues: "the core of the work is in the two sequels 'Funeral Speech-Plague' and 'Melian Dialogue-Sicilian Disaster'" (Strauss 1978: 227n39). Note how the social disintegration through the disease of internal cabals is a part of this second plot line. Similarly, White (1984) argues that the Athenian rhetoric of imperial interest destroys the capacity to form or to maintain "a larger community with others or to claim a consistent character for oneself: indeed it is to lose the power of practical reason. This is what Thucydides will show in the Melian dialogue" (White 1984: 76ff.). White sees the men of Melos as having died trying to preserve their own sense of identity; correlatively, he sees, in the collapse of the intercity culture of argumentation evident at Melos, the destruction of the cultural terms by which the Athenians defined their own identities and their own self-interest.[40]

Both interpretations are tragic ones. I suggest that the mathematics appropriate to these fact-consistent historical-political tragedies is not that of "mere power politics," but rather that of nature-linked dramatic plot possibilities, of comic or self-destructively tragic stories. An exploration of the relevant "structuralist" literature is Alker (1987).[41] It offers a mathematical-historical way of spelling out, in a testable fashion, how the suffered is the learned!

The most dramatic piece of evidence of Thucydides' dramatism, I have saved until last. It is the hardest, too, for twentieth-century scholars trained in the rigorous separation of facts and values, to appreciate. It makes the greatest sense once the clear scientific character of the Dialogue's analysis has been accepted – either as Classical

[40] Aron (1984: 23) makes these points more epigrammatically: "Politics is dialectic when it unfolds between men who mutually acknowledge each other. It is war when it brings into opposition men who ... wish to remain strangers to one another.... By the same token, we perceive why war is the completion of politics and at the same time its negation." To be valid at the intercity level these arguments require, what David Sylvan (1994) disputes, the existence in the argumentative *culture* of Thucydides' Greece, *and inter-city practices*, some kind of anarchical *society* built up by the states and their inhabitants.

[41] See Chapters 3 and 8 below.

dialectic or in some modern, e.g., Rescherian, reconstruction thereof. *At the same time that it is a turning point in Thucydides' entire "scientific history," the Melian Dialogue is pure drama.* To quote Cornford, at the point in the Melian conference where the dialogue begins, "the historian changes from narrative to full dramatic form, prefixing as in a play, the names – 'Athenians,' 'Melians' – to the speeches."[42] The dialogue was, in fact, a principal feature of Greek tragedy of the period, as practiced by Euripides and others. By Thucydides' shifting into this form, Cornford argues, the dramatic ironies of this pivotal turning point are highlighted. These concern the excessive emotions infecting both the Athenians and the Melians. When we understand that theater in Athens was an accepted part of the political dialogue, a way – like Thucydides' history – of attempting cathartically to instruct the Athenians about others' and their own tragic possibilities, the contradiction between "scientific history" and "drama" at least partly resolves. Aron similarly suggests that Thucydides' insertion of socio-logical analysis into his narrative allows him *"at the same time"* "the result of art" and "the reflection of reality" (Aron 1984: 28, his emphasis and mine).

It turns out, then, that the Melian Dialogue is a key scene in a scientifically written classical morality play about might and right, not simply an eternal statement of the mathematical truths of *Realpolitik*. Blind, insolent, arrogant, lustful Athens will soon pay for her failings with the lives of many of her citizens and eventually her independence as well. Like the most thoughtful modern realists, Thucydides joins both normative and scientific investigations pointed toward the suf-fering-based "learning" of moral lessons. Surely the oppressive, self-defeating hybris of those "strong" who "do what they must" is one such historical lesson.

On the appropriation of the classics

In a recent, post-modernist treatise, *On Diplomacy*, James Der Derian has attempted "to explain a[n international political] system by studying the genesis of its internal relations, which are seen as expres-sions of alienated *powers*." International relations are thus dialectical

---

[42] Relying heavily on Dionysus, Cornford (1971: 175ff.) gives a much more extensive analysis of the structure of the Dialogue. The treatment of Cleon, the victory at Pylos, the nonmentioning of Alcibiades' role in the Melian decrees all fit into his more elaborate conception of Thucydides' dramatic craftsmanship.

mediations of estrangement. A student of a leading classicist of our era, Hedley Bull, Der Derian, too, cites the authority of Thucydides as a support for his own approach, quoting a passage pointing (ironically, we have seen) to subsequent Athenian injustice: the Corcyrans say to Athenian and Corinthian representatives on the eve of the outbreak of the Peloponnesian War: "If the Corinthians say that you have no right to receive one of their colonies into your alliance, they should be told that every colony, if it is treated properly, honours its mother city, and only becomes *estranged* when it has been treated badly. Colonists are not sent abroad to be slaves of those who remain behind, but to be their equals" (Der Derian 1987: 2–6). Since our entire effort to reconstruct Thucydides' dramaturgical historical-political science has similarly sought to uncover the inner determinants, the identity-constitutive tragedies and comedies of an increasingly alienated realm of inter-state politics, certain aspects of a neoclassical orientation can legitimately be attributed to the present effort as well.

Neoclassical polimetrics

But there is a difference. Although virtually all serious students of international politics have read (and many have taught) Thucydides' classic work, whose implicit, dialectical methodology has been available in principle *since the dawn of scientific history*, they rarely or never suggest more can be done to improve upon its explicitness, its expressive and creative power, its testability. When the formalizations suggested are so incompletely in touch with the orienting epistemologies of such a classical approach, I can agree with their reluctance. But, against that view taken to extremes, and in the hope of enlisting the scientifically oriented (Zinnes 1975; Sergeev 1986), I reassert here that the above partly *formal* analysis of the Melian Dialogue seems full of methodological potential.

What classical political argumentation can do best, if grounded in a cooperative, uncoerced, moral-political, truth-seeking orientation and used skillfully to ask the right questions – those that critically probe the more fundamental justifications – is suggest the key determinants of sociopolitical identities, actions, policies or relationships, and constructively criticize such contingently variable and valuable human things. Methodologically, Thucydides may be said hypothetically to reconstruct his dialogues in order to discover what was "demanded" of his speakers at key turning points in their histories, to compare actually observed actions, situations and characters with such "demands," and then to derive moral-political "lessons" from an observation of both their inherent features and consequent developments on the basis of further critical discussion of the feasibilities, desirabilities and necessities shaping those demands.[43]

For one trained in the powers of formal analysis, the extended version of the above exercise suggests, in clear outline, what a truly classical polimetrics of political argumentation about practical public actions and contingent constitutional structures would look like. It would be a *reflective polimetrics focused on conduct, its practical-normative justifications, its institutional contexts and their experiential contents and consequences.* It would be a polimetrics grounded in experience and rigorous argumentation more than in (quasi-)experimental inference and conventional mathematical probability and statistics.[44] Neoclassical polimetrics sees theory testing in policy oriented ways, thinking of reforms humanistically as "arguments" rather than naturalistically as "experiments" (compare Campbell 1982 and Dunn 1982). In addition to close, constructively critical interrogations of policy-makers and their self-justifying documents, supporting argumentation might include thought experiments, hypothetical or asked questions about truthful reasons for observed actions, juxtaposed with careful, comparative historical studies. Polimetrics built up from a foundation in political argumentation can help reveal the underlying, contestably

---

[43] As an example of their continuing relevance, I think it is now possible to judge Karl Deutsch's argument in the 1960s, citing Athens' self-destructive democratic imperialism far away from home as a precedent against American involvement in Vietnam. His views were more historically justified than the claims of those citing pro-involvement Manchuria and Munich precedents from the 1930s.

[44] These remarks reflect critically on Alker (1965), where I translate classical Greek political syllogisms into modern bivariate and trivariate statistical relationships, as a step toward multi-equation Simon-Blalock causal modeling (Ando, Fisher and Simon 1963); they support my hermeneutically inspired later work on polimetrics (Alker 1975, 1984). They are not meant to imply that all statistical studies of argumentation practices, their claims or consequences are inappropriate. Indeed William Riker (1984) is particularly suggestive of places where creative moves and patterned regularities in political argumentation may be found, regularities susceptible to a variety of further qualitative and quantitative analyses. The more sophisticated Wittgensteinian argument that experimental methodology cannot adequately decipher causally the linguistically mediated internal relations constituting social action was most convincingly made for social psychologists in Harré and Secord (1972); in consequence, they propose a dramatically oriented ethnomethodological approach to the analysis of social interactions very appropriate to Thucydides which has been suggestive of my own reconstructive focus on participant roles and rules here.

legitimate and possibly changing political orders, or constitutions, the principled practices and constitutive relationships which, if known, will enable further, even more penetrating, policy relevant discussions of a critical and reconstructive sort.

Retraveling from past to future

Despite its abstention from formal modes of analysis, Der Derian's genealogical approach is still just as relevant. His own comparative study of the different "common senses" of different diplomatic eras is justified as an effort to refute the existence of any ahistorical, timeless, defining essence of international politics. To study discursively, genealogically, historically the internal relations of power politics is to deny its eternal reality. My own attack here against mathematical Realpolitik fits that concern. Many of Thucydides' modern interpreters have misappropriated his name to justify their own far too eternal and timeless sounding enterprises. Should we be against all such efforts at appropriating the past? No, at least not in principle. Rather, the thesis of the present chapter is that we should be more historically and epistemologically self-aware, so that we can do a better, more modest job in retraveling such roads. Locate oneself, like Thucydides did, in the midst of contending claims about inner and outer natures, the determining realities of world politics. Try to adopt, adapt and improve on the best modes of inquiry recoverable from the past. Critically value factual accuracy, contextual appropriateness and cautious generalizability in seeking to learn precedential lessons from the past and apply them to the future.

Thus we too may participate in the engaged, dramatic, but relatively objective and analytical kind of historical political analysis that Thucydides was engaged in. Like the Athenians at Sparta before the war, or the relatively peaceful relations between Athens and its allies and subjects at that time, we can scientifically appeal to dialectical judgments, relatively unconstrained argument and counter-argument, "impartial laws ... [and] differences settled by arbitration" (I.76–77). We can join different sides of the inner contradictions of barbarians and Greeks, enlisting Thucydides' or Euripides' insights in our own political-scholarly debates. By dialectically engaging ourselves in the endless, passionate search for objectively accurate, and motivationally superior historical accounts, we critically renew the past and help create the future.

63

2 Aristotelian political methodologies

> We've lost the idea that politics are part of the humanities.
> Martha Nussbaum (1989: 459)
> Politics was always, to the Greeks, an "art" as well as a "science."
> Ernest Barker (1958: xiii)
> Nature always strives after "the better."
> Aristotle, *On Generation and Corruption* (336b28)

Inspired by Thucydides' great study of the Peloponnesian war, in chapter 1 I suggested the possibility of a neoclassical Polimetrics, dialectically grounded in human experience, focused on contextually appropriate practical-normative standards of just conduct and institutional worth; its preferred dialectical "logic" would be modern argumentation theory. In the present chapter, I shall report on further explorations of the Western classical tradition for its insights into the appropriate tasks of political inquiry. I want to suggest how a methodological rereading of Aristotle can help us revise, enlarge and carry forward the neoclassical conception of politics and political methodology presented above. This rereading will find a multidisciplinary Aristotle employing and suggesting a variety of methodologies for sociopolitical inquiry. His approaches to Political Science will be found to be grounded in three characteristically different ideal types: an Ethical Aristotle, a Synthetic Aristotle, and an Aristotle for the ages – a Cosmological Aristotle.

Why pay special attention to Aristotle in a book on international studies? What purposes have I had in recovering contemporarily oriented, methodologically relevant Aristotles? Aristotle has been arguably the most influential philosopher/practitioner of scientific and humanistic studies in the history of Western civilization.[1] He wrote influentially on logic,[2] public rhetoric,[3] poetics, natural science (several treatises on physics, others on astronomy, meteorology, the history and parts of animals, the functioning of the soul or psyche, dreaming and prophesying), metascience,[4] ethics, constitutional law and public policy,[5] as well as comparative and international politics.[6] In my attempt to fathom the shape of a contemporary, rigorous but humanistic mode of sociopolitical inquiry, he is therefore an obvious possible source of valuable instruction. Even when we disagree with his findings or standards of inquiry, it is because he built such an enduring professional identity out of such different personae that I believe that all social scientists should treat Aristotle as an ancestral scholar worthy of critical yet appreciative imitation (contrast Wallach 1992: 634).

Much of what Aristotle thought and wrote was a response to Plato's

[1] I have used McKeon (1941) for a general overview of Aristotle's work, but have also found Barker (1958), Wallach (1992), Irwin's Notes and Annotated Glossary in Aristotle (1985), and Nussbaum (1990, 1992) extremely helpful.

[2] Many political examples and methodological insights can be found in Aristotle's books focused on the instrumentalities of thought – his logical writings, known collectively as the *Organon*. Included are the *Categories*, *On Interpretation*, the two formally oriented *Analytics*, the *Topics* and *On Sophistical Refutations*, two defining works in the tradition of informal logic, typically involving reasoning from "probable," i.e., weighty, opinions.

[3] Although the *Rhetoric* overlaps a good deal with the *Topics* in discussing the commonplaces appealed to in persuasive speech, and Rescher (1987: 113) follows Aristotle in placing it within a grouping of generally oriented logical writings, other writers would classify it and the *Poetics*, which it also overlaps, as belonging to literary or humanistic studies.

[4] I use the term "metascience" to avoid the heavy biases twentieth-century positivists associate with "metaphysics," because I want the reader to attempt, in part at least, to see Aristotle through Radnitzky's ontologically sensitive approach, briefly reviewed in the Introduction. Aristotle's *Metaphysics* even includes a discussion of the measurement of the unity, plurality, difference and contrariety of things (1052a15–1059a14). Unless otherwise noted, my quotations to Aristotle's works are from McKeon (1941). To facilitate cross-references to other editions, citations will be to the standard Greek texts.

[5] Of his collection of 158 constitutions only *The Athenian Constitution* survives. A reading of the Rhodes translation (Aristotle 1984), my standard source, makes clear that the work included not only elements of the formal laws of different poleis, but also critical historical commentaries.

[6] Although an older work, the Barker translation of the *Politics* (Barker 1958), like the Irwin translation of the *Nicomachean Ethics* (Aristotle 1984), has excellent notes and commentary. So I shall use each of them as my standard source for these works. Aristotle's writings on kingship and colonies, prepared for his most famous pupil – known now as Alexander the Great – have been lost.

extremely influential teaching; from this follows the partly true, but Eurocentric, claim that "intellectual history since the time of Aristotle has been largely or in part a debate between Platonists and Aristotelians" (McKeon 1941: xvi). It is of particular interest to the student of Thucydides' pre-Socratic dialectical approach, however, that Aristotle partly departed from Plato's own, related, dialectical mode of knowledge generation, preferring when possible a conception of demonstrative science founded on his newly discovered set of formally valid syllogistic inferences. But if in this way Aristotle's concept of rigorous science as a deductive system of universal laws or principles comes closer to modern, mathematicized natural science, Nussbaum (1978) argues that it was Plato's version of Socrates, but not Aristotle, who believed that a science of practical measurement would be the salvation of troubled humans.[7]

In what sense am I here using the term "methodology"? What is methodology? Von Wright (1971: 3) treats the subject of methodology as identical with the philosophy of scientific method, a subject which obviously includes, but is not limited to, the role of measurement. Because Aristotle practiced in what we now consider to be the arts, the humanities, theology, the natural sciences and the social sciences, an appropriate conception of his politically relevant methodologies should obviously include the arguable discussion of the ways such different disciplines ought to proceed.[8] Indeed, as we shall see, the Synthetic Aristotle considered many of the disciplines he helped found to be sciences of a sort, definable in terms of their distinctive,

---

[7] She argues against the view of Plato/Socrates in the *Protagoras*, that people would "agree that our salvation lay in the science of measurement" as opposed to some other science, and shows with some careful analysis of Aristotle's texts that Aristotle's principal schema for explaining purposive action in humans and animals, the practical syllogism, was not thought by him to be includable within a universally valid system of deductively organized moral rules, laws or principles.

[8] The supreme generalist, as well as a multidisciplinary specialist, Aristotle called upon all branches of knowledge in attempting to characterize and build any one of them. Hybrids are common. For example, fairly consistently he considers rhetoric to be an art, a practical faculty, a subject that can be treated systematically. Defined in contrast with what he and Plato describe as the practice of the Sophists, it is as "a combination of the science of logic and of the ethical branch of politics; and it is partly like dialectic, partly like sophistical reasoning." He cautions against refashioning it too much away from a subject dealing "simply with words and forms of reasoning," toward "a more instructive art and a more real branch of knowledge" (political science) (*Rhetoric*: 1359b). A better view of the Sophists' generalizing inclinations is suggested in Chapter 1 above.

specialized knowledges; others were primarily arts, while some were both arts and sciences. Accepting Aristotle's point that the humanistic disciplines like rhetoric, ethics and literature also have methodologies useful for knowledge cumulation should not trouble us, as any contemporary visitor to specialized seminars in such disciplines soon recognizes. How else would hybrid disciplines like journalism, legal studies, medical ethics, discourse analysis and public administration proceed?

A second modification of von Wright's philosophical conception of methodology is the present emphasis on its applied character. Like the many critics of "positivist" social science, e.g., Habermas (1971, 1973b), I disapprove of the tendency of many social scientists to try and pass as "mature scientists" by aping the practices of contemporary natural scientists, without being able rationally and persuasively to argue the relevance of such practices for their own subject matter. That criticism cannot be directed at Aristotle. On the other hand, like Aristotle, I am really interested in *doing* research well; I have tried to teach and apply what I have learned. Indeed, my understanding of the substantive, the philosophical and the technical aspects of political methodology has pushed me toward the adaptation, invention and application of methodologies, methods and techniques more appropriate for political inquiry than previously existing practices. A philosophically oriented political methodologist need not be a practical contradiction.

In sum, I shall stick with von Wright's philosophical conception of the field of methodology, giving it both an interdisciplinarily broadened, and a politically applied, character. Given that the different Aristotles, and subsequent Aristotelians, have had several distinguishable, subject-oriented research philosophies, my subject then in this chapter is politically oriented Aristotelian research methodologies.

After some remarks on why the apparent absurdity of rediscovering Aristotle might actually be desirable for contemporary methodologists, I shall review Aristotle's own arguments about the possibility of a political science and an associated "poli(s)metrics," producing three different, but related, Aristotelian answers. All three point toward the value of an often underappreciated Aristotelian tradition of social science. In conclusion, I shall offer an illustrated set of substantive and methodological standards recommended for contemporary neo-Aristotelian sociopolitical inquiry.

Discovering Aristotle again?

Mention was made above of my continued effort at *exploring* the classics. Among political theorists writing in the tradition of Leo Strauss, e.g., Harvey Mansfield, Roger Masters, Stephen Salkever and David Schaefer, Aristotle is, of course, neither lost nor in need of exploratory rediscovery; his contributions have repeatedly been publicly announced. Many other classically trained social and political theorists also know that "Aristotle has become a contemporary in the discourse of political theory" (Wallach 1992: 613; see also Bernstein 1983; Luhmann 1990; MacIntyre 1984; Nussbaum 1990; Salkever 1981).[9]

But, often, the recently minted "methodologist" whom one meets at professional social scientific meetings in North America has little time for social or political theory and their seemingly endless debates. She is likely, moreover, to think that neither Aristotle nor any other pre-Galileo social theorist was "serious" about methodological issues, as she defines them,[10] or that his writings are of no particular contemporary relevance.[11]

---

[9] Wallach (1992: 615–618, 635) knowledgeably describes recent turns to Aristotle in "the discursive games of liberalism versus communitarianism, virtue versus rights, teleology versus deontology/utilitarianism, or naturalism versus historicism." He describes four components of the contemporary neo-Aristotelian project, several of which I find attractive: (1) the appeal to practical reason or wisdom to reconcile nature/convention and universal/particular dichotomies; (2) the decontextualized treatment of his disagreeable, naturalistically argued prejudices as only contingent features of his system; (3) the opposite treatment of the attractive parts of his system as transhistorically valid or responsive to a historical epoch like our own in its sense of a declining capacity for democratic control of public affairs; and (4) the offering of a model for reasoning about political life superior to liberalism and/or Kantian morality, which can guide our judgments concerning the future well-being of our own and other political communities.

[10] Besides this truthful report, here is citeable evidence. Neil Beck's back cover endorsement for King (1989) rules out Kant, Marx, Weber, Lasswell, Simon and Donald T. Campbell as well as Aristotle as political methodologists: for Beck, King (1989) "is the first book to take the problems of political methodology seriously." Even if we limit "political methodology" as a field to quantitative data analysis – and all of *Rediscoveries and Reformulations* is an argument against that limitation – the Aristotelian tradition of scientific, interpretive and teleological inquiry is still seriously shortchanged by such a perspective. It should be added that neither Salkever nor Wallach emphasize the methodological contributions of Aristotle and his followers.

[11] As a counter-example to such reductive narrowness, I am happy to cite my MIT colleague, Zhiyuan Cui, who enthusiastically introduced me to *Love's Knowledge* (Nussbaum 1990). I had to buy and read the book to find again the passage on page 5

With this chapter, I shall try to show how the earliest author of a book on methodology,[12] whom Leo Strauss considered the discoverer of the idea of political science,[13] offers a particularly unified and challenging conception of political methodology, as well as a variety of specific methods of political inquiry, and why he and the tradition associated with him deserve contemporary consideration.[14] Were the literatures I shall touch upon here regularly included in psychology, political science, political economy, public choice, sociology or international relations training programs, I believe their students would be a little more modest about the advantages of a very small set of "the latest (and hence, by implication, the best)" "scientific" techniques, a little more skeptical about efforts to narrow their own disciplinary boundaries in ways that exclude humanistic (including narratively or argumentatively oriented) modes of inquiry, and a little more historically alive to the creative, contradictory syntheses of interpretive philosophy, constructive art and explanatory science implicit, at least since Aristotle, in phrases like "political science."

Actually, if we are to tolerate the use of an exploration metaphor with respect to the classics of one's own discipline, "*re*discoveries" is more accurate than "discoveries" in many cases; shifting away from "explorations" toward invention themes, "reformulations" might even better serve to help us recognize the novel methodological elements associated with creative recoveries of an important past. Indeed, not only do such rediscoveries reconstitute "traditions" or "disciplines" of inquiry, their brightest moments can be characteristic reformulations of great ages in many civilizations. As its commonly used name implies, the Renaissance – a great, if violent, defining moment in modern

that he enthusiastically pointed to: "certain truths about human life can only be fittingly and accurately stated in the language and forms characteristic of the narrative artist." Most, if not all, of the essays gathered together in this book were written in the search for replicable versions of that knowledge.

[12] Mentioned in lists of Aristotle's manuscripts, Aristotle's *Methodology* has, unfortunately, not survived.

[13] See the references in Wallach (1992: note 35). I am inclined to agree, however, with E.H. Carr (1964), who considers Chinese scholars writing about the same time as Socrates, Plato and Aristotle to have independently created the discipline of political science. I am indebted to a Chinese historian, Hermann Mast, for the observation that there are passages in Confucius' writings about virtue that are interchangeable with sentences in Aristotle's ethical/political writings.

[14] This investigation therefore offers a more positive view, expressed in its concluding suggested standards for sociopolitical inquiry, than Stephen Salkever's view that "Aristotelian social science yields no rules of method" (Salkever 1981: 503).

Western civilization – was a "rebirth," a "rediscovery" and an inventive "reformulation" of many of the most profound achievements of Greco-Roman civilization, including Plato's and Aristotle's works.[15]

Sensitivity to these differences suggests questions whether historically oriented students of sociopolitical relationships are of necessity less detached from, and more constructive of, their subject matter than the practitioners of the so-called "natural sciences." Is that more intimate connection necessarily bad? Are those primarily interested in social questions, politics, international relations or, most broadly, international studies, deserving of the label of "scientists" at all? More positively, to what extent is their quest for secure knowledge, or truth, a common enterprise shared with artists and humanists? Are social and political "truths" or "laws" in any way "natural" or strictly comparable to the powerfully explanatory "laws of nature" discovered by "natural scientists"? Do "social scientists" or "political scientists" ever really give universal, necessary, timeless, lawful explanations; do they ever do anything more than just reformulate earlier collective self-interpretations?

Was the study of politics a science for Aristotle, and if so, how?

The reading or rereading of Aristotle helps us to rethink such questions, including those about the epistemological status of the study of politics. But to put Aristotle's conception in the appropriate context, we need a preliminary understanding of his broader system of thought, and of the places of philosophy, the sciences and the arts within that system. Indeed civilizations and epochs can and should be compared and evaluated in terms of the extent to which such broad classifications differ, change and correspond (Rescher 1987). If one is curious about the scientific status of one's own training, should not one be curious about its comparative validity, exclusively or inclusively defined, *vis-à-vis* the scientific standing of other disciplines, epochs and civilizations?

In this regard recall Thomas Kuhn's amazement – indeed, his personal "discovery" of the coherence uncovering power of hermeneutical historical inquiry – on finally realizing that medieval Aristo-

---

[15] Galileo's mechanics, like his support for Copernican astronomy, was clearly influenced by Neoplatonic metaphysics. We shall return to the discussion of one of the Renaissance's concerns directly linked to Aristotle's *Politics* – civic humanism – in the discussion of Machiavelli and Las Casas in Chapter 4 below.

telian physics was coherent, even scientific, but based on a different ontology of the modes of being and becoming. One memorable, hot summer day, Kuhn "all at once perceived the connected rudiments of an alternative way of reading the texts" before him. Unlike Galileo, the Aristotelians' special subject was

> change-of-quality in general, including both the fall of a stone and the growth of a child to adulthood. In a universe where qualities were the "ontologically primary and indestructible elements," imposed on omnipresent neutral matter, qualities constituted individual bodies or substances. In modern physics bodies don't have identities [but rather ...] predictively essential state variable characterization, like spatio-temporal location, mass, velocity (momentum) and acceleration. But for Aristotle, since position was a quality, motion was a change-of-state corresponding to child development; identity was real, but preserved only in the "problematical sense that the child is the individual it becomes." (Kuhn 1977: xi–xii)

With this ontologically motivated cognitive gestalt flip – producing a new and deeper understanding of Aristotelian science – "strained metaphors often became naturalistic reports, and much apparent absurdity vanished" (*ibid.*).[16]

One of those "apparent absurdities," of course, is why child development and physics belong somehow in the same cluster of natural phenomena. As suggested by the clustered list of Aristotle's writings above, psychological development is governed in part by the inherent, natural tendencies of the soul; additionally it is governed by character and habit as shaped by education, a major public policy issue in the *Politics*. The Classical Greek word for nature, *physis*, is defined in what one could call a developmental way, with ontogenetic, evolutionary and even cosmological overtones.[17] So both disciplines,

---

[16] This paragraph is taken largely from the discussion of dialectical hermeneutics in Alker (1981); see also Table Intro.1 above.

[17] "[I]t is plain that nature [*physis*] in the primary and strict sense is the essence of things which have in themselves, as such, a source of movement" (Aristotle, *Metaphysics*, 1015a13). In the *Politics* Aristotle classifies constitutions as he would living types, and is "inclined toward the Ionian doctrine of 'becoming' – the genetic (or, we may even say ... 'evolutionary') doctrine of *physis*, according to which the substance of things, and of man himself ... is engaged in a process of movement from a primary natural potentiality to the formed and finished completion which is ... even more natural" (Barker 1958: xi, xxix, lxxiif).

Cosmological themes appear, *inter alia*, in the *Metaphysics*, in *On the Heavens*, and in the appeal to the sun's eternal, self-sufficient circularity at the end of *On Generation and Corruption*.

71

understood in a developmental fashion, are parts of Aristotelian natural science.

This explication points toward an additional, important preliminary insight concerning Aristotelian inquiry. What we would call the nature–nurture issue in contemporary social scientific theorizing, the Classical Greeks thematized as the *physis (nature)–nomos (law, convention)* debate about the relative importance of nature, natural law or merely local convention as sources of justice (Aristotle, *Nicomachean Ethics*: 1049b7–11, 1129b11, 1180b, Glossary 413–414). It is not unreasonable to expect a wise, synthetic scholar in either of these debates to deny an "either/or" position, and to support some version of a "both/and" view. To interpret psychology, and even politics, like astronomy and physics, as a matter of *physis*, is thus both for Aristotle and us a challenging possibility.

For those caught up by modern usage, it may be helpful as a third preliminary point to emphasize that, for Aristotle, philosophy and the different sciences overlapped. One reason for this was etymological: literally the "love of wisdom," philosophy sought to separate valid knowledge from mere opinion, while *episteme*, definitionally referring to a right thinking state of the soul or psyche, can be variously translated as "science," "knowledge," or "scientific knowledge." More epistemologically, in Classical Greece, philosophy was expressed in and through discourse in which participants' concerns, questions and needs were addressed and through which their minds or souls might themselves also be changed (Nussbaum 1990: 20). The sciences, on the other hand, the *epistemai*, were systematically organized, rationally justifiable and teachable bodies of doctrine, knowledge or instruction, alternatively classified in terms of their different subject matters or the kinds of inferences used in them (Aristotle 1985; Irwin's Annotated Glossary 424f–425). Clearly these conceptions did, and do, greatly overlap; in recognition of this ancient truth, our universities still give Doctor of Philosophy degrees in many different fields.

One finds the same overlap of philosophy, science and even political studies – subjects that our contemporaries put in different schools or faculties – in various classifications of the branches of the Aristotelian philosophical system and in Aristotle's own distinctions among the different truths and the different sciences. For scholars interested in sociopolitical questions, perhaps the most often discussed taxonomy is the one found in the *Nicomachean Ethics*. In a discussion of the particular virtues of thought, Aristotle distinguishes five states in which the soul grasps the truth in its affirmations or denials. These are craft [– knowledge, due to an art, craft or *techne*], scientific knowledge [*episteme*], intelligence [*phronesis*], wisdom [*sophia*] and understanding [*nous*]; for belief [*doxa*] and supposition admit of being false. (1139b15)

Comparably, Aristotle's Alexandrian editors distinguished three branches of Aristotelian philosophy: they grouped together logical studies (collectively, the *Organon*), the philosophy of nature (including the philosophy of inanimate and animate matter, i.e., physics, biology, psychology), and the moral/political philosophy of the ethical treatises and the *Politics*. Cicero restates these categories as branches of philosophy dealing with discourse, nature and living, respectively.

What can we make out of the incomplete overlap of these two classifications? First of all, let us take the cluster of studies known as the *Organon*, literally the "instrument." From a reading of its component books, it becomes clear that for Aristotle the general subject of discourse, or formal and informal logic, is a domain of specialized knowledges or sciences, i.e., *epistemai*, defined with respect to a group or class of instruments of knowledge – logic, language or discourse – rather than a specific substantive subject matter.

Another special group is composed of the practically oriented branches of knowledge, including ethics and politics; these seek *phronesis (intelligence)*, which is by him sometimes also interpreted as "right judgment" about *praxis (action)*, or deliberatively grounded practical intelligence about how to live a good life (compare Aristotle 1985: Glossary; Nussbaum 1990; and Walton 1990 for similar conceptions). As for other kinds of truth, *sophia (wisdom)* seems at times to come in both practical and theoretical, or philosophical, variants; and so does *nous (understanding or sense)*, either as practical perception, i.e., "common sense" understanding of non-rationalized situational particulars, including actions, that could be otherwise, or as the more or less metaphysical intuition of the necessary truths, the first principles of demonstrative sciences (*Nicomachean Ethics*, 1143b1–6, Glossary: 429).

The specific branches of natural philosophy in the Alexandrian taxonomy *mostly* correspond to recognizable natural sciences, then and now. An exception is metaphysics. Interestingly, the manuscript entitled by Aristotle's editors as his *Metaphysics* – a word which literally refers to a text coming "after," not "above," his *Physics* in some early manuscript collection – was then treated as a work on the philosophy of nature. It refers to a dialectically argued "science" or "first philosophy" or "theology" of both sensible and non-sensible (unmovable) substances in nature, of the variety of substances or beings and the corresponding discipline-constituting definitions and their generally or necessarily true first principles.

Philosophical knowledge of things means knowing their original or first causes. Thought of as answers to different "why" questions, the material cause is something's matter or substratum, its efficient cause is the source of its change, its formal cause is its defining essence or substance, its final cause, often in opposition to its efficient cause, is its purpose and good, the end of all generation and change (*Metaphysics*: 983a24ff.). Seeking the different kinds of causes ontologically constituting different kinds of being and change represents a direct and explicit methodological implication of this special science (McKeon 1941: xviii–xix).

A final preliminary point concerns the roles of formal and informal logic, intuition, induction and deduction in scientific work. If we customarily think of summary statistics as means for making inductive generalizations, induction for Aristotle sounds more informal and abductive in the sense of an act of hypothesis formation: induction is described in the *Topics* (105a13) as "a passage from individuals to universals, e.g., the argument that supposing the skilled pilot is the most effective, and likewise the skilled charioteer, then in general the skilled man is the best at his particular task." Hypothesizing and establishing general, or universal, and necessary, claims, and then logically, deductively, syllogistically[18] deriving new universal truths from them are the ways the theoretical sciences proceed.

---

[18] In the *Prior Analytics* (24a19–24, 25b) Aristotle defines "A syllogism is discourse in which, certain things being stated, something other than what is stated follows of necessity from their being so." He considers a perfect syllogism to be one where "nothing other than what has been stated" is needed to make this the case. His preferred format for valid scientific inferences or demonstrations is the universal syllogism in the first figure:

> "If A is predicated of all B, and
> B of all C,
> _____
> A must be predicated of all C."

There are a finite set of other possibilities connecting the three terms, some of which are valid; "all" may be "some" or "no," and "is/are" may be "is/are not" in this syllogistic formalism.

In the *Posterior Analytics* Aristotle speaks of a "congenital discrimi-native capacity which is called sense-perception" and is possessed by all animals. More advanced animals have the capacity to retain sense-perceptions, also described as intuitions, creating memories. Those with even greater capabilities can take a number of memories, organizing them further to constitute a single experience, identified in terms of the universal element within each of the particulars. Humans get to know primary premises inductively for "the method by which even sense-perception [of a particular man, Callias] plants the universal [man in general] is inductive" rather than scientific. "From experience again – i.e., from the universal now stabilized in its entirety within the soul – originate the skill of the craftsman and the knowledge of the man of science, skill in the sphere of coming to be and science in the sphere of being" (*Posterior Analytics*: 99b36–100a8).

Since "all scientific knowledge is discursive," arriving at the essential features of universal concepts (such as correct individual-genus-species relationships) from earlier, rudimentary universals appears to take place through arguments of both a dialectical (arguing from noncertain premises) and demonstrative sort. "And the originative source of science [especially accurate intuitive sense-per-ception] grasps the original basic premiss, while science as a whole is similarly related as originative source to the whole body of fact" (*ibid.*: 100a&b).

Aristotle's two different conceptions of science

Against this background it is relatively easy to see why Aristotle is of at least two minds concerning the "scientific character" of the study of politics (Aristotle 1985: Irwin's Glossary, 421–425). We have just seen a sketch of the evolution of universalistic and theoretical knowledge generation process from the *Posterior Analytics*; the next several sentences after the richly pluralistic and non-reductive "five truths" quotation above from the *Nicomachean Ethics* make very similar points. Sciences, rigorously defined, deal with necessary, universal, even eternal truths or laws, and new experiences, from which new truths are syllogistically derived. The initial, discipline-defining truths themselves must be arrived at through a dialectical and inductive mode of investigation. On these grounds, political inquiry about the usual, the contingent, the particular, and the taking of actions in concrete situations, is not strictly a science.[19]

On the other hand, Aristotle also uses the more relaxed notion of an *episteme* as a systematically and rationally oriented body of knowledge, productive of one kind of truth or another; in this sense, for Aristotle, there are many different, substantively oriented sciences. Included in this conception are more or less rationally organized arts or crafts like bridlemaking, generalship and medicine, practically oriented disciplines like ethics and politics, and non-substantively focused disciplines such as logic, interpretation, the investigation of topical commonplaces evident in dialectical reasoning, and rhetoric – itself a hybrid discipline as we have earlier noted.

Thought of in terms of their general or theoretical principles, these disciplines were sciences; in practice, as applied, they were arts. Each could have their different, more theoretical or more applied methodologies for analyzing political matters. Following the premise in the *Metaphysics* (1025b25) that "all thought is either practical [oriented toward producing *praxis* or action] or productive [as a *techne*, art or craft] or theoretical [as mathematics, physics and theology are]," the scientific status of such a heterogeneous set of disciplines and their associated methodologies depends on the "or"s in Aristotle's classification of truths not being exclusive.

Three kinds of Aristotelian political science

We now have the materials with which to answer in three overlapping but increasingly ambitious ways our previous question about whether, and methodologically how, the study of politics is a "science" in Aristotelian terms. Aristotle might call the differing conceptions of political science found in his writings an *aporia* or puzzle; to resolve such ambiguities he might suggest an exercise in classification based on essential similarities and differences in subject matter. Today we would call such an exercise an offering of overlapping ideal types.

In answering this question, I have found essential both the distinc-

[19] Compare Nussbaum's (1990: 54ff.) criticism of thinking of practical reasoning as scientific. Walton (1990) has an equally well-informed, quite similar reconstruction of practical reasoning (and therefore ethics and politics) as "goal-driven, knowledge-based, action-guiding argumentation" susceptible in large part to scientific analysis; his approach will be discussed further in Chapter 12 below.

tion between *physis* and *nomos* (nature vs. law or convention), and that between *techne, episteme, phronesis* (art or craft vs. science vs. practical intelligence). Awareness of these distinctions must be added to the etymological clarification just offered of the two meanings of *episteme*. Because individual ethical life for a Classical Greek presupposed, contributed to, was part of, was legislatively and educationally shaped by, and was fulfilled in the public moral life of, the polis it should not surprise us to find relevant definitional discussions in both the *Nicomachean Ethics* and the *Politics*.

Answer No. 1 (The Ethical Aristotle): Ethics and Politics, as classically taught and practiced, are primarily humanistic activities oriented around the development, production and use, in concrete deliberative decisions, of cultivated perception, practical reason and intelligence.

It is quite clear that ethics and politics are, for the Ethical Aristotle, primarily producers of practical knowledge, intelligence or *phronesis*. In this way, as producers of such reasoning, intelligence and decisions, ethics and politics are also productive crafts or arts.

According to Answer No. 1, Political Science is primarily an ethical-political discipline. If this conception of politics is strange to the contemporary social or political methodologist, then their puzzlement confirms Martha Nussbaum's above quoted remark, on a Bill Moyer's Public TV show, that "We've lost the idea that politics are part of the humanities." Nussbaum's books on classical thought (1978, 1986, 1990; Nussbaum and Sen, eds. 1993) develop this view and frequently elaborate on its methodological significance. In a particularly relevant recent study, she organizes her review of classical Greek ethical thought (Nussbaum 1990: 13–29) in terms of the key questions asked, the particular perceptions and concrete practical judgments involved, the diverse literatures considered relevant – including poetry and public dramas, and a discussion of their formal structures and emotional appeals. The key starting point of classical Greek ethics was, in her view, the question asked in Plato's *Republic*: how one should live. The Aristotelian answer, which of course requires further specification, is that "the best life is inclusive of all those things that are choiceworthy for their own sake [i.e., with] intrinsic value."

Nussbaum finds strong support for a humanistic reading of

Aristotle in the *Nicomachean Ethics*, one not without its methodological implications. To spell out more concretely what choices are choiceworthy, she argues that practical moral reasoning must address "what pertains to the end," i.e., both a clarification of appropriate ends and the means to best obtain them. As previously noted, she rejects the view that rule-based deductions or scientifically valid quantitative measurements of practical choices are possible. Aristotle's account of action via the practical syllogism is, however, presented as a general explanatory scheme for action, whose parts are both conceptually and logically related. The scientific aspect of this mode of reasoning is not identified with its reducibility to calculating rules, but with the force and logical necessity of its inferences when component elements are actively and appropriately combined in someone's mind.

Indeed, Nussbaum (1978: 176ff.) presents an impressive, synthetic exposition of Aristotle's practical syllogism as a schema for the teleological explanation of animal (including human) activity. In dialogue with von Wright's own impressive effort formally to reconstruct Aristotle's most famous contribution to interpretive ethical and political inquiry (von Wright 1971), she uses her reading of Aristotle's scattered treatments of teleological inference to clarify some ambiguities raised by certain passages in the *Nicomachean Ethics*. Labeling the human animal in question HA, his situation-specific belief B, and A and A_1 as possible actions of HA in the situation in question, her version of his practical reasoning schema is:

> HA's situational object of desire, or goal, G
> HA's belief B that A (or A_1) was necessary to bring about G
> _____
> HA did A (or A_1) because he wanted G and believed B

She argues that Aristotle employs this model, expanding it to allow human deliberation about internal constituents of the end or goal G, as well as about external means such as A or A_1. He also suggests elements of a deliberative procedure for selection of means from among the possible alternatives on various grounds and is clearly aware that both kinds of deliberation could involve further complexities in situation-specific relations among action possibilities or necessities and goal components.

Methodologically, in seeking the good, moral and political practical reasoning should only seek "the degree of exactness" warranted by their often difficult and contradictory subject matter. "Moreover, what is fine and what is just, the topics of inquiry in political science, differ and vary so much that they seem to rest on convention only, not on nature"; thus "it has happened that some people have been destroyed [an obvious bad] because of their wealth [a presumed good], others because of their bravery." In such cases we can only "indicate the truth roughly and in outline ... about what holds good usually [but not universally], it will be satisfactory if we can draw conclusions of the same sort" (*Nicomachean Ethics*: 1094b12–22).

There are truths reachable and sharable by a consensually oriented version of the argumentation processes described in a Rescherian fashion in Chapter 1, not unlike John Rawls' idealized justice-seeking argumentation. Methodologically, in this domain, the Ethical Aristotle tends to follow the practice of starting discussion from the major alternative positions seriously being advocated on a subject, and trying to keep as much of value in such positions as possible. Proceeding dialectically, then, ethical-political inquiry needs to use the

> inclusive dialectical method first described by Aristotle ... one that (continuous with the active searching of life) can provide an overarching or framing procedure in which alternative views might be duly compared, with respect for each, as well as for the evolving sense of life to which each is a response.   (Nussbaum 1990: 25)

Just as Habermas has expressed appreciation for an ontologically sensitive, critically hermeneutic, communicatively reformulated version of this methodology (Habermas 1973: Ch. 1; Bernstein 1983: 30–50, 175–196), Nussbaum calls upon us to seeek "reflective" or "perceptual equilibrium" through a "communal process of inquiry, reflection, and feeling with respect to important civic and personal ends" (Nussbaum 1990: 15); she argues that the "Aristotelian procedure tells us to be respectful of difference, but it also instructs us to look for a consistent and shareable answer to the 'how to live' question, one that will capture what is deepest and most basic ..." (*ibid.*: 28).

As one saw above in the dramatic commentaries on the Peloponnesian war performed in Athens while the war continued, comedies and tragedies were politically oriented, emotionally powerful arguments in this dialogue. This is only one of several complexifications of a rich, methodologically suggestive Aristotelian conception of politically relevant rationality that Nussbaum reformulates.[20] Much later in *Love's Knowledge* Nussbaum approvingly summarizes Aristotle's inclusive attitude toward literature, ethics and politics:

> [Aristotle's ethics ...] attempts to describe the limits and possibilities of that species-specific form of life, saying where, within those [human] good is to be found. This suggests, then, that good Aristotelian writing in ethics should call upon emotions, and upon narrative structures, enlisting their illumination – for through all of this we trace the outlines of our dependence and express our attachment to things outside ourselves ... Our pity and fear for imperfect heroes, and our fellow feeling with their story become ingredients in the recognition of human value. (Nussbaum 1990: 389)

As suggested by Wallach's translation of *politike* as "the science of the political art" (Wallach 1992: note 6), one can also find a second answer to our question. It is Ernest Barker's answer, also quoted at the beginning of this chapter, that "Politics was always, to the Greeks, an 'art' as well as a 'science.'" Spelling this out a bit gives:

Answer No. 2 (The Synthetic Aristotle): Politics is an art and a science, particularly to the extent that systematic knowledge can be developed concerning:
(a) political beliefs, argumentation, and rhetoric;
(b) desirable practices, e.g., virtuous actions, perceptive decisions, good policies and just laws;
(c) self-sufficient political systems, socially appropriate constitutions, enduring ways of life.
Evidence for or against generally or universally valid knowledge claims should be developed through comparative philosophical, legal/legislative and scientific studies of the natural and conventional facts of these subjects.

---

[20] Nussbaum (1990: 56–104) gives a brilliant exposition of a perceptually oriented Aristotelian conception of public rationality attentive to:

  (a) deliberative procedures appropriate for contradictory, incommensurable, plural values not measurable by any unitary quantitative standard;
  (b) the priority of the particular in rule-based judgments;
  (c) the rationality of emotions and imagination;
  (d) the value of claims generated by literary excursions of sympathy, pity and fear; and
  (e) the role of leadership and citizenship in a society of cultivated perceivers.

Succinctly, Answer No. 2 is an answer to our question suggested mostly by the *Rhetoric*, the *Politics* and the *Constitution of Athens*. But it is also stated in the language of contemporary empirically oriented, archive-supported, data making and analyzing research programs, as well as the vocabulary of systems theory (Richardson 1991). In the same, rather inductive vein, the Synthetic Aristotle ends the *Nicomachean Ethics* with some methodological remarks about the right approach to the legislative science which his predecessors have left largely uncharted. After a review of their scattered remarks on particular related topics, he suggests we

> study the collected political systems, to see from them what sorts of things preserve and destroy cities, and political systems of different types; and what causes some cities to conduct politics well, and some badly.
>
> For when we have studied these questions, we will perhaps grasp better what sort of political system is best; how each political system should be organized so as to be best; and what habits and laws it should follow.   (*Nicomachean Ethics*, 1181b17–24)

If we recall the expansive conception of the public domain in Classical Greek society, and recognize too that even today's liberal societies use governmental means to finance and direct most of the research and education that takes place in our advanced societies, and to regulate those economic activities they do not directly control, Answer No. 2 supports the expansive conception of political science as the ruling or leading science given at the beginning of the *Nicomachean Ethics*. Having assumed, in the end, the identity of "the good" and what actions and investigations aim at, and further accepting the Aristotelian metascientific notions of the supremacy of self-sufficient forms of collective being and of goods that are intrinsically ends in themselves, Aristotle argues for the importance of the science of the highest good as follows:

> Then surely knowledge of this [highest] good is also of great importance for the conduct of our lives .... It seems to concern the most controlling science, ... the ruling science. And political science apparently has this character.
>
> (1) For it is the one that prescribes which of the sciences ought to be studied in cities, and which ones each class in the city should learn, and how far.
>
> (2) Again, we see that even the most honoured capacities, e.g., generalship, household management and rhetoric, are subordinate to it.

> (3) Further, it uses the other sciences concerned with action, and moreover legislates what must be done and what avoided. ... For while it is satisfactory to acquire and preserve the good even for an individual, it is finer and more divine to acquire and preserve it for a people and for cities.   (*Nicomachean Ethics*: 1094a23–b10)

Perhaps even more troubling than its expansive sense of politics and political inquiry is the extent to which evaluative language is included in the defining phrases of Answer No. 2. Nonetheless, I think the Synthetic Aristotle wanted, carefully and scientifically, to use such evaluative language. That such language is appropriate follows from arguments and views I have associated above with Answer No. 1. Indeed, Nussbaum (1990: 35f) approvingly cites a Wittgensteinian critique of the metaphysical errors of philosophers (and methodologists?) dazzled by the methods of the contemporary natural sciences, that they "are irresistibly tempted to ask and answer questions in the [dehumanized] way science does ... [a] tendency [which] is the real source of metaphysics, and leads ... into complete darkness." A reading of Aristotle's richly supported catalogues of rhetorical moves, topical commonplaces and sophistical errors supports as well the interpretation that his readers were supposed to use all their distinctively human faculties in assessing the validity of his descriptions and judgments.

Reading the one – out of 138! – surviving entry in the Synthetic Aristotle's own comparative and historical political data program, his *Constitution of Athens*, suggests some large challenges for either classical or contemporary methodologists. Given practical questions like those just suggested, or their somewhat more theoretical versions addressed in the *Politics*, Aristotle's work suggests that we should seriously and rigorously treat as *data* comparable, critical, i.e., emotionally-morally evaluative, constitutional *histories*, including largely non-quantitative *textual information* on their origins, legal contents, applications, reforms, successes and failures in resisting both external and internal threats, as well as the other consequences of the procedures and practices they assume and mandate! Traditionalists have, of course, long tried to do this, following Aristotle's injunction against quantitative metricization of many-faceted, inexact, ethical-political matters.

More generally, there is a strong linguistic justification from the Synthetic Aristotle for focusing methodologically not only on the historical and comparative "constitutional" data-collecting efforts just mentioned, but as well on the political rhetoric and dialectic associated with such developments, the truths successfully appealed to, as well as their errors. This includes attention to the conduct of candidates and office holders, the moral-emotional appeals of public speakers and public dramas, the argumentation of law courts as well as democratic and representative assemblies, and more scholarly and philosophical arguments about politics. It is part of his famous argument that "man is by nature an animal intended to live in a polis' (*Politics*: 1253a). It is that nature "makes nothing in vain; and man alone of the animals is furnished with the faculty of language ... But language serves to declare what is advantageous [in one's interest] and what is the reverse, and it therefore serves to declare what is just and what is unjust." Human linguistic capabilities make possible their "association in [a common perception of] these things [what is just and unjust, etc.] which makes a family and a polis" (*ibid.*). Linguistically focused pol-i(s)metrics should therefore attend to these distinctive expressions of humankind's political sensibilities and capabilities.

But what does it mean that nature makes nothing in vain? Are human perceptions of, and deliberative discovery of, the good in any way natural? The ability to perceive and linguistically share common perceptions of justice and injustice, of good and evil, appears to Aristotelians in part to be biologically given. But how can a particular Greek political institution – the polis, about to become obsolete because of Macedonian and Roman cosmopolitan/imperial practices – be considered "natural"? These serious questions point toward another, very important but deeply controversial, research program explicit in Aristotle's writings, that programmatically informs his discovery and/or invention of political science. It is implicit in, but goes beyond, Answer No. 2.

Answer No. 3 (The Cosmological Aristotle): A Political Science worthy of the name can and must grow out of the seeking for perfection, the growth toward organized complexity, inherent in Nature. It should seek the necessary and universal truths functionally linking human knowledge as to what is virtuous, good and just, and the scientifically discovered and discoverable regularities of publicly-oriented human desires, beliefs, actions, practices, associations and institutions.

This is the Cosmological Aristotle, an Aristotle who at least in the long run is an optimist about human prospects, an Aristotle for the ages.

But he is not necessarily optimistic in the short run. Aristotle increasingly recognized that

> Man, when perfected [by the appropriate political policies and constitutional arrangements] is the best of animals; but if he be isolated from law and justice he is the worst of all ... man is furnished from birth with arms [such as, for instance, language] which are intended to serve the purposes of moral prudence and virtue, but which may be used in preference for opposite ends. ... Justice [which is his salvation] belongs to the polis.
>
> (*Politics*: 1253a34–37)

The Cosmological Aristotle motivates the Synthetic Aristotle, with his presumption that arts and science overlap and can further converge. Answer No. 3 suggests a deep reason why Aristotle likes to start his dialectical inquiries with a review of the best opinions and arguments available. It justifies the use of evaluative language in the concepts of Answer No. 2, giving them *in part* a natural, functional basis. It strengthens and makes more falsifiable the claimed-to-be inclusive lists of tasks and offices frequently occurring in his writings with the view that "All things derive their essential character from their function and their capacities" (*Politics*: 1253a); as will be further discussed below, the discovery of necessary functions is intended to apply both to the basic needs of individual citizens or families and to larger, more or less self-sufficient sociopolitical systems as well. The Cosmological Aristotle asks that we look critically but hopefully for the goods being served by existing or eventually emergent practices.

Unlike the more skeptical claim of seeming difference in the *Nicomachean Ethics* cited by Nussbaum, Answer No. 3 implies a claim that *physis (nature)* and *nomos (law and convention)* are intrinsically related, that they have a common, natural, richly human, politically relevant, scientifically discoverable, but contradiction laden core.[21] According to

---

[21] Stephen Salkever puts the Aristotelian view nicely: "Human beings are uniquely capable of, *and uniquely in need of*, a rational perception of their interest in order to live well, and such a perception (and therefore such a life) is dependent upon the presence of nomoi." Aristotle's recognized contradiction within this conception is that the human projects of living, living together (stably, in a socially integrated fashion) and living well (in a virtue-realizing, flourishing, city where citizens have enough leisure time to be politically active) often have contradictory empirically observable conditions. "Those nomoi which are best suited to producing the necessary conditions of political life are often not those which are best suited to the development of virtue" (Salkever 1991: 489, 494).

Answer No. 3, *physis* and *nomos* combine in complex, unsuspected ways. For example, like the above discussion of Answers No. 1 and No. 2, Alasdair MacIntyre argues that "man is in his action and practice, as well as in his fictions, *essentially* a story-telling animal. He is *not essentially*, but becomes through his history, a teller of stories that aspire to truth" (MacIntyre 1984: 216, my emphasis).[22]

I was led to Answer No. 3 textually by several quotations and coincidences. Obviously, there are the famous, strange, easy to spot quotations about every craft, investigation, action and decision leading toward some good (*Nicomachean Ethics* 1094a), from which Political Science derives its architectonic definition as the investigation of the ruling good. Less obvious but quite powerful was the realization that the same texts in the *Nicomachean Ethics* which its translator, Terence Irwin, cited as evidence of the prior *physis–nomos* controversy were also among the texts where Aristotle is defining Political Science! This coincidence suggests – the Cosmological Aristotle's leap of faith – that the possibility of an architectonic Political Science in the sense of the Cosmological Aristotle requires a discoverable core within this overlap.

Even despite Nussbaum's skepticism about ascribing universal teleology to Aristotelian nature (Nussbaum 1978: 95–99) I find such an evolutionary, cosmological conception in almost every work Aristotle wrote. As an impressive example, consider:

> Coming-to-be and passing-away will, as we have said, always be continuous, and will never fail ... And this continuity has a sufficient reason on our theory. For in all things, as we affirm, *Nature always strives after "the better."* Now "being" ... is better than "not-being" but not all things can possess "being," since *they are too far removed from the "originative source"* ... God therefore adopted the remaining alternative, and fulfilled the perfection of the universe by making coming-to-be uninterrupted: for the greatest possible coherence would thus be secured to existence, because that "coming-to-be should itself come-to-be perpetually" is the closest approximation to eternal being.
>
> (Aristotle, *On Generation and corruption*: 336b25–35, my emphases)

One sees here a Great Chain of Being notion (Lovejoy 1936) allied to

---

[22] Wallach (1992: 625–626) treats MacIntyre's version of Aristotle as traditional Aristotelianism, citing his positive attitudes toward Thomas Aquinas' theological and philosophical synthesis of Aristotelian and Christian views. In cultural terms, the Islamic tradition also has important links with the cosmological aspects of Aristotle's thought.

the stages of animal/cognitive evolution and development mentioned in the above summary of the argumentation at the end of the *Posterior Analytics*; there is also a sense of an encompassing cosmological order that includes the life of a small Mediterranean city. Compare this vision with Vernadsky's and others' attempts to create a new, multidisciplinary science of the Biosphere (Alker and Haas 1993). When adhered to, at the metascientific level, this conception supports in an appropriately qualified, non-reductionistic manner, the positivists' unity of the sciences position in the positivism–dialectics controversy reviewed briefly in the Introduction to this volume.

The exalted conception of Political Science offered in Answer No. 3 is a challenge which, if met, provides a worthy standard in terms of which Western, or any other, civilization could be judged. But I agree with critics of Aristotle and recent neo-Aristotelian development that Aristotle's teleological universalism, his metaphysical biology and cosmology, is a central claim in his system which must be either rationally defended or attacked, and surely requires contemporary reformulation. How much of the methodological wisdom implicit in the Ethical and the Synthetic Aristotle can be "saved" if the Cosmological Aristotle is overthrown is a difficult question; I think quite a lot remains, but in the more piecemeal fashion that goes with occasional historical footnotes and a broad tradition of analysis.

Moreover, too easily derived versions of Political Science No. 3 in the past have been the basis for Western nations' colonialism, and cultural chauvinism. Philosophical naturalism has equally fostered gender discrimination and racism (Haraway 1989). It is perhaps only now – when there are beginning to be truly global structures for social scientific and humanistic research which have the possibility of limiting political, cultural, racial and gender biases, and when biologically and socially oriented research have centuries of critically debated but also increasingly impressive discoveries to build on[23] – that this essentialist version of Political Science may be possible.

---

[23] Understanding better such research possibilities suggests a harder look at Roger Masters' pioneering, but lonely, work to fit together an Aristotelian philosophy and contemporary bio-political research on human nature (Masters 1989). Perhaps it is convergent with the novel sense of emergent complexity evident in the work of the Santa Fe Institute, e.g., Epstein and Axtell (1996), Kauffman (1995).

Some methodological standards from the Aristotelian tradition

The Aristotelian tradition

Alasdair MacIntyre (1984: 146) suggests that the notion of a *tradition of thought* implies "a very unAristotelian [i.e., an anti-essentialist] theory of knowledge according to which each particular theory or set of moral or scientific beliefs is intelligible and justifiable – insofar as it is justifiable – only as a member of an historical series." Hence, "to treat Aristotle as part of a tradition, even as its greatest representative, is a very unAristotelian thing to do" (*Ibid.*). Nonetheless, because Aristotle himself paid considerable attention to his Greek predecessors and borrowed from them, I shall follow historical realities, current usage and Georg Henrik von Wright in distinguishing two main traditions in the history of ideas about science, the *Aristotelian* and the *Galilean* (von Wright 1971: Ch. 1). Thus Von Wright shows how an appreciation of these research traditions can be helpful in dealing more adequately with a variety of methodological issues facing the humanistic and social scientific disciplines.[24]

Although von Wright provisionally accepts a methodological characterization of scientific inquiry as oriented toward the descriptive study of facts and the theoretically grounded attempt to predict, explain or make intelligible such facts, he obviously considers such distinctions to be tremendously oversimplified. Specifically, there is the philosophical issue whether such disciplines must accept the necessity of general laws for scientific explanation, especially in the realm of the human sciences. Von Wright additionally recalls the two traditions' contrasting positions with respect to the conditions which respectable explanations should satisfy. Going back beyond Aristotle to Plato, "[t]he Galilean tradition in science runs parallel with the advance of

---

[24] Anne Marie Ahonen (1994) has made an excellent application of the contrast of Galilean and Aristotelian traditions to the difference between Raymond Aron's and Kenneth Waltz's international relations theory. She shows how the hermeneutical and neo-Kantian influence of Dilthey on Aron's doctoral dissertation forms a necessary basis for understanding his differences from Waltz's more Galilean-Durkheimian structuralism. Phenomenologically grounded in *Erlebnis* (lived, historical experience) rather than the *Erfahrung* (sense data?) of J.S. Mill's British empiricism, Aron "became attached to the Aristotelian tradition for which human reality is by nature teleological [historically constituted] and cannot be subsumed to general laws" (Ahonen 1994: 82).

the causal-mechanistic point of view in man's efforts to explain and predict phenomena, the Aristotelian tradition with his efforts to make facts teleologically or finalistically understandable" (von Wright 1971: 2–3). The extended discussion of context-specific practical reasoning – a major focus of his own book on *Explanation and Understanding* – is just such an Aristotelian effort. So is his illuminating proposal to *quasi-causally* explain historical interactions as chains of causally interconnected practical reasonings (von Wright 1971: 143). I shall conclude this chapter by suggesting and illustrating some defining standards for contemporary political methodologists working in what can be called an Aristotelian tradition.

Seven neo-Aristotelian standards

Other than classically oriented policy "traditionalists" or ethical-political theorists, contemporary workers in the Aristotelian tradition are likely to have reformulated enough features of the three different Aristotles identified above to justify their being considered neo-Aristotelians. With this likelihood in mind I now propose seven neo-Aristotelian standards for guiding sociopolitical research.

Standard No. 1 (*Topical priorities*)

Because humans are by nature political animals capable of using their distinctive species capability for speaking about right and wrong, including just and unjust forms of political association, the most appropriate subject matter for political inquiry is the content of such political argumentation, the institutionally shaped and institution-shaping action (or praxis) it engenders, and the impact of such actions on the human lives, associations and institutions involved.

In simpler words, compare the most important arguments with the most relevant facts. That is, focus empirically, critically and constructively on practical arguments about, and associated with, decisions, policies, laws, associations, constitutions or other practices claimed to achieve some common or public good. As Aristotle's work still so brilliantly illustrates, and this chapter further exemplifies, the distinguishing feature of political methodologies should be their illuminating focus on these characteristic features of human political interactions.

Sociopolitical inquiry must always have an important inductive component, based on the recognition that political actions occur in concrete situations, and that political ends and systems change over time in important respects: they have both natural, contingent and constructed aspects. Hence, in light of the above review, a contemporary, Synthetic Aristotle should follow.

Standard No. 2 (*Data gathering priorities*)

Three especially important collections of materials for political scientific data programs of special interest to followers of the Synthetic Aristotle are:

(a) Comparable and accessible collections of the functionally described political systems or legally codified constitutions of towns, cities and states (or even of interstate systems) are needed. These should further be classified as to their division of offices, functional responsibilities and resources among the different socioeconomic classes; these analytical polity characterizations should be associated with critical histories of their uses, reforms, and changes *vis-à-vis* the achievement of various public goods.

(b) The Aristotelian student of political rhetoric, poetics, hermeneutics or dialectics must know not only what makes an argument demonstrative or worthy of belief, but also what role persuasion plays practically, in engendering or deterring actions. The Aristotelian student of rhetorical practice needs also to know how to make one's character appear right, and how to put one's hearers in the right emotional frame of mind, understood in terms of the feelings, expectations and moral bases associated with such emotional orientations.[25] Comparable and accessible collections of arguments, practical reasoning and conversational debates used in political decision-making groups, law courts, bureaucracies, public assemblies, elected bodies as well as electoral campaigns and other public ceremonies, should be collected. They should be classified as to lines of argument, users, examples, facts or generalizations cited; associated, often ideological, conceptions of a more general interest being served; general and situation-specific assessments of their validity; and actual or potential refutations.

(c) These two kinds of information or data ought to be connected via

---

[25] This list derives largely from Aristotle's *Rhetoric*. In Chapter 3 I shall review humanistic methods for inferring powerful underlying affective-moral meaning structures implicit in the readers of classical religious or political texts. A more general discussion of ways to uncover lesson-suggesting "story grammars" within sociopolitical texts is given in Chapter 8.

relevant fact gathering efforts, as well as accessible accumulations of relevant secondary literatures. Of great importance are facts and corroborated generalizations of relevance to the five main matters about which political speakers speak and citizens (or their leaders and representatives) deliberate: economic ways and means; the actual and hypothetical capabilities and practices of various political groups or states to make war and to negotiate for and maintain a peace; the actual and potential means of a state's defense; the internal and external bases of states' viability;[26] the availability and distribution of domestic sources and foreign trade relevant to meeting nutritional and other basic needs of their citizenry; and the comparative knowledge of decisions, policies, laws and constitutions, as they affect the general welfare.

Aristotle would never have treated all alignments of voters in some socially described space as equally likely, nor would he have reduced their views to (multidimensional) single-peaked preference curves. He believed that constitutional arrangements should be both described in terms of, and adapted to, the existing historical, socioeconomic, geographic and cultural situation of the citizens to be governed by and through them. His insistent but critical linking of decisions, policies and institutional practices to the public goods they arguably serve obviously challenges the way most of our existing data programs store the votes or decision-relevant opinions of our citizens, the significant actions of our legislators, public budgets, war dead, and economic activity indicators.

As a single, illustrative example of neo-Aristotelian data-making, I mention briefly the series of studies by Martha Nussbaum, Amartya Sen and their associates conceptually and methodologically elaborating upon a new, influential, functional-capabilities approach to the assessment of levels of popular and national development. (Crocker 1992 gives a 47–item bibliography; see especially Nussbaum and Sen, eds. 1993; Nussbaum 1992; Sen 1992; and the discussions of the Human Development Index and the measurement of human security in United Nations Development Programme 1994.) The approach suggests ways of measuring human socioeconomic development linked to providing the resources that meet the human needs which engender capabilities

---

[26] Aristotle treats as relevant for security concerns the knowledge of "how many different forms of constitution or polities there are; under what conditions each of these will prosper and by what internal developments or external attacks each of them tends to be destroyed" (*Rhetoric*: 359b-360a).

necessary for effective political participation. It forces a focused discussion on what, concretely, human well-being or flourishing or happiness consists of and requires. It thus artfully sidesteps, and I believe technically illuminates, at least some of the issues of internationally comparing political societies with different economic, social and political objectives.

The Synthetic Aristotle can be seen as a very early advocate of the epistemological unity of the natural and social sciences. Certainly his own contributions, and those of many of his followers since Ibn Khaldun, strive for that kind of unity. Thus, whereas Socrates dialogically dreamed of political salvation through measurement, Plato invented his eternal "Forms" because his dialectically developed essential definitions didn't quite fit the changing things of experience, and Democritus used a materialistic physical method of essential definition. According to McKeon, "Aristotle sought to combine the virtues of these two methods, to give the forms of Plato a material embodiment [to account more adequately for change] and to disclose formal traits beyond the [visual] peculiarities and combinations of the elements in the matter of Democritus." In subsuming the concerns of these and other earlier writers, including the preoccupation of the Pythagoreans with formal causes, "Aristotle considered his own peculiar contribution to be the discussion of efficient and final causes. ...." (McKeon 1941: xix).

This piece of intellectual history suggests that Aristotle's unifying approach was based on the acceptance of the reality of a variety of human-relevant causal explanatory concepts. Following James Bohman's post-Kuhnian reading of Aristotle as someone who, much more than Plato, recognized the indeterminacy and multiplicity of "causes" or "reasons" in natural and social life (Bohman 1993: 54), let me suggest an inclusive, pluralistic standard for contemporary neo-Aristotelians. It grows out of the humanly oriented quality of Aristotelian teleology.

Standard No. 3 (*A plurality of humanly-oriented causality notions*)

In analyzing polities – or alternatively, to use different translations of *politeia*, constitutions, political systems, cultures, or ways of life – seek to identify the engendering purposes, reasons, functions and causes. Specifically, look for: (a) their originating events and instrumental causes; (b) their material-activity bases; (c) their essential and definitionally constitutive forms, i.e., intrinsically related and politically constructed identifying features; and (d) their encompassing yet inherent, but analytically subdivisible, "functional" tendencies toward, or away from, "final systemic states." These latter may or may not be equilibria; they should as well be classified in terms of the realization and frustration of relevant human goals.

To the extent a sociopolitical system is self-sufficient, all four of these classes of "causes" should be both distinguishable, mutually compatible and even reinforcing of one another; but investigate both theoretically and empirically the extent to which these modes of accounting for human action do or do not help constitute self-sufficient modes of political life.[27]

Aristotle was one of the earliest "functional" theorists of political life. Both because, and in spite of, the critical view many contemporary social methodologists have about functional arguments (see the discussion and associated bibliography in Elster 1989: Ch. 10), systematic modelers of systematically organized social and political human interactions cannot get along without some versions of such arguments. For example, Brunner's version of Lipset and Huntington's political development theories – illustrated in Alker (1973) and extended to Barrington Moore's analysis of the social origins of dictatorship and democracy in Moy (1971) – transcends in formal rigor and empirical relevance much of the verbal theory in the political development field. Brunner empirically tested the first two theories *vis-à-vis* recent Turkish experience. Bremer (Bremer, ed. 1987) presents an ambitious, complex, empirically supported, cybernetic-functionalist account of the domestic and international functional interdependencies of more than twenty state systems; following earlier work by Bremer and Mihalka, Cusack and Stoll, and in the same territorially organized cybernetic modeling tradition as Epstein and Axtell (1996), Duffy (1992) has run 256 parallel simulated state system worlds. The cybernetic systems theories of Deutsch, Easton and von Neumann,

---

[27] In his *Ibn Khaldun's Philosophy of History*, Mahdi (1964) suggests that Khaldun thought of economic activities and urban institutions as the material causes of a culture or society, state institutions as its shaping formal cause, the shared sense of social solidarity as its efficient cause, and the resulting common good as its final cause. Since Ibn Khaldun himself gives very detailed and specific propositions about the rise and decline of particular dynasties, and broader civilizations, it would be a valuable cross-cultural scientific exercise to try and reformulate such arguments in contemporary vocabularies drawn from the Aristotelian social scientific tradition.

which influenced these studies, clearly embodied key elements of the Aristotelian tradition.[28]

Because the more refined comparative and historical study of constitutional possibilities and consequences is becoming popular both in law schools and certain versions of public choice theory, e.g., Elster (1991), Fung (1993) and Niou and Ordeshook (forthcoming), one must say the Aristotelian tradition continues to have contemporary sociopolitical relevance in several different lines of work, to differing degrees and in differing ways. Both these studies are unusual in that they make an effort to talk about concrete systemic effects, often anticipated, of differently defined and practiced constitutional features.

An Aristotelian sociopolitical methodologist has to try hard to catch the distinctively human capacities of speaking, reasoning abstractly and perceiving concretely, inferencing, arguing, remembering, building unified experiences out of memories, telling stories, and justifying actions with rational and/or emotional arguments.[29] Interpretation for Aristotle meant the logical/linguistic *parsing* of human claims into their basic linguistic/grammatical forms whose validity could be checked by appropriate disciplinary means. Rescher (1987:

---

[28] Reading Aristotle after having been taught by Karl Deutsch that government was cybernetically like steering – a metaphor Aristotle also uses – I am struck with how much, in particular, his uses of "feedback" were a quantitative reformulation of the Aristotelian notion of *phronesis*; cybernetic systems theory, with its hierarchies of feedback relationships and humanistically defined multicausality, is deeply teleological. In contrast with contemporary work focused on system equilibrium, the ethical component of Deutschean political cybernetics focuses on enhancing autonomy, self-determination and growth, achieved through a balanced attentiveness to outside stimuli and internally recalled memories; he also studied community development in terms of growth in responsiveness, adaptiveness, mutual predictability. Deutsch's commitment to developing data programs was also very much in the spirit of the Synthetic and even the Cosmological Aristotelian traditions. But his scientific reformulation of the nature of governance structures in "bit flows" language – like Jay Forrester's System Dynamics – lacked a full appreciation of later computational political models specified in terms of revisable, constitution-like systems of "rewrite rules" and discourse-oriented "conversations" (Deutsch 1963; Alker 1986a).

[29] The standard of humanly oriented causal analysis fits here, too, at the level of specific actions by individuals or groups. Today's voluntaristic social action theorists (see Alker 1974) tend to forget, or take for granted, that Aristotle's remarkably prescient conceptualization of action occurs in the ethical/legal context of judging the responsibility for, and/or involuntary nature of, an agent's act. He distinguishes the following list of relevant questions: " (1) who is doing it; (2) what he is doing; (3) about what or to what … ; (4) sometimes also what he is doing it with, e.g., the instrument; (5) for what result, e.g., safety; (6) in what way, e.g., gently or hard" (*Nicomachean Ethics* 1111a2–6).

113) even labels the Alexandrian-Aristotelian subpart of the *Organon* dealing with the grammatical analysis of propositions as *hermeneutics*. Should not today's political methodologists be trained in representing the inferential interconnections and substantive validity of practical sociopolitical arguments by linguistically appropriate means as well? The Ethical Aristotle challenges us to do no less. For the synthetically inclined Aristotelian should not rhetoric, dialectics, poetics – and their successor disciplines like hermeneutics, linguistics and discourse analysis – be the appropriate sources for relevant analytic and synthetic methodologies?

Standard No. 4 (*The linguistic imperative*)

Because sociopolitical writing and speaking exemplify distinctive human capacities for practical reasoning and argumentation, the student of politics should use, adapt and further develop the best formal or informal linguistic tools available for analyzing, synthetically recreating and empirically checking theories about such performances.

Since the historical role of the *Organon* has long justified their relevance for political inquiry, the truth-seeking student of politics need feel no disciplinary qualms in using the best linguistic tools available. Whatever their disciplinary origin, they should be used for analytically understanding, situationally explaining and synthetically recreating the failures and achievements of human practical argumentation. There are strong Aristotelian precedents for her focusing within such arguments on the narratives, the moral-emotional appeals, the rhetorical topics, the valid and fallacious inferences and the other elements of reasoning they inevitably contain. Moreover, she should judge superior those methodological tests and those theoretical models which focus not only on what side of an issue political figures come down on, but the *reasons* they give for doing so (e.g., Alker 1984; Carbonell 1981; Slade 1994).

Of those traditions of speech modeling that have clear Aristotelian themes, consider especially: (a) Abelson-Schank modeling of context-specific purposive cognition and action;[30] (b) the analytical

---

[30] In Alker (1984) I explicitly draw out connections between the Abelson–Reich conservative foreign policy belief system simulation and the Aristotelian tradition of modeling practical reasoning and humanly oriented multicausal assessment. As noted in the Introduction, Abelson himself noticed the similarities between the category schemes of Schank's Conceptual Dependency Analysis and Aristotle's *Categories*; I now see a more or less conscious fit between Aristotle's concern with

literature on practical and legal reasoning;[31] (c) Austin–Searle speech act theory and its extensions to the modeling of text acts and reciprocal communications;[32] (d) the literature on emotional-moral meaning structures;[33] and (e) the learning/evolutionary systems theory literature, including the newer literatures on the evolution of organized complexity, as applied to social rules or quasi-legal precedent cases.[34] Similarly, with the resources of computational linguistics and artificial intelligence, the micro-structure of linguistically mediated human communication relationships is now beginning to be better understood in a rigorous, yet empirical fashion.

When faced with a tradeoff between such richly qualitative descriptive or historical information and more reliably, but not clearly more validly quantified information, the Aristotelian methodologist should prefer the former. As Robert Abelson's studies of political ideology have long shown, however, where the ethicist sees the danger of thought become formulaic, the social scientist sees the ironic possibility of success in formally modeling stereotypical thinking. To try to escape this dilemma, whenever possible, she should try to develop linguistically-sensitive formal representations of information that do retain their rich descriptive content as fully as possible. Given the importance and complexity of concrete

---

Topics and Abelson's and Schank's concern with the "implication molecules," "schemas" or "scripts" within politically relevant belief systems. Wendy Lehnert's Abelson–Schank inspired method of exploring the emotional-moral content of affective stories, exemplified and extended in Chapter 3 below, fits closely Aristotle's analysis of specific morally and politically relevant emotions in his *Rhetoric*. The influence of the Abelson–Schank studies on my "Polimetrics" (Alker 1975) and "Can the End of Power Politics ..." in Chapter 5 below should also become evident. Other studies in that tradition of special interest to the politically oriented are Carbonell (1981), Slade (1994) and Schank, Kass and Riesbeck (1994).

31 To be reviewed more extensively in Chapter 12 below.
32 As signposts to this literature, read Austin (1962); Searle (1969); Bach and Harnish (1979); von Cransch and Harré (1982), which has an empirically suggestive, explicitly neo-Aristotelian conception of action; Winograd and Flores (1986), as discussed in Alker (1986a); Cohen, Morgan and Pollack, eds. (1990).
33 Additional discussion, with citations, occurs in Chapter 3.
34 As a reading of the early volumes of the *General Systems Yearbook* will confirm, an entire generation of general systems theorists were entranced with this idea, including Kenneth Boulding, Donald T. Campbell, Karl W. Deutsch, Herbert Simon and Anatol Rapoport. Relevant literatures for triangulating this field include Richardson (1991), Alker and Christensen (1972); Alker's 1974 and 1977 papers reprinted as Chapters 7 and 11 below; Axelrod (ed. 1976; 1984); Hudson, ed. (1991), which uses "organized complexity" as the theme of its Introduction; Taber (1992); Epstein and Axtell (1996).

moral perceptions, as argued by Aristotle and Nussbaum, a good Aristotelian methodological case can be made for using only *partly formalized* approaches to analyzing arguments and emotional-moral belief structures.[35] Such are ways of proceding methodologically so that rigor and relevance do not point in opposite directions.

The linguistically educated methodologists I know who may well agree with some version of Nussbaum's Aristotelian arguments are also likely to have been challenged by Alasdair MacIntyre's related conception of actions as "moments[s] in a possible or actual history or in a number of such histories." They further recognize that writing good history is inevitably a creative political act: "history is an enacted dramatic narrative in which the characters are also the authors" (both quotations are from MacIntyre 1984: 214–215). They have tried to respond methodologically and technically by adapting or developing new ways of *non-reductionistically* treating the descriptive content of arguments and narrative accounts, possibly even including their emotional-moral appeals, as data. Unlike standard numerical representations, and conventional events data, their representations of quantitative or qualitative particulars take place within holistic, networks of conceptually and temporarily interconnected events, actions or arguments. They have inventively done so in ways that creatively challenge the boundaries of conventional political methodology (Alker 1975; Hudson, ed. 1991;[36] Mallery 1994).

My contemporary exemplar of the Ethical Aristotle was Martha Nussbaum. She reminded us at the beginning of this chapter that "politics are part of the humanities." For the ethical humanist, every academic statement, every observation, every theory production or criticism exercise is a performance, in some larger sociopolitical context, on some larger stage.[37] Like Ernest Barker, the follower of the Synthetic Aristotle similarly sees sociopolitical studies as an Art and a Science. Methodologically, both perspectives suggest the following.

---

[35] Without having had the benefit of this insight in their formulation, the methodologies of Chapters 1 and 3 in this volume conform to this injunction.

[36] In their contributions to the Hudson volume, Duffy and Mallery use labelled, bidirectional semantic graphs generated from parsed and coreferenced texts by a complex system of artificial intelligence programs called *RELATUS*, rather than statistical or logical formalisms operationally and manipulably to represent, i.e., metricize, narrative content. Alker, Banerjee, Hudson and Mallery take, as well, a few steps toward representing and assessing the emotional-moral content of narratives.

[37] Jim George's whole review of international theory (George 1994), rediscovered as political practice, fits this humanistic moment of the Aristotelian tradition nicely.

Standard No. 5 (*The challenge of multiple human knowledge interests*)

Politics is a human endeavor, which humanistic disciplines like ethics, rhetoric and poetics, dialectics and hermeneutics, were developed to help us understand. A humanist finds it much easier to recognize and to affirm that there are different and multiple goals, perspectives, inferencing practices, methodologies and *knowledge interests* underlying the Galilean and the Aristotelian traditions of sociopolitical research.

Habermas (1971: 1973a) characterizes the positive knowledge interest as one oriented to prediction, explanation and control. Reducing phenomena to bits or bytes so that they can be causally explained by statistically identifiable stochastic process models is just such an important, naturalistic and positivistic concern. The from-independent-to-dependent-variables explanatory thrust of systems-oriented statistical inference is entirely consistent with this knowledge-engendering outlook.

The hermeneutic knowledge interest, on the other hand, is described as a *practical* human concern, habit, or striving for the reaching of understanding or agreement. In true Aristotelian fashion, it points toward what might become a rational basis for some future collective action. Both Rescher's and Nussbaum's treatments of argumentation and reasoning processes fall within this knowledge interest.

Reading Aristotle even helps to show how knowledge development can be deeply linked to individual and collective efforts to achieve and sustain autarchy, autonomy or self-sufficiency. When linked to an emancipatory interest in freeing individuals and collectivities from unnecessary impositions and constraints, the Aristotelian search for the "best and most complete" "good for man" provides a classical instantiation of what Habermas calls the emancipatory knowledge interest. This third knowledge interest deeply informs the modern, the Enlightenment, and the critical traditions of social theorizing.

Given the Aristotelian tradition's firm placing of most of political inquiry within the realm of practical reasoning about contingent truths, most contemporary political scientists have failed to address the related philosophical and methodological literatures squarely.[38] This avoidance has had several forms:

(a) the redefinition of practical and hermeneutic questions about

---

[38] The discussions of "Rescuing Reason ..." and the "The Return of Practical Reason" in Chapters 6 and 12 below do try to take the issue of practical reasoning seriously.

particular ethical/political situations as a search for universally valid principles and efficient means of instrumental action (Habermas 1973b)

(b)   the reduction of morally rich and complex descriptive accounts or situational evaluations to reproducible behavioral quantifications;

(c)   the reductive elimination of either the truths provided by the moral imagination, the moral affections, or morally powerful narrative understanding ("love's knowledge").

Hence a Political Science troubled by the relation of theory to practice must recognize the contribution of the arts and humanities to its substantive issues, and shape knowledge development strategies based on this hermeneutic recognition; an even more interdisciplinary field like international studies must do likewise.

Does the Cosmological Aristotle have anything of additional relevance to suggest to contemporary methodologists, other than a call to find unities of theory and practice in the literatures of chaotic, organized and evolutionarily complex systems? The cautionary discussion of the nasty cultural biases associated with civilization-justifying essentialist claims certainly belongs in any discussion of contemporary, internationally oriented methodological practice. But I think there is an important, more positive idea of real practical importance to contemporary methodologists. It comes from systems theory's efforts to reformulate the Cosmological Aristotle's insights in a scientifically productive way.[39]

Borges somewhere has a story of a map so large that it actually covers the territory it attempts to map. Obviously a model as large or as complex as the phenomena we use it to help us to understand defeats our purposes. But part of the Wittgensteinian fear of a physicalistic metaphysics mentioned above is an opposite concern: naturalistically condoned failures to recognize the complexities of the creative, practical dimensions of human activity. If we try to keep both perspectives in mind, an ontological-methodological Great Chain of Knowing/Acting/Being possibilities can still help us judge model-reality fits. It can give us a rough, naturalistic, evaluative hierarchy in

---

[39] "General systems theory offers a new approach. At first sight, it looks like Aristotelian theory. A general notion of the social system is used to define the *encompassing* system as a *special* case of social systems. The content, however, has changed" (Luhmann 1990: 175). See also Boulding (1956) and Campbell (1960), both reprinted in the *General Systems Yearbook*, edited by Anatol Rapoport.

Table 2.1   *The Great Chain of Knowing/Acting/Being*

Campbell's Hierarchy of Knowing Processes	*Aristotle's Grading* of "Continuous scale of ascent" from lifeless things to human animals
1 Genetic mutation and selective survival	world of plants
2 Bisexuality and heterozygosity	distinction between animals reproducing with/without male/female differentiation
3 Blind trial and error problem solving	greater or lesser capacity for motion and sensibility
4 Learning (retention of adaptive response patterns for future use)	animals with more intelligence and memories
5 Perception, i.e., visual exploration of potential locomotor alternatives	indistinct perception of sponges, other relatively immobile sea animals, etc.
6 Observational learning characteristic of social animals	distinct perceptual capabilities
7 Imitation based on perception	more intelligent, longer living animals living with offspring on a social footing
8 Linguistic instruction about the nature of the world and correct responses thereto	distinctive human capacity for speaking and reasoning (logos)
9 Thought, wherein potential locomotions are symbolically checked *vis-à-vis* mnemonically represented model of the environment	distinctive human capability to distinguish the universal in the particular, to codify memories into unified experience
10 Social decision making (pooling of partial observations into models)	the fulfillment of human nature in the polis
11 Modern science	some humans have a capacity for philosophy
12 Machines (a separate, parallel, Chomskean hierarchy)	Metaphysics: Platonic forms

Source: Campbell (1960, 1961); Aristotle, *The History of Animals*, 588a–589, and *Politics*, 1253a, in McKeon (1941).

terms of which to supplement "variance explained" assessments of model-reality fits.

Standard No. 6 (*Reducing model-reality insults*)

As matched against each other on the Great Chain of Knowing/ Acting/Being, tractable models which come closer to representing the characteristic features of the reality they address, *ceteris paribus*, are better.

Table 2.1 lists a correspondence between types of being and knowing identified by Aristotle, and a general systems hierarchy of knowledge modalities identified by a leading contemporary social scientific methodologist, Donald T. Campbell. Although models of artificially alive social processes are of course not really alive, they at least begin to explore new dimensions of social life which other traditions take for granted, and are to be encouraged.[40] As with all models, of course, some features of a complex reality are being high-lighted, while others are backgrounded. Standard No. 6 is suggested as a way of rethinking a related set of representational issues.

Although I agree with Onuf (1995) that the Great Chain of Being notion can help contemporary International Relations scholars rethink their appropriate "levels of analysis," I wish to suggest that the greatest methodological challenge suggested by this hierarchy is that we must significantly reduce avoidable insults to human nature which hide all too easily beyond the respectability of discipline-specific calls for scientific parsimony. When tractable modeling representations exist with characteristic properties closer in the Knowing/Acting/Being chain than one's own, disciplinary habit is a weak methodological justification. Standard No. 6 suggests an obligation to learn, to use, and to recommend them. Cohen *et al.*'s *Intentions in Communication* is, for example, much more representationally sophisticated about human memories, social discourse and symbolically encoded learning than Axelrod's *The Evolution of Cooperation*; if one wants to study human interactive learning, the former style of work insults human capabilities much less. If such representations are too difficult or complex to master, intermediate, but still linguistically based model representa-tions are available, as those reviewed in Hudson, (ed. 1991) and Taber

---

[40] This functionalist assessment stance will be further discussed in Chapter 5 below. The first of several conference proceedings on artificial life are published as Langton, ed. (1989); on this theme see also Boulding (1956); Simon (1962); Axelrod (1984); Arthur (1993); Epstein and Axtell (1996).

(1992). Historical studies of historical learning may well be the best of all currently feasible approaches, despite their lack of formal rigor!

Several especially troubling or inadequate features of these methodological suggestions should at least be mentioned; it is not my intention unreservedly to endorse Aristotelian approaches. Indeed, each of the examples we have looked at has revised the Aristotelian corpus, and I would expect subsequent methodologists motivated by the present discussions to continue to do so.

Standard No. 7 (*Sensitivity to the problematic areas of the Aristotelian tradition*)

Aristotle's work has become only a small part of an historically developed Aristotelian tradition of intentionally-oriented sociopolitical inquiry, whose relevance must be, and has been, adapted to current circumstances. Particularly important changes to take into account in reinvigorating this tradition include:

(a) The subsumption of syllogistically formalized modes of reasoning within twentieth-century revolutions in formal logic. Von Wright, for example, is very aware of Frege's, Whitehead and Russell's and Wittgenstein's contributions to logic; he even uses simple automata theory to excellent effect in reconstructing modal possibility arguments implicit within the discussion of alternative, counterfactual, practical historical possibilities. But there is an even more powerful set of relevant logical and linguistic formalisms – those associated with recursive, self-referring and self-compiling computer programming languages like COMMON LISP. These seem especially relevant for a formally rigorous "ruling science" of collective self-control (Batali 1988; Luhmann 1990; Kauffman 1995, ch. 12), if we are not overcome by the arrogance of mathematical political theorizing.

(b) Similarly, contemporary understanding of the pragmatic force of inferential arguments (Heidegger, Wittgenstein), of the elocutionary force of linguistic performances (Austin, Searle, Harré), and the metaphorically shaped character of scientific concepts and logical forms (Johnson 1987; Lakoff 1990) all challenge objectivist and phenomenologically essentialist readings of nature. The recognition of the cultural and bodily bases of our apprehending external reality, however, do not foreclose revised, inter-culturally validated versions of naturalist epistemologies, e.g., the one described in Wierzbicka (1992).

(c) Aristotle's evolutionary typologizing strategy and his culturally shaped sense of natural hierarchies have not stood the test of civilizational time. Already in his own day, his ex-student Alexander of Macedon was introducing cosmopolitan patterns of egalitarian human association that the Stoic and Judeo-Christian-Islamic traditions of philosophy were to adopt centuries later. Similarly, his treatment of natural laws, and natural hierarchies (e.g., rulers to ruled, masters to slaves, men to women) does not survive contemporary critical analysis.

(d) Moreover, his functionalist way of systemic thinking needs a careful rethinking, if not reformulation, in light of both recent critiques of functionalist thinking and emerging styles of natural language, using various degrees of analysis and argumentation formalization.

Substantively unified, technically diverse political methodology

Gary King wrote *Unifying Political Methodology* with the intention "to stimulate and centralize methodological debate in political science," in the "hope [that] a new and much needed subfield of political methodology will eventually emerge" (King 1989: xi). King wants Political Science's methodological and/or statistical subdisciplines to be autonomous from other disciplines: he calls for "uniform, discipline-wide methodological standards" (pp. 4–5). Because the disciplinary boundaries of sociopolitical inquiry have changed so much through time, and in relatively arbitrary ways – is ethics out, public choice in, econometrics out, likelihood maximizing statistics in, computational linguistics out, textual content analysis in, rhetoric out, cultural history in, the critical legal analysis of public institutions out? – I am wary of any such attempts to achieve uniformity in that broad, interdisciplinary set of concerns I have here labeled sociopolitical inquiry.

I applaud an integrative approach to the technical estimation and inference-oriented statistics literature recently being used by formally rigorous political methodologists. King's impressive knack for choosing interesting and revealing applications of the "likelihood theory" approach deserves emulation. But I must caution against identifying political statistics with political methodology and the implication that the integration of a class of statistical techniques is a unification of political methodology. In too many contemporary,

Platonic–Galilean, conceptions of methodology, there is little or no attention to alternatives like the Aristotelian tradition – its linguistic/pragmatic roots and its methodological contributions – or to the methodologically suggestive controversies inspired by its descendants: intentionalist, systems theoretic, interpretive and hermeneutic/dialectical philosophies of sociopolitical inquiry.[41]

Positively put, it has been the illustrated message of this chapter that the methodological approaches and the formal/technical tools of sociopolitical inquiry can and should be especially adapted, or developed, to reveal the crux of its sociopolitical subject matter. With its three different, but philosophically integrated, conceptions of inquiry – each with different methodological emphases and technical alternatives – the long-enduring, interdisciplinary, Aristotelian tradition offers evidence of a rationally based, substantively focused, epistemologically integrated, yet pluralistic research approach with such relevance. It is an ironic conclusion to a chapter dedicated to a sympathetic but critical reading of the conceptual and methodological suggestions of a Stagirian refugee who lived 2,400 years ago that this task is far from finished. For contemporary North American social scientists it has hardly begun.

[41] Compared with King (1989), for example, King, Keohane and Verba (1994) make real progress in recognizing the "descriptive inference" associated with the Aristotle/Weber/Geertz tradition of interpretive analysis. Although Weber is mentioned, no attention is given either to the traditions of analysis which he tried to synthesize – as summarized, for example, by von Wright (1971) and Apel (1984). This newer book does not encourage students to read further in the literature of the philosophy of social science, where provocative, well argued reformulations of the Geertzian position can be found. It also lacks any attention and footnotes to the alternative formal representations which von Wright, I and others have found so useful for rigorous, methodologically sophisticated treatments of questions arising from the Aristotelian tradition of sociopolitical inquiry.

3 Toynbee's Jesus:
Computational hermeneutics and the continuing presence of classical Mediterranean civilization[1]

In *The Uses of Enchantment*, Bruno Bettelheim argues that "our greatest need and most difficult achievement is to find meaning in our lives" (Bettelheim 1977: 3). Most Americans appear at least partially to have achieved this goal with the help of Jesus. In a recent Gallup sample of 1,509 Americans, nine-tenths said they had been influenced by Jesus as a moral and ethical teacher, three-quarters believed that Jesus was alive in Heaven today, 71 percent said that they were deepening their personal relationships with him: two-thirds held that a person must accept Jesus to gain eternal life. "The Gallup organization says a sample of 1,500 is subject to a margin of error of two to three percentage points" (Briggs 1983).[2]

The meaning of the Christian message is much more uncertain and variable than these sampling margins suggest. Few countries in the world are both as religiously Christian and as intellectually ignorant of the tenets of their dominant religion as the same Gallup poll suggests. Nearly three-fifths of the American survey panel did not know that Jesus delivered the Sermon on the Mount; 46 percent of the sample could not *name* the four Gospels considered by all scholars to be the single most important extant source on the life and teachings of Jesus. Moreover, a third of these Americans "believed it was possible to obtain everlasting life without accepting Jesus, and nearly a fourth

---

[1] This chapter excerpts, and revises Alker, Lehnert and Schneider (1985). Its original version was supported in part by the National Science Foundation, Grant No. IST-8217502. In deference to the very substantial earlier contributions of my coauthors, I have retained the first person plural in appropriate places, but not sought their approval of my revisions, from the infelicities of which they are thereby, in advance, exonerated.

[2] The quotations and the fractions in this paragraph are from the Briggs article, which refers to a report released by the Gallup organization.

thought it was possible to be a 'true Christian' without believing Jesus was divine" (Briggs 1983).

Were we to attempt to replicate these results outside of the United States, or to reconstruct analogous aggregations 100, 500 or 1,900 years ago, surely even more profound differences and diversities would have been found. On the other hand, and perhaps in part because of this diversity of interpretation, the Jesus story has been amazingly successful as spiritual guide, political propaganda or cultural ideal. No text in Western history, whether fictional or scientific, religious or secular, has more frequently, universally and lastingly given significance both to individual lives and/or great historical movements. With important modifications, its influence has spanned at least four fundamentally different modes of production (classical slavery, feudalism, early modern capitalism, and recent East European socialism).

As social and computer scientists reflecting on our own religious socialization, we are led to ask the following questions. In the light of both traditional and more recent scholarly approaches, what are appropriate, scientific ways to ascertain the meanings we and others see and feel within the Jesus story? What motivating power or charisma does this story, or "myth" contain?[3] What basic structure or structures, what infectious, self-replicating, "viral" qualities account for this power?[4] Can we replicably discover and empirically test some of the ways in which its deepest structure has been rewritten into different "surface" texts? Or do the "rewrites" that are discussed by many traditional scholars themselves differ in their fundamentals? Which versions of the Jesus story, thought of as an imitable hero story, have had more or less appeal in which personal, cultural, economic or political contexts, thought of in contemporary or historical terms? In particular, why do so many Americans and others find Jesus' story so personally meaningful even when their knowledge of Scripture is so superficial? How would we begin, methodologically, to map these

---

[3]   We use the words "myth," "hero story," "legend," "fairy-tale" and "folk-lore" as technical terms in the human sciences, without prejudice to the issue of the ultimate, religious validity of Christianity. More generally, we wish to be identified with the "humanistic" tradition which seeks autonomy in defining its subject matter and standards of scholarly inquiry concerning issues of religious significance, and with the humanistic or cultural sciences which claim autonomy *vis-à-vis* the knowledge interests, methodology and tools of the natural sciences.

[4]   Some of this biological terminology comes from a provocative, but flawed reverie on "Metamagical Themas: Virus-Like Sentences and Self-Replicating Structures," by Douglas Hofstadter (1983).

meanings – or that of other charismatic religious and political figures – across the different cultural and political boundaries of the world? The importance of these questions justifies our evidently humanistic and admittedly inadequate scientific efforts to answer them.

This chapter presents a synthetic rationale for our approach, which has concentrated until now not on survey data, but on the discovery of analytically reproducible, motivationally suggestive plot structures implicit in texts of the Jesus story, as they are read or heard by different individuals. In a critical hermeneutic way, two such independently coded, computer-assisted analyses will be presented and compared, without the prior assumption that only one true structure *really exists*. Lehnert's coding of the Jesus story derives from Arnold Toynbee's schematic outline in an Appendix to *A Study of History*; the longer Alker-Schneider coding relies as well on the Biblical verses cited by Toynbee (Toynbee 1946: 376–539).[5] Our conclusions will stress continuities between our own computer-assisted form of humanistic hermeneutical inquiry – computational hermeneutics – and more traditional forms of social scientific text analysis, in which Toynbee has been a pioneer. With needed improvements, and maintaining its mix of human and machine inputs, we believe the present approach can make a methodological contribution to the empirical, critical and constructive discussion of the many different ways that classical Mediterranean civilization is a continuing presence in our, and others' lives.

A new approach to an old topic

Given the enormous corpus of previous scholarly investigations of the meanings of the Jesus story, it would be hard to justify a new approach without finding certain continuities with, and lacunae in, previous approaches. Our approach addresses a cluster of concerns we have found in several venerable humanistic traditions – religious history, psychoanalysis and hermeneutical philosophy. It proposes and explores a marriage between the traditional search for mimetic plot structures and a novel, still evolving, computer science methodology of narrative summarization and affective plot unit analysis (Lehnert 1981; Lehnert, Black and Reiser 1981; Lehnert and Loiselle 1985).[6] It does this

---

5 Further Toynbee page references in the present chapter are to this volume.
6 A more extensive review of roughly comparable, and testable approaches to the summarization and interpretation of story structures is given in Chapter 8 below. In the 1970s and early 1980s, early versions of that chapter, first entitled "Fairy Tales and

in the hope that the explicitness, formal tractability and potential cumulativeness of computerized methods of text analysis may add new forms of constructive rigor to the critical examination both of classical texts, their more recent interpretations, and their cross-national and cross-cultural extent, variability and endurance.

Religious history

Religious history seeks to give meaning to its hearers or readers through its accounts of the purposes and actions of God (or the gods) and those divinely inspired. Of course, the impulse to see Divine Plan or Providence in the larger movements of history has not been unique to the Judeo-Christian tradition, where it is highly developed. The missionary fervor of early (and recent) Islamic civilization is well known; so is the ambiguous "Mandate of Heaven" legitimating early Chinese rulers. Hegelian philosophy sees history as the unfolding of Reason's self-understanding. Despite its atheistic stance, Marxian philosophy also has very Christian dramatical turning points: it foretells the replacement of an old order by a new one after an heroic struggle, in which the working class assumes the role of savior of humanity. All of these traditions, to varying degrees, have scripted histories within them, revered accounts of key individuals or groups whose life histories are suggested as vehicles for the follower's own increased understanding, and as models for their own lives. Johan Galtung has argued that developmental history, crisis turning points and history-ending appearances of God on Earth are, however, distinct features of Western, but not Eastern "social cosmologies" (Galtung 1980b).

For present purposes, what is particularly important about Toynbee's religious history is not so much his development of a multistage, comparative conceptualization of civilizational history in which various heroic figures do or do not succeed in shaping revitalizing responses to the challenges faced by their civilizations; rather, it is his derivative, more specific thesis and argumentation concerning the role

World Histories," were written before I came across Lehnert's work; so that even though finally published in 1987, after Alker, Schneider and Lehnert (1985), it may also serve as a comparative introduction to the present chapter. Lehnert and I had both studied with Robert Abelson, and we were admirers of the Schank–Abelson line of work on computational text understanding and Abelson's more particular interest in the dynamics of politically relevant belief systems, e.g., Abelson and Reich (1969), and Schank and Abelson (1977).

of the Gospels in the development of a unified, and relatively enduring Hellenic-Syriac-Christian popular culture within the Graeco-Roman world. Investigating the appeals of the Jesus story today is a way of studying continuities and transformations in such civilizational communities.

A comparison of elementary features of classical stories about Socrates and Heracles, heroic Spartan kings, Roman reformers (particularly the Gracchi), leaders of the slave revolts and Jesus leads to Toynbee's conclusion that "[t]he correspondences work themselves out into an identical drama which appears, at least in essence and outline, to underlie the whole of this group of hero-stories, pagan and Christian alike" (Toynbee 1946: 406). Why is this the case? "The Gospels contain, embedded in them, a considerable number and variety of elements which have been conveyed to them by the stream of [Hellenic, Syriac, etc.] 'folk-memory,'" out of "shifting subterranean currents of a perennially flowing primitive psychic life" (1946: 457). Out of these currents of primitive psychic life, "elements native to one culture can make their way into the life of another culture even at times when, on the sophisticated surface of life, the two cultures which are thus in effective communication [at the popular or proletarian level] ... are consciously antipathetic ..." (1946: 447). Taken together, these elements might properly be described as "the epic cycle of the Hellenic internal proletariat; and epic poetry is [somewhere] between the two mental realms of 'folk-lore' and history" (1946: 448).

Toynbee's heroic story frame cannot fit all reconstructions of the early Christian experience equally well. If the earliest Christian battles seem to have been primarily against Jewish authorities, the relative responsibility of Jewish and Roman authorities for the execution of Jesus remains an unanswered controversial question. An argument has been made that the Gospels' relatively unfavorable treatment of the Jewish authorities represent an explicit attempt to cover up Jesus' support for the Jewish "Zealots" rebelling against Rome (Brandon 1979).[7] But it is clear that the authority of the Roman emperor is the chief target of the early martyrs inspired by Jesus.[8]

Religious history also teaches the reflective scholar that Christian interpretations have given significance to very different political movements. A longer term, less millenary, less pacifist, more conservative

---

[7] We are grateful to Walter Dean Burnham for calling this study to our attention.

[8] A particularly vivid, insightful, text-based account of the martyrdom issue in the early Christian church is Elaine Pagels (1979: Ch. 4).

interpretation of Roman authority roughly coincides with the conversion to Christianity of the Emperor Constantine. The most serious enemy of Christian history then becomes those attacking (or defending themselves against) that empire. Medieval views of the gulf between the City of God and the City of Man support religious retreat into more perfect (but authoritarian) monastic communities and preparation for an all-important afterlife in Heaven or Hell. The modern era is associated with the redirection of religious energy from Christendom's Crusades against the "Infidel Turk" to total Holy Wars between Catholics and Protestants, or even persecution of one Protestant faction by another, as before and during the English Civil War (see especially Johnson 1975, 1981). Hence the flight of the Pilgrims and the founding of a New Jerusalem, "a city upon a hill." Other new cities were given names like Providence and Philadelphia. These events are prominent in American history books.

Psychoanalytic readings of fairy tales, myths, dreams and utopias

Despite many criticisms we or others might wish to make of Toynbee's monographic appendix, we find the scholarly attitude revealed there to be both exemplary of objectively disciplined humanistic scholarship and prophetic of much more recent work. For example, consider again Bruno Bettelheim's well-known psychoanalytic study of the role played by myths, fairy tales and folkloric legends in meeting our need for meaning in our lives. Without citing him, Bettelheim amplifies Toynbee's argument in a remarkably complementary fashion:

> Myths and closely related religious legends offered material from which children formed their concepts of the world's origin and purpose, and of the social ideals a child could pattern himself after.... These were the images of the unconquered hero Achilles and the wily Odysseus; of Hercules, whose life history showed that it is not beneath the dignity of the strongest man to clean the filthiest stable; of St. Martin, who cut his coat in half to clothe a poor beggar.... A myth, like a fairy tale, may express inner conflict in symbolic form and suggest how it may be solved.... The myth presents its theme in a majestic way; it carries spiritual force, and the divine is present and is experienced in the form of the superhuman heroes who make constant demands on mere mortals. (Bettelheim 1977: 24–26)[9]

[9] A different psychoanalytic treatment of heroic savior myths is Murray Edelman (1967:

Both the historian and the psychiatrist see the unconscious realm of individual psychology, with its powerful symbols, fundamental conflicts and integrative accommodations as relevant features of enduring religious myths. Drawing examples from both Hellenic and Judeo-Christian traditions, both see social needs – the revival of disintegrating civilizations or the socialization of future generations in their cultural heritage – as differentially met by the heroic stories of apparently childish or "primitive" folklore. Both appraise positively the search for integrative, directive meanings in human life through the analysis of legendary or literary narratives, as they interact with the lives of their audiences.[10]

Hermeneutic philosophy

As a pioneering proponent of the human sciences, Wilhelm Dilthey conceived of hermeneutics as the art of interpreting texts. Hermeneutic philosophy was given the related task, "the search for objective methods that can confirm intersubjectivity through a critical interpretation of human expressions" (Makkreel 1975: 258–60, 327, 345–357).[11] A distinguished contemporary practitioner of that art and that philosophy, Paul Ricoeur, has argued that "the narrative schematism 'is an art hidden in the depths of the human soul, and it will always be difficult to extract the true mechanism from nature in order to lay it open before our eyes'" (Ricoeur 1981).[12] Yet his mode of critical hermeneutic analysis exemplifies a third humanistic tradition, hermeneutical philosophy, particularly useful for us in the delineation of the Toynbee–Bettelheim realm of folklore and myth, somewhere between

217–228). Edelman argues that "Myths and metaphors permit men to live in a world in which the causes are simple and neat and the remedies are apparent. In place of a complicated empirical world, men hold to a relatively few, simple, classic, archetypical myths, of which the conspiratorial enemy and the omnicompetent hero-savior are the central ones" (1967: 228). Edelman's conformist view should be contrasted with the radical and conservative perspectives reviewed below.

[10] Toynbee's religious defense of his approach is worth noting: "But is it credible that God should have revealed himself in 'folk-lore'?... [I]t is in 'folk-lore' if anywhere – for it is certainly not on ballot-papers – that *Vox populi* becomes *Vox Dei*.... 'In that hour Jesus rejoiced in spirit and said: I thank thee, O Father, Lord of Heaven and Earth that thou hast hid these things from the wise and prudent and hast revealed them unto babes. Even so Father; for so it seemed good in Thy sight' (Luke x.21; Matt. xi.25–26)" (1946: 538ff.).

[11] In the present chapter, quotations and paraphrases are taken from these pages.

[12] Textual page references in the subsequent three paragraphs are also to this volume.

poetic fiction, depth-psychological symbolic meanings, scholarly history and cultural studies.

Like his predecessors, Ricoeur wants to discover the reality, the authentic truth of mythological or legendary stories about which adequate, empirically accurate historical analysis is not possible. He wants a demystified way of distinguishing history from fiction, yet preserving the larger unity and distinctive truth values of each. Ricoeur argues that "by opening us to what is different, history opens us to the possible, whereas fiction, by opening us to the unreal, leads us to what is essential in reality" (1981: 296).

His argument may be briefly sketched as follows. Having accepted some version of Gallie's thesis that "history is a species of the genus story" (as cited in Ricoeur 1981: 272), Ricoeur recognizes the difficult problem of conflicting possible psychoanalytic interpretations of the same evidence. Neither neopositivist accounts of historical explanation nor atemporal structuralist models of narrative structure are adequate. Ricoeur sees a configurative, sequential element of narrative within both historical and fictional writing, as well as the listener/reader's experience. A context sensitive (but not context bound) knowledge interest in communicative understanding is also presupposed by both forms of narrative.

Dilthey said that "The poet is a seer who intuits the sense of life." He would agree with Ricoeur's view that historical writing has its "poetic" qualities, and encourage his search for plot-like organizing schemes. For Ricoeur these involve four fundamental types of "emplotment" (Frye's romances, tragedies, comedies and satires), different formal arguments (positivist or dialectical laws), contrasting world hypotheses (such as Pepper's formism, organism, mechanism, contextualism), and alternative ideological mobilizing schemes (such as Mannheim's conservatism, radicalism, liberalism, anarchism). Fictional writing is Aristotelian *mimesis*, not merely imitative copying, but "productive imagination," "the reactivation of human actions," an "iconic augmentation" of the real, magnifying its essential possibilities. *Mimesis* occurs only when poetic activity constructs plots, such as the *mythos* ("meaning speech, fable and plot together") of a tragic poem. "We thus discover, with the *mythos* of Aristotle's *Poetics*, what is essential in our concept of plot in history: union of contingency and consequence, of chronology and configuration, of sequence and consequence" (1981: 292–294).

Ricoeur has recently deepened and modified his views on mimetic plot structures. But his latest books, including *La Metaphore Vive* and *Temps et Récit*, continue his concern with generative and synthetic semantic structures. Of narratives he says, "semantic innovation consists in the invention of a plot which is itself a work of synthesis: by virtue of the plot, ends, causes and accidents are joined together under the temporal unity of a total and complete action. It is this synthesis of *heterogeneity* which makes comparable narrative and metaphor."[13] Despite their obvious referential differences, very similar configurative elements connect fictional stories and traditional histories. Ricoeur reviews debates between Braudel, Dray, Gallie, Hempel and their followers, using an augmented, three-stage conception of *mimesis* – as prefiguring, configuring and refiguring imitations of life – to develop further his position.

A reformulated problematique

Although we have not exhausted humanistic insights relevant to our questions, the above synthetic review suggests a convergent focus for addressing them. If motivationally productive, mimetic, plot-like structures help give meaning to children's stories, religious myths and narrative histories, a major scientific goal must be their operational identification through careful textual analysis. Once identified, the way the "narrative schematism" projects them into the hearer/readers' lives must be investigated.

Even if this quest borrows from traditional approaches the hermeneutic route of close textual analysis and starts from Toynbee's schematic list of eighty-seven story elements, his schematic summaries of classical hero stories raise numerous issues for the computationally oriented text analyst. There are many questions not satisfactorily answered by his study. For example, how should we represent and identify the meaning components of the Jesus story? His numbered elements seem all to be rather complicated, but of varying degrees of complexity. Are there distinctive or crucial elements of his heroic version of the Jesus story that he has neglected, misstated or overemphasized? Are some more "essential," basic or primitive than others? Is a more parsimonious or deeper account of Toynbee's own

---

[13] Ricoeur (1983: 15), our translation. Ricoeur gives an extensive discussion of Aristotle's poetic theories, Gallie's notion of "followability" in narrative texts, Hempel's nomological treatment of historical laws and the "quasi-plot" of Braudel's history of structures, cycles and events (1983: 298ff.).

analysis possible? If we arrive at an appealing plot-like deep structure to this story, how do we know if it is correct, the deepest, the truest, the best or even the better interpretation of a complex "surface" text? Would different readers, from different cultural contexts but reading the same Gospels, find different contents in the episodes he chooses to emphasize? How can we test for the generalizations he makes about Mediterranean civilization at the level of individual lives? At what point should we challenge his cultural rereading of the Jesus story itself?

New ways of dealing with these lacunae may indeed be helpful. Hence a concern with the meaning of the Jesus story has brought us to the recent computationally oriented literature on narrative summarization and analogical or metaphorical reasoning, as exemplified by the present collaboration. It is our hope that working together we can provide certain answers to these questions with the assistance of the findings, the conventions, the techniques and the programs associated with that literature.

We can now more explicitly summarize this discussion in terms of several desiderata for the further scientific investigation of our problem:[14]

(1) To think of Jesus story elements positivistically, as problematically true or false assertions, misses their historically validated motivational appeal, at least partly exercised symbolically at the preconscious or unconscious psychic level. The story's affective structure needs further micro-investigation.

(2) Descriptive story elements should be readable as imitable and modifiable recipes for human behavior.

(3) The variety of historical contexts in which this motivational power has been exercised (on the basis of the same, or nearly the same, Gospel texts, but not always with the same effectiveness) argues strongly for one or more deep-structured representations of its essential elements, capable of being rewritten in many different, but not all particular situations.

(4) Some kind of mimetic plot structure may well be what we are looking for as a major underlying source of the infectious, viral, self-replicating power of the Jesus story.

(5) Once the existence of precise versions of basic texts has been

---

[14] The following list of desiderata, as well as the next section of this chapter, are adapted from the preliminary report on our studies: Wendy C. Lehnert, *et al.* (1983: 358–367).

assured, both operational strategies for discovering underlying plot-like structures and rationalized procedures for showing their relative merit as summarizers of more complex texts should be investigated.

(6)   If an inductive strategy for structurally characterizing such stories is utilized, procedures for recognizing and combining primitive thematic elements should be clearly and precisely explicated.

(7)   A useful way to explore competing and/or convergent interpretations of the motivational appeal of basic religious narratives is independently to subject these texts to replicable affective plot summarization procedures. Of course the resulting story summaries will not resolve age-old hermeneutical controversies; but they should provide explicit and rigorous bases for further discussion and further generalizing studies.

On meeting these desiderata with plot unit summarization procedures

The search for the mimetic plot structure of the Jesus story happily converges substantially, if not in every detail, with a research program on narrative summarization in terms of affective plot units initiated several years ago (Lehnert 1981). Not only does this line of investigation code narrative elements affectively, its inferences from detailed textual codings to summary plot structures are similarly substantive, unlike the syntactic models typical of the "story grammar" approach initiated by Rumelhart (1975, 1977). And it is an ontologically important property of any LISP-based manner of *describing* plot units that it readily allows recipe-like *procedural* interpretations. Hence the first two desiderata above seem potentially realizable within this approach.

What about our third and fourth desiderata: the mimetic adequacy of the plot-unit-based story characterization we arrive at and the prospects for generating "realistic" rewrites of such a deep structural characterization in at least idealized versions of various (but not all) personal or historical contexts? Preliminary empirical comparisons with story grammar representations have shown affective plot structures to predict remembered story summaries better than story grammar summaries (Lehnert, Black and Reiser 1981). This suggests that the affective organization of human story memories is indeed approximated by the Lehnert approach. We will have more to say below about the infectious, "virus-like" quality of plot unit summaries, but the extraordinary motivational appeal of the Jesus story undoubtedly has many sides to it. Given the gross affective discriminations now serving as the basis for our investigation into affectively based plot structures, and the radical reduction in cognitive content such coding ensures, closure cannot soon be expected. It will be remarkable indeed if previously developed procedures for inferring summary plot structures significantly and appealingly comprehend story accounts as complex as those dealt with by Toynbee.

Obviously, concrete explorations of mimetic (or "imitative") adequacy depend on the capacity to simulate context-specific plot rewrites and, within the limits of propriety, test for their evocative effects. Moreover, these effects will only yield to scientific analysis when the syntax, semantics and pragmatics of story generation and understanding experiences are well explicated. Because various such efforts have at least partly succeeded on the basis of other deep-structured plot characterizations[15] and progress is being made on the construction of generative story grammars for plot unit summaries (see the other chapters in Tonfoni 1985), we believe that such a generative testing of our text-based plot structures eventually will be both possible and likely to give positive and generalizable results.

Besides the facility with which its coding procedures can be compared empirically with others, Lehnert's narrative summarization approach has the additional merit of starting with amendable lists of explicitly defined primitive and complex plot components and an associated set of replicable procedures for inductively composing a more or less integrated plot summary of a given story text. These have been fully presented in her previous papers, particularly the Lehnert–Loiselle paper in the Tonfoni volume. Hence our fifth and sixth desiderata are reasonably met by these procedures.

Because the extremely interesting (and controversial) arguments made by Toynbee on the basis of his own narrative summary of the Jesus story, that schematic summary itself is an attractive text of reasonable length for our first narrative summarization effort. Whether his summary and our codings of it are independently replicable will then be explored in terms of a lengthier analysis of the Biblical texts

---

[15] Meehan (undated) cites earlier work by Sheldon Klein at the University of Wisconsin at Madison; we have also in mind work by Patrick Winston, Boris Katz and others at MIT. See Winston (1982).

cited by Toynbee in support for his summary account. Hence the final desideratum above may eventually be satisfied, but only within the context of larger hermeneutical discussions.

Our first search for mimetic plot structure

Lehnert's initial encoding of the Jesus story

When asked about the possibility of coding Toynbee's eighty-seven-element schematization of the Jesus story, Lehnert's response soon evolved into a two-pronged collaborative approach: she decided to code it herself and to train the first two authors of this chapter in the procedures involved so that an independent replication would be possible. We report our joint interpretation of her initial results here, followed in the next section by a brief report on the Alker–Schneider coding, which augmented Toynbee's schematic version of the Jesus story with a reading of the Biblical texts cited by Toynbee.

Affect states are not subtly distinguished; they mark gross distinctions between "positive" events, "negative" events, and mental events of neutral or null emotionality, but they are labeled from the perspective of each significant actor in question. Following the explicit procedures of her 1981 paper, Lehnert's first coding decision was to distinguish the following six distinctive actors in the story: God, the existing (Jewish) religious/political Authorities, the Hero (Jesus), the Masses (of Judea and Samaria) he early appeals to, his Disciples, the Traitor (Judas), the Foreign Potentate (Pilate) and the Enthusiast (Paul) who plays such an important role after the Hero's death.[16]

Then the resulting graph of thirty-seven positive affect states, twenty-eight negative affect states and fifty-five affect-neutral mental states was constructed, with these affect states appropriately connected by the five kinds of links plot unit analysis currently allows: motivation links (symbolized by "m"s), actualization links ("a"s), termination links ("t"s), state equivalence links ("e"s) and undifferentiated interpersonal

---

[16] This terminology, explicit in Toynbee's summary, suggests ways in which Toynbee seeks to generalize and compare the Jesus story with other hero stories of the period. Although there are general principles involved – related to their likely role as independent agencies influencing plot development – this decision did raise questions in our mind whether Toynbee's "Forerunner" role (John the Baptist) should have been independently coded, and whether the Roman soldiers (as potential converts to Christianity and symbolic members of the Graeco-Roman internal proletariat) should have been differentiated from the Judean masses and the Potentate.

Table 3.1   *Primitive plot units*

A. Monadic

M ↓a + SUCCESS	M ↓a – FAILURE	– ↓m M PROBLEM	+ ↓m M ACTIVATION	M ↓m M MOTIVATION
M ↑e M PERSEVERANCE	+ ↑e – MIXED BLESSING	– ↑e + HIDDEN BLESSING	– ↑e – COMPLEX NEGATIVE	+ ↑e + COMPLEX POSITIVE
– ↑t + RESOLUTION	+ ↑t – LOSS	+ ↑t + POSITIVE TRADEOFF	– ↑t – NEGATIVE TRADEOFF	M ↑t M CHANGE OF MIND

B. Dyadic

? ╲ – NEGATIVE REACTION	? ╲ + POSITIVE REACTION	– ╲ M EXTERNAL PROBLEM	+ ╲ M EXTERNAL ENABLEMENT	M ╲ M EXTERNAL MOTIVATION

links (the e-links of Lehnert–Loiselle, which are graphically unmarked). Table 3.1 shows which combinations of link types are syntactically allowed, and provides as well the mnemonic names for the primitive plot units of plot unit analysis. At this point it should be observed that those textual elements giving merely descriptive details (such as references to the hero's royal lineage and genealogy) as well as merely visual elements (Toynbee's tableaux) were explicitly ignored by her coding procedures.

Coding affective states and their linkages is a skilled procedure. Several comments are appropriate about this important step in Lehnert's analysis of Toynbee's schematic summary text. First, it should be stressed that plot units have been defined with an emphasis on affective and purposive behavior, such as individual success and failure, interpersonal cooperation and competition. The inclusion of any particular link is in effect a commitment to the existence of a primitive plot unit – one of the units in Table 3.1 – in the text being considered. It is from such affectively and purposively oriented elementary plot units that all more complex plot structures are constructed, using preestablished lists of possible complex units.

Secondly, research has shown that ordinary reader/listeners bring to any new text a set of higher-order or "top-level" knowledge structures used in interpreting that text. Therefore, skilled coders must be familiar with, and are expected to look for, a number of complex plot units. When done carefully, this kind of coding increases the chance that subsequent searching for higher order (or deeper) plot units will be successful.

Thirdly, an important grammatical constraint in the production of an affect state graph is the requirement that at most one link of each allowable kind may go into or out of a particular affect state. Novice coders often use up the limited options they have for certain such links – m-links in particular – before they realize the existence of more important story connections. As a result, they must make repeated recoding efforts.

On the other hand, sophisticated coders must still make difficult choices among the several possible connections symbolically suggested by certain texts. At the moment reasonably explicit and reliable heuristic and grammatical coding rules exist for most of this process, but no completely programmed and validated coding algorithms are available. Of particular interest in our own initial discussions of Lehnert's coding rules (which, under her supervision, Alker and Schneider applied to a well-known fairy tale before attempting Biblical texts) were the ways in which the "e"s allow symbolically rich affective equivalences and contradictions. Differences in the number and kind of e-links were perhaps the most important divergences in our coding practices at this stage; and such differences are likely to make substantial differences in the topological structure of plot unit inter-linkages at the focus of attention in later stages of Lehnert's analysis. As a result, one may argue there is still a need feasibly and explicitly to elaborate (and perhaps modify) certain constraints on the use of state equivalence links (the "e"s) beyond those possibilities noted in the Lehnert–Loiselle paper.

The automated inference of a summary affective plot structure

It is at this point that Lehnert's Yale version of the Plot Unit Graph Generator played an important role in our investigation. On the basis of a previously defined set of approximately forty-five possible complex plot units (mostly a subset of the more elaborate list of complex plot units in the Appendix to the Lehnert–Loiselle paper) all

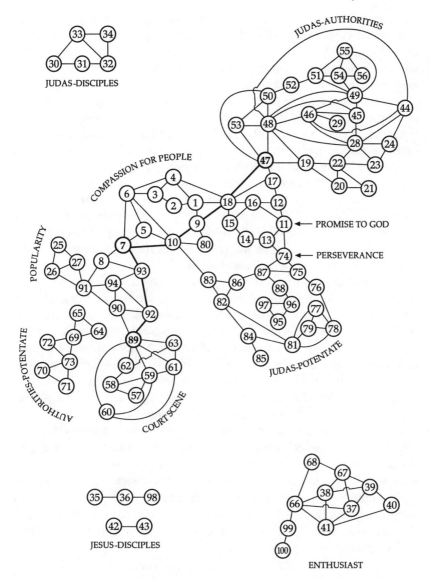

Figure 3.1 Six top-level plot unit clusters in Lehnert's coding of Toynbee's Christus Patiens

complex units contained in the affective state graph of the story were discovered computationally. There are 199 molecule-like structures of affective meaning in Lehnert's coding of *Christus Patiens*, of which the computer search algorithm further identified half (actually 100) as undominated, i.e., "top-level units."

Fortunately for our purposes, as seen in Figure 3.1, eighty of the top-level plot units implied by Lehnert's coding of the Jesus story are interconnected with each other, reflecting an obvious narrative coherence involving the central elements in Jesus' life. Five additional clusters of top-level plot units were found: ten connected units involving actions by the Enthusiast (Paul), a seven-units set of relationship between the Jewish Authorities and the Roman Potentate, two small clusters involving Jesus and his Disciples, and one involving Judas and the Disciples. The somewhat disturbing (but also simplifying) separateness of these clusters helped motivate the addition of transitive e-links to the current version of the PUGG program.

What is at the center of the main narrative cluster in Figure 3.1? Does this complex configuration have something we might think of as a basic string of motivational codons, a viral, highly infectious, self-replicating molecular core structure? (Hofstader, 1983) Following a strategy developed for summarizing the most motivationally significant elements in complex top-level narrative structures, Lehnert identified three top-level units as critical ones, in the sense that their disappearance would disconnect more than 10 percent of the top-level units from the rest of the major narrative cluster.

Three such plot units had this property: Jesus' MOTIVATION for calling to the masses, the authorities' SUCCESS-BORN-OF-ADVERSITY in finally getting Jesus arrested, and their RETALIATION against his exasperating responses in getting him put to death. These units and their minimal connecting path are emphasized in Figure 3.1 and summarized in Table 3.2. Graphically, at a more disaggregated level of detail, these three plot units (one atomic or primitive, the other molecular or complex) are shown as Figure 3.1a on p. 121.

The next step was to find the minimal path connecting these crucial plot units, as a way of inductively inferring a motivational core of top-level affective plot units. Although a computer program for this step does not yet exist, its results were unambiguously determined. Table 3.2 reports the highly suggestive results of this procedure. Not only do these eight plot units tell the essence of a story of Jesus being commissioned by God to do battle with the ruling, but illegitimate

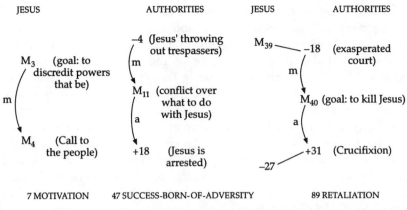

JESUS   AUTHORITIES JESUS   AUTHORITIES

M_3 (goal: to discredit powers that be)

-4 (Jesus' throwing out trespassers)

M_{11} (conflict over what to do with Jesus)

M_4 (Call to the people)

$+18$ (Jesus is arrested)

M_{39} — -18 (exasperated court)

M_{40} (goal: to kill Jesus)

$+31$ (Crucifixion)

-27

7 MOTIVATION 47 SUCCESS-BORN-OF-ADVERSITY 89 RETALIATION

Figure 3.1a The three most critical plot units in Lehnert's Jesus

authorities, there is also emphasis on Jesus' highly political conflict with the authorities and the religiously (and motivationally) significant connection of his goals to his own (unjustified) crucifixion. His death according to the practice reserved for rebels against Roman authorities turns out paradoxically to be a successful act *vis-à-vis* his original aspirations, which were originally coded by Lehnert to include being a savior with a religious following. Note especially the HIDDEN BLESSING associated with this self-sacrificial act, an e-link connecting his death to his subsequently being worshipped. One might hypothesize that this emotionally powerful feature of the Jesus myth will be found in many other Christian stories as well, although the "self-interest" aspect of martyr-like behavior will probably not be an agreed upon component.

A preliminary assessment of these results

Lehnert's version of the deep affective plot structure of the heroic Jesus story, then, turns out to be highly significant, a rather surprising discovery at least for those educated in Sunday schools that deemphasized radical political interpretations of the Jesus story. It corroborates both political and religious readings of the Jesus myth that have emphasized the divinely legitimated, revolutionary historical-political character of its imitable but modifiable recipes for meaningful action. In this sense we argued, in our earlier report, that we had approximated the infectious core structure of the "Jesus virus." (Our term, suggested by Hofstader, 1983.)

A quick review of certain historical conflicts suggests some cases where recipes, "viral texts," heroic models or mimetic plot structures of this sort have been fairly effectively employed: the early Christian break from Judaism; the resistance of the early Christian martyrs against Roman Authorities demanding that the emperor be treated as a god; early Lutheran and Calvinist Reformations directed against a corrupt papacy; Solidarity's resistance against Soviet–Polish Communist Party orthodoxy. Although we are inclined to discredit treatments of the Crusades in these terms (even the attempt to recapture Jerusalem), "liberation theology," the priest-assisted revolt against Somoza in Nicaragua and the attack of many Christian leaders against authorities advocating nuclear war-fighting strategies during the Cold War also come to mind.

This computationally assisted interpretation of Toynbee's Jesus story supports the psychoanalytic insight that religious myths are oriented primarily toward super-ego development. Id negatives (such as bodily suffering) are associated with moral and spiritual positives (such as righteous conduct). In Lehnert's affective graph, Jesus receives the spiritual reward of posthumous worship, representing the partial achievement of his top-level goals. Her top-level summary of this graph highlights a HIDDEN BLESSING molecule whose psychoanalytical significance we have just argued.

With this result, a first approximation to our quest for a multifaceted, mimetic plot structure of the heroic Jesus story has been achieved. It allows us to raise additional substantive issues about the Toynbee–Lehnert mimetic plot structure we have just reviewed. First of all, it is clear that the radical Puritanism of the structure in Table 3.2 coincides with the view that Christianity should work better in opposition to illegitimate authorities than in support of them. Thus Table 3.2 suggests the essence of what has become one of the most important "community-creating political myths" in the modern era.

Conservative religious thinkers will doubtless find objections to this view.[17] Voegelin, for example, might argue that Table 3.2 epitomizes the radical perspective of those Puritans (and their liberal and Marxist descendants) who believe in the "Gnostic fallacy" that "experiences of [revolutionary] transcendence ... belong to the nature of man."[18]

---

[17] In a helpful critique of an earlier draft, Aron Wildavsky complained to us of the Toynbee–Lehnert interpretation that it suggests that only radicals get to Heaven!

[18] These quotations are from Stephen A. McKnight (1978) and Hans Aufricht (1978).

Toynbee's schematic text and Lehnert's plot unit summary converge importantly in another way. Toynbee's schematic treatment of the heroic Jesus omits his resurrection, but includes the fact that he (like other classical heroes) was subsequently worshipped. The highly instrumental, purposive orientation of the Yale school of artificial intelligence is somewhat similarly reflected in the purposive, goal orientation of plot unit analysis. Thus it reflects what Weber would call the rationality of ends and means, rather than the logic of absolute ends. As a result, Lehnert could finesse the problematical issue of Jesus' goals in bringing about his own crucifixion (psychoanalytically, his self-destructive masochism; religiously, his belief in doing God's will, perhaps his own subsequent resurrection) by imputing an initial motivational state of "idealistic goals," from which she derived a subgoal of "buck the system." (The Alker–Schneider coding discussed below similarly imputed a goal of "being a savior.") Clearly the numerous negative events for Jesus, the "hidden blessing" and "success" molecules associated with our independent codings of the outcomes of the Jesus story point toward an internally contradictory, drama-inducing motivational complex. But neither Toynbee's classical hero story framework nor our codings of it nor psychoanalytic theory adequately comprehend the mysterious power of this drama. We shall return to the discussion of the comic, tragic, or tragicomic significance of these story endings in the concluding section of this chapter.

Hooker's derisive summary of Puritanism is approvingly cited by Voegelin and summarized by McKnight (p. 53) as follows:

> A political movement is started by somebody who has a "cause" and who strives to promote his cause by attracting "the multitude" through pointing to social evils and by criticizing severely the upper classes of society. Then he will direct the ill-will of the masses against the established government. After confidence in the established government has been sufficiently undermined, a new form of government will be proposed. The Puritan will formulate his "cause" in written or printed form so as to win adherents who blindly accept it.

The language is highly reminiscent of "liberation theology," the Toynbee–Lehnert account, as well as Pauline and Puritanical practice. It does not fully correspond to the actions of the "Jewish Christians" identified by Brandon (1979), who continued in association with the authorities of the Jewish Temple, believing not in Jesus' divinity, but that he was the promised Messiah of the Jewish people. Because of their apparent support for the Zealot-inspired revolt against Rome some years after Jesus' death, they were nonetheless totally wiped out at the time (70 AD) of the destruction of the Temple in Jerusalem.

Table 3.2 *Lehnert's deep structure of the heroic Jesus*

Links among plot units	Plot units (with agents)	Textual summary (with relevant Toynbee elements)
7*	MOTIVATION (Jesus)	The goal of discrediting the power that be motivates a call to the people. (T 7, 8, 9, 10)
9	ENABLEMENT (Authorities)	The recognition of their authority motivates a desire to maintain it. (T 18, etc.)
10	COMPETITION (Jesus vs. Authorities)	Jesus' motivated, principled behaviours flaunting authorities scandalize, i.e., compete with those desiring to maintain their authority. (T 7, 14, 18, etc.)
18	RETALIATION (God vs. Authorities)	God's lack of recognition due to the recognition granted to illegitimate authorities motivates his goal of regaining respect. His will is acted upon when Jesus throws out the trespassers. (T 7, 17, etc.)
47*	SUCCESS BORN OF ADVERSITY (Authorities)	Jesus' insulting acts leads to a conflict over what to do with him, which is resolved by his arrest. (T 17, 18, 49, etc.)
89*	RETALIATION (Authorities vs. Jesus)	Jesus' exasperating responses to the authorities motivate their goal to kill him, which succeeds with a crucifixion putting Jesus to death. (T 52, 53, 69, 74)
92	HIDDEN BLESSING (Jesus)	Jesus' being put to death is compensated for by his being worshipped. (T 69, 74, 76, 83)
93	SUCCESS (Jesus)	Jesus' early call to the people is rewarded as he is worshipped. (T 10, 76, 83)

* The removal of any of these critical nodes, emphasized in Figure 3.1, will disconnect at least 10 percent of the main graph structure of Figure 3.1

Our second search for mimetic plot structure

The Alker–Schneider coding of Toynbee's schema and associated biblical texts

Alker and Schneider's choice of "characters" was also largely in conformity to Toynbee's general language for the major roles in his Hero story frame, but they did include the Roman Soldiers and Jesus' Mother as distinct, but infrequently appearing characters. More importantly, Alker and Schneider's use of the cited Gospel passages – usually Mark or Matthew was given closest attention when multiple Biblical citations appeared in Toynbee's discussion – meant a considerable augmentation in the size of the affective state graph that they created. Also relevant to this increase was the way in which Alker and Schneider included Toynbee's tableaux, on the basis of the Biblical text surrounding them, whereas Lehnert had excluded them on the grounds that no actions were taking place.

Alker and Schneider spent several hours discussing their preliminary results with Lehnert, and were influenced by her criticisms on a number of points in the recoding of their graph. All in all, a graph of 109 positive affect states, 57 negative ones, and 149 affect neutral mental states was created. This meant a huge graph of 311 nodes, more than three times bigger than the one Lehnert had created; it cannot be pictured here. Of special note, Alker and Schneider had created more than 5 times as many M nodes as Lehnert.

In their coding effort it is noteworthy that Alker and Schneider rather naturally divided up their text and affectual interactions into a number of substantively motivated story parts, scenes or acts. These sometimes were tightly connected; sometimes several transitional nodes came between. In sequential order the scenic labels suggested were: Birth and Baptism; Early Ministry of Jesus; Authorities' (Elders') Attack and Judas' Betrayal; the Last Supper; Gethsemane and Jesus' Arrest; (First) Trial by Authorities; (Second) Trial before Pilate; (Third) Trial by Crowd; Crucifixion and Burial; Fulfillment.

As a basis for discussing the major differences in complexity involved, we present one scene or act from the Jesus story coded in two different ways. Positivistically trained social scientists see such comparisons primarily as ways of measuring the reliability with which coding procedures can be independently replicated. Not oblivious to such considerations, but aware of the hermeneutic point that different

Table 3.3   *Toynbee's five elements dealing with Jesus' trial by the authorities (with Biblical citations)*[a]

(T49)	The hero is arrested and is then immediately brought to an impromptu trial during the night.
	Matthew xxvi.57 Mark xiv.53 Luke xxii.54 John xviii.13, 24
(T50)	A true saying of the hero's is dishonestly twisted by his enemies into a misrepresentation which is extremely damaging to him.
	Matthew xxiv.1–2 Mark xiii.1–2 Luke xxi.5–6 Matthew xii.6 Matthew xxvi.60–1 Mark xiv.57–8
(T51)	The hero on trial is reproved by the authorities for contempt of court.
	Matthew xxvi.62–3 Mark xiv.60–1
(T52)	When a question is put to the hero which offers him a possible line of retreat, the hero does not take the opening, but gives, instead, an answer that is calculated to exasperate the court more than anything else that he could conceivably have said.
	Matthew xxvi.63–4 Mark xiv.61–2 Luke xxii.66–70
(T53)	On the strength of the hero's answers to the two test questions the court immediately passes the sentence of death upon him.
	Matthew xxvi.65–6 Mark xiv.63–4 Luke xxii.71

[a] Toynbee 1946: 393–395. Because he appears to use the King James version of the Bible, we have used it as well.

perspectives may validly read the same text differently, and also aware of the richer textual bases used in the Alker–Schneider effort, we present for comparative discussion Figures 3.2 and 3.3. Each is based on the text of Table 3.3.

Extracted from Toynbee's original list of eighty-seven components of the generalized Jesus story, Table 3.3 gives the five elements for Jesus' trial before the Jewish Authorities, along with associated Biblical citations. Although we have not written out the Biblical passages, it is clear to anyone from a perusal of the cited texts that several verses, often with somewhat different emphases, usually correspond to a single Toynbee element.

A very clear difference in the Lehnert and Alker–Schneider codings of the Toynbee eighty-seven-element schema can be seen with respect to how they each coded element T51 in the table, as it relates to the

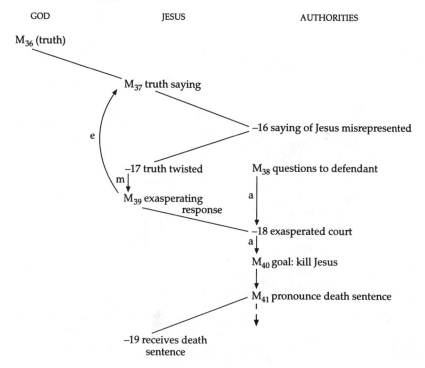

Figure 3.2   Lehnert's coding of the first trial scene

others. In Figure 3.2, Lehnert merges Jesus' contemptuous silence (T51) with his exasperating non-denial of divinity (T52). Her treatment of this merged action assumes that the motivation for making an exasperating response is Jesus' experience of false witnesses, and she further assumes that the court's reaction to Jesus' response is a new goal of killing him. None of these connecting or motivating links is evident in the Toynbee text, although each might be reasonably inferred.

Figure 3.3 conveys a rather different conception, based both on a more detailed decomposition of elements in the Toynbee scheme, and a reading of associated Biblical texts. First, note how it is organized much more scenically, in the sense that initial goals for the two major actors are stated at the beginning of the interaction. Secondly, two three-step tiers of M's connect general scene-character goals to a much more detailed, three-round account of Jesus' trial. According to Mark (xv.56) but not mentioned by Matthew, the false witnesses largely self-destruct because of their contradictory testimony – hence the – "sub

127

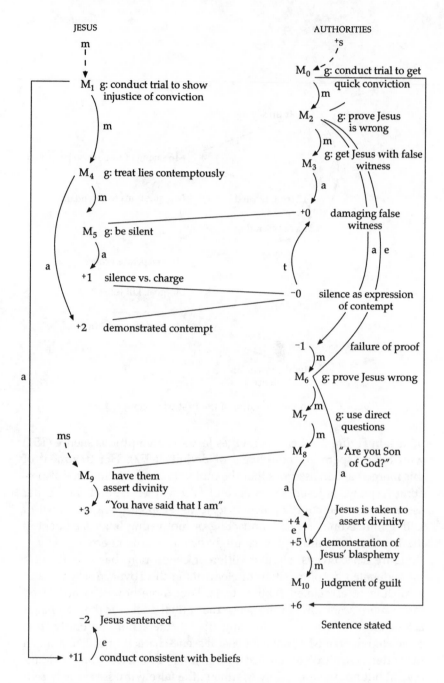

Figure 3.3 Alker–Schneider's coding of the first trial scene

one" state, causing an Authorities' FAILURE, going down from "M sub 2" in Figure 3.3. As for the contemptuous silence that Jesus displays, and that Alker and Schneider explicitly code, neither of the cited Bible passages (Matthew xxvi.62–3 or Mark xiv.60–1) explicitly indicate the judgment of contempt implied by Toynbee (T51), only the Authorities' annoyance at Jesus' silence, and their determination to explore another way of convicting him. Certainly their motivation to gain revenge on Jesus originates long before the middle of this scene.

The battle between Jesus and the Authorities is central to the Lehnert summary and to the scene-by-scene treatments of the augmented coding in which Alker and Schneider emphasize the continuities between scenes in motivations such as these. Hence they see "M sub 9," Jesus' motivation to have his divinity asserted, as also engendered much earlier. This link is indicated in Figure 3.3 by a minor, dashed line into "M sub 9," a node label which we shall sometimes abbreviate even more compactly as "M$_9$." In the Alker and Schneider coding, both Jesus and the Authorities persist, they persevere in the effort to realize their goals.

In the Alker–Schneider treatment, more of a dramatic quality is also present. Note the way they code the back and forth argumentative exchanges of Jesus and the Authorities. Consider Jesus' extremely powerful, rhetorical move in Mark xv.2, but not Matthew. He breaks his silence with "Thou sayest it" as a way of having them affirm his familial relationship to God, without himself committing blasphemy. Jesus gets his opponents to say this, in a way acknowledging that he is right. He "wins" the scene in pro-Christian eyes, even though he loses it in worldly terms (by getting convicted and crucified).[19]

Thus Jesus succeeds, as do the Authorities, each in their own way. The drama of antagonistic purposes continues. Moreover, a HIDDEN BLESSING for Jesus appears at the end of this scene (and several others in the augmented story). We are ritualistically reminded of Lehnert's

---

[19] According to Brandon (1979), in historical fact it was not necessary for the Jewish authorities to appeal for Roman support in all capital cases. They were able to impose death sentences by stoning, for example, for serious religious crimes. The centrality of the Pilate episode in the Jesus story may then be due to other reasons, including the importance of reconciling Jesus' death according to a punishment (crucifixion) reserved for political rebels with Christianity's desire to convert followers of the Roman state religion. Certainly our coding of the Pilate episode and its aftermath, not further discussed here, contains more favorable links between the Christians and the Romans than those between the Christians and the Jews. Thus it tends to confirm Brandon's interpretation of the Bible's reporting of Jesus' trial in these political terms.

overall plot summary: some version of its fundamental antagonism between Jesus and the authorities is followed by the latter's success, a success which Jesus somehow turns to his own advantage. Despite its collapsed detail, in at least one way Figure 3.2 succeeds better than Figure 3.3 in matching the thematic quality of Lehnert's overall narrative summary in Table 3.2: both her codings start with messages from God. Some of the mimetic quality caught by her summary seems to be reproduced in several of the story's individual scenes. We are struck by the deep self-replicating power of the narrative summary her first coding and synthesis produced.[20]

A mixed-method summary of the major Alker–Schneider connected subgraph

Given suggestive, but not entirely satisfactory summarization results for Jesus' first trial scene (Figures 4 and 5 in Alker, Lehnert, Schneider, 1985, not reproduced here), equivalent results could not be expected from the use of similar summarization procedures applied to the largest connected subgraph automatically generated from the Alker–Schneider coding of the entire Toynbeean version of the Jesus story. We should expect some methodological innovations might be required in order to make sense of the more complicated Alker–Schneider graph structures as well.

Problems were formidable in this enterprise, but the surprising coherence of the results makes us think they were worth the effort. What we present is only a summary tentative account. At least 504 plot units were identified in a first pass, of which 197 were top-level units, 138 of them in the major connected subgraph, which has as its first and last units God's and Jesus' SUCCESSes. A ratio of 138:80 suggests a structure whose top level is approximately twice as complicated as Lehnert's comparable structure in Figure 3.1. A computer run of nearly two hours was required for this mammoth analysis using the PUGG complex plot unit subset 2.0, flexible unit definitions, omitting the

---

[20] This monadic idea of a thematic part reproducing a cultural whole is of course central to the Judeo-Christian idea of a divine order, and to the Christian ritual of the Last Supper. A major idea in artistic studies of cultural unities, it appears in many episodic analyses of hero stories by Toynbee, Burke, Campbell and others. In particular see Umberto Eco (1976: 35), who says of Superman, "Nous voyons, aujourd'hui, dans son geste, la manifestation d'un *modèle de culture* unitaire capable de se renouveler dans chacun de ses moindres aspects."

complexities of e-link transitivities, and following the Lehnert-Loiselle convention of not treating primitive dyadic links as top-level units. Including the e-link transitivity option did not change our top-level structures very significantly. We shall summarize the results here. (See also the extended discussion of Figure 6 in Alker, Schneider, Lehnert 1985.)

A mixed method of scenic identification was undertaken, preliminary to plot summarization. It became apparent that pivotal meaning units had to be calculated specific to particular scenes (and maybe specific to particular actor perspectives). Then the centrality of Pilate in his "big scene" and that of Jesus in his, the Crucifixion, would seem more natural. Separate scenes were usually identified on the basis of their high levels of thematic interconnectedness. But there were real problems in defining the endings on one scene and the subsequent, but not necessarily immediate beginning of the next one, somewhat like the gaps noted by Alker and Schneider in their original scenic labeling of their coding of the Jesus story. For example, equivalence links that constituted goal reaffirmations often seemed to border new scenes and there is a moderately complex transitional sequence linking Jesus' first and second trials.

Introductory, transitional and postscript themes were identified by a qualitative effort to find critical or transitional nodes in the story. Rarely was one plot unit so decisively critical, but often two adjacent units seem to do almost all the filtering, the sequencing, the reaffirming of top-level goals. The direction of inter-unit connections, as when they pointed further into the heart of a new scene, sometimes was topologically helpful in defining these boundaries. As a last resort, in certain ambiguous cases, it helped to know the specific content of underlying plot units or affect states, in order more sharply to delineate scenes. The rough scenic boundaries, and associated titles – mostly similar to the previously suggested list – are given in Table 3.4. We use "acts" there to label the major scenes, to be more in harmony with the majestic scope and drama of the Jesus epic.

The central actors and plot units in Table 3.4 were identified by taking the maximally connected plot units in each of these acts; they make excellent sense. Ignoring for now the plot units indicated to be transitional, note the characters and plot units at the center, the core or the pivot of each scene. Most of the items in Table 3.4 are self-explanatory given the complex molecular definitions in Figure 3.3a (see also Lehnert and Loiselle 1985).

Table 3.4 *Some central and transitional plot units in the topical summary of Alker and Schneider's Jesus*

Act and label	Top-level plot units and their main characters
I Jesus' early Ministry	Jesus is MOTIVATED with goals of being Savior, to propagate new order, to claim divine kingship, and evidences PERSEVERANCE in doing so.
II Authorities Motivated to Seek Revenge	With goal of ruining Jesus, Authorities evidence PERSEVERANCE AFTER FAILURE, continued MOTIVATION to arrest and convict him.
TRANSITION	Jesus evidences PERSEVERANCE and MOTIVATION in goals of being Savior, undergoing unjust sacrificial death, preparing for capture and death.
III Last Supper	Goals for supper achieved leads to re-ACTIVATION of
TRANSITION	Jesus' goal of preparation for capture and death.
IV Betrayal in Gethsemane	Judas, with goal of making a "deal" with Authorities, undergoes RETURNED FAVOR of finding and identifying Jesus in return for 30 pieces of silver.
V Arrest and TRANSITION	Jesus evidences PERSEVERANCE in preparing for capture and unjust sacrificial death.
VI Trial by Authorities and TRANSITION	Authorities are KILLING TWO BIRDS in getting Jesus to assert divinity and commit blasphemy; simultaneously with goals of conducting himself so that his conviction appears unjust and his actions remain consistent with his beliefs, Jesus achieves NESTED SUBGOALS-2
VII Trial before Pilate and masses	Pilate's SEQUENTIAL SUBGOALS of being friendly ruler leads to judgment of innocence, plus reliance on customary choice of crowd.
VIII Crucifixion	Jesus evidences SEQUENTIAL SUBGOALS of conduct re: unjust conviction, consistency with beliefs, undergoing unjustified sacrificial death, dying like a savior; portents at his death.

Noting that the text for the NESTED SUBGOALS-2 meaning molecule on the far right of Figure 3.3a can be reconstructed from Figure 3.3, we suggest the reader use the details we have provided to try and reconstruct the operational bases for the Alker–Schneider Jesus summarized in Table 3.4. These details elaborate upon the summary of Table 3.4 in non-surprising ways. But the specific contents of the Arrest scene (Act V) are not well handled there. In Christian eyes, Jesus'

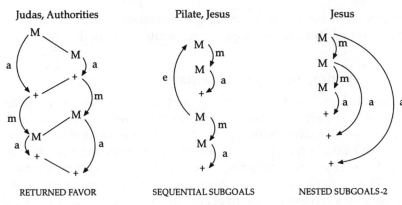

Judas, Authorities   Pilate, Jesus   Jesus

RETURNED FAVOR   SEQUENTIAL SUBGOALS   NESTED SUBGOALS-2

Figure 3.3a   Some complex plot units in Alker–Schneider's Jesus

perseverance again steals the scene – the location of surely one of his most table-turning, pacifistic sayings: "For all they that take the sword shall perish with the sword" (Matthew xxvi.52).

We here have broadened Lehnert's earlier structural focus on critical units to include those units or unit pairs which, if eliminated, would nearly (or completely) disconnect large blocks of the major connected subgraph. Identifying such critical or transitional units has not been an entirely rigorous topological procedure; it too has been assisted by a reading of the contents of the plot units possibly to be treated in this way.

Four critical or "transitional" nodes were identifiable in the complex figure (See Alker, Lehnert & Schneider 1985: 83ff., underlying Table 3.4). Quite remarkably it turns out that each of these critical links concerns Jesus' persistent, self-transcending motivation to achieve a situation-transforming victory even while losing, to "win" even in dying a humiliating death. We have thus found critically central to the Jesus story a resurrection theme, even when (following Toynbee) we have omitted Jesus' resurrection from it!

Were Jesus' incredibly persistent motivation to collapse at any of these points, it would change the story beyond recognition; that, at least, appears to be the substantive meaning of a critical or "transitional" node in the top-level plot unit graph. Since each of the critical/ transitional units involves persistent motivation, inferred by Alker and Schneider to fit the events of a particular scene or sequence of scenes, it is fair to say that human code-interpretations are as central to this version of computationally assisted hermeneutics as to classical text analysis; but the surprising finding, nonetheless, is the critical structural unity such motivations give to scene after scene of the Jesus story.

A comparative commentary

How different, how comparable, are the two interpretations, Toynbee-Lehnert and Toynbee-Alker-Schneider given above, based respectively on Tables 3.2 and 3.4? Although the texts coded were not the same, we may still ask, in the light of Toynbee's claim to be summarizing the cited Gospel passages, whether our second coding reliably validated or invalidated the first; or, more hermeneutically, we can ask about the different interpretive perspectives elicited by the discipline of graphing our cognitive-affective perceptions. Can we say something more about Toynbee's interpretation itself, as it gets expressed in affective plot unit terms? Several remarks are germane.

It has been a common assumption of the two interpretations that the story of Jesus' life was in fact his message. Not only is this an ontological tendency of Artificial Intelligence LISP programming – data may be thought of as procedures – it is an assumption that the Jesus text, properly understood, would be highly mimetic in many, but not all situations. There is the larger issue, then, of whether Jesus' life, as summarized here in action-oriented, morally suggestive, affective terms, or by Toynbee or in the Bible itself, is consonant with the messages, morals, parables, principles he actually appears to have preached.

As an approximation Lehnert's synthetic summarization procedures produced what we called a "viral text," infectious, capable of being reproduced elsewhere, but requiring other biological "hosts." Alker and Schneider did find some of this thematic structure reappearing in several independently coded scenes of theirs, but the copy was not exact: most suggestively HIDDEN-BLESSINGS and ironic, double successes frequently ended their scenes, as was illustrated in Figure 3.3. Additionally it should be reported that there are pluses and minuses, SUCCESSES and FAILURES at the end of their Jesus story affect graph, but – perhaps because the Resurrection is omitted – no really synthetic HIDDEN BLESSING.

The Alker–Schneider interpretation associated with Table 3.4 differed, however, in that its meanings were in several places: (1) in the critical/transitional molecules, mostly made up of humanly inferred goals within M-states; (2) in the scenic summaries, as in Table 3.4, written around the specific content summaries associated with central molecules located by cluster-oriented topological procedures, once scenes themselves had been properly identified; and (3) in the symbolic scenic titles, which like ritualistic Stations of the Cross, they used to indicate the progression of the scenes themselves.

Given the difficulty Alker and Schneider had in finding central high-level interpersonal meaning units from the Lehnert–Loiselle list that adequately summarized their version of the Toynbee story, more work on spelling out culturally specific and cross-culturally valid interpersonal themes is needed. Perhaps relaxing the assumption that forbids treating primitive interpersonal affect units as top-level entities might be explored; or these units might be more richly defined along lines like those to be suggested below. More explicitly stated encoding heuristics would probably produce more closely corresponding figures than the two codings of the first trial scene in Figures 3.2 and 3.3 above, but it would be unwise to expect complete agreement among all coders on the rules themselves, or on high-level codings made in terms of them. The great, hermeneutic strength of Lehnert's procedure derives from its individually oriented evocative nature: both affective plot relations and humanly specified substantive goal nodes are evoked from the humans employing the procedure; as a result, one should not expect on scientific grounds the same perceptual organizations *ought* to be uncovered.

One has the impression of a more complex, differentiated biochemistry of mimetic effects. It is almost as if the whole message of the story was in Jesus' mind, as well as his life story: his self-and situation-transcending commitments have been the focus of the Alker–Schneider interpretive synthesis. Theirs was a somewhat more inwardly oriented version of the Jesus story; Lehnert's was somewhat more outwardly, and revolutionary. Both reflect different themes in their Protestant socialization. A greater, multidimensional richness of recursive, self-replicating structure may be necessary for the full satisfaction of our reconstructive analytical purposes.

In exploring further the inner meanings of Jesus' life, we have been struck by the absence of a resurrection in each Toynbee-based code. Perhaps the tendency of the Alker–Schneider account to recreate this central "mystery" of the Jesus drama speaks also to its greater interpretive ambiguity, which lends itself to a variety of diverse personal and historical interpretations. For example, let us consider a variety of plausible "Christian" interpretations at the personal level, based on Sunday School lessons likely to be full of sayings and moral parables attributed to Jesus, plus hymns or testimonies dedicated to him. Christian soldiers are taught, like the Martyrs, to enter battles not fearing death. The sick marvel at Jesus' miraculous healing power, the "miracle" of rebirth. Young lovers know their own transcendent joy in the pronouncement that "God is love." Devout athletes think triumphantly of *Chariots of Fire* in performing superhuman feats. Radicals scorn unjust rulers, or think of evicting the money changers from the Temple. Mothers think of themselves as Mary in transcending their grief to care for a handicapped child.

A pietistic interpretation of the Jesus story suggests that Jesus is not just a revolutionary political figure transcending the limits of his situation (or not at all, some conservatives would say); rather, it suggests that the reverent imitation of Jesus transforms the meaning of ritualistic significance of our personal lives. Given the large complex of social and historical causes accounting for Christianity's rise and wane in America, functionally speaking, such an argument does help account for the paradoxical survey results at the beginning of this chapter. And it is a strength of the second interpretation above that its focus on forms of self-transcendence points in this direction, subject to the limits of non-self-referential plot unit meaning representations.

Almost absent throughout, however, in both interpretations are the contradictions in motives – the war inside Jesus' and the Authorities' minds – that it is reasonable to assume went on there. Surely the dramatic power of the Jesus story, its power to get inside and motivate its reader/hearers, comes in part from the dilemmas of principled action that he in particular faced. Although some of the richness of Pilate's contradictory goals of being a just ruler as well as one who could accommodate with the Jewish Authorities are in the Alker–Schneider coding of the Trial before Pilate scene, such an account of Jesus is largely missing in the account above; it is totally absent concerning the Jewish Authorities. Affective, non-cognitive mental states cannot do these reflective traumas justice: plot units do not sweat blood.

Specifically, and perhaps most importantly for political scientists, neither of our Toynbee-based interpretations brought out the conflict in the Jesus story between our coding of his *actions* as aggressive, competitive, even malicious and our interpretation of what he *said*, in particular the political pacifism of the Sermon on the Mount.

Concretely, we were not fully able to represent his voluntary submission at the time of his arrest. His own message is at least in part revolutionary politics; it was also, before being historically transformed into conventionalized religion, ethical, sacrificial, revolutionary non-violence that has appealed to such diverse figures as St. Francis, Gandhi, Martin Luther King, Jr., Lech Wałesa and Benigno Aquino. The Sermon on the Mount contains the paradoxical, but fervent injunction: "Love your enemies, bless them that curse you, do good to them that hate you, and pray for them which despitefully use you, and persecute you" (Matthew v.44). Lehnert and Loiselle's addition of SACRIFICE to KIND-ACT AND UNSOLICITED-HELP on the earlier list of complex plot units is a step in the direction of specifying the various mixtures of self-serving, self-denying and situation-transcending love; it hardly exhausts the topic.[21]

Next steps

Going beyond the present analysis, we should like to suggest some more general directions for subsequent work. None of them is very simple; each is occasioned by the present effort to discover mimetic plot structure in a powerful religious-political text. Each suggests new directions for artificial intelligence work oriented toward discovering and summarizing affective plot structures. In other words, we are speculating about further work in computationally assisted hermeneutics. If any point has been made clear by the previous two interpretive exercises, computers can help focus, clarify, criticize, explicate; they do not supplant the human interpreter.

One of the principal differences between the interpretations above was the greater emphasis the latter gave to the episodic structure of the story. Since grammatical rules concerning episodes sequences are the heart of modern story grammars, it appears necessary to merge them with the more substantively oriented plot unit analysis approach if we are to be able to distinguish "syntactic" from "semantic" content, formal and substantively important transitional plot units. It would help us, for example, to untangle the messy border identification problems encountered in the preliminary stages of the Alker–Schneider analysis. A synthesis of the two approaches to memory organization and narrative recall appears appropriate, at least for

---

[21] Suggestive readings on these interpretations are Yoder (1972) and Haley (1969).

some purposes (Black and Wilensky 1979: 213–229; Mandler and Johnson 1980: 305–312).

Recursive rewrite possibilities

The above discussion often required untangling sequential and nested goal structures so as to get at the content of the underlying atoms of meaning or affect. We are interested in exploring whether the search operations involved might be made more recursive, with partly defined molecules that have partly specified "slots" to be filled in the completion of an inferred meaning. Perhaps the variety of separately indicated plot units in the Appendix of the Lehnert–Loiselle paper could be reduced by some such approach. Certainly a lot of computational complexities might be engendered, but the idea is worth exploring (Abelson and Reich 1969).

Sometimes the inferred meanings discovered by normal summarization procedures involved reflections on the entire scene being considered. Mimetic plot structures were described as if they were able to generate new interpretations in some, but not all, new contexts. For such actions a kind of recursive rewrite capability is also required. We suspect successful story generation programs given some kind of motivational "viral text" will eventually have self-referential ways of reflectively rewriting themselves.

But it must be added that our preliminary explorations have suggested that the seminal ideas at the heart of important religious-political texts may not yield easily and totally to such efforts. A fertile, symbolic ambiguity helps mimesis by different people in different contexts. Religious faith and a commitment to political legitimacy may well not be content-free. The problem of adequate representations of moral, cognitive and affective content remains, complicated further by the need to explore what situational features help instill, evoke or prevent transcendent, collectively oriented action scripts.

Toward a richer affective taxonomy of emplotment possibilities

One of the strengths of Lehnert's affective formalisms is that they seem often to retrace the subterranean faults, the purposive and affective distinctions in terms of which our memories are organized. The method helps then to retrieve the morally or politically charged texts associated with affective and cognitive states centrally and critically important for subsequent actions. The results are subject to multiple interpretations; in this sense they are mimetically ambiguous, but hermeneutically and practically robust.

Consider, for example, the central role that the HIDDEN-BLESSING molecule has played in so many Christian stories – including "The Gift of the Magi," as analyzed in Lehnert's 1981 paper. We suggested above several different ways in which religious or political self-transcending and/or situation-transforming processes may succeed, and then get interpreted in such terms. But *substantive* differentiation among affective plot unit terms was difficult when persevering, nested and sequential goal sequences dominated structural representations.

Another problem arose when we tried to specify in affective plot unit terms whether the Jesus story was a "tragedy" or a "comedy" or, in case MIXED- or HIDDEN-BLESSINGS were involved at the end, a "tragicomedy." Have we adequately defined the meaning of these terms in plot unit terms? We suspect not. Recall Ricoeur's suggestion of that dimension of "emplotment" distinguishing comedies from tragedies, satires and romances. How do the latter two fit in?

Figure 3.4, based on Paul Hernadi's synthesis of the poetic literature on "genres," may be helpful in these regards. It relies on some of the same literary theorists that Ricoeur himself cites. Let us explain it and then suggest that it be used in a subsequent genera-tion of affective plot unit studies. The figure can be nicely interpreted in terms of the laughing and crying masks of Greek comedy and tragedy, distinguishing crying or laughing with, from crying or laughing at. Thus in his *Poetics* Aristotle characterizes tragedy in terms of an opposition and synthesis of the emotions of crying with (fear) and crying for (pity). One could not make such distinctions using current plot unit coding or analysis rules without adding at least another dimension.

The basis of Hernadi's continuous taxonomy of the emotional appeals of dramatic works, and therefore of the works themselves, may also be explicated somewhat differently as follows. Think of someone indulged or deprived, i.e., in a "+" or "−" affect state. Politically speaking, this distinction might be described in terms of "winners" and "losers," which usually, but not always, come in pairs. How do you, the reader, orient yourself toward these parties? In general, or in some particular case, do you identify with the winners or the losers? Put yourself in the upper half of the circle if you identify with the winners, the indulged, the fortunate; or, if you are aware of the (hopefully ennobling) endurance of pain and suffering by the losers, put yourself in the lower half of the circle.

Next ask yourself about self-transcending orientation toward the winners or losers: most basically, do you love them, share their happiness, their joy; or do you hate them, scorn and despise them? A second dimension of affective orientation has thus been introduced. As Hernadi describes it, it is eminently religious and political. Revolutionary commitments to change the world on one extreme are opposed to reverent, accepting, religious or personal self-redefinitions; both are types of self-transcending (and, potentially, situation-transforming) change. This distinction is remarkably similar to, if not identical with, a theme that emerged in our comparative discussion of differences in emphases between the Lehnert and Alker–Schneider analyses.

Continuously varying mixes of what Hernadi labels generically as fear, pity, joy and derision, account for all twelve of the affect states, or audience moods, in the figure. Conventional plot unit analysis is not nearly so rich oriented as it is only toward the indulgence-deprivation vertical axis in the figure.

We believe different types of mimetic emplotment can be distinguished in terms of the two component affect states we have described. In the light of the emotional taxonomy in Figure 3.4, for example, reread the list of diverse personal "resurrections" suggested above – ranging from the soldier's overcoming fear to the mother's transcendence of grief over a severely handicapped child. Hernadi himself offers classifications of many quasi-religious dramas in these terms; a selection of these and other plays are included in the figure to illustrate this reading of drama. Thus Faustian jousts with the Devil, Oedipus' martyrdom, Shakespeare's miraculous, rather Catholic *Tempest*, Shaw's radical and satirical *St. Joan* can be analyzed in terms of their distinctive affective appeals.

As with most other great epics, Jesus' story is tragicomic, with important elements of tragedy, comedy, social or political satire and romance. Read as drama, it suggests a rich variety of concrete emplotments. Surely the enduring meanings of Jesus' HIDDEN-BLESSING allows all of these interpretations. The ambiguity of the story as to moral standards, its entertainment and commitment appeals (Hernadi's terms) encourages it to be mapped onto all of the quadrants in the figure, festivities as well as martyr plays, satires and romances. We might suggest that the Toynbee-Lehnert interpretation offered above fits into the socially or politically satirical realm, while the Toynbee-

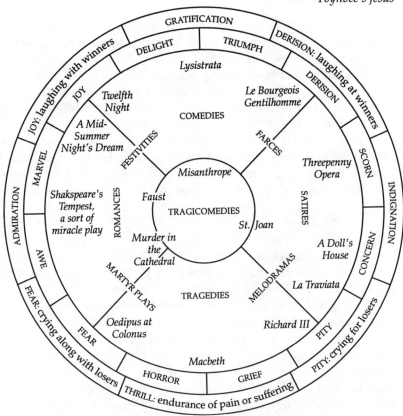

Figure 3.4 Dramatic genres classified continuously in terms of the
audience mood responses to their entertaining commitments

Notes: The up-down axis is one distinguishing indulgent vs. the inescapably
painful. It does so from a survival-oriented, self-assertive perspective. The left–
right axis is one of self-transcending commitments to change. On the right are
plays where socially or politically oriented remedial actions are suggested or
implied; on the left, personally or religiously oriented self-transcendence is
sought.

Source: The figure synthesizes materials from the text and two figures of Paul
Hernadi, "Entertaining Commitments: A Reception Theory of Literary
Genres," *Poetics* 10 (1981): 95–211.

Alker-Schneider interpretation, somewhat more tragicomic in its net
effect, sounded much more like a Faustian romance. Our research
activity has also been, in a way, a Faustian romance: our entertaining
commitment has been to unify a Promethean science (Artificial Intelligence or computational text analysis) and the ineffabilities of self-
serving and self-transcending love.

We have been sufficiently encouraged, and humbled by the above results to suggest in these last few pages ways to further and deepen our analysis. Further adding to our humility has been the realization that hermeneutic philosophers long ago defined the broad outlines of the interpretive route we have taken; we can at best hope to have provided ways of making a variety of such interpretations specifiable in a more explicit, testable fashion. In calling for objective methods which could confirm shared interpretations, Dilthey argues that the ultimate goal of hermeneutics was to analyze the starting point for any possible rules of understanding (Makkreel 1975: 259). This is what we have been doing in the development and application of a lexicon and grammar of plot unit analysis. Moreover, Dilthey went on to argue some eighty years ago that "if we want understanding to yield the greatest possible result for our knowledge of the spiritual world, it is most important that we affirm the validity of this form in its autonomy. A drama is performed ... Understanding is then directed at the context of the plot, the characters of the protagonists, the integration of moments which determine a change of fate" (Makkreel 1975: 327). How close our own understanding of computational hermeneutics has now come to this point of view!

Our suggested next steps derive both from our sense that plot unit analysis does effectively discover central, even generative meanings within a wide variety of narrative texts and from an awareness of its current limitations. Its crude affective distinctions and simplified combinatorial grammar, joined with the absence of specific cognitive contents in automated processing rules, limit the fidelity with which summaries like Figure 3.4 and Tables 3.2 and 3.4 can be confidently prepared. But given the enriched understanding we have undergone through making and revising the above interpretations, we are encouraged to call for further work on computational hermeneutics, and further applications of its improved methodology in cross-cultural contexts.[22] Through such studies, the extent, the variety and the limits

[22] Perhaps the most important connection so far in this regard is the expressed interest of Anna Wierzbicka, a linguist at Australian National University. From a rich, ongoing study of language primitives in many different cultural communities, she and her collaborators have identified both linguistic universals and cultural specificities stated in those universal terms (Wierzbicka 1992a,b). In a meeting Alker had with her in August 1993, she expressed an interest in attempting a specification of the message of the Jesus story, or at least some of his speeches, in her own universalistic version of cross-culturally validated cognitive-emotional language primitives. Her

of the ways in which the moral-political-religious exemplars of Toynbee's classical Mediterranean culture or civilization continue divergently to inform the lives of contemporaries can be more precisely, and empirically, established.

results to date confirm, with some interesting modifications, some of the Schankian primitives. Her efforts to express culturally specific feelings and morals in terms of a universally valid conceptual language has a Leibnizian cast that computational hermeneuticists must admire.

Part II
The humanistic science of the modern classics

4 The humanistic moment in International Studies:
Reflections on Machiavelli and Las Casas

As a student of international relations,[1] most of my ostensibly successful voyages of scientific discovery have ended up at the edges of a misnamed continent. Sailing under the non-national flag of "the pursuit of truth," I have come to see many of our concerns, theoretical models and methodological ways of defining research problems as parochial, scientistic, or even ethnocentric – crudely fashioned guides or tools for attempted "conquests" of already occupied and cultivated lands rather than the more innocent sounding "discovery and exploration" of a "New World."

Believing he had only found the eastern edges of an already known Eurasian landmass ("the Indies"), Columbus also long resisted such a description of his discoveries. For different reasons, many of us agree: the opening up in 1492 of an already occupied "New World" for European exploration and conquest was not the original human "discovery" of two continents. But it was a fateful shock for the "old orders" in Europe, Asia and the Americas; so we may rightly consider "1492" as a major world historical turning point, symbolizing a more complex transition from the pre-modern to the modern age. Today we are faced with the comparable challenge of making sense of a post-communist "new world order," in what some describe as a "post-modern" era.

The positivistic exploratory approaches of my early research now

---

[1] This slightly augmented version of my Presidential Address to the International Studies Association, given at the 1992 Annual Convention in Atlanta, Georgia, includes in Table 4.2 a set of Martin Luther King, Jr., quotations that were handed out at the meeting, but not published in the *International Studies Quarterly* version of the talk. Similarly, I have included an alternative version of the "Great Chain of Being" table handed out there as Table 2.1 above.

appear inadequate for addressing such challenging reorderings of both space, time and human lives. Like Christopher Columbus looking for an unfettered trading route to the limitless riches of the Indies, my preliminary epistemological map of the (inter-) disciplinary world of International Relations research (Alker 1968; compare Wright 1955) has proven to be too small by a third: as an "inferior" social scientist looking for the objective truths of the natural sciences, I have redis- covered instead different parts of a continent that was professionally unknown to me, "the Humanities."

Therefore, like Columbus' successors, I am eager to fill in a more accurate global map of international studies, one in which the human- ities, and the allied arts, play at least an intermediating, continental role. Hopefully those strange epistemological flora and fauna increas- ingly observable in my own publications – artifical intelligence, the "end of the power politics story," dialectical logics, reflective epis- temologies, "computational hermeneutics," plot structures, interpre- tive story grammars, historicity, emancipatory knowledge interests, "text models" and practical reasoning – or their more felicitously expressed descendents, will also eventually become recognized as normal parts of such a redrawn interdisciplinary, planetary landscape. And with such an improved map, as both a "naturalistic" and "humanistic" interdiscipline, International Relations may soon be more able fruitfully to get its bearings in "post-modern" time and space.

Since contemporary notions of "the humanities" derive directly from the recovery of the Ciceronian humanistic ideal during the Renais- sance, my historical curiosity suggests a review of several great humanists from that era especially interested in international relations. The present anniversary suggests including at least one who had an enduring impact on and in Columbus' "New World" of 500 years ago. To meet that requirement, and for other reasons, I have chosen the Italian bureaucrat and writer Niccolò Machiavelli (1469–1527) and the Spanish follower of the Conquistadores who became a New World friar, Bartolomé de Las Casas (1474–1566).

Why these two? In different cultures, Machiavelli and Las Casas have both become famous as Renaissance commentators on interna- tional relations. Both combined scientific and humanistic contributions in ways I believe to be suggestive for contemporary international studies. Like Alexander the Great, Machiavelli associated great glory with expansionary, conquering republics, kingdoms or empires; the

Renaissance historian Jakob Burchkardt saw him as the prophet of the conquest of the rest of the world by the European states and their interstate system. Many North American international relations scholars see him – too narrowly and exclusively in my view – as *the* founder of modern, scientific international relations. Las Casas also made significant scientific contributions to early modern Spanish international law and to multicultural international understanding. And he is widely recognized outside of the United States as "the first European to perceive the economic, political, and cultural injustice of the colonial or neocolonial system maintained by the North Atlantic powers since the 15th century for the control of Latin America, Africa, and Asia" (Ducelle 1980: 686). In this regard, Las Casas was as prophetically accurate as Machiavelli, although his prophecy of a post-colonial world order took several more centuries before it came to pass.

The juxtaposition of someone so well, if incompletely, known within English-speaking North America with someone much more widely known in the Latin American world also allows me to help correct an ethnocentric bias among many non-Hispanic North Americans unfamiliar with his work. For a scholarly association in the process of recognizing its North American character and about to meet jointly with Mexican and other Latin American international relations scholars (ISA 1992: 1, 15–17), a look at our shared, humanistic "New World roots" is both intellectually and institutionally appropriate.

Rediscovering the humanities: from post-modernity back to the Renaissance

Among the many humanists writing today about early and late modernity, perhaps it is Stephen Toulmin who has best expressed the civic spirit I wish to bring to the present enterprise: "As matters now stand, our need to reappropriate the reasonable and tolerant (but neglected) legacy of humanism is more urgent than our need to preserve the systematic and perfectionist (though well-established) legacy of the exact sciences; but, in the last resort, we cannot dispense with either" (Toulmin 1990: 180). Because he recognizes the excesses of recent modernity, he seeks to recover its humane, Early Modern roots from an era prior to the eighteenth-century triumph of scientific rationalism over the more moderate rationality claims of the humanities. Presciently, I believe, Toulmin thinks that the era defined by the identification of modernity with the "political supremacy of Europe" and "the hegemony of European ideas" is ending.

Havel's post-modern view of the post-Cold War world

As a "conversational partner" likely to be sympathetic with some but not all of Toulmin's humanistic views about early and late modernity,[2] I choose an expert and humane practitioner of international relations, the former president of Czechoslovakia, Vaclav Havel. Not only is he especially sensitive to the issues of "progress" or "evolution" in the post-communist world order, his interest in Heideggerian "onto-ethical political claims" (Elshtain, no date) resonates with, and responds to, those who argue that humanism is in crisis because the classical ontologies supporting humankind's special place in the world have been abandoned (Vattimo 1988: Ch. 2). In a recent article, Havel (1992) offers a provocative view of the post-Cold War world. For him, "the end of Communism" is "a message to the human race" about the "end ... to the modern age as a whole." It is a sign, a "serious warning" of a "final crisis" in modern thought – characterized by the belief that "the world ... and Being as such – is a wholly knowable system governed by a finite number of universal laws that man can grasp and rationally direct for his own benefit."

> This era, beginning in the Renaissance and developing from the Enlightenment to socialism, from positivism to scientism, from the Industrial Revolution to the information revolution, was characterized by rapid advances in rational, cognitive thinking. [There followed] the proud belief that man, as the pinnacle of everything that exists, was capable of objectively describing, explaining and controlling everything that exists ... an era of belief in automatic progress brokered by the scientific method. (Havel 1992: 15)

For Havel, the "collapse of colonial hegemony and the fall of communism" were "the two most important political events in the second half of the 20th century" (Havel 1994: A27). Communism was the "perverse extreme" of a much more general and widespread phenomenon: the pursuit by "arrogant, absolutist reason" of a single, objective truth, a universally valid theory or interpretation of the world and its history, "and thus a universal key to unlock its prosperity" (Havel

2 Even though I find Toulmin's periodizations especially persuasive, I shall not here use his convention of initial capitals for "Early Modernity" and the like.

1992). Even the revised, "post-hegemonic," Enlightenment-inspired Constitution of the International Studies Association, which abjures taking sides on international political questions, is unconditionally committed to "expanding, disseminating and applying knowledge of the interrelations of nations and peoples" (ISA 1992: 11). Are not Western believers in "the worldwide liberal revolution," the "directional history" toward it produced by "the progressive unfolding of modern natural science" and the fact that scientifically based "capitalism was in some sense inevitable for advanced countries" (Fukuyama 1992: 39ff., 89, 98) also subject to Havel's criticisms? (Compare the similar, if less apocalyptic, views of Toulmin 1990: 20.)

Havel's and Toulmin's provocative and perhaps puzzling humanistic concerns give us other, less personal reasons for looking back to Machiavelli, Las Casas and the early modern era in international studies. We need: to address Havel's critical conception of the origins and development of both communist and liberal/capitalist modernity; to better map, and recover, if possible, some of the humanistic aspects of international studies in an era when the sciences and the humanities were seen as complementary; and to clarify and defend the International Studies Association's revised constitutional statement of purposes.

Renaissance humanism

To proceed convincingly, I must first describe Renaissance humanism and early modernity. My understanding of Renaissance humanism as an historical, multi-faceted phenomenon derives most importantly from William Burckhardt (1990, originally 1860), Quentin Skinner (1978) and Weinstein (1980). Burckhardt emphasized four aspects of the Renaissance, each with humanistic aspects: most obviously, the political, cultural and epistemological-ontological "Revival of Antiquity" as a partial model for a reconstituted Italian present; secondly, "the Development of the [complete, fully capable] Individual"; thirdly, the unveiled rationalism of what Michelet called "the Discovery of the World and of Man" by explorers, scientists, poets, biographers and philosophers; and most provocatively, for present purposes, the novel, constructivist conception of "the State as a Work of Art."

As a reviver of antiquity, Petrarch (1304–74) was the first to think of [Western] history as having gone through a 1,000 years of "darkness," a "Middle Age" and then a "Renaissance" (a term first used in this sense by Vasari in the sixteenth century). In this then novel historical view, Roman ruins and decaying manuscripts became exotic, valuable traces of a distant "Golden Age." Historically, a radical, but cyclical decline was seen to have occurred from the astonishing literary culture and public virtue of classical Greece and Republican Rome. Petrarch, whom Burckhardt (1990: 9) describes as "one of the first truly modern men," and his contemporaries shaped a related, educationally influential, "myth" by stressing that recovery in that cyclic process depended on education in the classics, in Greek and Latin.

In a characteristically modern way, Petrarch and his followers saw true nobility as the achievement and exercise of virtue, not as an accident of birth; and they (like Galileo on another front) attacked Scholastics who parroted Aristotle for merely seeking the truth about virtue rather than having the will to acquire it. Although Aristotle and Cicero had both praised contemplative leisure – *otium* – when compared with the pursuit of useful activity – *negotium* – Petrarch and many other humanists followed Aristotle's commitment to an ethics defined in terms of public virtues, and recommended *negotium* as more desirable (Skinner 1978: I. Ch. 4, 202–203).

Burckhardt was obviously fascinated with Renaissance individualism, and the (supposedly sudden) appearance of "many-sided" or "complete" individuals like Petrarch, Da Vinci and Alberti. The latter harmoniously developed his "spiritual and material existence." Alberti's exceptionally successful career as an artist, architect, physicist, mathematician and prophetic historian is described as an important instance of the "recovery of th[e] classical dramatisation of the human condition" in terms of triumphs as well as tragedies (Burckhardt 1990: 101–104; Skinner 1978: I.38, 95).

The Renaissance humanists were also responsible, *inter alia*, for the typical Renaissance motif, the "claim that it is always open to men to exercise their *virtù* in such a way as to overcome the power of *Fortuna*" (Skinner 1978: I.98). The *vir virtutis*, the man of virtue, actively combined his classical learning and his rational mind in the life of his city or state; he would also fight bravely for its liberty and glory. It was this courageous, god-like, virtuous, gendered image of the complete man that became the ideal of a *uomo universale*, a "Renaissance man"[3]

---

[3] On the gendering of political and epistemological orientations suggested by this central metaphor in Machiavelli's *Discourses* and much of Renaissance political thought see Pitkin (1984), Brown (1988: Chs. 4–6) and Ashley (1989). For a different view, see the the the discussion of the civilizing, aggression-displacing role of *courtoisie* in early modern "proto-diplomacy" in Der Derian (1987: 87–92).

of general virtue and excellence. He possessed a kind of virtue previously denied by Pauline and Augustinian Christianity.

The discovery of the New World by an Italian sailor symbolizes an even more profound change in scientific and spiritual self-understanding by Italian man:

> In the Middle Ages both [the inward and outward looking] sides of human consciousness ... lay dreaming ... beneath a common veil ... woven of faith, illusion and childish prepossession ... Man was conscious of himself only as a member of ... some general category [like race, people, party, family, corporation]. In Italy this veil was first melted into air; an *objective* treatment and consideration of the state and of all the things of this world became possible. The *subjective* side at the same time asserted itself with corresponding emphasis; man became a spiritual *individual* ...
>
> (Burckhardt 1990: 98)

Burckhardt and Skinner agree that Renaissance humanism placed man – with his fully developed rationality, his many-sided creative powers, his ability to control his own destiny, his freedom of choice and associated responsibilities for the consequences of his actions – at the center of the universe. Burckhardt is unstinting in his praise for the universalistic and scientific humanism of Pico della Mirandola (1463–94). "He was the only man who loudly and vigorously defended the truth and science of all ages against the one-sided worship of classical antiquity" (Burckhardt 1990: 135). The "loftiest conceptions" and most thorough and profound understanding of mankind may be found in his famous *Oration on the Dignity of Man* (Mirandola 1965).

Pico della Mirandola believed he had found the same God in Greek, Roman, Muslim, Hebrew and Christian sources. God was "the master-builder" who has placed man at the "midpoint" or "center" of the world, "confined by no bounds," unlike other creatures governed by the laws of nature, able to "fix limits of nature for" himself. In the *Oration*, God says:

> Thou, like a judge appointed for being honorable, art the molder and maker of thyself; thou mayest sculpt thyself into whatever shape thou doest prefer. Thou canst grow downward into the lower natures which are brutes ... [or] grow upward from thy soul's reason into the higher natures which are divine.   (Mirandola 1965: 4–5)

Burckhardt says this "one single result of the Renaissance" – this truth about mankind, its capacities and responsibilities – "is enough to fill us with everlasting thankfulness" (Burckhardt 1990: 229).[4]

We can now better understand the sense in which Burckhardt described the contradictory Renaissance conception of "the State as a Work of Art." First of all, it is an essentially modern, if violent and tradition-disregarding, constructivist notion that extended from self-sculpting individuals to states and even – if we are to believe Machiavelli, Burckhardt's outstanding example – to empires. This conception, which has roots in the Aristotelean notion of the contingency of the political realm, was further, and famously, developed by Vico in the eighteenth Century and Herder and Marx in the nineteenth (Alker 1990).

Secondly, Burckhardt (1990: 20) clearly links "the state as a work of art" to its being "the outcome of reflection *and* calculation" (my emphasis). This art has results in "their inward constitution, no less than their foreign policy"; as Burckhardt's examples make clear, war, too, was a bloody work of art. If the adaptation of means to political ends is an essential feature of modernity, it is not all of the troubled "modern political spirit of Europe." The "new fact [the constructed state] appears in history" precisely when the free play of instincts, the "vicious tendency" of "unbridled egotism, outraging every right, and killing every germ of a healthier culture" is "*overcome or in any way compensated*" (*ibid.*, my emphasis).

Although Burckhardt and Skinner agree on the importance of calculation and ruthless instrumental action in the Renaissance, neither emphasizes the importance of political-economic factors more generally. From a culturally sensitive world systems perspective, the "Renaissance represents the climax of early commercialization in Europe, the formation of urban mercantile society, civilization as we have defined it, but dominated by an absolutist state-class. This is also the age of European expansion ... [based on the ontological model of] a

---

[4] The themes here are of course pre-Christian. Compare Aristotle's similar discussions (in *Historia Animalium*, Book VIII) of the "upward scale" from lifeless things to plants, the "continuous scale of ascent" from plants toward the animal. Among the animals, "the nature of man is the most rounded off and complete, and consequently in man the qualities or capacities [of a proto-human sort found in some animals] are found in their perfection." Aristotle continues with a highly gendered list of attributes distinguishing men from women, with the former excelling in courage and sympathetic helpfulness, while women are more jealous, querulous, scolding, prone to despondency, void of shame or self-respect, false of speech and difficult to rouse to action (McKeon 1941: 635–637).

civilized centre contra savage periphery, a model which is permeated by a great-chain-of-being mode of classification" (Friedman 1983: 35). We have already seen this ontological hierarchy in della Mirandola's placing man between beasts and angels, and we shall see it again below.

The multidisciplinary epistemologies of Renaissance humanism

We can add to the above thematically oriented discussion of Renaissance humanism a few preliminary epistemological clarifications as well, which I believe have methodological relevance[5] for the current concerns of our interdiscipline. First of all, Skinner suggests that "humanists" in Renaissance contexts were "the students and protagonists of a particular group of disciplines centered around the study of grammar, rhetoric, history and moral philosophy" (Skinner 1978: I.xxiii–xxiv). Skinner pays particular attention (especially 1978: I. Ch. 4) to the "civic humanists," who valued republican liberties, and advocated an activist philosophy of life; he cites Hans Baron's claims that "civic humanism" developed primarily out of Florentine resistance to external despotism in the late fourteenth and early fifteenth centuries.[6] It is this group of civic humanists whose knowledge-seeking approaches I shall next summarize.

Agreeing with Burckhardt in this emphasis, Skinner suggests that the major epistemological orientation of Renaissance humanism in general, and civic humanism in particular, sought for sustainable interpretations of a common good. Humanists attempted to combine rhetoric with true wisdom. This was so because understanding the

---

5 In the present chapter, epistemologies (philosophies of knowledge cumulation) are assumed to be grounded in ontologies (more or less metaphysical doctrines of "being"), and methodologies are thought of as applied epistemologies using particular techniques (Alker 1988b).

6 Skinner's impressive review of the ideal of republican liberty and the contributions of medieval French and Italian rhetoricians and scholasticism to Renaissance thinking about individual, ecclesiastical, republican and national liberties contradicts Burckhardt's overly nationalistic account of the origins of the Renaissance and Baron's relative neglect of twelfth and thirteenth-century roots of civic humanism; it allows for subsequent interpretations that have suggested the Renaissance to have risen gradually and unevenly from French, Italian and also, via Spain, certain Islamic sources (compare Halperin 1963). His discussion of the spread of the Northern Renaissance (including Erasmus and More) into Spain also connects my Italian and Spanish examples.

laws, values or history of a different culture on its own terms was to be done in imitation of the classics, interpretively, historically, linguistically. Weinstein (1980: 884) goes further: applied to archeological traces, including recorded speeches and other texts, Renaissance historians and rhetoricians believed in using *"grammatical understanding"* (my italics). As Botticelli tried to do in recovering truly Roman standards of painting and sculpture, using careful measurements to do so, Petrarch did in his grammatically based, deeper recovery of the practical standards of conduct and persuasion immanent in Cicero's rhetorical writings, perhaps the highest cultural achievement of Republican Rome. A genuine historical sensibility combining objective and evaluatively interpretive ways of seeing, was rediscovered; so were the works of classic historians like Tacitus and Thucydides.

Historical interpretation often had a critical thrust. For example, the relevance for free cities of the imperial Justinian Code had already been sharply questioned in the twelfth and thirteenth centuries. But it was Valla, using philological techniques, who decisively delegitimized the so-called Donation by the Emperor Constantine to the Bishop of Rome of dominion over the entire Western Roman empire by showing the glaring anachronisms the document contained.

Recall that Renaissance state building, according to Burckhardt, was based on both reflection and calculation. To interpretive, critically reflective modes of understanding and argumentation, applied in either philosophical or historical contexts, was often added reliance on statistical evidence and insight. With roots in Florentine and Venetian commercial and diplomatic practices, early sixteenth-century histories, especially that of Varchi, combined "scientific" and "civically humanistic" sides of human beings, as well as their characteristic modes of evidence and argumentation. A "statistical estimate of outward life ... [was] uniformly accompanied by the narrative of political events" (Burkhardt 1990: 69).

Machiavelli, Renaissance humanism and modernity

Machiavelli as a late Renaissance civic humanist

Among subsequent interpreters, Machiavelli remains both important and controversial. In particular, Berlin (1982: 25–39, 62) gives a rich historical review of different interpretations. (See also Pocock 1975;

Mansfield 1981; Pitkin 1984; Brown 1988: Chs. 5, 6; Augelli and Murphy 1988; Walker 1989; de Grazia 1989.) Berlin quite tellingly quotes Meinecke's famous saying that "Machiavelli's doctrine was a sword thrust in the body politic of Western humanity, causing it to cry out and to struggle against itself" and against the source of "the most violent mutilation suffered by the human practical intellect." But he then goes on repeatedly (like Skinner 1978: I. Part II; Weinstein 1980; de Grazia 1989) to describe him as a humanist.

Following these leads, instead of trying immediately to assimilate him to one or another of our contemporary scientific/theoretical schools, I suggest we think of Machiavelli as a late Renaissance civic humanist. Inspired by the republican ideals of earlier forms of Greek and Roman civic humanism,[7] in the face of a wrenching decline in the old order of things, Machiavelli was a humanist who was willing to innovate in the moral standards he advocated for attaining civic greatness. If Florence could not be ancient Athens or late Republican Rome, it nonetheless could still be great.

Against a background review of the ideal of liberty in the twelfth and thirteenth-century *Regnum Italicum*, Skinner's treatment (1978: I. Chs. 1–4) of other politically oriented Renaissance writers in the early and late fifteenth century shows in detail how many of Machiavelli's views were also held by his humanistic peers and forefathers. Their (and Machiavelli's) love for antiquity included a great admiration for the *republican* and the *imperial* features of Rome before the Caesars. To recall the Dacres translation (Skinner 1978: I.94), Machiavelli ends *The Prince* with famous and stirring lines from Petrarch:

> Virtue 'gainst fury shall advance the fight
> And it i' the combat soon shall put to flight;
> For the old Roman valour is not dead,
> Nor in the Italians' breasts extinguished.

Machiavelli, like many other of Burckhardt's Renaissance individualists, sought the *rebirth* of a passionate, this-worldly-oriented, heroic political ethos. For all his realism, Machiavelli was an utopian theorist of expansionist imperial republics,[8] for which a rather mythologized

---

[7] See in particular the discussion of Aristotelian political ethos and poli(s)metrics in Chapter 2 above.

[8] Although Machiavelli surely valued the glory that came from conquest, he did seem to agree, as Juvenal had much earlier argued, that "the acquiring of foreign lands" meant that Rome became too tempted by foreign customs, with the result that "in place of frugality and its other high virtues, 'gluttony and self-indulgence took

Ancient Rome was his greatest example. To quote Quentin Skinner again:

> he [Machiavelli] insists that "if you have in mind a Republic that looks to founding an Empire," then the people as a whole must be made the guardians of liberty ... "there has never been any other ... Republic so well adorned [as Rome.]" ... "Should a Republic be so fortunate as frequently to have men who by their example give fresh life to its laws, and do not merely stop them from going to rack and ruin, but restore their former vigour, such a Republic would last for ever."
>
> (Skinner 1978: 160, 170–171, 180; internal quotes to Machiavelli)

This clear evidence of Machiavelli's commitment to civic humanist republican goals – the furthering of the non-privately owned things or matters (*res*) of the public realm (*publica*) – puts him in a tradition going back to Cicero, Aristotle and Plato. It serves as well to introduce his more unconventional and distinctive contributions as a late Renaissance humanist.

Republics, of course, do not live for ever, even though the relative immortality of a "perpetual republic" might be seen as a substitute form of Eternity worth striving for by those who are no longer motivated to achieve Heaven in an afterlife. As the above quotation suggests, among *"humanists of the later Renaissance"* Machiavelli was unusual in his concern with, and analysis of, corruption in political life (Skinner 1978: I.128ff., 166ff.).

Indeed, Machiavelli accepted and greatly elaborated upon the civic humanist theme, evident in the quotation from Burckhardt above, that the corruption destructive of republican liberties results when the interests of particular groups of citizens are put ahead of the interests of the community as a whole. The following quotation, which is central to the argument and organization of Machiavelli's *Florentine Histories*, sketches his relatively distinctive approach:

> [S]ome divisions are harmful in republics and some are helpful. Those are harmful that are accompanied by sects and partisans; [and vice versa] ... One acquires [reputation] publicly by winning a battle, acquiring a town, carrying out a mission with care and prudence, advising the republic wisely and prosperously. One acquires it in private modes by benefiting this or that other citizen ... getting him

possession of it and avenged the world it had conquered.'" There seems to be no intrinsic reasons against coercive expansion. I follow here Skinner (1978: 163) who is quoting a passage from Machiavelli's *Discourses*.

unmerited honors, and ingratiating oneself with the plebs ... From this latter mode of proceeding, sects and partisans arise[;] ... the reputation ... not mixed with sects ... is founded on a common good ...   (Machiavelli 1988: 276–277)

Quentin Skinner and J.G.A. Pocock have described "the Machiavellian moment" both as a period in early modern Europe temporal self-understanding where classical republican ideas were revived, and as the problem complex that faced the relevant, secular, civically minded, republican thinkers within that period, whose view of the possibility of the glorious, near immortal life for their own Republics was in conflict with "a Christian time-scheme which denied the possibility of any secular fulfillment" (Pocock 1975: vii–x).

Corruption was clearly a major difficulty within this problem complex. In his third Discourse, Machiavelli argued that "wealth without worth" was invariably a source of republican civic corruption. Others before him stressed – as was embarrassingly evident from Florentine wars with Milan in which their merceneries switched sides – that greed for wealth could have an undermining effect on Florence's independence.

But there was also a quite remarkable, and novel, attitude to some forms of competitiveness and acquisitiveness in Machiavelli's other writings. Although Bruni, the Florentine humanist, had previously argued that there was a special connection between freedom and equality of opportunity, for greatness was supposed to raise especially able glory-seeking citizens within a commonwealth, Machiavelli went further in the *Discourses*, arguing that the "tumults" of class conflict in ancient Rome, the class conflicts between nobles and plebs, were "the primary cause of Rome's retaining her freedom." Moreover, "class-conflict is not the solvent but the cement of a commonwealth" (Skinner 1978: I.181). Although these conflicts could be interpreted as "corrupting" in either Machiavelli's classical or a very modern sense, they were also seen by him as providing, when appropriately balanced off by Rome's political institutions, a relatively effective way of combining particular interests and constructing a tolerable approximation to a Roman general interest.

Machiavelli's most distinctive contribution to this late Renaissance discussion was to give and elaborate upon a new answer to an old question, "Whether it is better [for a leader] to be loved than feared, or the reverse?" In *The Prince* he contradicted conventional, and earlier humanist, morality, in arguing "it is far better to be feared than loved if you cannot be both." As Isaiah Berlin has emphasized (Berlin 1982: 58–71, seconded by Skinner 1978: 135), Machiavelli's great and tragic originality, after 1,000 years of Christian civilization, was most force-fully to suggest its end of innocence by proposing an alternative, "secular, humanistic, naturalistic [and patriotic] morality."[9] Surely the "New Prince" that appears so dramatically in Machiavelli's writings follows a new moral code. Machiavelli's idealization of Cyrus, Moses and Theseus as principled but ruthless, and culturally sensitive, state builders also shows an alternative vision. These images fit as well Burckhardt's vivid conception of violent Renaissance artists con-structing glorious (Italian) states. And I believe this ruthless but patriotic morality should be considered a troublesome part of the Machiavellian moment.

Machiavelli challenged both Thomistic scholasticism's efforts to unify Greco-Roman and Judeo-Christian philosophies of life, and the more secular and optimistic, syncretically religious humanism of earlier Renaissance philosophers like della Mirandola. In the writers of antiquity, Machiavelli found a different world from the decadent, secularly-oriented religiosity of the Roman Church. Near the end of his *Discourses* Machiavelli used the language of Savonarola to prophesy that "whoever considers the foundations [of the Roman Church], and sees its present use, how diverse it is from them, would judge it to be, without doubt, close either to ruination, or the scourge [of God]" (as quoted in de Grazia 1989: 102).

His attack on the Christian religion for its subversion of civic life – in effect the sects and partisans referred to in his *Florentine Histories* – goes so far as to suggest that civic religions ought to promote "magnani-mity, bodily strength, and everything else that conduces to make men very bold" rather than define man's highest good in the medieval way as "humility, abnegation and contempt for mundane things." Machia-velli openly defies the Biblical view that "The wisdom of this world is the enemy of God," placing in his reformed and preferred Hell the famous learned men of antiquity, "Plato, Plutarch, Livy, Tacitus" among them (de Grazia 1989: 341).

Among "God's friends" in the present, or in his reconstructed

---

[9] I should mention here Harvey Mansfield, Jr.'s caveat (Mansfield 1981: 294–295, and Machiavelli 1988: xiv) that Machiavelli's "peculiar humanism" puts the morality of observed practice ahead of the "force of morality" in using the resources of classical humanism against itself. This sense of the contradictory elements in modernity will recur below in several different forms.

Heaven, are those capable of doing evil for the higher public good, "certain men – one of the Medici or a new prince or whoever will take up the barrier of Italy's redemption" (de Grazia 1989: 56). Indeed, one may think of Machiavelli's moral/political philosophy as a desperate response to a dying old order, as a ruthless, passionate, analytically reflective effort to identify with those changing economic, social and political forces around him which might ultimately sustain and support a strong, independent, republican, glorious, Italian state.

Machiavelli's ontological, epistemological and methodological contributions

Inverting della Mirandola's syncretic religious/philosophical idealism, Machiavelli suggests that "it is in fact indispensable for the ruler to become 'half beast and half man,' since 'he cannot survive otherwise'" (see Skinner 1978: I.136). Thus Machiavelli's great originality as a practical, state-oriented moralist has ontological dimensions. Going against his pre-modern sense of the cyclical rise and fall of states and civilizations, Machiavelli "repudiates the prevailing Christian doctrine that political life is subordinate to eternity" (Walker 1989: 36–38). He substitutes "spirited selfishness" for an immaterial "soul" (Mansfield 1981: 301–305). His "New World" is connected with a different evaluative ranking of the different modes of being, one where heaven and hell, as traditionally defined, are reversed.

Responding to the extremity of his situation with these extremely radical practical-ontological revisions, Machiavelli nonetheless used a style that we have come to associate with the rebirth of historical sensibilities among Renaissance humanists like Alberti. Like many other Renaissance *historians*, he wrote the *Discourses* to "draw those practical lessons which one should seek to obtain from the study of history" (quoted in Skinner 1978: 169).

An adequate epistemological characterization of Machiavelli's contribution surely should include his adoption and adaptation of the linguistic, grammatical and interpretive orientation of Renaissance humanism to his own purposes. Consider the *interpretive* character of Machiavelli's contemplative passion for antiquity (quoted in De Grazia 1989: 26):

> I enter the ancient courts of the men of antiquity where affectionately received by them I pasture on that food that alone is mine and for

which I was born, where I am not too timid to speak with them and ask them about the reasons for their actions; and they in their courtesy answer me; and for four hours of time I feel no weariness, I forget every trouble, I do not fear poverty, death does not dismay me; I transfer all of myself into them . . .

This is not science as the rational/virile domination of nature, it is Aristotelian poetic *mimesis*, the Renaissance's creative recovery of classical interpretive methodology.

Not able to afford much formal training from the rhetoricians, lawyers, classical linguists or other humanists of his time, Machiavelli nonetheless moves analytically toward a more scientific version of their modes of analysis. In this regard, he continues and goes beyond the synthetic Renaissance orientation toward qualitative and quantitative historical analysis mentioned above. Critical, rational, humanistic conversation tends to become reconstructive analysis capable of producing systematic, testable observations about human nature and human accomplishments. Machiavelli's partial success in unambiguously reconstructing the maxims of conduct of his greatest and most ruthless peers, his proto-science, belongs epistemologically within the transformative, historical discussion of *mimesis, hermeneutics,* and *rational theories of action and choice* (see Ricoeur 1981; Alker 1990; Hollis and Smith 1991).

Let us try responsively to project this approach into current times. Using whatever evidence or data which were reliably available, we can say that Machiavelli *treated the actions of those he reported on as texts* (Ricoeur 1981), inferring, as Meinecke observed, the existence of realistic, shockingly ruthless, cunning, statist *practical reasoning/inferencing* (Alker 1984) within the actions (including the deceptive words) of princes. With a keen eye and ear for provocative formulations, he built an imperfect[10] but prescient, proto-scientific, Petrarchean *grammar of emerging, but not eternal, modern power relations* (Alker 1977a, 1987, 1988a).

Machiavelli's politically ambivalent modernity

As a Florentine, Machiavelli experienced first hand the French invasion of a disunited Italy in 1494. According to Martin Wight (1977: 124ff.),

[10] I agree with Der Derian's treatment of Machiavelli (Der Derian 1987: Ch. 5) as a theorist of "proto-diplomacy" rather than "diplomacy," for reasons that include Der Derian's emphasis on Machiavelli's characteristically imperfect recognition of reciprocal relationships between fully sovereign actors.

1494 was the beginning of a slow but dramatic absorption by fledgling European Absolutist states of the glory-seeking, accumulation-supporting, sovereignty-asserting, power-balancing, quasi-anarchic rules and roles of the thereby subordinated and devastated Italian city-state system, an extremely bloody process that did not reach maturation, and a social order of mutually respecting sovereigns, until the Treaty of Westphalia in 1648.

This new world – with its new princes, growing principalities, and bloody birthing processes deeply colored by quasi-totalitarian wars of religion – Machiavelli both described, quasi-scientifically analyzed and prophetically anticipated. It was, like him, *modern* in several, ambivalent senses.

Modernity, according to one of the most thoughtful international political theorists of the subject, William Connolly (1989: Ch. 1), is a period or "order" in which the insistence upon taking charge of the world comes into its own. Machiavelli's own version of the *vir vs. fortuna* Renaissance theme in *The Prince* exemplifies the active seeking control over nature theme that Connolly, Pitkin and many others have seen as a characteristic feature of modernity. But this new, emerging concept of anarchic "order" is, as Wendy Brown has argued, a highly gendered image of Absolutist power, completeness and autonomy.[11]

Michael Shapiro (1991) suggests another important addition to Connolly's characterization of the "order of modernity." In a non-reductionistic, contextually and historically sensitive way, he proposes reconstructing the multiple orders of modernity as the results of charged, changing, intimate, identity-affecting, and sometimes opposed relations between sovereignty and exchange impulses.[12] I

---

[11] Because the argument carries over to Machiavelli and to our subsequent discussions of individuals or states seeking power and glory, it is also worth noting here that feminist writers like Pitkin (1984) and Brown (1988: Chs. 5 and 6) explicitly challenge this notion of "completeness" or autonomous self-fulfillment, based on a gendered degrading of the role of support roles often filled by women. Wendy Brown makes the point quite generally (1988: 107):

> Independence is the goal and articulation of power, yet power is generated through interdependent relations. Power is always obtained from somewhere or something – it is not autoinseminating – yet when power's purpose is more power, it necessarily repudiates or attempts to depower its sources. This is the contradiction at the heart of a masculinist politics in which power becomes its own end and thereby subverts itself.

[12] "The sovereignty impulse tends toward drawing firm boundaries around the self, unambiguously specifying individual and collective identities, privileging and rationalizing aspects of a homogeneous [recognizable] subjectivity ... constituting forms

would like to suggest that this political-economical problematization of modernity applies to the problems of self-definition facing those living within the Machiavellian moment of early modernity as well.

Indeed, one should suspect that many more reconceptualizations of modernity are possible, perhaps deeper and more balanced than that proposed by Havel, with which this chapter began. In the light of our previous appreciation of the interpretive advances associated with, or suggested by, Renaissance humanist thought, it is not surprising that Connolly goes on to argue that modernity has as well among its defining characteristics "the quest for freedom as self-consciousness," and an associated, contradictory, destabilizing "inability to endure its own impulse to self-consciousness." From its aspiration to know and "frame" itself derives an emancipatory, self-discovering, but incompletely achieved "aspiration to articulate the container into which its own discourse has been poured" (*ibid.*).

Machiavelli is clearly self-conscious, or reflectively modern, in the troubled sense suggested by Connolly, Shapiro, Pitkin and Brown. Recall his passage on conversing with the ancients already cited. His writings about Florence, Italy and the challenging new world coming from within and across their borders, embody these dimensions. His plays, we are told (de Grazia 1989: passim), are also comedies critical both of himself, his romancing and the degenerate church. Machiavelli's *Florentine Histories* book is more tragic, suggesting a sense of public, civic degeneration and corruption, only partly alleviated by the appearance of virtuous princes.

Indeed, Machiavelli dies in 1527 hopeful for new positions of power and responsibility in a revivified Florentine republic (1527–1530), but also, I suspect, fearful of Florence's and Italy's republican future. By 1530, Florence has disappeared permanently from the stage of world history as an independent republic, three years after the Medici Pope, Clement VIII, has crowned the Spanish Emperor Charles V, the King of Italy. Under "an increasingly effete succession of Medici Dukes" the

---

of ... otherness; and specifying and bounding both the spaces in which subjects achieve eligibility and those in which the collective as a whole has dominion.

In contrast, the exchange impulse encourages flows and thus (often) the relaxation of specifications of eligible subjectivities and territorial boundaries. The opposition between flows of exchange and the inhibitions of sovereignty is oriented around *issues of selfhood and location* and consequently involves an emphasis either on ownership and the maintenance of authority and control or on reciprocity, substitutability, and ... produc[ing] expanded domains in which things can circulate" (Shapiro 1991: 448; my italics).

Florentine Republic "dissolved into the Grand Duchy of Tuscany" (Skinner 1978: I.115).

Although Machiavelli's most important political offices were held during the years 1498–1512, in the service of a republican leader, Soderini, later on in his life he was obviously tempted to reidentify with anti-republican, nationally oriented, modern- (im)morality types, state-sculptors like the Medici. Living "in [the] Hell" of ruthless, early modern, sovereignty-seeking, state rationalities, seeking to hold up a mirror to "new modes and orders" in "unknown lands and seas," more stimulated by the great statesmen he admired who were condemned to Hell by conventional Christian morality, trying to "reform" Hell or at least make it inhabitable in his literary work, hoping that some charismatic reformer might follow the ruthless economies of power that he had proposed in the service of a better, presumably republican and united Italy, Machiavelli made his own exchanges. He "trad[ed] soul for country" (de Grazia 1989: 351–355). Machiavelli's famous affirmation of greater love for his country than for his soul unreservedly, if ironically, occurs in a correspondence with Vettori and Guicciardini, who are working desperately in 1527 with anti-republican but pro-Italian Papal/Medici forces to prevent the disintegrative conquest of Italy by foreigners.

Bartolomé de Las Casas as a humanist historian of the New World

Why Las Casas? Ask Machiavelli

For me, the attractions of now discussing Bartolomé de Las Casas are several, beyond the overlap in their lives, and their prophetic significance for subsequent international relations. Machiavelli's and Las Casas' connections are more intimate, more complementary, more contradictory, and even more prophetic than one might think.

Once we recognize Machiavelli as a late Renaissance humanist writer, advisor and historian, we can perceive Las Casas as an equally or more successful fulfiller of all of these roles as well.[13] Both tried

---

[13] Athough Las Casas was not involved with the Hapsburgs' efforts to conquer Italy and control the papacy, his side did win, ending Florence's republican independence in the process. On Indian affairs, Las Casas appears to have used the divisions existing between the nobility, the conquistadors and the king or emperor to his advantage, giving his rulers' principled arguments to supplement, rationalize and

actively and repeatedly to make real their political utopias; both oscillated between periods of activity and contemplation, with partial or total failures in the former being the most important proximate causes for their impressive triumphs of observant, if painful, historical learning in the latter.

Even more important than their differing national political allegiances and fortunes are some fundamental contradictions. Whereas the Italian Machiavelli early in *The Prince* magnanimously treats Ferdinand as "a weak king [who] has risen to being, for fame [honor] and glory, the first king of Christendom," and gives the Emperor Charles V a starring role in both *The Prince* and the *Discourses*, the Spaniard Las Casas, their loyal subject, nonetheless becomes their most famous critic. Partly due to Spain's position as a leading power of the Counter-Reformation, Las Casas is unlikely to argue for an anti-traditional morality like Machiavelli's; his radically egalitarian ontological affirmations argue one traditional source, the Bible, against another, Aristotle, rather than directly invert the traditional ontological hierarchies.

Had he lived longer and been exposed to the man and his writings, I suspect Machiavelli would have been both fascinated and appalled by his Spanish contemporary, and impressed by the exchange-based sharing of legitimizing and proselytizing roles uniting the Spanish church and state that his missionary accomplishments reflected. He would have easily recognized the importance of Las Casas' later writings as works of art that helped spawn an alternative new science (cultural anthropology), an alternative new ethic (a communicative, multicultural, universalist respect for human dignity) and an alternative new ideology (connecting collective human rights to self-determination with anti-colonialism). Looking back from the twentieth century, Machiavelli would have seen within Las Casas and himself two mixed versions of what we have come to know as "realism" and "idealism" in international politics. Machiavelli would have, perhaps secretly, told us to read Las Casas.

Writing a lived history of the New World

Las Casas had that profoundly modern Renaissance sense of someone who tried to take charge and make better the world he lived in, in a

revise ordinary political considerations. A colonial policy more viable in the intermediate term was a partial result.

critically self-reflective way. Identified with scholasticism, Thomism and the Counter-Reformation led by the Spanish emperor (Skinner 1978: II. Ch. 5; Pagden 1987), Las Casas nonetheless increasingly embodied in his life and scholarly work many of the most admirable aspects of humanistic modernity that we have so far identified. He had that special Renaissance humanist sensibility of attempting to live his life as a spiritually and materially integrated, rationally guided, and reflective work of art.

As an historian of the New World in which he lived for many years, as a responsible participant and maker of the history he was writing about, and as a critic of that history, Las Casas wrote what I shall call "lived history," always trying to derive valid and sharable lessons from his and others' successes and failures.[14] Because this type of humanistic scholarship is so powerful, yet seems strange to those of us more used to statistical "events data research," and because it too may help us rethink our contemporary epistemological positions (see also Alker 1987, 1992a), I shall discuss how such a lived history was composed and has since been read.

Most of what Las Casas did and said can be thought of as preparatory to, autobiographically reported in, spun off from, or commentary on his monumental *History of the Indies* (Las Casas 1877, 1971a, 1971b). Indeed, as an editor Sanderlin groups his selections from Las Casas' writings (Las Casas 1971a) as those of a historian, autobiographer, anthropologist and political thinker. In the translated excerpts from the *History* (Las Casas 1971a,b) one finds dramatic, religiously interpreted accounts of Columbus' voyages, the powerful remarks of Montesinos and Hatuey quoted in Table 4.1, autobiographical remarks about Columbus' first triumphal return to Spain and Las Casas' conversion to a pro-Indian position, elements of an often rather utopian anthropology of Indians, and insightful accounts of Cortes' Machiavellian maneuverings.

The third, partly anthropological set of Sanderlin's selections are all from *The Apologetic History*, or *Apologetica* – in its final form a 1350-page work, originally a part of the *History of the Indies*, only fully published in 1909. Related, partial treatments of Las Casas' famous

---

[14] With phraseology from Diodorus Siculus, Pagden (1991) offers the striking praise: "Las Casas had, indeed, succeeded 'in recording the common affairs of the inhabited world as though they were those of a single state' and had thus made his 'treatises a single reckoning of past events and a common clearing-house of knowledge concerning them.'"

Table 4.1   *Annotated chronology of Bartolomé de Las Casas' life and works*

1474–1512	**Seville**: Born as son to a small merchant of Jewish background
1493	**Seville**: Witnesses Columbus' triumphal return from New World; father and two uncles sail on Columbus' second voyage
1497	**Granada**: Serves as soldier fighting Moorish rebels
1498–1501?	**Seville**: Latin education at cathedral academy Has from his father an Indian slave later released by Isabella
1502	**Spain to Hispaniola**: Embarks as *doctrinero* with Nicolas de Ovando
1503–1505?	Having helped put down several Indian uprisings, given an *encomienda* by Adm. Diego Columbus; performs expected religious evangelization and has right to forced Indian labor in fields or mines
1506–1507	**Rome**: Visits Rome, and is made a deacon in the church
1511–1512	**Hispaniola**: Probably hears Dominican Antonio de Montesinos' sensational sermon attacking "cruel and horrible servitude" and slaughter of Indians, asking "Are they not men? Do they not have rational Souls? Are you not bound to love them as yourselves?"
1512–1513	**Hispaniola**: Perhaps first person in America ordained as a priest **Cuba**: Participates as priest in bloody conquest; given *encomienda*
1514–1515	**Cuba and Spain**: After further contact with Dominicans, converts to their view and preaches so; returns his Indians to Governor; returns to Spain; has inconclusive audience with dying Ferdinand
1516–1520	**Spain, Hispaniola, etc.**: Gets appointed Protector of the Indians by the court, and begins search for more humane alternatives; proposes "towns of free Indians"; goes back to New World with investigatory commission, but fails; succeeds in his recommendation to import black slaves for sugar mills, a suggestion he later regrets
1520–1522	**Spain and Venezuela**: Given grant to try out his utopian scheme of "Indian communities," as alternative to *encomienda* system; effort in Venezuela fails
1522–1527	**Hispaniola**: Retreats to the monastery, joins Dominicans, writes reform proposals to Court; begins *History of the Indies*
1531	**Hispaniola**: Writes *Council of Indies* (Madrid) attacking *encomiendas*
1534–1539	**Hispaniola, Nicaragua, Guatemala**: Pacifies Indian rebel Enriquillo, argues for voluntary conversion of Indians in *The Only Method of Attracting All People to the True Faith* and against considering them as "beasts who talk"; opposes *encomenderos* in Nicaragua; organizes mission in Guatemala

Table 4.1 *contd*

1540–1543	**Spain**: Learning from previous reverses, campaigns effectively for the New Laws of 1542; writes *Very Brief Account of the Destruction of the Indies*, which contains personally witnessed lurid details of wanton Spanish cruelty, and cacique Hatuey's remarks at the stake refusing baptism and Heaven: he would "rather [go] to hell so as not to be where Spaniards were"; also attributes Christians' killing of "infinite number of souls" to their "wish for gold"; Christian law forbids "that evil be done" "that good may follow"
1544–1547	**Mexico**: Consecrated Bishop of Chiapa, refuses absolution to *encomenderos*, organizes church behind his policies, provokes riots; denounced by Inquisition; New Laws are suspended; writes *Confesionario* arguing the illegitimacy of all conquest and calls for reparations; still possesses Negro slaves
1547	**New Spain to Spain**: Returns permanently
1550–1551	**Valladolid**: Debates Renaissance humanist scholar Sepulveda, 1551, before royally appointed panel of judges; Sepulveda argues justness of war versus Indians – according to Aristotle, Indians "are inferior to the Spaniards just as children are to adults, women to men, and ... apes are to men." In Latin *Apologetica* and Spanish *Defense* defends, in Aristotelian terms, the Indians as not natural slaves, superior to many old world nations in natural reason and the following of natural law; defends human sacrifice; quotes Cicero arguing "all the races of the world are men," "the entire human race is one," alike in creation, nature and free choice, with "capacity ... to be instructed, persuaded, and attracted to order and reason and laws and virtue and all goodness"
1552	**Spain**: Publishes seven treatises on Indians, including *Account*, which in pirated editions is used as propaganda by Spain's enemies
1554–1564	**Spain**: Defeats Peruvian bid for legitimization of *encomiendas* with *Letter to Carranza* calling for independence of Indians, despite offer of 7–9 million ducats from colonialists
1566	**Dominican Convert of Nuestra Senora in Madrid**: Dies, leaving will prophesying that "because of these impious, criminal and ignominious deeds perpetuated so unjustly, tyrannically and barbarically, God will vent upon Spain His wrath and His fury, for nearly all of Spain has shared in the bloody wealth usurped at the cost of so much ruin and slaughter."

Sources: Las Casas 1971a, b; Ducelle 1980; Todorov 1992.

disputation with Sepulveda[15] at Valladolid were published in 1552. The fourth section presents selections from Las Casas' political thought, including selections from the 1552 treatises, memorials and letters addressed to the Spanish King, his advisors or other officials. The most famous of these, widely republished and recirculated in the sixteenth and seventeenth centuries, is also historical writing, but in a polemical, rhetorical, ideologically charged way: a *Very Brief Account of the Destruction of the Indies*.

Contending ways of giving narrative sense to Las Casas' life and work

Hayden White (1987: 1–25) suggests that historical narratives both presuppose more, and do more, than the annals, medieval chronicles or behavioral event data sequences we may be familiar with. Narrative fullness in reporting on the happenings occurring to individuals in or outside of a group requires *shared* identifications with at least some of the protagonists, a kind of sociality which the achievement of historicality by a narrative presupposes. The narrative form – a beginning, middle and an end, where the beginning and the end are connected in some way – both appeals to the existence of a sociopolitical order, within whose morals that narrative call for completion, and helps to reproduce or amend that order. Table 4.1, largely prepared from standard sources, gives a somewhat more biographically and narratively coherent account than a mere chronology. Thus more actors, action rationales and reactions are identified than in Las Casas (1971a: 289ff.).

Take the five first entries in the table: what narrative significance do they suggest? Does being born into a Christian family said to be of Jewish background suggest both an especial sensitivity to discriminatory treatment? Is there a similar anticipatory quality in his early contact with Indian slavery and a queen willing to intervene against some of its excesses? Or, we might want to emphasize Las Casas' prophetic role as a chronicler of Columbus' life and discoveries (Pagden 1991), or his credentials as a (eventually repentant) Conquistador? Like the claims in his *History* of the providential character of

---

[15] Sepulveda was a chaplain to the emperor, the leading Spanish "humanist" of his day, translator of Aristotle's *Politics* into Latin, and defender of/apologist for Spain's wars against the Indians.

Columbus' discoveries, these beginnings set up a variety of related possible narrativizations of his lived history.

Another early theme is suggested by the mention of Las Casas' participation in a post-1492 mopping up operation against Moorish rebels and of Nicolas de Ovando as the leader of the 1502 expedition that brought Las Casas to the New World. The fall of the last Moorish/ Islamic kingdom of Grenada to Ferdinand and Isabella in 1492 liberated the resources that made financing of Columbus' original trip feasible. It also suggests that the harsh habits developed during the Reconquista of Spain, in which Ovando also participated, were likely to be reproduced in a peripheral context.

Consider next the puzzle of Las Casas' reported trip to Rome. Is it a sign of religious observance, or of God's favor? Or should we see here unconscious evidence of a spatialization and temporalization of a newly reinvigorated Great-Chain-of-Being ontology[16] which in the early modern era placed Rome or Europe at the center of the civilized world, identified distant peripheries with more ancient, primitive or barbaric aspects of its past? (Friedman 1983: 34ff.)

The famous quotation from Hatuey will be shocking for many religious readers. Methodologically, it and the other highly selective quotations in the table show what textual attributions of intentionality do to transform behavioral sequences of "events data" into meaningful, memorable and criticizable accounts of human conduct. Does not it also substantively qualify Las Casas' life story, or the *Very Brief Account* spun off from it, as international, or intercultural, relations?[17] Are not we fortunate that what Hatuey said has not only been preserved and translated, but that it stands for a vivid, symbolic affirmation of a larger pattern? This *Account* suggests synecdochically the larger message of the story for the Spanish. The mentioning of specific Indians helps

---

[16] See Lovejoy (1976: originally 1936). Following Aristotle or Ibn Khaldun, as cited in Chapter 2 above, let it suffice here to describe this classical ontological continuum as traditionally ranging from rocks, plants, lower and higher animals, to variously differentiated humans characterized by speaking, reflecting, thinking and spiritual or prophetic powers, to angels, and the divine.

[17] Las Casas was also an influential member of the Spanish Renaissance school of writers on international law and international society that sometimes gets mentioned in one's graduate textbooks as a major source of what is known as the Grotian tradition of international relations. Der Derian (1987: 101–102) argues that while "unable to halt the genocide of the native populations of Central America, Victora, Bartolomé de Las Casas, and many of the later natural law writers, were instrumental in freeing proto-diplomatic relations from the exclusive Christian mediation."

strengthen the anti-colonial tradition of scholarship concerned to give voices to the largely unheard from Indian and Mestizo populations of the fifteenth and sixteenth centuries (see Todorov 1992, originally 1982; Root 1988; Piedra 1989; Seed 1991 for English language entry points into this literature). It also crystalizes Las Casas' – always debatable – role as colonial "fixer" (*vis-à-vis* Enriquillo).

Todorov (1992) correctly criticizes much of Las Casas' activity and interpretations (and those of his Spanish and Indian contemporaries) as unidirectional, ethnocentric and monological; the treatment of native Americans as exotic, barbarian, heretical "others" deflects a process of mutual recognition, respect and toleration. One could go further, and argue along with David Campbell that the "exploration and interpretation of the New World is an historical moment" in the development of modern identity through the experienced intertextuality of interracial/ intercultural communications where ontologically grounded characterizations of "presence" and "absence" are not shared. For Campbell, "Las Casas' progressive position ... is still finally unable to shrug off a persistent [Eurocentric, phonological, ontological and epistemological] logocentrism" (Campbell 1992: 111–118).

In the middle of Las Casas' life (and Table 4.1) the identification of the *encomenderos* and the controversial attribution of economic motives to their activities – but not to those of Columbus – suggests a more economic "plot" and the protagonists, or the subplots, of a sharable story of inhumane treatment. The extent to which both social/moral failures of recognition and respect for others and of exploitation commingle in Las Casas' accounts may help explain their citability by subsequent commentators of various ideological orientations.

The brief verbatim excerpts from the lengthy Valladolid debate and associated documents do not do justice to their length, passion, erudition or complexity.[18] But their stirring language, which eloquently

---

[18] From the point of view of Las Casas' humanistic contribution to multicultural anthropology, political science and international studies, the form and content of at least one of Las Casas' major arguments should be mentioned. Arguing in classical dialectical/disputational fashion against Sepulveda's various theses, including the dehumanizing hierarchy given in Table 4.1, Las Casas turns Aristotle's own list of barbarian or subhuman characteristics in the *Politics* against Sepulveda. The Indians have kingdoms, royal dignitaries, jurisdiction, good laws and lawful government; hence they are neither barbarians nor the "natural slaves" that Sepulveda, using another Aristotelian phrase, had argued they were.

Secondly, against the charge that Indian cannibalism justified Spanish conquest, Las Casas heroically, and multiculturally, argued sacrifice was a sign of religiosity

invokes fundamental values of Western civilization, helps establish Las Casas' status as an aged but ageless Renaissance humanist – a heroically determined continuation of the voices of della Mirandola and Montesinos against the powerful voice of a higher status "humanist" scholar at least partly corrupted by the search for power and wealth.

One could call this recognition of, and respect for, universally/ naturally grounded, species-wide, creative human capacities, together with the recognition of the intrinsic worth of the differing, voluntarily based, cultural expressions of these capacities, the "Las Casas moment" in Renaissance humanist thought. The moment, i.e., the "universalistic humanism" characteristic of many of the Renaissance writers we have reviewed, is parallel to, equal in importance with, but – concerning involuntary imperial expansions – contradictory to the Machiavellian moment previously described.

Indeed, Hanke (1959: 116) concludes by arguing that Las Casas' moving assertion at Valladolid that "all the peoples/races of the world are men" prefigures the United Nations' Universal Declaration of Human Rights, which four centuries later asserts that "All human beings are born free and equal in dignity and rights. They are endowed with reason and conscience and should act toward one another in a spirit of brotherhood." This deep conviction forms the foundations of Las Casas' substantial, if flawed, and frequently utopian, social scientific accounts of Indian practices and institutions (Sevilla-Casas 1977).

It is especially significant from the perspective of the narrative completion of a lived history, and from the point of view of Las Casas' Renaissance humanist commitment to universal human dignity, how he concludes his magisterial *History*. In his last chapter, which only reaches the second decade of the sixteenth century, he attempts to characterize a then unnamed crime against collective human rights that we now call genocide, and he makes an effort roughly to quantify and explain the *despoblacion y soledad* of large parts of the previously populous Carribean. Moreover, like Valla, the Renaissance Italian critic of the Donation of Constantine, Las Casas (see Hanke 1974 and Todorov 1992, but not Las Casas 1971a or b) argues against there having been meaningful opportunities for peaceful persuasion of the Indians via various more or less hypocritical, state and church sanc-

and (sometimes, of remarkable, voluntary) selflessness, condoned both by natural law and the Bible (!) Human sacrifice was a "probable error" in Aristotelian terms, not the violation of natural law.

tioned opportunities for peaceful submission and conversion, *requerimientos* never communicated to them with an open ended chance to reason about them.[19]

Las Casas' last testament, like the end to his *History* and his radically anti-colonial letter to Carranza, reaffirms this profound criticism of Spanish conduct in attempting to impose their dominion over others (Pagden 1987). Adding the most memorable sentence from Las Casas' will to Table 4.1 fits as well our own interest in his predictive/ prophetic qualities. But it disturbs an account that could have peacefully and reverentially ended with Las Casas dying literally and figuratively within the arms/abode of Nuestra Senora in Madrid. It provides, too, a very anti-Spanish[20] way of completing the story, and suggests that the Spanish conquest has been a failure.

Might not a much more general, but differentiable, critique of the ethnocentric and colonial practices of each of the modern European (and non-European) states have been implied? Todorov's brilliant account of the development of the three stages of Las Casas' thought – from Conquistador, to caring colonialist, to other-respecting, anti-colonial, intercultural communicator – clearly transcends a Spanish focus for the discussion of imperial relationships with others, and provides a contemporary developmental version of the Las Casas moment of modern humanism (Todorov 1992). Views obviously differ in this regard, and require considerable further analysis. Nowadays, one could credibly argue against religious proselytizing in any form. For more general, and contrasting, interpretations of the New World experience, compare: Vargas Llosa's argument (1991) that Las Casas and the Conquistadores represented variants of autonomous, principled, individual conduct not possible within ant-like, totalitarian, Indian societies; Octavio Paz's reflective view (1987) that the Aztecs suffered fatally from the lack of biological and cultural contact with other civilizations; Todorov's (1992) provocative interpretation of the crucial role of inaccurate Aztec categorizations of their rapidly chan-

---

[19] Hanke (1974) and Todorov (1992) emphasize this point in their narrative summaries, but the more conventional summaries of Las Casas (1971a, b) do not.

[20] Dor-Ner (1991: 225–226), among others, has criticized the "Black Legend" that argues Spanish colonialism was worse than the other European or American variants. Hanke (1970, 98–100) also critiques this legend with citations to New Englanders in 1640 voting proclamations that "The Lord may give the earth or any part of it to his chosen people. ... We are his chosen people." Like these writers, Campbell (1992) also critically compares treatments of Negroes, Mestizos and Indians in Anglo-American and Ibero-American contexts without an anti-Spanish bias.

ging situation; and Dor-Ner's (1991: Chs. 5–7) ecologically grounded, multifaceted assessment of "A New People," "The Columbian Exchange" and a "World Made Whole."

The history of the early Conquistadors and the misnamed "Indians" of the New World is clearly much more complex than a two-page narrative can suggest. It includes accounts of cannibalistic wars and sacrifices that would turn the stomach of any humanist, and thus weaken some of his most powerful and astonishing arguments for human sacrifice, e.g., that Abraham and God both were willing to sacrifice their own sons, and God actually did so! These data, but not the evidence emphasized by Las Casas' black and white critics of his treatment of Negro slaves,[21] have been omitted from this table. Nonetheless, Las Casas' clustering of narratives deserves its classic status. His exceptional contributions to the temporally ordered self-understanding of a continuing society (Hispanic culture and Western civilization more generally) – to their historicality or historicity – derive significantly, I hope to have shown, from the powerful and sharable meanings his "lived" (and relivable) narratives construct and convey.

The Las Casas moment in contemporary International Studies

As Hanke's and Todorov's books, among others, make clear, the Las Casas moment of early modernity has survived, in various forms, into our own time.[22] Their analytical accounts draw appreciably on Las Casas' universalism and the respect and tolerance for other cultures that his later arguments evidenced (See also Said 1979).

Because of my belated rediscovery of Las Casas' scientific humanism, another line of research – on American ethnocentrism during the Vietnam War – has taken on new significance for me. I

---

[21] Like Hanke (1959: 9), Williams (1970) is particularly critical of Las Casas' (and Thomas More's) attitude toward (black) slavery. Nonetheless he places "Las Casas among the greatest gifts of Spanish civilization to the Caribbean and the world" (p. 406).

[22] Were I to have pursued the contemporary empirical exploration and testing of Machiavellian thought, in particular republican civic humanism recast in contemporary "reason of state" terms, the exercise would have been more familiar. Lake (1992) has both a provocative and "pro-American" civic humanist twist – suggesting democracies are more likely to win wars as well as less likely to fight them, especially against each other – and a good bibliography of recent, relevant literature. Were Lake's analysis linked to the overlapping, but sometimes contradictory arguments about imperial republics of the universal humanists, some extremely provocative and illuminating humanistic and scientific inquiry might result.

recall this work because its inspiration – the words of Martin Luther King, Jr. – have already become part of the "lived history" of my own generation.[23]

Developed from William Graham Sumner's 1906 study of *Folkways*, LeVine and Campbell's (1972) empirical concept of ethnocentrism includes "both the ingroup-outgroup polarization of hostility and the self-centered scaling of all values in terms of the ingroup folkways." The former includes variants of the (pre-Machiavellian) view that "Virtue consists in killing, plundering, and enslaving outsiders"; the latter theme elaborates on the "view of things in which one's group is the center of everything, and all others are scaled and rated with reference to it" (LeVine and Campbell 1972: 8).

Alker and Sylvan (unpublished) find sentences from Martin Luther King, Jr.'s famous 1967 address, "A Time to Break Silence" (Washington 1990: Ch. 40) to illustrate every one of the twenty-two component beliefs that Levine and Campbell use to operationalize their Sumner-based conception of ethnocentrism. Relevant quotations are in Table 4.2. The deep parallellism between these illustrative sentences and Las Casas' views as expressed in Table 4.1 is especially striking. To use King's doubly appropriate, anti-ethnocentric language, there are "strange liberators" in both the Caribbean and Vietnam; domestic political injustices (such as practices against Moors and Jews in Spain, and blacks in the United States) are being played out on foreign grounds. Like Hatuey, Ho Chi Minh's salvation from retaliatory hatred depends on a "sense of humor and of irony" concerning his own "aggression" when his poor weak nation is being heavily bombed by a rich and powerful country from far away.

The standards of a universalist, multicultural humanism are powerfully articulated in King's call that "Every nation must now develop an overriding loyalty to mankind as a whole in order to preserve the best in their individual societies." Like della Mirandola, King recognizes a syncretic "Hindu-Moslem-Christian-Jewish-Buddhist" belief in love as the "unifying principle of life." Given Sumner's roots in Social

---

[23] There are of course other, probably more enduring and broadly defined, contributions along these lines that should be mentioned. For example, Harff and Gurr's (1988) work also empirically explores the extreme consequences of ethnocentrism, and suggests operational conceptions of politicide and genocide. Perhaps the most comprehensive and challenging American overview (in the bicontinental sense) of related work on ethnic identification, ethnic rights, ethnic conflict and ethnodevelopment is Stavenhagen's (1990).

Table 4.2

Structured aspects of Martin Luther King Jr.'s anti-ethnocentrism[a]

1.1 *See selves as virtuous and superior* 1.2 *See outgroup as contemptible, immoral, and inferior*
p. 235: [The Vietnamese people] must see Americans as strange liberators ...
Even though they quoted the American Declaration of Independence in their
own document of freedom, we refused to recognize them ... support[ing]
France in its reconquest ... we again fell victim to the deadly Western
arrogance [p. 241: "of feeling that it has everything to teach others and nothing
to learn"]
1.4 *Sees selves as strong* 1.5 *Sees outgroups as weak*
Is our nation planning to build on political myth again [about Saigon's
democracy and NLF weakness] and then shore it up with the power of new
violence? Here is the true meaning and value of compassion and nonviolence
when it helps us to see the enemy's point of view, to hear his questions, to
know his assessment of ourselves. For from his view we may indeed see the
basic weaknesses of our condition, and if we are mature, we may learn and
grow and profit from the wisdom of the brothers who are called the
opposition.
1.12 *Cooperative relations with ingroup members* 1.13 *absence of cooperation with
outgroup members*
p. 242: All over the globe men are revolting against old systems of exploitation
and oppression and out of the wombs of a frail world new systems of justice
and equality are being born ... We in the West must support these revolutions.
... It is a sad fact that, because of comfort, complacency, a morbid fear of
communism, and our proneness to adjust to injustice, the Western nations that
initiated so much of the revolutionary spirit of the modern world have now
become the arch anti-revolutionaries.
1.14 *Obedience to ingroup authorities* 1.15 *absence of obedience to outgroup
authorities*
p. 231: ... surely this is the first time in our nation's history that a significant
number of its religious leaders have chosen to move beyond the prophesying
of smooth patriotism to the high grounds of a firm dissent based upon the
mandates of conscience ["our inner being"] and the reading of history.
1.16 *Willingness to remain as ingroup members* 1.17 *absence of conversion to
outgroup membership*
p. 242: Every nation must now develop an overriding loyalty to mankind as a
whole in order to preserve the best in their individual societies. This call for a
world-wide fellowship that lifts neighborly concern beyond one's tribe, race,
class and nation is in reality a call for an all-embracing and unconditional love
for all men.
1.3 *See own standards of value as universal, intrinsically true. See own customs as
original, centrally human*
p. 242: When I speak of love ... I am speaking of that force which all of the
great religions have seen as the supreme unifying principle of life. ... This
Hindu-Moslem-Christian-Jewish-Buddhist belief about ultimate reality ...
1.6 *Social distance [between ingroup and outgroup]*
p. 238: I speak as a child of God and brother to the suffering poor of Vietnam. I

Table 4.2 *contd*

---

speak for those whose land is being laid waste, whose homes are being destroyed, whose culture is being subverted.

1.7 *Outgroup hate*

p. 242f.: The oceans of history are made turbulent by the ever-rising tides of hate. History is cluttered with the wreckage of nations and individuals that pursued this self-defeating path of hate.

1.20 *Virtue in killing outgroup members in warfare*

p. 233: ... the tragic recognition ... that the war was doing far more than devastating the hopes of the poor at home ....they ... had to fight and to die in extraordinarily high proportions ... . We were [sending "crippled"] black young men to guarantee liberties in Southeast Asia which they had not found in southwest Georgia and East Harlem.

1.22 *Blaming of outgroups for ingroup troubles*

p. 242 (continued from 1.12–1.13): Therefore, communism is a judgment against our failure to make democracy real and follow through on the revolutions that we initiated.

Note: [a] Remarks from Washington (1990: Ch. 40) contrasted with fifteen (of twenty-three) italicized characterizations of ethnocentric attitudes and behaviors toward ingroups/outgroups (LeVine and Campbell 1972); examples of the remaining eight characteristics omitted for reasons of space.

Darwinism, the application of such criteria to United States foreign policies in the American–Vietnamese War suggests a similarly more general (and extremely tough) test for the performance of Western civilization in its own universalist humanist terms, a test that King's anti-ethnocentric remarks suggest it failed in that war.

Modernity, post-modernity and humanistic International Studies

Let me conclude by returning to four concerns raised in my introductory sections.

Root conceptions of humanistic International Studies

The most fundamental characteristic of the early modern/Renaissance scholars we have looked at (including Sepulveda) is their republican civic humanism, their civic engagement in *res* (matters) *publicae* (of public concern), with at least some genuine concern to achieve the common good of the people involved. All the early moderns we have looked at, especially Machiavelli and Las Casas, have been significantly motivated by such concerns, and identified with their larger communities. When one recalls that their characteristic disciplinary orientations were rhetoric (including training in persuasive speech and formal disputation), grammatically oriented language studies, history and moral philosophy, it is relatively easy to see contemporary descendents of these disciplinary specializations – argumentation theory, computational hermeneutics, case-based legal and political reasoning modeling (Mefford 1990), case method discussion teaching (Christensen *et al.* 1991), and the discourse analysis approaches of many contemporary ethnomethodologists (Boden and Zimmerman 1991) come to mind.

Adding the rigor and precision of contemporary scientific analysis need not change fundamentally the laudable civic humanist objective of participating in, making more complex or enlarging the public life and space of one's community. Both the larger sketch of Machiavelli's republican history, Las Casas' relivable "lived history," Todorov's brilliant *The Conquest of America,* and the applications of LeVine and Campbell's operationalizations of ethnocentrism have illustrated as well ways in which Toulmin's belief that humanist argumentation and anti-ethnocentric tolerance needs to be combined with the rigor of early or later modern scientific methods. Narratives or arguments that both define public directions, withstand critical investigation, and engage collective identifications and public sentiments are, and have long been, at the core of humanistic international studies. This is true whether public activism or objective and critical contemplative detachment is the orientation involved.

Epistemologically, humanistic knowledge seeking is not so separated from living. Havel (1992) tapped into the fundamentally *interpretive* character of humanistic endeavor when he said "We must try harder to understand than to explain" (see also Hiley *et al.* 1991). For humanists, describing, arguing, self-discovering, world disclosing, difference recognizing, policy proposing, state constructing, interpretation criticizing, collectivity mobilizing, historical sense making, lesson-drawing, explanation-seeking and consequence inferring activities fit within schemes of human purposes and value relevance.

Perhaps the deepest aspect of the modern search for reflective self-determination has concerned the never fully accomplished striving for balance, completeness, integration or understanding and control of one's material, intellectual, emotional, spiritual and ontological inner and outer worlds, even when they were undergoing fundamental changes. Maintaining one's integrity may also lead to the recognition of difference as the outcome of such a quest. Living participants in their own "End of History" – that of an independent, republican Florence and of pre-1492 Spain where centuries of battling Islam defined a militant, conquest-oriented Christian imperialism – neither Machiavelli nor Las Casas refused to grapple with the contradictory, emergent features of a new world; they recognized both unity and difference in their innovative interpretations.

What is modernity?

As a preliminary contribution to the modernity-post-modernist debate (see also Der Derian and Shapiro 1989; White 1991; Rosenau 1992), following the suggestions of Toulmin and Havel, it has seemed to me that we needed to know more about what modernity is – what it originally meant, what it has stood for, what it has become. The best short answer I have found came from the humanist domain of political philosophy: Connolly's (1987: 2) "In modernity, the [incompletely self-reflective] insistence upon [man's] taking charge of the world comes into its own." Within those disciplines concerned with increasing knowledge about individuals, nations, peoples and their interrelationships, modernity was taken in its beginning to be associated with a new, multidimensional, if gendered sense of human possibilities, conceived of in both a naturalistically scientific (Galilean or Cartesian) and a science respecting humanistic fashion.

I have tried to reilluminate one of the greatest periods in Western and world history, the transition from the medieval to the modern age, the Renaissance. Within this review, two or three distinguishable humanist moments have emerged: traditional civic humanism, the Machiavellian variant thereof attempting to immortalize virtuous republics in a *Realpolitik* world which included their own domestic and constitutional politics, and Las Casas' striving for universal, multi-cultural recognition of human dignity.

The synthesis of these later two moments, a synthesis including many earlier elements of civic humanism as well, I suggest calling "the humanistic moment" in International Studies. Thought of as a period, such a "moment of history" is largely coextensive with early modernity; thought of in terms of a set of complementary and contradictory world sculpting and rationalizing impulses, this "Humanistic

Moment" *is* a first approximation to the early modernity of International Studies. Connolly's contradictory conception of the modern attempt, with insufficient reflection, to take charge of the world may be seen similarly but more generally to embody both a humanistic morality and a statist one. Attempting to coordinate, balance or integrate both components of this specific "humanistic moment" (and that of its feminist critics) would give a more androgynous ideal of humane action than either of its rather gendered components, taken separately. Nonetheless, I am open to Rob Walker's characteristically incisive suggestion that these remarks might better have been titled "Humanistic Moments in International Studies."

Is modernity over?

This review suggests two ironic results concerning Havel's and others' critical dismissal of an absolutist, arrogant, scientistic, domineering modernity. First of all, our Toulminized Havel fits the Burckhardt–Skinner conception of a modern humanist very closely. To take only two of their criteria and apply them to Havel, we can say that he too has discovered a new world of inner and outer awareness, of Being and of personal experience, "an elementary sense of justice, the ability to see things as others do, a sense of transcendental responsibility, archetypal wisdom, good taste, courage, compassion and faith in the importance of particular measures" (Havel 1992). These rudiments of a prior civility are Havel's revival of antiquity.[24] Moreover, like the Renaissance humanists, Havel takes an activist, artistically constructive role toward the world, believing that "politicians should lead the way" because of their "changed attitude toward the world, themselves and their responsibility" (*ibid.*). The more general implication here is that at least some other "post-modernists" too should be thought of as radical late modern humanists, and their work judged accordingly.

Secondly, our recovery of "the humanistic moment" supports

---

[24] Recall the discussion of First Philosophy, Wisdom and Theology, alternative names for Aristotle's science of Metaphysics – in Chapter 3 above. In his later OpEd Havel (1994), suggests reflection on a new, i.e., post-modern, science of the cosmos. On the border between science and myth, the "anthropic cosmological principle" and the "Gaia hypothesis" that sees the earth system as a living, mega-organism inspire us with "the awareness of our being anchored in the Earth and the universe ... that we are an integral part of higher, mysterious entities against whom it is not advisable to blaspheme."

Toulmin's claim that eighteenth century Cartesian rationalism tended to wipe out many but not all traces of the earlier, more humanistic sensibilities of early modernity. But like the recognition of Havel's own humanistic modernity, this recovery, including but not limited to the variety of research approaches on "otherness" and ethnocentrism that were mentioned, defeats Havel's claim that modernity is over. If both the Machiavellian and Las Casas moments of early modernity are still very much with us, and Havel's own position can be likened to a variant of the latter, how can we argue that modernity is over?

Toward a more humanistically understood inter-discipline of International Studies

Hopefully this discussion will be seen as a helpful reformulation of the related, earlier, over-drawn controversies between "realist" *or* "idealistic" and "traditional" *or* "scientific" approaches to international studies. Despite the contradictory practical and philosophical moralities and radically contrasting ontologies these orientations sometimes entail, their interpretive, historical and rhetorical strategies all share an interpretive, meaning constituting, epistemological orientation common to the humanities. And if the examples I have given generalize, humanistic *and* scientific research practices can be greatly multiplied.

Out of loyalty to the modern/enlightenment goals of the International Studies Association, drawing on some of the principal inspirations of my own writings, supporting its new, North American commitment to being one among many international studies associations, I have suggested ways in which humanistic considerations in general, and the civic, Machiavellian, and multicultural humanistic moments in particular, can affect and improve international studies research.

Perhaps coming out of these discussions one can see emerging a new and better period of humanistically shaped international studies. It might reflect less imperialistic and ethnocentric, more genuinely pluralistic, morally tolerant ideals in the world around us as well. Fulfilling certain Renaissance and Enlightenment ideals, it would retain the classical humanistic, practical/moral concern for the common good, but enlarge that conception equally to include men and women, as well as ethnic and national communities around the globe. Multicultural respect for naturally or divinely endowed human dignity would ground this perspective.[25]

Virtue and glory would not be linked to conquest of "them" by "us." Visions of pluralistic, transnational, international and supranational structures of competition and cooperation are also apparent. And, as Havel emphasizes, there would be a moral-ontological openness to different individual and collective modes of being and doing, knowing and feeling. The over-exploited natural world would also be seen as transcending, encompassing and supporting us.

These ideals can be described either as the contradictory fulfillment of "the Humanistic Moment" of modernity within international studies, or its post-modern supercession. They might also be argued to be appropriate guides for a global inter-discipline of international studies attempting humanistically and scientifically to make sense of a very different, often less attractive, world. They should help us anticipate and make sense of major changes that are taking place in the world around us and inside of us. Which label one uses for this vision – late modern or post-modern – matters less than the deeper issues of intergroup relations, knowledge accumulation, and collective learning to which it points.

[25] For one familiar with the Cartesian/Chomskean variant of linguistic naturalism, the step from a remarkably endowed, universally defined human being to the multicultural appreciation and tolerance that Las Casas and Todorov advocate is bridgeable by a constructivist research philosophy and an enriched understanding of sociolingusitic generativity (Alker 1984, 1987, 1990). That is why the Las Casas moment is at the same time "universalist" and "multicultural."

5 Can the end of power politics be part of the concepts with which its story is told?
A Leibnizian reply

This chapter attempts to outline a methodology for committed peace research that dialectically synthesizes the virtues of positivist, radical (including Marxist) and more conservative (traditional) conflict resolution concerns. A necessary element in any such synthesis is the use of self-referential, strategy-suggesting, theory-imbedded, system-reflecting, narrative-oriented conceptualizations – as in my chapter title.

Both Bertell Ollman and Jon Elster have argued that Leibniz, Marx, Hegel and Whitehead adhered to an ontological philosophy that things are really "internal" relations. The first part of the chapter suggests an explication of this kind of "theory-laden" conceptualization in critical (primarily Marxist) perspectives on Absolutism; the second similarly reconstructs Leibniz's ironical labeling of Louis XIV as *Mars Christianissimus*. The third part outlines an "operational" conception of explanatory, interpretive and critical peace research. Its integrative vehicle, a recent artificial intelligence simulation of power plans by Roger Schank and Robert Abelson, illustrates how the critical, empirical application of descriptive concepts from either the Marxian or the Leibnizian tradition might be attempted.

The intellectual puzzle which this chapter addresses is elliptically summarized in its title: "Can the end of power politics be part of the [operational concepts] with which its story is told?" In the last decade or so, several such puzzles, some of them even more arresting, have come forcefully to my attention. Recalling them might better locate in the reader's mind the significance of such dialectical queries, and motivate the more abstract review of the philosophy of internal relations that these encounters provoked. Such a journey, which has carried me into the highly compressed depths of Leibnizian metaphysics and Marxian ontology, and which I am still continuing, has happily provided me with a provisional basis for understanding more fully my topical question and others like it. Since reproducibility is such a fundamental aspect of shared understanding and valid scientific analysis, I have tried of late to think how the transcendence of power politics may in concept and in deed be part of operational specifications of its brutal reality. Surprisingly enough, certain clearly operational computer simulations of power relationships, if correctly interpreted, appear to have many of the appropriate representational characteristics – hence, my desire to repeat publicly such an interpretation as a way of encouraging further work in this direction.

Three dialectical puzzles

At an MIT seminar quite a few years ago, a Canadian sociologist, John O'Neill, made the then stupefying remark: "This cup of coffee contains within it the entire history of imperialism."[1] The remark seemed, in context, an important one; the author was coherent, intelligent, even witty. Was he mad? What puzzled me most, if he was sane, was not that a radical might argue metaphorically that the coffee was a capitalistic product of an age of competing imperialisms: conservative politicians also took it as unproblematical that "dirty money" ought to be laundered, of late in Mexico; Lady Macbeth regularly and understandably saw blood where others noted only well-washed hands.

First of all, I didn't see how to resolve the manifestly contradictory use of the word "within." To my operational measurement sensibilities, *inside* the cup was only a dark brown liquid, which we conventionally call coffee. Secondly, why was it so important in O'Neill's talk that I *understand* the correct *description* of an *object*? My methodological training had emphasized various multimethod, multitrait, operational measurement procedures as ways of typing, clustering or dimensionalizing phenomena. But almost always these deep descriptive characterizations were not sufficient research results: one then should go on and do the best kind of correlational and, hopefully, causal analysis to account for, or *explain*, the distinctive variabilities thus uncovered.[2]

---

[1] I am paraphrasing here; and I now know that O'Neill was at the time probably paraphrasing a well-known remark by Marx of a similar cast.

[2] Such a research strategy is readily apparent in all the "quantitative international politics" texts and articles of the 1960s, including my own. In a letter commenting on an earlier draft of this chapter, Singer summarizes the conventional view well: "To use the familiar trichotomy, there are three classes of knowledge: existential, correla-

Finally, to one trained to think of the past as time series data and lagged explanatory variables, it was of course problematic what the "history" looked like that one might find in O'Neill's cup by wearing the right kind of observational spectacles.

The next similarly puzzling episode was really a series of discussions in Allende's Chile about the use of behavioral scientific models and methods. Talk soon turned to the philosophies, such as logical positivism, logical empiricism or contemporary analytic philosophy, which were used to justify these models and methods.[3] The theme I remember most vividly was that mathematical social science, including the Dahl–Harsanyi power model, distorts social relations to the extent that it participates in and mirrors our alienation under "capitalism." How could social scientific observation be part of the world it was trying objectively to observe? Derivative, partial explications of this view were claims that North American statistical studies were products of their era, and as such usually much too individualistic and mechanistic in their data theories; and that even simultaneous causal models with unmeasured variables were inherently invalid ways of representing the historically varied "structural determinations." Moreover, *dependencia* was to be taken as a peripheral expression of the reproduction of world capitalism which eventually could or would be transformed into a non-exploitive socialism. I had the

tional, and explanatory. The boundaries are quite permeable, but generally we have little choice but to begin with a 'causal' query and then work our way up from the existential/descriptive knowledge base, through the correlational ... and *then* go on to examine contending bodies of correlational knowledge in order to ascertain which of them offers the most compelling grounds for inferring 'causality.'"

A partially contrasting view, to which I want also to be responsive, says: "One of the major thrusts of modern social science has been the effort to achieve quantification of research findings. Utilizing the heavily narrative accounts of most historical research seems not to lend itself to such quantification. What then is the reliability of such data, and to what extent can one safely draw conclusions from the material about the operation of a system as such? It is a major tragedy of twentieth-century social science that so large a proportion of social scientists, facing this dilemma, have thrown in the sponge" (Wallerstein 1974). Chapters 3 and 8 of this volume directly address this concern.

3   Writings by A.J. Ayer (1952, 1959), Ernst Nagel (1961, 1957), Carl Hempel (1958), Karl Popper (1959, 1961) and Abraham Kaplan (1964) appeared to serve as the unbreachable standards to which one could refer, almost always in passing, without having the time or the inclination to discover or explore whole schools of alternative metascience, such as the dialectical-hermeneutic tradition of Apel, Habermas and Radnitzky, e.g., the latter's *Contemporary Schools of Metascience*. See the Introduction for more discussion of this alternative.

distinct impression that certain groups of Marxian social scientists were both defensive because of their lagging mastery of inaccessibly expensive research technology and, more importantly, genuinely committed to a coherently explicable epistemology different than logical empiricism,[4] one in which particular descriptive accounts could only fully be understood in terms of a global story of exploitation, conflict and emancipation.

A third episode, during a year on leave in Europe, produced a puzzle that was by then more familiar. In a Geneva seminar, J. David Singer told how his description of his operational dimensional analysis strategy for measuring the capability dimensions of power in the international system since 1815 had evoked from British peace researchers the accusation that his research approach gave evidence that he too was one of those "power politics types." Hence, like my Chile experience, Singer must be wondering: how was the scientific study of power politics, by someone very much opposed to it, in any way helping to reproduce the phenomenon itself?

From the point of view of traditional European scholars, one can imagine several typical reactions to Singer's epistemology, and his quantitative methodology. First, as previously noted, the great mass of qualitative, narrative historical knowledge and research that we associate with "traditional" International Relations (in the sense of Hedley Bull)[5] somehow gets put aside as speculative, unconfirmed or "pre-operational"; at best it may be gleaned for correlational hypotheses. Traditionalists of either Marxian, liberal or conservative political orientations must reject this treatment.[6] Traditionalists also usually follow Bull in arguing that *normative* concerns should be at the core of world politics research, and that a scientific model that bends

---

[4] It is not appropriate to comment on all these points here but, because of a major rash of quantitative studies of dependency by North American scholars (Caporaso, Duvall and Russett among them), it is worth mentioning Cardoso's published criticisms of such methodologies; at the time of these discussions I might add that I usually argued that quantitative Marxian mathematical political economy and qualitative, nonanalytic computer simulations like those by Abelson, Boudon and Brunner struck me as avoiding at least some of these problems. A fuller, and importantly revised, set of arguments on these questions is given in the main body of the present chapter.

[5] Hedley Bull (1977) is only the latest statement of a normatively oriented "traditional" approach, which Bull has repeatedly distinguished from the systems orientation of those like Morton Kaplan or David Singer.

[6] See Introduction, Chapters 11 and 12 for further discussion of Bull's "classical" approach.

over backwards to be positivistically objective defeats the peace researcher's own normative purpose. In particular, correlational generalities, even breakpoints like those Singer and Deutsch have found roughly between the nineteenth and twentieth centuries, do not convey sufficiently practical suggestions for how to make world politics more predictable or stable.

From a transnationalist peace research perspective (Burton *et al.* 1974), one suspects another important British critique of Singer's computation of quantitative capability measures derived from urban population, iron and steel production, military budgets and force sizes of diplomatically recognized nation-states. These units of analysis are too atomistic and too unproblematical; it is the constitution and reconstitution "in blood" by cross-national elites of such war-prone beasts that should be examined, even discredited, requiring a much different data base in which the (re)constituting of the *units* of analysis is a central, doubly problematical, dependent phenomenon, not merely an "operational" research procedure.

Broadening the list of ways in which Singer's positivist peace research strategy might be critiqued to include the alternate viewpoint of traditional European Marxism, one need not accept historical materialism to see the relevance here of Perry Anderson's basic political axiom that "it is the construction and destruction of States which seal the basic shifts in the relations of production, so long as classes subsist."[7] Peace research should be sensitive to the lesson of a tradition that opposes the " 'self-centered' modern state [in which] the principle of *bellum omnium contra omnes* can be formulated as if it possessed the elementary force, eternal validity and universality of the laws of nature" (Meszaros 1972). Too often, positivist methodology thinks these universally valid laws can simply be represented by its causal models. Surely one should consider seriously both the carefully documented methodology of comparative historical case studies Anderson uses as well as the story he tells: the birth of the [war-prone] Absolutist multilateral political order, from Westphalia onward, "as a

---

[7] Anderson (1974a: 10ff.). He argues that the dynamics of the rise of "Absolutism, the first international State system in the modern world," cuts across the rise and fall of particular national Absolutisms, as well as the "chronological monism" of Singer's 1815–1965 data frame: after Spain's fall, "English Absolutism was cut down in the mid-17th century; French Absolutism lasted until the end of the 18th century; Prussian Absolutism survived until the late 19th century; Russian Absolutism was only overthrown in the 20th century." Anderson argues (8) for theoretically informal case studies of the causality of both the "short run" and the "long run."

single field of competition and conflict between rival States, was itself both cause and effect of the generalization of Absolutism in Europe."[8]

Let us try briefly to unpack our topical title in the light of this last, partly hypothetical episode account, which we have expanded in order to make it more compatible with, and incorporative of, the previous two. Does it not ask: (i) how can we achieve operationally reproducible scientific explanations; (ii) problematizing appropriately both the internalized past, continuing existence and possible futures of our units of analysis; (iii) allowing for the mutual determinative significance of part and whole; (iv) within carefully constructed interpretive or narrative accounts ("true" stories); (v) developing empirically valid descriptive concepts not so ahistorically reflective of the absolutist or imperialistic tendencies of the age that they fail to (vi) suggest practical steps toward a peaceful epoch beyond the war-prone power politics of Absolutism, and the somewhat more indirect exploitations of imperialism and dependencia?[9]

[8] Throughout his book, Anderson emphasizes the war-prone nature of the noble class, whose interests were most fully represented in the Absolutist state, and the ruthless "Machiavellian" international order of "power politics" (my labels) it did much to create. For example, "the virtual permanence of international armed conflict is one of the hallmarks of the whole climate of Absolutism" (Anderson, 1974a: 33); hence, the insertion of "war-prone" in the above quote, taken from page 430. His argument for the generalization of the Absolutist system to include less developed Eastern Europe is not reductionistic: "It was the two intersecting forces of an uncompleted process of feudalization – which had started chronologically later, without benefit of the heritage of Antiquity, and in more difficult topographic and demographic conditions – and an accelerating military pressure from the more advanced West, which led to the paradoxical pre-formation of Absolutism in the East" (430–431). In fact, this thesis takes 800 pages to spell out, including a parallel study, *Passages from Antiquity to Feudalism* (1974b). Wallerstein's conception of the mutual determination of part and whole is remarkably similar. The development of a world system consists of the conflicting forces that hold it together by tension and tear it apart as each group seeks to remold it to its own advantage. States do not develop, and cannot be understood, except within the context of the development of the world system" (1974b, especially Introduction, and Chapter 7). In a Vicoesque sense, he asserts that "'Truth' changes because society changes" (9). Nonetheless, in seeking causal explanations, he tries to be objective and at the same time committed in his scholarship.

[9] In a massive review of the recent writings of Winch, Louch, MacIntyre, Taylor, Ryan, Pitkin and Habermas, Richard Bernstein comes to a similar conclusion about *The Restructuring of Social and Political Theory* (1976). "There is a common illusion that the history of thought proceeds in terms of clearly demarcated intellectual positions ... that can be characterized in terms of either/or ... either social and political theory *must* be explanatory and empirical ... or it is not genuine theory at all. Either the theoretical understanding of the social and political world *must* be interpretive, or it is totally inadequate. Either theory *must* be critical about the gravity of social and

189

Outline of a Leibnizian resolution

If our dialectical puzzles have turned into a problematique for contemporary peace research, their reinterpretation[10] has not pointed toward obvious ways in which such research must be fruitfully conducted.[11] Writing "traditional" comparative histories "with a message" about states and their state-systems appears an appropriate response, but how can that "traditional" approach be a "scientific" one, moving in a clear, reproducible fashion between descriptions of particular episodes and adequate historical explanations between plot outlines and fully interpreted scripts, from ought to is and back again to revised oughts plus feasible desirabilities?

One might think this task a hopeless one, the reconciliation of irreconcilables: "traditional," "fuzzy" hermeneutic-dialectical critique and "modern" positivistic science. My own recent research, however, into the epistemology actually employed on the technically advanced frontiers of positivistic social science, namely cybernetic simulations of human cognition, suggests "synthesis" is possible. Trying better to understand the contributions of Chomsky, Deutsch, Kaplan, Simon and Forrester has led me back to the cybernetics of Weiner, McCullough-Pitts, von Neumann and Shannon. As is so often the case, some of these pioneers have been quite openly reflective about their own intellectual roots. Whether one looks behind von Neumann's self-reproducing automata, or Weiner's teleological mechanisms, or

political life, or it is not theory. But as Hegel has taught us, the history of culture develops by the assertion and pursuit of what appear to be irreconcilable conflicts and oppositions. ... [T]here is an internal dialectic in the restructuring of social and political theory: when we work through any one of these moments, we discover how the others are implicated. An adequate social and political theory must be *empirical, interpretive*, and *critical*" (235).

[10] I owe the revised topical outline of this section in large part to Dwain Mefford, who has also read Heinz Holz (1958) on Leibniz for me. Suggestions by George Smith and a seminar by Jerome Lettvin have also been most helpful.

[11] Just as we have problematized the scientific analysis of Absolutist "power politics" before the age of capitalistic (and socialist) imperialisms, so we could continue the discussion into the present era with its imbalance of nuclear terror (seen in both East–West and North–South terms). Such a further analysis would move us, appropriately, into the reconceptualizations of sovereignty, power and peaceful survival strategies appropriate to our time, without falsely denying the possibilities of nuclear catastrophe. Important works recently contributing to this task include those already mentioned by Hedley Bull and Deutsch and Senghaas; also Hoffmann (1975), Rosenau (1963, 1970), Keohane and Nye (1977), Hoffmann (1975), Herz (1976) and Quester (1970, 1977).

McCullough-Pitts' logical "realization" of the ideas immanent in nervous activity (an important basis for von Neumann's computer design), one returns to Leibniz.

As Weiner says of cybernetics and society, "Leibniz, dominated by ideas of communication, is in more than one way the intellectual ancestor of the ideas of this book for he was also interested in machine computation and in automata" (Weiner 1956: 19). Reading Leibniz, and the modern corpus of Leibniz commentaries,[12] one is struck again and again by the strong commitment to scientific and non-contradictory logical rigor in a mind trying dialectically to resolve some of the deepest contradictions of his age.[13] Thus, rather than "logic without metaphysics," Leibniz says (according to Couturat in the Frankfurt collection) that his metaphysical principles and his logical principles are one.

Leibniz describes his elementary substances (monads) as windowless logical atoms, souls with meanings, entelechies with final causes, and living automata (from Aristotle to self-reproducing Turing machines via Christianity!); yet he denies Cartesian dualism, embedding incorporeal monads in material bodies.

Although independently existing, windowless and immaterial, his primary substances are not conventional things like coffee or states, nor the unobservable blackbox objects of behaviorism; nor are they the extensional (true or false), elementary (unanalyzable) sense data propositions of early Russellian logical positivism; nor do they support an epistemology of methodological individualism in its standard version. For monads are, in varying degrees, "active principles of unity" (Hacking 1976: 146) intentionally comprehending the world around them (Furth in Frankfurt, 1976: 103), indestructible but alienable unities of active teleological subject and manipulable object (Holz 1958). Not only may they be thought of as causal "generative relations" (Russell in Frankfurt 1976: 398), "mirroring" the past and the future world around them from their point of view, but also their identifying predicates are involved in the world and cannot be purely

---

[12] I have been most helped by Elster (1975) and Frankfurt (1976). The commentaries from the Marxist perspective of Hans Heinz Holz (1958) are not cited by either Frankfurt or Elster, however. Accessible primary sources are Leibniz (1976) and Leibniz (1972). In the following few pages, my brief exposition is not going to give the many, many footnotes to these works that they deserve.

[13] Why else would Marx praise Leibniz so effusively in one of his letters to Engels? "Du Kennst Meine Bewunderung für Leibniz," dated 10 May 1870 (Marx 1950), and cited in Holz (1958).

extrinsically conceptualized.[14] As impressed with mechanistic causal laws as any contemporary positivist social scientist, he strongly resists the elimination of teleonomy and organism from the natural world (so, ontologically "naturalistic" Weiner, von Neumann, Ashby and Bertalanffy cut the Gordian knot by reintroducing the forbidden entity: *living machines* capable of teleonomy, intentionality, adaptive self-organization and self-reproduction). And yet, using this scientific view, he opposes the coercive mechanistic degradation of both animals (vivisection) and political communities.[15]

Most often misunderstood, thanks to Voltaire's Panglossian stereotype, is Leibniz's deep but idiosyncratic commitment to the metaphysical principle of sufficient reason (everything has such a reason or cause at least in God's mind) with its anti-evolutionary corollary principle of plenitude (God left nothing undone in the original creation) from which it follows that ours is the "best of all possible worlds."[16] Read as a deep commitment to the possibility of genuine dialectical synthesis, i.e., harmony among opposites, this positive

[14] Thesis 79 of the *Monadology* argues that "souls act in accordance with the laws of final causes by appetitions, ends and means. Bodies act in accordance with the laws of efficient causes. ... The two realms ... of efficient causes and ... of ends are harmonized together." Riley (1972: 12) even goes so far as to characterize Leibnizian substances in Hegelian terms of "inner activity" and self-movement of its own active life! Ishiguro's "Leibniz's Theory of the Ideality of Relations" in Frankfurt (1976) is brilliant on this point, e.g.: "So long as there is more than one individual ... truths about any individual which we may describe by monadic predicates ... are inseparable from ["intrinsically bound up with"] the relational properties that are true of the individual. ... Every concept must involve relations and lead us from the subject to other things with which the subject is related," eventually "even to all others" (pp. 197, 194). Ollman's very (1976) similar insistence on the centrality of such "internal relations" in Marxian ontology thus connects Marx's with Leibnizian peace research at this point.

[15] "The unity of a clock is quite different from that of an animal, for the latter is able to be a substance endowed with a true unity like what one calls *I* in ourselves." Quoted by Ian Hacking (1976: 149). His conservative critique of Louis XIV's destruction of political communities seeking to maintain their independent viability will be explored more fully below.

[16] Elster (1975) is very telling on the timeless and evolutionary quality of Leibniz's mercantilist political economy. He emphasizes the capitalistic, dynamic, developmental quality of Leibniz's metaphysics and his ontology (monads *strive* for their fullest possible existence). Similarly, Hintikka talks of the metaphysical options associated with the possibility (in God's mind) of other worlds. Marxist narratives of Absolutism (like that of Anderson cited above) may be thought of as reversals in temporal ordering and real-world referents of Leibniz's pre-creation tale: "It cannot be denied that many stories, especially those we call novels, may be regarded as possible, even if they do not actually take place in this particular sequence of events

heuristic does not imply the invariably optimistic and apologetic conservatism one associates with such a view; on the positive side, it was a profound metaphysical source of his greatest strivings and accomplishments.

Leaving aside the many scientific issues on which Leibniz (and his contemporaries) now appear to have been seriously wrong,[17] let me try to restate his views on questions of sufficient reason and plenitude, at least as they bear on the possibility of a scientific yet engaged and interpretive peace research. Hintikka, in Frankfurt (1976: 155ff., 177–181), argues that Leibniz, who was trying to get Galileo's writings removed from the Index of forbidden books, must have objected to Galileo's critics' use of the principle of plenitude against him. (The critics argued that Galileo's views limited "God's power to particular effects.") Hence, Leibniz was clearly not a reactionary in his time.

Moreover, God's omnificent and omniscient perfection – as the monad of monads – made possible not only the existence of the universe but also of the world – reflecting capacities of every monad, including therefore the clearer perceptions and deeper reflections of logical scientific analysis.[18] With this version of the plenitude principle, Leibniz also reconciles contingency and necessity, and justifies (by the assumption of God's existence as a self-sufficient cause) the possibility of self-sufficient (we would say self-steering) agencies:

> just as all physical events must have efficient causes, so all conscious choices must have motivating reasons; and these reasons must lie in the apparent values inherent in the objects chosen. This proposition is for Leibniz an "eternal truth"; "a power of determination implies contradiction. ... It is metaphysically necessary that there be some such cause."   (Lovejoy 1976: 314)

that God has chosen." Leibniz is himself making fun of King Arthur and related myths. See Hintikka in Frankfurt (1976: 177) for sources and further analysis.

[17] Lovejoy argues that scientific empiricism opposes Leibniz's *a priori* plenitude-derived views on "the number of species, the continuity ... of the differences between them, the quantity and original distribution of matter, the existence or non-existence of vacua" because it views such matters as purely arbitrary (Lovejoy 1976: 308). Kauffman (1995), however has several Leibnizian themes.

[18] "The sufficient reason which has no need of any other reason must be outside the sequence of contingent things, and must be a necessary being, else we should not have a sufficient reason with which we could stop. ... [T]he 'sufficient reason' is nothing less than a logical necessity believed to be inherent in an essence; ... [thus] Leibniz speaks of God as the *ultima ratio rerum*." The first quote from Leibniz, and Lovejoy's commentary on it, are from Lovejoy (1976: 311).

Ultimately, as in God's mind, Leibniz believed that all [essential] truths were reducible to analytical, i.e., logical, expressions.[19] Moreover, Leibniz's deep belief in the fullness and continuity of both the contingent world and the necessary realm of logical possibility crucially motivated his invention of the calculus. He posits infinitesimals smaller than the smallest real number (and through division, larger than the largest integers), reconciling the finite and the infinite: arbitrarily small regions of a continuous line, infinitely small (monads), contain the whole real line within themselves.[20]

But what is frequently missed is that his invention of the calculus was only part of a broader program of developing an unambiguous and non-contradictory logic for metaphysics, and a universal language based on a small set of the alphabetical primitives of human thought (Russell 1976: 367). What for present purposes is even more important is the clear grounding of this program in an attempt to resolve the political, metaphysical and scientific disputes of the day.[21]

[19] C.D. Broad (1976: 1ff.) makes a useful reinterpretation of this claim. "In every affirmative proposition, whether it be necessary or contingent, universal or singular, the notion of the predicate is contained either explicitly or implicitly in that of the object. If it is contained explicitly, the proposition is analytic; if only implicitly, it is synthetic."

This program of analysis is very fundamental both to classical hermeneutics and modern linguistic analysis. Leibniz's search for the Alphabet of human thoughts, discussed below, is the motivational basis of conceptual dependence analysis underlying the Schank–Abelson simulation languages to be discussed below. (See Russell 1976: 367ff. for more details in Leibniz's program.)

Broad's sensible distinction between identifying (or essential) predicates and others allows contingent and particular truths to exist consistently in Leibniz's system; and it means that the ontological philosophy of internal relations characterizing Leibniz and Marx is to be disambiguated from the "dogma" of internal relations, brilliantly and reconstructively dissected by G.E. Moore (1920), that no relations are extrinsic.

[20] This ingenious conception is now said to be a logically consistent, modelable definition of hyper-real (nonstandard) numbers. It may be of as much dialectical significance in the history of scientific thought as the invention or discovery of negative, irrational and imaginary numbers. Robinson's fuller logical realization of the Leibnizian program, plus a few of its larger implications, are mentioned by Elster (1975); and discussed in H. Jerome Keisler (1976); and A. Robinson (1976). Mathematically, I am more impressed by nonstandard analysis than by the statistical principle of maximum likelihood, which is also clearly motivated by a different version of the principle of plenitude.

[21] The following paragraphs rely heavily on C.J. Friedrich (1976), and the previously cited works of Holz and Lovejoy. Toulmin's (1990: Ch. 2) independently derived analysis of Descartes' very similar, war driven, "metaphysical" interest in new, more precise, and more consensus producing ontological and logical foundations of knowledge and theology should be read comparatively with this analysis.

Born in 1646 just before the end of the Thirty Years War (1648) and Descartes' death (1650), Leibniz did not contentedly and passively observe the imperial, religious and dynastic wars of his age. He spent much of his life trying on the one hand to resolve the theological differences separating Catholic and Protestant (in part through the creation of new formal tools), and on the other hand he repeatedly involved himself in the politics of the day. In general he tried to protect the independence of the smaller German states through legal arguments in favor of a Christian republic of European states, and on occasion through fairly sophisticated and "realistic" power-balancing diplomacy, trying either to deflect France against the Turks or to build German–English alliances against her.

His normative ideals were quite explicit: until late in his life he argued for the feasibility and desirability of a return to a Holy Roman Empire format with temporal and spiritual sovereigns (the Emperor and the Pope). He preferred such a system of multiple loyalties, and many independent, non-absolute sovereign ties, eternally subject to the moral orders of the City of God. Thus Leibniz rejected Hobbes' Absolutist doctrine of law as the sovereign's command in favor of Roman and Christian universal jurisprudence. Like Hobbes, he defined the state in terms of "a large society whose end is the common security," but went on to emphasize its role in procuring happiness, well-being and the public good through a just system of institutionalized charity, and refused to treat it as a true (monadic) unity (Leibniz in Riley 1972: 29, 26). But if this was the desirable essence of a state, it was not the only observable reality.

His engaged, theory-based descriptions of Absolutist state action are nowhere more forcefully conveyed than in his sarcastic attack on Louis XIV, describing him in self-contradictory terms as "Mars Christianissimus, the most Christian war-God"![22] He ironically defends German liberties and wonders why the French are always needing more taxes from their citizens. The taking of Strasburg through the deceitful breaking of pledges is "the most violent and the most Ottoman

---

[22] Although not referred to by either Elster or Friedrich, this essay is reprinted in Riley (1972: 121–145), and discussed thoroughly by him. Its implicit explorations of Absolutist expansion are in terms of personalistic aggrandizement rather than due to socioeconomic causes, but its clear commitment to politics and negotiation on reasonable Christian principles is cogently conveyed. The implicit, preferred, but counterfactual, state system Leibniz has in mind must be inferred, however, on the basis of his other political and jurisprudential writings.

political act that a Christian prince has ever undertaken."[23] Clearly the damning force of his insincere praise is heightened by the implicit appeal to his normative ideals.

Although Leibniz is burdened by a doctrine of moral and political perfection that seems, with its emphasis on monadic immortality and state artificiality, to mitigate against political development of decay,[24] one can sketch something more of his political ideals in these terms. Essential human capacities for reasoned and charitable action and the desire to achieve happiness and well-being are innate in individuals, who thus necessarily strive for their realization in a variety of ways. On the other hand, the contingent capabilities of citizens, states and statesmen for realizing such objectives vary tremendously. A greater degree of compatibility among essential capacities for autonomous self-realization is neither possible nor realistically desirable in this "best of all possible worlds." All monads are essentially different, and thus more or less rationally individuated. Yet enormous room exists for the enhancement of contingent capabilities for producing the mutual enjoyment of such goods in the contemporary world of artificial, often exploitive and destructive, states. "The end of political science [and in our context peace research] with regard to the doctrine of forms of commonwealths ... must be to make the empire of reason flourish. ... Arbitrary power is what is directly opposed to the empire

---

[23] Leibniz in Riley (1972: 140). If Ottomans are worse than Christians, one may conversely ask whether Leibnizian "universal" reason is the Logos of domination, or capitalistic instrumental rationality. Bozeman (1960) has argued a basic similarity between the cultures on both sides of the sixteenth-century Mediterranean: one Christian, one Islamic.

[24] Nearly two decades after writing this chapter, I came across Nicholas Onuf's highly suggestive review of Wolff's eighteenth-century version of Leibnizian plenitude (Onuf 1994). Even though Wolff's Leibnizian treatment of natural law and Nature's design as objective reality has been largely forgotten, in part because of Kant's withering epistemological critique of his dogmatism, there seems to be considerable carry over in cosmopolitan international thinking from Leibniz through Wolff to Kant, Hegel and beyond. The notion of plenitude or perfection is associated with the pre-planned quality of Nature, its city-like organization. Kant's similar belief in Nature's inherent progressive qualities is evident in many of his political writings, but he locates the various architectonic principles of world citizenship and international organization mainly in the realm of subjective, human, moral law. Leibniz and Wolff are more faithful to classical Stoic and post-Machiavellian ideas of a virtually existent grand Republic (*civitas*) of Republics (*civitates*). Ontologically, "Wolff's *civitas maxima* is a virtual republic [in the sense of Giddensesque scientific realism]. As such it stands above all other *civitates*, which in their turn stand above other, ascending levels of association in 'the great chain of being'" (*ibid.*, 323).

of reason. But one must realize that this arbitrary power is found not only in Kings, but in assemblies ... and judges" (Leibniz, as quoted in Riley 1972: 23ff.).

Leibniz appeals to this ideal of the end of power politics in his mocking description of Louis XIV's excesses. His concept of coercive power recognizes many of its brutal realities without residually, at least, denying, as Habermas puts it, that "power springs from unimpaired intersubjectivity."[25] Here also we find a provisionally adequate description of states as contingently existing powers. As artificial composites, they are causally predisposed both to exercise terror and to produce well-being and security. They unidentically reflect the insecure world of which they are part. Power capabilities exist *within* these composites, historically ranging from empathetic, socially unconstrained and rational modes for understanding and resolving interstate conflicts to power-balancing and (worst of all) brutal deception; but they are only contingently exercised. In this rich conception, then, may lie Leibniz's chief legacy for the scientific, interpretive and critical political analysis of power politics.

Some operational implications

Two explications of how "the end of power politics can operationally be part of the concepts with which its story is told" have been noted. Beneath their sharp differences in language and political orientation, the reader should nonetheless have detected important similarities. Are they sufficient to resolve all differences between radical and conservative peace researchers, between scientific positivists and normatively engaged political theorists? I doubt it. Yet the insights generated as to real differences and possible compatibilities may have been worth the effort.

My third and final interpretation of our topical question will emphasize issues of conceptualizing power in a way allowing operational measurements and theoretical testability. It will rely heavily on writings by Elster and Ollman on Marxist and non-Marxist ontologies of internal relations; its operational vehicle will be a recently pro-

---

[25] Habermas (1977: 3–24, esp. 8). Arendt (*The Human Condition*) is then quoted: "What first undermines and then kills political communities is loss of power and final impotence. ... Power is actualized only where word and deed have not parted company, where words are not empty and deeds are not brutal, where words are not used to violate and destroy but to establish relations and create new relations" (9).

grammed computer simulation. My aim is not to argue that all radical traditionalists should immediately apply to the Pentagon for large research grants to conduct computerized studies of Absolutist power politics; nor do I feel that all positivist peace researchers should become expert in "computational" dialectics. Rather, my objective is to correct mistakes and to forge as many links of mutual understanding and concerted action as are objectively possible among researchers committed to scientific research, and to share my revulsion toward the political terror so pervasive in world politics.

In the postscript to *Alienation*, Bertell Ollman distinguishes three different ontological conceptions of the whole: (1) "the atomist conception, already present in Descartes and dominant in modern philosophy," according to which the whole is the simple logical or algebraic combination of "simple facts"; (2) "the formalist conception," visible in Hegel, Leibniz and most modern structuralists, which attributes a predominance and independent identity of the whole *vis-à-vis* its parts; and (3) the dialectical and materialist conception of Marx (often confused with the formalist notion) that views the whole as the structural interdependence of its relational parts" (events, processes, conditions). Our Leibnizian review has shown how Leibniz's monadic ontology has characteristically tried to span all three of these modern conceptions. One suspects Singer's "operational" philosophy of power measurement, on the other hand, to be based on neither the formalist nor the dialectical view but on an atomistic and extrinsically relational conception. Moreover, if Singer and his British critics are starting from differential *ontologies of social reality*, it is quite plausible to expect misunderstandings on what is involved in the operational measurement of power. On the other hand, the quantitative peace researcher, like the many positivist critics of Marx cited by Ollman, probably also understates the consistency and empirical content of careful, comparative, historical thinking.

Moreover, here is an important way in which Marx and Leibniz agree: for essential entities or relations, both subscribe to a philosophy of internal relations. In Leibnizian ontology, all non-composite things (monads) are "windowless," but nonetheless reflective of each other and of the rest of the world from their own points of view; they are "internally related" to each other through the mind of the Absolute which makes their existence real. For Marxists, all social relations in the Absolutist age are internally reflective of the organizing principles of an Absolutist political economy.

As Elster, Hintikka and others have argued, there is a very modern, logical interpretation of widowless, internally structured, Leibnizian monads, with practical implications concerning how power might differently be formally operationalized by radicals, liberals or conservatives. The *metaphysical-ontological* thesis that each individual monad reflects all other monads in the universe is now frequently translated *logically/linguistically* as the "thesis that *all* apparently monadic [attributes or] predicates have a hidden relational structure" (Elster, n.d.: 7; 1975: 12–16; 1978). Rather than an attribute or a thing (or a statistically weighted averaging of attributes in Singer's approach), *power should be thought of as a relation indicating ways in which a contextually specific universe of power exercise attempts have been, might have been, and/or might in the future be successful.*

The Harsanyi–Alker approach to *power measurement in a schedule sense* (Alker 1973: 372)[26] proceeds in this direction, and even refers to classical power measurement theory (of the sort inspiring some of Singer's diplomatic ancestors at the Congress of Vienna). One could move toward that position by starting with Donald Campbell's approach to criterion validity: before a statistical measure of an attribute or trait can be said to be valid, it needs to be shown to predict to some external criteria, like winning battles against less powerful opponents. The functional *relation* thus obtained may, in Harsanyi's terms, be thought of as a production *schedule* linking extents, frequencies, costs, scopes of compliance and/or defiance with resources, costs, intentions and strategies employed by influencers in a particular systemic context. Finding theory-based *causally valid structural* schedules of this sort is a complex problem of empirical theory development, neither easy nor *a priori* impossible.

A further logical/linguistic idea about power assessment is suggested by the frequent diplomatic use of "the powers" as a state-identifying label. As both Dahl and Singer among positivist theorists of power and influence agree, power is relational, perhaps in a schedule sense. But what does that mean? As used by them, in describing the extent to which A has power over B power is an external relation: neither A's nor B's identity is modifiable by the relationship itself. In Singer's case diplomatic recognition appears to be unrelated to the "power" position of sovereign status. Based on both the Marxian and

---

[26] It might be observed that this intentionalist, theory-laden approach to power assessment corresponds closely to Holz's radical interpretation of subject and object in Leibniz's pre-cybernetic ontological thought.

Leibnizian accounts of power politics given above, I would now argue that *coercive power* (or force) is an identifying internal relationship among all or most contemporary *state actors*. The "powers" are defined "in blood" by the system of which they are a part. *Yet Singer's measure* (a weighted sum of attribute values) *implies only an unessential, external relationship among actors and their attributes.*

Elster's formal reasoning on this point goes roughly as follows (Elster, n.d.: 18–29): "Internal relations are the relations without which one or both of the relata would not have been what they are, whereas external relations are such that we may abstract from them in thought without the relata losing their [essential] identity" (18). An operational interpretation in the tradition of modern Leibnizian scholarship would allow the *testing* of Leibniz's belief that all relations among particulars are external. *"Rab" is an external relation if there exist two (not necessarily unequally determined) predicates F and G such that "Fa and Gb" implies "Rab."* Furthermore, the reducing predicates F and G must either themselves be irreducible or, if reducible, the range of the variables that go into the full reduction of "Fa" must not include b, and the range of the variables that go into the logical rewriting of "Gb" must not include a. Elster illustrates these notions with statements like:

a has power over b	(1)
a has more power over b	(2)
a exploits b	(3)
a has more money than b	(4)

Singer's "liberal" power measures are like money, or coffee, described merely physically and quantitatively: statements (2) and (4) similarly suggest operationally comparing two (or more) magnitudes to determine if they are true. In the above formal definition of external relations, Fa and Gb would correspond to all such quantities; hence, dimensional comparisons or averaged conjoint measurement score differences, even if Singer were to add many other dimensions of data, would be external measures of "power" given what we know about the constitutive role of coercive power in maintaining or destroying the "recognized" identity of states in the modern era. According to either a Leibnizian or an Andersonian account one must conclude, therefore, that Singer's measures are false.[27]

---

[27] Were he to accept my application of his criteria as determining that power in the case of Absolutist states is an internal relation, Elster might also want to describe Singer's concept as fetishistic. "Une definition générale du fétichisme serait donc par la

Numbers (1) and (3) above suggest definitions in interactional (Ollman would say "inner actional") terms. If they are conceived of as internalized in, and constitutive of, actor A or B, the full schedule sense measurements of power previously alluded to may be treated as intrinsic or internal conceptions of power. Thus, their cost-extent relationships, *inter alia*, cannot adequately be described merely in monadic, Fa and Gb terms.

Let us assume a functional relationship of any computable sort is used to measure the power of a, e.g., Fa. It is a central result of modern logic, in particular recursive function theory (Rogers 1967),[28] that any computable function (relation) can be expressed in terms-generalized recursive functions which have the key recursive property of being definable in terms of themselves. A single actor's power assessment in these terms would also violate Elster's external relations decomposability definition if the F used in the recursive substructure of Fa referred relationally to b. Modern computational linguistics uses such self-referential capabilities for anticipatory and retrospective "self-simulations" of a–b interaction possibilities. Hence, such approaches, to which we now turn, also clearly belong in the realm of internal power relations, even if their ultimate logical (LISP) representations are the extrinsic formulas of an augmented quantified logic.

Recall how Leibniz conceived monads as computers embodying active principles of unity. The discussion of power *plans* in Schank and Nash-Weber (1976)[29] indicates one such treatment of a worker's power over his supervisor, or those who appoint plant supervisors. However, it is elaborated only in a very provisional fashion.

The building blocks of the power world of Figure 5.1 are internally structured "plans" – plans that contain, call upon, follow on or

négligence des relations implicites. Ainsi l'analyse marxiste du fétichisme de la Marchandise est une critique politico-grammaticale de l'illusion que la propriété d'être une marchandise appartient à la chose physique au même titre que sa couleur ou son poids" (Elster 1975: 113).

[28] I should note that my use of Elster/Moore's characterization of internal or intrinsic relations does not exactly parallel Carnap's (or Russell's) usage of intentionality as non-truth functionality (Carnap 1946).

[29] A slightly updated treatment is given in Schank and Abelson (1977). Marxist "plots" and "scripts" including noble-class domination and its subsequent transformations could be imbedded in the world models used to answer questions about resources and wants in Figure 5.1, as well as in its RECONSIDER procedure.

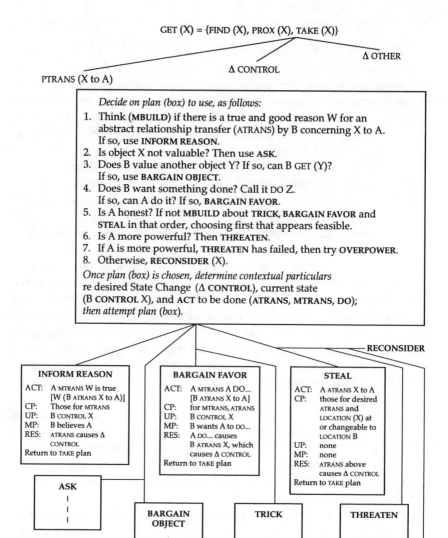

GET (X) = {FIND (X), PROX (X), TAKE (X)}

Δ OTHER

Δ CONTROL

PTRANS (X to A)

Decide on plan (box) to use, as follows:
1. Think (**MBUILD**) if there is a true and good reason W for an abstract relationship transfer (**ATRANS**) by B concerning X to A. If so, use **INFORM REASON**.
2. Is object X not valuable? Then use **ASK**.
3. Does B value another object Y? If so, can B GET (Y)? If so, use **BARGAIN OBJECT**.
4. Does B want something done? Call it DO Z. If so, can A do it? If so, **BARGAIN FAVOR**.
5. Is A honest? If not **MBUILD** about **TRICK**, **BARGAIN FAVOR** and **STEAL** in that order, choosing first that appears feasible.
6. Is A more powerful? Then **THREATEN**.
7. If A is more powerful, **THREATEN** has failed, then try **OVERPOWER**.
8. Otherwise, **RECONSIDER** (X).

Once plan (box) is chosen, determine contextual particulars
re desired State Change (Δ **CONTROL**), current state
(B **CONTROL** X), and **ACT** to be done (**ATRANS**, **MTRANS**, **DO**);
then attempt plan (box).

━━ RECONSIDER

INFORM REASON

ACT: A MTRANS W is true
 [W (B ATRANS X to A)]
CP: Those for MTRANS
UP: B CONTROL X
MP: B believes A
RES: ATRANS causes Δ
 CONTROL
Return to TAKE plan

BARGAIN FAVOR

ACT: A MTRANS A DO...
 [B ATRANS X to A]
CP: for MTRANS, ATRANS
UP: B CONTROL X
MP: B wants A to DO...
RES: A DO... causes
 B ATRANS X, which
 causes Δ CONTROL
Return to TAKE plan

STEAL

ACT: A ATRANS X to A
CP: those for desired
 ATRANS and
 LOCATION (X) at
 or changeable to
 LOCATION B
UP: none
MP: none
RES: ATRANS above
 causes Δ CONTROL
Return to TAKE plan

ASK
|
|
|

BARGAIN OBJECT
|
|
|

TRICK
|
|
|

THREATEN
|
|
|

OVERPOWER

ACT: A DO... B DO...
 B ATRANS X to A
CP: enabling conditions
 on DOs are known
 & handleable
UP: B CONTROL X
MP: B can't prevent
 A DO...
RES: Δ CONTROL
Return to TAKE plan

Figure 5.1   Getting power: A's plan for getting X from B
Source: Schank and Abelson 1977.

presuppose other plans. Like monads, the most basic of elemental plans, which are not themselves further decomposable, are called plan boxes; these are indicated in the figure by boxed lists, the first row of which gives the name of the plan box. These plan boxes, however, are not windowless. Inside them are the sequentially considered act(s) envisioned by the plan, their enabling conditions (divided into controlled preconditions, CP, uncontrolled ones, UP, and mediating ones, MP) and the assumed results. INFORM REASON, ASK, BARGAIN and OVERPOWER are such plan boxes, while GET, TAKE, CONTROL and RECONSIDER are more complex, non-elemental plans. This computationally operational conception of power exercise parallels, as well, the normative hierarchy of more or less attractive power exercise modes identified in Leibniz's nonexclusive desired goals, descriptions and practice. In Schank's power world, in fact, *getting* has both Machiavellian and Caesarian qualities – Machiavellian because of the large variety of deceptive and coercive modes for A to take a desired object X from B; Caesarian because of the zero-sum *veni, vidi, vici* sequential substructure of the GET macroplan: find X, get proximate to it, and then take it!

Macroplans, like basic plans, contain lists of appropriate actions below their name labels. In the TAKE (X) plan, for example, an actor (or computer) trying to execute an appropriate action (such as a physical transfer, or PTRANS of object X to actor A in the figure) moves from left to right when the leftmost act is not feasible. Special DELTACTS, such as CONTROL and OTHER, are listed within a macro plan, and are of use for making possible actions listed on the left, when they have not yet taken place. As the figure makes clear, DELTACTS may have rather complex, program-like inner structures. Note in particular how instruction 3 for deciding which basic plan box to call requires an anticipatory simulation of a GET macro plan within an action within the "higher order" GET plan at the top of the figure. Such a "recursive" GET within GET ... plan within plan within plan ... substructure is self-referential or reflexive in the sense of Hegelian or Marxian critique. It is also typical of list-processing computational linguistics modeling, and reminiscent of Leibniz's infinite plenitude of beings within beings within beings ... It thus parallels certain recent attempts to formalize Marxian or Hegelian dialectical logic.[30]

---

[30] Recent but partial bibliographies are given in Riegal (1976) and Varela (1979). Elster (no date) believes that dialectic logic is only an extension (like LISP) of ordinary Frege-Russell-Whitehead logic; Varela, like Von Forster, argues differently. I am intrigued

The careful reader will note another complexity in this, not well prefigured in Leibnizian thought and logic: the necessity of a separate, formal semantic system for describing basic macroplans. Thus PTRANS, MBUILD, MTRANS and ATRANS are capitalized in the figure not because they are plans but because they are assumed to be predefined primitive semantic predicates. Similarly, the careful reader of Figure 5.1 might have noted that TRICK has a basic plan as an argument rather than variables like A, B, X. This means that it may be thought of as a *rewrite* procedure for rewriting during operation the instructions within the plan of which it is a part.

Well into the power plan of Figure 5.1, note that the CONTROL "subroutine's" line 6 asks a key relational question: "Is B more powerful than A?" This instructional question implicitly also requires a recursive anticipatory simulation of overpowering action (the touchstone of *Realpolitik*) to see if threats might work because OVER-POWER's mediating precondition requires an anticipatory simulation of the possibility of B's *getting* A *not* to take overpowering actions, i.e., preventing A from doing so. Knowledge of economic or coercive capabilities (Singer-like component measures) is needed to fill in the determining conditions of these plan parts! *Thus, not only is our power/plan relation an internal relation by the above definition,* but it also satisfies Anderson's narrative practice in studying Absolutism and Ollman's Marxian maxim: "the story itself is thought to be somehow part of the very concepts with which it is told." Even more remarkable, perhaps, *this* POWER/TAKE *routine contains within it,* from A's point of view, a stored *knowledge world* ("called" in each anticipatory simulation) as well as its future (through the anticipatory simulations of preventable overpowering, for example). Until this world is called and the plan's variable slots are concretely determined, using Singer-type data, the power plan is still partly "pre-operational."[31]

From the point of view of the transcendence of power politics, we have imminent (prefigured) characterizations of the control conditions under which non-coercive reasoning (INFORM REASON) or requests (ASK) or non-coercive bargaining can effectuate goal realization: thus,

by the issue, but not yet able to resolve it. Chapter 1, written after the present chapter, takes further steps in this direction. So do Chapters 6 and 8, which present a less formalized version of Marxian historiography.

[31] A "story-plot" in this formalism would be a sequence of successful or non-successful plan efforts involving two or more actors.

non-coercive power relations are contained imminently in coercive concepts
and relations, as we argued peace researchers should want to be the case! Of
course, in a Machiavellian world the enabling conditions for INFORM
REASON are rarely met. And compared to our Leibnizian conception,
INFORM REASON is very underdeveloped. This plan box needs considerable elaboration plus greater reflexive possibilities for a self-conscious
awareness of how unequal material conditions of various actors may
constrain such rational possibilities. A modifying box: increased
reasoning capabilities for reaching agreement should be added as well.
A more adequately described power plan would thus elaborate and
update both DELTACTS and historical/systematic changes necessary for
non-coercive, reasoned goal attainment.

This example has for a third and final time shown how the end of
power politics can be part of the operational concepts with which its
story is told. My related critique of Singer's positivist power-measuring
strategy has been: stop ignoring implicit, internal relations in "operational" studies of power; and pay more attention to the problematical,
contingent identities of a system's operating units. More suggestive
theorizing points toward the existence within these unities of conceptual *deep structures* which imply both contextually varying interpretations of more superficial directly observable relationships and causal
histories of the unities and systems involved. Thus, Singer's treatment
of power relations could be redefined in terms analogous to the
Choucri–North interactive, dynamic causal models among demographic, economic and military variables, many of them close to those
used by Singer.[32] Thus, unlike certain rather vague core concepts in
much (but not all) Marxist theorizing, these deep causal *conceptualizations* are operationally testable *explanations*, revisable on the basis of
test results.

Such identity-constituting conceptual deep structures, like narrative
power plans or goals, should both remember their pasts and be
"pregnant with the future" by containing the conditions both for their
own utilization and their normatively preferred but not inevitable
transformations. Pragmatic inferences could be drawn at any time
about the situational range of probable, successful, survival-consistent

---

[32] No model that Singer has ever written is, in my opinion, more suggestive in this
regard than his 1970 work. A comparable treatment of power by Poulantzas (1968)
would thus be made falsifiable if its core assumptions about the maintenance of
ruling class dominance were dynamically and operationally defined in terms of a
theory about the conditions, modes and stages of power exercise.

self-realization strategies. These programs should regularly be subject to conceptual and empirical revision in terms of historical changes in the identity of powerful states and their interrelationships, and the possibilities of their peaceful transformation.

6   Rescuing "reason" from the "rationalists": Reading Vico, Marx and Weber as reflective institutionalists

That we disavow reflection is positivism.   Habermas (1971)

North American epistemological discussions in international studies in the 1960s and 1970s were frequently ahistorical and, in a variety of ways, unreflectively "positivistic."[1] Although positivistic behavioral, classical and dialectical/Marxist traditions of investigation flourished unequally in different parts of the world, it was hard then – and in the graduate programs shaped by professors who achieved senior positions during the Cold War, it is still difficult – to find discussions across these traditions, wherein all participants recognize the intellectual seriousness and scientific aspect of each tradition's best endeavors. Hence, readers of the 1988 Special Issue of *Millennium* on "Philosophical Traditions in International Relations," should have been refreshed and enriched, if not always pleased, by its "skepticism of monological answers, totalizing theories, and disciplinary ideologies posing as natural, self-evident truths." Having witnessed "a loss of awe for the grand theories of international relations," James Der

---

[1]   I use the term "positivistic" here as a short-hand way of conveying several meanings, including the optimistic/naturalistic/social engineering sense of Comte and Mill, as well as "prediction and control oriented," "preoccupied with seeking context-independent explanatory causal laws," and "claiming to be scientific in an objective, data-based, value neutral way." An informed, useful overview of "logical positivism" is given in Ayer (1969); (see also Alker 1982, excerpted in the Introduction above; Lapid (1989); plus responses by K.J. Holsti, T.J. Biersteker and J. George in the same volume). In criticizing various aspects or applications of positivistic research, I do not mean to imply that it is of no value; as suggested in the Introduction, I am most interested in the synthesis of "positivistic," "interpretive" and critical or "emancipatory" research approaches.

Derian calls for a reinvigorated "textual politics," the revalorizing of "a dialogical approach [to the monologue of tradition], recognizing the polyvalent, multicultural, and stratified nature of international relations" (Der Derian 1988).

As a contribution to this dialogue of traditions, which elsewhere I have argued *constitutes* the *international* and *interdisciplinary* study of international relations (Alker and Biersteker 1984), I here recharacterize what Robert Keohane has recently called the "reflectivist" approach to research on international institutions, distinguished in his view by its concern with intersubjective meanings and the embeddedness of contemporary international institutions in pre-existing social practices. Several sources of that tradition will be reread here as vintage exemplars of a critically and rationally oriented, but still historicist[2] tradition of social theorizing, from which derive the particular explanatory concerns noted by Keohane. Whereas Keohane emphasizes "reflectivists'" concern with unintentional or non-instrumental determinants of particular institutions, their desire to explain the preferences that rationalists assume, and their interest in endogenous patterns of change in general institutions, like the nation-state system, I wish to characterize the reflectivist *approach* in terms of an older *tradition* of theoretically guided social inquiry into the problems and prospects of modernity. With examples and arguments, I also hope to convey a more imaginative, dialogical, procedural and communicative conception of human rationality than the individualistic, instrumentalist, "substantive," and market-inspired conceptions evident in what Keohane calls the "rationalist" approach (Keohane 1988).[3] In contrast to Keohane's

---

[2] Practitioners of an "historicist" line of research explicitly recognize that human expressions, including theirs and others' scientific theories, are historically bounded in many, frequently non-obvious ways, some – but not all of which – they may be able correctively to take account of. This commitment to historical and contextual fallibilism, so well grounded in the historical sociology of the natural and social sciences, should not overly trouble contemporary Popperian "critical rationalists."

[3] Keohane is himself deeply influenced by the effort of J. March and J. Olson (1984) to synthesize rational choice and historical sociological approaches to institutional theorizing. Keohane adopts Simon's instrumentalist notion of "rational behavior" – "behavior that is appropriate to specified goals in the context of a given situation" – and characterizes economic "rationalists" in terms of their "substantive or objective rationality" – a view of "behavior that can be adjudged objectively to be optimally adapted to the situation."

In my own modeling work (e.g., Alker and Christensen 1972; Alker, Bennett, Mefford 1980; Alker, Duffy, Hurwitz, Mallery 1991) I have chosen to follow Simon's

positivist preoccupation with law-like explanations, I shall further emphasize reflectivists' concern with both the explanatory, the critical, the constructive and the meaning-constitutive functions of human language and reason, including history retelling, culturally shaped practical argumentation, scientific explanations and figurative descriptions.

In order better to bring out the historical roots and the more general significance of reflectively oriented modes of historical-cultural inquiry, a first step will be a restatement of Giambattista Vico's extraordinary early eighteenth-century vision of the domain and purposes of the soon-to-emerge, modern, social sciences. Inspired by Isaiah Berlin, this account will lead to another, Hayden White's Vico-based recasting of Marxian developmental historiography in a linguistic, figurative, tropological manner. A third retelling will be a brief, largely Habermasian reconstruction of Weber's critique of modernity. Habermas endorses both the emancipatory promise of communicative rationality and the claim that modern, capitalistic, economic, political and scientific practices have, in certain respects, curtailed the meaning-giving, legitimacy-creating potential of communicative action. All three "roots" will be found to have suggested related versions of the insecurity dilemmas of much concern to institutional "rationalists," dilemmas here redescribed as characteristic partial failures of modernity.

Vico's historical hermeneutics

Born in 1668, Giambattista Vico was a politically conservative Catholic, the holder of a minor Neapolitan Professorship of Rhetoric from 1699 to 1741. As a classical juridical scholar, he unsuccessfully aspired to a Professorship of Jurisprudence, and died in 1744, little recognized for either his attacks on his more famous predecessors and contemporaries – Descartes, Hobbes, Locke and Voltaire – or his highly original ideas

preferred "procedural" account of "the limitations of knowledge and computing power" of the rational choosing organism (Simon 1985: 294), augmented by Rescher's conception of dialectical reason: "Reasoning can proceed not just inferentially" (ampliatively from axioms) "but also dialectically" (reductively, argumentatively) from a complex, contradictory set of plausible initial positions. "There are two different sorts of cognitive disciplines – the hard (e.g., physics), for which the mathematical (ampliative model [of reasoning]) is doubtless optimal, and the soft (e.g., history), for which the dialectical/reductive model is optimal" (Rescher 1987: 40). For an even more comprehensive, communicative conception see Habermas (1984, 1987).

about the historical-cultural sciences. Yet the relevance of his thought for methodological descendents of Descartes, Locke and Hobbes accounts for interest in him today as much as his anticipation of several of Hegel's, Marx's and Dilthey's key ideas (Vico 1968, orig. 1725 and 1744).

Having first read about Vico in Habermas's penetrating essay on the classical doctrine of politics (Habermas 1973a),[4] I shall here content myself with citations to, and summaries of, Isaiah Berlin's wonderfully accessible reading of Vico's work, emphasizing his most arresting and time-defying claims (Berlin 1977),[5] following this with several of Hayden White's especially suggestive interpretations of Vico's connections to Marx. First, as Berlin rightly emphasizes, Vico countered Descartes' boldly modern criterion of truth: "that the judgments claiming to be true must be seen to consist of clear and distinct 'ideas,' ultimate constituents ...not further analyzable ... ultimate atomic entities of thought ... connected ... by 'necessary' logical links ..." (11) with a conception of his own.

To supplant this mathematical notion of truth, which neither Descartes nor Vico thought appropriate for the inexact, contingent, creative domain of human affairs – daily life as well as humanly crafted laws and institutions – Vico in 1708 first distinguished between "outer" and "inner" knowledge, a distinction later to be recognized by Hegel as between the outwardly oriented *Naturwissenschaft* and the *Geisteswissenschaft* (12). He then proposed, prophetically, that the clarity and certainty one experiences with mathematical reasoning is not because of its necessary connection with nature, but that, as "the free creation of our own minds ... mathematical propositions are true only because we ourselves have made them" (15).

Here enters Vico's famous syllogistic formula: *Verum et factum*

---

[4] In the present context, perhaps the most important point to make from Habermas' treatment is his focus on how Vico relies on the Aristotelian *episteme/phronesis* distinction to recommend an imperfect but more appropriate combination of rhetoric, ethics and topics to help determine not eternal truths but prudent actions, which neither he nor Habermas (but Hobbes and Bacon) wants to reduce to instrumental calculations. Habermas (1973a: 46) then quotes Vico's larger life task as "The reconciliation of the classical and the modern method."

[5] Berlin's own citations are to Vico (1968) and to his other writings. Note especially Berlin's summary (1977: xvi–xix). Elucidating remarks and quotations are taken either from this Introduction or the Vico part of this comparative essay (Berlin 1977: 3–142). Pages for longer citations will be indicated in parentheses in the next several paragraphs of this text.

convertuntur, meaning that "the true" and "the made" are convertible, i.e., exchanging these words as subject and predicate terms of a syllogism preserves its validity.[6] Traditionally, rereading the syllogism internally and agentively, this has meant that not only "what one creates one can fully know" but also, most provocatively, "the converse – that one can know [fully] only what one has created ... oneself" (16). In Vico's own words, "the rule and criterion of truth is to have made it" (Vico quoted, 126). From this it follows that "Since men in some sense make their own history ... men understand it as they do not understand the world of external nature" (Berlin 1977: xvi ff.).[7] *Mathematics and history* are then *superior to physics* in the degree to which they can be penetrated by the human mind: "truth is what has been made, and for this very reason we cannot [operationally] demonstrate physics *per causas* [genetically, causally] because the elements which compose nature are outside us" (Vico quoted, 17), known fully only to God, "opaque" nature's creator. Vico distinguishes between (outer or inner) nature and culture, between events and acts, between the nonhistorical and the historical in terms of what cannot and what can be entered by the human mind (140). Indeed, a sharp difference exists between the self-understanding sought by the humanities and the observable regularities (and their generative laws) sought by the natural sciences.

Related to this constructivist sense of historical development, human nature should not be seen as essentially fixed; those trying to understand and adapt their world to their physical and spiritual needs continuously transform that world and themselves. Similarly, knowable regularities of the created, invented world differ in principle from those of the natural world, because the former "obeys rules that they have themselves imposed on their own creations" (xvi ff.). This antiessentialist view allows for more fundamental historical changes in identities than pre-modern thinkers would expect; it exists, however, in tension, with a staged, or scripted, understanding of national/civilizational development and decay.

Indeed, Vico's *New Science* is the comparative, historical study of

---

6   A brief introduction to syllogisms is given in Chapter 2 above.
7   This is only the first of a number of citations or paraphrases wherein gendered language is likely to insult the sensitivities of the contemporary reader. With apologies, due to my attempt to render accurately the views and language of the older scholars whom I am discussing, I shall continue this practice where it is deemed inconvenient not to do so.

national/societal cultures, in many respects like Ibn Khaldun's *Muqaddimah*, a monumental, fourteenth-century comparative, historical-cultural study of regimes and civilizations written in Arabic, which he might have seen in some form.[8] Common styles, pervasive cultural patterns are seen in all the activities of a given society, "the thought, the arts, the social institutions, the language, the ways of life and action" (xvii, 138). Berlin believes that the transformative linking of the *verum/factum* formula to all of history – all that which men "have done and made and suffered; and arising out of it, the very conception of culture as a category of historical thought" – is Vico's greatest lasting contribution (117; see also xvii). Berlin also sees Vico as a forerunner of Herder and other historically, culturally and communicatively oriented theorists of nationalism.

As Weber later reformulated Dilthey's interpretive approach, proposing a comparative, historical sociology seeking explanatory understanding (*Verstehen*) of the characteristic uniquenesses of particular cultures, e.g., early modern capitalism,[9] so two centuries earlier Vico abductively reformulated classical inductive logic in emphasizing the important scholar role of human *fantasia*, the "unique capacity for imaginative insight and reconstruction" of other cultures in a self-reflective way that is nonetheless ultimately the "investigation of the *modificazioni* of our own minds" – the imaginative grasping of "their experience within the potentialities of our own human consciousness" (Vico paraphrased by Berlin, 102, 107ff.).

Vico's concern with the concrete particulars of individual societies is all the more remarkable, given that he also believed two bold and powerful positive research heuristics: "If the whole human race could speak as one man, it could perhaps remember all, and say all there is to be said" (82) and that "there must ... be a [researchable] mental language [of basic ideas, *voci mentali*] common to all nations which

---

8   Its first edition seems to have been a manuscript copy given to the royal library at Tunis in or before the year 1382 of the Christian calendar (Mahdi 1964: 52); on page 5, Mahdi describes Khaldun's opus as "a new science of culture."

   In a letter commenting on an earlier version of this chapter, Robert Cox has plausibly suggested that there were strong political/religious disincentives in the Italy of his time for Vico to acknowledge his familiarity with Arab/Islamic texts, even if he had seen some form of the *Muqaddimah*. Roy Mottaheddah confirms that Vico might well have known of Ibn Khaldun's work in some form, but might not have wanted to cite it.

9   A philosophically sophisticated account and selection is Dallmayr and McCarthy, eds. (1977).

uniformly grasps the essence of things feasible in human social life, and expresses it with as many diverse modifications as the same things have aspects" (Vico quoted, 48).[10] If the continuous self-transformation of man and of human institutions is common to all of humanity in the course of struggle to overcome human and natural obstacles, Vico's unifying idea of a national or civilizational culture has individuality and uniqueness associated with it, sufficient for us to recognize certain cultural possibilities as incompatible with Greek, Roman, French or medieval cultures (136–138).

Like many classical and religious historians before and after him, including Ibn Khaldun and Arnold Toynbee, Vico saw the history of particular societies as passing through particular stages: "first crude, then severe, then benign, then delicate, finally dissolute" (Vico quoted, 83). In other words, there was a *storia ideale*, an ideal eternal history, a cosmic wheel, a true theodicy immanent in the experience of each nation, a cycle of rise, development or progress, maturity, decay and fall (36, 81, 113). If the belief in cosmic harmony was translated by the Renaissance (and the Enlightenment) into the vision that the world can be made beautiful and rational, Vico's organic, Renaissance notion of the internal relationship between the individual microcosm and larger macrocosms also fits here: his *idée maîtresse*, later also found in Hegel, Piaget and their followers, of the "unity – and parallelism – which obtains between the necessary succession of the phases of a civilization and the development of mental attributes and powers in the [creative, as if divinely understood] individual" (16, 100).

Citing Collingwood, Berlin identifies this complex of developmental ideas, partly rooted in a dynamicized Platonism, as the first appearance of a full-fledged modern historicism. For Berlin, historicism is a doctrine whose empirical forms have, on the whole, been stimulating and enriching, but whose dogmatic, metaphysical forms have inhibited and distorted the historical imagination (36). Going beyond this historicism, the reader should recognize several even more general and fundamental features of "enlightened" modernity in these views.

---

[10] The most cross-culturally sensitive realization of this Leibnizian – even Aristotelian – idea I know is Wierzbicka (1992). What a challenge for mathematical modeling of social relationships, for those computer scientists specializing in "representation language languages": a formalizable fundamental alphabet for universal and culture-specific concepts! Comparisons with the semantic research program of George Lakoff and his associates suggests many challenging and as yet unsolved issues for such a research program.

Berlin also shows how this complex motivated Vico's attacks on Natural Law and social contract theorists, i.e., rationalists like Descartes and Spinoza, utilitarians like Hobbes and Locke, and even jurists like Grotius and Pufendorf (whom he nonetheless greatly admired). Their blindness to these dialectical features of development meant that they all assumed a fixed, unchanging human nature, fully developed psychological and moral structures, from which universal goals, interests, rights, laws and obligations flowed (34).[11] Even though modernity is at best a mixed blessing for Vico, he argues that gentile history does not show the reactionary's dream of a pre-existing "Golden Age." But neither is world cultural development simply progressive. Without actually using the concept of "incommensurability," Vico argues in a pre-Kuhnian fashion that neither the circumstances of the Renaissance nor the consequences of Greek development were completely conveyed by Roman language and experience.

Nonetheless, Vico's stages of civilizational development, organically linking individual microcosms and macrocosms, have a progressively more self-conscious linguistic, cognitive and communicative structure. "Man's effort to understand himself and his [humanly modified] world, and to realize his [changing] capacities in it" produce an "orderly procession (guided by Providence, working through men's capacities)." This orderly procession evidences "ever deepening types of apprehension of the world, of ways of feeling, acting, expressing, each of which grows out of, and supersedes, its predecessor" (34ff.).

In contrast with the Baconian experimentalism of some of his contemporaries, Vico argues that the three most incorruptible sources of historical knowledge are language, mythology and antiquities (41). Vico does not believe positivistically in the possibility of an unaltering, Leibnizian or Russellian, "logically perfect language constructed to reveal the basic structure of reality" (42), but he did grasp the "seminal and revolutionary truth" we today associate with names like Hegel, Marx, Vygotsky, Mead and the later Wittgenstein

---

[11] Here are unmentioned, much earlier sources for several of the "reflectivist" concerns summarized by Keohane in his Presidential Address. Berlin's reconstruction of Vico is clearly reflectivist:

> A static model like the social contract omits ... facts – the survival of the past into the present, the influence of tradition, of inherited habits and the shapes they assume ... [such myths as] the contract, or obedience to universal reason, or calculation of rational self-interest, placed at the centre of their systems by Hobbes and Spinoza, are, for Vico, merely the refuge of ignorance. (40ff.)

(Schmidt 1981; Habermas 1987; Holiday 1988; Mead 1934; Wertsch 1985), that "linguistic forms are one of the keys to the minds of those who use words, and indeed to the entire mental, social and cultural life of societies" (51).

Communicatively speaking, the earliest humans, primitive savages, signaled to each other using "mute acts" (or what Berlin and Mead would call "gestures"). In this "divine period," dominated by the senses, a poetic logic of "natural symbols" prevails, where thunder is a language in which the gods speak. "The next stage in the ascent of humanity is marked by the use of metaphors, similes, images and the like"; mythic characters are "imaginative universals" not yet fully abstracted general terms (43ff.). Indeed, language "tells us the history of things signified by the words" (Vico cited, 48); myths "are the concrete mode of expression of the collective imagination of early mankind" (53); and Hellenic "Fables are true histories of customs" (Vico quoted, 53), to be interpreted as coded representations of plebeian class conflicts with their aristocratic rulers (54ff.). Finally, the third, "human" period of history evidences reason and a language of "conventional signs invented and altered at will" as we now know them. Just as a grammatical metaphor helps capture the unique development of individual societies from a common ground containing a multiplicity of "well formed" possibilities, so a "morphology of a symbolic system" is seen to be unified "with the growth of the culture of which it is the central organ" (48).

No less astonishing than his prevision of key Hegelian–Marxist developmental ideas, in keeping with his conservative, religious and anti-democratic character, Vico also used concepts which would now be labelled "reification" and "alienation." The "common sense" of a society, "the judgment without reflection felt in common by the whole of a people, order, nation, or the whole human race" (quoted, 61) are exemplified in the "pride, avarice, cruelty" typical of every ruling aristocracy, including the heroic Homeric age and early Western feudalism. In such periods, "Primitive men are bound by [rigid] rules ... and can advance only if the rules seem to them made not by themselves, but to be objective and absolute ... external entities, demanding absolute obedience" (61). Here, reification – "Men fear death, and collectively invent gods stronger than death" – a form of alienation, enters historical analysis well before Hegel, Feuerbach, Marx or Freud (61).

The succeeding age, a more democratic one, has its own forms of alienation, referred to by Vico with the striking phrase of the "second barbarism of reflection (*la barbarie della reflessione*)" (quoted, 63). By this he means not the barbarity of youthful sensuality but "a kind of senility and impotence, when each man lives in his own egotistic, anxiety-ridden world, unable to communicate or co-operate with his fellows" (63). Plutocracy and democracy, of "free discussion, legal arguments, prose, rationalism, science" (62) leads to skepticism, loss of a socially cohesive faith, excess individualism, social disintegration, anarchy, "unchecked liberty," the melting away of civic virtue, violence and barbarism, as a cycle of decay completes itself (62ff.) in a way that Plato, Aristotle and Ibn Khaldun have similarly described.

Hayden White's version of Vico's stages, applied to Marx

In an affirmative discussion of "poetic wisdom" in his *New Science*, Vico recalls the famous Renaissance distinction among figurative tropes: metaphor, metonymy, synecdoche and irony,[12] stressing the continuities between mythic and (scientific) prosaic language, rather than their differences. In a highly informative review of subsequent historiography, Hayden White elaborates on Vico's use of these figurative tropes "for differentiating the stages of consciousness through which mankind has passed from primitivism to civilization" (White 1973: 32). Without subscribing to either of the more pessimistic cyclic readings of Vico's thought, emphasized by Berlin, or the more optimistic one that White uses to connect Vico to Marx, I think it opportune to re-present here this highly suggestive development of Vico's thought as well.

Following traditional poetics and modern discourse analysis, White is concerned with the way linguistic tropes make possible the characterization of different objects, indirectly or figuratively. Thus, in "Metaphor (literally "transfer") ... phenomena can be characterized in terms of their similarity to, and difference from, one another, in the

---

[12] In this subsection, I shall frequently cite White (1973: 32n). Pages 29–42 of White's Introduction, "The Poetics of History," are the basis for Table 6.1; his historiographical review, going back to the Renaissance, is most concentrated in Chapter 1, "The Historical Imagination Between Metaphor and Irony," pp. 45–80. Table 6.2 below derives from White's Chapter 8, "Marx: The Philosophical Defense of History in the Metonymical Mode," pp. 281–330. As with my retelling of Berlin's account of Vico, I shall preface references to his work with brief page citations in parentheses. Direct or translated quotations from other writers will be indicated explicitly.

Table 6.1 *A developmental typology of figurative tropes (after G. Vico, H. White, K. Burke)*

Name	Definition	Move (at literal and/or figurative level)	Examples
METAPHOR	Phenomena are characterized in terms of their similarity to, or difference from, one another.	REPRESENTATIONAL. Literal *identification* is to be taken figuratively, indicating entity's possessed qualities, e.g., analogy, simile.	my love, a rose
METONYMY	The name of a part of a thing is substituted for the name of the whole.	REDUCTIONIST. One part is prosaically reduced to an aspect, e.g., causal or agentive, of another, to which it is *extrinsically* related, e.g., merely mechanically.	"fifty sail" "the roar of thunder" "the thunder's roar"
SYNECDOCHE	A phenomenon is/ can be characterized by using the part to symbolize some *quality* [or essence] presumed to inhere in the totality.	INTEGRATIVE. As microcosmic replications, parts are seen as *intrinsically* (organically) related to some *qualitatively different* sum, whole or totality.	He is all heart.
IRONY	Entities can be characterized by way of negation.	NEGATIONAL. What is affirmed on the literal level is negated at the figural. The basic figurative tactic is catachresis (equating the observed with the manifestly absurd) or aporia (initial self-doubt, particularly re reality assessment inherent in one's language).	The above, applied to some manifestly cruel, unsympathetic person.

manner of analogy or simile, as in the phrase 'my love, a rose' " (34; see also Table 6.1). Relating to its etymology, meaning "name change," metonymy allows the substitution of a part of a thing for the whole, as when we use the phrase "fifty sail" to mean "fifty ships"; extrinsic relations between part and whole, in the sense that neither's identity is effected, are typically presupposed. Synecdoche, seen by some theorists as a form of metonymy, refers to the larger whole in terms of a quality assumed, dialectically, to be internal, or intrinsic, to it. Irony allows the characterization of objects "by way of negating on the figurative level what is positively affirmed on the literal level" (White 1973: 32; see also the summary in Table 6.1).

Although irony, metonymy and synecdoche can all be seen to be kinds of metaphor, they all perform different *reductions or integrations*, either effected at "the literal level of their meanings " or "by the kinds of illuminations they aim at on the figurative level" (34). Hence, in Table 6.1, we list the representational functions of metaphor, the reductionistic and integrative discursive functioning of metonymy and synecdoche, and the negational role of Irony (White 1973: 32ff.).

The reductionistic scientific role of act-agent and cause-effect metonymic reductions is particularly emphasized.[13] In a memorable passage, associated with a discussion of such metonymic reductions, White argues:

> as Vico, Hegel, and Nietzsche all pointed out, the phenomenal world can be populated with a host of agents and agencies that are presumed to exist *behind* it. Once the world of phenomena is separated into two orders of being (agents and causes on the one hand, acts and effects on the other), the primitive consciousness is endowed, *by purely linguistic means alone*, with the conceptual categories (agents, causes, spirits, essences) necessary for the theology, science, and philosophy of civilized reflection.   (35, emphasis in the original)

Already, one might doubt that the social sciences will endlessly progress under monopolistic figurative reductions of the social-historical-cultural world to mechanistic causality and instrumental agency.

---

[13] In emphasizing the reflective, developmental reading of Vico's thoughts on rhetoric and poetics, we can only briefly touch on the significant resonance that White and Burke find with Vico on this related theme, the role of poetic figures in prefiguring and constituting "realistic," or "scientific" descriptions and explanations. This "stylistic" feature of nineteenth-century historiography is a central theme in White's book. Indeed, in his rediscussion of one of Vico's earlier examples, White shows (see Table 6.1) how "the roar of thunder" treats atmospheric noise in cause–effect terms, while "the thunder roars" implies a reduction to an agent–act relationship.

Synecdochic integrations bring to attention shared or mutually interrelated qualities, identities or encompassing totalities. White's example in Table 6.1 (from 36) is a metonymic name change, "He is all heart," used synecdochically to convey a quality of compassion. Vico's treatment of "the particularly and individually true" as "the historically and culturally made" could also be described synecdochically, as a way of calling attention to the creative role of humankind in the making of their own history. "The aim of the Ironic statement is to affirm tacitly the negative of what is on the literal level affirmed positively, or the reverse" (37). A sarcastic "He is all heart!" exemplifies such usage.

The Ironic, in this sense, is more complex: it presupposes an absurdity recognizable by the reader or hearer. Irony (capitalized by White to signify the defined meaning) is a "linguistic paradigm" of a higher kind of thought radically self-critical "with respect not only to a given characterization of the world of experience but also to the very effort to capture adequately the truth of things in language" (37).

White respecifies the common understanding of Marx as a "conflict theorist" by claiming he "apprehended the historical field in the Metonymical mode.... [using prefigurative] categories of schism, division, and alienation" (281). He strongly distinguishes between two "orders" of history, a mechanistically/causally structured, and metonymically describable base of technological/economic means and modes of production, and a superstructure of consciousness and class-divided cultural/legal/political institutions syntactically determined by the base. The superstructure contains a rich variety of more or less self-aware and alienated consciousnesses, practices and institutions, whose histories can be synecdochically told as tragedies and comedies of class conflict. Marx's struggle is "to synthesize the tropological strategies of Metonymy and Synecdoche in a comprehensive image of the historical world" (285).

A further tension exists between a tragic emplotment of man's attempts to construct a viable human community within the historically shaped laws of his existence and a comic interaction which "progressively moves man toward a condition in which society itself will be [synecdochically] dissolved and a genuine community, a communistic mode of existence, will be constituted as his true [less naturalistically constrained, unalienated, morally free, acting according to just norms generalizable to all, self-consciously directed and collectively understood] historic destiny" (287).[14]

In introducing his book, citing Lévi-Strauss and Foucault, White suggests a sensitivity to the charge "that the historical consciousness on which Western man has prided himself since the beginning of the nineteenth century may be little more than a theoretical basis for the ideological position from which Western civilization views its relationship not only to cultures and civilizations preceding it but also to those contemporary with it in time and continuous with it in space" (2). He further contextualizes his rhetorical and historiographic analysis of nineteenth-century historians with a review of the "'Reflective' or 'critical' historiography" of the Enlightenment and its predecessors, a group in which Vico's criticisms of ahistorical rationalism find a special place.[15]

Indeed, Marx seems to have been anything but unique in his espousal of the ideal of some future, more rational society, joined to a recognition that the "Enlighteners" did not provide an adequate, "realistic" ground for the justification, or realization, of their rationalistic ideals. Marx's systematic commitment to an epistemological version of Vico's *verum/factum* conversion, his respecification of societal understanding in terms of the ability to change its own development, is more distinctive, as his poetic, Romantic, quasi-religious, even eschatological vision of a communist future.[16]

From a chapter fifty pages in length we shall summarize only two of

[14] This filled-in quotation is meant to suggest Marx's communist ideal, when a new and more perfect history or historicity is supposed to begin. More generally, when historicist understanding is self-reflective, historicity imperfectly results. In an analytically sensitive recasting, influenced by Husserl and Heidegger, Olafson (1979) explicates historicity traditionally as "the temporal self-understanding of a continuing human society." Marcuse (1987) begins (p. 1) with a more classical, Vicoesque conception: "Historicity is what defines history and thus distinguishes it from 'nature' or from the 'economy.' Historicity signifies the meaning we intend when we say of something that it is 'historical.' ... the meaning of the 'is,' namely the meaning of the Being of the historical." Marcuse's Marxian emphasis on "intersubjective world-constitution through work and action" (Benhabib's Introduction, p. xxix), may account for Heidegger's apparent rejection of the *Habilitationsschrift* that was the German language original of this book.

[15] See especially White's pp. 51–53 and the terminology quoted on p. 59 from Eduard Fueter (1911). Thus an explicitly labeled "reflectivist" tradition of critical historiography goes back at least eighty years. The focus on "reflection" can even more appropriately by linked back via Hegel to Kant's critical look at presuppositions (Roberts 1992), and perhaps earlier.

[16] Alker (1987), reprinted as Chapter 8 below, gives more details and citations.

the ways that White could be said to have strengthened and elaborated upon Vico's anticipation of Marx's arguments, and then briefly mention a third. First, the left column of Table 6.2 summarizes Marx's discussion in the early chapters of *Capital* of the *forms* of economic value. Just as Vico the classicist distinguished a meaningful "inner" domain from an "outer" physical one, so Marx distinguishes an inner domain of meaningful *contents* and true labor values from an external world of phenomenal, misleading and commodified *forms* superficiously described in terms of marketized use values. According to White, Marx's Vicoesque, critical analysis of the different types of value recognized by the language of commodities follows the developmental sequence and meanings of metaphor, metonomy, synecdoche and irony. White sees four (or more) stages implied by Vico's analysis where Berlin only emphasized three. His end purpose is to explain the paradoxical quality of money fetishism – capitalism's devoted commitment to a nearly useless generalized form of economic value, gold.

Recall Vico's discussion of primitive minds identifying themselves metaphorically with nature. According to White's close analysis of Marx's language in the early chapters of *Capital*, even before barter equivalence is established, the superficial equivalence of a certain amount of linen (B) and a coat (A), can be symbolized by the equation $A = B$. The equivalence is seen to be that of a visual simile, the coat *looking like* the linen in the sense of reflecting in a sublimated fashion the same amount of labor value input into its construction. Already use value is identified with the quantity and physical form of a thing, not its intrinsic, labor value.

The extended/total and generalized forms of economic value are described as in Table 6.2. The Metonymic reduction of an extended value to a particular formal equivalence is seen to reflect the organically constitutive quality of a general market system of commodified exchange relationships. These market valuations are extrinsic to the essential labor-generated value that particular commodities contain.

The absurd, ironic quality of a gold-based monetary system, typical of European capitalism in the later nineteenth and early twentieth centuries, is one of Marx's most famous rhetorical arguments. Notice how nicely it fits both the catachresis and aporia tactics of ironical negation described in Table 6.1. Here is palpable evidence – not of the immanent collapse of the gold standard, which indeed did not survive the most serious adjustments of the global financial system subsequent to Marx's prognosis – of the deeply figurative or tropological quality of

Table 6.2   *The figurative tropes associated with Marx's first four stages*

Trope	The succession of forms of value in capital	The succession of forms of society
METAPHOR	ELEMENTARY: Metaphorically, we say a coat (A) *looks like* a bolt of linen (B), or A = B, to express its sublimated, use/value *form* [as opposed to its intrinsic, labor value *content*] in concrete, bodily terms.	PRIMITIVE COMMUNIST: Here man is identified with himself, and with nature. He hunts and gathers like other animals, is organized in tribal societies, and exhibits only herd-consciousness.
METONYMY	TOTAL or EXTENDED: The relational value of two commodities, A = B, is seen as part of an infinitely extendable series of quantity equivalencies, A = B; B = C; C = D; etc.	SLAVE: A division of sexual labor, and of material and mental labor, combined with increased productivity, brings about (un)equal property relations between opposed families, with wives and children Metonymically reduced to slave-like roles in families.
SYNECDOCHE	GENERALIZED: Synecdochically, this extended value of a particular commodity is seen to reflect a general totality, a unified system of extrinsic, use-value oriented market relationships.	FEUDAL: A class division of hereditary nobles and serfs, integrated parts of a larger feudal order. Some serfs become chartered burghers, or free laborers. Internal and external contradictions develop within the intellectual, legal, spiritual and political superstructures of society, due to developments in its productive bases.
IRONY	MONEY: The ironic, absurd characterization of the intrinsic real/labor value of a commodity in terms of the quantity of extrinsically nearly useless (but fetishized) gold it exchanges in the advanced capitalistic market.	CAPITALIST: Class conflict between bourgeoisie and proletariat. The irony of bourgeois revolution is that its revolutionary accomplishments – egoistic calculation, ever-increasing productivity, social "realism" – are self-defeating. Increased consciousness of paradoxical social systems breeding poverty in the midst of plenty, war when peace is possible, the perception of the possibility of a labor-value oriented economy.

Source: White 1973, ch. 8.

222

Marx's analysis of value. The "extrinsic" market commodity relation-ship ironically hides an "intrinsic" reality of labor-based worth which "the language of commodities" has difficulty expressing.

Hayden White's concern with Marx's historiography is a double reflection: it self-consciously discusses how historians themselves reflectively write/make histories of an historical field from available historical records. In a linguistic/pragmatic way, White discusses both the economically grounded "grammar" of historical existence and the base-superstructure "syntax" of Marx's historical craft. Critically, he "plots" or scripts Marx's writing about his own time as both a bourgeois tragedy and a proletarian/human comedy in ways not unrelated to Vico's ironic view of historical progress in the era of the Enlightenment. Indeed his proposal is that the four stages of the classical comedy – *pathos, agon, sparagmos* (tearing or rending), fol-lowed by a recognition, or reflective reconciliation, *anagnorisis* – is contrasted with the ironic descent into bondage and alienated exploita-tion that Marxian tragedies always tell.[17]

The second main column of Table 6.2 fits the well known first four stages of Marxian developmental accounts: primitive communism, slave societies, feudalism and capitalism (followed of course by soci-alism and communism), into the developmental rubric just deployed. The overall transition from a society of unconscious metaphorical understanding to an era where capitalistic development is supposed to be undermining itself is a breath-taking, if hard to falsify, vision. In keeping with the conception of irony just reviewed, unsentimental, calculating capitalists, and the empiricist mentalities which capitalist modes of production foster, make realistically clear the age's paradox-ical ironies – poverty in the midst of plenty and costly wars when peace is both desirable for most citizens and obtainable. The more complex and ironically self-reflective aspects of this "last" historical stage before socialism fits well the ironic apprehension of intrinsic monetary values, and a socialist society oriented to meeting basic needs as prescribed by the labor theory of value.

---

[17] For the sake of brevity, I only note here the large section of White's chapter where he retells Marx's account of France's mid-nineteenth-century political-economic history in these terms. The generative structure of his mature, concrete histories – *The Eighteenth Brumaire* and *The Civil War in France* – are shown to reflect the same figurative definitions and dramatic emplotments as his early writings in *The Commu-nist Manifesto* and his most abstract economic analysis in *Capital*, enriched of course with his tragicomic, farcical account of Napoleon III.

Less clear from White's account is the basis for putting the forms of public consciousness associated with slave societies behind those of feudal ones. White's tropological account fits Marx's developmental typology to the extent that the exclusionary treatment of slaves – to the point where many of them cannot even reproduce – can be seen as reductive metonymy when compared to the more organic integration of feudal roles or class incumbents. But it leaves one with suspicions that the oligarchic social orders preceding the large-scale development of the slave economies of antiquity should be in the table. Similarly, late slave societies, with their impressive, if limited integrative achievements, might be placed closer to modernity than, at least, the dark, early ages of feudalism. Suffice it here to note that White emphasizes a multiplicity of metonymical and synecdochic paths dialectically leading from primitive social orders to advanced civilization.

Just as Vico's linguistic/figurative reflectivity helps clarify the ways in which Marx understood the poetic, reality-constituting features of bourgeois consciousness, so does his critical orientation toward the opacities of rationalistic historical self-understanding deepen our understanding of Marx's conceptions of commodity fetishism and worker alienation. Vico's anticipation of the creation of national and linguistic cultural communities, with their own ethnocentric blindspots additionally broadens and deepens the tradition of reflective, historical, social inquiry.

When one thinks of communism as an ideal culminating stage of history, one where human communities direct their own futures in terms of shared accounts of past forms of alienation and of successful revolutions against them, we can sense ways in which Marx's ideal future was a kind of communal historicity, the beginning of a new era of unalienated, unsuperstitious, unblocked collective action and shared self-understanding. Vico's similarly structured anticipation of the nationalisms of nineteenth-century Europe and the twentieth-century world system may nonetheless impress us as more prophetic. Marx's deep involvement with the reflective, critical views of the Enlightenment is clear, even if his suggestive, class-conflict-sensitive understanding of history problematically goes beyond those of other Enlightenment or post-Enlightenment thinkers.

Habermas' reflectively radicalized Weber

Just as Marx's literary, figurative mode of critical analysis is less known to positivistically inclined, non-sociologically educated international studies researchers, so their Weber literacy, if it exists at all, is likely to extend to bits of his methodological writing on *verstehen* and "value free" social science, or his substantive writings on bureaucracy or power. Among multi-paradigmatic, historically literate sociologists, however, Weber is often taught, along with Durkheim, Marx and sometimes Comte, as a founder of that modern discipline. Seen critically and comparatively *vis-à-vis* these alternative traditions, Weber is a major, comparatively and critically inclined, social theorist of modernity.

Although one can trace some of his epistemological views back to the nuanced positivism of Mill and Comte, one can more adequately treat Weber, like Vico and Marx before him, as a creative methodological synthesizer of positivistic, hermeneutic, dialectical and historicist traditions of social theorizing. Hegel's reflective, reason-centered theory of history, his brilliant, dialectical logic, and his phenomenology of consciousness – traceable back through the enlightener Kant to early modern writers like Leibniz, Newton and Descartes – are important parts of the story; so are the impacts on Weber of Kant's Enlightened critical rationalism, as mediated through the *Geisteswissenschaften* orientation of Dilthey and Rickert. Nietzsche's anti-Enlightener, anti-Christian, anti-hypocritical cynicism, set against the background of European *Realpolitik*, also clearly affected Weber's critical thought.[18]

Weber's critique of modernity

Comparable with the critical and appreciative orientations of Vico and Marx toward certain (sometimes different) aspects of modernity, one may expect Weber's historically alive, religiously focused, scientifically committed, liberal sensitivities to align him with certain critical perspectives on twentieth-century modernity:[19]

> The Puritan wanted to work in a calling; we are forced to do so. For when asceticism was carried out of monastic cells into everyday life and began [especially through the Protestant Ethic] to dominate

[18] Useful selections from, and discussion of, Weber's concepts and methodology include Gerth and Mills (1946), Weber (1949), Dallmayr and McCarthy (1977); Giddens' introduction to Weber (1989). The present discussion relies chiefly on Chapters 2 and 7 of Habermas (1984).

[19] The following two quotes from Weber (1989) are reprinted by permission of the publisher.

225

> worldly morality, it did its part in building the tremendous cosmos of the modern economic order ... In Baxter's view the care for external goods should only lie on the shoulders of the "saint like a light cloak...." But fate decreed that the cloak should become an iron cage. ... [V]ictorious capitalism, since it rests on mechanical foundations, needs its support no longer. The rosy blush of its laughing heir, the Enlightenment, seems also to be irretrievably fading, and the idea of duty in one's calling prowls about in our lives like the ghost of dead religious beliefs.   (Weber 1989: 189ff.)

The indictment of modern capitalism, especially in the United States, is especially stinging:

> In ... the United States, the pursuit of wealth, stripped of its religious and ethical meaning, tends to become associated with purely mundane passions, which often actually give it the character of sport. ... [O]f the last stage of this cultural development, it might well be truly said [quoting Goethe]: "Specialists without spirit, sensualists without heart; this nullity imagines that it has attained a level of civilization never before achieved."   (*Ibid.*: 182)

European social theorists are more likely to know these famous lines than North American methodologists. They suggest an eloquent intensity of normative concern closer to Marx and Engels' indignant criticisms of nineteenth-entury capitalism than to the "value free" social science normally associated by positivistic methodologists with Weber's writings.[20]

The communicative foundations of Habermas' reformulation of Weber

Indeed, Habermas' two-volume *Theory of Communicative Action* has as its most important substantive focus a radicalized, communicatively oriented version of Weber's eloquent, pained critique. My review of Habermas' book here takes advantage of the linguistic version of

---

[20] Collins' (1986) provocative reading of Weber emphasizes the similarities between his last, multidimensional treatment of capitalism (Weber 1981) and Wallerstein (1974, 1980, 1989). Weber's (1981) chapter on "Citizenship" ends with the Wallersteinian thesis: "as long as the national state does not give place to a world empire, capitalism also will endure" (p. 337). The closest Weber comes to the ironic interpretation of money emphasized above is his "Speculation reaches its full significance only from the moment when property takes the form of negotiable paper" (Weber 1981: 278), a sentence with which he dramatically concludes a chapter entitled "The Meaning and Presuppositions of Modern Capitalism."

Marx's ironic "fetishism of commodities" analysis already retold above.[21]

Recall Hayden White's Vicoesque (but post-Weberian) self-critical awareness of the possibly ideological character of exaggerated claims about Western reflective historical understanding. Like most other serious contemporary students of Weber, Habermas identifies the "universal-historical problem" at the center of Weber's scientific work as the careful, historical identification of the "characteristic uniqueness" of "Occidental Rationalism": "why, outside of Europe, 'Neither scientific nor artistic, nor political, nor economic development entered upon the path of rationalization peculiar to the Occident?'" (Habermas 1984 and 1987: II.157,[22] quoting Weber's *Vorbemerkung* to his studies in the sociology of religion.)[23] From an historicist vantage point,[24] the rationalized aspects of the modern are seen to occur in increasingly differentiated cultural, societal and personal worlds (II.167; also VI.119–152).[25] Habermas uses these distinctions in his respecification of Weber's critical treatment of modernity. This he summarizes as a claim of the loss of meaning

---

21 In achieving perspective on Habermas's massive two-volume work, I have found helpful Thomas McCarthy's writings, lectures at Harvard by Hillary Putnam and Daniel Bell in the fall of 1989 on this work, and Dallmayr (1989).

22 Here and hereafter I shall normally cite Habermas's two-volume work by chapter and page. Roman chapter numbers I–IV and xlii, plus 465 pages comprise volume 1; Chapters V–VIII and v, plus 457 pages make up volume 2. Weber quotations will be specially indicated.

23 In this late work of Habermas, Occidental Rationalism is seen to involve both cognitive elements (including modern natural science, universities, scientific enterprises and a capitalistic economy), evaluative elements (rational natural law, professionalized jurisprudence, modern governmental institutions, methodical-rationalized personal conduct, the worldly asceticism of the Protestant Ethic, and the bourgeois nuclear family), and expressive elements (including autonomous art production, criticism and trading practices).

24 Weber's historicist self-understanding is emphasised in Weber (1968: 184, 213; and 1985). I am grateful to Robert Hancke for the references.

25 Habermas defines the three, differentiated worlds of modernity as follows:

> I use the term *culture* for the stock of knowledge from which participants in communication supply themselves with interpretations as they come to an understanding about something in the world. ... *society* [stands] for the legitimate orders through which participants regulate their memberships in social groups and thereby secure solidarity. By *personality* I understand the competencies that make a subject capable of speaking and acting, that put him in a position to take part in processes of reaching understanding and thereby to assert his own identity.   (VI.138)

and freedom within modernity's scientifically enabled "iron cage" of economic and political institutions.

Habermas finds Weber's diagnosis of the strengths and pathologies of Western modernity rich, but inadequate; it is particularly inhibited by Weber's conceptionalization of modern, rationalized, action systems only in terms of cognitive-instrumental (or purposive) rationality. "[W]e could analyze the rationalization of action systems ... [also] by bringing in moral-practical and aesthetic-expressive aspects across the whole spectrum. I have attempted to meet this desideratum ... by elucidating such concepts as 'action oriented to mutual understanding,' 'symbolically structured lifeworld', and 'communicative rationality'" (VIII.303ff.). After a brief review of Habermas' use of these concepts, I shall return to his radical respecification of Weber's modernity problematique, critically perceived.

Communicative rationality distinguished from strategic rationality

Habermas's distinction between instrumental (including strategic) rationality and communicative rationality appears in his earliest writings.[26] Clearly its roots include the Kantian moral attitude against treating others instrumentally, rather than as ends in themselves.

In developing his latest version of this ideal-typical distinction between communicative and strategic orientations, Habermas starts with an argument that the "rationality of an expression" is based on "its being susceptible of criticism and grounding" (I.9). He distinguishes between actions oriented toward success or effectiveness, and those communicatively oriented toward understanding, agreement, rationally sharable truths. Following Piaget, Schutz and the brilliant American social psychologist George Herbert Mead, Habermas treats "rational expressions" as cooperatively oriented meaningful actions, symbolic expressions requiring linguistic capacities for their interpretation, more than animal-like gestures or signals.

---

[26] His distinction between "symbolic interaction" within an institutional framework and purposive-rational actions of an instrumental or strategic (involving others, treated instrumentally) sort is one such predecessor. Such distinctions are at the heart of my collaborative current work on SPD protocols, where we often find action that looks to be communicatively oriented, not merely strategic signaling behavior. See Chapters 9 and 10 below. Obviously, instrumental and communicative orientations can overlap.

*Reflective linguistic capacities and argumentative speech acts
as grounds for communicative rationality*

Language and communication are seen as profoundly social, requiring internalized reflective capacities. Indeed, "taking the attitude
of the other is an important mechanism in the emergence of
language" (V12). Behavioral responses are to be understood "in the
full dialogical sense of an 'answer' [within an internalized dia-
logue]"; language is additionally necessary "for achieving understanding via identical meanings because participation in real or
external dialogues already requires the use of linguistic symbols"
(VII.12ff.). The conditions of validity of symbolic expressions refer to
a background knowledge [a lifeworld] intersubjectively shared by
the communication community" (I.13). Communication is reflectively
anticipative and self-referring: "What is essential to communication
is that the symbol should arouse in oneself what it arouses in the
other individual. It must have that sort of universality to any person
who finds himself in the same situation" (Mead quoted by Habermas, V15). Although the extent to which the lifeworld is proposi-
tionally and criticizably available (it is always tacit and
presupposed) may be debated, the lifeworld context is seen to
contain normative standards at least partially shared within communication communities.

Habermas addresses the links between a multifaceted, wide spectrum, integrative rationality and communicative action grounded in
a pragmatic theory of reasoned argumentation. "In contexts of
communicative action, we call someone rational not only if he is able
to put forward an assertion and, when criticized, to provide grounds
for it by pointing to appropriate evidence, but also if he is following
an established norm and is able, when criticized, to justify his action
by explicating the given situation in the light of legitimate expectations" (I.15). This generalized notion extends well beyond instrumental action in the cognitive domain: "We even call someone
rational if he makes known a desire or an intention, expresses a
feeling or a mood, shares a secret, confesses a deed, etc., and is then
able to reassure critics in regard to the revealed experience by
drawing practical consequences from it and behaving consistently
thereafter" (I.15).

Reflective "media" and "attitudes" characterize deliberatively rational conduct in cognitive-instrumental, moral-practical, evaluative

and expressive domains (I.20).[27] "In practical discourse reasons or grounds are meant to show that a norm recommended for acceptance expresses a generalizable interest; in aesthetic criticism grounds or reasons serve to guide perception and to make the authenticity of a work so evident that this aesthetic experience can itself become a rational motive for accepting the corresponding standards of value" (I.20). Argumentative validity claims in these practical and aesthetic domains parallel those in theoretical/cognitive-instrumental and therapeutic/expressive domains. Corresponding validity claims correspond to "rightness of action norms," "adequacy of evaluative standards," "propositional truth" and "expressive truthfulness or sincerity." "The logic of argumentation does not refer to deductive connections between semantic units (sentences) as does formal logic, but to nondeductive relations between the pragmatic units (speech acts) of which arguments are composed" (I.22ff.).

The reproduction, evolution and normative development of a symbolically structured lifeworld

As in his earlier works, Habermas is deeply committed, as an upholder of the Enlightenment tradition, to the emancipatory power of reflective reason, formulated here more generally than by Weber, as communicative rationality. Communicative rationality is said to increase with learning in the personal, cultural and societal spheres (VI.147). Traditions too have a certain historicity; they too become reflectively rationalized with increased modernization:

> The renewal of traditions depends more and more on individuals' readiness to criticize and their ability to innovate. The [ideal] vanishing point of these evolutionary trends are: for culture, a state in which traditions that have become reflective and then set aflow undergo continuous revision; for society, a state in which legitimate orders are dependent upon formal procedures for positing and justifying norms and for personality, a state in which a highly abstract ego-identity is continuously stabilized through self-steering. (VI.146)

We see here how communicative rationality is treated as *a* source of modern development, with an emancipatory aspect. Indeed, Habermas has offered cognitively, normatively and legally oriented revisions of

[27] Politically speaking, Habermas endorses democratically structured deliberative rationality in an enlarged public sphere. For a remarkably similar conception, see Joshua Cohen (1986, 1989a, 1989b).

the classical Marxian stages theory already previsioned by Vico and recast by Hayden White in Tables 6.1 and 6.2 above.[28]

Speaking broadly, culture, society and personality are also treated as parts of the lifeworld – the arena of implicit, background knowledge that socialized individuals bring to their communicative interactions. Reproduction process can maintain interpretive schemes making possible consensus on valid knowledge, legitimately ordered social relations and personally socialized identities; loss of meaning, anomie and personal psychopathologies are pathological manifestations of reproductive breakdowns or crises (VI.142ff.).

Sociation of new members in a lifeworld fosters the historical connection of situations as well: "it secures for succeeding generations the acquisition of *generalized competencies for action* and sees to it that *individual life histories are in harmony with collective forms of life*" (VI.141). Like Vico and Mead, Habermas is strongly emphasizing the role of linguistically embedded knowledge and communicative interactions calling upon this background, in local, national or international community building.

Habermas' radicalized version of Weber's modernity thesis

Now we are ready to recast Weber's distressed picture of modernity's pathologies of meaninglessness and unfreedom in Habermasian terms. The key idea follows the critical Marxist literature on bourgeois class domination, commodity fetishism and the reification of economic and political relationships. "[T]he imperatives Weber connected with the idea of 'bureaucratization'" are seen negatively as "penetrat[ing] into communicatively structured domains of action, so that the space opened up by the rationalization of the lifeworld for moral-practical will-formation, expressive self-presentation, and aesthetic satisfaction does not get utilized" (VII.328).

---

[28] Earlier hierarchies remarkably like those of Tables 6.1 and 6.2 structure personal, cognitive, moral and ego development in Habermas (1979: Ch. 3). The general movement is from habitual, traditional or instinctive activity to self-reflective, principle-guided action. In *The Theory of Communicative Action*, vol. II, many aspects of this work are present. Figure 28, page 192, entitled "Forms of Mutual Understanding," suggests movement from sacred to profane domains of action, associated with differentiation between instrumental relations of success and validity-oriented movement toward mutual understanding, eventually further distinguishing scientifically objectivating, norm-conformative and attitude-expressive validity claims.

This penetration is effected by the media of money and bureaucratic power seen as facilitating systemic (functional and instrumental) integration (Marx's realm of necessity) rather than social integration (Marx's norm-based realm of freedom, where actions are subject to rational criticism). Like other commodities, money and bureaucratized authority become fetishized, disconnected from the history and practices underlying their production, making these practices relatively difficult to criticize with the standards of communicative rationality. Coordination is achieved more and more in terms of second order consequences of actions, not rational deliberation about public purposes. Hence follows the provocative and controversial thesis of "Internal colonization" of the lifeworld by the systems world, as in Lukác's "vision of an administered, totally reified world in which means-ends rationality and domination are merged" (VII.332ff.).

Weber's later work, in particular his *General Economic History*, focused on the international dynamics of the globalization of Occidental Rationality.[29] Some ideas of how this treatment would be handled in a Habermasian way are suggested by one of Habermas' earlier books. There, Habermas has described the development of post-Enlightenment moral/political identities as follows.

> The identity of world citizens obviously is not strong enough to establish universal conscription. A symptom of this can be seen in the double identity of the citizen of the modern state.... This competition [between the group identities of *homme* and *citoyen*] was temporarily silenced through membership in nations: the nation is the modern identity formation that defused and made bearable the contradiction between the intrastate universalism of bourgeois law and morality ...and the particularism of individual states....[30]

Thus the contradictory, war prone structure of the modern state system is also part of Habermas' generalized version of Weber's modernity problematique. In his view, the political philosophy of socialism is linked to a development in collective identity more fully compatible with universalistic, Enlightened ego structures.

> What the eighteenth century had thought of under the rubric of cosmopolitanism was now conceived of as socialism .... This was the

---

[29] Hedley Bull's similar, sociological account is reviewed in Chapter 11 below.

[30] Habermas (1979: 115). In his final work, Weber remains critical of capitalist evolution; in a chapter of the *General Economic History* entitled, "The External Facts in the Evolution of Capitalism," he makes the Marxian claim: "The conduct of war by the state becomes a business operation of the possessing classes."

first example of an identity that had become reflective, of a collective identity no longer tied retrospectively to specific doctrines and forms of life but prospectively to [political] programs and rules for bringing about something [new and improved]. (Habermas 1979: 115)

A second look at the reflectivist tradition of research on international institutions

This sympathetic, epistemologically oriented retelling of modern, reflectively oriented accounts of institutional development may have revealed as many meanings of "reflective" as there are of "paradigm" (Masterman 1970, discussing Kuhn). Nonetheless, a certain coherence of concern survives across these tradition-sensitive retellings. Roughly substitutable and partially overlapping conceptions of "reflective" include "non-positivist, dialectical, dialogical, critical, or communicatively rational," "cognitively or socially aware, introspective or self-conscious," "linguistically, cognitively, morally, normatively, developmentally, historically, politically or scientifically more advanced." These broadened epistemological, social scientific and philosophical conceptions of critical, self-conscious and communicative rationality are united by roughly parallel normative, interpretive and empirically testable developmental theories defined at the individual, the social, the national or international level.

A strong case can thus be made for identifying the "reflective" tradition of social theorizing in terms of its critical, and constructive, attitude toward the promises, the presuppositions and the limitations, the practices and institutions, of modernity. I have also emphasized the "reflective" tradition's more-than-instrumental, linguistically self-referential concept of interpretive and figurative communication, combined with a contextual and historicist conception of rationality. Even though each of our principal theorists has a different political orientation, these communalities are genuine. Traditions continue to exist in their reformulations, which may also provide bases for significant innovation, as we have also seen; *secondary* analyses, then, have been exactly right for present identificational purposes.

Based on these findings, I would like briefly to suggest a rather different view of the state of recent research on international institutions than that offered by Robert Keohane in his frequently cited Presidential Address (Keohane 1988). First of all, although Keohane may of course use any terms he chooses – and clearly the concern of his address is with international institutions – he does not make clear that the "critical or reflective" approach to social theorizing has a much broader and longer tradition than his citations suggest. Indeed, I have traced this concern back to the Enlightenment and its critics, and even back to the early modern period. Vico was a brilliant, if reactionary critic of the early years of the modern European experience, who used its rational and scientific tools in a highly creative, and reflective way. The tradition of critical and imaginative reflection about modernity, its meaning, its alternatives, its causes and its consequences, includes Vico, Marx, Weber, Berlin, White and Habermas. These modern scholars have all, to varying degrees, been reflective enough, using their uncoerced reason, to question the extent to which their own intellectual productions have benefited from, or been distorted by, the European-centered creation of the modern world.[31]

Evidencing a relatively positivistic preoccupation with explanatory theory, Keohane does not make clear the variety of critical, interpretive, emancipatory *and* explanatory "knowledge interests" – to use Habermas' term – that are part of this rich and venerable tradition of social theorizing. The emancipatory interest, in particular, is grounded in the rationalizing development of modern domestic and international society, whose tools of analysis include those developed both by the "reflectivist" and (instrumentally or substantively) "rationalist" approaches identified by Keohane. The Enlightenment was founded on a commitment to the rational criticism of social institutions, an attack on superstition and unreflected upon tradition, the transcendence of particularity. The associated universalizing knowledge interests are, and have been, constitutive of all the modern social sciences; to varying degrees, these orientations have also been shared by the best critics of the Enlighteners. An historicist attitude is an appropriate, critically reflective orientation applying reason against its own, blinded or particularistic, or fetishized applications within these sciences. Positivistic, equilibrium-seeking epistemologies of social science, such as those usually espoused by "rationalist institutionalists," are vulnerable, like any other scholarly approach, to such criticisms.

One must ask how much instrumentally oriented rationalist theories are parts of the problem of modernity, not answers to the questions of institutional design and reform that Keohane rightly concerns himself

---

[31] One could of course include here and discuss post-modern scholars of modernity; a beginning of such discussion is made in Chapter 4 above. More thoroughly see Habermas (1987).

with.[32] And an adherent to the reflectivist tradition, like myself, must call for the rescue of reason itself, in its communicative form, from its instrumentally impoverished, scientifically pretentious embodiments.

Keohane is correct to emphasize the sociological orientation of "reflective institutionalists," like Alker, Ashley, Kratochwil and Ruggie; but he does not extend it to the different, more comprehensive and developed concepts of practical and communicative rationality that they build their theories from.[33] Unfortunately, he does not clarify the linguistic bases of their orientation. Nor does he say how, from Vico to Marx to Mead to Habermas, language has been seen as a communicative medium as well as a constitutive force, both within the domestic and international societies and the international institutions he concerns himself with.

Language is a social institution par excellence; so are particular language games and discourse practices. Their critical, reflective investigation has long been a central issue in the reflective analysis and criticism of historical development. Hence linguistically oriented studies, such as those by post-structuralists he does cite, but also the whole cluster of then just emerging "post-modernist" critics (Der Derian 1987; Der Derian and Shapiro, eds. 1989) correctly belong at the heart of the contemporary study of the evolving and transforming institutions of international/world society.

This broader view of the "reflective or critical" tradition also suggests a very different sense than Keohane's of the research contributions of "reflectivist" and "rationalist" research programs to the understanding and reform of international institutions. If Weber was a "reflectivist," as he most assuredly was, then the sociological contributions of Weberians like Haas, Hoffmann and Aron surely belong in any adequate or instructively balanced list of works on international institutions.[34] So do the largely compatible sociological contributions

---

[32] Note how this question is a special variant of "Can the End of Power Politics be Part of the Concepts with which its Story is Told?" Chapter 5 above.

[33] Chapter 12 focuses on Kratochwil's uses of "practical reason."

[34] I should state that I am as concerned with the pedagogical implications of Keohane's forward-oriented juxtaposition of research approaches as with the adequacy of his then stated views about the relative lacunae of reflectivist research programs. Certainly he is exceptional in his efforts to understand and present both approaches, including my own reflectivist inclinations, fully and fairly. Although he barely cites the specific contributions of Weber, Haas, Hoffmann and Wallerstein, Keohane may reasonably be read as asking for more concrete descriptive and explanatory studies of particular international institutions like the United Nations, Exxon or the World Bank,

of Grotian internationalists like Hedley Bull, Karl Deutsch, Herbert Kelman, Anthony Smith and Martin Wight. So does the work of neo-Marxist and post-Marxist scholarship, not just Robert Cox whom Keohane cites, but also Immanuel Wallerstein and his hundreds of research program adherents around the world. The journal *Review*[35] is regularly full of articles on the inter and inner connections between domestic and international social and economic and political actors; these are all socially and institutionally conceived. And, the Marxian-inspired literature on nationalism, imperialism, dependency and its alternatives also addresses domestic/transnational/international issues and institutions in a powerful and frequently penetrating way. Thus, the "reflectivist" tradition has generated far more "research programs" than the economic and game theoretical lines of "rationalist" research, mostly in the United States, that Keohane mentions.

My final point is a self-critical one. Before engaging in the reading leading to this chapter, working within the narrower "reflective resolutions research program" or the Haas-Butterworth-Alker-Sherman line of research on collective security-seeking practices,[36] I did not fully realize the extent to which the "Prisoner's Dilemma" or the "security dilemma" have been central problems of modernization theory and its critics for more than two and one half centuries. Vico, Marx, Weber and Habermas all have criticized those social developments associated

by the next generation of reflectivist scholars, including post-structuralist or post-modernist critics of modernity. Given their preoccupations with reconstructively *understanding* linguistic practices and with the critical aspects of social theorizing, replicable, *explanation*-oriented, scientific research progams are indeed harder to find in their current work.

[35] Published by the Fernand Braudel Center for the Study of Economies, Historical Systems, and Civilizations, SUNY at University of Binghamton, Binghamton, New York.

[36] The most synthetic of my first generation of Haas-inspired studies of the UN Collective Security System was Alker and Christensen (1972). The most important second generation "security system" modeling research along these lines was James P. Bennett's Ph.D. dissertation, summarily reported on in Bennett and Alker (1977).

A proposal to the National Science Foundation from the Center for International Studies at MIT, dated Nov. 30, 1977, was entitled "Reflective Logics for Resolving Insecurity Dilemmas." I was the principal investigator; Dwain Mefford coauthored the proposal text. A rewritten version of the proposal, incorporating some of James Bennett's early efforts at Schank–Abelson style textual modeling, funded by NSF Grant No. 7806707, appeared as Alker, Bennett, Mefford (1980). The third generation of research in this line of work has required considerable data making and methodological effort. Progress is reported in the Duffy, Mallery and Sherman chapters of Duffy, ed. (1994).

with the extension of egoistic, historically blinded, strategically defined, exchange-oriented relationships. Even Robert Jervis' imaginative and insightful game theoretic retelling of Rousseau's parable of the "stag and hare" (Jervis 1978) misses the larger issues of rationality, modernity, deliberative democracy and legitimacy that Rousseau was concerned with (Williams 1989).[37] To think of such dilemmas as communicatively restricted, instrumentally rationalized, reifying objectifications of less than fully human interaction possibilities is to suggest that the best contributions of modern criticism are worth preserving for a post-modern age.

[37] One could say that Williams (1989: 194) rescues Rousseau's more hopeful realism from Waltzean and Jervis-style *Realpolitik*: "The stag-hunt represents a primitive form of rationality which Rousseau acknowledges, but which he argues is disastrously deficient and represents not the eternal form of reason dictated by the logic of the situation, but rather an immature and incomplete understanding requiring supercession." This theme is taken up again in Chapters 11 and 12 below.

7 An Orwellian Lasswell:
Humanistic scientist

First published in a volume focusing on the broader thematic relevance of George Orwell's *1984*, this chapter is, perhaps surprisingly, about Harold Lasswell. For most readers, Harold Lasswell is probably but a shadowy figure from the "distant past" of American Political Science – one might recall an association with Merriam at Chicago in the 1930s; some catchy titles like *Politics: Who Gets What, When and How*; some crude operational studies of propaganda content; his commitment to the policy sciences; or the jargon-filled years of the Yale Law School and his coauthorship with Myres McDougall and others of numerous, weighty tomes on international law. But I consider Harold Lasswell to be the most important "founding father" of American Political Science in the twentieth century, the professional contemporary whose work most closely rivals and complements Orwell's achievements, and a shining, if neglected, model for further critical studies of systems of international domination; so I write about him here.

The Lasswell you will read about, then, will not be the person who directly influenced a whole generation of my teachers – themselves influential scholars like Gabriel Almond, Robert Dahl, Karl Deutsch, Heinz Eulau, Robert Lane, Daniel Lerner, Ithiel Pool, and Lucian Pye; it will be my personal Lasswell. This chapter pays homage to a great teacher from one of his later students. Focusing on an especially appropriate, but independently developed, theme it tries to present an Orwellian Lasswell for 1984 and beyond. If this Lasswell is less known than other Lasswells, even by those who know his work less superficially than the typical graduate student or teacher of today, I take the resulting identity dilemmas as evidence for my thesis about Lasswell's unequaled influence in American Political Science. As a true founding

238

father, he was, in a very professional way, an inspiration for the right and the left; an Americanist, a European comparativist, a developmentalist, and an international scholar. He was a functionalist and an action theorist; a student of broad social processes and institutions as well as of the irrational minutiae of individual political behavior; a behavioral scientist, a policy analyst and a critical humanist; a "realist" and an "idealist"; a political scientist for all times, even post-1984.

To make my approach work I must show that there is an Orwellian Lasswell relevant for today, someone who not only shared many of Orwell's preoccupations but also as a political scientist shaped viable scholarly responses to them, responses we might expect Orwell himself to have tolerated or approved. This is not an easy task – Orwell profoundly distrusted intellectuals, and he disliked jargon. Lasswell trained Yale lawyers and political scientists, intellectual elites, in systematic political analysis. He was a scholar's scholar, able to define and defend disciplinary boundaries using difficult technical vocabularies. But a great commonality yet remained: they were both rational, humane citizens of the same tortured world.

With respect to "Orwellian" conceptualizations of the "institutionalized relations of global power and domination – their emergence, perpetuation, and possible transformation" – I accept Richard Ashley's interpretation of Orwell's *1984* as broadly suggesting:

1 potent imagery about the emergence of a new, totalitarian world order; and
2 appropriate intellectual and political commitments in an age whose desperate insecurities threaten to extinguish even "The Last man in Europe," Orwell's first projected title for that work.[1]

My reading of Orwell's work, like my understanding of the life that produced it, has been heavily conditioned by Bernard Crick's *George Orwell: A Life* (1980) and William Steinhoff's *George Orwell and the Origins of 1984* (1976).[2] "Orwellian" signifies for me not only the

---

[1] See Richard Ashley's undated "Section Description" for "Section 18: International Relations: Hierarchical Aspects of International Politics" of the 1984 American Political Science Association Program. I am responsible for my response in what was originally a section theme paper.
[2] Any quotations or paraphrases from the text of Orwell's *1984* will be taken either from these studies or the New American Library edition (New York, 1983), without further acknowledgment.

powerful, nightmarish world of *1984* but also the way of life and writing style of a man who "hated the power-hungry, exercised intelligence and independence, and taught us again to use our language with beauty and clarity, sought for and practiced fraternity and had faith in the decency, tolerance and humanity of the common man" (Crick 1980: 406).

World power hierarchies

What first suggested to me a compatibility of perspectives was teaching Lasswell's "The Garrison State" (Lasswell 1941) as a political science text to follow Orwell's *1984*. But in order to show how the two writers could come to such frightening, and similar, projections about world politics, I have to "unpack" Lasswell's conceptual and methodological orientation to such "developmental constructs" and show which aspects of the *1984* literary construct Orwell himself took seriously.

Lasswell's early political "realism"

In 1934 Lasswell began what he considered to be his most significant book, *World Politics and Personal Insecurity*, with a shocking, pithy, "realistic" account of "who gets what, when, and how" in world politics:

> Political analysis is the study of changes in the shape and composition of the value patterns of society ... Since a few members of any community ... have the most of each value, ... the pattern of distribution ... resembles a pyramid. The few who get the most ... are the *elite*; the rest are the rank and file. An elite preserves its ascendancy by manipulating symbols, controlling supplies, and applying violence.   (Lasswell 1934, 1950)

So far this conception maps quite clearly onto the cynical, power-oriented elites dominating *1984*, even if its Machiavellianism need not exhaust either Lasswell's or Orwell's views of the possibilities of human nature.[3]

---

[3] At this point Orwell's rejection of the rather similar political "realism" of James Burnham should be noted as a potential stumbling block in my efforts to construct a consistent Orwellian Lasswell. In his essay/pamphlet "James Burnham and the Managerial Revolution," Orwell (no date) admits the impressive projective plausibility of Burnham's thesis of an increasingly oligarchic managerial revolution (neither

Lasswell goes even further, however, defining significant changes in world history in terms of changing worldwide patterns of recruitment of elites, their symbolic self-understanding and their replacement possibilities.

> A *revolution* is a rapid and extensive change in the composition and the vocabulary of the ruling few; *world revolutions* are those which inaugurate new principles of elite recruitment and new reigning ideologies in the political life of humanity. No doubt the French and Russian revolutions were major innovations in the world history of rulers and ruling symbols. ... If the significant political changes of the past were signalized by revolutionary patterns which rose and spread until they were blocked or superseded by new revolutionary innovations, the future may follow the same course of development ... Correct self-orientation would therefore consist in discerning the principle of elite recruitment and the predominant symbols to appear in the next phases of world political change ... Developmental analysis construes particular details with reference to tentatively held conceptions of the elite-symbol changes toward which or away from which events are moving. (Lasswell 1950: 34)

1984 and "The Garrison State" as compatible developmental constructs

An "apprehensive" developmental perspective characterizes Lasswell's writing in 1941 – two years before Orwell first outlined *1984* –

socialist nor capitalist) leading at the international level to a world of three totalitarian superstates. But he rejects Burnham's Machiavellian political analysis, which we might paraphrase as: (1) Politics (the struggle for power) is essentially the same in all ages; (2) Power hunger is a natural instinct forever separating an unscrupulous ruling elite from an unpolitical, brainless mob of the ruled; (3) History is a series of swindles wherein elites lure masses into revolution with the false promise of Utopias, only to reenslave them after the revolt succeeds.

Orwell counters that the proper question is "Why does the lust for naked power become a major human motive exactly *now*, when the dominion of man over man is ceasing to be necessary?" He takes seriously the possibility "that the Machiavellian world of force, fraud, and tyranny may somehow come to an end," i.e. that democratic Socialism could happen. And he attributes to Burnham and many other intellectuals an unsavory and ultimately unrealistic form of power worship: "That a man of Burnham's gifts should have been able for a while to think of Nazism as something rather admirable, something that could and probably would build up a workable and durable social order, shows what damage is done to the sense of reality by the cultivation of what is now called 'realism.'" The problem of reconciling this later view, which I agree with, and Lasswell's earlier "realism" will be addressed in the second section of this essay (Orwell no date, 176–181).

about "the possibility that we are moving toward a world of 'garrison states' – a world in which the specialists on violence are the most powerful group in society" (Lasswell 1941: 455). His article suggests the same orientational concern as Orwell's, the desire to focus attention on a possible development of tremendous, negative value relevance. Listen to Lasswell's abstract of that article; it could almost equally well describe *1984*:

> The trend of the time is away from the dominance of the specialist on bargaining, ... the businessman, and toward the supremacy of the specialist on violence, the soldier. ... It is probable that the ruling elite of the garrison state will acquire most of the skills that we have come to accept as part of modern civilian management ... especially skill in the manipulation of symbols in the interest of morale and public relations. Unemployment will be "psychologically" abolished. Internal violence will be directed principally against unskilled manual workers and counter-elite elements who have come under suspicion. ... The practice will be to recruit the elite according to ability (in periods of crisis); authority will be dictatorial, governmentalized, centralized, integrated. ... The power pyramid will be steep, but the distribution of safety will be equalized (the socialization of danger under modern conditions of aerial warfare). ... The elites will seek to hold in check the utilization of the productive potentialities of modern science and engineering for nonmilitary consumption goods.
>
> (Lasswell 1941: 455)

Here is an independent, earlier version of *1984*, closer to it in outline than any of the book's literary precursors by Swift, Kipling, Wells, Huxley, Chesterton or Zamiatin. Globally a self-perpetuating militarized technocracy rules a world made up of garrison states. Objective standards of rationality partly govern the elite's actions; not so the masses. Frequent "war scares" mean that often unconscious fears of death are ceremonialized and ritualized. "This is one of the subtlest ways by which the individual can keep his mind distracted from the discovery of his own timidity" (Lasswell 1941: 466). We see as well an Orwellian deflection of economic capacity away from true improvements in the standard of living; military construction and expenditure are mentioned as ways of satisfying this need. The use of propaganda, a moderately egalitarian income distribution and drugs are suggested to be effective ways of undercutting criticism. Terror is also a routine instrument of domestic rule.

Although there is no explicit discussion of imperialism as a necessary feature of the garrison state in Lasswell's 1941 article, violent chauvinistic expansionism is associated with modern war crises in his earlier work. In 1934, Lasswell identified the pervasive, worldwide expectation of violence with the "drastic redefinition of the situation in directions gratifying to the underindulged, unreflecting, incautious, and spontaneous patterns of culture and personality," obviously including aggressiveness among them. In particular the "insecurities connected with the war symbol are partially disposed of by vigorously asserting the 'we' symbol at the expense of the 'they' symbol." Conditions for the maintenance of peace in an insecure world by a power-balancing process are investigated including the measurability of variations in power (conceived as fighting effectiveness), the convertibility and distributability of power among balances, the early visibility of power variations and the sentimentibility of the power estimation process and found not likely to be met in the modern age of complex technologies and highly mobilized mass publics. Rather, contemporary Great Power war crises are associated with a culture of chauvinism, an exacerbated "we/they" thinking, "the most extreme form of truculent assertion ... an excited demand for the limitless, violent expansion of the nation" (Lasswell 1950: 57, 74, 84).

Shared resistance to propaganda about inevitable and beneficial directions of political change

We see how Lasswell's developmental analysis of political hierarchies in the world crisis of the 1930s led him to the same preoccupations as Orwell. But the similarity was even closer: both Lasswell and Orwell took a hard, critical look at the political *myths* (including the utopias) by which all polities, including imperialist democracies and totalitarian states, sustain themselves. Both studied the self-deceiving justifications of imperialism (Orwell's *Burmese Days* and Chapter 6 of Lasswell's *World Politics and Personal Insecurity*); Orwell's devastating study of the betrayal of socialist revolutionary principles, *Animal Farm*, corresponds in many ways to Lasswell's functionalist, at times empathetic, but ultimately sardonic treatment of the Russian revolution as the "second bourgeois revolution, conducted in the name of the proletariat" (Lasswell 1965 [originally 1951b] 29). Their criticisms extended to Marxist arguments about the inevitability of proletarian victories under socialism. When a hierarchical alternative was considered – a totalitarian world of collectivist oligarchies or a world of garrison states – these also were treated as possibilities, not inevitabilities. Both Orwell and Lasswell lived rationally in a world of limited but distinct political possibilities.

Let me consider in more detail this correspondence of views on the possibility of coercive, hierarchical world order alternatives to genuine international proletarianism. In *1984*, Goldstein's heretical/anarchist treatment of the anti-proletarian Ingsoc regime is entitled "The Theory and Practice of Oligarchical Collectivism"; the major world powers are treated as without significant ideological differences. Through an examination of Orwell's essays we can easily verify that both of these literary constructions were thought by Orwell to represent objective world tendencies. Reviewing favorably Franz Borkenau's *The Totalitarian Enemy*, in 1940, he was to treat the Hitler–Stalin pact as evidence that National Socialism *is* revolutionary socialism, but a socialism that crushes both the property owner and the worker. As a result, the communist and fascist regimes, "having started from opposite ends, are rapidly evolving toward the same system – a form of 'oligarchic collectivism'" (Orwell 1940, cited by Steinhoff 1976: 182).[4] In an essay for the *Observer* written in 1948, the same year as *1984*, Orwell argued that "the Russian Communists necessarily developed into a permanent ruling caste, or oligarchy, recruited not by birth but by adoption" (Orwell 1948, as cited by Steinhoff 1976: 182). Orwell feared the coming of a hierarchic world order of two or three superstates, with a semidivine caste at the top and something like slavery at the bottom; each state might be able to overcome any internal rebellion, but not to conquer the others, perpetuating itself through complete severance from the outside world and the crisis atmosphere of a continuous phony war.[5]

As early as 1934, Lasswell saw Marxism as "the strongest protest symbolism with revolutionary demands and universal claims" (Lasswell 1950: 129) to historical and scientific supremacy. Writing in 1951, shortly after *1984* was finally published in the United States, Lasswell was to focus and sharpen his very similar argument about the communist elites in the Soviet Union and elsewhere:

---

[4] Crick is right to stress (1980: 260–263) the importance of "Inside the Whale" for understanding Orwell's gloomy views about the rise of totalitarianism, in part through the corruption of power-hungry, inexperienced intellectuals. That essay is reprinted in Orwell & Angus (eds. 1968: 493–527).

[5] I am paraphrasing an Orwell quote given by Steinhoff (1976: 183).

From the Communist standpoint there is no doubt about the truth: we are moving from capitalism to socialism, from the primacy of the bourgeoisie to the supremacy of the proletariat. However, the Marxist tradition is interpreted in many different ways. Machajski suggested that the most important development of our epoch is the rise to power, not of the working class as a whole, but rather of the intellectual worker, whose capital is his knowledge. Relying upon the superiority of knowledge, the intellectual wins the support of the manual workers, whom he exploits mainly for his own benefit. Of all theories of the place of the intellectual in history this is the most uncongenial to those who claim to speak in the name of the masses.

(Lasswell 1965: 29)

In a more general analysis of the correlates of a Cold War trend toward bipolarization of the world, and its associated basic characteristic of the "expectation of violence," Lasswell zeroes in on the Soviet elite as follows: "If we apply these categories to the bipolar situation, we find that the ruling elite of the Soviet world has the problem common to dictatorship of 'externalizing hostility' against the outside environment. Hence the ruling elite enjoys a continuing gain in internal power by sustaining a perpetual crisis" (Lasswell 1965: 69–70).

As a committed democratic socialist, Orwell did not mean his literary destruction of "the last man in Europe" as a prophecy, nor as an anti-leftist diatribe. It was a warning about likely consequences of an era of total (but artificially drawn out) war from whose effects English-speaking countries were not immune.[6]

As his more general analyses of bipolarity and chauvinistic responses to war crises suggest, Lasswell, too, thought in terms of more general trends and multiple options facing all of the major states. For example, *World Politics and Personal Insecurity* contains a delightful scenario for world unification in the interest of professors of social science, an "elite based on vocabulary, footnotes, questionnaires, and

---

[6] Both Crick (1980: 395) and Steinhoff (1976: 199) cite similar statements, offering interpretations similar to the one made here. To quote Orwell selectively from their citations: "Specifically the danger of the present trend toward a world like 1984 lies in the structure imposed on Socialist and on Liberal capitalist communities by the necessity to prepare for total war with the USSR and the new weapons, of which of course the atomic bomb is the most painful and the most publicized." "I believe also that totalitarian ideas have taken root in the minds of intellectuals everywhere, and I have tried to draw these ideas out to their logical consequences. The scene of the book is laid in Britain in order to emphasize that the English-speaking races are not innately better than anyone else and that totalitarianism, if not fought against, could triumph anywhere."

conditioned responses, against an elite based on vocabulary, poison gas, property, and family prestige" (Lasswell 1950: 20). More seriously, the last chapter is a hard-headed yet idealistic psychiatric discussion of the prerequisites of a just and (therefore more) stable world order. In his 1941 article, Lasswell recognizes four contending major world-symbol patterns: national democracy, the antiplutocratic thrust of the "axis" of National Socialistic powers, the Soviet-led version of the world proletariat and a truer world-proletarianism hostile to all the above alternatives. His sketched transition to a world of garrison states suggested their probable order of appearance as "Japan in China, Germany, Russia, United States of America" (Lasswell 1941: 467–468). Although his 1951 monograph elaborates most tellingly variants of Machajski's hypothesis about "the world revolution of the middle income skill groups," also referred to as the "unnamed revolution" and the "permanent revolution of modernizing intellectuals," Lasswell juxtaposes Orwellian trend statements about totalitarianism, militarization, and bipolarization with a contrary tendency toward the worldwide interdetermination of human actions. And he is open, indeed more positive than Orwell, about our new world of intellectual elitism in the sense that from "the standpoint of human dignity the probable result cannot be foretold with confidence" (Lasswell 1965: 92).

The fearsome novelty of new totalitarian state forms

It should be emphasized, against those political scientists who want to treat all modern nation states as the same, that both Orwell and Lasswell saw something fundamentally new occurring in the twentieth century. It was founded in the development of technical civilization and modern propaganda, combined in the unprecedented, highly controlled mobilization of popular enthusiasm for total wars. Thus even Orwell's discussion of the "future England" recognizes the fundamental role of newer skill groups, people of indeterminate social class:

> The old pattern is gradually changing into something new .... To that new civilization belong the people who are most at home in and most definitely *of* the modern world, the technicians and the higher paid skilled workers, the airmen and the mechanics, the radio experts, film producers, popular journalists and industrial chemists. They are the indeterminate stratum at which the older class distinctions are beginning to break down. (Orwell 1941 in Crick 1980: 27)

The conspicuous role of symbol manipulators in these newer social formations is worthy of comment. But Orwell went further, arguing in 1939 that:

> The terrifying thing about the modern dictatorships is that they are something entirely unprecedented. Their end cannot be foreseen ... it may be just as possible to produce a breed of men who do not wish for liberty as to produce a breed of hornless cows. The Inquisition failed, but then the Inquisition had not the resources of the modern state. The radio, press censorship, standardized education and the secret police have altered everything. Mass-suggestion is a science of the last twenty years, and we do not yet know how successful it will be.[7]

He recognized that war "is the greatest of all agents of change" (Orwell 1941: 94, discussed in Crick 1980: 275). Indeed, he saw as frightening and new the emergence of total states at war with one another and, as we have seen, feared such developments were likely in England after the war even if Hitler was defeated.[8]

As we have seen, these themes are also Lasswellian; Lasswell's sense of revolutionary change corroborates Orwell's on all these points. Not only was his first book on revolutionary war propaganda, he was deeply interested in the role of intellectuals (once defining them as "symbol specialists") (Lasswell 1951: 85–86). He considered totalitarianization as a world trend, defining it as "the subordinating of society to government, and the concentration of all governmental power into a few hands, perhaps ultimately in the hands of a self-perpetuating caste of police officers." Since centralization was a function of perceived common threat, war obviously had a lot to do with the trend. Technically, the most important "developments in this connection are the devices for abolishing privacy" (Lasswell 1965: 77). How strongly these trends point in the direction of the totalitarian states of *1984*!

Science, commitment and power

Among their various shared concerns – science fiction utopias, the genuinely emancipatory outcomes of revolutionary struggles around the world, and the pathologies of power-hungry individuals, but not

---

[7] "Review of *Russia Under Soviet Rule* by N. de Basily," reprinted in Orwell and Angus (1968, 1: 378–381). Both Crick (1980: 247–249) and Steinhoff (1976: 183–185) cite and discuss this review.

[8] I accept Crick's judgment (p. 307) about Orwell's views concerning future post-war totalitarian possibilities; it correlates with numerous statements by Orwell, including his essay "Inside the Whale."

political psychiatry *per se* – several more correspondences between Orwell and Lasswell will be discussed here. Since Orwell was a writer and a journalist and Lasswell a political scientist, obviously their professional engagements were not identical. But both men had a lot to say about the hierarchy-renewing temptations of power, as well as the honesty, detachment and political commitments of intellectuals.

The corruption of intellectuals

Several elements of Orwell's indictment of his fellow intellectuals have already been mentioned or implied: their self-serving betrayal of egalitarian revolutionary ideals; their lack of the experience that ordinary people have had in practice with the totalitarian ideals (like "necessary murder") that many intellectuals of his time theoretically espoused; the corruption of their honesty or moral decency by power or the hunger for power. One quotation from his essays will suffice: "It was only *after* the Soviet regime became unmistakably totalitarian that English intellectuals, in large numbers, began to show an interest in it ... . The American James Burnham ... is really voicing their secret wish: ... to destroy the old, equalitarian version of Socialism and usher in a hierarchical society where the intellectual can at last get his hands on the whip" (Orwell 1968: 179).[9]

This quotation suggests some of the bitter forces behind Orwell's critique of power-corrupted intellectual work, a major theme in much of his political writing. His implicit critique of this tendency in *1984* is given specific content through his literary construction of doublethink. It is therefore worth repeating some of the book's analysis of the central generating principles of public intellectual life in Oceania. The analysis for "Ignorance is Strength" starts with a great falsehood itself: a theory – like those James Burnham and the early Lasswell subscribed

---

[9] An anonymous reviewer of this essay has suggested that Lasswell's commitments to "value free," empiricist social science reinforced his own "corruption as an intellectual," his empathetic, power-oriented complicity with the "treason of the clerks" that Julian Benda, Orwell and, more recently, Noam Chomsky have so brilliantly and passionately criticized. Indeed, in Chomsky (1969), some of Lasswell's closest associates – Daniel Lerner, Ithiel Pool and Lucian Pye – and Lasswell himself are effectively targeted. Accepting much of the force of such criticisms, my essay nonetheless attempts to suggest several ways Lasswell's own intellectual development, his historical sensitivity, and his uniquely influential disciplinary self-understanding may be seen as profound responses to them. There was, I believe, an underappreciated, Orwellian moralist inside Harold Lasswell as well.

to – that there are three eternally existing classes whose interests are entirely irreconcilable with each other. This is contradicted within a page or two in Goldstein's *Theory of Oligarchic Collectivism* by the admission that authoritarian political theories had done their best to discredit revolutionary beliefs in the rights of man, freedom of speech and equality before the law just at the time when technical progress made it possible to realize these ideals: "The earthly paradise had been discredited at exactly the moment when it became realizable." One is led to infer that the ignorance of the masses is their strength, but only within a powerful, regimented and hierarchical state based on lies (the denial of the existence of objective reality, the continued mutation of the past, and total ignorance about the real people of the other superstates) serving the interests of the powerful elite.

"War is Peace" is given a similar, devastating analysis. When it became clear that "an all-round increase in wealth threatened the destruction – indeed, in some sense was the destruction – of a hierarchical society," perpetual, potentially disastrous but never decisive imperialistic warfare evolved as a way of killing the expectation and reality of increased material well-being for the proletarian masses. By thus preventing revolutionary protest, it gave the party elites and most of the proles (outside the imperialistic battlegrounds) a kind of anxiety-full peace. Of the two central war aims of the party, neither was realistic; yet doublethink encouraged their passionate, self-contradictory pursuit. The first, the desire to conquer the entire earth, destroyed the surplus products of human labor; it was neither feasible nor based on an objective vital national interest other than elite perpetuation. The other, the extinguishing "once and for all of the possibility of independent thought," was mightily encouraged by "war hysteria" (producing something like Lasswell's chauvinistic "drastic redefinitions" of the objective conflict situation); it flew in the face of the need of party managers for rational assessment.

Finally, for "Freedom is Slavery," I offer my own, Orwellian reconstruction. This self-contradictory slogan ironically contradicts the major emancipatory thrust of Western civilization. That thrust might briefly be characterized as movement toward materially supported, life-serving, rationally redeemable, self-realizing, mutually supporting forms of individual and collective self-determination. Consistent with the political economic analysis of the previous paragraph, this liberating thrust being is equated with obsessive compulsive adherence to an imposed ideal: such goals are to be given up by Oceanians,

just as they have been given up by the collectivist death worshippers of
1984's Eastasia. *1984* for many of its less politicized readers is most
importantly the totalitarian, statist destruction of Winston Smith's
human identity by his forced renunciation of the intimate, idiosyncratic
intensely personal fulfillment, self-understanding and interpersonal
commitment achieved through his love for Julia.

One might even take Orwell's irony one level higher: the party elite
of Oceania is itself obsessively enslaved by the constant "necessity" of
combating the potential freedom of thought and action of those
amongst or outside their numbers who might revolt against them. The
"autonomy" which Oceania "enjoys" in perpetuating itself is at the
same time the slavery of *all* its subjects. Like Hegel's lord-bondsman
relationship, the "free" dominion of the master enslaves both the
master and his serf.

In concluding this brief review of the generating principles of
doublethink, I shall not list lots of contemporary examples of Oceania's
obfuscating Newspeak. Any citizen of our society can, with care, fill in
examples: limiting myself to the Reagan Administration, "Ignorance is
Strength" vividly came to mind when Admiral Poindexter told
millions of American citizens that there are important things about
how their government is conducted "that they don't want to know,"
and "War is Peace" achieved renewed resonance when Secretary of
Defense Weinberger called mass-murdering MX missiles "Peace-
makers." That Soviet leaders practiced similar deceptions is evident
from the degree of misunderstanding Soviet citizens regularly exhibited concerning the "defensive" character of their government's own
force buildup. It is worth quoting Crick's judgment of Orwell's
transpartisan, intellectual consistency: "Orwell did not denounce intelligence or possibly intellectualism .... He was no anti-intellectual as
such, only against most of the self-styled intellectuals of the 1930s
vintage," whose loss of objectivity and critical independence he so
viciously attacked (Crick 1980: 274–275).

It is perhaps more surprising to discover that, at least in the last
years of his life, Lasswell, too, found intellectuals to have been severely
deficient, in particular with respect to the perpetuation of the power-
oriented war system, sustained by and contributing to a continuing
worldwide pattern of expectations of international violence. The most
eloquent statement of these views, which can be found in several of his
papers from the late 1960s, occurs in a paper given first to the
American Psychological Association, entitled "Must Science Serve

Political Power?" (Lasswell 1969). Presumably Lasswell chose a non-political science audience as more likely to be sympathetic to such views. Given that "science works for power," his explanatory focus is on the inner reward structure of knowledge institutions, those that cement parochial relationships of mutual interest within the societies where they reside. Scientists do not do much better than the "militantly competitive elites of the opulent and knowledgeable powers." On the basis of prototypical contextual considerations, he concludes that in the aggregate scientists "contribute more directly to the service of war and oligarchy than to world security and the welfare of the whole community" (Lasswell 1969: 5). In part, Orwell's tendencies have actually been realized.

Beyond power-hungry personalities

The careful reader of this essay (and its footnotes) will recall a particularly problematical point in my attempted reconciliation of Orwell and Lasswell, on the basis of which I want to argue how problems of international hierarchy might fruitfully be studied. Like Goldstein's partly fabricated theory of the eternal three classes and Burnham's analysis of politics as a perpetual swindle of the occasionally revolutionary masses, Lasswell's early Machiavellian political "realism" clearly conflicts with Orwell's belief in the possibility of democratic socialism by personalities far different from those allowed to survive in garrison or totalitarian states. Here, too, a remarkable essay on "Democratic Character" represents an evolution in Lasswell's perspective, one much more consistent with Orwell's most mature views (Lasswell 1951a). Lasswell's famous formula for political man,

$$p \} d \} r = P$$

suggests how private motives (p) are displaced onto public objects (d), followed by rationalization (r) in terms of certain positions about the public interest.[10] His discussion of the structure of the democratic character is motivated by a long quotation from *The Authoritarian Personality*, the first part of which confirms this projective formula:

---

[10] Lasswell (1950: 39n) gives both this formula and earlier citations. At this point I must note that both Lasswell and Orwell regularly used the now outdated, and to my mind chauvinistic, linguistic convention where "man" refers to "man or woman." Because of the frequency of such quotations, in the present essay I have resisted giving "The last woman in Europe" and "political woman" their due.

"Thus a basically hierarchical, authoritarian, exploitive parent-child relationship is apt to carry over into a power-oriented, exploitively dependent attitude toward one's sex partner and one's God and may culminate in a political philosophy and social outlook which has no room for anything but a desperate clinging to what appears to be a strong and disdainful rejection of whatever is relegated to the bottom." The tendency toward rigid, convention-bound, dichotomous handling of ingroup-outgroup cleavages resonates with Lasswell's much earlier discussions of the chauvinistic consequences of war crises. But a more democratic alternative is also identified by the author of *The Authoritarian Personality*. "There is a pattern characterized chiefly by affectionate, basically egalitarian, and permissive interpersonal relationships ... encompassing attitudes within the family and toward the opposite sex, as well as an internationalization of religious and social values. Greater flexibility and the potentiality for more genuine satisfactions appear as results of this basic attitude" (Lasswell 1951a: 508, citing Adorno *et al.* 1950: 971).

No longer is political man prototypically Machiavellian. Lasswell's extraordinarily creative and affirmative response to the preoccupation in American intellectual circles with the authoritarian personality is to formulate an empirically assessable democratic alternative and discuss the conditions affecting the likelihood of its emergence and persistence. Given a newly articulated commitment to human dignity defined operationally in terms of the wide sharing of many values, democratic character is now said to be "cast into relief" by its alternative, *homo politicus*, who relishes the pursuit of power by the use of power, which definitionally for Lasswell involves the capacity to invoke severe sanctions. "Since we understand that power relationships have, or are assumed by the participants to possess, the element of severe deprivation, it is apparent that the human being who is fascinated by power is out of harmony with our basic concept of human dignity" (Lasswell 1951a: 498). The self-system of the democratic character, because it has not been crushed by pervasive experiences of low self-esteem, evidences "deep confidence in the benevolent potentialities of man." How antithetical to *1984*! Its value demands are multiple; it is "disposed to share rather than hoard or to monopolize." Its "open ego" is "warm rather than frigid, inclusive and expanding rather than exclusive and constricting," capable of friendship and "unalienated from humanity." Its energy system is free from anxiety, having "at its disposal the energies of the unconscious part of the personality" (Lasswell

1951a: 514). In his old age Lasswell, too, seems to have become more democratic, more optimistic, even idealistic about the potentialities of his fellow man: "Can the violence system be changed into a nonviolent system? Can this transformation be brought about nonviolently? The answer, I submit, is yes" (Lasswell 1968). Corresponding to Orwell's internationalism, Lasswell's old, idealistic search for a world-unifying myth and technique has been fulfilled.

Political commitments: patriotism and internationalism

Orwell considered himself a radical patriot; though a supporter of the British war effort, he saw World War II as a revolutionary socialist opportunity in England and steadfastly opposed British imperialism in India and Burma. He was an anti-nationalist, and therefore in some sense an internationalist. These terms are most fully defined and illustrated in his 1941 volume on "The Lion and the Unicorn: Socialism and the English Genius," and in his 1945 essay "Notes on Nationalism." "By 'patriotism' I mean devotion to a particular place and a particular way of life, which one believes to be the best in the world but has no wish to force upon other people." "Nationalism" means "first of all the habit of assuming that human beings can be classified like insects and that whole blocks ... of people can be confidently labeled 'good' or 'bad.'" Secondly, nationalism refers to "the habit of identifying oneself with a single nation or other unit, placing it beyond good and evil and recognizing no other duty than that of advancing its interests." Thus a "nationalist is one who thinks solely, or mainly in terms of competitive prestige." The "nationalist" is broadly defined; the concept is meant to refer as an overdrawn extreme type to neo-Toryism, communism, pacifism, ethnic nationalisms, class feelings, etc. It has extremely negative connotations: "Nationalism is power hunger tempered by self-deception. Every nationalist is capable of serving something bigger than himself – unshakably certain of being in the right" (Orwell and Angus 1968: 362–363). In extreme cases nationalism is characterized by high degrees of obsession with the superiority of one's own power unit, the instability of political loyalties to it, and indifference to belief-contradicting reality. Telling illustrations include the varying attitudes of different British intellectuals toward the political capacities, the economic performances, and the atrocities committed by Allied and enemy powers before and during World War II.

One is reminded of Lasswell's indictment of chauvinism, his critique of national imperialistic movements as driven in reality by the demand for supremacy. In 1934 he characterized "modern national imperialism" as "a mass demand for permanent control over peoples of alien culture, to be attained by force if necessary, and justified by allegations of mutual advantage" (Lasswell 1950: 117). But Lasswell went further toward a communitarian internationalism than even Orwell. Distinguishing between a world *public order* sustained by potentially violent sanctions and a world *civic order* relying on non-violent sanctions in support of concerted action, he called for a transnational World Community Association to foster "metro-global community, meaning a world organized as voluntarily as possible among the emerging metropolitan centers of the globe." His varied set of economic, social, educational and political activities for this association he described as "the preparation of a new world within the framework of the old" (Lasswell 1968: 122–123). Proposing an attack on the war system, he attacked the world public order's nationalistic biases by advocating "the break up of national power monopolies by dividing the giant powers into small powers and consolidating an international organization strong enough to maintain at least minimum public order and to prevent barriers to the movement of persons and goods" (Lasswell 1967: 14).[11]

Both Lasswell and Orwell patriotically supported their governments during World War II, Lasswell working for the Office of War Information and Orwell orchestrating broadcasts to India by the BBC. But as we have seen, their patriotism did not prevent them from taking, at one time or another, radically revisionist attitudes toward world order. Our Orwellian Lasswell sounds more like Richard Falk, their radical internationalist descendant, than Machiavelli, Vilfredo Pareto or Henry Kissinger!

Political commitments: decency, dignity and democratic socialism

Against power-hungry intellectuals Orwell regularly appealed to the decency and morality of the ordinary citizen. He made no secret of his

---

[11] This essay, along with the call for simultaneity in revolts against the war system, suggests (p. 2) "The obvious hypothesis ... that unless the war system were supported by the socio-economic system, and the socio-economic system were supported by the war system, the institution of war would long since have disappeared from human culture."

political commitments. In the famous essay "Why I Write," which was written in 1946 and chosen to introduce his *Collected Essays*, Orwell states that "every line of serious work that I have written since 1936 has been written, directly or indirectly, *against* totalitarianism and *for* democratic Socialism, as I understand it" (Orwell and Angus 1968: 5).

Lasswell, on the other hand, despite his democratic "repugnance and apprehension" toward the garrison state, did not to my knowledge identify himself as a socialist. Moreover, his political commitments and his professional scientific work were argued to be rigorously separate. Thus he emphatically introduced his influential conceptualization of political analysis, *Power and Society* (1950), by first recognizing "the existence of two distinct components of political theory – the empirical propositions of political science and the value judgments of political doctrine." He then went on to state flatly that "only statements of the first kind are explicitly formulated in the present work" (Lasswell and Kaplan 1950: xiii). If Lasswell were consistent across his writings, this would be a sharp difference in political and professional orientation between Orwell the journalist and Lasswell the political scientist. But Lasswell was not consistent.

Orwell was active in the League for the Dignity and Rights of Man, which tried to define democracy in a multivalued way, going beyond nineteenth-century liberalism (Crick 1980: 344–345). Lasswell's concern for the multivalued democratic character correlated with a new commitment of his own in the post-World War II era to the policy sciences of human dignity. Personality and culture were inwardly dependent, often mutually reinforcing. Therefore, along with a commitment to democracy comes a commitment to a kind of personality most likely to realize and perpetuate such values. "A democratic community is one in which human dignity is realized in theory and fact. It is characterized by wide rather than narrow participation in the shaping and sharing of values" (Lasswell 1951a: 523–525).

Notice what, operationally, these vague standards are supposed to mean. "Power is shared when in fact there is general participation in decision-making," when it is assumed that "office-holders can be criticized without fear of serious retaliation," and "there is a presumption against the use of power in great concentration, particularly in the form of regimentation, centralization, and militarization."

Although there is to be a strong presumption of the widest possible scope for voluntary choice and privacy, the political myth of a democratic community "emphasizes the desirability of congenial human relationships."

In economic terms, both in expectation and reality, democracy means "security of basic income is guaranteed in theory and fact," that "opportunities are open to every capable person to earn more than the basic income. A balanced, graduated distribution of income is valued and realized, preventing a division of the community into 'rich' and 'poor.'" An expectation of continuing economic growth is also part of Lasswell's democratic myth. Although this may be associated in many minds with liberal "trickle down" rationalizations, it should be recalled that in *1984* these expectations were killed by wealth-consuming perpetual warfare; the consequence was the easier justification of a hierarchical society on the basis of a presumed scarcity of economic rewards (Lasswell 1951a: 476–477).

Orwell's democratic socialism was non-Marxist and atheoretical. It allowed for altruistic, non-material motivational elements in human nature. It connoted "liberty, equality and internationalism," or "political democracy, social equality and internationalism." In his famous phrase, "Liberty is the right to tell people what they do not want to hear" (Crick 1980: 306, 362 and Orwell no date). Operationally speaking, with Lasswell's commitment to basic needs-oriented economics, and Orwell's distrust of centralized, bureaucratic socialism, are these two political commitments really very different after all?

One may still ask whether these remarkably similar value commitments extend fully into their professional attitudes toward political commitment. In his writing Lasswell at times seems, like most behavioral political scientists, to follow the model of value neutrality supposed to guide the scientist; Orwell clearly belongs in the tradition of the critical humanist. Even acknowledging the importance Orwell placed on logical argument (symbolically the absurdity of $2 + 2 = 5$ in *1984*, a slogan actually blazing forth from Moscow apartment buildings during the Stalin era) and an objective truth (which totalitarian ideologies tend to distort or deny), my "convergence" thesis seems in real trouble.

This difficulty disappears, however, when the Orwellian Lasswell speaks out movingly at the end of his powerful, affirmative essay on democratic character:

To some extent descriptive probing into the processes of political life has been held back by inapplicable analogies from the natural sciences. It is insufficiently acknowledged that the role of scientific work in human relations is *freedom* rather than prediction. By freedom is meant the bringing into the focus of awareness of some feature of the personality which ... has been operating "automatically and compulsively." The individual is now free to take the factor into consideration in the making of future choices. This enlargement of the scope of freedom is the most direct contribution of the study of interpersonal relations to democracy. Hence it is the growth of insight, not simply of the capacity of the observer to predict the future operation of an automatic compulsion, or of a non-personal factor, that represents the major contribution of the scientific study of interpersonal relations to policy. From the classical inheritance we have no static tradition, but a vast panorama of inspiration and suggestion for the reshaping of all civilizations and all cultures toward the goal of free men in a society at once universal and free.

(Lasswell 1951a: 523–525)

Lasswell may be more grandiose than Orwell; his prose may only approximate Orwell's eloquence on rare occasions. But Lasswell's political psychiatry is grounded in the same tradition of critical and constructive humanism as Orwell's. The deep emancipatory interest of both men in a world order transcending imperialistic power politics and diminishing the resulting hierarchical patterns of domination shines through their work.[12]

Democratic possibilities after 1984

Having established at least several non-contradictory identifications, expectations, and demands characteristic of the Orwellian Lasswell, I must now answer the question, "What does he say to the post-1984 world?" Do not the preoccupations of World War II and its aftermath seem long out of date? Has not international political science progressed to the extent that the journalistic writing and psychoanalytically informed hypotheses of the 1930s and 1940s are obsolete? I hope

[12] Emancipation is discussed as well in Lasswell's much earlier work (1934: 98), where its "fullest psychological sense" is limited "to the achievement of release from an internalized symbol of authority." What a change some fifteen years later! I am reminded of the curious convergence between the "iron cages" of Orwell and Weber. Nothing is a more powerful symbol of dehumanizing totalitarian terror in *1984* (see Chapter 6).

the title of this concluding section does not suggest too narrowly partisan a view.[13]

An Orwellian Lasswell is a scholar committed to a world of greater human dignity, of wider value-sharing as an overriding objective of his or her political analysis, patriotic but internationalist. The oligarchic collectivism of swollen military establishments, the bureaucratically entrenched and corporate wealth has little attraction at home or abroad. Now that 1984 has come and gone, it is clear that Orwell's worst case of a hierarchical world of totalitarian garrison states, of invulnerable, deeply hypocritical, war-based reproductive mechanisms has *not* been *fully* realized. For that we should be thankful.

Detailed discussion of the degree of movement toward or away from that conception are worth continuing analysis. Compared to 1941 or 1944, I believe we have moved back from that nightmare. Comparing 1984 and 1948, before the end of the Cold War, I was not so sure of the direction of movement, especially if we take the boundaries of Oceania for such comparisons: England plus the Americas.

Cold War hysteria was again alive and well. The terror used by elites to control the peripheries of these regions over the last several decades had been enormous. The partial demilitarization of the "Southern cone," ironically in part due to revanchist colonialism in Britain concerning Gibraltar and the Malvinas, was being compensated for by the Vietnamization of Central America. Cuba's export of doctors and educators was unfortunately matched by military assistance, not all (viz., Grenada) oriented strictly toward the increase of human dignity. A small fraction of the arms expenditures in the region since 1948 could have ended poverty there by 1984. Freedom of speech was still paid for with one's life, one's job, or personal independence in too many places.[14]

---

[13] The next few pages reflect their 1984 APSA origins. On the state of international relations research in the United States then, see Alker and Biersteker (1984) and Ashley (1984).

[14] See the publications of Ruth Sivard and of the Bariloche group for further relevant quantitative analyses, particularly Amílcar D. Herrera, *et al.* (1976).

On the more journalistic side, an excellent, informed critique of the "distortions, disingenuous statements, tortuous interpretations, half-truths" (and outright lies) of congressional testimony and public declarations by American policy-makers concerning Central America, so reminiscent of Vietnam, is Raymond Bonner (1984); the quotation is from p. 9. We learn how American Presidents have certified progress in human rights to have occurred even when Archbishop Oscar Arnulfo Romero is publicly assassinated with apparent impunity for such "communistic" views as the claim, surely consistent with human dignity, that "the root of all violence is

But an Orwellian Lasswell committed to real democracy had the right, indeed the obligation, to cry out: America, where has your commitment to human dignity, to decency gone? Right-wing authoritarians solicitous of the economic privacy of their richest supporters are not "dignified" by that respect for "freedom," which can mean virtual economic slavery for most of their fellow countrymen and women. Our foreign policies promote the same bimodalization of world income that we are seeing at home.[15] The Soviet Union avoids large redistributional aid programs by blaming all inequalities on capitalism, yet through its allies it competitively contributes to the militarization of Asia, Africa and even (to a much lesser extent) Latin America. Compared even to the oil-rich Arab states, the United States gives less real developmental aid, and sells many more weapons. In perhaps half the receiving countries such "assistance" is not primarily justifiable by external threats to national security. Compared to 1960, militarization of the Third World has probably increased (Falk 1981). For too many of the rural poor, family sizes are still too large because development has stagnated. One of the few arenas of cooperation among the superpowers is in their fated attempt to limit the monopoly of nuclear terror to the great powers. Terrorism of the weak competes on unequal terms with the state terrorism of the strong. There are many more affronts to human equality and dignity in the Cold War world of 1984 that need to be criticized.

Surely an Orwellian Lasswell has something important to say as well about "realism" as an intellectual style of political analysis, especially when promoted nationalistically, as it often is by those whose preoccupation with power-prestige tends to make them argue that military self-help is a universal necessity. Let us accept that in the 1930s too many idealists ignored the ominous implications of the foreign policies of the United States, Britain, Japan, Italy, France, the Soviet Union and Germany. But one who is moved to change a world political order that is in many ways a continuing affront to human dignity should not treat it merely as a natural phenomenon, a tragic necessity whose harmful effects might hopefully be minimized. Elite

institutional violence. The situation in the country is lamentable, particularly among peasants and slum dwellers. The rich are getting richer, the poor are getting poorer" (p. 43).

[15] The domestic evidence on bimodalization is assessed in Joshua Cohen and Joel Rogers (1984) and Thomas B. Edsall (1985). Relevant international evidence is in the book cited in the previous note.

authoritarianism, "realist" national security priorities, and exploitive, systemic role-rule structures *inner-act*, more often in a mutually supportive than a self-contradictory way. By not recognizing the role realist foreign policy practices play in the legitimating of international domination, such scholars become apologists for the systemic status quo. The conditions for the reproduction of such systems need continually and contextually to be studied; practices that constructively undermine them need to be identified and explored.

An Orwellian Lasswell speaks as well to the fashioning of concepts we use to comprehend and steer ourselves through the often difficult and insecure world of international politics. Sanctioning power is an essential feature of world politics; economics can not be fully separated from politics. Using thought models from instrumentalist, utilitarian economics obscures the coercive underside of supposedly free and voluntary market exchanges. Their costs and benefits are more than economic; they include effects on the autonomy and dignity of national and subnational actors. Yet so many of our best modelers misunderstand themselves as riding starward the chariots of "high mathematical science" when what they are really doing might better be described as circling above congested unsafe airports, burning up precious fuel, going nowhere but up and down through clouds of ideological distortion, leaving many of their student passengers feeling more than a little queasy.

The narrative immediacy of Orwell, the configurative contextualism of Lasswell, and the systemic possibilism of my Orwellian Lasswell all suggest giving substantive names to contending possible sources of order in world politics. These names would be conceptually keyed to the varying recruitment, legitimation and perpetuation practices of these candidate orders. Surely, the organizing principles of international actions by and through major states deserves special attention. Liberal conceptions of utilitarian action are likely to be inadequate and inappropriate in much of the modern world. The extent to which communist, fascist, "friendly fascist," democratic nationalist, democratic socialist, neo-imperialist or totalitarian systems of practice are emerging, retreating and/or renewing themselves deserves special attention. As knowledgeable observers we must not be squeamish about criticism or rigidly parsimonious in the choice of conceptual equipment. We should look for winners *and* losers among contending world powers; see if together they make up a larger, coherent, extendable pattern of order; and go beyond the limiting grammar of utilitarian realism and the structuralism of power rankings in describing what is happening.

Nothing could be a more immediate reflection on the previous biographical construction than the urgency of orienting oneself, as concerned citizen or scholar, toward the emergent possibilities among the major contenders for world power. The extent to which these actors reflect, coproduce or reproduce newly emergent patterns of political practice is particularly noteworthy; the obsolescent, partial renewal of other concerted efforts, like nineteenth-century power balancing, must also be taken into account. Lenin used such a strategy in his brilliant, polemical, yet scientifically suggestive reconceptualization of turn-of-the-century imperialism. We have seen how hierarchical constructs like "oligarchic collectivism" and a world of "garrison states" were critically generalized reflections by Orwell and Lasswell of communist double-dealing in Spain and the Stalin–Hitler pact of 1939. The same could be said of totalitarianism, a concept and practice used by the losing German General Staff at the end of World War I, and borrowed, with amplifications, by Mussolini and Hitler later on. Totalitarianism's genuine novelty and unpredictability have been less at the focus of attention of international relations scholars than modern comparativists. On the other hand, Hannah Arendt, among others, has argued that Khrushchev's reforms helped end totalitarianism as the dominant mode of political life in the Soviet Union (Arendt 1968: Preface to vol. II). If this argument was more valid in the Gorbachev era, then "nationalistic" we/they rhetoric about "freedom vs. totalitarianism" was partially suspect. There is the possibility that a different kind of more authoritarian pluralism might be developing in world affairs, even after Soviet communism has ended.

Although mathematical modelers may have particular difficulties in paying attention to multiple, emergent-order possibilities, it is important to be able to empathize with the legitimating appeals of serious contenders without succumbing to them. Otherwise, all the biasing effects of nationalism (in Orwell's sense) will be at work. Neither are simple projections of short-term trends (like the non-aggression pact of Nazi Germany and Soviet Russia, or Germany's later advances in Russia that so impressed James Burnham, or the popularity of Reagan's foreign policy style) necessarily good indicators of longer-term trends. Orwell's writing had a peculiar cogency for ex-communists and Socialists; his books were even highly sought after by certain elites within the communist states of the Stalinist era.

They helped play a crucial orienting role. Lasswell's treatments of the betrayal of communist myths has more cogency for other leftists because of his acknowledgment of (and analysis of the reasons for) Marxism's enormous appeal. When he showed how democratic nationalism helped restrict, and in turn was partially incorporated by, the international relations of the Soviet Bloc, Lasswell benefited from his previous, analyses of National Socialism. Such states were partly changing into older, recognizable forms of tyranny and imperialism.

Patriotic political scientists are especially susceptible to the distorting temptations of national power or the fetishism of the state. After all, if we were not interested at least vicariously in the successes of the powerful and/or their supersession by the formerly powerless, we probably would not be very good at our jobs. But in an era riven by the expectation of violence, indeed the cataclysmic threat of aerial nuclear warfare, objectivity and decency were very hard to maintain. The "mental cheating" of doublethink was especially tempting in a jingoistic time.[16] But the self-righteous nostalgic hegemonism of imperial democracies, the rosy glow of Pax Britannica or Pax Americana, the superstate fetishism of English (and Russian) language international relations research have been serious problems for genuine self-understanding for a longer time than the language of the 1984 presidential campaign in the United States. They infected 1984 otherwise admirable scholarship. More academically speaking, self-serving theories and question-begging treatments of opponents – cheap putdowns directed toward those of alternative metatheoretical orientations – were too often the rule, especially toward the Marxist tradition of scholarship, which had much more scientific vigor in the First, Second, and Third Worlds than most behavioral "neorealists" were willing to admit.

Serious, uncoerced engagement with intellectuals from opposing and dominated states, as well as other traditions of interpretive scholarship, is both patriotic and scientifically defensible. Such activities can help finally correct such self-serving biases if only we come to realize that an international science of international politics oriented

---

[16] Alexander Zinoviev (1979, 1980) is the living political writer of my acquaintance who comes closest to continuing the Swift-Voltaire-Orwell tradition. Two profound and provocative semiformal, dialectically inspired treatments of Soviet doublethink are Jon Elster (1980) and Vladimir A. Lefebvre (1982). On the roots of American jingoism, see Michael Hunt's (1987) historical treatment.

toward the universalization of human dignity was possible in the late Cold War, where it had remarkable effects on Soviet intellectual elites unable to reciprocate such open self-critical engagement. It is possible now, in a world where many in the West see militant Islam as a fundamentalist threat. My Orwellian Lasswell, who tries to write and speak English that ordinary people can appreciate and understand, would argue that real freedom *transcends* slavery if by that we mean unending, proud, non-imperialistic dedication to the cause of a more democratic world order.

Part III
Contemporary humanistic reformulations

8   Fairy tales, tragedies and world histories:
Testable structuralist interpretations

A fairy tale fulfills the role of a social utopia.

Roman Jakobson (1973)

But like any living thing, the tale can generate only forms that resemble itself. If any cell of a tale organism becomes a small tale within a larger one, it is built ... according to the same rules as any fairy tale.

V. Propp (1977)

Essence is expressed by grammar.

Ludwig Wittgenstein (in Gier 1981)

Troubled times breed reflective thinkers. As inhabitants of such an era we join those from other ages, other disciplines and even other civilizations in the search for historical understanding. We try to make sense of the world we live in, in order to distinguish what we can change and what we cannot, to illuminate the choices we may make, to inspire informed hope and counsel reasoned caution in our descendants, giving dignity to our own brief lives, our contemporaries and those before and after us.

As a teacher of an historically oriented interdisciplinary course on theories of international relations, I am struck both by the centrality of these purposes in the literature I have recently assigned to my students, and the unsatisfactory nature of the interpretive accounts they provide. Among scholarly studies of our multifaceted predicament written in the last decade or so, perhaps the most attention catching have been:

    (a) the global modeling studies evoked by the Club of Rome's amplification of debates occasioned by Jay Forrester's *World Dynamics*;[1] and

    (b) the *Annales* style of modern world systems studies stimulated by Fernand Braudel's exemplary writings, starting with *La Méditerranée à l'Epoque de Philippe II*.[2]

Forrester offers a neo-Malthusian picture of the contradictory possibilities of further world growth that both complements and contradicts the post-Marxian image of the contradictory development of exploitive capitalism out of slowly changing feudal market relations and even more basic material-environmental rhythms offered by Braudel and his followers. Writers following either exemplary study are now exploring Kondratieff cycles (or other structures of long duration) and dynamic mechanisms of capital accumulation, innovation and exhaustion to try and account for the present troubled times of the world economy.[3]

I take it one of the reasons for the relative "success" of such studies is the extent to which the authors or their fellow workers have combined drama-like readability with an impression of historical and/or scientific trustworthiness and the quasi-metaphysical, almost inevitable grandeur to which seekers after encompassing truths are especially susceptible.[4]

---

[1]   Jay Forrester's (1971) Chapter 2 is entitled "Structure of the World System," while Chapter 4, titled "Limits to Growth," provides a key concept in consequent debates. Relevant commentaries included Karl W. Deutsch, Bruno Fritsch, Helio Jaguaribe, and Andrei S. Markovitz (1977); Christopher Freeman and Marie Jahoda (1978); Donella Meadows, John Richardson, and Gerhart Bruckmann (1982).

[2]   Published originally in 1949 in France (second revised edition, 1966), this work was described at its original thesis evaluation as "an epoch in world historiography." Based on the second revised edition, translated by Sian Reynolds, the English version, *The Mediterranean World in the Age of Philip II*, appeared in 1972. Samuel Kinser (1981) gives the citation for this quote at pp. 103ff. His otherwise bibliographically rich review of Braudel's influence makes no mention, however, of Braudel's considerable following among radical economists, sociologists or political scientists.

[3]   A rich body of relevant citations are given in Joshua Goldstein (1986). Three especially relevant alternative theoretical treatments of many of the same issues are Geoffrey Barraclough (1964), Richard Ashley (1980), and Johan Galtung (1980b).

[4]   Compare the somewhat similar treatment of the compulsive appeals of communist, democratic, nationalist, and fascist "myths" in Chapters 2 and 11 of Harold D. Lasswell's pioneering *World Politics and Personal Insecurity* (1950, originally, 1934). This book is also relevant to the highly dangerous myths about invincibility in total, including nuclear, war. Selected quotes include: [In a war crisis] "The flight into action is preferable to treatments of insecurity; the flight into danger becomes an insecurity to end insecurity" (75). "The dash into ... the war pattern offers supposed opportunities for the ... release of the blocked aggressions. The war crisis proceeds by redefining the world in terms of ... impending dangers" (pp. 82ff.).

Forrester's Systems Dynamics methodology provides highly explicit and precise deductive inferencing from hypothetical premises stated as non-linear integral-differential process models. Unfortunately these often are not or cannot be empirically tested against plausible alternatives using empirical data. Braudel's scientific style allusively combined extraordinarily rich, mostly narrative detail with necessarily fragmentary quantitative data on long-term ecological and economic rhythms of Mediterranean life. Although the regulating hypothesis of economic determinism often serves Braudel and his followers as a productive positive research heuristic because such movements do often influence or condition the world of macropolitical events, the impacts of the Renaissance, the Reformation and the often associated major wars and dynastic unifications of the early modern period are not given sufficient autonomous credit.

Neither approach appears to leave much room for individual or group responses to the enormous moral, economic and political issues raised by their accounts. It is hard work to generate testable hypotheses from either. Men and women may indeed make history, as Marx said, constrained by the contexts and choices history allows them. How and why they actually do so in many different particular situations is not yet very clear in these accounts.

One is reminded of Arnold Toynbee's monumental *A Study of History*, which succeeded in capturing the imagination of many throughout the English-speaking world during the decades of the 1940s and 1950s, characterized in 1956 by one of its critics as "undoubtedly the most widely known work of contemporary historical scholarship."[5] Despite Toynbee's claims to be scientific, and the incredible gathering of evidence presented in his volumes, most critics seem to have found Toynbee's arguments lacking in logical consistency and vulnerable to contrary interpretations. His formula of "challenge and response" and his stages theory of civilizations may be too mythical, too vague adequately to explain or foretell civilizational advances and declines, but at least it suggested important possibilities for heroic forms of human choice.

Life is not a myth or a fairy tale with a guaranteed happy ending;

---

[5] Ashley Montagu, ed. (1956: vii) The original study (Toynbee 1934–1954) contains ten volumes. D.C. Somervell's abridgement in two volumes (Toynbee 1960), has an especially analytical summary of Toynbee's "Argument," pp. 355–393 of the second volume, which makes clear the strong, but now neglected ecological themes in Toynbee's work.

neither is it an inevitable tragedy, one that encompasses all of Western civilization or the human species. Nor are most political or cultural leaders successfully heroic. Should one then refrain from attempting to give meaningful interpretations to world history? Or should one only try to refrain from being "ideological" in making such efforts, if it is indeed possible to do so? Can we indeed refrain from mythical, poetic or moralistic and ideological elements in writing scientific histories of the challenges, the limits and the potentialities of our times?

Despite the obvious and lasting value of a certain degree of scholarly detachment, I believe that in the last analysis all social-scientific research paradigms or theoretical traditions do have mythopoetic or moral-ideological elements explicitly or implicitly embedded in their "models of men" and of what they, and women, can or should become.[6] For example, Thucydides' classical "objective" study of the *Peloponnesian War* can convincingly be interpreted as a morality play in which vengeful gods or goddesses punish Athens for her moral *hubris*.[7] Like all other great story tellers, Marxists and Malthusians also have their moral and poetic aspects, which are revealed in the ways they try scientifically or unscientifically to interpret consistently, intelligibly and didactically the historical facts they have uncovered.

If some such argument is accepted, then we may ask these questions another way: Is there some improvement possible in the way historical accounts can be made testable as they approach value questions, structural constraints and human choice possibilities? Is there a way of making world historical accounts empirically revisable while at the same time allowing them to have the reflective character and dramatic force of a tragic morality play or the ironic happiness of a Russian fairy tale? Can our accounts of the significance of historical events somehow allow or even facilitate the evident ability of the greatest historical writers to catch our moral and political imaginations, and comment profoundly on the choices before us without losing our hard-won professional commitment to falsifiable scientific theorizing?[8]

Further reflection on the Braudel, Forrester or Toynbee examples

---

[6] The role of "models of men" (and women!) in research paradigm complexes is argued in both Alker (1982) and Alker and Hurwitz (1980: Ch. 2).

[7] These arguments are reviewed and supported in Chapter 1 above.

[8] Terminologically I here follow Imre Lakatos' impressive "rational reconstruction" of Kuhnian philosophy of science, *i.e.*, his "sophisticated methodological falsificationism," as discussed in Alker (1982) and the Introduction above. See also Alker (1984).

suggests additional epistemological and methodological questions. As Immanuel Wallerstein – the leading American proponent of the Braudelian approach – has provocatively suggested of an important difference in scientific styles: "Using the heavily narrative accounts of most historical research seems not to lend itself ... to quantification. ... It is a major tragedy of twentieth-century social science that so large a proportion of social scientists, facing this dilemma, have thrown in the sponge" (Wallerstein 1974: 8).

I do not think quitting is the right response to Wallerstein's challenge, just as I do not find entirely adequate the endless repetition of the often telling criticisms of Forrester's succumbing to neo-Malthusian ideology and his avoidance of superior econometric standards and procedures (which his historical data, however, often cannot support). Nor do I think that "quantification" is the only mode of formalization necessary or appropriate for the logical and empirical rigor and tractability that mathematical representations have given to so many of the natural and social sciences. We must broaden and deepen the universe of scientifically relevant modeling approaches appropriate for the formal analysis of interpretive and theoretical world histories. Historical evidence, much of it textual, should not *a priori* be reduced to quantitative time series, or otherwise ignored.

In developing novel scientific approaches to the great social scientific questions – the causal explanation of social actions, the interpretive understanding of historical patterns or the emancipatory realization of a higher level of human self-fulfillment – I propose to rely on the more systematic, increasingly formalized but still humanistic, critical and largely qualitative accounts of narrative possibilities suggested by writers like Propp, Jakobson, Breymond, Burke, Campbell, Foucault, Frye, Lakoff, Lukács, Prince, Ricoeur, Todorov, Schank and Abelson and other contemporary literary critics, cognitive scientists or text linguists.[9]

Rather than argue the view, common among East European scholars, that Marxian theories can also be formalized in ways mathematically equivalent to Forrester's System Dynamics, my emergent proposal is that historical limits and possibilities are better understood in terms of

[9] Had I read George Lakoff's unpublished MIT bachelor's thesis (Lakoff 1962) before I wrote the first version of this chapter, it would have saved me a lot of time! It contains many of the basic ideas independently developed here. A comprehensive, more recent introductory bibliography of text linguistics is Robert de Beaugrande and Wolfgang Dressler (1981). See also Breymond (1973) and Ricoeur (1983).

such formal constructs as Schank–Abelson scripts (Schank and Abelson 1977), Lehnert-Ricoeur-White plot summarizations,[10] or the context-sensitive, transformational story grammars of Lakoff, Prince, Todorov, Mandler and Johnson, Berke, etc.

These mathematical constructs have their origins in nineteenth-century Biblical criticism – notably the hermeneutics of Von Hahn and Rank[11] – and early structuralist accounts of Russian fairy tales – notably Propp's pioneering work (Propp 1977, originally 1928, in Russian), as well as recent work in logic, philosophy, mathematical linguistics and computer science. And since both qualitative and quantitative causal relationships may be expressed within them, they have the potential at least, of subsuming world modeling efforts within a less deterministic, more choice-oriented, possibilist mode of scientific understanding.

Of course, we cannot expect such narrative models to fit perfectly all the complexities of our recorded past: world history is not reducible to a few qualitative or quantitative essential formalisms. Postmodernists like Jean-François Lyotard (1984) have argued against both the historical adequacy and the ethical desirability of the great "metascripts" of the world religions, of liberalism, romantic nationalism, Marxism and the Enlightenment, including even Kantian universal peace-seeking. The extraordinary richness of history's human subject matter and of the grammatical possibilities within natural human languages for describing that history deny the ultimate adequacy of any such over-simplified account of individual or collective human social actions.

Similarly we can recognize the likely historical-empirical importance of a rich variety of literary genres, both tragic and comic, which world literature has given us in our search for context-transcending modes of personal significance without assuming any one genre or taxonomy of genres is universally, eternally or essentially valid. Nor must we assume that genre distinctions or taxonomies are solely properties of the texts they obviously infuse. Following the pragmatic turn in post-Wittgensteinian philosophy, we can look for "essences" not simply in texts, but in the practical grammars of human language use, including but not limited to standard or exceptional text interpretations.

---

[10] See Chapters 3, 5, 6 above; the Lehnert approach will be simply illustrated below.

[11] Johann Georg von Hahn listed various formulas of folk narratives in 1864, and afterwards; Otto Rank published his psychoanalytic *The Myth of the Birth of the Hero* in 1909; both writers are briefly discussed in Alan Dundes' introduction to Lord Raglan (1965).

According to Jonathan Culler, "genres are no longer taxonomic classes but groups of norms and expectations which help the reader to assign functions to various elements in the work, and thus the 'real' genres are those sets of categories or norms required to account for the process of reading" (quoted in Kent 1991: 300). The question becomes one of the most intriguing topics of cross-cultural and historical empirical inquiry. (Alker 1986a begins one such discussion in a Japanese context based on the analyses of this present chapter.)

Nevertheless – and because the "metascripts" of past eras are being severely challenged – several related, relatively new, quasi-grammatical approaches to explanatory, interpretive and evaluative/emancipatory understanding appear promising from an empirical testing or methodological falsificationist perspective. Script-based interpretive procedures and, more generally, story grammars are currently undergoing intensive investigation in text linguistics, cognitive psychology and artificial intelligence.[12] This work suggests many research programs capable of further elaboration and improvement. Their quasi-grammatical constraints are being supplemented by a related set of pragmatically oriented narrative generation and summarization techniques. Because these focus squarely on the realm of human aspirations, intentions, actions and their causal constraints, and because they can encompass both qualitative and quantitative plot-like historical possibilities, my bet is that in the long run the new critical, cognitive and textual sciences will produce better, more open-ended, humanly relevant "world" models using such devices. Focusing on narrative scripts and their underlying plots and associated transformational grammars not only helps reconstitute international relations within the dialectical-hermeneutic tradition as a reconstructive but fallible science of human possibilities, it also reasserts that concept of scientific international theory which grounds itself in practical striving toward world community.[13]

---

[12] For international studies, two especially interesting books doing such work are Hudson, ed. (1991) and Wierzbicka (1992b). See also George Lakoff's direct application of the substantial, cross-cultural Lakoff-Johnson-Turner research program on metaphorical meaning generation to the Gulf War (Lakoff 1991). Despite differences between Lakoff's and Wierzbicka's approaches, surprisingly many of the components of Schank–Abelson textual pragmatics and Searle's post-Austin and post-Wittgenstein speech act pragmatics appear to have cross-cultural validity.

[13] For Karl Deutsch's seminal contributions to this alternative to the realist tradition, see Richard Merritt and Bruce M. Russett (1981), especially the chapter by Arendt Lijphart, and Chapter 11 below. By way of productive contrast, see also Johan Galtung (1980a).

From fairy tale morphology to "simple" story grammars consistent with affectively relevant plot summaries

In his commentary "On Russian Fairy Tales," Jakobson (1973: 636ff.) recounts various efforts since Pushkin to uncover the essence of Russian prose in the role structures and functional sequences of classic fairy tales. He recounts Propp's "arresting conclusion" that despite an enormous variety of tale plots, "all fairy tales are uniform in their structure." Because Propp's argument prefigures contemporary formal accounts of the components of interpretive scripts and story grammars, let me briefly review the basis for this conclusion, quoting both from Jakobson's essay and from Propp's original monograph.

Propp's morphology

As seems intuitively plausible, Propp detects seven fundamental dramatis personae in Russian fairy tales, with corresponding spheres of action. These main actor types or roles are: hero, villain, donor (or magical devices), helper (also assisting the hero), princess with her father, dispatcher (of the hero) and false hero (who typically falsely claims the rewards intended for the true hero). Propp's thesis of the unity of all Russian fairy tales is a structural-functional claim, argued in terms of thirty-one *functions* of the seven classes of dramatis personae.

By "function" Propp means "the deed defined from the viewpoint of its signification for the plot." Table 8.1, a summary of Chapter 3 of V. Propp's *Morphology of the Folktale*, lists what these functions of the dramatis personae might be. Both the function numbers and symbols are his, although at points I have recast or paraphrased his summary descriptions.

Propp's thesis is derived from and tested against Afanasev's classic collection of Russian folktales, which was first published in 1855–64, and has gone through many editions in several languages.[14] "The action of all tales included in our material develops within the limits of these [thirty-one] functions" (Propp 1977: 64ff., 105ff., 128ff.). The functions are said not to exclude each other, but to develop out of each

---

[14] Unfortunately, the Pantheon edition (Afanasev 1973) does not give numbers corresponding to those cited by even the second revised edition of Propp's study.

other "with logical and artistic necessity." The exhaustive, ordered set of functions in the table offers a scheme (or, in more contemporary terms, a script or frame) that is "a *measuring unit* for individual tales."

One of the simplest examples of such an assessment is of tale number 131 in the sixth Russian language Afanasev edition. It also illustrates the kidnapping of a princess by a dragon, which is for Propp a very basic fairy tale. I reproduce here Propp's qualitative measurement, or coding, of the functionally abbreviated text of this tale, as well as his summary formula (1) for it:

> A tsar, three daughters (α). The daughters go walking (β^3), overstay in the garden (δ^1). A dragon kidnaps them (A^1). A call for aid (B^1). Quest of three heroes ($C \uparrow$). Three battles with the dragon ($H^1 - I^1$), rescue of the maidens (K^4). Return ($\downarrow$), reward (W^0).

$$\beta^3 \, \delta^1 \, A^1 \, B^1 \, C \uparrow H^1 - I^1 \, K^4 \downarrow W^0 \tag{1}$$

The formula consists of a certain number of Greek letters, indicating elements of the preparatory section of the tale, followed by one pass, or move, through the H–I "struggle, then victory" theme. One might want to have a triple repeat of this H–I thematic, but at least Propp considers this a single move tale. The subscripts and superscripts refer to more specific versions of the general functions in Table 8.1. This A^1 is a particular kind of villainy – the kidnapping of a person – while H^1 refers to a fight in an open field, rather than a game of cards, etc., and the final W^0 indicates a monetary or other material gain rather than the full "wedding and accession to the throne," which would not be possible for a king with three daughters!

Propp tabulates schematizations like (1) above for forty-six such stories, many of them with several moves; he also discusses many other stories and challenges his readers to apply his approach to the remaining tales in Afanasev's collection. After his discussion of the preparatory sections, Propp uses a "variable scheme," formula (2), to reduce all of his analyzed tales to a single structure:

$$A \, BC \uparrow D \, E \, F \, G \, \frac{H \, J \, I \, K \downarrow Pr - Ps^0 L}{L \, M \, J \, N \, K \downarrow Pr - Rs} \, Q \, Ex \, T \, U \, W * \tag{2}$$

This formula makes clear that there are two distinctive move classes;

Table 8.1 *Propp's fairy tale frame*

	α	INITIAL SITUATION
I	β	ABSENTATION Family member absents himself.
II	γ	INTERDICTION An interdiction (suggestion) to hero is made or ordered.
III	δ	VIOLATION Hero violates interdiction. Villain enters.
IV	ϵ	RECONNAISSANCE Villain attempts reconnaissance (or hero does).
V	ζ	DELIVERY Information about victim delivered to villain.
VI	η	TRICKERY Villain attempts deception of victim to possess him/his belongings.
VII	θ	COMPLICITY Victim submits to deception, unwittingly helps enemy including preliminary misfortune.
VIII	A	VILLAINY Villain causes harm, injury to a family member.
VIIIa	a	LACK A family member either lacks or desires something.
IX	B	MEDIATION, CONNECTIVE INCIDENT Misfortune or lack (for victim hero) made known to seeker and others. The latter is approached with request or command. He is allowed to go or is dispatched.
X	C	BEGINNING COUNTERACTION Seeker/hero agrees to, decides on counteraction.
XI	↑	DEPARTURE Hero leaves home. Optional. Provider, donor appears.
XII	D	DONOR'S FIRST FUNCTION Hero is tested.
XIII	E	HERO'S REACTION to the actions of the donor (maybe positive, maybe negative).
XIV	F	PROVISIONAL RECEIPT OF MAGICAL AGENT Hero acquires its use.
XV	G	GUIDANCE Spatial transference of hero to whereabouts of an object of search.
XVI	H	STRUGGLE Hero and villain join in direct combat.
XVII	J	BRANDING Hero branded, often in and/or before battle, by princess.
XVIII	I	VICTORY Villain is defeated.
XIX	K	LIQUIDATION* Peak of narrative. Initial misfortune, lack is liquidated.
XX	↓	RETURN Hero returns.
XXI	Pr	PURSUIT Hero is pursued.
XXII	Rs	RESCUE Hero rescued from pursuit.
XXIII	O	UNRECOGNIZED ARRIVAL of hero either at home or in another country.
XXIV	L	UNFOUNDED CLAIMS BY FALSE HEROES* Hero at home.
XXV	M	DIFFICULT TASK This is proposed to false or true hero.
XXVI	N	SOLUTION The task is resolved; preliminary solution may occur.
XXVII	Q	RECOGNITION Hero is recognized, often by use of branding (XVII).
XXVIII	Fx	EXPOSURE False hero or villain is exposed.

Table 8.1 *contd*

XXIX	T	TRANSFIGURATION Hero is given new appearance or possessions.
XXX	U	PUNISHMENT Villain (of 2nd move, or false hero) is punished. Villain (move 1) punished only if no battle or pursuit.
XXXI	W	WEDDING Hero is married and/or ascends the throne, etc., rewards.

Note: * My label. Propp (1977) uses * and numerical sub/superscripts to further differentiate his action/function types.

those containing a H–I "struggle, then victory" theme or those with a M–N "solution of a difficult task" movement. After preparatory discussions, stories may have zero, one or more moves of each of these types. The simple tsar with three daughters story above, summarized in formula (1), clearly fits within the possibilities of formula (2). Rarely, however, are all or even most of the thirty-one functional elements present; in his Appendices, Propp also introduces symbols for "leave-taking at a road marker," transmissions of a signaling device, motivations, positive and negative results of functions, connectives (which can be triply repeated), inessential (non-functional) and unclear or alien forms.

Mandler and Johnson's story grammars

For comparative purposes, we include here two more recent alternative structural accounts of virtually the same story, this time called the King Story and told to contemporary American children as part of a cognitive psychological study of story structure and recall. The first will be Mandler and Johnson's "story grammar" approach to identifying particular story structures and the larger classes of possible stories to which they belong. The second will be Wendy Lehnert's affective plot unit analysis and synthesis of the King Story's plot structure.

Table 8.2 should first be read to see the textual similarity just referred to, as well as its translations, elaborations and contractions. The text associated with formula (1) above does not give details about why the daughters overstayed their walk in the woods, nor how the heroes heard of the daughters' plight.

Associated with the King Story "data" of Table 8.2 and the story grammar "theory" of Table 8.3, we have given in Figure 8.1 Mandler and Johnson's highly successful "grammatical" reconstruction of that story.[15] Looking not just at the bottom of the figure, whose numbers correspond to the story elements in Table 8.2, we see that it represents a kind of grammatical parsing of the story's eighteen previously distinguished elements. Immediately associated with each of these elements is a "state" or an "event" node. If they are considered to be "external," states refer to a current condition of the world; internal states indicate emotions or other states of the mind. "External events include actions of characters and changes of state in the world. Internal events, or happenings, include "thoughts and plans, perceptions, and such peculiar phenomena as forgetting" (Mandler and Johnson 1977: 115). Although they have not further distinguished events and states in their article, Mandler and Johnson do call attention to a kind of event they call an "appraisal," rather like Propp's noticing that the transmissions of a signaling device should be formalized in a particular way.

Moving further into the body of the story tree, we come to what are called non-terminal nodes in such a structure. These must be elaborated upon before terminal events or states, corresponding to observable textual elements, can be accounted for. To understand how these are constructed, it may be simpler to start from the base of the tree, the most general, abstract or "deepest" level of nodal structure. This shift in perspective amounts to thinking about how the fairy tale was generated, or recalled, as a way of understanding its deeper meaning and structure. The first branching of the tree in Figure 8.1 distinguishes an initial setting of the scene (corresponding to Propp's preparatory section, functionally described with the Greek letters of Table 8.1) from the body of the tale, called its event structure.

Once the setting, or preparatory aspect of a story is defined, how does it develop, what are the allowable possibilities from which the observed one is realized? Here is where some of the most amazing claims are made by Propp's structuralist approach. Both his main story lines in formula 2 develop from villainy or lackings of some kind; either the villain must be overcome or the lack resolved through the

---

[15] Mandler and Johnson (1977). The origins of this rigorous form of story grammar in Chomsky's transformational syntax, and problems of properly adapting his formalisms to semantic content are ably discussed in Ryan (1979); in particular, note her critique of Prince (1973). Invernizzi and Abouzeid (1995) go an important step further to suggest quasi-experimental story recall evidence from Papua New Guinea and the United States for the nonuniversality of Mandler–Johnson story grammars.

Table 8.2   *The King Story*

1	There was once a king
2	who had three lovely daughters.
3	One day the three daughters went walking in the woods.
4	They were enjoying themselves so much
5	that they forgot the time
6	and stayed too long.
7	A dragon came
8	and kidnapped the three daughters.
9	As they were being dragged off they cried for help.
10	Three heroes heard the cries
11	and set off to rescue the daughters.
12	The heroes came
13	and fought the dragon,
14	and they killed the dragon
15	and rescued the maidens.
16	The heroes then returned the daughters safely to the palace.
17	When the king heard of the rescue
18	he rewarded the heroes.

Source: Mandler and Johnson, 1977. Reprinted by permission of the author and publisher, Academic Press.

completion of some difficult tasks; in multimove stories both types of resolution are often required. Discussing the ways in which different themes or variants of themes may be selectively composed out of the thirty-one functional elements, their substitution instances and move sequences, Propp argues that it would be "possible to artificially create new plots of an unlimited number" (Propp 1977: 111). Moreover, "were we able to unfold the picture of transformations" in themes and their variants, one could show "that all of the given tales can be morphologically deduced from the tales about the kidnapping of a princess by a dragon ..." (Propp 1977: 114). One is reminded of Aristotle's claim in his *Posterior Analytics* that all valid syllogisms can be deduced from the First Figure.

Propp recognizes that this incredible creativity, or generativity, of the fairy tale teller is subject to important dependencies or constraints: (1) the overall sequence of functions governing move development; (2) story subjects or objects chosen for a particular function may limit substitution possibilities for other story elements, absolutely or relatively; (3) not all personages have attributes appropriate for particular functions; (4) a "certain dependence exists between the initial situation and the functions which follow it" (Propp 1977: 112). As he puts it

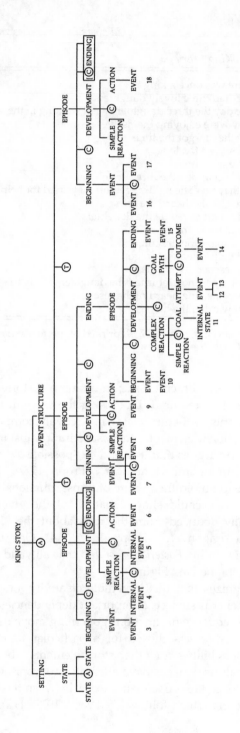

Figure 8.1 The underlying structure of the King Story

Note: Underlying nodes which have been deleted from the surface structure are enclused in brackets.
Violations of canonical structure are enclosed in boxes.
Source: Mandler and Johnson 1977 (122), copyright 1977.

earlier: "But like any living thing, the tale can generate only forms that resemble itself. If any cell of a tale organism becomes a small tale within a larger one, it is built ... according to the same rules as any fairy tale" (Propp 1977: 78).

Propp's profound Leibnizian vision of the monad-like reproduction of tales within tales suggests that the essence of a tale is something like the genetic structures of Formula 1 or 2.[16] Within acceptable limits and conventions, it does appear that Propp's approach to fitting these formulae to given folktale transcriptions quite readily allows falsifications; hence his achievement is an impressive scientific demonstration of DNA-like regularity. But he admits that he is not yet able to specify how the generative transformations, or rewrites, take place.

Fortunate to be working in a later era when the mathematics of Chomskean transformational rewrite rules is well established, Mandler and Johnson give us some concrete theoretical proposals about what Propp called the "logical and artistic necessity" developmentally connecting setting and event structure with "terminal" nodes or story elements. Looking at the figure again, we see that they break down the body of the single move King Story into three episodes. The first corresponds to the preparatory $\beta^3 \delta^1$ sequence of Formula (1). The second, comprising events 7 through 15, corresponds to the A^1, B^1, $C \uparrow$, $H^1 - I^1$ and K^4 sequence at the heart of the story's single "move." Events 16 through 18 correspond to the "return and reward" functions in Propp's characterization. These macro story parts are combined by separately coded AND and THEN connectives, indicated by circled A's and T's respectively.

Roughly, the three episodes give a beginning, a middle and an end to the King Story, although the corresponding grammatical rule in Table 8.3 sets no limit on the number of episodes possible within a story's event structure. A repetition of this triadic structural pattern occurs in the "beginning causes development causes ending" rule for rewriting episode elements whenever they occur in the elaboration of a story's event structure. Graphically symbolized by a circled C, the causal connective used by Mandler and Johnson to bind episode elements together translates the notion of a prior node providing a "sufficient reason" for the subsequent node to occur. It represents their attempt, probably not the final one, formally to identify just what

---

[16] On the role of this Leibnizian perspective in communitarian theory, see Alker (1981b) and Chapter 5 above.

makes up and distinguishes simple (and certain more complex) stories from other kinds of more open-ended narrative texts.

Since it provides a "story grammar" for our exemplary fairy tale, Table 8.3 suggests, but does not yet fill out, this section's advertised transition from morphological basic scripts to testable "simple" story grammars. Several sets of comments are in order. Looking more carefully at the rewrite rules in the table, first note that although the universe of concern, simple stories or "fables," does not exactly correspond with Russian fairy tales, both types of story appear to have "morals" embedded in them. Secondly, getting down a "goal path" appears, at a higher level of abstraction, to be what Propp's H–I and M–N moves have in common; thus it appears that the rules in Table 8.3 could be used to predict at least the formal sequence of states or events envisioned by Propp's formulae 1 and 2! Thirdly, the use of either/or type paths, symbolized in the figure by braces enveloping several exclusive alternatives, is also common to this and Propp's formalism. Fourthly, the AND, THEN and CAUSE connectives, amplified by the use of parentheses repeated n times, gives a richer version of Propp's connective ideas. Fifthly, their use of boxed nodes to show exactly where elements predicted by the grammar *do not* appear gives greater precision to Propp's concern with unclear or alien forms (which he symbolized with the letter X); it also puts this kind of generative and interpretive modeling squarely within the "falsifiable theorizing" tradition of scientific analysis. *Note that only two "ending" nodes in Figure 8.1 do not fit the story grammar of Table 8.3.* Sixthly, the infinite variety of possible instantiations of this grammar is associated with a set of rewrite rules that allow events, states and episodes to reoccur, theoretically without limit, within themselves: here we have a more adequate formal way, through the use of what are called recursive or self-calling logical functions, of generating an infinite variety of thematic variations, as well as tales within tales within tales ... as Propp had desired.

A second set of comments concern the adequacy of the Mandler–Johnson proposal in particular, and the more general idea of story grammars. Despite the greater technical sophistication of the Mandler–Johnson approach, it clearly is only an intermediate step in an ongoing field of contemporary research. Beyond the need to better understand the ways in which story functions or grammatical elements might be meaningfully suppressed, there is the need to discover the deeper meanings affecting the moral force of such stories. Thus the grammar seems better at conveying text composition syntax than the semantic or pragmatic "dependencies" among story elements that Propp noted. Intuitively speaking, somehow the next-to-terminal elements in the story tree of Figure 8.1 do not have much of the richness of a similar translation of Formula 1, even using the restricted set of labels in Table 8.1.

As Mandler and Johnson have elsewhere argued,[17] the meaning and use of particular terminal story elements is context-sensitive; technically, then, more adequate rewrite rules for generating (or interpreting) surface texts in terms of more basic deep semantic structures should also take such interdependencies into account. Just as Propp tried to introduce motivations and positive or negative function results, one is tempted to recast their way of summarizing story structure in the Schank–Abelson "conceptual dependency" tradition along lines developed either by Meehan (1976) or Lehnert (1981).[18] After all, motivationally appealing deep semantic structures are what move men and women interpretively to constitute or reconstitute the political realm.

Lehnert's affective plot units

Coming from an interest in narrative summarization, Wendy Lehnert has developed affective plot unit analysis and synthesis procedures partly as a reaction to the psychological inadequacies of story grammars like those proposed by Mandler and Johnson.[19] Her concern has been to access the higher levels of affectively charged and central concepts that are somehow found within the plot summaries we are readily able to recall, and from which story tellers can regenerate elaborated story forms as well. Indeed some evidence (Lehnert, Black and Reiser 1981) suggests that such representations of story structure are more readily remembered than the deepest, but rather abstract nodal structures typical of story grammar representations like the one in Figure 8.1. Because her plot unit methodology is highly suggestive of qualitative ways of formally analyzing certain basic concepts in

---

[17] Mandler and Johnson (1980), a response to Black and Wilensky (1979), which gives a provocative Chomskean argument for the necessity of context sensitivity in the construction of adequate story grammars.

[18] Both Meehan and Lehnert are Schank students. See also literature by Carbonell and Dyer generated by Schank and Abelson (1977).

[19] See previous citations, plus Lehnert, Alker and Schneider (1983), a prelude to the more intensive study of Chapter 3 above.

Table 8.3   *Summary of rewrite rules for a simple story grammar*

FABLE →	STORY AND MORAL
STORY →	SETTING AND EVENT STRUCTURE

SETTING → $\left\{ \begin{array}{l} \text{STATE}^* \text{ (AND EVENT}^*) \\ \text{EVENT}^* \end{array} \right\}$

STATE* → STATE ((AND STATE)*)

EVENT* → EVENT (($\left\{ \begin{array}{l} \text{AND} \\ \text{THEN} \\ \text{CAUSE} \end{array} \right\}$ EVENT)*) ((AND STATE)*)

EVENT STRUCTURE → EPISODE ((THEN EPISODE)*)

EPISODE → BEGINNING CAUSE DEVELOPMENT CAUSE ENDING

BEGINNING → $\left\{ \begin{array}{l} \text{EVENT}^* \\ \text{EPISODE} \end{array} \right\}$

DEVELOPMENT → $\left\{ \begin{array}{l} \text{SIMPLE REACTION CAUSE ACTION} \\ \text{COMPLEX REACTION CAUSE GOAL PATH} \end{array} \right\}$

SIMPLE REACTION → INTERNAL EVENT
((CAUSE INTERNAL EVENT)*)

ACTION → EVENT

COMPLEX REACTION → SIMPLE REACTION CAUSE GOAL

GOAL → INTERNAL STATE

GOAL PATH → $\left\{ \begin{array}{l} \text{ATTEMPT CAUSE OUTCOME} \\ \text{GOAL PATH (CAUSE GOAL PATH)}^* \end{array} \right\}$

ATTEMPT → EVENT*

OUTCOME → $\left\{ \begin{array}{l} \text{EVENT}^* \\ \text{EPISODE} \end{array} \right\}$

ENDING → $\left\{ \begin{array}{l} \text{EVENT}^* \text{ (AND EMPHASIS)} \\ \text{EMPHASIS} \\ \text{EPISODE} \end{array} \right\}$

EMPHASIS → STATE

Source: Mandler and Johnson (1977: 117). Copyright 1977. Reprinted by permission of the authors and publisher, Academic Press.

political texts, and because it should be possible some day to combine valid elements of the story grammar approach with plot unit analyses, I shall briefly summarize and illustrate it here.

Recall that Mandler and Johnson distinguished external and internal states. Similarly, Lehnert starts from a gross taxonomy of external events positively or negatively evaluated by a particular actor (symbolized + or − respectively), and distinguishes all of these from internal mental states (symbolized by M's) which can be goals, perceptions or other cognitions. She exhaustively defines a set of atomic or primitive plot units on the basis of five types of links among these events and states: motivation (m), actualization (a), termination (t), equivalence (e) and affective or communicative causality between two characters, symbolized by diagonally slanted dashes. Like its predecessor in Chapter 3, Table 8.4 lists the twenty primitive plot units that may be defined in her system using these elementary components.

According to a number of reasonable coding conventions, Lehnert is able to code the affective structure of simple stories with moderate reliability. Figure 8.2 illustrates what one of these looks like, the King Story again. Notice immediately that actors are not treated as abstract role types (which for Propp may have several, changing incumbents); rather those actors or classes of actors (such as the three daughters and the three heroes) are distinguished only when their action patterns are different. Notice also that only one arrow of each type may go into an M or + or − state, and that each such event or state is separately identified and associated with a textual summary of its significance.

Figure 8.2 illustratively completes the analysis of affective relationships in its story; it only hints at the synthetic, computer-assisted summary interpretations that Lehnert's procedures suggest. To appreciate these synthetic possibilities, one needs to define more complex sets of molecular plot units on the basis of the primitive ones in Figure 8.2. Our own subsequent analysis is based on a set of forty-seven of these, on the basis of which forty non-primitive plot units were found in Figure 8.2, fifteen of which were unsubsumed by any others, hence considered top level units. Others, with different interpretive perspectives, could define their own more complex meaning units (as well as giving the primitive plot units in Table 8.4 different names). What Lehnert's computer programs do is to uncover all such pre-defined plot units in the affect state graph, find the "top-level" plot units in such a complex interpretive structure, represent them and their interconnections, and discover which units are most connected to others, the structure of narrative centrality and cohesion, etc.

Two results of such computations are given in the configuration of Formula 3 below, from which we may derive a third. The most highly connected top level plot unit is the heroes' sequential subgoals of rescuing the king's daughters, while the most pivotal top level plot unit is the heroes' nested subgoal structure for doing so, where pivotal plot units are those whose omission would disconnect a sizeable body of top plot units. Connecting up such central or pivotal units suggests plot summaries very much like those human subjects actually recall. In the present case, the top level plot units most closely connected, the

Table 8.4   *Primitive plot units*

A. Monadic

M ↓a + SUCCESS	M ↓a − FAILURE	− ↓m M PROBLEM	+ ↓m M ACTIVATION	M ↓m M MOTIVATION
M ↑e M PERSEVERANCE	+ ↑e − MIXED BLESSING	− ↑e + HIDDEN BLESSING	− ↑e − COMPLEX NEGATIVE	+ ↑e + COMPLEX POSITIVE
− ↑t + RESOLUTION	+ ↑t − LOSS	+ ↑t + POSITIVE TRADEOFF	− ↑t − NEGATIVE TRADEOFF	M ↑t M CHANGE OF MIND

B. Dyadic

?⟍ 　　− NEGATIVE REACTION	?⟍ 　　+ POSITIVE REACTION	−⟍ 　　M EXTERNAL PROBLEM	+⟍ 　　M EXTERNAL ENABLEMENT	M⟍ 　　M EXTERNAL MOTIVATION

Source: Lehnert, Alker, Schneider (1983).

maximal and pivotal units, start with a COMPETITION between the heroes and the dragon, followed by the overlapping, SEQUENTIAL and NESTED SUBGOALS just referred to, concluding with the heroes' ENABLED SUCCESS and their subsequent REWARD by the king. The closeness of approximation of this sequence, highlighted as Formula 3, to the semantic content of Propp's original functional frame (in Table 8.1) is highly gratifying!

$$
\text{COMPETITION (H, DR)} \quad
\begin{cases}
\text{SEQUENTIAL SUBGOALS (H)} \\
\text{NESTED SUBGOALS (H)} \\
\quad \text{ENABLED SUCCESS (H)} \\
\quad\quad \text{REWARD (K, H)}
\end{cases}
\tag{3}
$$

Finally, granting that the above illustrations make plausible the possibility of constructing *partial* world history grammars that look something like story grammars built around semantically and motivationally suggestive plot units, one is entitled to know what thoughts scholars like Propp, Jakobson, Mandler and Johnson or Lehnert have had about *why* their relatively simple formulae, graphs or grammars work so well. What really is going on?

Briefly put, one could argue that simple tales are such a pervasive part of many different cultures because they are especially meaningful, and structured so as to be especially easy to remember. Table 8.1, as well as Formulae (2) and (3) and Figures 8.1 and 8.2 show different versions of the extremely simple and memorable structures involved. Such structures were probably necessary for such tales to survive and be transmitted by an oral story-telling culture.

But that still leaves the issue open as to *why* the tales have been such a pervasive feature of even highly literate cultures. With an implicit link to Jung-like discussions of unconsciously grounded archetypes, Propp makes the suggestion that "the basic, vivid moments of our essentially very simple scheme also play the psychological role of a kind of root." But he also recognizes that the majority of the Russian fairy tales' elements – "miraculous births, interdictions, rewarding with magical elements, flight and pursuit, etc." – "are traceable to one or another archaic cultural, religious, daily, or other reality" which must be used contextually for the fuller, comparative understanding of the significance of a particular tale (Propp 1977: 112–115).

Jakobson goes further. Citing authorities on both sides of the Russian Revolution, he argues that "A fairy tale fulfills the role of a social utopia." Thus Lenin is quoted as saying "he could write from this material beautiful studies about the hopes and longings of our people." Under this influential materialist reading, one might treat Propp's schema as utopian grammatical essences![20] And Jakobson recalls Trubetskoy's comments on Afanasev's collection of tales as

---

[20] In a chapter on "Holism and Internal Relations," Nicholas F. Gier (1981) argues (p. 89) that "Wittgenstein believes that all necessity is 'grammatical' and is not tied to formal logic. ...." Unlike logical propositions, grammatical propositions are always synthetic *a priori*. He then goes on, in the frontispiece to the next chapter (p. 91) to provide quotes that convey much of the Leibniz-Propp-Jakobson perspective of the present paper:

> "So in philosophy all that is not gas is grammar."
> "Essence is expressed by grammar."
> "Philosophy as the custodian of grammar can in fact grasp the essence of the world, only not in the propositions of language, but in the rules for this language which exclude nonsensical combinations of signs."

attempts to delineate heaven or Paradise, another realm, "a better place" with "easy bread." "In pursuit of this aim the good fellow has to master a 'cunning science,' or maybe, simply to 'follow his eyes'" (Jakobson 1973: 650ff.).

Jakobson tells of efforts after the Soviet revolution to collect new and authenticate old fairy tales on the basis of peasant judgments. This methodology is justified by the argument that the folk tale is typically collectively owned. "The socialized sections of the mental culture ... are subject to much stricter and more uniform laws than fields in which individual creation prevails" (Jakobson 1973: 641). If collective cultural products are structured according to discoverable grammatical laws, can the various "meanings" attributed to world histories by Toynbee-like communitarians, neo-Marxians, neo-Malthusians (or modern liberals) be far beyond?

Tragedies and comedies about the weak and the strong

What gives Forrester's neo-Malthusian mathematics, Marxist world histories, Braudelian epics of the *longue durée* or Toynbee's vision of civilization's development and decay their dramatic character, the grandeur of heroic quests that succeed or fail with quasi-metaphysical inevitability of necessity? Does our sense of time, direction and historical possibility itself change from era to era? (Maier 1987). Can we somehow partake scientifically of the tragic or comic force of great histories while still leaving open constrained possibilities that the world we make will really be different because of what we have done, might do, or somehow failed to do? Is there a contextually sensitive, yet possibilist science of ecological, historical, political development? (Sprout and Sprout 1965). Can it apply to ordinary people, both the weak and the strong, not just the heroic, the magical and the mythical?

The implication of Propp's, Jakobson's and Wittgenstein's views cited above is that "necessity" and "dramatical force" come from something like story grammars, grammatical internal relations that constitute the identities of the actors, sentences, stories, dramas or histories they help generate. Fairy tales following the scheme of Formula (2) somehow *must* have happy endings; tragedies too convey a haunting inevitability of failure despite the valiant efforts of their protagonists to avoid such tragic endings. Somehow, motivationally,

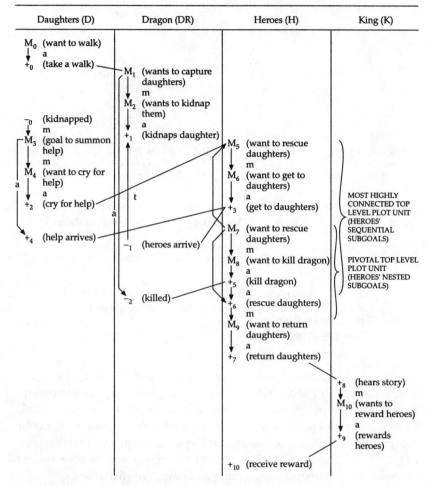

Figure 8.2 Lehnert's affective state graph for the King Story

comedies make us happy, restore our faith in life, while tragedies provide also a kind of emotional purging or catharsis, the need for which should be better understood. The "essence" of the story is thus not merely in the text or the performance, but in our cognitive-emotional reactions to it.

What then is the "formula" or scheme that seems for so many of us to underlie valiantly resisted, but somehow "inevitable" tragic failure? Is there a similar mythic or poetic deep structure engendering the expectation of success? Why do such formulae move us so?

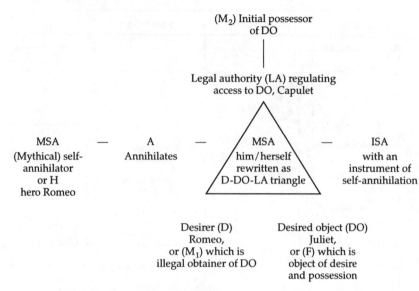

(M₂) Initial possessor
of DO

Legal authority (LA) regulating
access to DO, Capulet

MSA — A — MSA — ISA
(Mythical) self-   Annihilates   him/herself   with an
annihilator   rewritten as   instrument of
or H   D-DO-LA triangle   self-annihilation
hero Romeo

Desirer (D)   Desired object (DO)
Romeo,   Juliet,
or (M₁) which is   or (F) which is
illegal obtainer of DO   object of desire
and possession

Figure 8.3 Berke's basic tragic plot sentence subject to initial transformations and subsequent character identifications for first Romeo and Juliet plot

Source: Berke 1982 (28–32, 66ff.)

Since mathematical deduction also carries with it an air of inevitability (at least for those who feel the premises in use are secure and that standard deductive logic is the only appropriate mode of valid inference), we might look to systematic and formal theories of poetic genres (which include romances and epics as well as comedies and tragedies) for answers, bearing in mind our earlier qualifications about the need for pragmatic interpretations of narrative structures.

Northrop Frye has made a strong case for distinguishing comic from tragic plots on the communitarian basis of whether "the hero becomes isolated from his society" (a tragedy) or "he is incorporated into it" (a comedy) (Frye 1971). Thus comedies, like fairy tales, have socially happy endings, tragedies sad ones. Bradley Berke gives a more active version of the same distinction, which will help answer the above questions: "The tragic thinker 'stages' the destruction of the social order in the imaginary realm of myth. We shall call this destruction of the social order by the individual 'self-annihilation'. ... Whereas the 'Hero' represents the active, antisocial aspect of the mythical self-annihilator, the other actants represent, jointly, the passive social aspects of this imaginary figure" (Berke 1982: 9). Citing many of Chomsky's early writings on transformational grammars, as well as Todorov's book-length grammatical treatment (1969) of Boccaccio's *Decameron*, Berke shows how the tragic structure of many of Sophocles', Racine's and Shakespeare's dramas can be understood as the "inevitable" or necessary consequence of a large, possibly infinite variety of possible rewrites of the same basic tragic formula, given in Figure 8.3. The core idea is volitionally or actively induced self-destruction: *a typically mythical self-annihilator (MSA) annihilates (A) him/herself with an instrument of self-destruction (ISA)*. Figure 8.3 suggests that this act of self-destruction involves society as well – for Berke, Propp plus Mandler and Johnson, the self is an abstract role, an actant, not just a particular individual. Berke redefines his MSA as made up of a desirer (D), its desired object (DO) and a legitimate authority (LA) regulating access to the desired object. Internal id, ego and superego components of the same individual's personality are also suggested by this rewrite of the direct object in the basic tragic plot sentence.

Before commenting on the various world histories we have discussed, let us illustrate Berke's "tragic story grammar" approach with one of his most elaborated examples, the major (but not the only) plot of Shakespeare's *Romeo and Juliet*. Actually, this play also includes comic elements (Romeo does marry his love, but only for one night) which are tragically overwhelmed by their adolescent impetuosity and the intense hostility of Montague–Capulet Verona.[21]

As possible sources for the tremendous identity we feel with these beautiful, heroic, but star-crossed lovers, one might suggest our own adolescent experiences along the same self-destructive lines, or our identification with an age of great tragic output and self-awareness, such as fourth-century Athens or the early modern era, when an old ruling order (or aristocratic class) has lost its power inevitably to bring happiness to us. Less exalted, but pervasive self-defeating tendencies are familiar to us all. Existentially, Berke views tragedy's cathartic power as due to its promise of release from such traumas, of Nirvana,

---

[21] Berke's analysis of *Romeo and Juliet* is centered around the technical analysis summarized by Figures 8.3 and 8.4 below, derived from his pp. 66–73. Tzvetan Todorov (1969), *Grammaire du Decameron* is obviously one of Berke's exemplars. Todorov's earlier work cites Propp, Greimas, Breymond and J. Harris (a transformational grammarian and teacher of Chomsky) as relevant studies earlier than his own. The most thorough review and extension of this post-Propp, largely French literature is perhaps still Claude Breymond (1973).

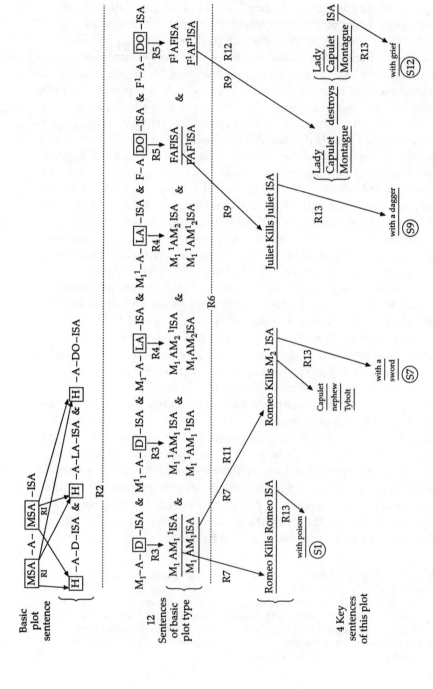

Figure 8.4 Aspects of a Romeo and Juliet plot generated by Berke's tragic grammar

Source: Berke 1982 (67, 71).

of peace and death (Berke 1982). The basic mythical and poetic forms of comedy and tragedy, of heroic epic and endearing romance, clearly appeal to deep levels of our conscious and unconscious experience.

The identifications in Figure 8.3 may be used, and should be reviewed, before trying to make sense of the abbreviated summary of Berke's reconstructive analysis in Figure 8.4. Looking at this figure, it may best be understood as a partially explicit portrayal of the grammatically permitted transformations which turn the basic tragic plot sentence at the top into the four key instances of self-annihilation at the bottom (S1, S7, S9, S12), which together provide an important plot summary of *Romeo and Juliet*. Each of the five rows in the table represents a stage in this process; the numbered R's, associated with the corresponding rewrite arrows when they are not too complicated to draw, refer to explicit grammatical rewrite rules given in Berke's text (his Chapter 3, fifty pages long). As in the Mandler and Johnson story grammar of Table 8.3, these rewrite rules are possibilistic, not deterministic; grammatical theory puts constraints of possible instantiations, but does not pre-determine them.

Not to get lost in the details, some of which are suggested by the content and notation of these two figures, the main thrust of the rewrite rules involved is to elaborate the basic tragic plot sentence into a twelve-sentence-long basic plot type (at the middle of Figure 8.4), and then to delete and complete these sentence forms to give the concrete particulars of self-annihilation characterizing a particular plot. In his text, Berke spends approximately nine pages elaborating twenty-seven possible variants of the twelve-sentence plot types, all generated by different possible variants of the subject and object actants in the basic plot sentence. Near the bottom of the figure, possible completions are suggested involving large numbers of deletions as well as specific proper names for subjects and objects and one or more concrete variants of annihilation ("banishing" or "disturbing" are formally as good as "killing") and of instruments therefor (e.g., a sword or dagger or knife, poison, grief).

At this point we should note that story grammars often downplay realistic or sensible constraints of a semantic or pragmatic character. Clearly someone cannot banish someone with grief or poison them with a non-dipped dagger; and the relevant actor needs to be enabled or capable of undertaking the chosen annihilating act. The relevant repertoires must be there, possibly having been suggested by one's surroundings; situational constraints should not be overpowering. The same kinds of problems might have been raised concerning both the Propp and Mandler–Johnson examples. True action possibilities in life, like in drama, can only be appreciated adequately when the context of conditions surrounding them is well understood. If the motivating power of poetic forms comes in part from their ability to appeal to our deeper selves, abstracted from our everyday contexts, the scientific promise of those forms must be realized through these contexts.

Can historical, *non-mythical* self-annihilators be the actants of Berke's formulae? Can poetic forms, with their many unrealistic features, apply to everyday life? Here again, Northrop Frye has a very helpful typology that both distinguishes and relates literary forms to ordinary people. Recall his distinction between the tragic and the comic in terms of the hero's separation from or integration into society. Add to this a fivefold distinction in terms of whether the hero's power of action is greater than ours, less, or roughly the same (Frye 1971: 33–52). Frye's ten types of comedy and tragedy (with subvariants and illustrations) are given in Table 8.5.

These categories are immensely suggestive. To see our reality as mostly of the "low mimetic mode" corresponds in a way to the recent rise in literary works about ordinary, middle-class people, who may be no weaker or stronger than ourselves. Like the rise to maturity of each individual, the stages of our civilization have been increasingly democratic, but not exclusively identified with the lower literary modes in this array. Eras of radical optimism concerning social and political developments also may be more frequently or deeply linked with happy, associative, comic outcomes; or they may be driven by deeply sensed tragedies of the lonely human condition, only alterable when basic scripts or plot possibilities, or our appreciation of them, are changed.[22] Conservative orientations allow similar complexities, with less hope of realistic ameliorative change.

[22] Compare Frye with the complementary views of Joseph Campbell (1972):

> Occidental judgment is founded on a total misunderstanding of the realities depicted in the fairy tale, the myth, and the divine comedies of redemption. These, in the ancient world, were regarded as of higher rank than tragedy, of a deeper truth, of a more difficult realization, of a sounder structure, and of a revelation more complete.
> The happy ending of the fairy tale, the myth, and the divine comedy of the soul, is to be read, not as a contradiction, but as a transcendence of the universal tragedy of man ....
> Tragedy is the shattering of the forms and of our attachment to the forms; comedy, the wild and careless, inexhaustible joy of life invincible.

Table 8.5 *Frye's typology of fictional modes*

Hero's power *vis-à-vis* ours	Tragic fictional mode	Comic fictional mode
superior in *kind* to others and environments, e.g., divine	myths, death of Dionysus	mythical comedy of assumption or salvation. Christ or Apollo
superior in *degree* to these	romance, legends, folk tales	romantic comedy, as in elegiac, idyllic past
superior in degree to us but sharing our environments (hero as leader)	high mimetic mode of most epics and classical tragedies (leader falls)	high mimetic comedy, as those by Aristophanes; blends heroic and ironic
they are on our level	low mimetic tragedy, pathos	low mimetic comedy, new comedy; humorous breaking or irrational or absurd
they are beneath us	everyman as ironic or hapless victim; close again to myth, e.g., Charles Chaplin	ironic, with driving out of scapegoat

To see the human possibility of occasionally heroic transcendence of our natural environment need not suggest that we all follow hopeless causes. That there are transcendent, symbolic or even mythical social or political purposes, social utopias, in search for which we *collectively and legitimately* are willing to kill or die, dramatically *constitutes* the most essential political actions. When we describe political or social actors in terms of laughable inadequacies or ironically criticize them for redeemable failures, we place them beneath us. We suggest the possibility of improving on our lot by taking our collective destiny in our own hands. Hence ironic criticism as well as heroic leadership and mythic interpretive forms have social roles to play, if properly disciplined, in motivationally suggestive critical and constructive historical analysis.

Finally, now we can see some important sources of Forrester's or Braudel's or Toynbee's historical appeal. (We shall leave to a concluding section some thoughts on improving the scientific character of their kinds of world historical analysis.) Highly aggregated, abstracted or impersonal forces (heroic saviors founding new religions, classes, forces and relations of production, macroecological shifts) are like mythical actants. Whether the interpretive stories they tell are comedies preservative of existing society's virtues or tragedies about alternative developments, motivational appeal comes both from the reader's identification with such decontextualized and at least partially mythical actors. Deeper explanations, more moving and satisfying interpretations, sociopolitical change productive of emancipatory fulfillment all come more fully when the shared insights of multiple perspectives are uncovered and the real differences among them more accurately explored.[23]

For example, Forrester's studies almost invariably support the conservative moral that liberal reform efforts are self-annihilating (because of the unanticipated consequences of non-linear feedbacks, etc.). The confrontation of multiple computerized thought models of the same phenomena must be encouraged, even if populist technocrats might wince at the loss of certainty such openness implies. Neo-Marxist writers somehow must identify capitalism as the most basic, quasi-mythical self-annihilator; the working class, or its vanguard, somehow must play an heroic role; only the most skeptical can see the vanguard party as a *possible* self-annihilator. Toynbee's discussions of the joint effects of internal and external proletariats on imperial decline are enormously suggestive, but his call for super-human saviors (or the belief in their existence) as the price of the renewal of civilizations in crisis may be too optimistic or pessimistic as futurology. Imposing logical rigor or overwhelming historical evidence add necessity and inevitability to mythic appeal. Each author enriches our understanding of how the individual, the group and larger social and ecological forces interact and "inner-act" with each other. To challenge these basic features of each historical interpreter is not to disallow the research generating possibilities of research heuristics that are not directly falsifiable; it is to call attention to alternative possibilities and the need on occasion seriously to explore, to convert to, to critically revise and to synthesize among them.

[23] The implied criticisms here and the examples of the next paragraph are of course illustrative, not exhaustive nor fully developed. In addition to the critical studies of global modeling efforts and Toynbee's magnum opus mentioned above, I would like to cite as directly relevant to the discussion of Marxist themes in the present paper: Ernst Bloch's writings; Kenneth Burke (1969), especially his Marxian dramatist grammar of pp. 211–214; Harold Rosenberg's (1965) "The Heroes of Marxist Science" in his *The Tradition of the New*; Jack Zipes (1979); and the extremely suggestive analysis of the internal ties between Marx's several volumes of poetry (!) and his later work in Leonard P. Wessell, Jr. (1979).

How interpretive story grammars may discipline the writing of theoretically informed world historical narratives

This chapter has assumed that improved efforts at writing world histories are in order, efforts that will not be falsely restricted to merely the descriptive and explanatory functions of supposedly non-interpretive, objective history. It has been based on the additional recognition that the primary but not exclusive materials of the historian are textual, and that historical works, when completed, are narrative in form. A deeper, more controversial homeomorphism has been the one assumed to exist between the forms of fictional texts – stories or dramas – and of scholarly historical narratives. This correspondence has been elsewhere justified, and will here be briefly reviewed as a way of recapitulating the argument so far. Then some new steps toward more rigorous historical studies, based on some politically suggestive historical scripts, will be briefly proposed. Thus the above path from basic scripts to possibilist historical grammars incorporating affectively suggestive comic or tragic plot structures may reproduce itself in subsequent work, even if the exercise involved is only partially or hypothetically realized.

As philosophical commentators about historical writing, both Paul Ricoeur and Hayden White have made a strong case for essential correspondences between fictional and historical narrative forms.[24] A synthesis of their arguments generalizes to a conception of scientific historiography consistent with and rationalizing of the previous emphases of this chapter.

One may acknowledge with Gallie that "history is a species of the genus story," about major achievements or failures of people living and working together, in societies or nations. Moreover, one may think about narrating history as a Wittgensteinian language game, which must be constituted or reconstituted grammatically. Clearly some degree of interpretation is involved in the generation of such narratives. Nonetheless fitting historical evidence into a coherent narrative qualifies as an objective contribution, a "narrativist" explanation, "because it is empirical and subject to techniques of verification and disconfirmation in the same way that theories in science are." At the

---

[24] Hayden White (1978: Ch. 2); Paul Ricoeur (1981: Ch. 11). Both authors cite Aristotle, Gallie, Frye; Ricoeur cites White as well.

same time the art of narrating, like the corresponding art of following a story, requires that "we are able to *extract a configuration from a succession.*" But history, although it shares with fiction interpretive patterns consistent with facts, works toward the appropriate unifying form of narrative, that poetic activity which consists precisely in the construction of plots. "Just as there can be no explanation in history without a story, so too there can be no story without a plot by which to make of it a story of a particular kind." However the informing pattern of the historian's book, which is his *mythos* or plot, is secondary, a constructed achievement on the basis of available evidence, while for the poet, detail is secondary.

Interpretation occurs both at the historical and the meta-historical level. Just as interpretation consists of providing a plot structure appropriate to a sequence of events so that their nature is revealed as a "story of a particular kind," the historian at a more fundamental level needs to identify and choose the "kind of story" he or she wishes to tell from among those types (comedy, tragedy, romance, epic, satire) and modes of explanation (idiographic, contextualist, organicist or mechanist) available to him or her in our culture. Additionally, different formal argument types (deductive positivist or more open-ended, dialectical inferences) and contrasting world hypotheses (such as Pepper's formism, organism, mechanism and contextualism) may be implicit or explicit in one's historical practice. "Emplotment" may be thought of as embodying all four of these choices.

If scientific history writing is thus admitted to be a poetic, fictional activity, the mimetic character of fiction must be emphasized as applying to scientific history as well. Mimesis is a metaphoric or "iconic augmentation of the real," imitating not the effectivity of events, but their logical structure and meaning. Tragic mimesis (or what Frye would call the high mimetic mode) seeks, as Aristotle said, to represent human action in a magnified way. Thus the world of fiction leads us to the essential heart of the real world of action by playing the unreal, while true histories of the past open up buried potentialities of the present or future.

I shall just briefly mention two projects illustrative of the further work suggested by the present line of inquiry. The reader should be able to think of many more "story-oriented" studies in popular media or in the foundational works of any major tradition of sociopolitical theory. The first area of application is still partly folklore, but also partly history: the interpretation of the Biblical story of Jesus and its comparison with similar and different heroic "life and death" stories of his era. The second example bridged Marxian and Malthusian discussions of long-wave thinking, with more than a hint of serious quantifiable relationships, but still with a strong narrative character.

Surely a suggestive research strategy based on the insights of the present chapter is one leading to more explicit characterizations of basic, motivationally important plot structures in major political narratives. Figure 8.2 and Formula (3) pointed briefly in that direction, since they suggested how one might go about identifying centrally connected top-level plot units, the already interconnected building blocks of Lehnert's affectively suggestive summary plot structures.

Table 8.6 gives one of Toynbee's more suggestive arguments for the equivalence of heroic saviors in the Graeco-Roman world: numerous, sequentially organized, corresponding elements in recorded versions of the life and death of Socrates and Jesus.[25] It cried not only for detailed, hermeneutic investigation of sources, translations, purposes, but also for plot unit analysis. The motivating question for such investigations would be the nature of the emotional appeal, its molecular structure, if you will, that has so engaged many millions throughout the last two millennia, but which now seems to be on the decline, being replaced by other "savior myths," either Marxian or Islamic or nationalistic in character. Of course, such investigations need supplementing, just as this methodology itself could be augmented significantly to incorporate recognition of a greater variety of non-Western dramatic forms.

Similarly, the Marxian account of Kondratieff long cycles in Table 8.7 is especially intriguing because it suggests in narrative form, against a quantitative pattern of fluctuations, a typical historical pattern of interpretation that could be used as a basis for much more substantial comparative research (Mandel 1980).[26] As one might expect, Mandel's argument appears to save capitalism because of exogenous features in the situation, not any endogenous, self-renewing power. This translation of the idea of capitalism's tragic self-destruction in its *contingent* or exogenous renewal bears further reflection, even in the post-Cold War era. So does the rise of global ecopolitical

[25] Toynbee (1934–54, vol. vi, Annex entitled *"Christus Patiens"*). An 87-element scripted account of the heroic Jesus story, not closely fitting to Propp's list, but inclusive of almost all elements in Table 8.6, has been analyzed in Lehnert, Alker and Schneider (1983), and in Chapter 3 above.
[26] This paper is discussed comparatively in Joshua Goldstein (1986).

Table 8.6 *Shared elements in the "Lives and Deaths" of Jesus and Socrates*

1	Before reaching the age of manhood the hero wins his spurs in a disputation with some of the foremost living wits of an older generation.
2	The hero is recognized and accepted by a forerunner as the latter's successor and superior.
3	The hero is proclaimed by the voice of God to be unique among Mankind.
4	The hero inveighs against the powers that be.
5	In his domestic life the hero takes hardship and good cheer as they come, and shows himself capable of standing extremes of either of them without turning a hair.
6	By his refusal to go to extremes of asceticism – which he combines with a readiness to keep company with people of all sorts and conditions – the hero causes scandal.
7	The hero is publicly declared by one of his disciples to have within him something divine.
8	The hero claims to be divinely inspired.
9	The hero refrains on principle from trying to evade the operation of the Law of the Land.
10	The hero is brought to trial.
11	A true saying of the hero's is dishonestly twisted by his enemies into a misrepresentation which is extremely damaging to him.
12	The hero on trial is reproved by the jurors for contempt of court.
13	When a question is put to the hero which offers him a possible line of retreat, the hero does not take the opening, but gives, instead, an answer that is calculated to exasperate the court more than anything else that he could conceivably have said.
14	On the strength of the hero's answer the court immediately passes sentence of death upon him.
15	A tableau of the hero holding a death-cup, with a small party of intimate companions grouped round him.
16	When the hero is in articulo mortis, the friends who are with him weep – not for the hero, but for themselves because they are losing him – and then the hero tells them to restrain their tears.
17	In laying down his life, the hero demonstrates, by a triumphant response to the severest possible ordeal, that Righteousness has a supreme intrinsic value.
18	The hero is better appreciated by foreigners than by his own countrymen.

Source: Toynbee 1934–54 (vol. vi, 486–495).

Table 8.7 *Handel's causal narrative of world history*

"Depressive" long wave	"Expansionary" long wave	"Depressive" long wave
Prolonged underinvestment has led to abundance of money capital available	Increase in organic composition of capital begins to flatten out rate of profit at relatively high plateau	Rationalization investments (second phase) of technological revolution, vulgarization of innovations, disappearance of technological rents further saps average rate of profit)
Accelerated research for new labor-saving and rationalization inventions	Strong increase in employment strengthens labor and flattens out increases in the rate of surplus value	Monetary instability increases
Positive outcome for capital in intensified class struggles impeding introduction of new labor processes tied to new techniques	Strong demand for raw materials upsets relative price relationship to manufactured goods	Rates of investment and accumulation decline
Strong environmental changes inducing a sudden upturn in the rate of profit (several elements of a, b, c, d, and e over a period of time)*	Monetary stability shaken by credit explosion necessary to maintain pace of growth in spite of growing contradictions	Search for new sources of raw materials and new ways to reduce labor costs, but without immediate important results
Emergence of hegemonistic capitalist power on world market underwriting relative monetary stability	Intensification of class struggle	Sharpened crisis of capital valorization spreads into prolonged social and political crisis
Long-term upsurge in rate of profit and in rate of capital accumulation	Intensification of international competition	Devalorization of capital accentuates
Massive upsurge of investment allows technological revolution (first phase)	World hegemony of given hegemonic power undermined; further erosion of monetary stability over-accumulation	
Increase in relative rate of surplus value and technological rents give additional spur to rate of profit	Beginning of long-term decline in rate of profit	
Sustained economic growth favors huge international migration, which enables reproduction of reserve army of labor in spite of increased and heavy accumulation of capital	Attempts to increase the rate of surplus value further sharpens class struggle	
Spread of new labor processes leads (with time lag) to new forms of resistance and organization of proletariat		

Time sequence →

Source: Mandel. Reprinted with permission.
* a, b, c, d, and e refer to the five processes counteracting the decline in the rate of profit, as indicated in (1980: 74–75).

thinking (Alker and Haas 1993). But the availability of non-Malthusian ecological alternatives to Forrester's arguments, phrased in somewhat comparable, concrete terms, as summarized in the Alker–Haas review, is a step forward in the search for emancipatory ecological self-understanding.

In conclusion, although the last example does suggest multiple models of possible historical development, and the previous one at least explicitly contrasts one basic hero myth (Jesus–Socrates) with another (Propp's), it is not claimed that story grammars will soon replace or become the world models of the future. Rather, I have argued that measuring actual historical sequences and thinking of possible world historical developments in terms of alternative story grammars can enlighten and orient us toward a better future of constrained, but multiple possibilities.

9 Beneath Tit-for-Tat:
The contest of political economy fairy tales within SPD protocols[1]

Even mathematical economists tell stories (McCloskey 1990). And in doing so, they join themselves with the rest of the human race which has, since before recorded history began, made sense of their lives in such terms. The tales they tell are often fanciful ones; many have long-term ideological pedigrees. Sometimes they seem like mathematical fictions. In any case, we find it suggestive to think of such tales as political economy fairy tales. They are a pervasive, long enduring, and often little noticed aspect of our lives.

With a lively and contestational historical sense, we wish here to investigate the relationships between story telling, human motivations and economic activity in the particular context of Asymmetric Sequential Prisoner's Dilemma (ASPD) games. These relationships – and the history that they embody – are frequently unobserved by those fascinated by the prominence of Tit-for-Tat strategy[2] in SPD game play, no doubt because of its strength as an empirical generalization, and because of Axelrod's impressive (1984) but not fully formalized demonstration of its competitive advantages.

---

[1] With the title "Fairy Tales Can Come True: Narrative Constructions of Prisoner's Dilemma Game Play," this unpublished paper was originally coauthored with Karen Rothkin and Roger Hurwitz. Despite their very significant contributions, they are absolved from any responsibility for the changes I have made in order to include the paper in the present collection. In most places the "we" of the text continues to refer to this joint authorship, and extended collaboration, for which I am most grateful.

[2] Technically, a "Tit-for-Tat" strategy is one where a player initially "Cooperates" and then on the next move replies, "Tit-for-Tat" with the same "C" or "D" move that the other player made on her previous move. One may also, as is done in this chapter's title, extend the name "Tit-for-Tat" to refer to game histories where such strategies of play are much in evidence by one or both players.

Fairy tales in the humanities and the social sciences

Going beyond its primary reference to the fanciful tales of children with their "happily ever after" endings and of lovers whose "fairy tales" can come true, we must realize that "fairy tales" can, as justifications, also help deprive or kill people.[3] We are using the term "fairy tales" here in several related senses:

(1)   The wishful/fearful imaginative (and sometimes untrue) story telling constituting both popular culture and ordinary language use, even that evident in experimentally generated human game playing protocols;

(2)   The idealized, often emotionally and ideologically valenced narrative abstractions (or "fictions") found within all of the "great" and "awful" books of the humanities and the social sciences, as well as most of the normal scholarly literature of these disciplines; and, in a more specialized and sometimes pejorative specialization of the previous meaning;

(3)   The highly idealized, unreal, depersonalized or objectified, but still narrative-suggesting, formal/mechanistic representations of human interactions, i.e., the "model platonisms," that both inspire, inform and sometimes misguide our social scientific theorizing. (Alker 1987; Hurwitz 1989)

Associated with all three senses of "fairy tales" are two important theses and a derivative epistemological directive. First, economic, social and political activities are typically structured by, and re/deconstructive of, contextually appropriate "myths," "tales," "narratives" or "stories"; these convey to their tellers and recipients both sense, order, identity and practical lessons about ideal, typical or to-be-avoided possibilities. Secondly, as argued at the beginning of Chapter 8, the pervasiveness of fictional narratives in their literatures suggests, provocatively, that each of the social sciences, even economics, is irreducibly, or "essentially based on myth" (see also McCloskey 1990). Hence, an adequate discussion of the truthfulness of "scientific" theories must address the interpretive and fairy-tale-like character of their originating traditions and current practices.

---

[3]   George Lakoff (1991) begins with the elliptical but powerful: "Metaphors can kill." The rest of the paper unpacks the justificatory metaphor system that was part of the United States intervention in the Gulf War.

It is of course falsely "positivistic" to think that "objective" data-making can be completely free of either the human propensity to storify their significance, or the ideal/mythical patterns of human relationship deeply embedded in major traditions of social theorizing. But it is also poor scientific practice not to attempt to falsify scientific hypotheses and to test (more indirectly, perhaps) the interpretive power of their affiliated narrative accounts in terms of "fits" with relevant, reliably collected data.

Hence, good scientific practice is possible which adequately recognizes its roots in (re/de-) constructive human activity and related humanistic modes of historical inquiry (Alker 1985, 1987, 1992b). It needs, however, to be critical of inappropriate or untruthful representations of scholarly selves or of the contextually understood phenomena under examination, as well as failures to recognize or improve upon inadequate "fits" of the data of experience with competing theoretical and narrative expectations. That is how fairy tales, like great ideologies, can come true, at least partially, and for a limited set of times, peoples and places, historically or scientifically.

Although a certain kind of objectively oriented, disciplined detachment from the "subjects" of social scientific investigation is surely appropriate, we want as a final preliminary point to affirm the necessary roles of narratives in any reflexive (self-referring) social science. In a democratic society, "better" or more "truthful" stories must be repeatedly judged by informed and educated public opinion. The stories social scientists tell about their "subjects," and the arguments they are intermingled with, should be critically compared by the scientist with the discoverable accounts of the "subjects" themselves; the reciprocal criticism of scientists' accounts by their subjects, as well as other scientists, can and should be expected to occur in potentially valuable ways. From the vantage point of the more inclusive societies of which both researcher and research subjects are members, all such accounts are stories by their members about themselves.

Capitalistic fables, fairy tales and nightmares

Even if it is conceded that capitalism has achieved fantastic successes, relatively speaking, in recent world history, this contingently successful modern story may still be described as the triumph of a set of ideological beliefs about the power and imagined promise of liberal political institutions and capitalistic market processes. We shall try to make the study of Asymmetric Prisoner's Dilemma Games even more suggestive for historically oriented economists by comparing ASPD narratives of various sorts with some of the more interesting "fairy tales" and "nightmares" used to support and criticize capitalism.

Mandeville's Fable of the Bees

Perhaps the most famous ideological "fairy tale" prophetically antici-pating, in a rather conservative fashion, the triumph of capitalism, is Mandeville's *Fable of the Bees* (published in different forms between 1705 and 1733; the 1924 edition was reissued in 1988). Its practical "Moral" is explicit:

> Fraud, Luxury and Pride must live,
> While we the Benefits receive:
> Hunger's a dreadful Plague, no doubt,
> Yet who digests or thrives without? ...
> So Vice is beneficial found,
> When it's by Justice lopt and bound;
> Nay, where the People would be great,
> As necessary to the State,
> As Hunger is to make 'em eat.[4]
> Bare Virtue can't make Nations live
> In Splendor ...
>
> $\qquad\qquad\qquad\qquad\qquad\qquad\qquad\qquad$ (*ibid.*, I.36–37)

For Mandeville, virtuous action means that "Man, contrary [to] the impulse of Nature, should endeavor the Benefit of others, or the Conquest of his own Passions out of a Rational Ambition of being good" (*ibid.*: xlvii). The large domain of action following self-serving "natural" impulses or passions is therefore "vice." Then follows Mandeville's provocative thesis that vice is the "foundation of national prosperity and happiness."

It is also worth noting that an author renowned as a defender of *laissez faire* political economics was, as the above quotation already intimates, anything but a libertarian, politically speaking. One finds in Mandeville's writings an almost Hobbesian nightmare of an egalitarian world, whose baleful consequences require a strong state:

---

[4] Although George Bush's presidency cannot be identified with a global, anti-hunger policy position, his leadership in defining a military intervention by UN-authorized forces in Somalia for "humanitarian" purposes suggests – at least for a time – important historical distancing from Mandeville's "fable." Some recent research on hunger, famine and the equilibrium analysis of food supply related economic interdependencies is touched on in Sen (1987, especially Ch. 1).

For if by Society we only mean a Number of People, that without
Rule or Government should keep together out of a natural Affection
... then there is not in the World a more unfit Creature for Society
than Man; an Hundred of them that should be all Equals, under no
Subjection, or Fear of any Superior upon Earth, could never Live
together awake Two hours without Quarrelling. . . .   (*ibid.*, I.347–348)

For Mandeville, the ideal Society to be constructed is a "Body Politik"
which subdues Man to "become a Disciplin'd Creature, that can find
his own Ends in Labouring for others." Here "under one Head ... each
member is render'd Subservient to the Whole," and they "by cunning
Management are made to Act as one" (*ibid.*, I.347). The multiple
passions and forms of self-interested behaviors need, then, to be
shaped by both persuasion and force to produce such a society.[5]

Hirschman's alternative accounts

These associations bring to mind a second set of arguments for
capitalism, those reviewed by Albert Hirschman in *The Passions and the
Interests* (1977). His book shows how a medieval Augustinian problematique of achieving "civil virtue" through the repression (or harnes-
sing) of vices like pride, avarice, the desire for honor, and ambition
was slowly reformulated and eventually transformed in the early
modern era. He shows how Machiavelli's sixteenth-century advocacy
of vicious but virtuous conduct in the interest of an imperial, mercantile state was subsequently recast into the economic domain. By the
eighteenth century Montesquieu, Vico and Stewart had narrowed such
arguments even further in their advocacy of the calming effect of
coolly calculated self interests, particularly economic or commercial
ones, on the acquisitive passions of arbitrary rulers. Ever so gradually,
and not according to some preordained plan, action taken according to
calculated, contractually based, economic self-interest was rehabilitated
from a position of disdain, to one of honor and esteem.

[5] This problem seems a rather heavy handed version of the "anarchy problematique"
of contemporary realist thinking in International Relations, which focuses on the
establishing of a secure public order out of the self-interested actions of its sovereign
member units, by a mixture of reasoned persuasion and focused fear. But among
states, one would never describe a power-balanced system as one where each
member state was "render'd Subservient to the Whole." Neorealists similarly talk of
the "security dilemma" as an N-Person "Chicken" or SPD game, and the creation of
security as a public good, in the modern, Samuelsonian sense (Alker and Hurwitz
1980; Axelrod 1984; Keohane 1986).

It is hard to realize how great a constructive reversal of popular wisdom this gradual reversal represents. Here we wish only to emphasize the imaginary, counterfactual (and thus fictional and speculative) quality of each of these deliberative constructions, which largely predate the related, more well known liberal, Smithian *visions* of the efficient, everlasting wealth production of market-oriented, property-respecting, entrepreneurial, division-of-labor enhanced, governmentally-regulated nations.

Socialist fairy tales

A third, more radical, but equally constructivist, tradition links the creation of a stable and prosperous modern political-economic order to the revolutionary overcoming of the alienation and exploitation of workers by capitalistic practices, through the *visionary* creation of *social* or *socialized* production relations (Alker and Hurwitz 1980; Johnson 1988; Alker 1990). Traceable back through nineteenth-century social thinkers like Kant, Comte, Marx and Engels to the classical egalitarian beliefs of Mediterranean civilization, this tradition finds expression in twentieth-century social democratic, socialist, and communist thought and practice. SPD researchers are likely to appreciate its Scandinavian peace research variant, with anti-Machiavellian roots in both Lutheran and social democratic thought. In opposition to the *laissez faire* myth, the social democratic "fairy tale" claims that secure, peaceful and prosperous public orders require the ending of inequitable "structural violence" with respect to basic human needs, as well as the development and application of newer technologies for democratically determined public purposes, i.e., just, non-violent and efficient social and economic arrangements (Wallensteen ed. 1988: esp. Ch. 1).

These brief sketches suggest a variety of contrasting, "fairy-tale-like" beliefs or understandings more or less explicitly embedded in and presupposed by modern conservative, liberal and socialist/social democratic traditions of writing about liberal/capitalist political economy. The horror of triumphs by the alternative traditions of thought and practice is similarly bound to images or negative visions we shall call "nightmares" in order to suggest their surreal, narrative-like qualities. Hirschman (1991) summarizes West European reactionary conservative rhetoric in a similar fashion.

Surprisingly, they additionally treat the challenge of liberal/capitalist market relations within a broader political-economic context.

Whether Machiavelli, Hobbes or Rousseau gets cited, each tradition's major images, as briefly presented here, involves the construction and maintenance of systems of public order. Moreover, each tradition sees different, potentially conflictful relations between private actors and public authorities to be at the heart of this public order problematique, whether it is Mandeville's attempted reconciliation of "private vices and public virtue," Montesquieu's vision that commercial interests would soften and balance the passion-induced, frequently bad actions of the powerful, or social democratic calls for the collective ending of structural violence against the less fortunate members of liberal societies.

Asymmetric SPD games as contemporary, political-economic narrative construction, discovery and completion exercises

Without positing the prideful and fearful individuals of Hobbes' or Mandeville's imaginative theoretical works, Andrew Schotter (1981) has convincingly shown that a Prisoner's-Dilemma-like structure is latent in all economic exchanges (see also Johnson 1988: 229ff., Rose 1984). Short-term individual self-interests are in conflict with overall or longer term public or common interests. An enduring, institutionalized exchange structure mimics both the "consensual production interdependence" achieved by, and required of, democratically legitimate governance structures, and the indivisibility and non-excludability of public consumption goods emphasized by economic theorists (Alker 1977b: 34–43). Control relations are particularly interdependent, requiring cooperative or exchange-like behavior before joint individual payoff maximizing behavior can be realized (Alker and Hurwitz 1980: Chs. 4 and 5). According to Ostrom (1990: 217, note 1), the verbalized version of the Prisoner's Dilemma story – involving a district attorney offering (T)emptation payoffs and threatening (S)ucker payoffs to incommunicado prisoners as alternatives to the lesser (R)ewards of tacit inter-prisoner cooperation and the failure of joint (P)enalty sharing – was developed by Merrill Flood and Melvin Dresher around 1953, after the gaming exercises reported in Flood (1952).

Although economists have usually discussed SPD game strategies without attempting either to test the empirical validity of their normative proposals, or interpretively to make empirical sense of experimental players' own resolutional practices,[6] they could, and we believe they should, do so. Symmetric and asymmetric games, like the one in Figure 9.1 below, could be thought of as scenario development/narrative completion exercises whether or not they are associated with an unfinished, storied interpretation of the payoff matrix. Whereas Hobbesian conservatives are likely to identify with the coercive state apparatus wielded by the district attorney, or lament its absence in an "anarchic" world of power politics, liberals like Axelrod will try to paint such "anarchy" in a better light, and leftists will typically emphasize anti-statist, or anti-exploitation solidarity themes. In either case, choice-linked narrative protocols greatly facilitate such deliberative constructions, deconstructions or reconstructions of the options faced by states or players in analogously structured situations.

Indeed, we can use narrative-generating ASPD games to explore the relative sense-making power or truthfulness, for particular player populations, of the narrative structures generated by all three of the political-economic traditions reviewed above, as well as the empirical frequency or adequacy of the "solution concepts" or "strategies" proposed in the technical scholarly literature.

A 1952 RAND preview of our subsequent research

Although the norm for SPD experiments during the 1960s and 1970s[7] was not to collect, report, analyze or make available verbal protocols of

---

[6] In our literature reviews, we have found that most story completion/retelling exercises undertaken by economists try to preserve the identity of the main characters as economically rational individuals. Carol M. Rose is a brilliant partial exception, whose work independently supports and complements our approach. Having argued that "the claim of ownership" is "a kind of assertion or story, told within a culture that shapes the story's content," she suggests that Locke and Blackstone had to appeal to stories to make their liberal version of property plausible. Since – as has earlier been pointed out by others – a property regime has the structure of a common or public good, "there is a gap between the kind of self-interested individual who needs exclusive property to induce him to labor and the kind of individual who has to be there [a situation she describes as a SPD game] to create, maintain, and protect a property regime." The culturally gendered nature of the "Mom" or "Good Citizen" roles necessary for such caring sustenance suggests a large terrain for a feminist restructuring of the foundations of economics (Rose 1994, especially 25, 37–38).

[7] This was determined by the behavioristic science and the statistical conceptualizations of Atkinson and Suppes, Rapoport and Chammah (1965) and Morton Deutsch, among others; see Alker and Hurwitz (1980) for more details.

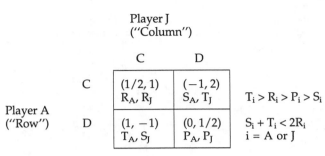

Player J
("Column")

		C	D	
Player A ("Row")	C	$(1/2, 1)$ R_A, R_J	$(-1, 2)$ S_A, T_J	$T_i > R_i > P_i > S_i$
	D	$(1, -1)$ T_A, S_J	$(0, 1/2)$ P_A, P_J	$S_i + T_i < 2R_i$ $i = A$ or J

Figure 9.1   Flood's 1952 game represented as a Prisoner's Dilemma

SPD game play, Flood (1952) does report, for the earliest recorded SPD game of which we are aware, verbal accounts for Players AA and JW. Recast in language corresponding to the conventional designations of Figure 9.1 above, these are presented, along with the cumulative move-payoff graphs characteristic of Alker's (1985) research program, in Figure 9.2 and Table 9.1.

We spend the time and paper necessary for this report of a single game for several reasons, beyond its evident historical interest. First, it helps, along with our brief discussion, to suggest the interpretive (including the strategic) richness made possible by the use of verbal accounts in the dramaturgical study of social interactions (Alker and Hurwitz 1980: Ch. 6, citing Harré and Secord 1972, especially Chs. 9–11). Indeed, Alker and Hurwitz concluded their literature review of SPD games with the suggestion that SPD games be dramaturgically reconceptualized as miniature "moral and political dramas on constricting social scientific stages." This they did as a way of attacking those purely behavioristic or economistic approaches to the "dilemma resolution" issue then prominent in the literature; if game play is understood as more or less skilled, meaning revealing, creative and always play-like performances by socialized, responsible and self-monitoring human beings, then conflicting performative interpretations – with "plots" and casts of passionately motivated characters such as those imaginatively constructed above – should be found in appropriately represented action descriptions.

Secondly, we present this example in some detail because of its prophetic quality with respect both to contemporary American political-strategic-economic culture and to our experimental investigations. We shall link the dramatic tension implicit in the non-shared protocol accounts of this exercise to the larger processual dilemmas

Table 9.1 *Running comments from first published SPD game*

Play No. Subject AA (Row)	Subject JW (Column)
1 JW will play D – sure win. Hence if I play C – I lose. [Ds]	Hope he's bright. [Cs]
2 What is he doing?!! [Ds]	He isn't but maybe he'll wise up. [Cs]
3 Trying mixed? [Ds]	OK, dope. [Ds]
4 Has he settled on D? [Ds]	OK, dope. [Ds]
5 Perverse! [Only C in first 11 moves]	It isn't the best of all possible worlds. [Ds]
6 I'm sticking to D since he will mix for at least 4 more times. [Ds]	Oh ho! Guess I'll have to give him another chance. [Cs]
7 [Ds]	Cagey, ain't he? Well … [Cs]
8 [Ds]	In time he could learn, but not in ten moves so. [Ds]
9 If I mix occasionally, he will switch – but why will he ever switch from D? [Ds]	[Ds]
10 Prediction. He will stick with D until I change from D. I feel like DuPont. [Ds]	I can guarantee myself a gain of 5 [by 10 Ds], and … that Player AA breaks even (at best). On the other hand, with nominal assistance from AA, I can transfer the guarantee of 5 to Player AA and make 10 for myself too [in a CC pattern]. This means I have control of the game to a large extent, so Player AA had better appreciate this and get on the bandwagon. [Ds]
11 [Ds]	With small amounts of money at stake, I would (as above) try (by using C) to coax AA into mutually profitable actions. With large amounts at stake I would play D until AA displayed some initiative and a willingness to invest in his own future. One play of C by AA would change me from D to C, where I would remain until bitten. On the last play it would be conservative for me to switch to D, but I wouldn't do so if the evidence suggested that AA was a nice stable personality and not in critical need of just a little … cash. Probably learned by now [Cs]

Table 9.1 contd.

12	[Cs]	I'll be damned! But I'll try again [Cs]
13	[Cs]	That's better. [Cs]
14	[Cs]	Ha! [Cs]
15	[Cs, then Ds on play 16]	(bliss) [Cs]
17	[Cs]	The stinker. [Ds]
18	[Cs]	He's crazy. I'll teach him the hard way. [Ds]
19	I'm completely confused. Is he trying to convey information to me? [Ds]	Let him suffer. [Ds]
21	[Ds]	Maybe he'll be a good boy now. [Cs]
22	[Cs]	Always takes time to learn. [Cs]
23	[Cs]	Time. [Cs through 26]
27	[Cs after a D]	Same old story. [Ds]
28	He wants more Cs by me than I'm giving. [Ds]	To hell with him. [Ds through 30]
31	Some start. [Ds]	Once again. [Cs]
32	JW is bent on sticking to D. He will not *share* at all as a price of getting me to stick to C. [General comment, associated with Cs on 32 through 40]	—, he learns slow! [Cs]
33		On the beam again. [Cs through 38]
39	[Cs after D on 38]	The —. [Ds twice]
41	[Cs]	Always try to be virtuous. [Cs]
42	[Cs through 48]	Old stuff. [Cs through 49]
49	*He will not share.* [D]	
50	[Cs, then Ds on 51]	He's a shady character and doesn't realize we are playing a 3rd party, not each other. [Ds]
52	[Cs 52 through 59]	He *requires* great virtue but doesn't have it himself. [begins long C series]
58	He will not share.	A shiftless individual – opportunist, knave. [but continues Cs]
59	He does not want to *trick me.* He is satisfied. I must teach him to share. [Ds]	Goodness me! Friendly! [Cs]
60	[Ds]	[Cs]
62	[Cs 61 through 66]	

Table 9.1 contd.

Play No. Subject AA (Row)	Subject JW (Column)
67 He won't share. [Ds]	
68 He'll punish for trying! [Cs]	He can't stand success [Ds for 3]
70 I'll try once more to share – by taking. [Ds]	[ends D series]
71 [Ds but then Cs through 80]	This is like toilet training a child – you have to be very patient. [Cs] [begins C series through play 81]
80 [Cs, then Ds on 81]	Well.
82 [Cs through play 98]	He needs to be taught about that. [Ds]
91 When will he switch as a last minute grab of (2). Can I beat him to it as late as possible?	[Cs from 83 to 99]
92 [Cs]	Good.

Notes: Column and row designations have been added and "play" options redescribed in terms of conventional C(ooperate) and D(efect) labels. Corresponding move information has been included; punctuation has been changed. Protocols have been represented in parallel, quasi-conversational form.
Source: Flood 1952 (39–52), who reports that the two subjects AA and JW are friends.

generated by inequitable reward structures in our society. From our summary narrative of this game, we shall also extrapolate to the larger population of games and game players which, since 1979, we have subjected to ASPD game play.

The first published RAND ASPD game

The first RAND SPD games were asymmetrical ones, played for pennies, without direct communication.[8] Looking at Figure 9.2, one finds initial confusion concerning the cumulative direction the game would take, followed by a stabilized, but uneven, jointly determined movement in the cumulative "+, +" direction. Despite the absence of

---

[8] Poundstone (1993) gives interesting background information on RAND's fascination with game theory, and the names of the players of the Flood game, but his interpretation of the game records I have adapted for presentation and discussion here does not match our own on several points.

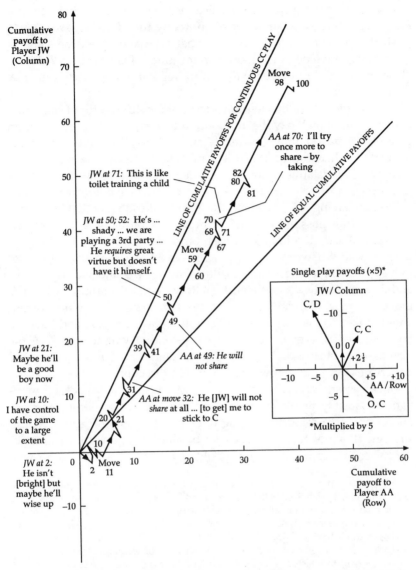

Figure 9.2 A cumulative payoff graph for the earliest published SPD game

Source: Flood 1952 (18–19).

315

opportunities for explicit communication, there seems to have been a reoccurring but irregular series of efforts by the "Row" player AA to push the cumulative totals nearer what we have called the "line of equal cumulative payoffs" shown on the graph. Plays/moves 7, 16, 31, 38, 49, 60, 67 and 81 evidence this effort, regularly retaliated against by Column Player JW.

The significance of this tension – indicated by the sector of the figure between the equal payoffs line and the unequal, pure cooperation cumulative payoff line – is much more clearly brought out by the simulated "dialogue of the deaf" in Table 9.1. On the basis of an analysis of his relative control/guarantee relationships (at play 10), JW justifies his favored position *vis-à-vis* his more social democratic RAND colleague, having already noted the Mandevillean view that this "isn't the best of all possible worlds" at move 5. Gradually, but unevenly, AA and JW develop images of each other and of the game's likely or desirable story-like development. At move 32, AA shows the first sign of his increasing preoccupation with "sharing" the unequal payoffs – 1 and 3 respectively – associated for "Row" and "Column" with a CC move.[9] Like a Mandevillean conservative, Player JW, who patronizingly refers to his friend as not "bright" (plays 1 and 2) and "a good boy" (move 21), is evidently fairly consistently trying to teach AA the virtues of a steady CC course. He regularly punishes AA for DC departures from their movement in the CC direction.

Quite remarkably, JW refuses to recognize the equity-seeking motivation plausibly linked to AA's occasional DC effort, demeaning AA on several occasions. Interestingly, at move 50, there is the typical strategic move of trying to get inferior allies in line with a solidarity appeal to a supposedly joint "Cold War" effort – note the "we"

---

[9] AA's remark more or less (self-)consciously fits the socialist "fairy tale," given a realistic cast by Johnson's (1988) claim that "[a]mong players in a dynamic PD a common interest in mutual cooperation is irredeemably conditional." As evidence, Johnson cites Elster (1982, 468), the "history of the working class shows ... that cooperative behavior typically is conditional – motivated by a concern for doing one's share rather than by the spirit of sacrifice or disregard of actual consequences."

The extent to which AA and JW, described as friends, were "role-playing" their game play and transcript articulations is unclear, but probably not negligible – not too many friends would be as condescending toward each other as JW appears to be to AA. It is thus particularly interesting that JW invokes an earlier classical language of virtuous conduct (move 50, Table 9.1) in justifying in a self-righteous and self-serving way a long string of cooperative moves. This argument, and JW's consistent sanctioning behavior for equity-seeking departures from a stable CC-pattern, both fit our previous Mandeville quotations in several key respects.

associated with play 50 – against some supposedly hostile third party (presumably not the Russians, perhaps the game instructor or his uneven payoff matrices). This approach, the impossibility of communication, and JW's demeaning sanctioning strategy, keep him from thinking about the equity/sharing issue increasingly preoccupying AA.

Dramatically, then, the unequally shared expanding pie of game payoffs reveals and replays a fundamental, historically shaped moral and political conflict over the distribution of benefits from jointly cooperative productive enterprises. Associated with an uneven movement in the direction of jointly positive outcomes is a frustrated dialogue – JW does not receive or interpret AA's "messages" very accurately – over such fundamental distributive/redistributive issues.

But the role orientations available within American culture for strategically interdependent game play also have particularly American roots. In the Conclusion to her acclaimed study of American culture, on the basis of completely different conversational evidence than here presented, Livia Polanyi offers a stylized narrative of ambivalences nearly equivalent to those we have just seen:

> The story of America is, very largely, a prolonged, complex, and sometimes tragic exegesis of those few lines from the *Declaration of Independence* "All men are created Equal." Yes, all MEN are EQUAL, but who *exactly* are [they]? ... what Rights ... have those who ARE NOT quite ADULTS?
> The question remains as painful, as perplexing, as ever: EXACTLY which INDIVIDUAL PEOPLE are ENTITLED to LIVE LIFE FREELY PURSUING HAPPINESS as EQUALS of other MEN. (Polanyi 1989: 193f.)

Polanyi's Declaration of Independence "story" frame is thus a liberal/democratic "fairy tale" in exactly the same controversial, but not necessarily pejorative sense that we described earlier.

The contest of order-building resolutions in our 1979–1983 exercises

According to procedures described elsewhere (Alker 1985; Hurwitz 1991), over a decade ago, Alker, Etheredge and Hurwitz conducted thirty-one asymmetric SPD student games using the same payoff matrix. It has a structure rather similar to that of Flood's matrix given in Figure 9.1:

		Column Player	
		C	D
Row Player	C	(1, 3)	(−6, 4)
	D	(6, −4)	(−1, −3)

Alker and Hurwitz wanted to go beyond Rapoport and Chammah's (1965) behavioristic concern with trends in individual C, D or collective CC, CD, DC and DD propensities, to get closer to the moral and political dramas they expected to find there. They were looking as well at the social and historical development of their minimally communicative, experimental, mini-"societies" (defined roughly in the Mandeville sense, which suggests that self-interested "defections" against the other "Prisoner" facilitate public virtue). The tendency of SPD players to become a "pair" of players who act less and less independently of each other, and match responses near the end of the game more than 90 percent of the time (Rapoport and Chammah 1965: 299), was a suggestive quasi-societal development in this regard calling for further clarification. Also needing explication were the operative rationales behind "Tit-for-Tat" propensities (used more often by males) and the divergent but individually stable outcomes referred to as "CC" and "DD" lock-ins, the former being more frequent among Michigan students repeatedly exposed to the payoff matrix's total value (Rapoport and Chammah 1965: Ch. 14).

As summarized in Hurwitz (1991), they found an enlarged dramatic/historical repertoire, largely describable in terms of the tendencies already hinted at by Flood, Rapoport and Chammah. With a variety of initial scenario specifications, we have found more comedies than tragedies in our dramaturgically oriented analyses of SPD games. Given the same, moderately asymmetric payoff matrix, a larger fraction of Boston area (mostly MIT) student players "succeeds" at ASPD games in getting long-term cumulative positive payoffs, and a smaller fraction fails, typically getting "locked in" to an anarchic "war of all against all" of their own making. Quantitatively speaking, nineteen out of thirty-one ASPD games produced stabilized outcomes ("story endings") pointed cumulatively toward either straight. CC lock-ins or equity-adjusted CC lock-ins. Only five relatively stable DD lock-ins were identified, along with three unresolved games and, surprisingly, four games appearing to end in either a CD or a DC pattern.[10]

Behaviorally speaking, for a large subset of the thirty-one games, "continuity" of move predictions (r = 0.79) and "matching" the other's expected choice (r = 0.76) gave slightly better empirical fits with actual behavior than a Tit-for-Tat model (r = 0.74) (Alker 1985: B-2-3).

But in the incompleteness, inefficiencies and instabilities of their "resolutional understandings," the mutually beneficial outcomes have often had disappointing or even quasi-tragic plots or subplots. That twelve of the nineteen "comic" outcomes were CC-type lock-ins, while only seven of them showed versions of equity adjustments, fits the somewhat more tragic story "line" or "plot" – self-defeating elements associated with glimpses of personal awareness and responsibility, as well as overwhelming larger necessities – which the Flood game would lead us to expect.

Using a systematic battery of questions every four moves, an effort was made to get behind these cumulatively focused patterns. Rather than present one of our "Hobbesian nightmares," a socially constructed DD "anarchy" which usually seemed "natural" or "inevitable" to our MIT players, we offer Figure 9.3 as almost ideally typical of the equity-sensitive CC lock-in tendencies of the 1979–83 games. Unlike the Flood game of Figure 9.2, the "fairy tale" coming true in Figure 9.3 is a social democratic one, constructed, ironically, by Row and Column players who described themselves at the start of the game as "conservative" and "moderately conservative" respectively.

Our brief comments will serve, moreover, to suggest some rather powerful disconfirmations of the empirical adequacy of "Tit-for-Tat" as a performatively adequate description of either male or female game play (Rapoport and Chammah 1965; Axelrod 1984). Since Amartya Sen's theoretical analyses of the identity, morality and choice issues implicit in SPD games come closer to the analyses offered by most other economists, we shall also briefly suggest some ways in which our games validate some of his insights, as well as ways in which his

---

[10] Although the four remaining ASPD games tended to point, surprisingly, toward CD and DC lock-ins, these only occasionally revealed real dramatic tension. For example, the 10 vs. 37 game ended its 52 moves with Column refusing to defect and Row trying harder and harder, but unsuccessfully, to get Row to defect. It reads a bit like a Christian martyrdom play. Several of the other CD or DC lock-in outcomes are associated with misread game specifications.

perspective requires even further, interdisciplinary development (Sen 1982, 1985, 1986).

First, note that even though this game (and many others like it) show highly coordinated behaviors, the mechanisms generating such reciprocity are not the "Tit-for-Tat" strategies discussed by Rapaport and Chammah (1965) and explored in an evolutionary fashion by Axelrod (1984) and, among many others, Nowak and Sigmund (1992). Players 52 and 57, equivalently designated Row and Column, do not start with well defined Tit-for-Tat strategies in mind; nor, more generally, as conventional game theory would have it, do they, or AA and JW before them, stick to the same strategy throughout the game. The mechanism of innovation is not fixed, "evolutionary" selection from among individuals or their progeny each following fixed, but often different, pre-programmed strategies.

Rather, despite the physical communication barrier, the players attempt practically to reason together. They reflectively explore their historically developing situations, and frequently (re-) construct their social relationships and (eventually multi-move) strategies as the game proceeds, until a stable pattern of play, based on mutually supporting interpretations, has developed. Row's strategy of trying regularly to bring about five CC's followed by one DC does not appear before move 17, and it is quite distinct from the strategy – better described as a moderately reflective heuristic rule of thumb since it does not cover all possibilities – of protective Ding evident in 52's remarks at move five. Column's interpretation of the emergent pattern is as a simple CC pattern at move 13, but a more complex, more equitable mix on play 17. Row's deeply suspicious attitude toward Column's double-cross intentions, evident in move 21 and debated at play 33, only slowly gives way to a stable expectation of nearly equal ultimate cumulative payoffs.

Presented in an early argumentation graphics format reported on in Chapter 1, the practical argumentation representations in the appendix to this chapter support and elaborate upon these interpretations. Figure 9A there shows Devereux's rational reconstruction of Column's reasoning at moves 1, 26 and 32. Thus notice *the complete change in meaning* associated with the C and D choices (or "behavior") at the later two points in the game. There is the expectation that actions that even "the scores a little bit" are justified by a joint commitment to a pattern of peaceful coexistence. Even a two point differential between cumulative payoffs is justified as the result of a "lost" "fight" at the beginning of the game. Comparing the differently rationalized "D" moves of move 1 and move 32 highlights how "D" "behavior" in Tit-for-Tat patterns can be differently interpreted as "action" in a more thoroughly understood ASPD game.[11]

Although 52 and 57 indeed never talk to each other, they can truthfully be described (Hurwitz 1991: 223ff.) as being practically engaged in historically changing "conversations for action," where moves are usually both instrumental and communicative at the same time. The "conversation" pragmatically converges on the "peaceful co-existence" first enunciated by 57 on move 9, and described at trial 33 by 57 as a shared effort "to maintain the point balance." Historical patterning is evident in the tell-tale "zig-zag" equity pattern, in the dramatic increase in correct predictions of each other's moves after about the first thirteen trials/moves, and, more subtly, in the increasingly shared understanding of what "peace" or the mutually improvised "game plan" is all about. If we look at the slightly longer 7th "tooth" in Figure 9.3 and connect it to the discussion of trials 43 and 45, we see an adaptive adjustment pattern at work, maintaining an internalized, equitable ideal.

The *shared meaning* of a "D" move, when out of the 5 C–C, D–C pattern, has changed from that of an act of "aggression" to that of a "mistake." This is not merely the changing significance of the same "behavior" when interpreted as *symbolic, instrumental and expressive social action*, it exemplifies what Max Weber (1978: 19–33) in *Economy and Society* would refer to as the construction of a legitimate socio-political *"order"* through sociopolitical action and interaction.[12] In the

---

[11] The Appendix also provides an illustration of the Aristotelian practice – described in Chapter 2 and mentioned further below – of interpreting human interactions as chains of practical syllogisms. Devereux's ability to reconstruct rationales is obviously contestable as well, but nonetheless very impressive in the way he hermeneutically explicates "surface" traces of the reasoning involved. Using computerized routines to make such history-sensitive reconstructions is not yet possible; I doubt it ever will fully be so.

[12] "Social action ... may be oriented to the past, present, or expected future behavior of others.... Overt action is non-social if it is oriented solely to the behavior of inanimate objects. [It is 'social' when] the actor's behavior is meaningfully oriented to that of others." "The social relationship thus consists entirely and exclusively in the existence of a probability that there will be a [mutually] meaningful course of social action" which may be oriented toward either usage, custom or self-interest. Legitimate orders are social relationships where "conduct is, approximately or on the average, oriented toward determinable 'maxims.'" Legitimacy means the maxims are "in some way obligatory or exemplary" (Weber 1978: 19–33).

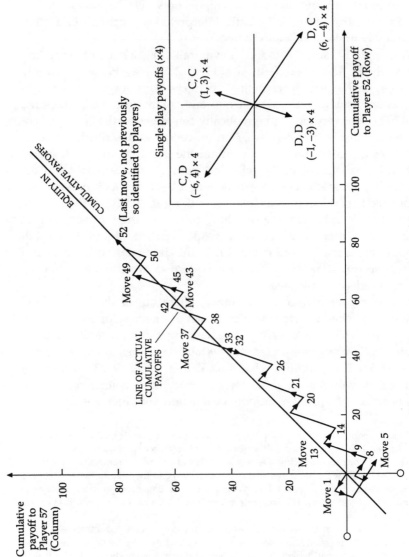

Cumulative
payoff to
Player 57
(Column)

EQUITY IN
CUMULATIVE PAYOFFS

52 (Last move, not previously
so identified to players)

50

Move 49

45

Move 43

42

38

LINE OF ACTUAL
CUMULATIVE
PAYOFFS

33
32

Move 37

26

21

20

14

Move
13

9

8

Move 5

Move 1

Single play payoffs (×4)

C, C
(1, 3) × 4

C, D
(−6, 4) × 4

D, D
(−1, −3) × 4

D, C
(6, −4) × 4

Cumulative payoff
to Player 52 (Row)

100

80

60

40

20

Figure 9.3   The Player 52 (Row) vs. Player 57 (Column) ASPD game

language of even more contemporary socioeconomic theorizing, it is a kind of quasi-historical, *"creation of traditions"* (Schelling 1960: 106–107, with extended italics) or the *"invention of tradition"* (Johnson 1988: 230–231, borrowing from Hobsbawm).

Within this socioeconomic understanding, narrative and history play crucial roles. What the behaviorally minded might describe as "path dependence" in sequential game play, is to us even clearer evidence of socially constructed *historicity*, definable as the shared temporal self-understanding of a continuing human society (Alker 1984, 1990, 1992b). Notice how a *shared narrative* has become part of the *shared identifications and common interests* of the 52–57 mini-society, symbolized compactly by Column's use of "the status quo" in move 49. As Sen has emphasized, collective purposes and rule-following behavior, as well as changed identifications and the moral principles linked to them, are part of this explanatory story (Sen 1985, 1986). What he nowhere mentions in these papers, however, is the ways in which individual and collective *identities and interests* are shaped and crystallized by *shared stories* of past moral, political and economic choices.

Historicity, then, is a crucial property of any emergent social order. It helps define the present and the future in terms of the past, its realized or failed collective possibilities. When we see in Figure 9.3 each of the components of a mutually oriented, maxim-based, mutually enforced, historically self-aware, sociopolitical order (in the Weberian sense), the constructivist understanding of social arrangements is fully realized. And we are entitled to argue what neither Axelrod nor Sen fully realizes, that human SPD games are, at least sometimes, narratively guided, social construction and/or reconstruction exercises in ways that strategic or evolutionary equilibrium models seriously, dramaturgically, underspecify.

The current round: Communication and cash facilitate equitable resolutions

Our current round of ASPD experiments are focused on the effects of motivational determinants, allowed communication, and cash payments on game play. Moreover, we have begun to explore ways of coding achievement, power, affiliation and intimacy motivations within the game summary narratives that players are asked to prepare, and on independent testing instruments (Winter 1991; Stewart 1982). This way we should eventually be able to examine the role of the situationally specific (Burns 1992) motivational determinants within the conversations for action clearly observable within our games, even when verbal communication is not allowed. The return to the great arguments about passions and interests supporting or undermining capitalism, or other socioeconomic and political arrangements, should thus be facilitated within the micro-worlds of ASPD games.

Drawing on Rothkin (1992: 31) and subsequent research, we can summarize the current, computerized round of ASPD research with the following figure:

	End Region	Game Instances	Total
	CC	Y Y	2
	CD		0
	DC		0
	DD	Y N N	3
Redistribution (includes equity)		Y Y Y N $Y $Y $Y $Y	8
Unstable		N N	2
			15

Figure 9.4   End regions for 15 recent ASPD exercises

Note: "Y" and "N" refer to allowance of communication; "$" refers to 10 cents per point cash awards.

Even though the number of games is still small, the pattern in Figure 9.4 clearly supports the expectation that the possibility of exchanging up to two short computer messages per move greatly increases the chance of achieving cooperative, equity-oriented, redistributive outcomes. And, as we found before, experimentally increasing chances for quasi-historical written reflections on the cumulative tendencies of game play tends to make for faster "positive, or comic resolutions" of game dilemmas. Surprisingly, monetary payoffs, in the few games we have used them, seem to do the same. Hence, the existence of social market-like relationships appears, as the *laissez-faire* fairy tale would have it, to facilitate virtuous public outcomes!

Now look at Figure 9.5 and Table 9.2. We have elicited or constructed for the game of Players 100 and 102 five narrativizing summary accounts: first the annotated cumulative graph, which shows many reverses and only a very grudging and unstable move toward the CC direction. Then, we present in Table 9.2 two summary narra-

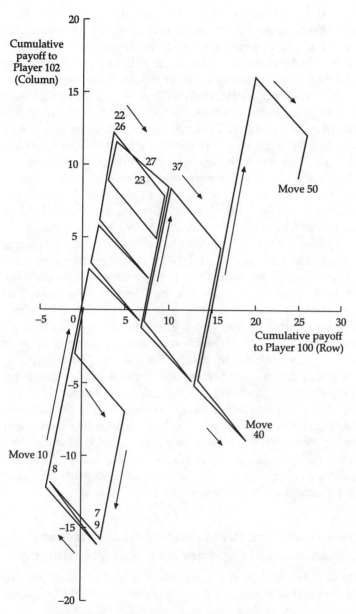

Figure 9.5 A cumulative payoff graph for a non-communication game: player 100 vs. player 102

tives composed by Players 100 and 102 immediately upon finishing their game. Taken together with audio recordings of post-game debriefing sessions, and carefully prepared "ethnographic" reconstructions of game histories, these provide a rich source of narrative materials for further, contextually sensitive modes of analysis.

Specifically, Table 9.2 contains as well power, achievement and affiliation motivation indicators from the story-based thematic apperception tradition of David McClelland and his coworkers (Stewart 1982), as coded by a professional coder, Samantha George. When compared with Hurwitz's ethnographic motivational account of 100 vs. 102 play (not included), the suggested interpretations of motivational bases for player actions can be seen to converge. Row's tough but peace-loving "foreign policy" surely fits the imagined world of liberal realism held by many American Cold Warriors. Somehow, as suggested by the movement of joint play out of the Hobbesian, collectively self-defeating world of DD lock-in nightmares into the mutually rewarding, Smithian realm of cooperative competition, the upper right hand quadrant of Figure 9.5, the "Cold War" has ended, or at least been transformed.

Not only are many of the generalizations about ASPD play's constructive character suggested above confirmed by this case, there is a remarkably clear example of the "softening" or "balancing" of domination oriented power motivations by economic achievement and affiliation motivations. Affect-neutral calculations of "interest" seem to be involved, but it appears better to note reasons within the passions (Frank 1988), and the ameliorative effects of economic achievement motivation on Row's (100's) power drive, once his goal of relative point superiority[13] is no longer threatened. At least in our micro-world, Hirschman's reconstruction of the Montesquieu–Stewart imagined arguments for capitalism have come true!

How ASPD narratives research historicizes and humanizes contemporary sociopolitical economy

More generally, this chapter has promoted the fruitful integration of narratively oriented humanistic inquiry and the empirically grounded

---

[13] Experimental instructions carefully stress that players should attempt to maximize their own payoff scores; this evidently did not stop Player 100 from relativizing his aspirations. Note also how, as in the Fudenberg and Maskin (1986) folk theorem, at least for a while, Player 102 can "beat the other guy out cold."

Table 9.2   *Player 100 vs. Player 102: player summaries*

A Player 100 (Row)
There were two turning points in this game. The
first was when I decided that *I had gained enough*   POWER – EITHER
relative points over the opponent to start cooperating.   STATEMENT
Once that happened, I realized that I *could let* the
other person come close and *let him* gain
confidence.
   I was not stimulating any scenario/strategy. I
didn't want the other person to have more points
than me, my whole strategy was based on that.
Well, there was some sense of role playing because   POWER
after a while I had the upper hand and *I knew I
could beat the other guy out cold* and so I began to
play with a little arrogance, I guess. (like a *superpower*)
   I think the opponent was basically reacting to my
moves which put him (the four persons were all
male) in a big disadvantage. The matrix basically
HELPED me too.
   Well, we *could have made the points gaining* MUCH   ACH-SCORED
MUCH *more efficient by cooperating* and then letting   EVEN IF HYPOTH.
me catch up (since a C by me and a C by the
opponent is +4 overall and a D by me and a C by
the opponent was + so I could have like let him
gain 10 points over me and then do a D (which will
even out the dis-parity) and then continue from
there. That's optimum but it's hard to convey and I
gave up once I had the upper hand.
   When I started I didn't really think of strategy. I
guess it all came together after a while and when *I*   ACH
began thinking about it I raced through the scores => ...

B Player 102 (Column)
I was the player that benefited from peace the most,
so I had to be almost suicidally hard-assed in the
beginning to avoid being kicked on a lot later. This
got us stuck in d–d mode until the other player
offered c; also meant that *any d's by other player had*   POW – ACTION → EFFECT
to be reacted to (and were). I was trying to just play
the game, *setting up a scenario* for the other player
where all-c's was optimal, but tended to think of it as
war and peace – *I was the peace-loving country* that
had to have *a strong deterrence*, even at great   AFF - POW
sacrifice. The other player *played about optimally* for   ACH – EITHER
the matrix – true, all-c would have been better, but   STATEMENT
he wanted to see if he could get away with a few
unresponded-to d's to *rack up big points* (and a
different strategy by me would have rewarded
that). Role playing as such was not clear on his

327

Table 9.2 contd.

part. Communication would have allowed me to explain my inflexible strategy to the other player, and hence probably stabilized things faster; also we could have struck deals like letting him do a d every now and then to make things more symmetric (I could make a deal like that only with communication – the game was too short for us to feel that out, especially as *"wars" had to be a bunch of turns long enough for them to be effective deterrents*, due to the lopsided matrix).	POW – HYPOTHETICAL

Note: ACH – 12
POW – 3
AFF – 1

theory-building activities of economics and its sister social sciences. Following in the humanistic footsteps of Montesquieu, Marx, Weber, Hirschman, Sen and McClelland, we have tried to illustrate how narratively sensitive ASPD research can both historicize and rehumanize *homo economicus*. In our experiments, looked at dramaturgically, or performatively, we have found quite a few of the major alternative arguments, "fairy tales" and passions associated with the triumph of capitalism over the last several centuries. Phenomenologically, experimental games are not considered as tests of unreal models; they have been redescribed as episodic, lesson-suggesting, monad-like dramas abstracted from a larger historical world which they microscopically reflect. This has been possible because we have refused, pseudo-scientifically, to treat social scientific "subjects" in experimentally isolated contexts as devoid of history, culture, language and previous human experience. Nor have we treated our greatest economic theorists as wholly isolatable from their own, similar contexts. Hopefully others will go further along these paths.

A. First Move

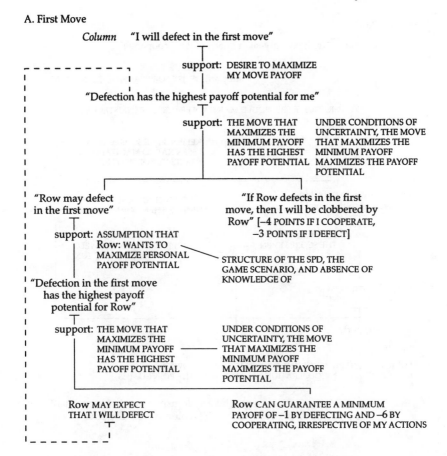

Figure 9A-1   A chain of practical syllogisms: practical argumentation in the player 52 (row) vs. player 57 (column) ASPD game

B. Move 26

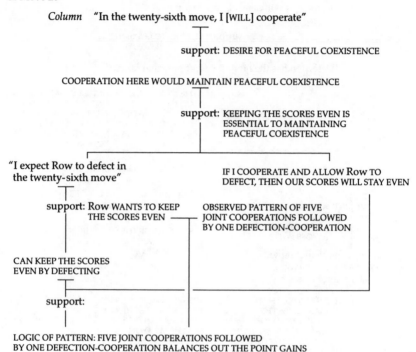

Figure 9A-2 A chain of practical syllogisms: practical argumentation in the player 52 (row) vs. player 57 (column) ASPD game

C. Move 32

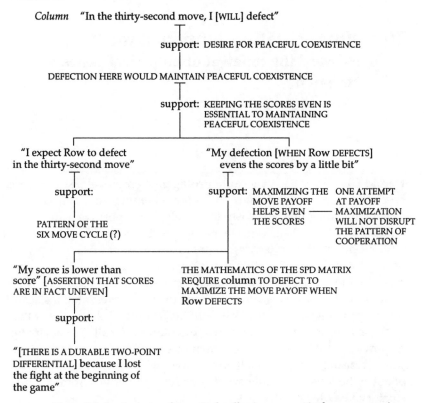

Figure 9A-3   A chain of practical syllogisms: practical argumentation in the Player 52 (Row) vs. Player 57 (Column) ASPD game

10 Emancipatory empiricism:
Toward the renewal of empirical peace research

Harold Guetzkow has long cautioned against empirical peace research becoming too "data bound." Without claiming to have captured exactly his intentions, I wish to develop the positive side of this injunction. How, then, can we recognize the actualities in our data without hiding the underlying, more or less just and peaceful possibilities? Assuming that there are various truths in our data, are there ways to find those special truths that can help unbind us, make us free – from past falsehoods, possibility-distorting representations, continuing oppressions, even war itself? In this chapter, I shall answer these questions in terms of a research orientation I call "emancipatory empiricism."[1] Although this research orientation is more general than peace research itself, I shall argue that it fits peace research well because the latter's disciplinary distinctiveness derives from an emancipatory knowledge interest.

One can conceptualize social scientific research orientations in general, and peace research in particular, at three increasingly comprehensive and concrete levels:

> *ontology* – their (metaphysical) doctrines of being – reality, actuality, necessity and possibility in the realms of human action and experience;
> *epistemology* – their philosophies of scientific knowledge generation and the methodologies (applied epistemologies) developed for discerning the real;

[1] My title reflects both the emancipatory impulses often evident in Karl Deutsch's systematic empiricism (which recognizes both inductive and deductive moments of social scientific development and points in an Aristotelian sense toward enhanced collective self-determination), and Johan Galtung's more dialectical conceptions of social research, spelled out most explicitly in his *Essays in Methodology* (Galtung 1977).

disciplinarity – the institutionalized disciplinary matrices (including research sponsors, professional organizations, research programs and knowledge interests) guiding research, teaching and applications of a field of knowledge.

After some orientational remarks about the relevance of its emancipatory knowledge interest for peace research's distinctive disciplinary self-understanding, I shall characterize emancipatory empiricism somewhat more generally. Adopting such an orientation, this chapter then offers twelve epistemological guidelines for emancipatory peace research, concluding with a call for non-emancipatory empiricists to rethink their social ontologies.

During a period when quite a few younger researchers are skeptical about, or disillusioned with, the empirical methodologies pioneered by Burton, Deutsch, Galtung, Guetzkow, Haas, Lasswell, Rapoport, Richardson, Singer and Wright, this contribution will serve critically to reawaken interest in them. My practical purpose in doing so is to help renew and develop a style of peace research that is both *empirical and emancipatory*.

How its emancipatory knowledge interest distinguishes peace research

I believe, and shall argue, that peace research's inherent, emancipatory knowledge interest – more strongly evident in some contexts than in others – forms a most important basis for peace research's disciplinary distinctiveness. What, then, is an emancipatory knowledge interest?

Habermas has described it as "an attitude which is formed in the experience of suffering from something man-made, which can be abolished and should be abolished." He believes the emancipatory interest to be more than a mere "subjective attitude which may or may not guide this or that piece of scientific research"; rather it is something profoundly ingrained in certain of our social structures, the "calling into question, and deep-seated wish to throw off, relations which repress ... without necessity" (Habermas 1986: 198).[2]

Let us accept for now a provisional characterization of peace research both as research in the service of war avoidance and as research organized in the interest of coercion-minimizing social justice

---

[2] The classic account of "surplus repression" by an earlier member of the Frankfurt school is Marcuse (1966).

(including, importantly, a variety of mutually consistent forms of self-realization and the avoidance of what Galtung has called structural violence).

How does peace research qualify for such an emancipatory knowledge interest? First of all, by demonstrating, as Margaret Mead long ago argued, that war is evidently "man-made," an invention rather than a necessity (Mead 1940).[3] Secondly, by arguing that war – and the coercive, militaristic way of life it supports – should be abolished. Thirdly, by attempting to establish that, like slavery, this way of life, and its most deleterious consequences, can be ended. Indeed, to the extent that its work is consistent with these or analogously functioning arguments, peace research is an appropriate, partly institutionalized, increasingly global embodiment of such a knowledge interest, and thus an apt candidate for exemplifying emancipatory empiricism.

Accepting the approximate appropriateness of this emancipatory characterization of the disciplinary focus of peace research points one (controversially) toward the distinctiveness of such an orientation *vis-à-vis* alternative research traditions (paradigms, programs and theories) and academic fields of study centering their investigations on war and peace. Here, then, is the major thesis I wish to sketch in this section: peace research's disciplinary distinctiveness derives most importantly from this emancipatory interest.

Consider peace research's major alternative with a similar focus, the realist tradition of international relations research. In the above characterization, there is already evident a basis for serious disagreement – in fact a conflict of interests – between the realist tradition of international relations (including programs of research on "strategic studies" when defined within that tradition) and peace research. With varying degrees of critical distance, the realist tradition defines itself in terms of state interests, conceived in terms of enhanced or maintained levels of power; in the twentieth century it has often been associated with the search for the eternal laws of power politics.[4] Order (not peace) is given precedence over justice, domestically and internationally.

---

[3] Given her view, Mead does not subscribe to the genetic necessity arguments involving male sexual hormones. Elshtain (1987) is a more recent, thoughtful feminist account of the roles contemporary women play (and can play) in sustaining (and undermining) war as a contemporary institution.

[4] See Chapter 1 above. The inadequate "realism" associated with "eternal necessity" arguments appears to be the all too influential conjunction (found in many other behavioral peace researcher's works) of Morgenthau's (anti-"idealist") "realism" and Hume's probabilistic "empirical realism." Bhaskar (1986) may be read as a 300 page

Even when made more "rigorous" by the adoption of scientific practices borrowed from the natural sciences, mathematical economics or statistics, behavioral "neo-realism" suffers directly or indirectly from difficulties similar to those of its realist progenitor. Claims of scientific neutrality with respect to policy issues may or may not be justified, but they get in the way of explicit criticisms of realism's too comfortable relationship with power holders, and inhibit the reasoned advocacy of the elimination of war, militarism, structural violence, ecological exploitation and other forms of social or natural injustice that are constitutive of the openly avowed commitment of emancipatory peace research to social change.

Similarly, despite this commitment, there are actual and potential conflicts of interest between peace research and Marxian scholarship defined entirely in terms of the interests of a particular coalition of classes, if that coalition excludes many others. Despite the emancipatory thrust of Marxist analysis and its optimistic view about the possibility of achieving more just, prosperous and peaceful communities, Marxist theory too can become (and has, on important occasions) a justification for unnecessary violence and repression on much too large a scale to be considered easily compatible with peace research's emancipatory interest; consistent, determinate intellectual bases for judging what is good and what is bad about the peace bringing or maintaining capacities and accomplishments of existing institutions are very hard to come by within that tradition.

Finally, consider the alternative candidate tradition concerned with war and peace perhaps even closer to peace research than Marxism *per se*, viz., international law. Its interests are mixed with respect to conflict resolution. Surely its contribution to social justice and peaceful conflict settlement needs recognition. But its use (and abuse) by rationalizers unwilling or unable to submit matters at hand to a legal settlement process seems quite distant from peace research's distinctive knowledge interest. Private and state interests can easily transcend peaceful ones in the shaping and unequal application of genuinely shared normative standards, which themselves often embody historical biases.

None of these oppositions need be conceived as total, nonnegotiable, so to speak. There are variants of "liberal realism," "behavioral

constructive critique of the "empiricist ontology" at the root of this version of empiricism, the Humean notion that "the objects of sense-experience are atomistic events constantly conjoined in determinate ways" (see especially pp. 39 and 96).

neorealism," "Marxian peace research" and "international law" that have made significant contributions to knowledge and practice recognized by many peace researchers. Nor is peace research itself devoid of the problems of conforming its interests in peace, justice and academic viability which the above characterization is designed to help clarify. But the above sketch represents, I believe, a *prima facie* case for peace research's disciplinary distinctiveness.

Given peace research's distinctive emancipatory interest, which sometimes places it in an uneasy relationship with certain other disciplinary orientations within the behavioral, social and ecological sciences, it is indeed appropriate to ask whether there is anywhere else outside of academia that one can find that same emancipatory interest? Are there possible allies in the social and political contexts of contemporary peace research with which peace researchers might or should make common cause? Were there no other peace-promoting movements or institutions, the practical import of its emancipatory task would be overwhelmingly difficult, and one would have grounds for suspecting the bona fides of peace researchers.

Late in what Raymond Aron has called "The century of total war" (Aron 1955), however, peace movements are widespread – some with state support, some without. Moreover, I believe that some of our other social institutions – the global collective security system of the early post World War II years, the defensive military establishments of certain nonaligned states – have rightly called war into question in a similar way. Domestically, the "welfare state," to the extent that it has eclipsed the "warfare state"[5] and promotes the dignity and mutually

---

[5] An empirically disciplined account of special relevance here is Ted Gurr (1988), which I find impressive, but overly pessimistic. Rewriting Lasswell's "garrison state" construct, Ted Robert Gurr elaborates two empirically discernible developments, externally oriented "militarized states" and domestically oriented "police states," both of which clearly over-rely on coercive state capacities. His suggestive conclusion that "only homogenous democracies with low power capabilities and limited alliance obligations are insulated from the development of the institutions and political culture of militarized and police states" is tempered by the sobering reflection that "chronic international conflict undermines the maintenance of non-coercive means of managing internal conflict both in specific countries and in the international system as a whole." His final remark that " 'idealistic' paths to a national and global future with diminished reliance on violence for the management of conflict ... do not follow from the realistic propositions and models advanced here" belies the "mixed message" of these two generalizations, which broadly might be said to be consistent with Richard Falk's structural reform proposals for the inter-state systems and those of Anthony Giddens (1985: Ch. 11).

compatible well-being of its citizens, is another positive development. Another such domestic institution, perhaps, is the law-abiding, conflict-managing police force.[6] The broadly international instances of legitimate police practice are also, on the whole, positive remnants of the UN collective security system.[7] The tougher question, and one where realists, Marxists, international lawyers and peace researchers are likely to disagree, concerns the extent to which the modern, Western state system is itself necessarily or unnecessarily war prone. It must remain central to the agenda of emancipatory peace research, especially because of the growth in this century of overly coercive "militarized" and "police" states within that system.

How emancipatory empiricism connects to peace research

The above line of reasoning points toward a broader epistemological stance for peace research, grounded in its distinctive emancipatory knowledge interest. I call such a stance "emancipatory empiricism," and intend now to show how it gets its name.

Institutionally, empiricism is widely identified with the heavily inductive, externally funded collection of scientific data – data-making claimed to be both objective, reliable and value-neutral – followed by statistical analyses searching for timelessly and universally valid probabilistic laws. Philosophically, such empiricism is often contrasted with "rationalist" philosophies of science that emphasize natural possibilities more than quantitative probabilities, the role of human intentionality in the shaping of experience, and the importance of theoretical reasoning in scientific analysis.

Sometimes empiricism is understood as one of several research programs within a larger discipline, or the argument is made (as Karl Deutsch and Harold Lasswell have done) that at a particular period in

---

[6] News reports on American Public Radio from Haiti in the Spring of 1987 suggested the existence of a more civilized, post-Duvalier regime should include the restoration of police functions to a domestic police force, rather than the partly secret armies theretofore involved in domestic security operations. The unevenly reciprocated patterns of social expectation concerning "domestic," "terrorist" and "international" violence is obviously of great scholarly interest in an era where "sovereign" states no longer have a monopoly on "legitimate" coercion, and foreign "aid" involves training ideologically committed "police forces" prone to intervene in domestic politics.

[7] Relevant discussions of the UN Collective Security system include Alker and Sherman (1982), Bull (1977), Haas (1983), Vayrynen (1985), Azar and Burton (1986).

its history a discipline needs renewal through extensive data-making efforts. More exclusively, the view is sometimes argued (or assumed) that only this inductive style of research (possibly combined with what Galtung describes as the Teutonic style of deductively oriented mathematical theorizing) is truly scientific, deserving the disciplinary privileges of tenured appointments, research grants, etc.

Conceived of as especially relevant to the behavioral, social and ecological sciences, "emancipatory empiricism" is more "rationalist" than "empiricist." But I keep (and redefine) the "empiricism" label because emancipatory empiricism pays very serious attention to the data of experience, and its proper collection, practical interpretation and reconstructive analysis. Thus emancipatory empiricism is especially interested in practical possibilities which can be hidden by "normal" regularities, in transformations that cannot always be captured by statistical probabilities, in emergent breakthroughs to preferable, sometimes novel psychological, social and ecological orders.

Institutionally, emancipatory empiricism aligns its knowledge-generating activities and its disciplinary self-understanding with historically changing and spatially contingent emancipatory knowledge interests. That such knowledge interests have influenced and can shape the disciplinary activities and self-understandings of peace researchers has just been argued. A more detailed epistemological exposition is offered by the guidelines below.

Twelve epistemological guidelines for emancipatory peace research

The following twelve epistemological (and methodological) guidelines distill some of my own learning from a fairly lengthy period of empirical research on the successes and failures of the UN collective security system, as buttressed conceptually and methodologically by related work on Sequential Prisoner's Dilemma games.[8]

---

[8]   In particular, see Alker, Bennett, Mefford (1980), Alker (1985), Alker, Duffy, Hurwitz and Mallery (1991), Alker (1993) and the research reported on in Chapter 9 above.

A second source of these reflections has been my involvement over the last several years in the Data Development in International Relations project, led by Richard Merritt and Dina Zinnes, which is both renewing and rethinking data collection efforts in the international relations and foreign policy field. See Merritt, Muncaster and Zinnes (1993) and Duffy (1994).

A third source of these ideas are the arguments and conversations I have reported on in Chapters 5, 6, and 11.

One may begin a sequential exposition of guidelines for a peace research governed by emancipatory empiricism by asserting that the data of human experience should continually be reinterpreted and respecified in the emancipatory interest of discovering and improving upon determinative possibilities for conflict management and conflict resolution that justly avoid civil and international wars. Taking seriously rationalist critiques of empiricism and the call for ontological depth of emancipatory realism (Sylvan and Glassner 1985; Elshtain 1979; and Bhaskar 1986), one can recast the empirical thrust of creative data making, interpretation and analysis. Basically, one must look for peaceful possibilities *within the data*, always remembering that data recordings are but manufactured traces of history, that these actualities of practical human experience stand in complex relationships with real but not directly observable, alternative possibilities – with a past, present and future of their own. Among such possibilities are movements beyond power politics, toward peace and community.

Lesson 1. Data coding procedures should be considered key dependent variables in an emancipatory peace research because they often (sometimes unconsciously) reflect just those social and political forces affecting war and peace that are supposed to be the objects of investigation.
Let me begin with a true story, which is all the more important because it apparently has nothing to do with the content of coding operations, only their procedural implementation. In the pioneering article by Lincoln Moses, Richard Brody *et al.* (1967) on the quantification of levels of cooperation and conflict in international events data, one graduate student coder (out of about five) was a non-American, a citizen of a Third World country, a woman. Her codings did not "reliably" agree with those of the others, and were discarded for most purposes. She then went on to cofound a new paradigm of international conflict research, lateral pressure theorizing, which redefined the meaning and significance of imperialism as it has been experienced by domestic populations within the Great Powers, their unequal allies, and Third World countries.[9]

---

[9] The source of the information I have used here, but not necessarily my interpretation of it, is Nazli Choucri, the discarded coder. Major books in the lateral pressure research program are Choucri and North (1975), Ashley (1980), and Choucri, North and Susumu Yamakage (1992).

Since Thomas Kuhn's writings have become very popular it is easier to argue that "new ways of seeing" can become scientifically significant; distinguishing them from "random error," as some naturalistically inclined behavioralists might label this deviation, is more difficult. The differences one might expect are both paradigmatic, orientational and nationalistic. The necessity of regularly choosing coders from among the informed citizenry of differently aligned world countries seems as evident a precaution as it is difficult to realize in practice. Orientational differences, e.g., between men and women, among different occupational or ethnic groupings, may be subtler biases, harder to detect, requiring corrections not as easily prescribed. Paradigmatic differences, e.g., among "liberal realists," "structural Marxists," and "dialectical peace researchers," should be more familiar to interdisciplinary scholars, even if an appropriate response to such differences is also controversial. Relevant methodological research requires the new dependent variables here mentioned.

Lesson 2. Always include the case inclusion and exclusion rules in the (augmented if necessary) specification of the coding rules for a conflict/ cooperation data set.

Now let us consider the definition of our cases, the units of data included in a particular collection. The most remarkable difference between the definition of conflict cases I have experienced in studies of conflict management precedent logics came in discussions of Akihiko Tanaka's thesis (see Tanaka 1984). Because he was (re-)-coding data from *The People's Daily* of China, he noted a tendency for episodic conflict cases to be conceptualized in terms of longer term, essential, on-going conflicts. Non-violent periods of moderate duration, the stuff of Western coders' case or phase distinctions, were less likely to be treated as evidence of hostility or conflict termination.

Although this editorial practice clearly fits (and can be justified by) the scholarly Marxist understanding of the continuing reality of (sometimes) unobservable social contradictions, the Chinese press's practice has merit for a variety of other reasons of well. Thus the Haas–Butterworth tradition tends to define case boundaries according to the international lawyer's dispute management practice of separating out manageable "cases," an operational practice that tends to obscure what Azar might call the underlying "protracted social conflicts" (see

Azar's Chapter 2 in Azar and Burton 1986).[10] Add to this the behavioral scientist's dubious tendency to increase the sample size of purportedly "independent" cases (in Stanley Hoffmann's language, treating history as if it were a field of daisies waiting to be stripped).

Another issue immediately related to case definitions concerns the extent to which universes of data collection consciously or unconsciously reproduce partitions of a larger reality that a more emancipatory empiricist would want directly to investigate. David Singer and Melvin Small initially focused on major power wars and then on wars among central system members (Singer and Small 1972). Civil (and some colonial) wars came later (Small and Singer 1982). Certainly an initial focus like this can be justified on the grounds of data availability and resource limitations, but the theoretical justifications for continuing the earlier focus are more slippery.

Why should a peace researcher consider as valuable what Great Power statesmen think is important? Should we accept either the "Cold War" or the "anti-imperialist" characterization of the principal international post-1945 conflict just because one of the superpowers officially condones such labeling?

Beyond the analytically important distinction loosely suggested by the distinction between "cold" and "hot" wars, there are deep issues concerning "structural displacements" of central system conflicts into the peripheral, more overt areas of competition, such as occurred before World War I. In frequency terms, there is a rich variety of evidence suggesting a greater incidence of what might be called "North–South" conflicts in post-war conflict patterns. And, ironically, there is similar evidence of diminished UN conflict management activities outside the areas and issues of direct interest to the major powers.[11]

Since exemptions from international scrutiny and accountability concerning imperial/colonial affairs have in the past two centuries often been legally argued in terms of "domestic jurisdiction," and the executive branches of major power governments have all sought

---

[10] Azar and Havener (1976) pose the related sociological measurement question of how to tap those often unobservable integrative/disintegrative processes whereby social objects are created and dissolved, processes that event data research in particular does not adequately (and continuously) reflect.

[11] Four empirical studies emphasizing conflictful North–South interaction patterns in various parts of the twentieth century, from very different paradigmatic perspectives, are Wallensteen (1973), Kende (1978), Doyle (1986) and Russett (1993).

secrecy concerning the conduct of foreign affairs on "national security" grounds, must not we be especially on our guard not to be affected by correlated data nonavailabilities in identifying the root causes of war? To put it in discourse analysis language, do not the "silences" in the data speak as powerfully as the observations we have been able to gather? In my early paper on "Can the end of power politics be part of the concepts with which its story is told?"[12] I referred to the "bloody ordination" that Great Powers conferred on new system members with their acts of diplomatic recognition. Should not the standards of conduct implicit in related scholarly definitions (by Singer and his associates) of their universes of investigation be equally carefully and critically scrutinized for tendencies unreflectively to reproduce a repressive status quo?

Perhaps the most dramatic finding along these lines that I have been associated with is contained in Frank Sherman's enhanced SHERFACS data set (Sherman 1994). Whereas Alker and Sherman (1982) together identified the possibility of easily observing agenda "non-decisions" in UN conflict management activities, Sherman's effort to code "domestic quarrels" and "international disputes," by relying primarily on other sources than the international organizations themselves doubled or tripled what might be argued to be "internationally relevant" conflicts. The gestalt flip encouraged by this finding – these silences in the Haas–Butterworth data which my research team had processually recoded – is to see conflict management practices by the extended UN system (including both regional and *ad hoc* management agents) as more like the tip of an iceberg of internationally unrecognized and unmanaged conflicts.

One should also note that the critique of inclusion or exclusion rules can have politically relevant consequences. Not only do "success batting averages" change, one may also find more sense in views one previously held suspect. I now see, for example, my own partially latent dissatisfaction with the watered down, "conflict management" research program that Ernst Haas originated[13] as having a certain resonance with much harsher criticisms of the United Nations from American academic ambassadors like Moynihan and Kirkpatrick. Indeed, the emphasis on the UN's failure to resolve conflicts – they

---

[12] Printed as Chapter 5 above.

[13] Haas' first related conceptual analysis on the subject that I am aware of is Haas (1955). The first empirical report is Haas (1968). Later empirical assessments include Haas (1983).

have claimed that it exacerbates some of them – resonates with the criticisms that John Burton would make from a much more anti-statist conflict resolution perspective.[14]

Lesson 3. Collect, try to reproduce, compare, confront, match different "scientific" treatments of the same conflict events (cases, disputes, crises, wars, agreements, peace breakthroughs).

If one recognizes the strong, if sometimes unconscious, tendency for scholars to reflect the biases of their research-originating traditions and contexts, then the obvious first step for the empirically minded is to check for such biases by undertaking the comparative and synthetic investigation of paradigmatic, orientational and political perspectives. Scholars from all sides of the Cold War need each other, as do those from different research traditions and orienting perspectives, for this reason.

If one allows that differences in scholarly perspectives are not simply private, unbiased conceptual or topical preferences of the "sovereign" research scholar, then the discovery and operational definition of international realities is more complicated. The more data sets of good quality one can find that embody different scholarly perspectives, the more one can "learn from the data" about these reality assessing perspectives. I have tried, where honest and reproducible differences among serious scholars of different research traditions may be found, to think of a larger, more coherent, yet often contradictory totality of conflict descriptions synthesized from the sometimes contradictory perspectives of these scholars. This totality includes the interplay of perspectives, a range of possibility-actuality relationships discursively implied by alternative coding schemes, and the inner relations of "participants" and "observers" (who can never be totally disinterested) to the conflict itself.

There are several, even deeper ontological issues here, seen from an emancipatory, dialectical-hermeneutic perspective. First of all, a dispute *description* is not completely separable from the cognitive practices or *procedures* that produced it. The real contenders for the "social scientific construction of international reality" are these different coding procedures, which, according to Lesson 1, are for this and other purposes appropriately treated as dependent variables.

Coding practices (including case exclusion rules) can best be compared operationally by incorporating both them and the raw data texts

[14] See Burton's contributions to Azar and Burton (1986).

343

they were applied to, into a word modeling software system like RELATUS, Gavan Duffy and John Mallery are developing, that can both interpret and apply coding rules to textual information sources (Alker, Duffy, Hurwitz, Mallery 1991). This would amount to a rigorous – empiricists would say operational – yet dialogical examination of complementary and contradictory scholarly practices, a necessary step on the way toward a socially achieved (rather than simply posited) scholarly universality.

The related ontological issue concerns the existence (and reliable discovery of) emergent social relationships of a collaborative or conflictful sort. New social emergents occur where previous determinations break down, where emancipatory restructuring of social relationships are possible. They emerge out of, and can be found within, overlapping perspectives. Hammarskjöld's role as UN secretary general in eliciting support from the super powers and General Assembly majorities for UN interventions in the Suez and Congo crises would be such an example. Belated Soviet and American groping in 1987 for some coordinated ways of containing the impacts of the Iran–Iraq war on their naval and commercial interests would be another. But for such evolutions to take place, they must be shared across a range of international actors.

Lesson 4. Progress toward genuine scholarly universalism can be usually achieved by making explicit – even recoding to make explicit – the normative bases, procedural preferences or political allegiances informing coding practices.

Obviously, such differences in orientation are major factors affecting differences in coding practices. Surely it will help the empiricist to delineate the different, value-relevant dependent and independent variables of concern. For me, normative clarification has had a much greater impact than such a modest clarification of research hypotheses. It has changed the paradigmatic ways I have tried to study alternative pasts and futures for international conflict management practices.

Twenty years ago, after my empirical study of UN voting patterns, prompted by Ernst Haas' pioneering empirical studies of the UN collective security system, I became especially interested in the evolutionary development and decay, the organization learning, ossification and decay of the UN concerning peace-making activities (see also Haas 1990). The attempt to use econometric time series models and/or Markov learning models of UN management actions eventually led me to a double discovery of heuristic significance. First of all, it turned out that the Congo Crisis, which helped precipitate the most serious UN constitutional crisis of that period, was more than an outlier, a deviant case in the tracking of these models. Indeed Christensen found statistically significant "breakpoints" before and after that episode in my causal models. What did this signify?

The United Nations Operation in the Congo was everywhere compared with the United Nations Emergency Force deployed at the time of the Suez crisis. This debatable "precedent," creatively deployed by the secretary general and his supporters, suggested the emergent possibility of decisive action by the United Nations on the basis of superpower agreement with Assembly majorities, even when other veto powers (Britain and/or France) disagreed. Trying to model that kind of relationship – i.e. processually match the Congo Crisis to the Suez Crisis in the search for relevant actions that might be taken, and, similarly, to explain why the UN seemed to know what actions to try in 1945 and 1946 without any directly relevant previous experience – was not working. Using the most advanced system for computerizing social science data analysis I then knew of (SPSS, TROLL, ESP, Ithiel Pool's ADMINS), it was impossible to code and include in my analysis (the search for) precedential similarities without writing my own rather lengthy programs for that purpose. It turned out that these search algorithms, which evolved into a precedential seeking and applying simulation model, roughly paralleled organizational memory processes. Not only did I invent for political scientists and international lawyers the subfield of formalized "precedent logics," through an analysis of residuals, I operationally rediscovered a normative level of political engagement theretofore only implicit in the data I was (re-) analyzing.

Let me talk about precedent logics first.[15] When I found (in my work with Christensen) that there was an "operational Charter" implicit in my early set of post-1945 conflict management cases, I knew that it would be better to model explicitly the norm application and revision process. This meant shifting to a research tradition, Artificial Intelligence, with appropriate representation, modeling and analysis techniques. It turned out that these (oversimplified) precedent

---

[15] This paragraph recalls my paper (Alker 1974), which evoked considerable resistance from conventional empirical methodologists at the time of its authorship and eventual publication in a European journal: it argues that the positive answer to its title question implies following the paradigmatic shift of Herbert Simon's own career.

seeking "procedures" (modeled in PL1), when included in the analysis, generated outcome-involvement residuals with no statistically significant breakpoints near the Congo Crisis as well. I soon noticed that Herbert Simon (in his work with Gregg on concept attainment and his work with March and Newell on organizational problem solving) had been there before me: Simon largely stopped writing about causal modeling, path analysis, structural modeling and conventional econometric methodologies more generally when many others were just beginning to do so, because he found – what many sociological and political scientific methodologists have yet to discover – something more intellectually challenging, and empirically appropriate for the problems he was interested in, viz. psychologically and organizationally relevant Artificial Intelligence, or Cognitive Science.

There was also an ontological shift implicit in this rejection of conventional behavioral scientific methodology, my going "from causal modelling to artificial intelligence." In doing so, I recognized a deeper level of reality and a new kind of scientific data relevant to it – the diplomatic debates about Charter revision that were at the center of international attention as the Congo and Suez-related UN financial crisis matured.[16]

As I was helped to see by Harold Lasswell's invitation to report my work with Christensen and Greenberg to the American Society of International Law, the negotiated, legal-normative aspect of conflict management is not merely instrumental searching for excuses, it may be constitutional politics as well. And it has a crucial parallel at the

---

[16] In making now a similar, explicit methodological challenge to quantitative peace research, I am suggesting that those who consider formal operationalization and measurement a *necessary* condition of science need to make such moves for cogent analytical (and representational) reasons. But since teaching methodology in Chile in 1971 and 1972, I have come more fully to appreciate the "techno-rational domination" aspects of very rigorous and expensive standards of scientific practice. Epistemologically, historically oriented *dependencia* theorizing was much more mature and sophisticated scientifically than the quantitative SPSS approaches to survey data analysis then being introduced there (and funded) from the United States. Even though natural language Artificial Intelligence modeling is distinctly superior to statistical operationalizations, and can be adapted to a sensitive, multicultural, hermeneutic-dialogical perspective, I do not believe that carefully employed natural language analysis is "subscientific," "preoperational" or obsolescent. Indeed the intensive investigation of grammar-based modeling approaches induces a Chomskean cum Wittgensteinian awe at a much more widely and equitably distributed resource: adult human ordinary language capabilities.

levels of practical reasoning and institutional learning about policy alternatives. There follows:

Lesson 5. Precedential reasoning about the relevant past is an integral part of diplomatic realities. To ignore the normative-empirical dynamics of defining a "case" (e.g., in Charter terms), or those of norm-based precedential learning ("drawing a lesson") in one's data making is seriously to diminish the likelihood that practically significant lessons can be drawn from that data.

The rationale here is both profound – concerning the difficulties behaviorally minded scholars have in getting at the constitutive level of political relationships in their data – and practically obvious. Have you tried to talk to diplomats about the "lessons" you have learned from behavioral research? Always, they want to relate your "lessons" to theirs. Unless you have already juxtaposed and simulated how your findings relate to their collective, practical self-understandings, you will talk past one another. Habermas might say that the realm of discursive, practical will formation must be distinguished from the world of adaptive or maladaptive systemic functioning of the sort causal modelers typically model.

But there was another "lesson" here that has not been so obvious to my readers, even though I soon was able to illustrate it in the 1975 "Polimetrics" chapter in the *Handbook of Political Science*. There I applied Lazarsfeld–Sills "reason analysis" to the dialectical process whereby a remarkable consensus was achieved in the Security Council for coercive UN intervention in the Congo (see Alker 1993). In my econometric data residuals, I had rediscovered metapolitics, constitutional politics, the fundamental, discursively mediated, dialectical process of structuring and restructuring international political institutions toward, and, as happened, away from supranationality.

Noting in passing the ontological character of this claim about the multiple layers of reality within my data, let me state two important additional lessons:

Lesson 6. In the construction of new data sets on international conflict, be sure to include the reasons actors give for the actions they take (or avoid), and the precedents they cite (or avoid) for justifying such (in)actions.

Lesson 7. If you have not coded conflict resolutional efforts (and their successes and failures) as part of your conflict data, get such information or include such information from other studies.

Here we have a crucial difference between those following realist categories of analysis and those deriving theirs from the communitarian

347

tradition. Following in Richardson's footsteps, but failing to rethink Richardson's injunction that his differential equation models were only adequate for projecting behavior if statesmen "did not stop to think," Singer and Small have not done this either in any of their data making concerning wars or militarized international disputes. The Haas tradition and Azar's COPDAB project, on the other hand, like the Behavioral Correlates of War project (to which Singer and Russell Leng made early contributions), are more inclusive in this regard, collecting rich data on conflict and cooperation activities. The reasons for my preferences on this matter are obviously related to my emancipatory interest in war avoidance and conflict resolution. Peace researchers have very few reasons for any longer continuing to replicate "war only" data-making. As communitarians, they are paradigmatically predisposed to see any war short of total war as only a partial breakdown of normally non-antagonistic forms of social communication and interaction which they are trying to discover how to reinvigorate.

Lesson 8. Going beyond the idea of "deviant case analysis," and the empiricist search for analytical-empirical accounts of behavioral regularities concerning peace-making successes and failures, approach case data from what Habermas calls a "reconstructive" perspective: take the best or the worst cases of conflict resolution outcomes and use them to uncover the practical grammars of action (and habit) making such outcomes possible.

Our work on successes and failures of UN conflict management has only looked intensively at a few cases, in particular the Congo Crisis, a turning point away from UN supranationality. But the Sequential Prisoner's studies are going further: Roger Hurwitz's dissertation (1991) looks at player generated protocols (supplemented by the narrative game histories players were asked to write) for two exceptional classes of SPD games, those evolving into stable cooperative patterns and those degenerating into stable defection relationships. These represent, if you will, historically contingent evolutions (or devolutions) of "community" and of "anarchy," not "naturalistic" or "inevitable" outcomes of either sort realists and some extreme idealists speak of. Hurwitz identifies those reflective redefinitions of the other player, his or her actions, and the game situation that account for turning points in overall, cumulative trajectories in game payoffs.

Less optimistically, look at the late Cold War world, or the post-Cold War world after the first blush of increased UN activities occurred. The major behavioral generalization from Haas' late Cold War study

(1983), supporting Sherman's unpublished analyses, is the decline in the effectiveness of the UN system, including its reformulation and weakening through the use of regional and *ad hoc* conflict management agents. The deep causes of this "regime decay" – which is still manifested in the UN's chronic budget deficits – require investigation in an analytical/empirical mode; surely they include the rise in "protracted social conflicts," in "domestic," multiethnic, "recognition" or "identity" conflicts as Burton might describe them. How the Cold War and its aftermath have catalyzed the remilitarization of the Third World, must be carefully investigated. But I have no doubt that selective (perhaps situationally matched) studies of exceptional successes and failures at conflict management or conflict resolution by the UN conflict management system will shed new light on possibilities for, and conditions of, significant improvements in that system.

There is an equally important methodological conclusion implicit here. I believe the information lost by quantitative attempts at coding such qualitative accounts of conflict initiation and termination successes and failures to be tremendous. Compared to Butterworth's coding of his two page narrative account of UN failures to manage the 1956 Hungarian crisis, information summarized quantitatively in two or three IBM cards worth of bits, John Mallery's highly structured semantic representation takes something like a half a megabyte of LISP encoded storage, for example. The moral here is:

Lesson 9. Structured narrative accounts of conflict developments are a crucial, necessary component of any data set on conflict (and its resolution attempts). (When integrated accounts can be constructed from partially convergent interpretive perspectives, they are especially valuable representations of the contradictory, yet social nature of political reality, including its emergent conflict resolutional possibilities.)

The values of narrative accounts, structured and retold from the multiple perspectives of the key participants, mentioning their practical understandings of their (and others') actions, incorporating the multiple sets of theoretically significant phenomena attended to by the relevant paradigms of empirical research, are numerous. For one thing, they can be behaviorally recoded in the future in different ways with far less work. Secondly, the significant meanings of key events are much more clearly conveyed in partial story forms. Thirdly, precedential analogies are more holistically discussable in such terms. Fourthly, process modeling methods are now becoming available that treat entire narrative accounts operationally, as data. Fifthly, the practical, hermeneutic process of building consensual understandings of the bases for collective political actions, are described and analyzed (both causally and reconstructively) on the basis of such narrative accounts. The "reason analysis" of partially convergent practical understandings of the Congo Crisis, mentioned above, exemplifies crudely such possibilities.

Can one be more specific and rigorous about such possibilities? What do greatly enriched semantic encodings allow?[17] Mallery has constructed his formalized account of the Hungarian crisis so that it can be metaphorically matched with other accounts of the same intervention and other Great Power interventions. He wants to compare the case descriptions in the manner that Pat Winston has compared Shakespearean plots, a subject of similar interest to me in my Abelson and Lehnert-inspired work on story summarizations; he is also developing ways to merge standard event data codings with more fully narrative accounts. Jim Bennett talks about the Artificial Intelligence modeling of precedential "data stories" as part of the history of the Vietnam war and the evolution of the strategy of "extended deterrence." Dwain Mefford sees such stories as potentially usable, quasi-legal, learnable (non-)intervention precedents (Mefford 1990).

Lesson 10. Think of conflict and cooperation case descriptions as LISP encodable data stories. These descriptions are then executable programs, situation specific practical accomplishments, procedural enactments that constitute the cases, analogous to, but possibly different from the practical actions constituting the observed realities they refer to.

Finally, we are directly at the ontological level of discussion. I think it helpful here to emphasize the formal properties of LISP encoded descriptions one more time. LISP is a computer language in which each description is procedurally executable. Each conflict and cooperation case description is then a context specific program, or recipe, of action and interaction, potentially available in individual or institutional memories for subsequent modification and implementation.

Ontologically, I think of data stories as cell-like organisms, inter-

---

[17] For relevant examples of newer approaches see Bennett (1984), chapters by Mallery, Sherman and Duffy in Duffy (1994), and Chapters 3 and 8 above. "Data stories," Bennett's phrase, encapsulates nicely many aspects of my earlier suggestion that the end of power politics (as well as other possibilities) should be part of the operational concepts with which peace researchers, at least, mapped the history of power politics.

acting monads, pieces of world history often externally revealing traces of the historical processes that internally or constitutively generated them. As cited in Chapter 8, V. Propp had the same vision when he said that "If any call of a tale organism becomes a small tale within a larger one, it is built ... according to the same rules as any fairy tale." (By the way, the reason why econometric models of "dependent reproduction" in the Third World will never adequately represent the phenomena they seek to explain is right here. Scholars using such representations do not recognize the linguistic, organic, parasitic, reproduction-prone, identity constituting, internal "essences" of the phenomena they study.)

Once the identity of a case description with its constitutive and engendering processes is recognized, learning from the data inductively becomes searching its external, visible traces for its internal, constitutive, yet contradictory essences. It is very important to recognize the multiple possibilities according to which that episodic case history (or tale) might have unfolded. Otherwise the freedom to intervene, to change, to avoid "that which represses without necessity" is obscured. Emancipatory empiricism requires that "the end of power politics" be a possibility within "the concepts with which its stories are told."

Lesson 11. More generally, think of historical events data as external traces of internal contents: the multiple layerings of contradictory and complementary determination to which they owe their hidden unities, divergent meanings, and possible futures.
One must conceptualize one's codings to reveal the multiple practical perspectives and institutional relationships that determine them.

Here Marxist research can do much more than just problematize liberally oriented neo-realists' definitions of international reality. It challenges their avoidance of ontological issues by offering a more potent alternative to the skeptical, conventionalist or probabilistic "empirical realism" they are wont to retreat to. I shall try to respond constructively to this challenge.

An ontologically robust reading of the Marxist tradition suggests that present and past class conflicts have generated multiple layerings of directly or indirectly observable reality. The ontological sharpness of this tradition, with its emphasis on identity-constitutive "internal" relations, was epitomized for me when John O'Neill gave a lecture at MIT in the mid-1970s, arguing that "This cup of coffee *contains* the

351

history of imperialism!" How much more should that be true of comprehensive narrative accounts of American interventions in Vietnam or Central America and Soviet invasions of Hungary or Afghanistan!

Not to be sensitive to these layerings (and others) is to miss the historical impact of the multiplicity of psychological, social, political and ecological structures determining and constituting contemporary reality, including its emancipatory constraints and possibilities. Everywhere the sensitized observer can see traces of prior class dominations; *but there are also traces of multi-class collaborations and other social conflicts and solidarities.* Classical "idealism," the Grotian realism of Hedley Bull, and behavioral peace research on the growth of ethnic, national, transnational and international societies and communities all attest to such achievements.

When both internal and external relations affect case relationships, case matching or "precedent seeking" efforts become more complicated and historically more interesting. Similarity matching and dissimilarity contrasting of procedurally specified data stories are "external" comparisons unless the attributes used in such efforts are in some sense essential, characteristic, case-identifying ones. Obviously one wants to relate essential characteristics. The analytical problem, then, for which statistics can only be moderately helpful, is to develop ontologically cogent distinctions between essential and inessential properties of the case descriptions.

One approach is to think of actor identities in terms of their processually important self-symbols or the characteristic (or high crisis) action propensities, such as the defense of dominance and exploitation relationships. In more complex multi-actor events or episodes, one looks for story-like significances, holistic descriptions in terms of key conflict or cooperation variables, plot-like structures that take actor identities and key interaction propensities into account.

Sometimes, indeed often, data stories are internally related. One cannot properly appreciate a case unless its constitutive inner-relations with other cases are appreciated. Hammarskjöld's creative, personally tragic role in precedentially connecting the Suez and Congo crises is one such inner relationship. The strange mixture of external and internal features of the Tibet and Korean conflicts is one of Sherman's most distinctive contributions to the Alker–Sherman paper. A related point is his insistence that the Dominican intervention by the United States must be seen – as indeed Lyndon Johnson has said – as negative learning from the Cuban Missile Crisis, which Johnson did not want repeated. Within such intentional relationships one can find the true and imperfect historicities binding together our larger political societies and communities.

International histories, written in an ecologically sensitive way, are the biggest such stories yet recorded about our species. Over the past few years I have been debating with Robert Keohane, Stanley Hoffmann and others about the historical constitution of international society, the "anarchical society" as Hedley has brilliantly described it. I have argued that game-theoretic representations of international interactions have too often ahistorically obscured the dynamic sociality, the continuous extension, stretching, tearing and repairing of the practical/normative fabric of that society. Peace researchers should be able to display ways in which pluralistic security communities arise and decline within and through the reproductive-transformative processes of that society. Hence:

Lesson 12. Code conflict-cooperation case descriptions in instrumental and expressive ways that reveal their internal and external connections. Otherwise historicities in the development of international society that point toward peace and community, rather than the renewal and extension of power politics, will never be revealed.

I can restate, and perhaps crystalize, the perspective of emancipatory empiricism in the interest of just war avoidance with this concrete data-making question. How would, or should, you code a piece of text from the mouth or pen of a foreign minister of a major power, privately associated with a new Third World coercive intervention, a statement that read: "the strong do what they can and the weak suffer what they must"? With fatalistic acceptance; as ahistorical, instrumental meta-talk; as the overriding of contrary recommendations (if discoverable); or as ironic and tragic, a remediable failure?

Towards emancipatory ontology

Both my deepened understanding of constitutional meta-politics during and after the UN's Congo Crisis, the tracking of imperialism's powerful reproductive mechanisms, and my arguments for the precedential historicity of international community formation reflect a slowly growing awareness of the importance of ontological depth in empirical peace research. My emphasis in this chapter on the possibilities of emergent social orders, of peace breakthroughs and regime decays reflects this concern. Perhaps they can be generalized.

When major changes in scientific thinking occur, they are sometimes associated with changes in the understood reality of things. The Reformation and the Renaissance brought an end to medieval Aristotelianism, replacing spiritual understanding with mechanical understanding of the nature of the physical world. Such a transformation is needed now if we are to escape the defeatist, flat, empiricist, nature exploitive conception of reality underlying too much contemporary behavioral science and empirical peace research.

One can take from Roy Bhaskar's brilliant *Scientific Realism and Human Emancipation* a very clear statement of the guiding motivation of such a newer conception: emancipatory peace research epistemologically directs its "learning from the data" toward the emancipatory "uncoupling [of] the present from the causality of the past," replacing "depotentialising (disempowering, oppressive)" psychological, social and ecological structures by "potentialising (empowering, enhancing)" ones. Conceiving of *emancipation* as a "special qualitative kind of becoming free" that "consists in the self-directed *transformation ... from an unwanted and unneeded to a wanted and needed source of determination*," Bhaskar argues that it "is both causally presaged and logically entailed by explanatory theory, but that it can only be effected in *practice*."[18]

---

[18] Bhaskar 1986 (142, 171). Italics in the original. This book agrees to a remarkable extent with Johan Galtung's *Essays in Methodology*, which he does not cite. It also provides, in its second and third essays, a rich summary of the ways in which scientific reasoning is more than purely ("Teutonically" Galtung would say) deductive.

11 The presumption of anarchy in world politics[1]
On recovering the historicity of world society

There be other names of government, in the histories, and books of policy ... For they that are discontented under *monarchy*, call it *tyranny* ... so also, they which find themselves grieved under a *democracy*, call it *anarchy*, which signifies want of government.

Hobbes, *Leviathan* (1651: Ch. 19)

Hedley Bull's World Society Problematique vs. the Cooperation under Anarchy Problematique

I do not agree that "Nations dwell in perpetual anarchy" because "no central authority imposes limits on the pursuit of sovereign interests."[2]

---

[1] Revised from delivery as a Griffith Lecture at American University, March 10, 1986. The topic was, at my suggestion, a reflection on a 1985/86 Harvard/MIT seminar series on rational choice and international institutions, directed by Robert Keohane. Since this unpublished paper has been commented on in the literature I am publishing it here in substantially its 1986 version.

[2] Oye (1985) begins with the presumption that "Nations dwell in perpetual anarchy, for no central authority imposes limits on the pursuit of sovereign interests." Recognizing its prescriptive and explanatory aspects, he then poses the "perennial Question": "If international relations can approximate both a Hobbesian state of nature and a Lockean civil society (where sovereign "states can realize common interests through tacit cooperation, formal bilateral and multilateral negotiation, and the creation of international regimes"), why does cooperation emerge in some cases and not in others?" Oye's key explanatory conditions are "payoff structures," future expectations concerning iterated games ("the shadow of the future"), and the "number of players." Quoted language is rearranged from, but preserves the sense of, the first page (plus the abstract) of that article.

In subsequent papers, an impressive array of mostly younger scholars apply Oye's "Hypotheses and Strategies" and Duncan Snidal's "The Game *Theory* of International Politics" (1985b) to a variety of economic and security affairs. Conclusions and implications are then drawn by Robert Axelrod and Robert O. Keohane in a paper

My objection to this hoary, but still fashionable bromide of international relations can be stated in terms of either of "anarchy's" two primary dictionary meanings: (1) a "confused," "disordered," "lawless," "unregulated" state of affairs; and (2) (more technically, but indiscriminately) a state of affairs "without rule, authority or government." In terms of the first definition the statement is historically incorrect; in terms of the second, its causal argument incorrectly denies the possibilities of order, law and regulation inherent in pluricentric or polyarchic sociopolitical systems. Therefore, I do not think subsequent scholarship should start with these *presumptions* – both senses of the term "presumption" are intended: "the taking for granted of such a characterization" in scientific research or policy formulation, and the "overstepping of proper bounds" I believe such an unwarranted assumption to be.

The immediate occasion for the development of this argument was the appearance of the October 1985 issue of *World Politics*, an issue dedicated to the scientific explanation and prescriptive promotion of "Cooperation under Anarchy," from whose introduction I have just quoted. The presumption that world politics are inherently anarchic is quite explicit and highly visible in this work. "'Cooperation' 'under' 'Anarchy'" seems to have been appropriate conceptual terminology in that journal at least since the January 1978 issue, which had two more stimulating and influential articles by Robert Jervis and Oran Young reflecting upon such themes.

With occasional inputs from microeconomic theory, all of these sources rely primarily, if not exclusively, on the theory of non-cooperative games – those where binding agreements are not possible. It appears natural for such authors to interpret sovereignty in a way that implies "anarchy," interpreted as a state of being subject to no binding, *externally enforced* agreements. These citations thus bound and exemplify most specifically the *cooperation under anarchy problematique* that I shall criticize here: recent attempts by North American scholars game theoretically to elucidate successes and failures at international cooperation along with efforts to understand and promote the institutionalization of the successes – efforts undertaken against the presumption that international relations are perpetually anarchic, in a way that can

entitled "Achieving Cooperation under Anarchy: Strategies and Institutions" (Axelrod and Keohane 1985).

fruitfully be modeled using the representational devices of liberal economics and non-cooperative game theory.[3]

The best critique is a constructive one, one that includes within it sufficient references to an attractive alternative approach to the same questions (or a reformulated, deeper version thereof). Given the recent availability of Stanley Hoffmann's extraordinarily compelling retelling of Hedley Bull's life work on (and beyond) the "anarchical society," I shall rely heavily on this work for that constructive aspect of my critique. Indeed, most of the objections I have to make against the "cooperation under anarchy" perspective are already explicit or implicit in that paper. Doubtless some of my own views will show through,[4] but hopefully they will not get in the way of the constructive, critical task I have set myself. Were the issues not so central to the future of the theory and practice of international relations on this planet, I would not otherwise take the unusual step of criticising younger scholars (and their teachers, who deserve more blame, but are less vulnerable). Except for their bad arguments (and because of their

---

[3] Economic theory and game theory are mentioned in both Robert Jervis (1978) and Young (1978). Jervis' first subhead in "Cooperation under the Security Dilemma" is "Anarchy and the Security Dilemma," but I would describe his invocation of anarchy at best as perfunctory. This description does not extend to his extremely rich discussion of offense-defense balances and differentiations, which somehow does not get adequately integrated into the analytical framework of the October 1985 volume, even though Jervis is a senior contributor to that issue as well.

In the 1985 *World Politics* volume, Snidal's article is the most committed to a deductive, theoretical version of the anarchy problematique, Oye's somewhat less so. The Axelrod–Keohane treatment uses Oye's framework heuristically, but not Snidal's deductive theorizing style, emphasizing instead practical institution building possibilities. In the 1978 issue, Young is more deductively oriented than Jervis, but his wide-ranging reflections are not presented as a unified, deductive theory.

The "anarchic" quality of international politics has been, of course, a standard theme of American neorealism, e.g., Waltz (1974, 1979). I have not tried to cover here related critiques of that work, some of which are collected (with Waltz's response) in Robert O. Keohane, ed. (1986).

[4] My own efforts in the area of the present discussion are mainly of two sorts. My efforts to review and develop alternatives to the "games and decisions" research paradigm complex for analyzing mixed interest, non-cooperative games (of which the "cooperation under anarchy problematique" is a particular component) may be traced from Alker (1974) through Alker and Hurwitz (1980) to Alker (1985), a research program continued in Chapter 9 above. Secondly, my collaborative work with Tahir Amin, Tom Biersteker and Takashi Inoguchi on *The Dialectics of World Order* is previewed in Alker (1981a) and Alker and Biersteker (1984). A more explicitly political statement containing some of the same themes of the present article is my "An Orwellian Lasswell for Today," Chapter 7 above.

willingness to make them publicly), I respect and admire the people I criticize here.

Briefly, and without incessant footnote acknowledgments, let me restate Bull's preferred research problematique, and put it in the perspective of his views on the contemporary world scene and on the discipline of international relations. Such a review may also serve to preview much of the subsequent argument.

Bull's consuming effort was historically to study the development, decay and transformations in international society, and responsibly to promote evolutions in that society consistent with humanistic, Western values. That society was constituted by its common interests and values, its common rules and institutions, which need careful, histori-cally accurate delineations. Because war has played a recognized, if changing role there, Bull thought that international society should not be equated with the typical domestic society within a modern state claiming exclusive monopolies on the exercise of legitimate violence. On the other hand, an international society of sovereign states – an "anarchical society" – does exist. Note the restricted use of "anar-chical" here to refer to the absence of a superordinate government, without the additional inference that no other bases for order, no other forms of rule are possible.

Bull's "anarchical society" was originally created in the West, and its practices have reflected to varying degrees common interests in its survival (which balance of power practices have sometimes served) and a distinctive moral-cultural basis: including, but not limited to, a widely shared respect for life, property and the keeping of agreements. Sympathetic to the Grotian tradition of natural law, Bull rejected the generalized Hobbesian view that only superordinate powers create societies, that international relations is an "anarchical" war of all against all, citing the Commonwealth as a counter-example.

Thus "society" for Bull falls in between "anarchy" in the pejorative Hobbesian sense, and "community," which to some extent it presup-poses. Indeed, in the absence of a supranational world authority, Bull called upon usually partisan states interpretively to seek as wide a consensual basis as possible in attempting to act in favor of their common interests and/or incompletely shared cosmopolitan ideals of individual rights and a world common good. The need is to reconcile sovereign states' rights with responsibilities to the global human community, to find and develop a feasible new order with certain "domestic" elements, *within* the anarchic state system, *and beyond* it. I

358

call this interrelated set of historical and normative concerns Bull's World Society Problematique.

Bull's problematique obviously subsumes the "cooperation under anarchy" problematique. But its greater cogency springs in large part from the extraordinary breadth and depth of historical vision from which it derives, one I would call "traditional," "communitarian" and even "dialectical." Although Hoffmann correctly recalls Bull's "realistic" attacks on various "utopian" or "revolutionary" proposals for a new world order, he spends less time emphasizing Bull's almost Lasswellian recognition of the transformative role of the great world revolutions on world society, including the French and Russian revolutions. Bull's recognition of the revolutionary development of the modern state system and what Barraclough has called the twentieth century's great "Revolt against the West" is equally profound, and genuinely global. Despite his Western values, Bull's analytical vantage point is not that of a Cold War partisan; he saw advantages and limitations to the bipolar superpower system that North Americans rarely acknowledge, and recognized global social consequences created by America's decline from hegemony. In the contemporary era, he recognizes the profound contradictions in international practices symbolized by Aron's concept of an heterogenous system. Most distinctively, in a world where nuclear and ecological common interests have outrun cultural homogenization, he saw an historically special opportunity for an independent Western Europe to accommodate post-Soviet and Third World differences with the United States.

Rather than (like Waltz) reduce international relations to the realist concern with "the politics of states in their external aspects," Bull's disciplinary approach is thoroughly multidisciplinary. He further denies reductionistic "realist" treatments of the bases of state action in instrumentally rational strategic power calculations – historically developed cultural beliefs are important. International order has both security, community, economy and ecology aspects. And his multidisciplinarity goes far beyond relatively tepid efforts to integrate security studies and international political economy within a game-theoretic, microeconomic framework. Bull's preferred multidisciplinary framework is historical, cultural, legal, sociological and political-diplomatic before it is technical and economic.

Methodologically, Bull accepts the traditional argument (made by Aristotle and rejected by Hobbes) that politics is not a realm of deductive certainties. At best it is a dialectical realm of argument and counter-argument, of "reasonable" policy formulation and criticism, not "rational" policy calculation. Interpretative understanding of policy practices and of the collective action possibilities within a frail and ambiguous normative consensus always have an artistic element; undue precision should not be sought. Indeed, essential issues are often not reducible to quantitative formulations. Bull's most original contribution, his sustained historical, conceptual and normative development of the idea of an "anarchical society," is clearly a dialectical synthesis of apparently opposed conceptions.

I do not accept all aspects of Bull's (or Hoffmann's) anti-scientistic critique of North American behavioral science,[5] from which I would infer their likely critical attitude toward the cooperation under anarchy problematique. Being quantitative is not the only way to be logically rigorous unless one accepts the Leibniz–Newton calculus as the preferred language of rigorous theorizing, deductive reasoning using game theory and microeconomics as proper instances of that kind of mathematics, and conventional probabilistic statistics as the only acceptable framework for empirical research. I do not;[6] and concerning the cooperation under anarchy problematique, I believe Bull's criticisms, and others akin to them, have considerable force.

Nor do I think Bull would be fully comfortable with an epistemological critique of the cooperation under anarchy problematique stated in anti-positivistic, anti-economistic terms. But it is toward these kindred criticisms – my own, not Bull's – that I am headed, always bearing in mind Bull's alternative world society problematique.

The meaning of anarchy as an issue of world politics

"Anarchy" is a negatively loaded political term, whose denotations and connotations have long been contested by Hobbesian conservatives, classic liberals and socialist revolutionaries. Bull himself, as we have seen, uses the concept rather carefully. He would be appalled, I believe, at the thoughtless, ahistorical way it is usually invoked by adherents to the cooperation under anarchy problematique; he was opposed to surreptitious dragging in of hidden value premises, espe-

---

[5] Indeed, Chapter 12 below spells out further my views on this issue.
[6] Again, this is an implicit reference to alternative formalization approaches, such as those from Artificial Intelligence suggested in Chapter 5 above and V. Hudson, ed. (1991).

cially when this was done in the name of "science." Where would a traditionalist like Bull or Hoffmann turn for a better understanding of such a concept? Obviously, to the history of scholarly, philosophical discussions of that concept.

I would like to argue that a look at an unabridged, historically organized dictionary often can serve many of the same purposes. My reader may take such an exercise as a preliminary test of some of the arguments, criticisms and distinctions made so far. Indeed, a look at related definitions in the unabridged *Oxford English Dictionary* (1933, 1972 Supplement)[7] authenticates such an understanding.

In the context of the primary denotative meanings quoted and synthesized from various dictionaries at the beginning of this chapter, one can find additionally in the *OED* that "anarchs" were thought of in the seventeenth century as "leaders of revolts," that Milton thought of Satan in such terms, much like many North Americans think of Central American "communists." Recognizable political conservatives are given credit for more paradigmatic usages of "anarchy" and its cognates than revolutionaries, liberals or Roundheads: Burke, Carlyle and Spencer are so credited. Bentham's utilitarian liberalism gets paradigmatic dictionary respectability with his anti-radical cite from 1791 (the era of the French Revolution) about the "anarchist ... [who] denies the validity of the law ... and calls upon mankind to rise up in a mass, and resist the execution of it."

Only recently, i.e. not in the 1933 edition of the *OED* but in the 1972 supplement, has the rule-respecting "self-righteousness of the sour, young anarch" been belatedly (and, one suspects, begrudgingly) recognized. (The dictionary refers to its source as the *New Statesman*, 1966.) At last, in 1972 the proper English speaker was authorized by the *OED* to use the alternative, but secondary definition of "anarchy" as "the theoretical social state in which there is no governing person or body ... but each individual has absolute liberty (without implication of disorder)." He or she may now additionally and properly recall that in 1884 "anarchy" was noted as "the favorite social remedy of the Russian revolutionary party," a clear reference to what would now be called the "terrorists" of that conspiratorial time; Fabian socialist references to "scientific Anarchists" in 1889 are also belatedly recognized. And

---

[7] The visible economism of my hometown library – unfortunate in many other respects
– happily suggests two ordinal measures of the relative prominence of alternative
meanings of "anarchy" and its cognates: rank orders in definitional listings and
belated recognition – inclusion of alternate meanings only in a supplemental volume.

supplementarily we learn that in 1892 the *Daily News* reported (but doubtless did not approve) that anarchy means to some "the placing in common of all this world's riches to allow each to consume according to his needs. Anarchy is a great family where each will be protected by all and will take whatever he required." In the 1972 Supplement to the *OED* the connection of anarchism with anarcho-syndicalism and revolutionary socialism (neither of them majority positions in British society) is at last clearly established, even if the fascinating accommodations and tensions among revolutionary anarcho-syndicalists and revolutionary socialists are not.[8]

These linguistic traces of past thought suggest further that the English language has sedimented more conservative victories over our consciousness than those won by radical anarchists. These sedimentations are a likely cause of the rather implicit, almost surreptitious way in which the cooperation under anarchy problematique presupposes (and thus helps reproduce) a conservative reality. Like "realist," connotatively "anarchy" is overwhelmingly (but contestably) bad!

[8] I have in mind Kropotkin's exchange with Lenin (Kropotkin 1973: 332). Lenin is there reported to have said, "We don't need the struggle and violent acts of separate persons. It is high time that the anarchists understood this and stopped scattering their revolutionary energy on utterly useless affairs. Only in the masses, only though the masses and with the masses, from underground work to massive red terror if it is called for, to civil war, to a war on all fronts, to a war of all against all – this is the only kind of struggle that can be crowned with success."

Aware of "anarchy's" word politics, the Marxist–Leninist scientific tradition (whose word politics are most worthy of extended comment at some other place) appears (by the later 1980s) partially, subsumptively, to have recognized the heterarchical reality in a less polemical way:

(1) admitting the possibility of co-occurring yet contrasting modes of production in the socioeconomic "bases of international relations";
(2) recognizing related, "genetic dependencies," such as the claim that "economic development is the crucial element in the configuration of forces in East–West relations," while at the same time insisting on the "functional superiority of politics over economics" in the conditioning of the "intensity, form and substance" of these relations;
(3) conceiving international class struggle as a competitive and collaborative "process of coexistence";
(4) "the final feature of the international system is the *decentralization of the international social environment* ... manifested in the absence of one supreme regulator of social life and the domination of coordination over subordination in relations among members of the international collectivity" (his emphasis).

Because internationally power is divided among independent, rivalrous units, relations of power and subordination "do not dominate the organization of international relations" (Kostecki 1985: 19–21).

Similarly, "sovereignty" is connotatively good. Since, as Oye suggests, one concept is internal (by definition, connotatively) opposed to the other, the doubled rhetorical force of "realist learning-to-live-under-anarchy" problematiques is that a world of "realistic," power-max-imizing "sovereign" rulers is good. Almost by definition, anyone – especially radical communitarians like myself – opposed to the per-petuation of such practices is both "unrealistic," "utopian" *and* bad!

By comparison, Bull's synthesis of conceptual elements from the realist, Grotian and revolutionary-cosmopolitan traditions is of a much higher order of argument. Many sides of the debate are reflected in the richness of the dictionary's historical definition list; many related perspectives are sources of Bull's conceptualization. Ironically, he does this as one who accepts "realist" criticisms of such "utopian" thought. Yet, to confound another inadequate dichotomy, I think it appropriate to think of Bull as a "utopian realist," a "realistic utopian." Although the standard textbooks would not have it this way, in fact, were not Machiavelli and Hobbes two of the very greatest of modern utopians?

Hobbes vs. Grotius vs. Kant, replayed

From these dictionary alternatives, listed neatly and sequentially, we have entered the traditional realm of contesting political theories. Our purposes are the same as Bull's might have been: from a fresh, contextual discussion of alternative scholarly traditions, to discover the critical and constructive insights they generate concerning the coopera-tion under anarchy problematique, as well as alternatives covering similar ground. We shall now take this path, this time treating Bull primarily as a Grotian, downplaying his cross-traditional synthesizing achievements. Our typology for circumspection will be Bull's: we shall contrast "Hobbesian" realists, Grotian internationalists (such as Bull and Deutsch), and Kantian revolutionary cosmopolitans.

Not very surprisingly, we shall find scholarly efforts resonating with anti-democratic usage and anti-revolutionary rhetoric in their ritualistic presumption of international "anarchy," efforts that nonetheless try to ameliorize in certain ways the tradition of "realist" scholarship. Who wins most of the battles here is already suggested by the contemporary linguistic fact that the North American anarchy problematique locates anarchy in a threatening, powerful position "above" states – a kind of "anarchy *über alles*" reminiscent of the threatening cartoons evoked by post-hegemonic, roughly contemporary American losses in Vietnam,

363

OPEC market actions, increases of the Soviet nuclear arsenal, Soviet intervention in Afghanistan, Cuban interventions in Africa and the ignominious holding of American hostages by Iranian revolutionaries.

North Americans do not need a self-deluding "restoration of pride"; they need some fresh insights from those not so troubled by our egoistic, self-righteous, hegemonic preoccupations. Take, for example, the untypical phrasing of a highly relevant British treatment of anarchic domestic and international relations that appeared just before the "anarchy problematique" in *World Politics*, Hedley Bull's neo-Grotian *The Anarchical Society: A Study of Order in World Politics* (1977), Charles Taylor's game theoretic yet surprisingly resonant *Anarchy and Cooperation* (1976) and Charles Beitz's more analytically refined critique of Hobbesian presuppositions applied to international relations (1979). Of course, the alternative usage in these citations is not new in contemporary scholarship – indeed, Oran Young cited approvingly Taylor's work – but Taylor's work does give us a plausible alternative conceptualization highly relevant to present concerns: "anarchy *and* cooperation" – not "cooperation *under* anarchy."

Indeed, Bull, Taylor and Young clearly speak to the real issue evoked by classical theorists of political anarchy – how can policies be coordinated or collective actions pursued in the absence of solutions imposed from above, *without assuming that nonhierarchical forms of collective self-rule (e.g., democracy or polyarchy) cannot exist*? I would like to draw upon these sources further to criticize the conservative bias and the reductionist interpretations already suggested by my analysis of the "word politics" of the anarchy problematique.

Although Hobbes actually focused the relevant discussions on domestic politics, Oye, Bull, Taylor and many others cite Hobbes as the exemplary seventeenth-century theorist of international anarchy. From a multitraditional perspective, I want to begin to unpack some of the genesis amnesia we have with respect to his work, and to criticize his contemporary descendants in terms of such recollections. In some ways, even Hobbes will be seen not to subscribe to the views now associated with his name; in other ways, he was more profound (and more ambiguous) than most contemporary game theory aficionados. Yet, from the perspective of other traditions, his distortions of social, economic and cultural relationships, plus his anti-democratic passion are sufficiently offensive yet undeniably profound to require considerable rethinking. For, as the most penetrating traditional realists have realized: "the very institution of the state – celebrated as the source of order, liberty, and morality for citizens – has also turned out to be a source of international chaos and consequently of physical danger and moral agony" (Hoffmann 1966).[9]

All scholars of world politics have heard of Hobbes' description of the "war of every one against every one" outside of the civil state, where no society exists and "the life of man" is "solitary, poor, nasty, brutish, and short." The better educated among us know he was really talking of a pessimismal ideal type, a mythic model of complete *domestic* disorder. Because states were far stronger than individuals, and not so equal, Bull is correct in arguing that Hobbes" view of international reality was less stark, even at a time when Holland's economic and political power approached hegemonic proportions. Moreover, we should be easily persuaded that Hobbes was quite aware of the politically loaded, anti-democratic connotations of "anarchy," a term he himself did not use in the chapter from which I just quoted, presumably for that reason (cf. the quote at the beginning of the chapter).

And some of us can recall from memory – as I cannot – Hobbes' definition of "the posture [or 'state'] of war":

> though there had never been any time, wherein particular men were in a condition of war one against another; yet in all times, kings, and persons of sovereign authority, because of their independence, are in continual jealousies, and in the state and posture of gladiators; having their weapons pointing, and their eyes fixed on one another; that is, their forts, garrisons, and guns upon the frontiers of their kingdoms; and continual spies upon their neighbours.
>
> (Hobbes 1962, originally 1651: 98–102)

How prophetically this anticipates at least the common American view of the central political dramas of the twentieth century, its world wars and its Cold War between "East" and "West" as we (but not many Asians) like to define these terms!

Hobbes' highly selective preference for Thucydides among classical writers is only slightly less known. But I want to review it here in order to suggest some of the anti-democratic political biases inherent in what Bull names – and also rejects – as Hobbesian realism, biases we are less often likely to recall. We do not live in the age of the Stuarts (Hobbes' employers for a time, while he was in exile during the Cromwellian era), or of a pro-revolutionary Locke and Milton. We are not Absolutist

---

[9] This article is full of thoughtful comments on Rousseau, Hobbes and Locke.

apologists embarrassed by Aristotle's advocacy of mixed forms of democratic government ("polities"). We do not think of Pericles' rule as "in effect monarchical," or take pains to demonstrate Pericles' royal lineage; we do not feel the need to treat Thucydides' preferred Athenian government of 4,000 arms-providing citizens as a natural aristocracy. But we do clearly speak from within the Hobbesian realist tradition when we define "anarchy" internationally in terms of the absence of a central government (British or Dutch or American "hegemony" rather than "monarchy" is what we have most often in mind).

On the other hand, we do recognize the "great licentiousness" and fearful breakdown of civil order in the plague of Athens as a precursor of Hobbes' terrifying pictures of "intestine disorder"; similarly we do see Hobbes' connection of equality, fear and class war in his rendering of Thucydides' account of the precedent-setting Corcyrean revolution, caused by "*desire of rule*, out of *avarice* and *ambition* and the zeal of contention from those two proceeding," a contest between two factions, "one the *political equality of the multitude*," the other the "*moderate aristocracy*."[10] As globally privileged North Americans, as middle (or upper) class scholars, like most of our leaders, we share Thucydides' fear of lower-class revolutions, the threat of victory by democratic "equality" in a bloody "civil war" that always exists in the Hobbesian subconscious. We are thus very tempted, in Bull's terms, to prefer international order over international distributive justice.

But most of us would not *defend* the Melian massacre the way Hobbes does as "not unlike to divers other actions."[11] Why is that?

---

[10] These anti-democratic biases are noted by Richard Schlatter in his introduction to *Hobbes's Thucydides* (Schlatter, 1975). Hobbes' own Introduction within this volume is indeed revealing. Cleon (the expeller of Thucydides) and Alcibiades (the likely author of the Melian decrees) are treated by Thucydides as instances of *democratic* degeneracy, not immoderate *hubris* or the corruption of imperial power. The quoted citations in the paragraph above are from Hobbes' translation, which in respect to civil war and the Athenian plague corresponds in tone to more modern renderings of the original Greek.

[11] Relying on both conservative and radical commentaries, in Chapter 1, I argue that Thucydides did not approve of the Melian massacre, and in this respect he is misinterpreted by Hobbes, who at one point noted the total absence of normative restraint in Spartan conduct as well. Many contemporary neorealists see that occasion as an instance of Thucydides' objective empiricism concerning the realities of power politics; I (and most classicists, but few contemporary neorealists) stress the culturally conditioned interpretation which sees a tragic moral drama in Thucydides' condemnatory account of Athenian degeneracy in that episode and in the subsequent Sicilian disaster.

Does not our rejection mean that we also do not accept his famous, fearful description of the "state" of war? Hobbes *presumes* there to be "no society" in the solitary, brutish "state" of war so he then could *argue* deductively ("geometrically") that in such a state there is no injustice or justice.

> To this war of every man against every man, this also is consequent; that nothing can be unjust. The notions of right and wrong, justice and injustice have there no place. Where there is no common power, there is no law; where no law, no injustice. Force, and fraud, are in war the two cardinal virtues. Hobbes (1962: 101)

Most of us would disagree with Hobbes here, believing that the Melian massacre was wrong, that war was even then a socially recognized institution, with limits on its proper conduct that would have led most disinterested Greeks to condemn the Melian massacre. We lament the absence of sufficient moral restraint and the associated political restraint that might have deterred such barbarity. We do not publicly praise the unrestrained utilization of force and fraud as virtues. At least since Nuremberg we, most peoples and nation-states of the world, have recognized that, like the killing of ambassadors, genocide falls outside the limits of civilized conduct. And from hindsight, and a Grotian perspective, we can note the tragic failures in the building of a Greek political community that the Peloponnesian War represents. To the extent that such arguments are persuasive to those concerned, we, Oye and his collaborators, and most other North American students of international relations – now follow Grotius, Locke, Kant, Bull or Deutsch more than Hobbes.

Oye's introductory citation of Locke suggests a sensitivity to the debate in classical liberal political theory about the "brutishness" of the state of nature, and the kind of "social contract" appropriate between rulers and their subjects in the establishment of a political order. Lockeans do not see international relations as a zero-sum war of all against all. As their framework suggests, Oye and his collaborators would thus be quite willing to see non-zero-sum possibilities for collaboration where reactionary Hobbesians would not. Indeed, that is an important reason for calling their anarchy problematique "liberal realism."[12]

---

[12] Bull (1977: 25ff.) contrasts Kantians with Hobbesians concerning the existence of "a purely cooperative or non-zero-sum game," confusing two different aspects of formal games. But his subsequent elaboration of the revolutionary Kantian perspective makes quite clear why it must oppose the anarchy problematique. According to this

Nonetheless, the anarchy problematique repeatedly makes assumptions at odds with key insights of the Grotian and Kantian traditions; it misses opportunities to find common ground among these traditions, common ground from which Bull probably derived his much richer and more profound world society problematique.

Hobbesian realists reject the Grotius-Bull-Deutsch tradition; although not *formally* forbidden from doing so, no non-cooperative game theorist specializing in international relations has included – to my knowledge – "international injustice norms" in the extensive or normal form representations (and payoff vectors) which are supposed to embody all the "rules of a non-cooperative game." None of the payoff matrices in the October 1985 issue of *World Politics* do so; no systematic search for normative constraints on behavior is invited. No

revolutionary perspective "[c]onflicts of interest exist among the ruling cliques of states, but this is only at the superficial or transient level of the existing system of states; properly understood, the interests of all peoples are the same." A fundamental ideological conflict "divides human society into two camps – the trustees of the immanent community of mankind and those who stand in its way...." Moral imperatives exist that "enjoin not coexistence and cooperation among states but rather the overthrow of the system of states and its replacement by a cosmopolitan society" (p. 26). It should be clear that this tradition is defined in a way that clashes with the Grotian willingness to find order in a more pluralistic, international society of mutually recognizing sovereign nation-states.

Hoffmann (1986) differs from Bull on Kant's revolutionary cosmopolitanism, seeing Kant as more of an internationalist liberal, with Grotian overtones. Along similar lines, Keohane has called to my attention Michael W. Doyle's thoughtful, empirically supported treatment of Kant as a prophetic liberal, perhaps the exemplary spokesperson for a tradition that has both *laissez-faire* conservatives and progressive "social democrats" within it. Doyle gives strong (but controversial) empirical evidence for the absence of inter-state wars among developed liberal states since 1815. (These states are operationally identified in terms of capitalistic economies, externally sovereign polities, juridical rights for individual citizens, and "republican" – including constitutional monarchy – forms of government.) Doyle (1983) also suggests that liberalism transcends realism's dire predictions – at least as they apply to relations among liberal states – but that an externally oriented accommodation is possible between liberalism and realism. Oye's Hobbes–Locke distinction is thus at least partly supported by a Doyle–Keohane–Hoffmann reading of the liberal tradition.

As a cautious cosmopolitan, I see some merit in each view: Bull's contextual one, correctly interpreting Kant as a radical spokesperson for the new modes of rational, liberal thought "released" and "exported" by the British and French revolutions and soon to become hegemonic throughout the European-centered world; Hoffmann's and Doyle's textual one, which assimilates these revolutionary views a century and a half later to Bull's Grotian realism and Hoffmann's own – for our day moderate – variant of liberal realism. The matter may be resolved by answering for oneself the extent (and periods for which) one wants to consider Lenin a "Kantian cosmopolitan."

society or social system is formally defined as undergirding, shaping or limiting these interaction opportunities. Yet it is a very widely held view outside the reactionary variant of Hobbesian thought (which nowadays sees an external world consisting mainly of friendly "authoritarians" and ruthless "communists," "totalitarians" or "terrorists") that domestic and world revolutions centrally involve such fundamental social questions of justice, identity-recognition and reciprocal respect – those larger collective "causes" for which citizens of one party or country are willing to kill or to die.

Similarly, neither the Grotian internationalist nor the more revolutionary universalist Kantian tradition identifies the absence of a central government (or monarch, or hegemon) with the absence of an international social or moral order. *Advocates of both traditions would balk at any set of definitions that do not distinguish social-normative integration from power centralization.* And they would resist the claim that no moral imperatives exist in international relations, that there is no international or universal human society.[13] Even if it were used to model decisions to give or to withhold diplomatic recognition – which is tantamount to state membership in that society – game theory cannot represent the mutual, intentional, rule-governed, self/other recognition process that is *the essence of the social*, domestically or internationally. Figure 11.1 below presents a much fuller implementation of such a two-dimensional conception than is evident anywhere in that issue.

Even though one could conceivably model certain aspects of persuasive communication game theoretically, anarchy-derived noncooperative game trees cannot represent formally the non-strategic communicative aspects of negotiations pragmatically oriented toward consensus seeking – the reaching of agreements. Nor can noncooperative game theory or microeconomic models formally give adequate attention to the shareable and contentious value orientations – including notions of just and unjust conduct in war and peace – which are the infectious and allergenic stuff of politics. They shape and express economic and political interests; they can help us make up our minds about the political programs we oppose or

---

[13] It should be noted that, on the realist side, Axelrod and Keohane avoid "Hobbesian" misrepresentations of anarchy by giving a different definition than the one the October 1985 *World Politics* issue begins with, referring to "a lack of common government in world politics, not to a denial that an international society – albeit a fragmented one – exists" (p. 226).

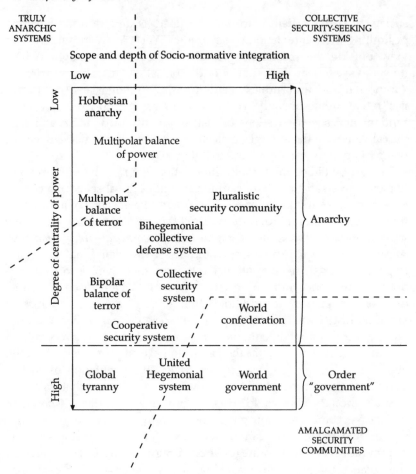

Figure 11.1 A communitarian sketch of alternative security systems

identify with. Political discourse and communicative action more generally require other scientific formulations.[14]

Previously noted Kantian or Leninist intuitions of underlying, yet transnationally realizable common interests may also be seen in this light. Clearly such normative structures are sometimes decisively

[14] John Mallery, for example, has recently proposed incorporating the Grosz–Sidner (1986) treatment of Discourse structure in the RELATUS text-analysis system at MIT (Alker, Duffy, Hurwitz, Mallery 1991). My own efforts to represent generatively potent justice/injustice ideals using Wendy Lehnert's affective plot unit algebra are reported in Chapter 3 above.

appealed to, abductively or adductively, in real political argument and action; hence they need explicit representations.[15] When Lenin was arguing with Kropotkin about anarchism and the world revolutionary situation (see footnote 5) he agreed with Kropotkin about the evils of bureaucracy and the desirability of cooperative worker organizations, he disagreed with the conservative class biases of syndicalism, and he doubted that anarcho-syndicalism was politically strong enough to destroy capitalism. But his synthesizing attitude toward Kropotkin and anarcho-syndicalism – he proposed the republication within Russia of Kropotkin's *History of the French Revolution* – is noteworthy as partly successful political collaboration and appropriation. He suggests an effort to build, broaden and strengthen, within the Soviet Union and beyond, popular identification with the *revolutionary tradition* of modern French republican thought and the Kantian Enlightenment.

The problematical legitimations of state rulers – their ways of overcoming within themselves and before others the "moral agony" of their actions – are necessarily exogenous to game theoretical representations of unitary state actors. Thus besides being unable to represent the crucial, contradictory imperatives of morality and interest that such actions sometimes face, two-party game representations – even if non-zero-sum games – reinforce the statist conservatism of Hobbesian realism when those parties are treated as unitary national actors. Conflict (like anarchy) is almost always *outside* the state, rather than cross-cutting interests and arguments that both social democratic pluralists and Marxist–Leninists see as primary sources of, and hindrances to, international cooperation. What *realistically* should be modeled as subnational and transnational groups, classes and coalitions seeking greater material advantages, but also increased legitimacy, power and community, never gets formally represented that way in an international 2x2 game. Allowing N-person formalisms, and exploring their consequences as the cooperation under anarchy problematique does, only compounds such problems when the "persons" are "states."

[15] Not only Lenin and Pierce, but classical realists like Thucydides, Machiavelli, Clausewitz, Carr and Aron (at times) may be assimilated to a dialectical view that both political arguments and phenomenologically valid conceptual models of political process rarely even approximate deductive certainty. This is not to argue that abductive or adductive inferences (or analogous political processes) cannot be formally modeled. See the Introduction and Chapter 1, 3 and 8 above for additional citations on the formalization political reasoning processes.

The real sources of social cohesion in an assumed world of possessive egoists must be exogenous to a deductive scientific model that postulates the opposite of what its users are trying to establish. As Ashley has put it, the "power" of realist power politics comes from the strength – such as it is – of the international *community* of realists, who must deny both the existence of, and their self-interest in the existence of, such a community.[16] As such, defenders of the practical import of the Cooperation Under Anarchy Problematique will actually be promoting in the guise of science a preferred pattern of international order – a world made safe for possessive individualists and expansionist states – which their problematique presumes.

Finally, let me develop further Taylor's highly perceptive account of Hobbesian reasoning *and* anarchist thought. I do so not because I wish to be fully identified with the Hobbesian tradition, which I do take seriously, but because I think Taylor's study better shows how research in the games and decisions research paradigm can sometimes be used constructively to illuminate fundamental political issues, without making most of the errors of the Cooperation under Anarchy Problematique. And Taylor's account allows me to try and rescue Hobbes' rationalist (but not merely instrumentalist) "domestic peace problematique" from his modern descendants, thus preserving its profundity (hopefully in a revised form) for Hobbesians, Grotians and Kantians alike.

Taylor discusses carefully Hobbes' argument in Chapters 14 and 15 of the *Leviathan*. He presents the argument as Hobbes does, one about natural laws discoverable without divine revelation by human reason. Although the issue as to whether such natural reason might be seen as existing in the "state of nature" (or international society) is not raised, Hobbes' derivation of the desirability of conditional cooperation *even in the state of nature* is emphasized (Taylor 1976: 100–111).

Hobbes' state of nature is a world of egoistic, prideful, expansionistic, possessive individuals. Since it is a fundamental "right of nature" that every man there has a "right to every thing" there that he is strong enough to get and keep, there follows rationally Hobbes' first law of nature: "that every man, ought to endeavor peace, as far as he has hope of obtaining it; and when he cannot obtain it, that he may seek, and use, all helps, and advantages of war." The second law of

---

[16] See Ashley (1987). An earlier version of this same chapter is the source of the "genesis amnesia" argument I adapt to the anarchy problematique below.

nature follows from the first: "that a man be willing, when others are so too ... as for peace, and defence of himself he shall think it necessary, to lay down this right to all things; and be contented with so much liberty against other men, as he would allow other men against himself." The third law of nature is "that men perform their covenants made,"[17] Hobbes' rather minimal conception of justice. The laws of nature are "eternal"; they "dictate peace." Seventeen more laws follow in Hobbes' analysis, including the advocation of mercy, moderation, equity, the lack of pride, etc., as well as a rational rule (cited with Biblical authority) by which all of these and others can be deduced: "Do not that to another, which thou wouldest not have done to thyself." Why isn't this moral standard, which Hobbes apparently derives from his motivational assumptions, in the Lakatosian core of all neo-Hobbesians' anarchy problematiques?

Hobbes argues that "The laws of nature oblige in conscience always, but in effect then only when there is security." Taylor goes on to argue that Hobbes' definition of the state of nature corresponds to an iterated N-person Prisoner's Dilemma (others might want to call this an assurance game or a coordination game). Hobbes' prescription of contingent cooperation is argued to fit the "Tit-for-Tat" strategy identified by Rapoport and others early on in the game theory literature as particularly important and efficacious.[18] It is consistent with my characterization of his most important objective being domestic peace and personal security, not the modern realist's concern for the maximization of the national interest defined as power.

But Hobbes' problematique is more complex than even Taylor acknowledges in his interesting exploration of the effects in such games of egoistic, altruistic and envious (status-sensitive) utility functions, modeled using different linear combinations of payoff functions.

[17] The emphasis in my Hobbes quotations is in the original.

[18] Taylor's argument is reviewed in Alker and Hurwitz (1980). It is imaginatively developed, with Hobbes' and Taylor's crucial discussion of social conventions, in Axelrod (1984). Russell Hardin and Duncan Snidal have more recently developed such insights further (Snidal 1985a).

I of course agree with those following the "anarchy problematique" that where possible it is often useful to distinguish among different kinds of non-zero-sum games. But I believe that such treatments of normative evolution, by starting (consistent with the anarchy problematique) from the assumption that no norms exist, and limiting player actions to instrumental rationality, do violence to our species being and history, to the reality of student game play in SPD-like situations, and to international society as well.

373

As Joshua Cohen has taught me, Hobbes' has a double level design problem. Recognizing that motivational support is necessary for subjects within a state to follow the dictates of their natural reason, and that passions may also distort their reasoning capabilities, *Hobbes wants somehow to create a political order that shapes people's emotions so that they will want to be peacefully rational, and it will be situationally appropriate for them to be so.* In other words, Hobbes wants to induce the right kind of fear and nonprideful desire so that the basic individual interest in survival is achieved by cooperative means. He wants to work with and shape the *passions* in order to achieve human *interests* in peace and prosperity.

Hobbes proposes, constructs and tries to justify an Absolutist state, the Leviathan, on instrumental, individualistic grounds. In the words of the Book of Job, he wants "a king over all the children of pride." He fails to achieve fully his goals, I would judge, because his presumptions of anarchy are too extreme, his "anti-anarchism" too rabidly anti-democratic, his assumed motivations of possessive individualism too absolute. Political orders, by their nature, are not wholly instrumental beings. Political orders cannot be *deduced* on instrumental grounds either. Yet true to his insistence on their interest in survival, Hobbes argues that individuals can never have their right to life taken away from them. In such a case the sovereign cannot be judged absolute or always effective.

It is on a related point that Hobbes is crucially ambiguous, in a way that raises (but does not resolve) the problematical possibility of polyarchic rule. In Hobbes' mechanical view, the Leviathan is an artificial mechanism, an automata, "in which the *sovereignty* is an artificial *soul*." But since the sovereign may be either one man, an aristocratic subset, or all men within a certain place, *the absolutization of the sovereign's power that Hobbes seeks could logically refer to the absolutization of a polyarchic form of rule.* At least a logical possibility, Hobbes does not fully pursue this concession to the republican (in the British case largely puritanical) thought of his time.

Besides their failure to recall this ambiguity, other cases of contemporary, conservative "genesis amnesia" include the presumption that asocial possessive individualism is eternal in European history and human nature. All the anthropology I know suggests such traits to be variables, not constants in human history. Moreover, society exists when a baby is first cared for. John Ruggie's account of the origins of the modern world polity also denies such a characterization as adequate for the medieval European system and for today's era of fundamental change. Modern "anarchy" was constituted by modern "sovereignty," and vice versa. Corporatist models of European and Asian society, the hegemonic pluralism of the Soviet world socialist system all support the dropping of such an ideological, self-serving, ahistorical assumption (Ruggie 1983; Scott 1976; Solomon 1982; Montagu 1978).

Nonetheless, Hobbes' failure is more impressive than the successes of many of his modern imitators. What I want to suggest here is that liberal realists should draw explicitly but critically on Hobbes' writings, leaving neither him nor them to their reactionary compatriots. Table 11.1 summarizes the Hobbesian peace problematique, as I have adduced it from Hobbes' writings. It may not be as compelling as Bull's world society problematique, but it certainly exceeds the cooperation under anarchy problematique in richness and depth.

Positivism, economism and capitalism

Despite its ambiguities, Hobbesian realism typically presumes – it rarely carefully tests or attempts to falsify – many of its crucial claims about international reality. By increasing our awareness of alternative perspectives that Bull would have called Grotian internationalism and Kantian universalism, I have tried both to clarify and question certain of the politically biased traditional presumptions (assumptions and heuristics) of that tradition. Many of them consciously or unconsciously will affect, I suggest, those scholars working within the cooperation under anarchy problematique. Hopefully, my analysis so far has also made plausible my claims as to the conservative, statist, central power serving, anti-popular biases of the large section of the realist tradition tracing its roots back to Hobbes.

Because of their mutually reinforcing character, dropping or modifying just a few of Hobbes' presumptions – as done by the investigators of the cooperation under anarchy problematique – will not fundamentally change its basic political character. Rather than urge them to abandon their own tradition, I have so far urged academic liberal realists – who are mostly neither anti-democratic nor conservative in American terms – to undertake a deeper, more critical, and historically self-aware appropriation of Hobbes' domestic peace problematique, preserving his institutional design orientation, expanding upon his ambiguities concerning the possibility of polyarchic rule,

Table 11.1 *The Hobbesian domestic peace problematique*

I	Definition of (Domestic) State of Nature "Anarchy"		
		1	Possibly but not necessarily "Zero-Sum" world of possessive individuals
		2	Inherent right of every man to every thing
		3	No society or external normative order
		4	A "state of war" (actual or expected)
II	Causal Assumptions		
		1	Equality breeds fear; each can kill each other
		2	Threat of civil war is responsibility of anti-monarch (democratic) forces
		3	Superior power is necessary to end fear, create society and order
		4	Covenant, if motivationally binding, can create context where VI.1 works

III Normative/Prescriptive Orientation

	A	Motivational Bases	
Hobbes'	A.1	Fear of violence and	
"Anti-Anarchism"	A.2	Fear of equality	
	A.3	Fear of democracy/preference for monarchy	
	A.4	Fear of Civil (class) war provoked by democratic Anarchs	
The "Possessive	A.5	Individual's desire for life	
Individualism"	A.6	Individual's desire for private property	
of human nature	A.7	Individual's prideful desire for more	
	A.8	Individual's desire for security of unequally distributed private property	
	B	Natural Laws (Located within Individual)	
	B.1	Obligation to endeavor peace, if possible; permission to use war	
	B.2	Willingness to lay down natural rights to all things, if others will for peace	
	B.3	Keeping of covenants (justice)	

IV	Law Evaluation Standard	1	Negative Golden Rule
V	Preferred Mode of Inference	1	Calculation of interest, "geometric" deduction
VI	Prescriptive Maxims "Natural Laws"	1	Conduct according to *reason* is preferable
	"Prudence"	2	Cooperate if expectation of security is reasonable

Table 11.1 *contd.*

VII Problematique (A Double-Level Social and Political Design Problem)

1 Covenant in a way that evokes human fear, pride and possessiveness so that prudent rationality still occurs, and political security is rationally to be expected, hence cooperative conduct results.

extending the inferential logics and rationality modalities they employ, including socio-emotional identity and status considerations, recognizing the problematical existence of international society in their initial formulations, controlling for the unitary, statist, conservative biases of their theoretical synthesis by focusing more explicitly on continuing problems and processes linking and shaping domestic and international politics. Walking in Hedley Bull's footsteps, I have tried to preserve the overlap among traditions that game-theoretic realism obscures, in the interest of developing a more broadly grounded, intellectually profound and truly international discipline of International Relations.

But my purposes go further, beyond where Bull himself would probably want to go. In this section, I want to note and criticize some more general epistemological tendencies evident in the anarchy problematique, tendencies toward positivism, economism and the *de facto* legitimization of an international system of capitalistic power balancing (euphemistically, "global interdependence"). Variants on this conception are characteristic world order models of liberal realism. I believe these epistemological tendencies fly in the face of the distinctive historical character of the twentieth century, and thus militate in a more general way against the sustained production of globally useful knowledge by that tradition. Thus an even stronger case could be made – Bull's own multitraditional practice supports it – for the greater global appropriateness of approaches to international collaboration that do not *presume* epistemological positions that on the global stage are, or have been, hotly contested.

Is there a characteristic pattern of international practices in the contemporary world? More dialectically, could not there be several, some more pervasive and dominating than others? As I suggested at the outset, world disorder is not anarchy. Rather, I see multiple world order contenders capable of maintaining and projecting a certain degree of internal and external order (and less justice). Relations across such major orders and outside them may be both cooperative and conflictual; they do have many of the features of international society that Bull suggests. The United States, Western Europe, Japan, the Soviet Union and the People's Republic of China are central poles of unequal strength and penetrating power in this system. Subregional leaders in the Latin, African, Middle Eastern and South Asian worlds could also be identified. Jockeying among the polar states and their unequal allies conforms to some of the maxims of classical power balancing relationships. Global financial institutions and interregional trading relationships more closely resemble the capitalistic economic relationships visible within the trilateral OECD world than the socialist economic arrangements characteristic of the Soviet and Chinese spheres. Hence I see "capitalist power balancing" as the most dominant among several distinctive patterns of world order practice taking place within the unevenly realized parameters of international society.

But here I deviate even farther from the classical realist picture of the absolute separability of "orderly" domestic affairs and "anarchical" international ones than does Bull. Not only are the international relations in question subject, to varying degrees, to the orderly regulation of the "anarchical society," the boundaries between domestic and international have become seriously eroded. Thus "foreign" affairs will not be entirely "external" because of the global orders interpenetrating each other and their peripheries to varying degrees. The realms of domestic and international moral constraint are thus overlapping, not essentially distinct. Indeed, just like "independent" and "dependent," "external" and "internal" have lost their simple territorial definitions to a striking extent. Mighty hegemonic contenders clearly don't respect many such boundaries; transnational actors are extremely adept at crossing through them; demographic, technological and ecological processes have drastically reshaped political boundaries and identities in a single lifetime. That is an important additional class of reasons why Bull can look for international morality *within* and *beyond* the anarchical society of sovereign states.

Specifically, our century has experienced total wars between liberal, militarist-fascist and socialist systems of order; and we have learned from the briefness of the post-war American hegemony – a period of rapid decolonialization around the world as well as increasing but now stagnating Soviet strength – that it could be wrong to treat any state as the singular victor in the world wars. As Robert Keohane has emphasized in *After Hegemony*, the decline from the United States'

378

hegemony need not be described as anarchical in the sense of being devoid of cooperative regimes, or as anti-American, just because of its increasing pluralism. This kind of pluralism has affected the Soviet regional hegemony as well.

Nor has cooperation with the war's other victors been impossible: Bull's international society has fitfully transcended even the Cold War. Periods of accommodation, *cold* war and even détente have been observed. For all its revolutionary, anti-imperialist rhetoric, the Soviet system of influence has exhibited both hegemonic and conservative tendencies. Dialectically, even though its internal economic relationships do not fit capitalistic patterns, it has substantially turned away from the ideals Lenin once claimed for it. Liberal realists are right, but not wholly so, that the Soviet Union has become reasonably adept at capitalistic power balancing roles.

For those like Bull whose interpretive lenses are not deeply colored by the Cold War, it has become increasingly clear that our century has also seen an unprecedented "revolt against the West,"[19] the partial rejection of each and every one of these Western systems of order and their self/other understandings. Bull is right to focus on this problem in his later work because of its tremendous, long-term significance. And his qualified optimism about current trends in the Third World seems justified.[20] Islamic internationalism, with its Sunni and Shi'ite poles, is neither "anarchical," "communist," nor full of "terrorists." Even "East" and "West" have different meanings than they had during the Cold War. A European or American vantage point pre-

---

[19] "The Revolt Against the West" is a chapter title both in Geoffrey Barraclough's brilliant *Introduction to Contemporary History* (1976) and in Bull and Watson, eds. (1984) – a chapter written by Bull. This similar perspective should be contrasted with Michael Doyle's much more positive assessment. Doyle (1983) argues that the number of mature liberal states has greatly increased in the world since 1900 and since 1945. The "interventionist" tendencies of "liberal imperialism" are acknowledged; the depth and magnitude of the reaction against it is not.

[20] After discussing the revolt against the West in the twentieth century, including the influence of Leninism and the Islamic revolt, Hedley Bull and Adam Watson conclude, *inter alia*, that the "source of the anarchy and disorder is in large measure to be found in factors that would be having their effect on the Western, industrialized world, even if it had not had to cope with the problem of adjusting itself to a resurgent Third World.... Indeed, the most striking feature of the global international society of today is the extent to which the states of Asia and Africa have embraced such basic elements of European international society as the sovereign state, the rules of international law, the procedures and conventions of diplomacy and international organization" (Bull and Watson 1984: 433).

sumed in the use of such terms no longer fits global understanding. The Islamic revival defines itself, as many Americans do also, as anti-Western – despite its roots in the Judaeo-Christian and Graeco-Roman traditions. Yet it certainly is not "communist."

Seen against this larger context of order-building practices in contemporary world politics, the epistemological biases of the cooperation under anarchy problematique are particularly glaring. Though they are not the same as Hobbes' anarchical state of nature, his motivational "anti-anarchism" and "possessive individualism," they are strikingly analogous. One can see an unreflective appropriation of some of the characteristic styles of thought in the liberal world, rather than a truly global attempt to transcend them.

First of all there is the ahistorical positivism of the anarchy problematique. The realist presumption that international society does not exist, that anarchy only need be defined as the absence of a central (or hegemonic) supranational power is "positivistic" in the general sense of being "historically unreflective." After all, Hobbes and Grotius were contemporaries of great renown, whose contradictory contributions to political science and international law both deserve, and have received, continued discussion. In that case why not start with social and political aspects of world politics in one's definitions, in order to assess their relative importance and allow integrative transformations to be endogenous issues within one's problematique?

Defining a research program in terms of greatly impoverished context representations – simple non-cooperative game matrices whose only rules define instrumental alternatives for predefined egoists unable to make binding agreements – and then proposing three unhistorical explanatory variables – the number of game players, their (actuarially discounted) iterated game futures and the degree to which their interests conflict – is also "positivistic" in the sense of mimicking the "parsimonious," deductive, universally valid, law-like explanations one would find in the ahistorical natural sciences. This avoidance of previously existing social relationships, of contextual complexity and of explanations in terms of the contradictory "burdens of the past," of arguable precedents that both hegemons and game players regularly talk about, infects even one of the most interesting questions in the "anarchy under cooperation" problematique, Tit-for-Tat reciprocity.

Let me first say that I applaud the attention given to this paradoxically potent strategy – it seems to suggest that "liberal/feminine" "cooperation" can have higher payoffs than "conservative/masculine" "defection" in a macho world of competitive egoists. Discovered by a game learning research program, most deeply explored by social psychologists interested in experimental situations that deflect its application, and acclimatized to an actuarial (or evolutionary) rationality by behavioral game theorists like Taylor and Axelrod, this theme enters the October 1985 *World Politics* volume as a conditional strategy of cooperation whose conditions of successful application are worthy of further study (Oye 1985: 16–18; Axelrod and Keohane 1985).[21]

Because, *qua* orthodox, non-cooperative, utility-maximizing game players, national decision-makers are *amoral*, this normative concern with Tit-for-Tat play cannot affect the basic "models of men and women" assumed by the problematique. It thus cannot reach the core status of the Negative Golden Rule heuristic in Hobbes' peace problematique. Consequently, the focus in *World Politics* is on *conditions* like "recognition" of "defection" and "control" of state actions that are necessary for Tit-for-Tat policies to induce "egoists" to cooperate (i.e., coordinate policies) while remaining egoists, *not on changes in identity, character, preference or moral priority*. Processes whereby social and political identities are recognized, changed or maintained are exogenous, presumed at the start by the game-theoretic definition of the game and its players. Norms cannot be considered sources of reciprocal conduct without assuming an international or world society of previously socialized beings in which such standards of conduct already exist. Thus a world of possessive egoists is not recognized to be a social order in itself.

Only *instrumental rationality* is presumed to be at work; yet it is *expressive rationality* – the search for honor, identity, mutual respect – that may well be more important.[22] It does not make sense in such a

---

[21] Some of my impressions about the use of "Tit-for-Tat" by "the anarchy problematique" are based on Robert Axelrod (1985), which was a lead-off paper at the Harvard–MIT study group/seminar in the fall of 1985.

[22] One can find variants of the expressive-instrumental distinction, *inter alia*, in Aristotle, Veblen, Turner, Murray, Goffman, Habermas and Harré. A related distinction contrasts expressive aspects versus practical aspects of social activity. Harré finds most illuminating Goffman's dramaturgical analysis of institutions as stagings "for dramas of character and for the living out of moral careers" (p. 7). He then proposes an expressive, "neo-Hobbesian theory" of the way social coherence is established and maintained "by a mechanism of ritually created obligations and commitments, mediated by the meanings conventionally associated [rhetorically] with certain acts and actions" (p. 18). Citations are from Harré (1980).

In the Harvard–MIT seminar, Stanley Hoffmann distributed Aron 1966 (767–781) as

world to ask of scholars, game-players or national role-players how or why they "present themselves" as possessive egoists or as liberal political economists (or neither). With such assumptions one can never learn to be more than an egoist.

Oye, Axelrod and Keohane have a related problem with the conceptualization of rational cooperation when they limit themselves to instrumentally defined non-cooperative games. For if they want to know "when is cooperation, defined in terms of conscious policy coordination, necessary to the realization of mutual interests?" they cannot treat this kind of underspecified coordination as a "more narrow" case of the effects of "payoff structure" (Oye 1985: 5).[23] As Habermas has persuasively argued, communicative, rational action oriented toward the reaching of agreement (and by extension, coordination) is not the same as instrumental, strategic action assumed by non-cooperative game theory.[24] Have we not moved into that analytically difficult world – not modeled at all by the cooperation under anarchy problematique – of what Paul David called "weakly cooperative games"?

A related problem occurs concerning these authors' commendable desire to provide and employ a "unified analytical framework" derived from elementary non-cooperative game theory and microeconomics. The goal is challenging – the identification of communalities and intrinsic differences in the politics of war, wealth or welfare.[25] The difference between "low politics" (economic welfare issues) and "high politics" (vital national security issues) might be conceptually transcended. The problem is that technical (instrumental), economic, social, legal and political rationality are not reducible to each other. Even

a contribution to our discussions of rationality. Aron there approvingly quotes Huizinga's famous study of the dramatically expressive play-element in culture (*Homo Ludens*): "Even in highly developed cultural relations, and even if the statesmen who are preparing the conflict interpret it as a question of power, the desire for material gain remains, in general, subordinate to [expressive] motives of pride, glory, prestige and the appearance of superiority or supremacy." This rather Hobbesian quote corroborates Harré's analysis, which (like Aron's) allows that the brutalization of conflict also may occur.

23 Axelrod and Keohane assume this definition of cooperation in their concluding essay.
24 See Habermas (1970), and the further discussion of, and citations to, his and Kratochwil's related views in Chapters 10 and 12 of this volume.
25 At the Harvard–MIT seminar, Joseph Nye and Robert Keohane defended Oye's "unified framework" (Oye 1985: 2) and Axelrod and Keohane (1985) largely on heuristic grounds, and because of their unified analytical framework capable of handling both economic and political/security issues.

worse, a cooperative sociopolitical order – necessarily the product of creative *social* and *political* rationality – is being pursued on the false Hobbesian belief that it can be positivistically *deduced* from a parsimonious set of entirely economic assumptions about an asocial world.[26]

Continuing to work with presumptions that other scholarly traditions seriously question supports the claim that such "scientific" activities are actually "promotional" ones in disguise, consciously or unconsciously reinforcing the self-understandings and tactics of only one pattern of world order-building practice.

But it is in a third (related) sense that I want most generally to characterize the anarchy problematique as "positivistic," namely in the sense that its dominant knowledge-generating interest is neither "hermeneutic" nor "emancipatory," but "positivistic" in Habermas' sense of being oriented toward prediction and control. The genesis amnesia of game players characterized in these ways corresponds to the genesis amnesia of the liberal realist tradition more generally, as described above. The emphasis on *calculated action* overwhelms the hermeneutic search for *consensually shared, contextually appropriate, reinterpreted standards of conduct* – which Bull's global society problematique is searching for, and which Ashley refers to as "shared background understandings, skills, and practical dispositions." Realism is no longer a living, critical tradition of statecraft searching for reasonable

---

[26] I take these concepts according to Paul Diesing's remarkable (pre-Habermas), but under-appreciated *Reason in Society* (1976, originally 1962). Without defining technical, economic or legal-moral rationality – each the subject of a chapter by Diesing – let me give a brief summary of social and political rationality in his terms. Both are variants of Weber–Mannheim organizational (functional) rationality, which occurs when any organization "is so structured as to produce, or increase, or preserve, some good in a consistent, dependable fashion" based primarily "on an internal structure which is able to continue effective operation through variations of personnel and through changes of environment" (3ff.). Contrasting integrative with equilibrium-oriented selective-evolutionary processes, Diesing defines "social rationality" as integration-enhancing action within a social system. "A social relation is integrated when the obligations, expectations, beliefs, and ideals of each role are consistent with one another and with the feelings and desires of the person taking the role, and when both role and both sets of feelings fit together and support one another" (76). For Diesing, "political decisions" are concerned "with the preservation and improvement of decision structures" (198). Politically rational actions creatively seek group self-mastery of freedom, in ways analogous to the social pursuit of mental health (233ff. and final chapter). This ordering elaborates on, and enriches, my understanding of the "low politics"/"high politics" distinction: a good argument could be made, for example, that the OPEC oil crisis involved a number of high political decisions in Diesing's sense.

policies[27] in the prudent pursuit of national interest. Payoff matrices appear as given, prior, objectivized outcome valuations. The emancipatory restructuring power of utilitarian self-interest, perfected private properties rights, and diminished transaction costs – as these new ideals were once argued against the "weight" of the feudal past – is largely forgotten or taken for granted by the game theoretic modeler.[28] *In a world where these liberal, capitalistic standards of conduct are now immensely controversial, their continued emancipatory content is problematical; they should neither be ignored nor assumed.*

With respect to the dominant positivism of the anarchy problematique, I am reminded of Habermas's moving lament:

> [T]he positivist self-understanding of the *nomological sciences* lends countenance to the substitution of technology for [rationally] enlightened action. It directs the utilization of scientific information from an illusory viewpoint, namely that the practical mastery of history can be reduced to technical control of objectified processes. The objectivist self-understanding of the *hermeneutic sciences* is of no lesser consequence. It defends sterilized knowledge against the reflected appropriation of active traditions and locks up history in a museum. Guided by the objectivist attitude of ["pure"] theory as the image of

---

27 From a reading of their previously cited works, it is clear that Aron, Bull and Hoffmann believe that the methodological precision appropriate for international political questions supports reasonable policy arguments, not scientifically calculated "rational strategies." On this issue they argue against the deductive, calculating spirit of Hobbes, so evident in Snidal as well (Snidal 1985b). An aside (p. 210) of his 1978 article suggests Jervis too is on the side of the traditionalists.

It is unfortunately characteristic of positivistically trained political scientists that they are both uninformed and skeptical of any claims contrasting favorably dialectical and standard formal logic. See relevant discussions in Chapters 1, 2 and 12 of this volume. As a "scientific traditionalist" on this issue, I agree with the preference for "reasonable policy" of the "traditionalists," as well as their critique of typical behavioral modes of demonstrating strategic rationality through calculation or deductive inference. But I side with the "scientific" side of the argument in believing that powerful formal tools are available (but not often attended to by political scientists) for the representation, modeling and analysis of "reasonable" policy inferences.

28 I am not saying that these variables are ignored. Robert Keohane makes good use of the lowered transaction costs concept in his *After Hegemony* (1984), as an argument for continuing old regimes into the post-hegemonic present. And Duncan Snidal has written a brilliant critical review of the literature on "Public Goods, Property Rights, and Political Organizations" (Snidal 1979). What is lost, however, in the positivistic self-understanding of these scientists is the ability explicitly and scientifically to make hermeneutic use of the liberal tradition in the way that Lenin did with Kropotkin, using, from outside, his internal understanding of the anarchists' own revolutionary tradition.

facts, the ... latter displace our connection with tradition into the realm of the arbitrary, while the former, on the leveled-off basis of the repression of history, squeeze the conduct of life into the behavioral system of instrumental action. The dimension in which acting subjects could arrive at agreement about goals and purposes is surrendered to the obscure area of mere decision among reified value systems and irrational beliefs.   (Habermas 1971: 316)[29]

The key point here for the interpretatively oriented social scientist is that the "possessive individualism" of game-modeled egoists is ideologically and theoretically controversial and therefore should be treated as such. When close to half of the people of the world, and perhaps a third of the world's states, consider themselves "socialist," it is too late to presume that all economic and political actors in the world-economy and the territorially organized state system are possessive individualists. Just because a scientific modeling tradition – game theory – has distilled the positivistic self-understanding of one of the major world order tendencies – indeed, still the dominant one – does not preclude its being of scientific worth. But it is obviously biased to continue to *presume* what perhaps half the world is trying to *transcend* – the unequal economic, the interventionist political, and the dignity-challenging cultural features of that system. Testing rather than presuming such models of instrumental action versus other, non-game-theoretic ones is highly recommended. Otherwise, the scientific ideal of universal truth becomes, more and more, substituted for by the cultural reality of what Geertz has called "local knowledge."[30]

Richard Ashley has made a very similar critique of "economism" in

---

[29] Habermas' writings and Kostecki's (cited previously) should be carefully studied as well, for different conceptualizations of "anarchical" patterns of international relations. In this spirit, Nicholas Onuf and Frank Kling have written a particularly impressive study, further discussed in Chapter 12 below, of "Paradigms of Rule" (i.e., their preferred translation of *Herrschaft* as used by Hegel, Marx, Weber and Parsons). They suggest and develop systematically an alternative classification to that offered by liberal realism. In their preferred conceptualization, "heteronomous rule" partly corresponds to the liberal realist conception of anarchy.

[30] I have in mind as practical alternatives the more dramaturgical, expressive, identity-affirming analyses of game play introduced in Alker (1985). A supportive quote for Asian contexts is Clifford Geertz's: "The Western conception of the person as a bounded, unique, more or less integrated motivational and cognitive universe, a dynamic center of awareness, emotion, judgment, and action organized into a distinctive whole and set contrastively both against other such wholes and against its social and natural background is, however incorrigible it may seem to us, a rather peculiar idea within the context of the world's cultures" (Geertz 1986: Chapter 3 at 59).

a recent article. "The new statism is, in short, an apology for the worldwide hegemony of a deadly logic of economy in determining social and political outcomes" (Ashley 1983). Having defined "variable economism" in terms of exclusively economic causal accounts – not a problem with the cooperation under anarchy problematique – he defines "logical economism" as "the reduction of the practical inter-pretative framework of political action to the framework of economic action: the reduction of the logic of politics to the logic of economy." When "one collapses political logic within economic logic, politics is portrayed as mere technique" and commits oneself to "the justification of the given order of domination." He further links a "closed union of economistic theory and economistic practice," historical economism, to modern, realist forms of statist capitalism and a Habermasian critique of the "scientization of politics." Should we not conclude, where Bull and Ashley agree, that

> it is necessary to replace the currently dominant concept of the states system as a vectoring of power and interests among multiple states-as-actors obeying technical-rational logics of action. It will be neces-sary to replace it with a conception of the state system as the political face, the habitually authorized public sphere, of a global *social system*. In effect, the state system should be seen as the public sphere of a pluralistic *insecurity* community – a social system in which the generalized expectation of mutual insecurity is coreflectively recog-nized, anchored in habits of compliance, and helps to secure the integrity of the system as a whole.   (Ashley 1983: 491)[31]

Toward pluralistic security communities

Having discharged my stated goal of constructively criticizing the positivistic, ahistorical qualities of the cooperation under anarchy problematique – hopefully in a response engendering way – I will not offer an alternative program to Bull's global society problematique. Rather, directing my remarks to the more scientifically inclined pos-sible adherents to the cooperation under anarchy problematique, I would like to conclude with some insights about the historicity of world society, and some thoughts on how pluralistic security commu-nities might be achieved within and beyond that society. The scientific

---

[31] The notion of an "insecurity community" is partly presaged in Bennett and Alker (1977) and Lasswell (1950, originally 1935), both of which Ashley was exposed to as an MIT graduate student. See also Chapter 7 of this volume.

questions involved are to me very challenging; I hope my readers/
hearers will want to answer them.

Of course I do think conventional sociological approaches to the
building of cooperation in world politics are extremely fruitful, and
often underappreciated by realists. After all, sociologists specialize in
the study of social conflict and its resolution, integrative and disintegrative processes, the dialectical supercession of old orders by and
within new ones. But my real disciplinary preference for future
scientific studies of international cooperation is – much like Bull,
Wight, Aron, Hoffmann, Deutsch, Braudel or Wallerstein – a multidisciplinary, historical one. In a phrase, we need to be able to generate
multiple possible histories of peace, on the basis of rigorous historical
studies of the psychological, social, cultural, moral-legal, economic and
political aspects of previous attempts from within international societies to form international political communities.

The scientific tasks involved are not what conventional behavioral
scientists might assume. I have always cherished Stanley Hoffmann's
witty attack against treating history as if it were a field of daisies to be
stripped![32] Indeed, as someone who taught econometric methods for
ten years, it has long been clear to me that history is more than time
series data. Thus as a social scientist I have long believed that the
simple stochastic models we fit to historical data should be thought of
as reductionistic null models, useful for identifying degenerative
organization, random complexity and deviant cases.[33]

What exactly makes history more than a concatenation of simple
stochastic processes? What is the valid kernel of Hegelian "Historicism"? As a continuing graduate student, I have learned rather recently
what others have known for decades: that there is a highly relevant
answer to these questions. What makes modern world history "historical" is its "historicity." That is why we need scientifically to study the

---

[32] This quotation resides in my memories from the late 1950s and early 1960s. Hoffmann
(1960: 45), cites approvingly Barrington Moore's resistance to the quantitative
"dismemberment of reality, due to the mistake of treating history ... as a 'storehouse'
in which facts are piled up as separate and discrete units."

[33] The following paragraphs are adapted from my memo on "Historicity for Beginners,"
that I wrote for the Harvard–MIT study group in response to the group's discussion
of Paul David's article on the suboptimality of the QWERTY keyboard (David 1985),
an impressive study group reading assignment chosen by Robert Keohane. It gave me
an opportunity to link David's concern with suboptimal path-dependent processes
and Frederick Olafson's *The Dialectic of Action* (1979). Page references in the text are to
that book.

historicity of the anarchical society, in order to learn how it was achieved, the seriousness of threats to its existence, and how some day it might peacefully be transcended by a fuller realization of international community.

My recent introduction to this literature came from Frederick Olafson's *The Dialectic of Action*, which I shall briefly summarize here (see also Alker 1984 and Chapter 6 above). Olafson's most fundamental hypothesis sees the humanities (including history) as "typically concerned with accounts of what human beings, whether fictive or real, have done and said and believed and desired." Such accounts "are therefore heavily committed to the conceptual instruments by which these human acts are symbolized," thus intentionally incorporating the language of mental acts and teleological explanations in terms of such beliefs and desires (p. 19). In the Husserlian sense, intentionality refers beyond the usual notion of purposefulness to "the mental act taken in its dimension of objective reference and as carrying within it the conceptual design of the object to which it is addressed, an object which it constructs through the appropriate logical operations or 'syntheses'" (16ff.). Historical events are typically "complex" events – like doing and knowing – in which other events (usually from the past, sometimes from the intended or feared future) are deeply embedded (82).

Both historical and fictional narratives, in Olafson's view, take shape from the dialectical interactions of intentional persons, whose consciousness performs both the semantic and object constituting functions of intentionality mentioned above. This conception allows Olafson to make his key definition:

> A sequence of actions ... may ... be called a dialectic ... [if] each action responds to another which is imputed to the partner in the exchange, and it creates a new situation to which the latter then has to respond itself. As in conversation – the original model for the concept of dialectic – there is no guarantee that the partners involved in such a series of exchanges will understand one another correctly.... (159)

The dialectical aspect of the historical movement of a society through an option tree (a game in normal form) "would have to be represented by a kind of [dialectical-hermeneutic] interlacing of the branches of two or more such trees" (159). This dialectic can be one of cooperation or conflict. Prisoner's dilemmas are cited as examples of such inner-actions.

Olafson argues against the adequacy of strictly deductive historical accounts or policy inferences as well. "In its most abstract logical form the progress of a narrative sequence is ... a chain of practical syllogisms in which the conclusion of each prior syllogism, as modified by whatever failures of execution the agent may not have been able to avoid, provides one of the premises for its successor."[34]

Olafson's treatment here relates rather directly to the economism discussed above. In arguing against both the automatic validity of individualistic psychologism (explanation in terms of an "independent calculus of satisfactions") and the privileged or logically compulsory character of the individual's identification with social norms, Olafson makes room for "the possibility ... [of] an espousal of the social norm by an individual that is not the product of mystification or of confusion as to the latter's self-interest and that really does effect an identification between individual and social interest" (107). He thus transcends the false dichotomies of egoism/altruism that the anarchy problematique is struggling with. Surely March and Olson's "choice" and "duty" frames (March and Olson 1984) for understanding action are also socially unified here.[35]

Reminiscent of the tradition of Grotius, Deutsch, Bull and Habermas, Olafson goes on to argue for the validity of histories written in terms of a plurality of institutional agencies, of which markets and states are two of the most important examples, referring to them as sometimes within the "subjacent generative order of society" (123). "The more highly developed a form of institutional agency becomes, the more likely it is that it will have achieved access to its own constitutive rules and that it will have claimed for itself the right and the capacity to modify them in various ways" (127).

Even more dialectical are those changes in the ways a society recapitulates and critiques its past experience. When reinterpretation is recognized for the historically critical act it really is, "the relationship to tradition becomes much more self-consciously free," allowing the picking and choosing of appropriate elements from that tradition, i.e., a "tradition of the new" (163ff.). The "Machiavellian moment" of

[34] Olafson 1977 (49). I believe Abelson's themes, scripts and "dremes" are defined in just such terms. In my "Historical Argumentation..." paper I dialogically encode an historical exchange between Reagan and Thatcher where the former's views on Grenada seem to be syllogistically abducted from a right-wing "No Win" implication molecule identified by Abelson a dozen years earlier, as discussed in the Introduction above and Alker 1984.

[35] This significant, multiparadigm paper was discussed in the Harvard–MIT seminar at Keohane's suggestion.

Renaissance Florence is cited intriguingly in this respect, as is the history of the Roman republic and empire. I am reminded of the creative (but not sustained) rewriting of the UN Charter that took place during the Suez and Congo crises.

Against the long tradition of humanist history, e.g., Machiavelli's history of the Florentine republic, Olafson argues that historically observable interactions at best allow imperfect or degraded versions of the interpretations in terms of moral or dramatic (plot-like) unities characterizing good literature. Does not this bring to mind in an American audience the self-constituting tales of the American civic religion, as described by Robert Bellah, which have been used by American presidents and contemporary hegemonists to justify our special role as God's chosen people? (Bellah 1967).

Olafson associates historicity with the appearance of cumulativeness in history (88), as a "comprehensive designation of the opening upon the past (and the future) as a common domain of reference" (95). Specifically the complexity of historical events in both the participant's and the historian's eyes refers to the sense that "other prior events are intentionally embedded in them through the capacity that each has for reference to events in his own past" (96). History in the sense of historicity begins in cosmic or natural processes "at that point at which intentional access is gained, on some reasonably stable and continuing basis, to prior events in that same process." Metaphorically, historicity occurs at "the point at which a process of events in time 'doubles back' on itself and is thereby enabled to live off itself" (101).

There are many inferior analogues to this crucial, humanistic idea in the natural and the social sciences. This doubling back on itself, whether conscious or unconscious, seems to be an aspect of legal-diplomatic traditions of practical argumentation going back at least to Thucydides and the pre-Socratics, of Hegelian reason, of path-dependent stochastic process notions, of cybernetic treatments of non-ergodic development, of electromagnetic hysteresis (defined by Webster as "the influence of the previous history or treatment of a body on its subsequent response to a given force or changed condition"), the non-monotonic inference of artificial intelligence, and Chomsky's derivation-dependent parsing – seven different versions of the same complex, developmental, dialectical idea.

Historicity for Olafson is essentially social. His argument goes beyond the obvious fact that its subject matter is usually social, addressing the partial unification of individual time frameworks. It involves the doubling back mentioned above. A form of intentionality, "historicity, in its full sense, is just this dimension of *shared self-temporalization among members of a continuous human society* of some kind" (my emphasis) (104, 109).

My experimental subjects in SPD games sometimes undergo the same experience in their smaller, artificial, experimental worlds. Similarly, I have tried to model precedential reasoning in the evolution and the decay of the United Nations collective security system. The "sense of community" that sometimes emerges within international societies – a shared self-understanding of a collective capacity for peaceful accommodation and change – must also flow from the historicity of those societies.

The significance of Olafson's conception goes beyond my attempts to wed Bull's world society problematique to other programs of research on cooperative game play or the formation of pluralistic security communities. For those not interested in any of the problematiques that I have mentioned, Olafson's analysis suggests even more generally a reconceptualization of the content and dynamics of academic research traditions. Political (or scholarly) traditions, like political communities, can be understood as "a corpus of norms, interpretative principles, and background beliefs of a great variety of kinds"; they represent "a kind of extended historicity" (162).

Olafson does not see adequately the connections that could be drawn between this emancipatory conception of historicity and the communitarian (and revolutionary rationalist) traditions of international thought. But his argument is very suggestive at this multitraditional level of analysis – the one where Bull excels – as well. Unfortunately, Olafson has become entrapped in the false dichotomies perpetrated by the false historicity of contemporary realism. Without citations to the work of Bull or Deutsch, he applies his conception of historicity in ways that clearly accept realism's self-serving distinction between realists and "unrealists," i.e., "idealists" or "utopians." He sees a collective self-temporalization of human society in the idealistic trend that "the ideal of a noncoercive and potentially universal human community based on the exercise of creative and intellectual powers has gradually taken form" (130). He is at pains to argue "the ultimate mode of contestation of our actions is that of force, which thus becomes a kind of implicit coefficient of every action that a society undertakes." The fact that "human history is a history of war" (161) is acknowledged.

He does not see that realists have been working hard to shape the historicity of the power politics community of statesmen and their acolytes that they belong to, the existence of which they are disposed to deny. Denying the reality of efforts by Grotius, Kant, Wilson or Lenin to transform this socially constructed (and reproduced) reality, Olafson accepts the realists' preferred world historical picture: "human history as a whole has often struck observers as a grandiose act of self-frustration on the part of mankind" (160). "Once the kind of social organization that makes war possible is in existence and the availability of war as the ultimate form of action is established in the human repertory of responses, it dominates all the relationships of societies with one another in a way which no one has yet found a way of significantly modifying" (161).

The denial of historicity to the communitarian tradition's own account of the past is almost palpable. (My calling Machiavelli a utopian idealist, for instance, repeats Toynbee.) Olafson's views here are derivative of a biased literature search into the field of international politics, one reflected in many course lists, that often exclude the communitarian and universalist-rationalist traditions altogether, or deny the historicity of their development, or deny the historicity of realism's own interconnections with these other traditions, which truly are "moments" of each other (in the Hegelian sense of innerrelated aspects).

So let me conclude by once again trying to overcome the genesis amnesia of realist self-understanding, offering some more optimistic thoughts about pluralistic community formation in the modern historical period, selected from contemporary writers in the Grotian and the Kantian traditions (Deutsch *et al.* 1957; Bozeman 1960; Walker, ed. 1984; Curtin 1984; Braudel 1981–5; and Rosecrance 1986).[36] First of all, I think it fair to characterize Bull's sustained demonstration of the life history of the anarchical society and its partial transcendence as a

---

[36] Like Ruggie (1983), Rosecrance's argument is worth further consideration for those who see anarchy (in the two-dimensional sense of low normative integration and power decentralization) as necessarily inherent in international politics:

> The transformation of the medieval into the modern can be depicted in at least two ways ... [Besides the consolidation of the territorial state,] it represents a reordering in the priority of international and domestic realms. In the medieval period, the world, or transnational environment was primary, the domestic secondary. Within states (prior to state consolidation) or between lords of the manor there was chaos or anarchy. External to the state, however, the pope, emperor, ecumenical Catholic Church, and the hierarchical obligations of feudalism created a certain order.   (Rosecrance 1986: 77)

scholarly contribution to the historicity of world society. This work deserves successors.

Secondly, isn't Braudel's magnificent *Le Temps du Monde* – his historical demonstration of cyclic movements in the cores and peripheries of the world-economy – at least as dazzling a radical contribution to the shared self-temporalization of world society? Asian scholars have noted its "pro-Western" bias in starting its tale in the European dark ages at a time when Islamic and Chinese civilizations were in full splendor; but is that the reason why its subsumptive analysis of the modern, capitalist, power-balancing system is so little known to contemporary North American students of international relations? Shouldn't the pervasive, exploitative inequities that Braudel has revealed be recognized by all of us?

Finally, in his studies of the formation of international communities, Karl Deutsch and his collaborators stressed the surprising ease with which pluralistic security communities had been formed in the North Atlantic Area. Security communities were treated as groups of people who had become integrated, i.e., attained an historical *sense of community* that led them to expect that they could solve their future problems without the appeal to the widespread use of violence. Conditions necessary for such developments most importantly were the compatibility of major values, the capacity of the political units involved to act responsively (e.g., more equitably) to others within the community, and the possession of mutual predictability (based of necessity largely on historical understanding). Clearly, a number of established habits, institutions and consultative relationships made this possible; they form part of the international regional society of the North Atlantic area. Analogous nation-building and community-building efforts may be discovered in other areas as well. Deutsch has thus shown us that the road to pluralistic security community is through and beyond the historicity of Bull's anarchical society and of Braudel's exploitative world economies.

12 The return of practical reason to international theory

Twenty-five years after Hedley Bull and Morton Kaplan debated in the pages of *World Politics* the relative merits of "scientific" and "classical" (or "traditional") approaches to the study of international relations,[1] the nearly simultaneous appearance of Kratochwil (1989), Onuf (1989), Hollis and Smith (1991), each of them a philosophically self-aware effort to redefine the discipline of international relations, allows a reconsideration of some of the key issues involved. Because Hollis and Smith rely heavily for their philosophical framework on Hollis' earlier text in the philosophy of social science, *The Cunning of Reason* (Hollis 1987), and that book also clarifies the connections between Hollis and Smith, and Kratochwil and Onuf, I have included it too in this review.

Contrary to earlier, self-flattering, largely North American "scientific" scholarly self-assessments,[2] the evidence of these four mature works of international relations scholarship supports the interpretation that neither side has yet decisively won the debate.[3] Rather, it now

[1] Two *World Politics* articles, by Bull (1966) and Kaplan (1966), as well as others from the period by scientific notables like J. David Singer, Richard Brody, Robert Jervis, Marion Levy Jr. and Robert North are reprinted in Knorr and Rosenau, eds. (1969).

[2] J.D. Singer (1969: 62–86, at 85) says prematurely that "The War is clearly over" and that "there is no longer much doubt that we can make the study of ... world politics ... into a scientific discipline worthy of the name." But he finds little ground for exultation and graciously and prophetically suggests that the scientific and the "Substantive, normative and judgmental end" of a continuum can learn from, and converge toward each other. Greenstein and Polsby's edited *Handbook of Political Science* (1975) has chapters on the scientific study of international relations by Kenneth Waltz and Dina Zinnes, but no "traditional/Classical" counterpart.

[3] In fact, since both Onuf and Kratochwil are legally trained, interpretively oriented, "post-positivist" scholars interested in achieving communitarian ideals, one could say that the earlier "Great Debate" between "realists" and "idealists" has also not yet

appears that all the mentioned authors have made considerable, interdisciplinary progress in *combining both classical and contemporary social scientific theorizing modalities* to address the key judgmental issues that Bull emphasized as central to the classical approach.

They have done so, I wish to show, by following the lead of post-Wittgensteinian philosophy in resurrecting, with reformulations and against considerable intellectual resistance, the Aristotelian notion of "practical reason." They deploy their renewed sense of practical activity for a variety of purposes, including the productive reframing of realists' "perennial" problem of anarchic order. This interpretation strongly suggests an even larger thesis, which here I can illustrate with only a few examples: "Great Debates" are defining parts of the historicity of any scientific discipline, especially an historical one; they are never "over." Their longer run effects on defining, broadening and restricting the accepted discourses of the discipline should be seen as of greater importance than the short-term "victories" as judged by certain contemporary audiences. In this spirit, I shall conclude with several reflections on the interdisciplinary significance of the observed "return."

Judgment and practical reason in the Bull–Kaplan debate

When as a traditionalist Bull refers to newer American research emphases as "scientistic,"[4] but then decides more politely to refer to them in terms of their (unrealistic) scientific aspirations, he is invoking (in a muffled way) a key epithet from a century-old debate. Central to this debate are the distinctive features of, and appropriate methodologies for, the "humanistic," "constructivist" or "artificial" cultural,

been decisively "won." Onuf and Kratochwil, like Bull and Wight before them – see Bull and Wight's introductory and concluding contributions to Wight (1992) and the discussion below – prefer to think about the balancing and synthesis of three or more different traditions, rather than the overly simplistic realist/idealist dichotomy.

    Moreover, like Bull and Wight, Onuf and Kratochwil and Hollis and Smith *simultaneously* address the central issues of what Kaplan calls International Relations' First and Second Debates, and Yosef Lapid (1989) refers to as "The Third Debate: On the Prospects of International Theory in a Post-Positivist Era."

4   The best relevant explication I can find of this epithet is Karl-Otto Apel (1984: 15ff., 33–39, 63, 143–158, 199ff). The gist of the implicit claim is that behavioral "scientists" are falsely appropriating the concepts, methods and epistemologies of the natural sciences into international relations.

social, historical and moral–legal sciences, as opposed to those taken to be characteristic of, and appropriate for, the physical, chemical and biological "natural" or "positive" sciences.[5] A reading of Apel, von Wright and Anscombe[6] on this controversy suggests more specifically and explicitly what "scientistic" was intended to convey: following the Galilean lead in downgrading the "internal" or "subjective" aspects of human activity, behavioral-empirical scholars have attempted causally to explain that activity without hermeneutically/ interpretively attending to or judging the practical "bad or good reasons" agents do or could give for their actions, thereby reducing occasionally creative and sometimes irresponsible intentional action, and all other quasi-Aristotelian expressions of human purposiveness, to caused behaviors, thus too radically separating understanding from explanation and the humanities from the scientific study of human nature and human social achievements, which study can never be totally "value free."

Although Bull is emphatic that methods should be appropriate to the phenomena, he does not wholly condemn the largely American empirically oriented studies, preferring to recommend over against a *scientific* orientation a *classical approach*. The classical approach offers "theorizing that derives from philosophy, history, and law, and that is characterized above all by the explicit reliance on the exercise of judgment and by the assumption that if we confine ourselves to strict standards of verification and proof there is very little of significance that can be said about international relations" (Bull 1966: 361). His preference is for what could be called an Aristotelian conception of the realm of international politics as one of contingency, uncertainty, hard-to-find judgmental middle ways. Thus Bull wants to preserve a sense of disciplinary work that relies on the "scientifically imperfect

5   J.L. Richardson (1990: 140–85) clearly places Bull's "debate with the behavioralists" in this larger context.

6   Apel's book length discussion of what Weberians will know as the *Verstehen-Erklaren* controversy suggests that contemporary, post-Wittgensteinian discussions of inter-pretation-oriented vs. explanation-oriented conceptions of social science are a third round of a controversy going back at least to John Stuart Mill's *A System of Logic* (1843) and Johann Gustav Droysen's *Grundriss der Historik* (1858). He presents the post-Kantian, post-Nietzschean arguments we usually associate with Weber, and which again reappear in the post-Wittgensteinian arguments of Anscombe, von Wright, Winch and their critics. Apel is responding at length to Georg Henrik von Wright (1971), who in turn is taking up and further explicating G.E.M. Anscombe's (1957) discussion of *Intention* in human affairs.

process of perception," leading to "tentative and inconclusive" results, a mode of inquiry that is nonetheless genuinely "cumulative" (Bull 1966: 369) and "scientific in the sense of being a coherent, precise, and orderly body of knowledge and in the sense of being consistent with the philosophical foundations of modern science" (Bull 1966: 375).

In retrospect, Kaplan appears as an insightful defender of systems theory and partly formal modeling approaches (including game theory), which Bull clearly dislikes; he emphatically rejects "traditional" as opposed to "scientific" scholarly research. Nonetheless, scholars like Raymond Aron are seen to employ methodologies not so far from scientific approaches, and Bull's work on arms control is considered "solid." Suggestively, Kaplan identifies Bull's approach as humanistic and, with explicit reference to Aristotelian syllogistic reasoning, contrasts favorably apodeictic inferences from necessary premises (in his view a characteristic of theoretically structured sciences) with inferences in the arts which attempt to build from less certain premises: "The humanist who wants to substitute in human events a verbal process called reason or understanding for a verbal and/or mathematical process called science has confused intuition with the articulation of communicable knowledge."[7]

Kaplan is somewhat less willing to call "traditional" analyses of the non-necessary (contingent, humanly constructed and hence practical) social and political domain "scientific" than Bull is to treat Kaplan, Deutsch or Russett as scientists; but he does view Aron's work as quite close to meeting scientific standards. Bull, on the other hand, sees their best insights as deriving not from their models or quantitative data, but from traditional judgmental investigations.

As a formal modeler of qualitative, practically oriented argumentation processes,[8] I think both scholars misstated their respective cases. Kaplan can be faulted for not foreseeing artificially intelligent

---

[7] Kaplan 1966 (4). In "The Humanistic Moment in International Studies: Reflections on Machiavelli and Las Casas," Chapter 4 above, I used the Hegelian concept of "moment" there to suggest the continuing play of the humanities in classical, modern and post-modern conceptions of international and comparative inquiry; here I shall emphasize the contributions of the authors under review to defining an interdisciplinary field of inquiry that is both scientific and humanistic.

[8] The Rescher-inspired style of argumentation modeling that, with Eric Devereux and others, I have tried to develop since the mid-1970s derives explicitly from the classical, Aristotelian tradition, and quite possibly could be extended to the Buddhist and other non-Western traditions. See Chapter 1 above.

mathematical models of what he called "the verbal process of reason or understanding"[9] but he has been vindicated for his preference for mathematical approaches (such as that of Von Neumann and Morgenstern) grounded in, or at least evolved from, the post-Fregean quantified predicate calculus of Whitehead and Russell. Formal systems deriving from their *Principia Mathematica* can be said, in many but not all ways, to have supplanted Aristotelian syllogistic reasoning: both the von Neumann–Morgenstern formal theory and the computational languages like C++, PROLOG and LISP – which are heavily used by modelers of human language, cognition and action processes – belong in this category.

Similarly, were he alive today and sufficiently well read, Bull could argue that contemporary students of language, cognition, communication and action – especially since the writings of the later Wittgenstein, Austin, Chomsky and Searle – have vindicated reformulated versions of his positions. Many familiar with twentieth-century British, French and German social philosophy knowledgeably criticize overstated formalist claims; similarly, historians of post-Enlightenment German social thought like Apel, Bernstein and Roberts are increasingly citing the relevance of practical reasoning in everyday social life, law and politics.[10]

Moreover, as a sometime teacher of philosophies of social science courses, I note with disapproval that, like many of my own contemporaries, in their debate neither Bull nor Kaplan paid more than passing attention to the highly relevant literature in the philosophy of the

---

[9] Since much of the formal modeling of "verbal" foreign policy "understanding" derives from the Abelson–Schank literature reviewed in Alker (1984) and above, I additionally cite here some excellent books on mathematically modeling verbal "reasoning." Douglas N. Walton (1990) is particularly impressive for his clear, synthetic mastery both of the philosophical sources of my earlier footnotes and the relevant earlier cognitive science/artificial intelligence literatures (including Nilsson, Miller, Galanter and Pribram, Sacerdoti, Simon, Schank and Abelson, Wilensky). A technically more difficult but impressive volume is Kevin Ashley's (1990). See also the difficult but rewarding, multidisciplinary Philip R. Cohen, *et al.* (1990); and the intriguingly relevant debate in *Cognitive Science* 17 (January–March 1993).

[10] An exceptional account of post-Kantian German language developments focusing on Frege, Husserl, Heidegger, Wittgenstein, Jürgen Habermas and the Erlangen School of the logic of dialogue is Julian Roberts (1992). The discussion of practical reasoning figures prominently and accessibly also in Richard J. Bernstein (1983). A learned, especially early, and hence neglected review of much of European logically oriented philosophy of language ending up in related, more post-modern francophonic perspectives on discourse practices is Michael Shapiro (1981).

historical or social or legal sciences on practical reason, judgment, lawful explanation in history, or scientific cumulativeness.[11]

Nonetheless, I think it fair to conclude that both sides vaguely recognized some kind of scientific middle ground between their positions. Hence they left open the possibility – already argued in the earlier chapters of this present volume – of a philosophically literate synthesis of naturalistic and humanistic modes of international relations research. In a fashion largely independent of, but complementary to, the arguments of the earlier chapters in this volume, I shall argue later that the books here being reviewed together achieve such an interdisciplinary reconstruction grounded in classical concepts of intentionality and practical reason. In order to make this case, and to use the contributions of Hollis and Smith, plus Kratochwil and Onuf, to support that interpretation, I need some hopefully consistent prior characterizations of "practical reasoning."

Practical reasoning in classical and contemporary guises

Because Hollis and Smith clearly pattern their book on von Wright's *Explanation and Understanding*, and his lucid inquiry acknowledges Elizabeth Anscombe's *Intention* as having both "made the notion of intentionality central to subsequent discussion of the philosophy of action" and "drawn attention to the peculiar logical character of [intentionality like] reasoning called in traditional terminology *practical syllogisms*" (von Wright 1971: 26), I start my discussion of intentionality and practical reasoning with Anscombe. Eventually, I shall suggest why I am focussing somewhat more on situationally oriented practical reasoning notions than their sibling ideas of teleology, purposiveness,

---

[11] To mention but four frequently discussed books from the English language literature of the late 1950s and the early 1960s, I cite G.E.M. Anscombe (1957), W.H. Dray (1957), P. Winch (1958), T.S. Kuhn (1962). Singer cites Popper and Reichenbach and disparagingly dismisses Bernard Crick's Wittgensteinian criticism of American behavioral science; Brody and others cite Kuhn. There is, however, almost no serious attention to claims of fundamental differences between the natural and social or humanistic sciences.

As J.L. Richardson has shown (1990: 140–185), Bull was *trained* in philosophy. Since Kaplan has elsewhere written knowledgeably on philosophy of history and social science issues, my criticism here is more of the way their famous, but poorly footnoted articles have been misused by my peers as *substitutes* for lengthier exposure to literatures which Bull and Kaplan may well have been familiar with.

performative speech acts, intentionality and language games, defined more generally.

From a review of what Wittgenstein called the "enormously complicated tacit conventions" that accompany our understanding of ordinary language, Anscombe delineates the common element in ordinary uses of "intention" as reference to actions about which it would be appropriate to ask of their agent "Why?" and expect in reply to be given "reasons for action," including references to nonobservable "mental causes." Indeed "a great many of our descriptions of events effected by human beings are *formally* descriptions of executed intentions" (Anscombe 1957: 6–7, 16–17, 78–86).

What brings Anscombe back to Aristotle's remarkably similar concept of practical reasoning within the schematic form of the practical syllogism[12] is the similarity of the meaningful orderings of an otherwise bewildering variety of different action descriptions each notion implies. From a review of Aristotelian examples, she concludes that the analogous "mark of practical reasoning is that the thing

---

[12] In the *Nicomachean Ethics* Aristotle treats virtuous character as the source of right ends, and practical reasoning as the deliberative, virtue-linked discussion of appropriate means to possible ends. After discussing how both scientific, practical and artistic reasoning can derive results from appropriate combinations of universal and particular premises, he distinguishes practical inferences as those resulting in action. Some of his simpler examples of the use of the practical syllogism ("the syllogism which deals with acts to be done" Book VI, 1144a, 30) suggest a deductive inferential quality:

"everything sweet ought to be tasted" and
"this is sweet: ..."
"the man who can act and is not prevented from [doing so]
must at the same time ... act accordingly." (VII.1147a, 25–37)

Despite this deductive quality to his simpler examples, his surrounding discussion of the problem of "weak conviction" and "incontinence" (1146b, 1147a), of conflicting principles ("the universal opinion ... in us forbidding us to taste [unknowns,]" (1047a), the recognition that the relevant opinion or knowledge must somehow be *active* in us (*ibid.*), and his sensing that the mere mouthing, as on a stage, of valid formalism gives us neither real knowledge of, nor explanations of, decisive deliberative actions (*ibid.*) all argue against a strong deductionist interpretation. Anscombe, von Wright, Apel and Walton, in their previously cited works, all elaborate upon this schema, and its dynamic use in *processes* of practical reasoning. For now it is sufficient to quote Anscombe to the effect that the "practical syllogism is not a form of [axiomatic, deductive or apodeictic] demonstration of what I ought to do [... but] a different kind of reasoning from that of the proof syllogism, but this has been misunderstood in modern times." Compare Nussbaum's somewhat different analysis in Chapter 2 above.

wanted is *at a distance* from the immediate action, and the immediate action is calculated as the way [a human being, or more generally a social agency has] of getting or doing or securing the thing wanted [or intended]." Since Aristotle, she goes on to argue, practical reasoning has regularly been distinguished from "scientific reasoning," and linked to formal reasoning schema and argumentative linguistic practices which are not of a strictly deductive character, but which nonetheless provide significant, putatively adequate bases for individual or collective human conduct. She argues that modern philosophy, with "an incorrigibly contemplative conception of knowledge" has blankly misunderstood the *practical knowledge* that it produces (Anscombe 1957: vii, 57).

For present introductory purposes it is especially useful to mention briefly two more generalized, yet traditionally grounded, conceptions of practical reasoning consonant with Anscombe's conceptualization of the discursive purposiveness of practical reason. In the first of these, Jacob Hintikka suggests:

> By practical reasons I shall simply mean reason in so far as it is occupied with human action, human doing and making, and with the results of such action .... "Maker's knowledge" is here supposed to cover also "doer's knowledge," for no distinction between *poiesis* [production] and *praxis* [practice] is intended.
>
> (Hintikka 1974: 83–102, at 83ff.)

Hintikka likens this notion to Maimonides' medieval vision of the "knowledge of the producer," Vico's New Science, and the work of Hobbes, "for whom the superior knowledge connected with a maker's 'practical reason' is demonstrative [classically, apodeictic] knowledge" (Hintikka 1974: 86). One could say that Hintikka's constructivist understanding of human actions and social relationships is the other side of the classical recognition of their contingent, alterable character; it obviously includes, and goes beyond, more restricted economic notions of production relationships.

Because it is well grounded in Wittgensteinian ordinary language philosophy, cognizant of the constructivist themes of Hintikka's perspective, and especially open to similar developments in cognitive science and artificial intelligence now actively being pursued by international relations researchers (Alker 1984 and Hudson, ed. 1991), I also introduce here the expanded notion of practical reasoning offered by Douglas Walton in his previously cited book on *Practical Reasoning:*

Goal-Driven, Knowledge-Based, Action-Guiding Argumentation. Reordering one of his lists to fit more exactly his subtitle, one can say that *practical reasoning is a type of argumentation* which:

(1) contains goals [preferentially stated as intentional claims] which it aims toward [and is committed to] realizing;

(2) is a knowledge-based type of reasoning, which ... takes its [open to revision] premises [and precedents] from a [variable,] particular situation or domain of relevant knowledge;

(3) ends or concludes in actions [changed commitments,] or a practical imperative that directs a reasoner to action;

(4) is a dynamic kind of [deliberative, self-critical] reasoning that can be evaluated both at a global or local level, in a sequence where a chain of goals and actions fit (or mesh) together;

(5) is a useful kind of [interactive, dialectical] reasoning because it fits into various [ethical, political, economic, aesthetic, dietary or medical] contexts of dialogue [including language game rules and sociological role expectations];

(6) takes side effects of contemplated courses of action into account, insofar as these ... can be anticipated.[13]

Practical reason returns to scientific international theory

Hollis and Smith's book is intended to introduce advanced undergraduate or graduate students in international relations to the contemporary literature on the philosophy of social science. Supplemented by selections from Hollis' earlier work, I would suggest that it successfully does so. One of their most interesting efforts in this regard is their largely parallel discussions of "Roles and Reasons" (Hollis and Smith 1991: Ch. 7) and "Reasons and Roles" (Hollis' Chapter 10), where they link policy decisions to bureaucratic roles and action-inducing reasons, with concrete examples taken from Carter Administration decision-making on the Iranian Hostage Crisis. The responsible, dissenting resignation of Cyrus Vance, and the end-running of his Deputy, Warren Christopher, by the interventionist majority are important, timely, even ironically tragic aspects of this account. Theoretically and

---

[13] Walton (1990: 310), in his synthetic, summary ninth chapter entitled "A Pragmatic Theory of Practical Reasoning." The terminology I introduce parenthetically in this list is taken from other parts of Walton's book. Compare Chapters 1 and 2 above.

empirically, they "settl[e] for elements of flexibility in roles and of judgment in reasons, which offer scope for both [causal] explaining and understanding [in terms of conscious, in-order-to reasons]"[14] (Hollis and Smith 1991: 179).

Besides suggesting numerous ways in which the "judg[ing of] the shrewdest course of action," non-computable "rational judgment," and "reasoned role-playing" are at the center of the bureaucrat's deliberations and decision-making practice (Hollis and Smith 1991: 159, 161, 165), they focus on what Hollis calls "activating reasons for action" or "good (enough) reasons for it" (Hollis 1987: 167, 204). Although this (and subsequent arguments) are precise paraphrases of the classical Aristotelian notion of practical reason, in the sense that contemporary philosophers like Anscombe have given it, neither Hollis nor Hollis and Smith explicitly use the term.[15]

But it is instructive that Hollis' whole book is a carefully developed argument for the inadequacy of instrumental economic accounts of human social activity in the increasingly complex "Garden of Eden" (and its successor environments!) which he theoretically and philosophically explores. In a fashion largely parallel with Anscombe's, Hintikka's or Walton's expositions, Hollis moves gradually from economic to sociological and moral-political models of Adam's interactions clearly linked to Kant and Rousseau. He treats instrumental economic models of action as "hopelessly indeterminate," arguing that intelligent role-players still have reasons for action, but they are role-related reasons . . . :

> Judgment is the role-player's judgment of how best to satisfy the demands of office, perhaps tempered by a refusal to heed only those demands. The effect is to make rationality less a matter of maximizing

[14] The first ten pages (171–181) of Chapter 8 are devoted to "practical Other Minds problems" an explicitly Wittgensteinian reformulation of "The Games Nations Play" as role-linked but society-creative language games whose regulative and constitutive rules are not reducible to game-theoretic representations.

[15] Hollis' apparent reasoning for not coming to terms with "the long line of Aristotelian thinking" in his admittedly non-exhaustive approach is his desire, as a social constructivist, to set "our animal nature aside in order to concentrate on the hermeneutics of culture" (1987: 206). But if he is clearly more willing appropriately to cite Pico della Mirandola, Vico, Kant, Weber, Elster or Wittgenstein, the above quotations, his Walton-like admission that "it is not plain that 'workable commensurability' is a name for [deductively calculable] maximizing [by businesses with plural goals] when there is such ambivalence about aims" (120), and his positive discussion of "social action" (134ff., 174–192) all tie him securely to the major notions used above to characterize "practical reasoning."

> [through a determinate deductive calculation] the value of a variable
> and more one of playing a role or game well.   (Hollis 1987: 170ff.)[16]

It is particularly interesting that Hedley Bull's key classical term, "judgment," only enters Hollis' argument at this late stage in Hollis' book. The better, policy-oriented, academic literature on foreign policy-making refuses to drop such terms.[17] Hollis' possible reasons for this partial reluctance we shall explore further below.

I certainly do not want to claim that Hollis in particular has somehow unknowingly skipped an important period of conceptualization in the history of philosophy: his whole book is grounded in Pico della Mirandola's classically oriented "Renaissance humanist vision of man as special in the cosmos" (Hollis 1987: 1).[18] In this vision Adam is told by his Maker that he has been made "neither heavenly nor earthly, neither mortal nor immortal, so that like a free and sovereign artificer you might mould and fashion yourself into that form you yourself shall have chosen." His whole book is "intended both to secure a robust sense in which Adam can be the sovereign artificer of his own life and to leave him the subject of a social science which respects the logic and power of decision-theory" (Hollis 1987: 92). This "sovereign artificer" reappears regularly throughout *The Cunning of*

---

[16] Since Hollis is contrasting non-deductively calculable reasoning with maximizing modes of action, it is worth noting that Walton (1990: 102–113) articulates with flowcharts versions of "satisficing" and "maximizing" which are *all* instances of practical reasoning. Hence it is not right for rational choice modelers to try to reduce "practical reasoning" to Simonesque satisficing and further assimilate practical reasoning to economizing where information searches are so costly that satisficing is a strictly optimal economic policy. The basic inference schema of practical reasoning used repeatedly by Walton expands upon Aristotle's three and four-step examples to include Intention, Alternatives, Selection, Practicality and Side Effects Premises; this five-part inference schema can be fitted into the six component knowledge-based, discursively interactive conceptual framework summarized above.

[17] Vertzberger (1990) starts out very behaviorally, but gets increasingly complex and synthetic, as in his chapter on "Decisionmakers as Practical-Intuitive Historians: The Use and Abuse of History." Alexander George (1993: 3–29, 147–150) has an excellent, explicit discussion of historical-political complexities and judgmental aspects of policy-making. I think it would be an especially valuable exercise to bring together the qualitative frameworks of these policy-making-focused writers, plus that of Neustadt and May (1986), together with the more formal treatments in Hudson ed. (1991), using Hollis' and Walton's rich articulations of the components of practical reasoning processes as coordinating lenses. These processual understandings would benefit further from critical appreciations along the Habermasian lines of Chapter 6 above, and the Kratochwil–Onuf perspective reviewed below.

[18] Compare this paragraph's discussion of Pico della Mirandola's 1484 *Oration on the Dignity of Man* with my Chapter 4 above.

Reason, embodying Vico–Hintikka style constructivism, and shaping even the creative enactments of State Department role incumbents!

Kratochwil's book examines rules and norms – particularly legal norms, values and principles – in domestic society and international life, especially in decision situations when no logically compelling solution seems more persuasive than others. With this focus, he presents his work as a limited contribution to social theory, jurisprudence (proper judging), and international relations, but one with potentially discipline-redefining implications for the latter of these fields (Kratochwil 1989: 1–20).[19]

Like Hollis he reveals classical roots in asserting "at least from Aristotle on, that the human world is one of artifice." He is aided in his analysis by citations to Aristotle's claim in his *Politics* that man is a political animal whose distinctive feature is "the power of reasoned speech" which "serves to indicate what is right and what is wrong," "just or unjust," and makes possible "the sharing of a common view in these matters that makes a household or a city." In a Wittgensteinian mode he is at pains to emphasize that ordinary language makes meaning, communication, remembrance and planning possible. If "human action" in general is "rule-governed," "action words" (especially directive or commissive speech acts), together with rules and norms, both "regulate" and, with their elocutionary force, "constitute" social practices. "Neither the model of instrumental rationality nor that of empathy, reconstructing the purposes of the actor, adequately explains a practice such as promising ... a correct analysis will have to capture both the intentional as well as the *conventional* [institutional] aspects of such a speech act" (Kratochwil 1989: 27ff.).[20] "The binding character of contracts, as mutual promises, depends for its validity not on the 'reliance' which one of the contracting parties might have placed on the promise of the other, but on the [constitutive *'elocutionary force'* of] the institution itself."

Kratochwil emphasizes his central reliance on the classical notion of practical reasoning with his subtitle; the book explores in depth the conditions or situations in which it is used. Indeed, his definition of

---

[19] He does so quite self-consciously within a discussion of "historical recognition and the establishment of 'fields.'" Unless otherwise specified, quotations in the next several paragraphs are from this extremely dense and provocative introductory chapter.

[20] Also the source of my next quotation. The reference is to John R. Searle (1969). See also Searle (1979, 1983).

practical reasoning recapitulates Anscombe's key insights, explicitly draws on Aristotle's argument in the *Nicomachean Ethics* as explicated by von Wright, and buttresses Hollis and Smith's hard won efforts to reintroduce practical reasoning and judgment back into scientific International Relations discourse: "Practical reasoning not only deals with issues of action but also investigates the formal properties of arguments which satisfy neither the conditions of induction nor those of deduction, and in which value-considerations figure prominently beyond the ends-means nexus of instrumental rationality" (Kratochwil 1989: 12).[21]

Within this communicatively/discursively constituted domain, law is a rule-guided choice, decision or judgment process wherein justice norms are applied to a controversy and reasons in defense of a decision are appraised; it is a "practical association" stylistically "united by the recognition of rights and practices but [it] is not organized for the pursuit of a common vision of the good life" (Kratochwil 1989: 18, 256). Hence we are intellectually empowered to look for law at work both inside and outside of courtrooms, within and between nations!

It should by now not be surprising that "judgments," as elliptically referred to by Bull, and dramatically introduced late in their arguments by Hollis and Smith, are the key units in Kratochwil's penultimate, processual treatment of "The Path of Legal Arguments" (Chapter 8). Thus, in "most, if not all legal systems, a judgment not only has to contain at a minimum the 'decision' reached but has also to provide reasons in support of the particular choice made by the judges" (Kratochwil 1989: 212).[22] The chapter explores "the logical structures of the two most important logical [and rhetorical] figures of practical reasoning, i.e., enthymeme and analogy." We should now be clearer that Bull's original phenomenological focus on "judgment" corresponds to an equally classical concern with human practical reasoning.

Kratochwil's philosophical and legal erudition is remarkable, especially when it is juxtaposed with his evident command of much of the recent economically oriented theorizing about international

---

[21] He emphasizes in the associated footnote 12 (266), that von Wright's "actionist" conception of causality does not sufficiently deal with "the problem of deliberation." Anscombe's grounding of her conception of intentionality in conversational terms, Hintikka's extended work on dialogue games, and Walton's developmentally inclusive paradigmatic reformulation of practical reasoning from goal-directed non-deductive inference, to a knowledge-based deliberative process, to a multi-actor, pragmatically defined reasoning dialogue (or dialectic) all spell out similar enrichments. See Chapters 1 and 2 above.

[22] The next quotation in the text (247) comes from the same chapter.

cooperation, regimes and institutions. He is equally at home with Kant's argument in his *Critique of Practical Reason* that human will inhabits a space of responsible freedom, with Weber's philosophical writings on social science, with Habermas' historically informed development of hermeneutic philosophy and his construction of a kindred theory of "communicative rationality" (Habermas 1987). More than anyone else, Kratochwil deserves credit for the return of a properly named and described practical reason to international theory; within its creative, norm-guided, attitudinal sweep, processes of legal reasoning can again engage and challenge the more reductionistic forms of scientific scholarship.

Onuf's basic organizing theme for the first half of his book, like that of its title, *World of Our Making*, is the constructivist appreciation of rule-governed makers' and doers' knowledge.[23] Both human agents, social meanings and social institutions are mutually "constituted in or through recurrent practices" arising out of "practical consciousness [which] consists of knowing the rules and the tactics whereby daily social life is constituted and reconstituted across time and space" (Onuf 1989: 58ff.).

Onuf clearly understands and uses the post-Wittgensteinian tradition of writings on intentionality and practical reasoning. In his second chapter on "Law and Language" he explicitly invokes, with qualified approval, Kratochwil's discursive, "post-positivist" efforts to redefine the realm of legal reasoning as that of a special kind – neither inductive nor deductive and therefore necessarily rhetorical – of practical reasoning.[24] But Onuf wants to go beyond this. He wants not to

---

[23] Onuf's first chapter on "Constructivism" starts (at 35) with Wittgenstein's Goethe-inspired observation that "Language ... is a refinement ... in the beginning was the deed." My text paraphrases the early themes of this chapter.

[24] Onuf 1989 (76–78), which is also the primary source for the phrasing of my next several sentences. His criticisms of Kratochwil's earlier formulation of law as "practical reasoning in public settings and for public purposes" seem to have apparently encouraged Kratochwil's current, domain-extending, "pragmatic" view "that the legal character of rules and norms can be established when we are able to show that these norms are *used* in a distinct fashion [according to the specific application of principles in the rhetorical "styles" wherein lawyers are trained] in making decisions and in communicating the basis for those choices to a wider audience." This characterization of law avoids coming up with positivistic demarcation criteria, extends its relevance beyond obviously relevant third-party judgment contexts, and is "independent of formal institutions, [or] levels of analysis" (Kratochwil (1989: 42, Ch. 7). By going the pragmatic route, focusing on interactive dialogue like Walton does, Kratochwil has helped overcome this criticism of his earlier work.

conflate principles with rules of high specificity and wants to include in his concept of law diverse "rules ranging from principles to procedures that work and look like law, even though convention holds that they are not."

The remarkable closeness of Onuf's ambitious and impressive argument to Kratochwil's and Hollis'[25] clearly suggests his book belongs in the current review; but his purpose is even more ambitious than Hollis and Smith's or Kratochwil's: to provide a new theory of "Rules and Rule" in international relations. Following a reinterpretive method he acknowledges as going back to Aristotle, Onuf grounds his "disciplinary construction project" for international relations in the "operative paradigm" of "political society," which has two general and pervasive properties: "One is the pervasive presence of rules which, in guiding, but not determining, human conduct, gives it social meaning. Whenever rules have the effect of distributing advantages unequally, the result is rule, which is the second general property of political society" (Onuf 1989: 21ff.).[26]

Onuf wants to define his social theory of international relations in terms of the performative roles of language in contexts not necessarily limited to practical reasoning.[27] His analysis suggests and richly elaborates upon categories of rules derived in a Wittgenstein-

[25] Now that Kratochwil's and Onuf's discussions of practical and legal reasoning have been introduced, compare how similarly Hollis argues that acts must be identified in terms of "the agent's intention in its context of conventions" and "legitimating reasons" (1987: 184–192), that reasons must be recovered and judgments judged "since the merit of the actor's reasons affect the residue for further explanation" (192), that Weberian ideal-typical "good reasons *explain* action" and justification-relevant "good (enough) reasons" help us to *understand* it as well (191, 201, 204), that the "Cunning of Reason" "in practice" means that the rational agent "satisfices with an eye to the forum in which it will be most urgent to justify himself afterwards, while thus leaving something over to satisfy other claims with" (203), that "rules vary from town to town and time to time [and country to country where] they enable and constrain the life of the inhabitants" (194), and that "I am taking up Rousseau's suggestion that the social contract creates the persons who, so to speak, make it" (212).

[26] Other phrases quoted or paraphrased in this paragraph and note come from 20–24. Onuf's notion of the paradigm of political society comes from Wolin; it refers to an "ensemble of practices and beliefs," of "institutions, laws, structure of authority and citizenship, and operative beliefs," which are paradigmatic "in the sense that society tries to carry on its political life in accordance with them." Onuf is here quoting S. Wolin (1980: 160–191, at 183ff.).

[27] Although he sees all behavior as rule-governed, and social practices as defined by rules in these ways, like his exemplar Giddens, Onuf never reduces social action, bureaucratic activity or social practices merely to their linguistic dimension.

Anscombe-Austin-Searle fashion "from a consideration of language as enabling people to perform social acts and achieve ends by making statements of assertion, direction, and commitment." In a remarkable chapter on "Cognition, Judgment, Culture," Onuf characteristically links these types of speech acts and rule statements respectively with the practices of "priests and professors," "warriors and diplomats" and "physicians and merchants." With suggestive, empirically linked references to gender and cultural differences, he argues that "Practice and consciousness taken together yield judgment" (Onuf 1989: 119).

Although I have some objections to Onuf's trinitarianism regarding faculties of experience and speech act typologies, I must admit it combines brilliantly with his Rules/Rule orientation in Part II's Chapter 5, a Pocock-inspired reformulation of the civic and international order in terms of "Virtues, Rights, Manners."[28] Here he develops the centrality of "might *and* right," or the fusion of rule and force, in Machiavelli's conception of virtuous civic life (grounded in the norm of doing no harm, but responding proportionately to injury); he grounds the Hobbes–Locke liberal tradition of order in the basic principle of the rights tradition, "that promises shall be kept"; and he links Burke, Hume and Gibbon to a political society constitutionally ordered in part by the common-law norm of telling the truth, at least as it is consistent "with what custom or manners expect," together with more controversial hierarchical patterns of power and privilege. Onuf is "confident that Pocock's formulation, or something quite like it, is the right one, that it exhaustively lists the primary categories of political practice in any society [including complexly structured international societies], and that these categories are mixed or even fused in practice but fully independent and mutually exclusive in conceptual terms."[29]

---

[28] That the whole book is well summarized by an appended "Synoptic Table" of "Paradigms of Experience" crossed by tripartite "Faculties of Experience" (1989: 290–293), is both an organizational strength and a weakness. Other conceptual and empirical attempts to organize the phenomena of international experience and the literatures of international relations often, but not always, have a tripartite structure, such as Kratochwil's searching exploration in his fourth chapter of the contributions of Hume, Hobbes, Durkheim and Freud to our understanding of compliance with norms; I have too much of a sense that the triad of categories of "existence" in space and time, "material control," and "discretionary endeavor" is preordained to triumph as the book unfolds.

[29] I have concluded this summary of Onuf (1989: 169–183) with a quote from 183.

How practical reasoning theorists transcend the presumption of anarchy in world politics

Having suggested how each of the books under review nonreduction-istically reframes the understanding of international relations in terms of post-Wittgensteinian conceptions of language use and language games, intentionality, practical reasoning, and judgment, I shall synthetically illustrate their approach to a characteristic and difficult problem of international relations, the securing of order (and justice) in situations which game theorists usually presume to be "anarchic."[30] Hollis and Smith in effect reopen the Bull–Kaplan debate when they begin their discussion of "International Games" with Green and Rapoport's indictment of Game Theory that "the use of these [scientific] methods [has] ignored the centrality of moral judgments in politics" (Hollis and Smith 1991: 130ff.).

The problems of anarchy, or Hobbes' problem of order for insecurity-spreading individuals/states, is often described by game theorists as a Prisoner's Dilemma. Like other well read political theorists,[31] they see what Hollis calls the "Leviathan Trap," to be transformable into an Assurance Game of coordinating expectations if either consensual norms or coercive norms (Hobbes' own, problematical solution of a contract-policing state set up by a voluntary social contract) bring about trusting relationships. And they recognize that Hobbes' view of international order was *not* the "warre of all vs. all"; his primary *domestically oriented* rhetorical/propagandistic purposes have in turn been used by statist rhetoricians for their own domestic and international legitimating purposes.

The further discussion of norms brings us several steps closer to the opening of the Leviathan Trap. Players grammatically able to rank

---

[30] See Chapter 11 above. The Wittgensteinian critique of game theoretic abstractions is that cooperative/conflictual "activities are not attempts to capture and define something which exists [Platonically, as a matter of "parsimonious" disciplinary ontology] independently of them" (Hollis and Smith 1991: 177).

The most important sources for the following synthesis, which I feel justified in making because of an at least partially demonstrated commonality of their views, are Hollis (1987: 40–44, 56–58, 63–65, 91–94, 210–212); Hollis and Smith (1991: 120–142, 155–170, 176–181, 188–195); Kratochwil (1989: 1–28, 67ff., 256–62); Onuf (1989), Chapter 5 (actually entitled "The Presumption of Anarchy"), and Chapter 6 (written with Frank F. Klink) on "Political Society." Hence, the "they" in my text.

[31] See the richly supportive bibliography and discussion of Russell Hardin (1991), "Hobbesian Political Order."

their rankings of preferences can be said to have "dispositional preferences" or reflective "values," conceived of as passionately held, second-order, dispositional attitudes. The socially coordinated internalization of appropriate resolutional "dispositional preferences," or rationally intertwined "normative expectations" is likely to involve, in actual historical situations, elements of rule-based trust and of socially institutionalized claims (rights or entitlements) to anticipated benefits.

But if the internalization of interaction-constitutive norms and the coordination of such expectations requires linguistic socialization through practical interactions, the possibility of a just resolution requires even more, a space for autonomous moral agency, within which good reasons can have independent force. Here, following in Anscombe's footsteps, the authors' use of anti-Humean, Kant-inspired distinctions between what I, modifying Hollis, shall call "passion-external reasons" and identity-related "passion-internal" reasons, is crucial.

Passion-internal reasons are more like self-constituting operatic themes, passionate value commitments, heroic Schank–Abelson scripts, or multi-stage Humean life "projects" which can enslave reason to the passions; they can even include commitments to painful or risky choices which, once successfully accomplished, can spring the Leviathan Trap. In doing so, a Rousseauian identity transformation of selves and societies, a world of reformed sovereignties can result.

Partially autonomous moral agents also may choose to follow passion-external reasons for action, even as they creatively enact the roles/personalities suggested by their intergroup relationships. Objectively good reasons, including but not limited to Sen-style rankings on preference rankings, or generalizable Kantian standards for self/other-regarding interest definition, can be internalized. The resulting principled identities of rational individuals or bureaucracies can noninstrumentally be expressed within subsequent deliberative and judgmental conduct. The actual content of identities and interests, the complex mix of passion-internal and passion-external reasons governing, and enacted in our lives, can only be discovered by concrete investigations of criticizable, intersecting, identity-linked and transformable chains of practical reasoning.

A myriad of imagined and actual social *practices*, then, *can* resolve prisoner's or assurance dilemmas in concrete situations whose contexts are richly enough described to include the relevant practical resources and expectations; they need not and will not necessarily do so. A great value of the books in question is the wide variety of abstract and concrete examples in which practical reasoning brings about, or fails to accomplish (as in some economic and security contexts) such resolutions, plus the associated discussion of the necessary and sufficient conditions in particular contexts for such an occurrence in the different cases.

Such problems are of course not all resolved in some abstract world where the resources, ontological presuppositions, theoretical concepts and practices sufficient for their resolution are presumed not to exist; it might rather be said that they are *demystified by being reframed as concrete practical reasoning problems in a multi-disciplinary world* in which resolution-appropriate identities, interests and conduct can – but need not – occur.[32] In every case, the *reframing* of the game/dilemma involved is from an abstracted, asocial world to a concrete, linguistically and historically described, heteronomous, social and political one; this has required a shift from a presumed to be isolated *homo economicus* to a contextually located *homo collocutionis, historicus socialis et politicus* capable, with some degree of autonomy and responsibility within porously bounded political societies, of *practically arguing for, or enacting* his passionate commitments, beliefs, loyalties, principles and interests. And in those societies which have significantly overcome gendered exploitations, "sovereign artificers" can be given both male and female names. Let us hope that a *homo humanitatis* routinely capable of *practical reasoning* can be included in a revisable core of the operating paradigm for a more genuinely interdisciplinary and historically nuanced field of International Relations.

Obviously, the approach should connect up with existing major literatures on the international system, its contingent and constructed character, as discussed at length in earlier chapters of this volume. It does, for reasons that should be increasingly clear. In retrospect, Morton Kaplan's own, constructivist and historical orientation toward political-legal rule systems seems assimilable here too (Kaplan 1957; Kaplan and Katzenbach 1961). The leap from Onuf's Weberian, Lasswellian, Giddensesque analysis of international systems to Alex Wendt's (1992) "Anarchy is What You Make of It: The social construction of power politics," is very short.[33] Kratochwil's brief historical

---

[32] Parallels with the analyses of Chapters 6 and 11 might be mentioned, since Onuf uses a phrase from the first one as the title of his Chapter 5.

[33] Indeed, Hollis and Smith, Carlnaes and others have recently furthered the discussion of Wendt's ontological realism and philosophical idealism in the *Review of International Studies*, among other places.

treatment of the "balance of power" as the boundary-conscious historical *exception*, built *up* from a *practical-legal ground* of mutually recognized rights, responsibilities and customs echoes Martin Wight's historical insights into the modern system of states. Supported by intriguing quotations from Frederick the Great, his argument that neorealist theorists like Waltz and Gilpin have failed to account, *inter alia*, for the tolerance-supporting *content* of the post-war modern European system is extremely rich. The legitimational dynamics of modern "sovereignty" construction, the expressive shaping of "national interests" that look neither like those evident in the Melian Dialogue nor the nearly empty theoretical categories of Waltzean systems theory are major achievements referred to, or suggested by, his concluding chapter.[34]

Even the epitome of economic thought, the market itself, gets reunderstood in such a perspective as anything but normless and ungoverned ("anarchic"); it is a pluricentered institution embedded within other institutions, such as the largely consensual, sometimes unstable, legally and politically shaped institutions of money and property which, as any contemporary European knows, it presupposes. Onuf says of the market what all of our authors would agree more generally of insecurity relationships, that the

> principle of utility supplies that theory with an ethical interpretation of its presumption [of anarchy] (masquerading as prediction) that unimpeded individual efforts to maximize utility yield the largest possible utility for all. Normativity is conventionalized out of sight, and largely out of mind. What utility did for liberalism, Bentham's conventionalized view of law [or legal positivism more generally] did for the state. (Onuf 1989: 195)

Indeed, the international relations world of Hollis and Smith, Kratochwil and Onuf seems to be a scientifically more articulated variant

---

34 Kratochwil (1989), entitled "The International Legal Order, International Systems, and the Comparative Analysis of the Practice of States." It is a real shame that Kratochwil's extraordinarily impressive historical-theoretical studies "On the Notion of Interest in International Relations" (1982), "Of Systems, Boundaries, and Territoriality: An Inquiry into the Formation of the State System" (1986), and his analysis of neorealism's weaknesses in explaining the end of the Cold War, summed up in Koslowski and Kratochwil (1994), are not more fully included in his final section. A revised edition illustrating in detail the power of his historical-interpretive-systematic approach with this material would both epitomize and conclusively demonstrate in a single volume the broad-ranging, cumulative, yet still practical synthesis of humanistic and scientific perspectives that I see in the present studies.

of the concrete, heteronomous, "anarchic society" whose globalization, and whose progressive and regressive moral-political judgments and practices, Hedley Bull was so eager historically to map![35]

Removing obstructions on the long road to cumulative international theory

I take it for granted that a large proportion of my readers not already personally familiar with Kratochwil or Onuf will agree with me that "practical reasoning" has not been a concept explicitly at the center of their recent theoretical or empirical activities. That "practical reason" was at the center of classical international discourse in what Kaplan would call the "traditional" or "pre-scientific" era is also clear, either because of the augmented version of Kratochwil's explicit arguments to that effect given above or because of the review of Aristotelian political methodologies in Chapter 2 above. Therefore these two facts require historically minded students to account for the return of practical reason in the present, scientifically oriented volumes. If they wish not to be enslaved to "false necessities," reality-truncating naturalizations, or exclusionary discipline-constituting power games, current students, researchers and teachers ought also to clear away as many of the remaining cumulation-blocking obstructions on the long, rocky road to cumulative international theory as they can.

All of the writers in question have critically increased our understanding of the "Hobbesian" attempt to "kill" domestic and international history and society with misleading, and very gendered, social contract myths.[36] Their efforts apply to a Hobbes better reunderstood both as a propagandistic rhetorician *and* a scientific theorist, as well as to contemporary neorealism. Their critical historicizing of the agonistic triumphs and the inegalitarian failures of liberal political economy is a similar powerful and useful antidote to capitalistic triumphalism.

But something else obstructive has been going on during the later years of the Cold War, when these books were written, which has not

[35] I have in mind, of course, his *Anarchical Society*, his *The Expansion of International Society* (edited with Watson), and his *Justice in International Relations* as appreciatively elaborated upon in Chapter 11 above and J.L. Richardson's previously cited contribution to the Miller–Vincent memorial volume.

[36] The leap to or from J. Ann Tickner's (1992) *Gender in International Relations* is also small. A two-way connection is worth making for both practical reasoning theorists and feminist international relations specialists.

yet been well understood, nor adequately pushed aside. Their transcendence of neorealist instrumentalist/strategic rationality even during the Reagan–Thatcher–Bush years needs greater recognition than I have given it so far. When "power politics" is partially, and geopolitically, being redefined, when neorealism has suggested very little of deep worth concerning the end of the Cold War and the shape of a post-Cold War era full of global economic dynamics and parochial, boundary-transcending identity conflicts, the appreciation of this emancipatory achievement should be easier to share. Its recognition should be a part of the critical historiography of international theorizing of the Cold War era in particular.

More generally, as already reviewed in Chapters 6 and 11 above, the modern meaning of "reason" has been fought over for centuries. Of special relevance to the present treatment, Norman O. Dahl has provocatively argued that Hume's instrumentalist conception of enslaved reason meant that practical reason (no longer) existed: "Practical reason exists if and only if reason by itself motivates people to act" (Dahl 1984). The prodigious journeys of Hollis and Smith's effort to understand the limited but real creative possibilities of bureaucratic decision-making within the often contradictory pressures of systemic and individual considerations are related, successful steps in a much larger, long-term effort to revivify refined notions of practical reasoning. So are Kratochwil and Onuf's Herculean, and to my mind both refreshing and successful efforts to reintroduce rules, norms and law (via sociolinguistic practices and practical reasoning) into scientific international theorizing about practices that reproduce, evolve and transform international systems.

The "return of practical reason" to Scientific International Theory is a neoclassical revival in the sense of Part I of this book. It is at the same time a reassertion of the independent and substantial importance of rules, norms, judgments and laws in a scientifically conceived interdiscipline of International Relations. Hollis' recovery of "passion-external" reasons is presented as an argument in the Kantian tradition; Kratochwil's Chapter 5 on "The Discourse on Grievances" similarly criticizes utilitarian conceptions of rule following, Kantian arguments about categorical imperatives and Grotian notions of natural law in terms of Pufendorf's version of the institutional rules and rights implied within moral or contractual assertions.

At stake are the core ontological/phenomenological assumptions of what Hedley Bull and Martin Wight call the Grotian and Kantian traditions of International Relations (Wight 1992). More such steps toward a fuller conception of communicative and strategic rationalities are clearly needed if our late modern era is to achieve early modernity's most worthy initiating political aspiration – rationally guided, dignity-respecting, world politics.[37]

Practical understanding, theoretical explanation and interdisciplinarity in the "Third Debate"

Hollis, Smith, Kratochwil and Onuf's focus on the constitutive and constructive aspects of practical reasoning as a compensatory readjustment to instrumentalist economic rationality points further to a set of problems in the guts of the current "post-positivist" battle for the hearts, minds and bodies of the social sciences (including International Relations).[38] Within International Relations, all of the present writers can be identified with the post-positivist "search for interpretive understanding" side of Lapid's "Third Debate" rather than the "naturalistic," or "positivistic" side's search for universal and timeless causal laws. Indeed, I have suggested that their advocacy of "practical reasoning," plus a network of related post-Wittgensteinian conceptualizations, amounts to an effort to redefine the disciplinary self-understanding of International Relations (and the social sciences more generally) in a more humanistic fashion. Because there is so much rigorous, richly supported, highly relevant work in the sciences of human communication,[39] I have further supported Quincy Wright, as reviewed in the Introduction to this volume, and the classicists by claiming that the resulting, redefined discipline should, as both Quincy Wright and Raymond Aron also argued, be considered part of the social sciences *and* of the humanities.

To show how the current, "Third Debate" is again replaying, and trying to transcend, the "understanding vs. explanation" theme, let me briefly recall Hollis and Smith's discussion of reasoned role playing as it might be reinterpreted in the language of Weber, Apel and

---

[37] See Chapter 4 above for a discussion of the overlapping but contradictory ways in which Machiavellian and Las Casas "moments" have attempted to realize the early modern promises of Pico della Mirandola style humanism.

[38] The detailed reconstruction of critical and reflective reason in Chapter 6 of the present volume is a remarkably similar effort.

[39] Recall the rehabilitation of the Aristotelian tradition of political communication studies suggested in Chapters 2 and 3 above.

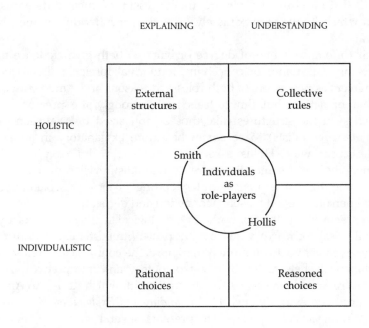

Figure 12.1   Hollis and Smith within their schema of 2R approaches

Habermas, primary sources for Onuf and Kratochwil's own theoretical elaborations.

Hollis and Smith end their volume with a dramatic disagreement: within a Weberian–Wittgensteinian orientational synthesis of interpretive/humanistic and scientific traditions, of causal explanations from outside and interpretive (Anscombe would say mentally causative) understandings from inside, they differ empirically on the degree to which "individuals take the stage in a social capacity" as makers of history or subordinates to some larger social whole (Hollis and Smith

417

1991: 2–5, 214–216). The picture they present of their differences, within which I have approximately located their individual names, is given above.

Their difference is one of degree or balance: both give credence to the freeing importance of conceiving individual foreign policy decision-makers as possessors of both roles and reasons and a modicum of freedom of action, but Smith feels more strongly the pressure of external systemic structures (like those emphasized by Waltzean or Marxian structuralists) to be somewhat more explanatory in an external, causal way. Hollis asserts, within the realm of practical, reasoned choices, a somewhat more individualistic vision of practical choices, requiring interpretive understanding in terms of role-linked but still personal "good reasons" for action and decision.

Quite remarkably, this contradictory, dialogical synthesis has exactly the dialectical form explicated by the post-Wittgensteinian literature review given above. Even more remarkably, the contradictory unity of simultaneously held contradictory explanatory and interpretive positions in a reasoned dialogue is the construct with which Karl-Otto Apel concludes his previously cited *Understanding and Explanation: A Transcendental-Pragmatic Perspective*. He presents several summary reflections on the latest stage of the *Verstehen-Erklaren* controversies, two of which put the significance of the Hollis–Smith opposed resolution in a much more general perspective:

> 1 ... [I]n a sufficiently isolated world system, the concept of the causal necessity of changes of state presupposes the concept of experimental action. This argument led to insight into an onto-semantically and transcendentally-pragmatically grounded complementarity involving the mutual exclusion, and hence supplementation, of language games and of phenomenal domains corresponding to them. ... [viz.] the description of objects of nature and the explanation of events, on the one hand, and, on the other, the understanding of action, an understanding that, in principle, does not concern objects but rather can only be a reflective theme.
>
> 2 ... [T]he purposive-rational understanding of subjective, nature-manipulating actions and their results must be linguistically articulable even to be comprehensible to the individual subject of knowledge. ... [It] presupposes intersubjective, communicative understanding. ... The distinction between ... the domain of "theoretical reason" within which, according to Kant, there can be no "constitution" of the object domain of the *Geisteswissenschaften* or social sciences and the domain of "practical reason," for which such

418

an object domain can be a practical theme, though never a scientific one [w]e can now modify. ... [H]ermeneutics can ... make society and history its theme as the subject-object of scientific knowledge ... [T]he "communicative experience of signs" seems epistemologically decisive ... [suggesting] a distinctive synthesis of "sensuousness" [empathy or *Verstehen*] and the understanding of intentional or conventional "symbols." (Apel 1984: 234–237)

In more homely English, recognizing the practical domain of interpretable human action within experimental inquiry rehumanizes the communicative experiential foundations of the causally oriented natural sciences. More comprehensive interpretive modes of analysis focused on the action engendering experience of signs and symbols similarly transcend the merely subjective understanding of social and historical phenomena, making possible social sciences like International Relations. A humanistic "unity of the natural and social sciences" can in this way be achieved by a recognition of the inner connections between the exclusive but complementary worlds of interpretive understanding and causal explanation, the worlds of "practical" and "theoretical" reasoning and knowledge.

Following the lead of Stephen Toulmin's (1990) enormously suggestive *Cosmopolis: The Hidden Agenda of Modernity*,[40] I want to conclude with the following "Late Modern" suggestion. It concerns the exclusionary paradigmatic lenses and deductive logical commitments – including the restrictive "positive and negative heuristics" of our Lakatosian research programs – with which we scientifically view concrete, often creative human endeavors. Treating mathematics, axiomatic reasoning and deductive logic (key elements of logical empiricist/positivist scientific validity) as cosmological givens, incontrovertible, or at least untouchable components in the "core" of the modern social sciences' Lakatosian research programs eventually

---

[40] Toulmin (1990) provocatively suggests that in the early seventeenth century there was a "Counter-Renaissance" revolt against the undogmatic, skeptical and tolerant version of Renaissance variants of practical reasoning evident in modernizing classical scholars like Erasmus and Montaigne. He suggests that Leibnizian and Cartesian metaphysics cosmologically substituted written, axiomatic, deductive, clearly grounded, universalistic, logical-mathematical argumentation for spoken, contextual, timely, case-specific practical argumentation; this was in significant part a reaction to the radical anxieties associated with the Thirty Years War in Europe. Hence my preference for the "practical reasoning" node as the identifying label for the larger complex of post-Wittgensteinian conceptualizations this chapter has explored under that label.

create, Toulmin implies, a degeneracy characteristic of several late modern social sciences.[41]

In this perspective, for example, the difficulty of the needed transformation in International Relations disciplinary phenomenology is not primarily empirical; it is logical, ontological-phenomenological and epistemological. The suggestion of the present writers is that practical reasoning logics, historically-linked discursive social ontologies, and a renaissance of interpretive/explanatory epistemologies are appropriate for our times and our theorizing practices.[42]

If the "Sovereign Artificer" can *only* today be located in the "virtual realities" of post-structuralist discourse analyses, International Relations is in deep paradigmatic trouble. Hollis and Smith, Kratochwil and Onuf have suggested another, more productive possibility. Extended into the realm of specialized methodologies it amounts to this: Like the formal logic of *Principia Mathematica*, the N-nation non-cooperative games of Game Theory, the successor versions of Kaplan's cybernetic systems theories, Schank–Abelson or Ashley–Cohen computational models of linguistic understanding, judgmental inferences and policy practices, historical-dramaturgical narrativizings of shared meanings, reconstructive discourse analyses, regime models, *and* Hintikka–Walton's, Hollis–Smith's and Kratochwil–Onuf's versions of practical argumentation are *each* redescribable as situationally specialized, pragmatically oriented, language games. The

---

[41] See the discussion and citations to Toulmin and Havel in Chapter 4. In pre-modern Australian aboriginal terms suggested by the Australian origins of the earlier version of the present chapter (Alker 1994), one can say that the effort to cumulate scientific knowledge from axiomatic, deductive inferences and incremental complexifications of a discipline's specific, non-falsifiable core assumptions is a majestic, ritualistic "walkabout" characteristic of much of the modern world. And we can observe that such efforts often go into infinite, degenerate loops and never *deductively* and cumulatively return to a discipline's better understood origination point when a body of cooperating scholars is not allowed, at least occasionally, revolutionary respecifications of its core logical, ontological and epistemological assumptions. This seems to be the "lesson" of Robert Keohane's impressive *After Hegemony* (1984). But Keohane doesn't give us, like Hollis and Smith, Kratochwil and Onuf, *homo humanitatis* and *practical reasoning* as alternate starting points for subsequent, perhaps more modest, more practically successful, *late-modern* partial world walkabouts by semi-sovereign student-participants in its affairs.

[42] In the Prisoner's Dilemma/Leviathan Trap domain, the needed paradigmatic trick is to *re-vision* how game players personally *enact*, *perform* or practically *accomplish* their achievements. Hollis, Smith, Kratochwil and Onuf all partake in this discursive, ontological, ethnomethodological transformation of contexted seeing. More concretely, see Chapter 9 above.

420

multi-disciplinary scientist of international relations should knowledgeably consider *all* of them as potentially relevant and appropriate to the phenomena of the field. In this way the *Verstehen-Erklaren* controversy can at last be productively transcended, when appropriate, experientially grounded syntheses of these approaches result.

The title of this concluding chapter is inspired by a book and a movie, *The Return of Martin Guerre*.[43] It seems there were two Martin Guerres in late medieval/early modern France, one traditional, unsympathetic, originally impotent and later militaristic and oppressive (when linked with the French monarch and the authority of the Catholic Church), the other a self-taught imposter, but a loving partner in a simulated, modern marriage that was fecund in children, Protestant in morality and capitalistic in its enhanced economic productivity. The historical incident, like the movie, contains at its core a debate before a tribunal of judges as to which man is the "real" Martin Guerre. Because the return of the original Guerre ultimately results in the execution of the second Guerre, and subsequent religious conflict results in the death of the most insightful memorializer and most clearly proto-Protestant of Guerre's judges, their lives have both a tragic and a triumphant character. One senses that the second Martin Guerre's loving but violence-evoking "return" is both a renewal and a portent of things to come.

Similarly, half a millennium later, while writing this review, I have had the powerful feeling of being the bearer of an ancient, pre-modern wisdom, what Aristotle called *phronesis*, or practical wisdom. I share with Hollis and Smith, Onuf and Kratochwil the exhilaration of their long journeys of rediscovery and reformulation. Practical reasoning's return is part of the historicity of the social sciences, containing the possibility (but not the Hegelian necessity) of a new (yet very old) kind of rationality, with enormous, but uncertain healing potential. Whether that means we bearers of the newer forms of practical reasoning are writing unredemptive epitaphs to the modern era, signaling the possibilities of a new renaissance of practical reasoning within late modernity (my personal belief), or are the harbingers, like so many others, of a new, unnamed, post-modern epoch not yet able to be born, I cannot be sure.

---

[43] The book was written by Natalie Zemon Davis (1983); she was also listed as a consultant in the credits of the French, César-winning movie.

References

Abelson, Robert P. (1973) "The Structure of Belief Systems." In Roger C. Schank and Kenneth Colby, eds., *Computer Models of Thought and Language*. San Francisco: W.H. Freeman.

Abelson, Robert P. and Carol M. Reich. (1969) "Implication Molecules: A Method for Extracting Meaning from Input Sentences." In D.E. Walker and L.M. Norton, eds., *Proceedings of the International Joint Conference on Artificial Intelligence*. Boston: Mitre Corporation.

Adey, G. and D. Frisby, eds. (1976) *The Positivism Dispute in German Sociology*. New York: Harper Torchbook.

Adorno, T.W., E. Frenkel-Brunswik, D.J. Levinson and R.N. Sanford. (1950, 1969) *The Authoritarian Personality*. New York: W.W. Norton.

Afanasev, Aleksandr. (1973) *Russian Fairy Tales*, translated by Norbert Guterman, Commentary by Roman Jakobson. New York: Pantheon Books.

Ahonen, Anne Marie. (1994) "The Contemporary Debate in International Relations Theory and Raymond Aron's Epistemology and Ontology," *Cooperation and Conflict* 29/1: 77–94.

Alker, H.R., Jr. (1965) *Mathematics and Politics*. New York: Macmillan.

(1968) "The Long Road to International Relations Theory: Problems of Statistical Nonadditivity," *World Politics* 18/4 (July 1966): 623–655. Reprinted in revised form in Kaplan, ed., *New Approaches to International Relations*. New York: St. Martin's Press, 1968.

(1973) "Political Capabilities in a Schedule Sense: Measuring Power, Integration and Development." In H.R. Alker, Jr., K.W. Deutsch and A.H. Stoetzel, eds., *Mathematical Approaches to Politics*. Amsterdam: Elsevier.

(1974) "Are there Structural Models of Voluntaristic Social Action?" *Quality and Quantity* 8: 199–246.

(1975) "Polimetrics: Its Descriptive Foundations." In Nelson W. Polsby and Fred I. Greenstein, eds., *Handbook of Political Science*, VII, pp. 139–210. Reading, MA: Addison-Wesley.

(1976) "Individual Achievements Rarely Sum to Collective Progress" (Autobiographical Reflections). In J. Rosenau, ed., *In Search of Global Patterns*, pp. 38–58. New York: Free Press.

(1977a) "Can the End of Power Politics be Part of the Concepts With Which Its Story is Told?" Paper delivered at the meeting of the American Political Science Association (APSA), 1977. Unpublished.

(1977b) "A Methodology for Design Research on Interdependence Alternatives." *International Organization* 31: 29–64.

(1981a) "Dialectical Foundations of Global Disparities," *International Studies Quarterly* 25/1: 69–98.

(1981b) "From Political Cybernetics to Global Modeling." In R.L. Merritt and B.M. Russett, eds., *From National Development to Global Community*. London: George Allen & Unwin, pp. 353–378.

(1982) "Logic, Dialectics, Politics: Some Recent Controversies," pp. 65–93. In H.R. Alker, Jr., ed., *Dialectical Logics for the Political Sciences*. Amsterdam: Rodopi.

(1984) "Historical Argumentation and Statistical Inference: Towards More Appropriate Logics for Historical Research," *Historical Methods* 17/3 (Summer 1984): 164–173. *Erratum* 17/4: 270.

(1985) "From Quantity to Quality: A New Research Program on Resolving Sequential Prisoner's Dilemmas." Revised version of a paper delivered at the Annual Meeting of the American Political Science Association, New Orleans (August 1985).

(1986a) "Bit Flows, Rewrites, Social Talk: Towards More Adequate Informational Ontologies," published in the proceedings of the Centennial Conference of Todai University, "Information and its Functions," October 1986. Reprinted in M. Campanella, ed., *Between Rationality and Cognition*. Turin: Meynier.

(1986b) "The Presumption of Anarchy in World Politics." Citable text of Griffith lecture, American University, Washington, DC. Republished in a slightly updated version in the present volume.

(1987) "Fairy Tales, Tragedies and World Histories: Towards Interpretive Story Grammars of Possibilist World Models," *Behaviormetrika* 21: 1–28.

(1988a) "The Dialectical Logic of Thucydides' Melian Dialogue," *American Political Science Review* 82:3 (September). An earlier draft was published in Russian by Progress Publishers in 1988.

(1988b) "Emancipatory Empiricism: Towards the Renewal of Empirical Peace Research." In Peter Wallenstein, ed., *Peace Research: Achievements and Challenges*. Boulder & London: Westview Press, Inc., pp. 219–241.

(1990) "Rescuing 'Reason' from the 'Rationalists': Reading Vico, Marx and Weber as Reflective Institutionalists," *Millennium* 19/2 (Summer): 161–184.

(1992a) "Historicity for Beginners: Can It Be Rightly Taught?" Prepared for the Karl Deutsch issue of Wissenschaft Zentrum publication, *WZB-Mitteilungen* 56 (June): 45–47.

(1992b) "The Humanistic Moment in International Studies: Reflections on

Machiavelli and Las Casas," International Studies Association, 1992 Presidential Address. *International Studies Quarterly* 36: 347–371.

(1993) "Making Peaceful Sense of the News: Institutionalizing International Conflict-Management Event Reporting Using Frame-Based Interpretive Routines." In Richard L. Merritt, R.G. Muncaster and D.A. Zinnes, eds., *International Event-Data Developments: DDIR Phase II*. Ann Arbor: University of Michigan Press.

(1994) "The Return of Practical Reason," Working Paper, Department of International Relations, Research School of Pacific and International Studies, Australian National University, Canberra. A revised version appears as Chapter 12 of the present volume.

Alker, H.R., Jr., James Bennett and Dwain Mefford. (1980) "Generalized Precedent Logics for Resolving Insecurity Dilemmas," *International Interactions* 7/2: 165–206.

Alker, H.R., Jr. and Thomas J. Biersteker. (1984) "The Dialectics of World Order: Notes for a Future Archeologist of International Savoir Faire," *International Studies Quarterly* 28 (1984), 121–142. Reprinted in James Der Derian, ed., *International Theory: Critical Investigations*. New York: New York University Press, 1994.

Alker, H.R., Jr. and C. Christensen. (1972) "From Causal Modelling to Artificial Intelligence: The Evolution of a UN Peace-Making Simulation." In LaPonce and Smoker, eds., *Experimentation and Simulation in Political Science*. Toronto: University of Toronto Press.

Alker, H.R., Jr., Karl Deutsch and Antoine H. Stoetzel, eds. (1973) *Mathematical Approaches to Politics*. New York: Elsevier.

Alker, H.R., Jr., G. Duffy, R. Hurwitz and J.C. Mallery. (1991) "Text Modeling for International Politics: A Tourist's Guide to RELATUS." In V. Hudson, ed., *Artificial Intelligence and International Politics*. Boulder, CO: Westview.

Alker, H.R., Jr. and P.M. Haas. (1993) "The Rise of Global Ecopolitics." Prepared for 1991 Meeting of the Mexican Association for International Studies. In Nazli Choucri, ed., *Global Accord: Environmental Challenges and International Responses*. Cambridge, MA: MIT Press.

Alker, H.R., Jr. and Roger Hurwitz. (1980) *Resolving Prisoner's Dilemmas*. American Political Science Association (Fall 1980).

Alker, H.R., Jr., R. Hurwitz and K. Rothkin. (1993) "Fairy Tales Can Come True: Narrative Constructions of Prisoner's Dilemma Game Play," paper presented at annual meeting of American Economic Association, Affiliated Social Science Associations, Anaheim, California, 1993. Unpublished.

Alker, H.R., Jr., Wendy G. Lehnert and Daniel K. Schneider. (1985) "Two Reinterpretations of Toynbee's Jesus: Explorations in Computational Hermeneutics." In Graziella Tonfoni, ed., *Artificial Intelligence and Text-Understanding: Plot Units and Summarization Procedures. Quaderni di Ricerca Linguistica*. 6.

Alker, H.R., Jr. and Frank L. Sherman. (1982) "Collective Security-Seeking

Practices Since 1945." In Daniel Frei, ed., *Managing International Conflict*. Beverly Hills, CA: Sage.

Alker, H.R., Jr. and David J Sylvan. (1988) "Foreign Policy as Ethnocentric Tragedy: The 1965 Commitment of US Troops to the Vietnam War." Revised panel paper presented at the International Society of Political Psychology, 1988.

Anderson, Perry. (1974a) *Lineages of the Absolutist State*. London: New Left Books.

(1974b) *Passages from Antiquity to Feudalism*. London: New Left Books.

Ando, Albert, Franklin Fisher and Herbert Simon. (1963) *Essays on the Structure of Social Science Models*. Cambridge, MA: MIT Press.

Anscombe, G.E.M. (1957) *Intention*. Oxford: Blackwell.

Apel, Karl-Otto. (1984) *Understanding and Explanation: A Transcendental-Pragmatic Perspective*. Translated from the German by Georgia Warnke. Cambridge, MA: MIT Press.

Arendt, Hannah. (1958) *The Human Condition*. Chicago: University of Chicago Press.

(1968) Preface, *Totalitarianism*, vol. II of *The Origins of Totalitarianism*, 3 vols. New York: Harcourt, Brace & World.

Aristotle. (1954) *Rhetoric*, translated by W. Rhys Roberts, and *Poetics*, translated by Ingram Bywater. Introduction and Notes by Friedrich Solmsen. New York: The Modern Library.

(1964) *Prior and Posterior Analytics*. Edited and translated by John Warrington. New York: Dutton.

(1984) *The Athenian Constitution*. Translated with introduction and notes by P. J. Rhodes, who suspects the book was in fact mainly written by Aristotle's students during his Athenian period, 332–322 BCE. London: Penguin Books.

(1985) *Nicomachean Ethics*. Translated with Introduction, Notes and Annotated Glossary by Terence Irwin. Indianapolis: Hackett Publishing Co.

Arnhart, Larry. (1981) *Aristotle's Political Reasoning*. DeKalb: Northern Illinois University Press.

Aron, Raymond. (1955) *The Century of Total War*. Boston: Beacon Press.

(1966) "Final Note: Rational Strategy and Reasonable Policy." In *Peace and War*. Garden City: Doubleday, pp. 767–781.

(1978) "Thucydides and the Historical Narrative." In his *Politics and History*. New Brunswick, NJ: Transaction Books, pp. 20–46.

Arthur, W. Brian. (1993) "On the Evolution of Complexity." Preprint dated April 11, 1993. Originally presented at an Integrative Themes Workshop at the Santa Fe Institute, Santa Fe, New Mexico.

Ashley, Kevin. (1990) *Modeling Legal Argument*. Cambridge, MA: MIT Press.

Ashley, Richard K. (1980) *The Political Economy of War and Peace*. London: Frances Pinter.

(1983) "Three Modes of Economism," *International Studies Quarterly* 27/4: 463–496.

References

(1984a) "International Relations: Hierarchical Aspects of International Politics." "Section Description" for Section 18. American Political Science Association Annual Meeting.

(1984b) "The Poverty of Neorealism," *International Organization* 38 (Spring): 225–286.

(1987) "The Geopolitics of Geopolitical Space: Toward a Critical Social Theory of International Politics," *Alternatives* 12: 403–434.

(1989) "Living on Borderlines: Man, Poststructuralism, and War." In J. Der Derian and M.J. Shapiro, eds., *International/Intertextual Relations*. Lexington: Lexington Books.

Aufricht, Hans. (1978) "A Restatement of Political Theory: A Note on Voegelin's *The New Science of Politics*." In Stephen A. McKnight, ed., *Eric Voegelin's Search for Order in History*. Baton Rouge, LA & London: Louisiana State University Press.

Augelli, E. and C. Murphy. (1988) *America's Quest for Supremacy and the Third World: A Gramscian Analysis*. London: Pinter.

Austin, J.L. (1962) *How to Do Things with Words*, 2nd ed. Edited by J.O. Urmson and Marina Sbisa, 1975. Cambridge, MA: Harvard University Press.

Axelrod, Robert. (1984) *The Evolution of Cooperation*. New York: Basic Books.

(1985) "Modeling the Evolution of Norms." Paper presented at the Annual Meeting of the American Political Science Association; subsequently revised and published as "An Evolutionary Approach to Norms," *American Political Science Review* 80/4 (1986): 1095–1111.

Axelrod, Robert, ed. (1976) *Structure of Decision: The Cognitive Maps of Political Elites*. Princeton: Princeton University Press.

Axelrod, Robert and Robert O. Keohane. (1985) "Achieving Cooperation Under Anarchy: Strategies and Institutions." *World Politics* 38/1: 226–254.

Ayer, A.J. (1952) *Language, Truth and Logic*. New York: Dover Publications.

(1959) *Logical Positivism*. Glencoe, IL: Free Press.

(1969) "Introduction" to A.J. Ayer, ed., *Logical Positivism*. New York: Free Press.

Azar, Edward E. and John W. Burton. (1986) *International Conflict Resolution: Theory and Practice*. Boulder: Lynne Rienner Publishers.

Azar, Edward E. and Thomas N. Havener. (1976) "Discontinuities in the Symbolic Environment: A Problem in Scaling," *International Interaction* 2: 231–246.

Bach, Kent and Robert M. Harnish. (1979) *Linguistic Communication and Speech Acts*. Cambridge, MA: MIT Press.

Bagby, Laurie M. Johnson. (1994) "The Use and Abuse of Thucydides," *International Organization* 48/1: 131–153.

Banks, Michael. (1985) "The Inter-Paradigm Debate." In M. Light and A.J.R. Groom, eds., *International Relations: A Handbook of Current Theory*. London: Pinter.

Barker, Ernest. (1958) *The Politics of Aristotle*. Translated with an Introduction, Notes and Appendices. New York: Oxford University Press.

426

Barraclough, Geoffrey. (1964, 1976) *Introduction to Contemporary History*. Harmondsworth: Penguin Books.

Barth, E.M. and E.C.W. Krabbe. (1982) *From Axiom to Dialogue: A Philosophical Study of Logics and Argumentation*. Berlin: de Gruyter.

Batali, John. (1988) "Reasoning about Self-Control." In P. Maes and D. Nardi, eds., *Meta-Level Architectures and Reflection*. Amsterdam: Elsevier Science Publishers.

Becker, Werner and Wilhelm K. Essler, eds. (1981) *Konzepte der Dialektik*. Frankfurt: Klostermann.

Beitz, Charles R. (1979) *Political Theory and International Relations*. Princeton: Princeton University Press.

Bellah, Robert. (1967) "The American Civic Religion," *Daedalus* 96/1: 1–21.

Bennett, James and H.R. Alker, Jr. (1977) "When National Security Policies Bred Collective Insecurity: The War of the Pacific in a World Politics Simulation." In K.W. Deutsch *et al.*, eds., *Problems of World Modeling*. Cambridge, MA: Ballinger.

Bennett, James P. (1984) "Data Stories: Learning about Learning from the US Experience in Vietnam." In Donald Sylvan and Stephen Chan, eds., *Foreign Policy Decision Making: Perception, Cognition and Artificial Intelligence*. New York: Praeger.

Berke, Bradley. (1982) *Tragic Thought and the Grammar of Tragic Myth*. Bloomington: Indiana University Press.

Berlin, Isaiah. (1977) *Vico & Herder: Two Studies in the History of Ideas*. New York: Random House, Vintage Books.

(1982) "The Originality of Machiavelli." In Isaiah Berlin, *Against the Current: Essays in the History of Ideas*. New York: Viking-Penguin, pp. 25–79.

Bernstein, Richard J. (1976) *Restructuring of Social and Political Theory*. New York: Harcourt, Brace, Jovanovich.

(1983) *Beyond Objectivism and Relativism: Science, Hermeneutics, and Praxis*. Philadelphia: University of Pennsylvania Press.

Bettelheim, Bruno. (1977) *The Uses of Enchantment: The Meaning and Importance of Fairy Tales*. New York: Random House, Vintage Books.

Bhaskar, Roy. (1986) *Scientific Realism and Human Emancipation*. London: Verso.

Black, J.B. and R. Wilensky. (1979a) "An Evaluation of Story Grammars," *Cognitive Science* 3: 213–229.

Boden, D. and D.H. Zimmerman. (1991) *Talk and Social Structure: Studies in Ethnomethodology and Conversation Analysis*. Berkeley: University of California Press.

Bohman, James. (1993) *New Philosophies of Social Science*. Cambridge, MA: MIT Press.

Bonner, Raymond. (1984) *Weakness and Deceit: U.S. Policy and El Salvador*. New York: Times Books.

Boulding, Kenneth. (1956) "General Systems Theory: The Skeleton of a Science" *Management Science* 2: 197–208. Reprinted in General Systems Yearbook I (1956): 11–14.

References

Bozeman, Adda B. (1960) *Politics and Culture in International History*. Princeton, NJ: Princeton University Press.

Brandon, S.G. (1979) *The Trial of Jesus of Nazareth*. New York: Stein & Day.

Braudel, Fernand. (1981–5) *Civilization and Capitalism: 15th-18th Centuries*, especially vol. III, *The Perspective of the World*. (In French, *Le Temps du Monde*.) New York: Harper & Row.

Bremer, Stuart, ed. (1987) *The Globus Model: Computer Simulation of Worldwide Political and Economic Developments*. Boulder, CO: Westview.

Breymond, Claude. (1973) *Logique du Recit*. Paris: Editions du Seuil.

Briggs, Kenneth A. (1983) "Gallup Poll Finds Image of Jesus Somewhat Murky." *New York Times* (Sunday, April 3).

Broad, C.D. (1976) "Leibniz's *Predicate-in-Notion Principle* and Some of Its Consequences." In Harry G. Frankfurt, ed., *Leibniz: A Collection of Critical Essays*. Notre Dame, IN: University of Notre Dame Press.

Brown, W. (1988) *Manhood and Politics*. Totowa, NJ: Rowman & Littlefield.

Bull, Hedley. (1984) *Justice in International Relations*. 1983–84 Hagey Lectures. Waterloo: University of Waterloo Publication Distribution Service.

   (1966) "International Theory: The Case for a Classical Approach." *World Politics* 18 (April): 361–377.

   (1977) *The Anarchical Society: A Study of Order in World Politics*. New York, Columbia University Press.

Bull, Hedley and Adam Watson, eds. (1984) *The Expansion of International Society*. New York, Oxford: Clarendon Press.

Burckhardt, Jacob. (1990[1860]) *The Civilization of the Renaissance in Italy*. London: Penguin.

Burke, Kenneth. (1969) *A Grammar of Motives*. Berkeley & Los Angeles: University of California Press.

Burns, T.R. (1992) "Two Concepts of Human Agency: Rational Choice Theory and the Social Theory of Action." In P. Sztompka, ed., *Human Agency and the Reorientation of Social Theory*. New York: Gordon & Breach.

Burton, John, *et al.* (1974) *The Study of World Society: A London Perspective*. University of Pittsburgh: Occasional Paper (No. 1) of the International Studies Association.

Campbell, David. (1992) *Writing Security: United States Foreign Policy and the Politics of Identity*. Manchester & New York: Manchester University Press.

Campbell, Donald T. (1960) "Blind Variation and Selective Retention in Creative Thought as in Other Knowledge Processes," *Psychological Review* 67/6: 380–400.

   (1961) "Methodological Suggestions from a Comparative Psychology of Knowledge Processes." General Systems *Yearbook* 6: 15–29.

   (1982) "Experiments as Arguments," *Knowledge* 3: 327–337.

Campbell, Joseph. (1972) *The Hero with a Thousand Faces*. Princeton, NJ: Princeton University Press.

Carbonell, Jaime. (1981) *Subjective Understanding: Computer Models of Belief Systems*. Ann Arbor: University of Michigan Press.

Carnap, Rudolph. (1946) *Meaning and Necessity*. Chicago: University of Chicago Press.

Carr, Edward H. (1964[1939]) *The Twenty Years Crisis 1919–1939: An Introduction to the Study of International Relations*. New York: Harper Torchbook.

Chomsky, Noam. (1956). "Three Models for the Description of Language." *IRE Transactions on Information Theory* IT-2 (1956): 113–124.

(1969) *American Power and the New Mandarins*. New York: Pantheon.

Choucri, Nazli and Robert North. (1975) *Nations in Conflict*. San Francisco: W.H. Freeman.

Choucri, Nazli, R. North and S. Yamakage. (1992) *The Challenge of Japan: Before World War II and After*. London & New York: Routledge.

Christensen, R.C., D.A. Garvin, A. Sweet, eds. (1991) *Education for Judgment: The Artistry of Discussion Leadership*. Boston: Harvard Business School.

Cochrane, C.N. (1929) *Thucydides and the Science of History*. New York: Oxford University Press.

Cogan, Marc. (1981) *The Human Thing: The Speeches and Principles of Thucydides' History*. Chicago: University of Chicago Press.

Cognitive Science 17 (January–March 1993). "Special Issue: Situated Action."

Cohen, Joshua. (1986) "An Epistemic Conception of Democracy," *Ethics* 97: 26–38.

(1989a) "Deliberation and Democratic Legitimacy." In A. Hamblin and P. Petit, eds., *The Good Society*. New York & Oxford: Basil Blackwell.

(1989b) "The Economic Basis of Deliberative Democracy," *Social Philosophy and Policy* 6/2: 25–50.

Cohen, Joshua and Joel Rogers. (1984) "After the Fall," *Boston Review* 9 (August): 18–20.

Cohen, Philip R., Jerry Morgan and Martha E. Pollack, eds. (1990) *Intentions in Communication*. Cambridge, MA: MIT Press, Bradford Books.

Collins, Randall. (1987) *Weberian Sociological Theory*. Cambridge: Cambridge University Press.

Connolly, W.E. (1989) *Political Theory and Modernity*. Oxford: Blackwell.

Cornford, Francis M. (1971[1907]) *Thucydides Mythistoricus*. Philadephia: University of Pennsylvania Press.

Crick, Bernard. (1980) *George Orwell: A Life*. Boston: Little, Brown & Company.

Crocker, David A. (1992) "Functioning and Capability: The Foundations of Sen's and Nussbaum's Developmental Ethic," *Political Theory* 20/4: 584–612.

Curtin, Phil. (1984) *Cross-Cultural Trade in World History*. New York: Cambridge University Press.

Dahl, Norman O. (1984) *Practical Reason, Aristotle, and Weakness of the Will*. Minneapolis: University of Minnesota Press.

Dallmayr, Fred R. (1989) "Lifeworld and Communicative Action, Habermas." In *Critical Encounters: Between Philosophy and Politics*. Notre Dame, IN: Notre Dame Press, Ch. 3.

Dallmayr, Fred R. and Thomas A. McCarthy, eds. (1977) *Understanding and Social Inquiry*. Notre Dame, IN: Notre Dame Press.

References

David, Paul. (1985) "Clio and the Economics of QWERTY," *Economic History* 75/2: 332–337.

Davis, Natalie Zemon. (1983) *The Return of Martin Guerre.* Cambridge, MA: Harvard University Press.

de Beaugrande, Robert and Wolfgang Dressler. (1981) *Introduction to Text Linguistics.* London & New York: Longman.

de Grazia, S. (1989) *Machiavelli in Hell.* Princeton: Princeton University Press.

de Romilly, Jacqueline. (1963) *Thucydides and Athenian Imperialism.* New York: Barnes & Noble.

Der Derian, James. (1987) *On Diplomacy: A Genealogy of Western Estrangement.* Oxford: Basil Blackwell.

(1988) "Introducing Philosophical Traditions in International Relations," *Millennium* 17/2: 189–194.

Der Derian, J. and Michael Shapiro. (1989) *International/Intertextual Relations: Postmodern Rereadings of World Politics.* Lexington: Lexington Books.

Deutsch, Karl W. (1958) "Science and Humanistic Knowledge in the Growth of Civilization." In K.W. Deutsch *et al.*, eds., *Science and the Creative Spirit: Essays on Humanistic Aspects of Science.* Toronto: University of Toronto Press, pp. 1–51.

(1963) *The Nerves of Government: Models of Political Communication and Control.* Glencoe: Free Press.

Deutsch, Karl W., *et al.* (1957) *Political Community and the North Atlantic Area.* Princeton: Princeton University Press.

Deutsch, Karl W., Bruno Fritsch, Helio Jaguaribe and Andrei S. Markovitz, eds. (1977) *Problems of World Modeling: Political and Social Implications.* Cambridge, MA: Ballinger.

Deutsch, Karl and Dieter Senghaas. (1975) "The Fragile Sanity of States." In Martin Kilson, ed., *New States in the Modern World.* Cambridge, MA: Harvard University Press.

Devereux, Erik A. (1985) "Game Strategy as Argument: Modeling Generative Role Logics in Dramaturgical SPD Data." Paper delivered at the Annual Meeting of the American Political Science Association, New Orleans. Unpublished.

Diesing, Paul. (1976, originally 1962) *Reason in Society: Five Types of Decisions and Their Social Conditions.* Westport, CT: Greenwood Press.

Dor-Ner, Z. (1991) *Columbus and the Age of Discovery.* New York: Morrow & Company.

Dougherty, James E., and Robert L. Pfaltzgraff. (1981) *Contending Theories of International Relations.* New York: Harper & Row.

Doyle, Michael. (1983) "Kant, Liberal Legacies, and Foreign Affairs," Parts 1 and 2, *Philosophy and Public Affairs* 12/3–4: 205–235, 323–353.

(1986) "Liberalism and World Politics," *American Political Science Review* 80/4: 1151–1170.

Dray, W.H. (1957) *Laws and Explanation in History.* New York: Oxford University Press.

Droysen, Johann Gustav. (1858) *Grundrisse der Historik.*

Ducelle, E. (1980) Bartolomé de Las Casas, *Encyclopedia Britannica*, 15th ed., vol. 10, 684–686.

Duffy, Gavan. (1992) "Concurrent Interstate Conflict Simulations: Testing the Effects of the Serial Assumption." *Mathematical and Computational Modeling* 10: 241–270.

Duffy, Gavan, ed. (1994) *New Directions in Event Data Analysis.* Special Issue of *International Interactions*, vol. XX, 1–2, 1–167.

Dunn, William N. (1982) "Reforms as Arguments," *Knowledge* 3: 293–326.

Eco, Umberto. (1976) "Le Mythe de Superman," *Communications* 24: 24–40.

Edelman, Murray. (1967) *The Symbolic Uses of Politics.* Chicago: University of Illinois Press.

Edsall, Thomas B. (1985) *The New Politics of Inequality.* New York: Norton.

Elshtain, J.B. (no date) "Don't Be Cruel: Reflections on Rortyian Liberalism." Mimeographed.

(1979) "Methodological Sophistication and Conceptual Confusion: A Critique of Mainstream Political Science." In J. Sherman and E.T. Beck, eds., *The Prison of Sex: Essays in the Sociology of Knowledge.* Madison: University of Wisconsin Press, pp. 229–252.

(1987) *Women and War.* New York: Basic Books.

Elster, Jon. (1975) *Leibniz et la formation de l'esprit capitaliste.* Paris: Aubier Montaigne.

(1978) *Logic and Society.* New York: Wiley & Sons.

(1980) "Negation Active et Negation Passive," *Archive for European Sociology* 21.

(1982) "Marxism, functionalism and game theory," *Theory and Society*, 11:453–82.

(1985) *Making Sense of Marx.* Cambridge: Cambridge University Press.

(1989) *Nuts and Bolts for the Social Sciences.* Cambridge: Cambridge University Press.

(1991) "Born to be Immortal: The Constitution-Making Process." Unpublished manuscript of the Cooley Lectures, University of Michigan Law School.

(n.d.) "Logical Foundations." Unpublished, but see Elster (1978).

Epstein, Joshua M. and Robert L. Axtell. (1996) *Growing Artificial Societies: Social Sciences from the Bottom Up.* Washington, DC: Brookings.

Fairfield, Michael and Bruce B. de Mesquita. (1976) "Choosing Sides in Wars." University of Rochester, mimeo.

Falk, Richard. (1981) *A World Order Perspective on Authoritarian Tendencies.* New York: Institute for World Order.

Finley, John. (1939) "The Origins of Thucydides' Style." *Harvard Studies in Classical Philology* 50: 35ff.

(1942) *Thucydides.* Cambridge, MA: Harvard University Press.

Flood, M. (1952) "Some Experimental Games," RM-789. Santa Monica, CA: RAND Corporation.

Forrester, Jay W. (1971) *World Dynamics.* Cambridge, MA: Wright-Allen Press.

References

Frank, R. (1988) *Passions Within Reason: The Strategic Role of the Emotions.* New York: W.W. Norton.

Frankfurt, Harry G., ed. (1976) *Leibniz: A Collection of Critical Essays.* Notre Dame, IN: University of Notre Dame Press.

Freeman, Christopher and Marie Jahoda, eds. (1978) *World Futures: The Great Debate.* London: Martin Robertson.

Freiberg, J.W. (1977) "The Dialectic in China: Maoist and Daoist." *Bulletin of Concerned Asian Scholars* 9: 2–19.

Friedman, J. (1983) "Civilizational Cycles and the History of Primitivism," *Social Analysis* 14.

Friedrich, C.J. (1976) "Philosophical Reflections of Leibniz on Law, Politics, and the State," in Frankfurt, Harry G., ed., *Leibniz: A Collection of Critical Essays.* Notre Dame, IN: University of Notre Dame Press.

Frye, Northrop. (1971) *Anatomy of Criticism: Four Essays.* Princeton, NJ: Princeton University Press.

Fudenberg, D. and E. Maskin. (1986) "The Folk Theorem in Repeated Games with Discounting or Incomplete Information." *Econometrica* 54/3: 533–554.

Fueter, Eduard. (1911) *Geschichte der neuren historiographie.* Munich: Oldenbourg.

Fung, Archon. (1993) "Making Rights Real: Roe Impact on Abortion Access." *Politics and Society* 21/4: 465–504.

Galtung, Johan. (1977 on) *Essays in Methodology,* 3 vols. Copenhagen: Eijlers.
   (1980a) *The True Worlds.* New York: The Free Press.
   (1980b) "Western Social Cosmologies," an invited presentation. Cambridge, MA: MIT, Department of Political Science.

Garst, Daniel. (1989) "Thucydides and Neorealism," *International Studies Quarterly* 33/1: 3–28.

Geertz, Clifford. (1986) " 'From the Native's Point of View': On the Nature of Anthropological Understanding." In Geertz, *Local Knowledge.* New York: Basic Books, Ch. 3.

George, Alexander L. (1993) *Bridging the Gap: Theory & Practice in Foreign Policy.* Washington, DC: US Institute of Peace Press.

George, Jim. (1994) *Discourses of Global Politics: A Critical (Re)Introduction to International Relations.* Boulder: Lynne Rienner.

Gerth, H.H. and C.W. Mills, eds. (1946) *From Max Weber.* New York: Oxford University Press.

Giddens, Anthony. (1985) *The Nation-State and Violence,* vol. II of *A Contemporary Critique of Historical Materialism.* Berkeley & Los Angeles: University of California Press.

Gier, Nicholas F. (1981) *Wittgenstein and Phenomenology: A Comparative Study of the Later Wittgenstein, Husserl, Heidegger, and Merleau-Ponty.* Albany: State University of New York Press.

Gochman, Charles S. and Zeev Maoz. (1984) "Militarized Interstate Disputes, 1816–1976," *Journal of Conflict Resolution* 28/4: 585–617.

Goldstein, Joshua. (1986) *Long Cycles in War and Economic Growth.* Cambridge,

MA: MIT, Ph.D. dissertation. Subsequently published in book form by Yale University Press.

Greenstein, F. and N. Polsby, eds. (1975) *Handbook of Political Science*. Reading, MA: Addison-Wesley.

Grosz, Barbara J. and Candace L. Sidner. (1986) "The Structures of Discourse Structure." In B. Grosz, *et al.*, eds., *Readings in Natural Language Processing*. Los Altos, CA: Morgan Kaufmann.

Gurr, Ted Robert. (1988) "War, Revolution and the Growth of the Coercive State," *Comparative Political Studies* 21: 45–65.

Haas, Ernst B. (1955) "Types of Collective Security: An Examination of Operational Concepts," *American Political Science Review* 49.

(1968) *Collective Security and the Future International System*. Denver: University of Denver Monographs.

(1983) "Regime Decay: Conflict Management and International Organizations, 1945–1981," *International Organization* 37/2: 189–256.

(1990) *When Knowledge is Power: Three Models of Change in International Organizations*. Berkeley & Los Angeles: University of California Press.

Habermas, Jürgen. (1970) "Science and Technology as Ideology." In his *Toward a Rational Society*. Boston: Beacon Press.

(1971) *Knowledge and Human Interests*. Translated by Jeremy J. Shapiro. Boston: Beacon Press.

(1973a) "The Classical Doctrine of Politics in Relation to Social Philosophy." In J. Habermas, *Theory and Practice*. Boston: Beacon Press, pp. 41–81.

(1973b) *Theory and Practice*. Translated by John Viertel. Boston: Beacon Press.

(1977) "Hannah Arendt's Communications Concept of Power," *Social Research* 44/1 (Spring): 3–24.

(1979) *Communication and the Evolution of Society*. Boston: Beacon Press.

(1984 and 1987) *Theory of Communicative Action*, 2 vols. Translated by Thomas McCarthy. Boston: Beacon Press.

(1986) "Life Forms, Morality and the Task of the Philosopher." In his *Autonomy and Solidarity: Interviews*. Edited and Introduced by Peter Dews. London: Verso, pp. 191–216.

(1987) *The Philosophical Discourse of Modernity: Twelve Lectures*. Cambridge, MA: MIT Press.

Hacking, Ian. (1976) "Individual Substance." In Harry G. Frankfurt, ed., *Leibniz: A Collection of Critical Essays*. Notre Dame, IN: University of Notre Dame Press.

Haley, Jay. (1969) *The Power Tactics of Jesus Christ and Other Essays*. New York: Avon.

Halperin, M. (1963) *The Politics of Social Change in the Middle East*. Princeton: Princeton University Press.

Hanke, L. (1970, originally 1959) *Aristotle and the American Indians*. Bloomington: Indiana University Press.

(1974) *All Mankind is One: A Study of the Disputation Between Bartolomé de Las Casas and Juan Gines de Sepúlveda in 1550 on the Intellectual and Religious*

Capacity of the American Indians. De Kalb, IL: Northern Illinois University Press.

Haraway, D. (1989) *Primate Visions: Gender, Race, and Nature in the World of Modern Science.* New York: Routledge.

Hardin, Russell. (1991) "Hobbesian Political Order," *Political Theory* 19, 156–180.

Harff, B. and T.R. Gurr. (1988) "Toward Empirical Theory of Genocides and Politicides: Identification and Measurement of Cases Since 1945," *International Studies Quarterly* 32/3: 359–371.

Harré, Rom. (1980) *Social Being.* Totowa, NJ: Littlefield, Adams & Co.

Harré, Rom and Paul Secord. (1972) *The Explanation of Social Behavior.* Totowa, NJ: Rowman & Littlefield.

Havel, Vaclav. (1992) "The End of the Modern Era." *New York Times,* OpEd page (March 1).

(1994) "The New Measure of Man." *New York Times,* OpEd page (July 8).

Hempel, Carl. (1958) *Fundamentals of Concept Formation in Empirical Science.* Chicago: University of Chicago Press.

Herrera, Amílcar D., *et al.* (1976) *Catastrophe or New Society? A Latin American World Model.* Ottawa: International Development Research Centre.

Herz, John. (1976) *The Nation-State and the Crisis of World Politics.* New York: David McKay Co., Inc.

Hiley, D.R., J.F. Bohman and R. Shusterman. (1991) *The Interpretive Turn: Philosophy, Science, Culture.* Ithaca: Cornell University Press.

Hintikka, Jaakko. (1974) "Practical vs. Theoretical Reason – An Ambiguous Legacy." In Stephan Korner, ed., *Practical Reason,* Bristol Conference on Critical Philosophy. New Haven: Yale University Press.

(1976) In Harry G. Frankfurt, ed., *Leibniz: A Collection of Critical Essays.* Notre Dame, IN: University of Notre Dame Press.

Hirschman, A. (1977) *The Passions and the Interests: Political Arguments for Capitalism Before Its Triumph.* Princeton: Princeton University Press.

(1991) *The Rhetoric of Reaction: Perversity, Futility, Jeopardy.* Cambridge, MA: Belknap Press.

Hobbes, Thomas. (1962, orig. 1651) *Leviathan.* Edited by Michael Oakeshott. New York: Collier Books.

Hoffmann, Stanley. (1960) *Contemporary Theory in International Relations.* Englewood Cliffs, NJ: Prentice-Hall.

(1966) "Rousseau on War and Peace." In his *The State of War.* New York: Praeger.

(1975) "Notes on the Elusiveness of Modern Power," *International Journal* 30/2: 183–206.

(1977) "An American Social Science: International Relations." *Daedalus* 106/5: 41–60.

(1986) "Hedley Bull and His Contribution to International Relations," *International Affairs* 62/2: 179–195.

Hofstadter, Douglas R. (1983) "Metamagical Themas: Virus-Like Sentences and Self-Replicating Structures." *Scientific American* 218/1 (January): 14–26.

Holiday, Anthony. (1988) *Moral Powers: Normative Necessity in Language and History*. London & New York: Routledge.

Hollis, Martin. (1987) *The Cunning of Reason*. Cambridge: Cambridge University Press.

Hollis, Martin and Steve Smith. (1991) *Explaining and Understanding International Relations*. Oxford: Clarendon Press.

Holsti, Kal. J. (1985) *The Dividing Discipline*, London: Allen & Paul.

Holz, Hans Heinz. (1958) *Leibniz*. Stuttgart: Kohlhammer Verlag.

Homer-Dixon, Thomas F. and Roger S. Karapin. (1989) "Graphical Argument Analysis: A New Approach to Understanding Arguments, Applied to a Debate about the Window of Vulnerability," *International Studies Quarterly* 33 (1989): 389–410.

Hudson, Valerie, ed. (1991) *Artificial Intelligence and International Politics*. Boulder: Westview Press.

Hunt, Michael. (1987) *Ideology and Foreign Policy*. New Haven: Yale University Press.

Hurwitz, Roger. (1989) "Strategic and Social Fictions in the Prisoner's Dilemma." In J. Der Derian and M. Shapiro, eds., *International/Intertextual Relations*. Lexington, MA: Lexington Books.

(1991) *Reason and Resolution: Strategic and Social Rationality in Resolving Prisoner's Dilemmas*. Ph.D. dissertation, Department of Political Science, M.I.T.

International Studies Association. (1992) *International Studies Newsletter* 19/,4.

Invernizzi, Marcia A., and Mary P. Abouzeid. (1995) "One Story Map Does Not Fit All: A Cross-Cultural Analysis of Children's Written Story Retellings." *Journal of Narrative and Life History* 5/1: 1–19.

Ishiguro, Hidé. (1976) "Leibniz' Theory of the Ideality of Relations." In Harry G. Frankfurt, ed., *Leibniz: A Collection of Critical Essays*. Notre Dame, IN: University of Notre Dame Press.

Jaeger, Werner. (1976) *Paideia: The Ideals of Greek Culture*. Translated by G. Higet. New York: Oxford University Press.

Jakobson, Roman. (1973) "Commentary." In Aleksandr Afanasev, ed., and Norbert Guterman, trans., *Russian Fairy Tales*. New York: Pantheon Books.

Jervis, Robert. (1978) "Cooperation Under the Security Dilemma," *World Politics* 30,1/2: 167–216.

Johnson, J. (1988) "Symbolic Action and the Limits of Strategic Rationality: On the Logic of Working-Class Collective Action." In *Political Power and Social Theory* 7: 211–248.

Johnson, James Turner. (1975) *Ideology, Reason, and the Limitation of War*. Princeton, NJ: Princeton University Press.

(1981) *Just War Tradition and the Restraint of War*. Princeton, NJ: Princeton University Press.

References

Johnson, Mark. (1987) *The Body in the Mind: The Bodily Basis of Meaning, Imagination, and Reason*. Chicago: University of Chicago Press.

Kagan, Donald. (1975) "The Speeches in Thucydides and the Mytilene Debate." In Donald Kagan, ed., *Studies in the Greek Historians*. Yale Classical Studies, XXIV. Cambridge: Cambridge University Press.

Kaplan, Abraham. (1964) *The Conduct of Inquiry*, San Francisco: Chandler.

Kaplan, Morton A. (1957). *System and Process in International Politics*. New York: Wiley & Sons.

   (1966) "The New Great Debate: Traditionalism vs. Science in International Relations," *World Politics* 19 (October): 1–21.

Kaplan, Morton A., and Nicholas deB. Katzenbach. (1961) *The Political Foundations of International Law*. New York: Wiley & Sons.

Kauffman, Stuart. (1995) *At Home in the Universe*. New York: Oxford University Press.

Keisler, H. Jerome. (1976) *Foundations of Infinitesimal Calculus*. Boston: Prindle, Weber & Schmidt.

Kende, Istvan. (1978) "Wars of Ten Years (1967–1976)," *Journal of Peace Research* 15/3: 227–241.

Kent, Thomas. (1991) "Hermeneutics and Genre: Bakhtin and the Problem of Communicative Interaction. In Hiley, Bohman and Shusterman, eds., *The Interpretive Turn*, pp. 282–303.

Keohane, Robert. (1983) "Theory of World Politics." In Ada W. Finifter, ed., *Political Science*. Washington, DC: American Political Science Association.

   (1984) *After Hegemony*. Princeton, NJ: Princeton University Press.

   (1988) "International Institutions: Two Approaches," *International Studies Quarterly* 32/4: 379–396.

Keohane, Robert O., ed. (1986) *Neorealism and Its Critics*. New York: Columbia University Press.

Keohane, Robert O. and Joseph P. Nye. (1977) *Power and Interdependence*. Boston: Little, Brown.

Khaldun, Ibn. (1969[1377]) *The Muqaddimah: An Introduction to History*. Translated by Franz Rosenthal, edited and abridged by N.J. Dawood. Princeton: Princeton University Press.

King, Gary. (1989) *Unifying Political Methodology: The Likelihood Theory of Statistical Inference*. Cambridge: Cambridge University Press.

King, Gary, Robert O. Keohane and Sidney Verba. (1994) *Designing Social Inquiry: Scientific Inference in Qualitative Research*. Princeton, NJ: Princeton University Press.

Kinser, Samuel. (1981) "Annaliste Paradigm?" *American Historical Review* 86/1 (1981): 63–105.

Knorr, Klaus and James Rosenau, eds. (1969) *Contending Approaches to International Politics*. Princeton, NJ: Princeton University Press.

Koslowski, Rey and Friedrich V. Kratochwil. (1994) "Understanding Change in International Politics: The Soviet Empire's Demise and the International System," *International Organization* 48: 215–247.

Kostecki, Wojcieck. (1985) "A Marxist Paradigm of International Relations," *International Studies Notes* 12/1: 19–21.

Kratochwil, Friedrich. (1982) "On the Notion of Interest in International Relations," *International Organization* 36 (Winter): 1–30.

(1986) "Of Systems, Boundaries, and Territoriality: An Inquiry into the Formation of the State System," *World Politics* 39 (October): 27–52.

(1989) *Rules, Norms, and Decisions: On the Conditions of Practical and Legal Reasoning in International Relations and Domestic Affairs.* Cambridge Studies in International Relations. Cambridge: Cambridge University Press.

Kropotkin, P.A. (1973) "Conversation with Lenin." In Kropotkin's *Selected Writings on Anarchism and Revolution.* Cambridge, MA: MIT Press, pp. 324–333.

Kuhn, Thomas S. (1962) *The Structure of Scientific Revolutions.* Chicago: University of Chicago Press.

(1970) *The Structure of Scientific Revolutions,* 2nd, enlarged ed. Chicago: University of Chicago Press.

(1977) *The Essential Tension: Selected Studies in the Scientific Tradition and Change.* Chicago: University of Chicago Press.

Lakatos, Imre and A. Musgrave, eds. (1970) *Criticism and the Growth of Knowledge.* London & New York: Cambridge University Press.

Lake, D.A. (1992) "Powerful Pacifists: Democratic States and War," *American Political Science Review* 86/1: 24–37.

Lakoff, George. (1962) "From Shakespearean Myth Criticism Toward a Grammar for Narrative." MIT Bachelor's Thesis supervised by N. Holland. Available from MIT Archives.

(1990) *Women, Fire and Dangerous Things.* Chicago: University of Chicago Press.

(1991) "Metaphor and War: The Metaphor System Used to Justify War in the Gulf," *Journal of Urban and Cultural Studies* 2/1: 59–72.

Langton, C.G., ed. (1989) *Artificial Life: The Proceedings of an Interdisciplinary Workshop on the Synthesis and Simulation of Living Systems...1987.* Reading, MA: Addison-Wesley.

Lapid, Yosef. (1989) "The Third Debate: On the Prospects of International Theory in a Post-Positivist Era," *International Studies Quarterly* 33/3 (September): 235–54.

Las Casas, Bartolomé de. (1878) *Historia de las Indes.* Mexico City: Biblioteca Mexicana.

(1971a) *A Selection of His Writings.* Translated and edited by George Sanderlin. New York: Knopf.

(1971B) *History of the Indies.* Translated and edited by A. Collard. New York: Harper and Row Torchbook.

Lasswell, Harold D. (1934, 1950) *World Politics and Personal Insecurity.* Reprinted in Harold D. Lasswell, Charles E. Merriam and T.V. Smith, *A Study of Power.* Glencoe, IL: Free Press.

(1941) "The Garrison State," *American Journal of Sociology* 46 (January): 455–468.

References

(1951a) "Democratic Character." In *The Political Writings of Harold Lasswell.* Glencoe, IL: Free Press, pp. 465–525.

(1951b, 1965) *The World Revolution of Our Time,* reprinted and augmented as Chapter 2 of Harold D. Lasswell and Daniel Lerner, eds., *World Revolutionary Elites: Studies in Coercive Ideological Movements.* Cambridge, MA: MIT Press.

(1967) "The Social and Economic Framework of War and Peace." In Carmine D. Clemente and Donald B. Lindsley, eds., *Aggression and Defense.* Berkeley: University of California Press, 317–325. Previously available as a University of California Medical School, Brain Research Institute, Los Angeles conference paper, November 17, 1965.

(1968) "Toward World Community Now." In *Alternatives to Violence: A Stimulus to Dialogue.* New York: Time-Life Books, pp. 118–126.

(1969, 1979) "Must Science Serve Political Power?" Paper for the American Psychological Association (31 August 1969). In Harold Lasswell, Daniel Lerner and Hans Speier, eds., *Propaganda and Communication in World History,* vol. III, *A Pluralizing World in Formation,* pp. 3–15. Honolulu: University Press of Hawaii, 1979.

Lasswell, Harold D. and Abraham Kaplan. (1950) *Power and Society: A Framework for Political Inquiry.* New Haven: Yale University Press.

Lefebvre, Vladimir. (1982) *Algebra of Conscience: A Comparative Analysis of Western and Soviet Ethical Systems.* Dordrecht & Boston: Reidel.

Lehnert, Wendy G. (1981) "Plot Units and Narrative Summarizations." *Cognitive Science* 4 (1981): 293–331.

Lehnert, Wendy C., Hayward R. Alker, Jr. and Daniel K. Schneider. (1983) "The Heroic Jesus: The Affective Plot Structure of Toynbee's *Christus Patiens.*" In Sarah K. Burton and Douglas D. Short, eds., *Proceedings of the Sixth International Conference on Computers and the Humanities.* Rockville, MD: Computer Science Press.

Lehnert, Wendy G., John B. Black and Brian J. Reiser. (1981) "Summarizing Narratives." *Proceedings of the 7th International Joint Conference on Artificial Intelligence.* Vancouver, British Columbia.

Lehnert, Wendy G. & Cynthia Loiselle. (1985) "Plot Unit Recognition for Narratives." In G. Tonfoni, ed., *Artificial Intelligence and Text Understanding, Quaderni di Ricerca Linguistica* 6 (1985): 49–94. Parma: Edizione Zara, Via Toscana, 80.

Leibniz, G. (1972) *The Political Writings of Leibniz.* Translated, edited, and with introduction by Patrick Riley. Cambridge: Cambridge University Press.

(1976) *Monadology and Other Philosophic Essays.* Translated by Paul and Anne Martin Schrecher. Indianapolis, IN: Bobbs-Merrill.

LeVine, R.A. and D.T. Campbell. (1972) *Ethnocentrism: Theories of Conflict, Ethnic Attitudes, and Group Behavior.* New York: Wiley.

Lorenzen, Paul and Kuno Lorenz. (1978) *Dialogische Logik.* Darmstadt: Wissenschaftliche Buchgesellschaft.

438

Lovejoy, Arthur O. (1936, 1964, 1976) *The Great Chain of Being: A Study of the History of an Idea*. Cambridge, MA: Harvard University Press.

(1976) "Plenitude and Sufficient Reason in Leibniz and Spinoza." In Harry G. Frankfurt, ed., *Leibniz: A Collection of Critical Essays*. Notre Dame, IN: University of Notre Dame Press.

Luhmann, Niklas. (1990) *Essays on Self Reference*. New York: Columbia University Press.

Lyotard, Jean-François. (1984) *The Postmodern Condition*. Minneapolis: University of Minnesota Press. With an introduction by Frederic Jameson.

Machiavelli, Niccolò. (1988, 1990) *Florentine Histories*. Translated by L.F. Banfield and H.C. Mansfield, Jr., Introduction by H.C. Mansfield, Jr. Princeton: Princeton University Press.

MacIntyre, A. (1981, 1984) *After Virtue*. South Bend, IN: University of Notre Dame.

Mahdi, Muhsin. (1964) *Ibn Khaldun's Philosophy of History: A Study in the Philosophical Foundation of the Science of Culture*. Chicago: University of Chicago Press.

Maier, Charles S. (1987) "The Politics of Time: Changing Paradigms of Collective Time and Private Time in the Modern Era." In Charles S. Maier, ed., *Changing Boundaries of the Political*. Cambridge: Cambridge University Press.

Makkreel, Rudolf A. (1975) *Dilthey: Philosopher of the Human Studies*. Princeton, NJ: Princeton University Press.

Mallery, John. (1994) "Beyond Correlation: Bringing Artificial Intelligence to Events Data." *International Interactions* (Autumn).

Mandel, Ernest. (1980) *Long Waves of Capitalist Development: The Marxist Interpretation*. New York: Cambridge University Press.

Mandeville, Bernard. (1988) *The Fable of the Bees: or Private Vices, Publick Benefits*, 2 vols., with a commentary critical, historical and explanatory by F.B. Kaye. Oxford: Clarendon Press. Reprinted by Liberty Press/Liberty Classics, Indianapolis, from the 1924 edition published by the Clarendon Press, Oxford.

Mandler, Jean M. and Nancy S. Johnson. (1977) "Remembrance of Things Parsed: Story Structure and Recall," *Cognitive Psychology* 9: 111–151.

(1980) "On Throwing Out the Baby with the Bathwater: A Reply to Black and Wilensky's Evaluation of Story Grammars," *Cognitive Science* 4: 305–312.

Mansfield, H. (1981) "Machiavelli's Political Science," *American Political Science Review* 75/2: 293–305.

March, James G. and Johan P. Olson. (1984) "The New Institutionalism: Organizational Factors in Political Life," *American Political Science Review* 79: 734–749.

Marcuse, Herbert. (1966) *Eros and Civilization*. Boston: Beacon Press.

(1987) *Hegel's Ontology and the Theory of Historicity*. Translated and Introduction by S. Benhabib. Cambridge, MA: MIT Press.

Marx, Karl and Friedrich Engels. (1950) "Du Kennst Meine Bewunderung für Leibniz," *Briefwechsel*, Band IV. East Berlin.

Masterman, M. (1970) "The Nature of a Paradigm." In Imre Lakatos and R. Musgrave, eds., *Criticism and the Growth of Knowledge*. London & New York: Cambridge University Press.

Masters, Roger. (1989) *The Nature of Politics*. New Haven: Yale University Press.

McCloskey, D.N. (1990) *If You're So Smart: The Narrative of Economic Expertise*. Chicago: University of Chicago Press.

McKeon, Richard. (1941) *The Basic Works of Aristotle*. Edited with an Introduction. New York: Random House.

McKnight, Stephen A. (1978) "The Evolution of Voegelin's Theory of Politics and History, 1911–1975." In Stephen A. McKnight, ed., *Eric Voegelin's Search for Order in History*. Baton Rouge, LA & London: Louisiana State University Press.

McKnight, Stephen A., ed. (1978) *Eric Voegelin's Search for Order in History*. Baton Rouge, LA & London: Louisiana State University Press.

Mead, George H. (1934) *Mind, Self & Society: From the Standpoint of a Social Behaviorist*. Chicago: University of Chicago Press.

Mead, Margaret. (1940) "Warfare is Only an Invention – Not a Biological Necessity," *Asia* 40/8: 402–405.

Meadows, Donella, John Richardson and Gerhart Bruckmann. (1982) *Groping in the Dark: The First Decade in Global Modeling*. New York: John Wiley.

Meehan, J.R. (1976) "The Metanovel: Writing Stories by Computer." New Haven: Yale University, Department of Computer Science Research Report 74.

(undated) "Using Planning Structures to Generate Stories," *American Journal of Computational Linguistics*, Microfiche 33: 78–91.

Mefford, Dwain. (1985) "Changes in Foreign Policy Across Time: The logical analysis of a succession of decision problems using logic programming," pp. 401–423. In Urs Luterbacher and Michael Ward, eds., *Dynamic Models of International Conflict*. Boulder: Lynne Rienner.

(1990) "Case-Based Reasoning, Legal Reasoning, and the Study of Politics," *Political Behavior* 12: 125–158.

Menendez Pidal, R. (1963) *El Padre de las Casas: Su Doble Personalidad*. Madrid: Espasa-Calpe.

Merritt, Richard L. and Bruce M. Russett, eds. (1981) *From National Development to Global Community*. London: Allen & Unwin.

Merritt, Richard L., Robert G. Muncaster and Dina A. Zinnes, eds. (1993) *International Event-Data Developments: DDIR Phase II*. Ann Arbor: University of Michigan Press.

Meszaros, Istvan. (1972) *Marx's Theory of Alienation*. New York & London: Harper Torchbooks.

Mill, John Stuart. (1980[1843]) *A System of Logic*. Charlottesville, VA: Ibis Publishing.

Miller, George, and Noam Chomsky. (1963) "Finitary Models of Language

Users" In Duncan Luce *et al.*, eds., *Handbook of Mathematical Psychology*, vol. II. New York: J. Wiley & Sons, pp. 468–488.

Montagu, Ashley. (1978) *Learning Non-Aggression*. New York: Oxford University Press.

Montagu, Ashley, ed. (1956) *Toynbee and History: Critical Essays and Reviews*. Boston: Porter Sargent.

Moore, G.E. (1920) "External and Internal Relations," *Proceedings of the Aristotelian Society* 20: 276–309.

Morgenthau, Hans. (1978) *Politics Among Nations*, 5th ed. New York: Knopf.

Moses, Lincoln, Richard Brody, *et al.* (1967) "Scaling Data on Inter-Nation Action," *Science* (May 26).

Moy, Roland F. (1971) *A Computer Simulation of Democratic Political Development: Tests of the Lipset and Moore Models*. Beverly Hills, CA: Sage Publications.

Nagel, Ernst. (1957) *Logic Without Metaphysics*. Glencoe, IL: Free Press.

 (1961) *The Structure of Science*. New York: Harcourt, Brace & World.

Neustadt, Richard E., and Ernest R. May. (1986). *Thinking in Time: The Uses of History for Decision-makers*. New York: The Free Press.

Niou, Emerson M.S. and Peter C. Ordeshook. (forthcoming) "Notes on Constitutional Change in the ROC: Presidential versus Parliamentary Government." *Chinese Political Science Review*.

Nowak, M. and K. Sigmund. (1992) "Tit for Tat in Heterogeneous Populations," *Nature* 335 (January 16): 250–253.

Nussbaum, Martha C. (1978) *Aristotle's De Motu Animalium*. Text with translation, commentary, and interpretive essays. Princeton, NJ: Princeton University Press.

 (1986) *The Fragility of Goodness: Luck and Ethics in Greek Tragedy and Philosophy*. Cambridge, UK: Cambridge University Press.

 (1989) "Martha Nussbaum, Classicist and Philosopher." Interview with Bill Moyers in Betty Sue Flowers, ed., *Bill Moyers: A World of Ideas*. New York: Doubleday, pp. 447–459.

 (1990) *Love's Knowledge: Essays on Philosophy and Literature*. New York: Oxford University Press.

 (1992) "Human Functioning and Social Justice: In Defense of Aristotelian Essentialism," *Political Theory* 20/2: 202–246.

Nussbaum, M. and A. Sen, eds. (1993) *The Quality of Life*. Oxford: Clarendon Press.

Olafson, Frederick. (1977) *The Dialectic of Action: A Philosophical Interpretation of History and the Humanities*. Chicago: University of Chicago Press.

Ollman, Bertell. (1976) *Alienation: Marx's Conception of Man in Capitalist Society*. Cambridge & New York: Cambridge University Press.

Onuf, Nicholas G. (1989) *World of Our Making: Rules and Rule in Social Theory and International Relations*. Columbia, SC: University of South Carolina Press.

 (1994) "Imagined Republics." *Alternatives* 19/3: 315–338.

 (1995) "Levels." *European Journal of International Relations* 1/1: 35–58.

References

Orwell, George. (1940) "Red, White, and Brown." Review of Franz Borkenau, *The Totalitarian Enemy.* In *Time and Tide* (4 May 1940).

— (1941) *The Lion and the Unicorn: Socialism and the English Genius.* Reprinted in Orwell and Angus, eds., *The Collected Essays, Journalism and Letters of George Orwell,* vol II, *My Country Right or Left, 1940–1943.* New York & London: Harcourt Brace Jovanovich, 1968, pp. 56–108.

— (1943–5) "Notes on Nationalism." In Orwell and Angus, eds., *The Collected Essays, Journalism and Letters of George Orwell,* vol. III, *As I Please, 1943–1945.* New York & London: Harcourt Brace Jovanovich, 1968, pp. 361–380.

— (1948) "Marx and Russia," *Observer* (London), 15 February 1948.

— (no date) "James Burnham and the Managerial Revolution," in Orwell and Angus, eds., *The Collected Essays, Journalism and Letters of George Orwell,* vol. IV, *In Front of Your Nose.* New York & London: Harcourt Brace Jovanovich, 1968, pp. 160–181.

Orwell, Sonia and Ian Angus, eds. (1968) *The Collected Essays, Journalism and Letters of George Orwell,* 4 vols. New York & London: Harcourt Brace Jovanovich.

Ostrom, Eleanor. (1990) *Governing the Commons.* Cambridge: Cambridge University Press.

The Oxford English Dictionary, unabridged ed. (1972) Oxford: Clarendon Press, 1933. Plus *Supplement to the Oxford English Dictionary* similarly published in 1972.

Oye, Kenneth A. (1985) "Explaining Cooperation Under Anarchy: Hypotheses and Strategies," *World Politics* 38/1: 3–24. The entire issue of *World Politics* has been separately published by Princeton Press (1985) as Kenneth A. Oye, ed., *Cooperation Under Anarchy.*

Pagden, A. (1987) "Dispossessing the Barbarian: The Language of Spanish Thomism and the Debate over the Property Rights of the American Indians." In A. Pagden, ed., *The Languages of Political Theory in Early-Modern Europe.* Cambridge: Cambridge University Press, pp. 79–98.

Pagden, A. (1991) "Ius et Factum: Text and Experience in the Writings of Bartolomé de Las Casas," *Representations* 33: 147–162.

Pagels, Elaine. (1979) *The Gnostic Gospels.* New York: Random House.

Patomäki, Heikki. (1992) *Critical Realism and World Politics.* Turku: Department of Political Science, University of Turku.

Paz, Octavio. (1987) "Food of the Gods." *New York Review of Books* 34/3 (February 26): 3–7.

Pico della Mirandola, Giovanni. (1965[1484]) *Oration on the Dignity of Man, On Being and the One, Heptaplus.* Indianapolis: Bobbs-Merrill.

Piedra, J. (1989) "The Game of Critical Arrival." *Diacritics* (Spring): 34–61.

Pitkin, H.F. (1984) *Fortune is a Woman: Gender and Politics in the Thought of Niccolo Machiavelli.* Berkeley: University of California.

Pocock, J. G. A. (1975) *The Machiavellian Moment: Florentine Political Thought and the Atlantic Republican Tradition.* Princeton, NJ: Princeton University Press.

Polanyi, Livia. (1989) *Telling the American Story: A Structural and Cultural Analysis of Conversational Storytelling*. Cambridge, MA: MIT Press.

Pollock, John L. (1992) "How to Reason Defeasibly," *Artificial Intelligence* 57: 1–42.

Popper, Karl. (1959) *The Logic of Scientific Discovery*. New York: Basic Books.

(1961) *The Patterns of Discovery*. Cambridge: Cambridge University Press.

Poulantzas, Nicos A. (1968) *Pouvoir politique et classes sociales*. Paris: F. Maspero.

Poundstone, William. (1993) *Prisoner's Dilemma*. New York: Anchor Books, Doubleday.

Prince, Gerald. (1973) *A Grammar of Stories*. The Hague: Mouton.

Propp, V. (1928, 1977) *Morphology of the Folktale*, 2nd ed. Austin & London: University of Texas.

Quester, George. (1970) *Nuclear Diplomacy: The First Twenty-Five Years*. New York: Dunellen Co.

(1977) *Offense and Defense in the International System*. New York: Wiley.

Radnitzky, Gerard. (1973) *Contemporary Schools of Metascience*, 3 vols. in one ed. Chicago: Henry Regnery.

Raglan, Lord. (1965) "The Hero of Tradition." In Alan Dundes, ed., *The Study of Folklore*. Englewood Cliffs, NJ: Prentice Hall, pp. 142–157.

Rank, Otto. (1964[1909]) *The Myth of the Birth of the Hero*. New York: Vintage.

Rapoport, Anatol. (1960) *Fights, Games and Debates*. Ann Arbor: University of Michigan Press.

Rapoport, Anatol and A. Chammah. (1965) *Prisoner's Dilemma: A Study in Conflict and Cooperation*. Ann Arbor, MI: University of Michigan Press.

Reichman, Rachel. (1985) *How to Get Computers to Talk like You and Me*. Cambridge, MA: MIT Press.

Rescher, Nicholas. (1977) *Dialectics: A Controversy-Oriented Approach to the Theory of Knowledge*. Albany: State University of New York at Albany Press.

(1987a) "Philosophical Taxonomy as a Philosophical Issue." In his *Forbidden Knowledge and Other Essays on the Philosophy of Cognition*. Dordrecht: D. Reidel Publishing Company, Chapter 10.

(1987b) "Rationality and Consistency." In his *Forbidden Knowledge and Other Essays on the Philosophy of Cognition*. Dordrecht: D. Reidel Publishing Company, Chapter 10.

Richardson, George P. (1991) *Feedback Thought in Social Science and Systems Theory*. Philadelphia: University of Pennsylvania Press.

Richardson, J.L. (1990) "The Academic Study of International Relations." In J.D.B. Miller and J. Vincent, eds., *Order and Violence: Hedley Bull and International Relations*. New York: Oxford University Press.

Ricoeur, Paul. (1981) *Hermeneutics and the Human Sciences*. Edited and translated by John B. Thompson. Cambridge: Cambridge University Press, Chapter 8.

(1983) *Temps et recit*, Tome I. Paris: Editions Du Seuil.

Riegal, Klaus. (1976) "The Systematization of Dialectic Logic for the Study of Development and Change," *Human Development* 19: 321–324.

References

Riker, William. (1984) "The Heresthetics of Constitution-Making: The Presidency in 1787, with Comments on Determinism and Rational Choice," *American Political Science Review* 78/1: 1–16.

Ristad, E.S. (1993) *The Language Complexity Game.* Cambridge, MA: MIT Press.

Roberts, Julian. (1992) *The Logic of Reflection: German Philosophy in the Twentieth Century.* New Haven: Yale University Press.

Robinson, A. (1976) *Non-Standard Analysis.* Amsterdam: North-Holland Publishing Co.

Rogers, Hartley. (1967) *Theory of Recursive Functions and Effective Compatibility.* New York: McGraw-Hill.

Roig, Charles. (1977) *Symboles et Sociétés.* Zurich & Las Vegas: Laing.

Root, D. (1988) "The Imperial Signifier: Todorov and the Conquest of Mexico," *Telos* 75 (Spring): 197–219.

Rose, Carol M. (1994) "Property as Storytelling: Perspectives from Game Theory, Narrative Theory, Feminist Theory." In her *Property and Persuasion: Essays on the History, Theory and Rhetoric of Ownership.* Boulder: Westview, pp. 25–45.

Rosecrance, Richard. (1986) *The Rise of the Trading State: Commerce and Conquest in the Modern World.* New York: Basic Books.

Rosenau, James N. (1963) *Calculated Control as a Unifying Concept in the Study of International Relations.* Princeton, NJ: Center for International Studies, Woodrow Wilson School of International Affairs, Princeton University.

(1970) *Adaptation of National Societies.* New York: McCab-Seiler Publishing Company.

Rosenau, P. (1992) *Post-Modernism and the Social Sciences: Insights, Inroads, and Intrusions.* Princeton: Princeton University Press.

Rosenberg, Harold. (1965) *The Tradition of the New.* New York: McGraw-Hill.

Rothkin, K. (1992) *Communication and Coordination in Asymmetric Sequential Prisoners' Dilemma Games.* B.S. Thesis, Department of Political Science, MIT.

Ruggie, John G. (1983) "Continuity and Transformation in the World Polity: Toward a Neorealist Synthesis," *World Politics* 35/2: 261–285.

Rumelhart, Donald F. (1975) "Notes on a Schema for Stories." In D.G. Bobrow and A.M. Collins, eds., *Representation and Understanding.* New York: Academic Press.

(1977) "Understanding and Summarizing Brief Stories." In D. Laberge and S. Samuels, eds., *Basic Processing in Reading, Perception, and Comprehension.* Hillsdale, NJ: Lawrence Erlbaum Associates.

Russell, B. (1976) "Recent Work on the Philosophy of Leibniz." In Harry G. Frankfurt, ed., *Leibniz: A Collection of Critical Essays.* Notre Dame, IN: University of Notre Dame Press.

Russett, Bruce. (1993) *Grasping the Democratic Peace: Principles for a Post-Cold War World.* Princeton, NJ: Princeton University Press.

Ryan, Marie-Laure. (1979) "Linguistic Models in Narratology: From Structuralism to Generative Semantics," *Semiotica* 28/1–2: 127–155.

Said, Edward. (1979) *Orientalism.* New York: Vintage Books/Random House.

Salkever, Stephen. (1981) "Aristotelian Social Science," *Political Theory* 9/4: 479–508.

Schank, Roger C. and B.L. Nash-Weber. (1976) *Theoretical Issues in Natural Language Processing*. Association for Computational Linguistics.

Schank, Roger C. and Robert P. Abelson. (1977) *Scripts, Plans, Goals and Understanding: An Inquiry Into Human Knowledge Structures*. Hillsdale, NJ: Lawrence Erlbaum Associates.

Schank, Roger C., Alex Kass and Christopher K. Riesbeck, eds. (1994) *Inside Case-Based Explanation*. Hillsdale, NJ: Lawrence Erlbaum Associates.

Schelling, Thomas. (1960) *The Strategy of Conflict*. Cambridge, MA: Harvard University Press.

Schlatter, Richard. (1975) *Hobbes' Thucydides*. New Brunswick, NJ: Rutgers University Press.

Schmidt, Alfred. (1981) *History and Structure: An Essay on Hegelian-Marxist and Structuralist Theories of History*. Cambridge, MA: MIT Press.

Schotter, A. (1981) *The Economic Theory of Social Institutions*. Cambridge: Cambridge University Press.

Scott, James C. (1976) *The Moral Economy of the Peasant*. New Haven: Yale University Press.

Searle, John R. (1969) *Speech Acts: An Essay in the Philosophy of Language*. New York & London: Cambridge University Press.

(1979) *Expression and Meaning*. London: Cambridge University Press.

(1983) *Intentionality*. London: Cambridge University Press.

Seed, P. (1991) " 'Failing to Marvel': Atahualpa's Encounter with the Word." *Latin American Research Review* 26/1: 7–32.

Sen, Amartya. (1982) "Choice, Orderings and Morality." In A. Sen, *Choice, Welfare and Measurement*. Cambridge, MA: MIT Press, Chapter 3.

(1985) "Goals, Commitment, and Identity," *Journal of Law, Economics, and Organization* 1: 341–355.

(1986) "Rationality, Interest, and Identity." In A. Foxley, M.S. McPherson and G. O'Donell, eds., *Development, Democracy, and the Art of Trespassing: Essays in Honor of Albert O. Hirschman*. Notre Dame, IN: University of Notre Dame Press.

(1987) *On Ethics and Economics*. Oxford: Basil Blackwell.

(1992) *Inequality Reexamined*. Oxford: Clarendon Press.

Sergeev, Victor. (1986) "Strucktura politicherskoy argumentatsii v 'Meliyskom dialoge' Fukidida" (The structure of argumentation in Thucydides' Melian dialogue). In B.M. Kloss, ed., *Matematika v. izuchenii srednevekovykh povestvovatel'nyich istochnikov*. Moscow: Nauka.

Sevilla-Casas, E. (1977) *Western Expansion and Indigenous Peoples: The Heritage of Las Casas*. The Hague: Mouton.

Shapiro, Michael. (1981) *Language and Political Understanding: The Politics of Discursive Practices*. New Haven: Yale University Press.

(1988) *The Politics of Representation: Writing Practices in Biography, Photography, and Policy Analysis*. Madison: University of Wisconsin Press.

(1991) "Sovereignty and Exchange in the Orders of Modernity," *Alternatives* 16: 447–477.

Sherman, Frank L. (1994) "SHERFACS." In G. Duffy, ed. (1994).

Simon, Herbert A. (1962) "The Architecture of Complexity," *Proceedings of the American Philosophical Society* 106/6. Variously reprinted.

(1985) "Human Nature in Politics," *American Political Science Review* 79: 293–304.

Singer, J. David. (1969) "The Incompleat Theorist: Insight Without Evidence." In Klaus Knorr and James Rosenau, eds., *Contending Approaches to International Politics*. Princeton, NJ: Princeton University Press.

(1970) "Escalation and Control in International Conflict: A Simple Feedback Model," *General Systems* 15: 163–173.

Singer, J. David and Melvyn Small. (1980) "Patterns in International Warfare, 1816–1965," *Annals* (September): 145–155.

(1972) *The Wages of War: A Statistical Handbook.* New York: Wiley.

Skinner, Q. (1978) *The Foundations of Modern Political Thought*, vol. I, *The Renaissance*, vol. II, *The Age of Reformation.* Cambridge: Cambridge University Press.

Slade, Stephen. (1994) *Goal-Based Decision Making: An Interpersonal Model.* Hillsdale, NJ: Lawrence Erlbaum Associates.

Small, Melvyn and J. David Singer. (1982) *Resort to Arms: International and Civil Wars, 1816–1980.* Beverly Hills, CA: Sage.

Smith, C.P., et al. (1992) *Motivation and Personality: Handbook of Thematic Content Analysis.* New York: Cambridge University Press.

Snidal, Duncan. (1979) "Public Goods, Property Rights, and Political Organizations," *International Studies Quarterly* 23/4 (December 1979): 532–566.

(1985a) "Coordination versus Prisoners' Dilemma: Implications for International Cooperation and Regimes," *American Political Science Review* 79/4: 923–42.

(1985b) "The Game *Theory* of International Politics," *World Politics* 38/1: 25ff.

Solomon, Susan G. (1982) *Pluralism in the Soviet Union.* New York: St. Martin's Press.

Sprout, Harold and Margaret. (1965) *The Ecological Perspective on Human Affairs.* Princeton, NJ: Princeton University Press.

Stavenhagen, Rodolfo. (1990) *The Ethnic Question: Conflicts, Development, and Human Rights.* Tokyo: United Nations University Press.

Steinhoff, William. (1976) *George Orwell and the Origins of 1984.* Ann Arbor: University of Michigan Press.

Stewart, A.J., ed. (1982) *Motivation and Society: A Volume in Honor of David C. McClelland.* San Francisco: Jossey-Bass.

Strauss, Leo. (1978) "On Thucydides' War of the Peloponnesians and the Athenians." In his *The City and Man.* Chicago: The University of Chicago Press, pp. 139–242.

Sylvan, David. (1994) "Before Security and Foreign Policy: War and Diplomacy in Ancient Greece." Paper presented at the Annual Convention of the International Studies Association, Washington, DC.

Sylvan, David and Barry Glassner. (1985) *A Rationalist Methodology for the Social Sciences*. Oxford: Blackwell.

Taber, Charles S. (1992) "POLI: An Expert System Model of U.S. Foreign Policy Belief Systems," *American Political Science Review* 86/4: 888–904.

Tanaka, Akihiko. (1984) "China, China Watching, and CHINA WATCHER." In Donald A. Sylvan and Stephen Chan, eds., *Foreign Policy Decision Making: Perception, Cognition and Artificial Intelligence*. New York: Praeger.

Taylor, Michael. (1976) *Anarchy and Cooperation*. London: John Wiley & Sons.

Thucydides. (1910; reprinted 1950) *History of the Peloponnesian War*. Everyman's Library edition, translated by Richard Crawley. New York: E.P. Dutton.

(1951) *The Peloponnesian War*. Revised Crawley translation, introduced by J.H. Finley, Jr. New York: Modern Library.

(1972) *History of the Peloponnesian War*. Rex Warner translation, introduced by M.I. Finley. New York: Penguin Books.

Tickner, J. Ann. (1992) *Gender in International Relations*. New York: Columbia University Press.

Todorov, Tzvetan. (1969) *Grammaire du Decameron*. The Hague: Mouton.

(1992 [1982]) *The Conquest of America: The Question of the Other*. New York: Harper & Row.

Tonfoni, Graziella, ed. (1985) *Artificial Intelligence and Text-Understanding: Plot Units and Summarization Procedures*. Quaderni di Ricerca Linguistica 6. Turin: Edizioni Zara.

Toulmin, Stephen. (1958) *The Uses of Argument*. Cambridge: University of Cambridge Press.

(1990) *Cosmopolis: The Hidden Agenda of Modernity*. New York: Free Press/ Macmillan.

Toynbee, Arnold. (1934–54) *A Study of History*. 10 volumes. London: Oxford University Press.

(1946) "Christus Patiens." In *A Study of History*. London & New York: Oxford University Press. (Annex II to Part V.C (ii)(a), volume VI, pp. 376–539).

(1960) *A Study of History*, 2 vol. abridgment by D.C. Somervell. London: Readers' Union and Oxford University Press.

United Nations Development Programme. (1994) *Human Development Report 1994*. New York: Oxford University Press.

van Eemeren, Frans H. and Rob Grootendorst. (1992) *Argumentation, Communication, and Fallacies: A Pragma-Dialectical Perspective*. Hillsdale, NJ: Lawrence Erlbaum Associates.

van Eemeren, Frans H., Rob Grootendorst and T. Kruiger. (1987) *Handbook of Argumentation Theory*. Dordrecht & Providence: Foris Publications.

van Eemeren, Frans H., Rob Grootendorst, S. Jackson and S. Jacobs. (1993) *Reconstructing Argumentative Discourse*. Tuscaloosa & London: University of Alabama Press.

References

Varela, Francisco J. (1979) *Principles of Biological Autonomy, Series Vol. 2.* New York: Elsevier North Holland, Inc.

Vargas Llosa, M. (1991) "Questions of Conquest: What Columbus wrought, and what he did not." *Harper's Magazine* (December): 45–53, and letters in the April 1991 issue.

Vattimo, G. (1988) *The End of Modernity.* Baltimore: Johns Hopkins University Press.

Vayrynen, Raimo. (1985) "Is There a Role for the United Nations in Conflict Resolution?" *Journal of Peace Research* 22/3: 189–196.

Vertzberger, Yaacov Y. I. (1990) *The World in Their Minds.* Stanford: Stanford University Press.

Vico, Gimbattista. (1968 [1725 and 1744]) *The New Science of Giambattista Vico.* Revised translation of the 3rd edn, 1744. Ithaca: Cornell University Press.

von Cransch, Mario and Rom Harré. (1982) *The Analysis of Action: Recent Theoretical and Empirical Advances.* Cambridge: Cambridge University Press.

von Wright, Georg Henrik. (1971) *Explanation and Understanding.* London: Routledge & Kegan Paul.

Waldrop, M.M. (1992) *Complexity: The Emerging Science at the Edge of Order and Chaos.* New York: Simon & Schuster.

Walker, R.B.J. (1989) "'The Prince' and 'The Pauper': Tradition, Modernity, and Practice in the Theory of International Relations." In Der Derian and Shapiro, eds., *International/Intertextual Relations: Postmodern Rereadings of World Politics.* Lexington: Lexington Books, pp. 25–48.

Walker, R.B.J., ed. (1984) *Culture, Ideology and World Order.* Boulder: Westview.

Wallach, John R. (1992) "Contemporary Aristotelianism," *Political Theory* 20/4: 613–641.

Wallensteen, Peter. (1973) *Structure and War: On International Relations, 1920–1968.* Stockholm: Raben & Sjogren.

Wallensteen, Peter, ed. (1988) *Peace Research: Achievements and Challenges.* Boulder: Westview.

Wallerstein, Immanuel. (1974, 1980, 1989) *The Modern World-System,* 3 volumes New York: Academic Press.

(1974) *The Modern World: Capitalist Agriculture and the Origins of European World Economy in the Sixteenth Century.* New York: Academic Press.

Walton, Douglas N. (1990) *Practical Reasoning: Goal-Driven, Knowledge-Based, Action-Guiding Argumentation.* Savage, MD: Rowman & Littlefield.

Waltz, Kenneth N. (1974) "International Relations Theory." In Fred Greenstein and Nelson Polsby, eds., *Handbook of Political Science.* Reading, MA: Addison-Wesley.

(1979) *Theory of International Politics.* Reading, MA: Addison-Wesley.

Washington, J.M., ed. (1990) *A Testament of Hope: The Essential Writings and Speeches of Martin Luther King, Jr.* New York: Harper Collins.

Weber, Max. (1949) *The Methodology of the Social Sciences.* A reader edited by E.A. Shils & H.A. Finch. Glencoe, IL: Free Press.

(1968) *Gesammelte Aufsatze zur Wissenschaftslehre*, 3rd ed. Tübingen.

(1978) *Economy and Society*, vol. I. Berkeley & Los Angeles: University of California Press.

(1981) *General Economic History*. New Brunswick & London: Transaction Books.

(1985) *Roscher and Knies: The Logical Problems of Historical Economics*. Edited and translated by Guy Oakes. New York: Free Press.

(1989) *The Protestant Ethic and the Spirit of Capitalism*. Introduction by Anthony Giddens. Translated by Talcott Parsons. London: Unwin Hyman.

Weiner, Norbert. (1956) *The Human Use of Human Beings: Cybernetics and Society*, 2nd ed., rev. Garden City, NY: Doubleday.

Weinstein, D. (1980) "The Renaissance." In *Encyclopaedia Britannica*, 15 ed., XV: 660–71.

Wendt, Alexander. (1992) "Anarchy is What You Make of It: The Social Construction of Power Politics," *International Organization* 46 (Spring): 391–425.

Wertsch, V. (1985) *Vygotsky and the Social Formation of Mind*. Cambridge, MA: Harvard University Press.

Wessell, Leonard P., Jr. (1979) *Karl Marx, Romantic Irony, and the Proletariat: The Mythopoetic Origins of Marxism*. Baton Rouge & London: Louisiana State University Press.

White, Hayden. (1973) *Metahistory: The Historical Imagination in Nineteenth-Century Europe*. Baltimore: Johns Hopkins Press.

(1978) *Tropics of Discourse*. Baltimore: Johns Hopkins University Press.

(1987) *The Content of the Form: Narrative Discourse and Historical Representation*. Baltimore: Johns Hopkins University Press.

White, James Boyd. (1984) "The Dissolution of Meaning: Thucydides' History of His World." In *When Words Lose Their Meaning: Constitutions and Reconstitutions of Language, Character, and Community*. Chicago & London: University of Chicago Press, pp. 59–92, 299–313.

White, S.K. (1991) *Political Theory and Postmodernism*. Leicester: Leicester University Press.

Wierzbicka, Anna. (1992a) "Defining Emotional Concepts," *Cognitive Science* 16: 539–581.

(1992b) *Semantics, Culture, and Cognition: Universal Human Concepts in Culture-Specific Configurations*. New York: Oxford University Press.

Wight, Martin. (1977) *Systems of States*. Leicester: Leicester University Press.

(1978) *Power Politics*. Edited by Hedley Bull and Carsten Holbraad. New York: Holmes & Meier.

(1992) *International Theory: The Three Traditions*. Edited by Gabrele Wight and Brian Porter, with an introductory essay by Hedley Bull. New York: Homes & Meier, for the Royal Institute of International Affairs.

Williams, E. (1970) *From Columbus to Castro: The History of the Caribbean 1492–1969*. London: André Deutsch.

Williams, Michael C. (1989) "Rousseau, Realism and *Realpolitik*," *Millennium* 18/2: 185–203.

References

Winch, P. (1958) *The Idea of a Social Science and Its Relation to Philosophy.* London: Routledge & Kegan Paul.

Winograd, Terry. (1980) "Extended Inference Modes in Reasoning by Computer Systems," *Artificial Intelligence* 13: 5–26.

Winograd, Terry and Fernando Flores. (1986) *Understanding Computers and Cognition.* Norwood, NJ: Ablex.

Winston, Patrick H. (1982) "Learning New Principles from Precedents and Exercises," *Artificial Intelligence* 19: 321–350.

Winter, D.G. (1991) "Measuring Personality at a Distance: Development of an Integrated System for Scoring Motives in Running Text." In A.J. Stewart, J.M. Healy, Jr. and D.J. Ozer, eds., *Perspectives in Personality: Approaches to Understanding Lives.* London: Jessica Kingsley.

Wolin, S. (1980) "Paradigms and Political Theories." In G. Gutting, ed., *Paradigms and Revolutions.* Notre Dame, IN: University of Notre Dame Press.

Wright, Quincy. (1955) *The Study of International Relations.* New York: Appleton-Century-Crofts.

(1965) *A Study of War,* 2nd ed. Chicago: University of Chicago Press.

Yoder, J.H. (1972) *The Politics of Jesus.* Grand Rapids, MI: Eerdmans Publishing Company.

Young, Oran. (1978) "Anarchy and Social Choice: Reflections on the International Polity," *World Politics* 30/1–2: 241–263.

Zinnes, Dina. (1975) "The Scientific Study of International Politics." In F. Greenstein & N. Polsby, eds., *Handbook of Political Science,* vol. VIII. Reading, MA: Addison-Wesley.

Zinoviev, Alexander. (1979) *The Yawning Heights.* New York: Random House.

(1980) *The Radiant Future.* New York: Random House.

Zipes, Jack. (1979) *Breaking the Magic Spell: Radical Theories of Folk and Fairy Tales.* Austin: University of Texas Press.

Index

Abelson, Robert, 4–5, 7, 11, 94, 95, 202, 271, 272, 283
  see also Schank, Roger C.
Absolutism, 163, 184, 188–9, 195, 198, 199, 374
  see also power politics
actions, 7, 16, 17, 27, 62, 73, 76, 88, 93n, 96, 162, 231, 396, 411
  communicative, 209, 228–9
  and dialectics, 388
  experimental, 418
  and Great Chain of Being, 98–100
  in Jesus story, 136
  and practical reason, 30, 402, 405
Adam, 403, 404
Adorno, T., 6, 8–10
affective states, 114, 120, 131, 135
  coding of, 116–18
  in King Story, 283–7
  taxonomy of, 138–43
  see also motivation; plot unit analysis
agents, 396, 407, 411
  see also actions
Alberti, L.B., 152, 161
Alcibiades, 52, 54, 58
alienation, 60, 61, 215–16, 219, 224
Alker, H.R., Jr., 7, 17, 24, 31, 59, 62n, 92, 154, 235, 273, 301, 304, 308, 309, 311, 318
  and peace research, 342
  and power measurement, 199
  see also Alker–Schneider coding
Alker–Schneider coding, 118
  compared with Lehnert, 126, 127, 134–7, 140
  and Jesus story, 106, 123, 125–30
  summary of, 130–4
ambiguity, 135, 138, 139, 140

anarchy, 8–10, 310, 371
  and balance of power, 377–8
  and co-operation, 355ff., 364, 375
  definitions of, 356, 360–3, 366
  and epistemological problems, 377–86
  and historicity, 388, 392
  and practical reasoning, 410–14
  presumption of, 18, 355ff., 410ff.
  and sovereignty, 374–5
  and world politics, 355–6
Anderson, Perry, 188–9, 204
animals, 84, 85, 86, 99, 191
Anscombe, Elizabeth, 396, 399–401, 406, 409, 417
Apel, Karl-Otto, 6, 8–10, 396, 398, 416, 418–19
appeals, moral-emotional, 94, 96, 139
  see also affective states
archetypes, 287
argumentation, 7, 79, 88, 89, 93, 94, 209, 320, 329–31, 390
  analysis of, 96
  culture of, 52
  cumulative, 32
  dialectic in, 27
  evaluation, 37–8
  failures in, 38
  formalization of, 32–7, 39–48
  and polimetrics, 61
  practical, 402
  and speech acts, 229–30
  terminology of, 39
  theory, 27, 30, 64, 177
  see also practical reasoning
Aristotle, 5, 11, 12, 13, 18, 29, 45, 111, 139, 152, 158, 166, 279, 298, 359, 366, 397, 405, 406
  functional arguments in, 92, 102

Index

Aristotle (*cont.*)
  and Great Chain of Being, 98–100
  importance of, 64–5
  methodology of, 66–7, 69
  on nature and politics, 83–6
  and Plato, 66
  and political science, 69, 70, 72, 73, 75,
    76–86
  on practical reasoning, 17, 88, 400–1, 421
  rediscovery of, 68–70
  and science, 70–6
  and synthesis of art and science, 80–3, 91
  tradition of, 87–8, 101–3
Aron, Raymond, 13, 19, 23, 60, 336, 397, 416
Artificial Intelligence, 14, 95, 123, 134, 184,
    273, 345, 346, 350, 390
  see also computer models
arts, 20, 66, 67, 70, 76, 77, 154, 397
  and political science, 80–3, 98
  see also humanities
Ashley, Richard, 385–6
assertions, 34–6, 38, 43
Asymmetric Sequential Prisoner's
    Dilemma (ASPD) games *see* SPD
    games
Athenians, 28–30, 40–5, 47, 51, 53, 54–5,
    58–9, 61, 63, 366
Austin, J.L., 95, 101
automata, 190–2
  see also computer models; cybernetics
Axelrod, Robert, 303, 310, 320, 323, 381
Azar, Edward E., 340–1, 348

balance of power, 377–8, 413
barbarism, 216
Barker, Ernest, 80, 96
base and superstructure, 219
behavior, 16–17, 113, 186
being, 85–6, 181
  see also Great Chain of Being
Beitz, C., 364
belief structures, 96
Bennett, Jim, 350
Berke, Bradley, 290–4
Berlin, Isaiah, 15, 157, 209, 210ff., 216, 221,
    234
Bettelheim, Bruno, 104, 109
Bhasker, Roy, 354
Bible, 166, 272
  see also Gospels
Braudel, F., 112, 268, 269, 295, 393
Bremer, S., 92
Britain, 258
Bull, Hedley, 18, 61, 187, 236, 361, 377, 378,
    379, 389, 391, 392, 404, 414

on the anarchical society, 355–9
on Hobbes, 358, 363–75
on Kant, 367–8n
multidisciplinary approach of, 359
and practical reason, 395–9
world society problematique of, 359–60ff.
Burckhardt, William, 151–4, 156, 160, 181
bureaucracy, 10, 89, 225, 231, 232, 402, 415
Burke, Kenneth, 56, 57, 58, 217, 271
Burnham, James, 240–1n, 248, 251, 261
Burton, John, 343
Butterworth, 349

calculation, 154, 156
calculus, 35, 194, 360, 398
Campbell, David, 172
Campbell, Donald T., 99, 100, 199
capitalism, 151, 185, 186, 212, 221, 222, 223,
    226, 268, 299, 371, 414
  and fairy tales, 304–9
  and limits of anarchy problematique,
    375–86
  and SPD games, 324, 325, 328
case rules, in peace research, 340–4, 350–1,
    353
causation, 74, 88, 91–4, 97, 185, 186, 192,
    205, 419
change, 74, 91, 211, 214
Charles V, emperor, 164, 165
Chile, 186
China, 340, 378
Chomsky, N., 4, 5, 183n, 190, 281, 291, 390,
    398
Christensen, R.C., 345
Christianity, 102, 104–5, 108–9, 122, 135–6,
    153, 160, 195
Cicero, 152, 156, 158
civilizations, 98, 107, 108, 143, 154, 155,
    213–14, 220, 269, 296
class conflicts, 159, 219, 351, 352
classical tradition, 12–14, 49, 64, 68, 106
  appropriation of, 60–3
  and dialectics, 28–31
  and practical reason, 399ff.
  revival of, 151–2, 157–9
codings
  of Hungarian crisis, 349
  of Jesus story, 116–37
  of King story, 283–7, 289
  in peace research, 339–44, 347–8, 353
coercive irrationalities, 30–1
Cogan, M., 50, 51
cognitive psychology, 273, 277
Cold War, 3, 150, 245, 256–9, 316, 325, 341,
    343, 348, 379, 414–15

452

CAMBRIDGE STUDIES IN INTERNATIONAL RELATIONS